EIGHTH EDITION

BEHAVIOR MODIFICATION
What It Is
and
How to Do It

Garry Martin
Joseph Pear

University of Manitoba

PEARSON

Prentice
Hall

Upper Saddle River, New Jersey 07458

Library of Congress Cataloging-in-Publication Data

Martin, Garry
  Behavior modification : what it is and how to do it / Garry Martin, Joseph Pear.—8th ed.
      p. cm.
  Includes bibliographical references and index.
  ISBN 0-13-194227-1
  1.   Behavior modification.   I. Pear, Joseph II. Title.
  BF637.B4M37 2005
  155.2'5—dc22

                                                                          2005033059

Senior Editor: Jeff Marshall
Editorial Director: Leah Jewell
Editorial Assistant: Jennifer Puma
Director of Marketing: Brandy Dawson
Marketing Manager: Jeanette Moyer
Marketing Assistant: Alexandra Trum
Assistant Managing Editor (Production): Maureen Richardson
Production Liaison: Jan Schwartz/Kathleen Sleys
Manufacturing Buyer: Sherry Lewis
Cover Design: Kiwi Design
Cover Image: Joel Nakamura/Stock Illustration Source, Inc.
Director, Image Resource Center: Melinda Reo
Manager, Rights and Permissions: Zina Arabia
Image Permissions Coordinator: Joanne Dippel/Jennifer Puma
Composition/Full Service Project Management: TechBooks/Shelley L. Creager
Printer/Binder: Courier Companies

Photo Credits: Page 22, Aaron Strong/The Stock Connection; p. 34, Michael Newman/PhotoEdit;
p. 55, David Young-Wolff/PhotoEdit; p. 83 (top left) Yellow Dog Productions/Getty Images Inc.-Image
Bank; (top right) Laura Dwight/PhotoEdit; (bottom left) Will Faller; (bottom right) Elizabeth Crews
Photography; p. 104 (top) Garry L. Martin; (bottom) Bueno Technologies; pp. 168, 194, 221, 237, 318,
Garry L. Martin; p. 263, Skjold Photographs; p. 384, Spencer Grant/Photo Researchers, Inc.

Pearson Education Ltd.   Pearson Education Australia Pty. Limited
Pearson Education Singapore, Pte. Ltd.   Pearson Education North Asia Ltd.
Pearson Education Canada, Ltd.   Pearson Educación de Mexico, S.A. de C.V.
Pearson Education—Japan   Pearson Education Malaysia, Pte. Ltd.

PEARSON
Prentice
Hall

10 9 8 7 6

ISBN 0-13-194227-1

To
Jack Michael, Lee Meyerson, Lynn Caldwell,
Dick Powers, and Reed Lawson, who taught us so
much and made learning so enjoyable
and
Toby, Todd, Kelly, Scott, Tana, and Jonathan,
who live in a better world because of such
dedicated teachers

Brief Contents

Contents

PART III   SOME PRELIMINARY CONSIDERATIONS FOR EFFECTIVE PROGRAMMING STRATEGIES

17   CAPITALIZING ON EXISTING STIMULUS CONTROL: RULES AND GOALS

18   CAPITALIZING ON EXISTING STIMULUS CONTROL: MODELING, GUIDANCE, AND SITUATIONAL INDUCEMENT

19   MOTIVATION AND BEHAVIOR MODIFICATION

PART IV   DEALING WITH DATA

20   BEHAVIORAL ASSESSMENT: INITIAL CONSIDERATIONS

Contents

Preface

This eighth edition of *Behavior Modification: What It Is and How to Do It*, like its predecessors, assumes no specific prior knowledge about psychology or behavior modification on the part of the reader. Those who want to know how to apply behavior modification to their everyday concerns—from helping children learn life's necessary skills to solving some of their own personal behavior problems—will find the text useful. Mainly, however, this book is addressed to two audiences: (a) college and university students taking courses in behavior modification, applied behavior analysis, behavior therapy, the psychology of learning, and related areas; and (b) students and practitioners of various helping professions (such as clinical psychology, counseling, education, medicine, nursing, occupational therapy, physiotherapy, psychiatric nursing, psychiatry, social work, speech therapy, and sport psychology) who are concerned directly with enhancing various forms of behavioral development.

From our separate experiences over the past 39 years in teaching members of both groups, we are convinced that both groups learn the principles of behavior and how to apply them most effectively when the applications are explained with reference to the underlying behavior principles on which they are based. For this reason, as our title implies, this book deals equally with both the principles and the tactics (i.e., the rules and guidelines for specific applications) of behavior modification.

Our goals, and the manner in which we have attempted to achieve them, can be summarized as follows:

1. To teach the elementary principles and procedures of behavior modification. Thus, we begin with the basic principles and procedures, illustrate them with numerous examples and applications, and increase the complexity of the material gradually. Study Questions at the end of each chapter promote the reader's mastery of the material and ability to generalize to situations not described in the text. These questions can also be used for examination purposes in formal courses.

   2. To teach practical how-to skills, such as observing and recording; recognizing instances of reinforcement, extinction, and punishment and their likely long-term effects; interpreting behavioral episodes in terms of behavioral principles and procedures; and designing, implementing, and evaluating behavioral programs. To accomplish this, we provide Application Exercises, involving others, which teach the reader about analyzing, interpreting, and developing programs for the behavior of others; self-modification exercises, which encourage the reader to analyze, interpret, and develop programs for his or her own behavior; and guidelines for specific applications.

   3. To provide advanced discussion and references to acquaint readers with some of the empirical and theoretical underpinnings of the field. This material is presented in the Notes and Extended Discussion section at the end of each chapter. These sections can be omitted without harm to the continuity of the text. Separate study questions on the notes are provided for those instructors who wish to use them and as aids for students who wish to broaden their understanding of behavior modification. The information given in the extended discussion sections can also be used by instructors as springboards for lecture material.

   4. To present the material in such a way that it will serve as an easy-to-use handbook for practitioners concerned with overcoming behavioral deficits and excesses in a wide variety of populations and settings.

   The book is divided into six parts:
   Part I (Chapters 1 and 2) introduces the behavioral orientation of the book and describes major areas of application of behavior modification techniques for improving a wide variety of behaviors of individuals in diverse settings.
   Part II (Chapters 3–16) covers the basic principles and procedures of behavior modification. Each of the chapters begins with a case history drawn from the fields of child development, developmental disabilities, childhood autism, early education, coaching, or normal everyday adult adjustment. Numerous examples of how each principle operates in everyday life and how it can operate to the disadvantage of those who are ignorant of it are also given.
   Part III (Chapters 17–19) provides more sophisticated perspectives on the principles discussed in Part II. Chapters 17 and 18 discuss ways in which to combine and apply the principles. Chapter 19 provides a behavioral view of motivation and includes insights on applying various motivational operations.
   Part IV (Chapters 20–23) presents detailed procedures for assessing, recording, and graphing behavior. Methods for conducting functional assessments and behavioral research are also described. Many instructors prefer to present much of this material quite early in their courses—sometimes at the very beginning. Therefore, we have written these chapters so that they can be read independently

of the rest of the book; they do not depend on any of the other material. We recommend that students be required to read these chapters prior to carrying out any major projects for their courses.

Part V (Chapters 24–28) deals with how the basic principles, procedures, and assessment and recording techniques are incorporated into effective programming strategies. In keeping with the rigorously scientific nature of behavior modification, we have placed heavy emphasis on the importance of empirically validating program effectiveness.

Part VI (Chapters 29 and 30) expands the reader's perspective of behavior modification. It presents an overview of the history of behavior modification and contains a discussion of the ethical issues in the field. Although some instructors might think that these chapters belong near the beginning of the book, we believe that the reader is more prepared to fully appreciate this material after obtaining a clear and thorough knowledge of behavior modification. We placed ethical issues at the end of the text not because we believe that this topic is less important than the others. On the contrary, we stress ethical issues throughout the book, and, thus, the last chapter provides a reiteration and elaboration of our views on this vital subject. We hope that after reading the concluding chapter, the reader will be fully aware that the only justification for behavior modification is its usefulness in serving all humanity in general and its recipients in particular.

CHANGES IN THE EIGHTH EDITION

In response to developments in applied behavior analysis, we have added a new chapter on motivation (Chapter 19). This chapter discusses strategies for using motivating operations in the design of behavior modification programs in order to enhance their effectiveness. Chapter 27 was completely rewritten to incorporate new developments in cognitive behavior modification, and to include discussion of mindfulness procedures and Acceptance and Commitment Therapy. Chapter 28 was also largely rewritten in order to provide an updated overview of behavior therapy treatments with some of the most common clinical problems with outpatients.

Other chapters have received considerable revision in accordance with reviewers' comments and recent developments in this rapidly expanding field. To Chapter 1 we added a section on behavior modification and related terms, and added discussion of dimensions of behavior. To Chapter 2 we added new references on areas of application. To Chapter 3 we changed the subsection "Establishing Operations" to "Motivating Operations" (to be consistent with the new motivation chapter), and we added a discussion of the pitfall of overly simplistic attempts to explain behavior due to positive reinforcement. We revised Chapter 4 to include additional examples of conditioned reinforcers. To Chapter 5 we added strategies for dealing with extinction bursts and aggression as side effects of extinction. To Chapter 6 we clarified the application of schedules of reinforcement to free-operant versus discrete-trials procedures. To Chapter 7 we added a section on differential reinforcement of alternative behavior. To Chapter 9 we added discussion and a table to distinguish more clearly between different types of prompts. To Chapter 10 we added a table listing the dimensions of be-havior that can be shaped, with an example of each. To Chapter 11 we added dis-cussion and a table to distinguish more clearly the three major training methods, and added examples of superstitious behavior and adventitious chains. To Chapter 12 we added a symbol, S^{Dp}, to refer to a discriminative stimulus for a re-sponse that will be punished, and we added additional discussion of considera-tions concerning use of punishment by parents and others. To Chapter 16 we added the general case approach as a strategy for programming generalization. In Chapter 18 we described stimulus control procedures for treating insomnia. To Chapter 20 (formerly Chapter 19) we added examples of the types of questions typ-ically asked by a behavior therapist during an intake session, and added a sample of a self-report problem checklist. To Chapter 26 (formerly Chapter 25) we added discussion of how consideration of response effort and motivating operations can enhance self-control. To Chapter 30 we added some new information concerning why, in the early years, the term *behavior modification* evoked a negative reaction.

Throughout the book we have added examples to better illustrate the applica-tion of behavior principles in everyday life, and have added many new references to reflect recent developments in the field. We also added a number of new notes to the Notes and Extended Discussion sections and deleted old notes where warranted.

INSTRUCTOR'S RESOURCE MANUAL WITH TESTS AND PRACTICA

One of our goals is to help students learn to think about behavior modification critically and creatively. Thus, in the Instructor's Resource Manual to accompany this text, we have included operational definitions of higher-order thinking based on Bloom's taxonomy in the cognitive domain, and have applied these definitions to the Study Questions in the text. Taking these thinking levels into account, we have provided an answer key to all of the Study Questions (including those on the Notes and Extended Discussion sections), indicating how students are expected to answer these questions on tests and exams in order to achieve a high level of think-ing about the material. A pool of multiple-choice and/or true/false questions has also been provided on a chapter-by-chapter basis. Finally, included in the Instructor's Resource Manual are 15 in-class practica or mini-lab exercises that have been developed and field tested. Each exercise is designed to be completed by a group of two or three students during a regularly scheduled class. After students have studied and been examined on relevant chapters, completion of a practicum helps them learn to talk about and apply behavior modification principles. Feedback from students indicates that the exercises constitute an excellent teaching tool.

ACKNOWLEDGMENTS

The writing of the eight editions of this book was made possible by the help of many individuals. We gratefully acknowledge the cooperation and support of the staff at the Manitoba Developmental Centre and Dr. Carl Stephens and the staff at the St. Amant Centre. Much of the material in this volume was generated while the authors were involved in these institutions; without the support of these staff members, this book would not likely have been written.

Grateful acknowledgment is due to our many students for their constructive feedback on earlier editions. We also thank Jack Michael, Rob Hawkins, Bill Leonhart, and Iver Iversen and his students for their many excellent suggestions for improvements. We also wish to thank Vikki Wood, Kendra Thomson, and Aynsley Verbeke for their cheerful and efficient word processing of this edition.

We are grateful to the following reviewers, whose helpful criticism improved this eighth edition:

Shirley Albertson Owens
Vanguard University

Ngoc H. Bui
University of La Verne

Thomas G. Brown
Utica College of Syracuse University

Page Anderson
Georgia State University

Norman H. Cobb
University of Texas at Arlington

Kirk M. Lunnen
Westminster College

Otto MacLin
University of Northern Iowa

Finally, we express our appreciation to the very capable editorial and production team at Prentice Hall. In particular, we want to thank Jeff Marshall, editorial assistant. We also want to thank Shelley Creager, project manager, of TechBooks, and Lynne Lackenbach for her very careful copyediting.

Completion of this book was facilitated by a research grant from the Canadian Institutes of Health Research (Grant No. MT-6353) to G. L. Martin and a grant from the Social Sciences and Humanities Research Council to J. J. Pear.

TO THE STUDENT

This book is designed to help you learn to talk about and apply behavior modification effectively. You need no prior knowledge about behavior modification to read and understand this text from beginning to end. We are confident that students at all levels—from beginners to advanced—will find the text informative and useful.

Behavior modification is a broad and complex field, with many ramifications. Realizing that some students will require or want a deeper knowledge of behavior modification than others, we have separated the more elementary material from the material that demands more thought and study. The former material is presented in the main body of the text. The latter material is presented at the end of each chapter in the section called "Notes and Extended Discussion" (N & ED). The numbers in the margin of the main text refer you to the corresponding numbered passages in the N & ED sections. How you use these sections is up to you and your instructor. You can ignore them altogether and still obtain a good working knowledge of the principles and tactics of behavior modification, because the main text does not depend on the material in the N & ED sections. We believe, however, that many students will find these sections very informative and that many teachers will find the material useful in stimulating class discussion and imparting additional background information.

Another major way in which we have attempted to help you learn the material is by providing guidelines on the use of all the behavior modification methods discussed in the text. These guidelines should prove useful as summaries of the material as well as in helping you to actually apply the methods described in the text.

Numerous study questions and application exercises (including "self-modification" exercises) are also presented in most chapters. The study questions are intended to help you check your knowledge of the material when preparing for quizzes and exams. The application exercises and self-modification exercises are intended to help you develop the practical skills you will need to carry out behavior modification projects effectively.

To help make your study productive and enjoyable, we progress from the simpler and more intrinsically interesting material to the more difficult and complex material. This is also true of the writing style. But a word of caution: *Do not be misled by the seeming simplicity of the earlier chapters*. Students who conclude that they are skilled behavior modifiers after they have learned a few simple behavior modification principles unfortunately end up proving the old maxim that "a little knowledge is a dangerous thing." If we personally had to pick the most important chapter in this book, in terms of the knowledge and skills that define a competent behavior modifier, it would probably be Chapter 24. We therefore strongly suggest that you reserve judgment about your abilities as a behavior modifier until you have mastered Chapter 24 and all the preliminary material on which it is based.

We would also point out that—as emphasized in Chapter 30—organizations that regulate behavior modification have appeared and gained in stature and influence in the past few years. If you are considering applying behavior modification on any level, we strongly recommend that you check with the Behavior Analyst Certification Board to determine how you may obtain the necessary qualifications. (Their Web address is www.bacb.com.)

With those words of caution, we wish you much success and enjoyment as you pursue your studies in this exciting and rapidly expanding field.

G.L.M.
J.J.P.

1

Introduction

Many of society's best achievements, as well as some of its most pressing health and social challenges—from racism to heart disease to AIDS to terrorism—are firmly rooted in behavior. According to a recent study in the *Journal of the American Medical Association,* approximately half of the deaths in the United States are caused by unhealthy behaviors. These facts led more than 50 scientific organizations in the United States to declare the first 10 years of the new millennium as the "Decade of Behavior." But what is behavior? Before attempting an answer, consider the following:

1. *Child with withdrawn behavior.* A class of nursery school youngsters is in the playground. While most of the children are playing, one little boy sits quietly by himself, making no effort to join in the fun. A teacher tries conscientiously, as he has many times before, to coax this child into playing with the others. But the boy steadfastly maintains his social isolation from the other children.
2. *Tardiness.* Cathy is a 7-year-old girl with very poor visual–motor coordination. She attends a school for children with developmental disabilities. Although she is able to take off her coat and boots and put them in their proper place each morning, she takes a great deal of time to do so, often spending as much as an hour in the coatroom. Her teachers fear that this slowness is interfering with Cathy's development of self-reliance. However, they are at a loss as to what to do about the situation, since all their urgings do not make the child move any faster.
3. *Littering.* Tom and Sally have just arrived at the place where they intend to set up camp and are looking in disgust and amazement at the litter left by previous campers. "Don't they care about the environment?" asks Sally. "If people keep this up," Tom says, "there

1

won't be any nature left for anyone to enjoy." Sadly they tell each other that something should be done about the problem, but neither can say what would solve it.

4. *Ineffective studying.* With two term papers due next week and a midterm exam at the same time, Sam is wondering how he is ever going to make it through his first year at university. The week before the exam he gets practically no sleep because of cramming every night, and just barely manages a C-minus on the test. But neither term paper is finished, and he is almost sure to lose marks for lateness even if his professors accept his overdue papers.

5. *Writing a novel.* Karen works in a bank, but her real ambition is to write a novel. Although most of her evenings and weekends are relatively free, she has not yet begun to write. Instead she spends all her spare time watching television, sewing, cooking, visiting friends, and going out on dates. Unfortunately, it is becoming more and more apparent that Karen's ambition will never be realized.

6. *Speeding.* Accidents frequently occur on the highway approach into Pleasant City. Despite clearly posted signs to reduce speed, many motorists fail to slow down until they are well within the city limits, and there have been quite a few close calls in which cars speeding into the city have just narrowly missed a child. If this continues, eventually some child is going to be seriously hurt or killed.

7. *A Phobia.* Albert is a normal, healthy young man, but he has one quirk: He is terrified of airplanes. If you were to ask him why he is afraid of airplanes, he would not be able to tell you. Rationally, he knows that it is unlikely that anything bad will happen to him when he is in one. Not only is his airplane phobia inconvenient, it is also very embarrassing since his friends do not seem to understand why he will not ride in an airplane to go on vacation with them.

8. *Migraines.* While preparing dinner for her family, Betty was vaguely aware of a familiar feeling creeping up on her. Then, all at once, she felt nauseous. She looked around fearfully, knowing from past experience what to expect. "Tom, Joe," she called to her sons watching TV in the living room, "you'll have to finish fixing dinner yourselves—I'm having another attack." She then rushed up to the bedroom, quickly drew the blinds, and lay down on the bed. Finally, after about 6 hours of almost unbearable pain, her symptoms subsided and she was able to rejoin her family. But the threat of "another one of Mom's migraines" that could occur again unpredictably at any time still hung over the heads of Betty's family.

9. *Staff management.* Jack and Brenda were having coffee one morning at the Dairy Queen restaurant they owned. "We're going to have to do something about the evening staff," said Brenda. "When I came in this morning, the ice cream machine wasn't properly cleaned and the cups and lids weren't restocked." "That's only the tip of the iceberg," said Jack. "You should see the grill! Maybe we need some kind of a staff motivation program. We need something!"

10. *Athletic performance.* A young gymnast performs her routines extremely well at practices. But she's easily distracted at competitions, has trouble focusing on her performance, and usually performs below potential. Neither she nor her coach knows how to solve the problem.

11. *Adapting in a personal care home.* Mary's Mom is 88 years old, and has lived alone for the past seven years. Unfortunately, it has become increasingly clear that she can no longer care for herself. Mary has made arrangements for her Mom to move to a personal care home, but her Mom is extremely anxious about "living with strangers." Mary doesn't know how to help her Mom cope with the anxiety.

Close inspection shows that each of the above involves some sort of human behavior. Together, they illustrate the range of problems with which specialists in behavior modification are trained to deal. In fact, if you read this book very carefully, you will find each of these types of behavioral problems discussed somewhere in the following pages. Many other types of cases will also be discussed. Behavior modification, as you will see, is applicable to the entire range of human behavior.

WHAT IS BEHAVIOR?

Before we can talk about behavior modification, we must first ask, what do we mean by **behavior?** Some commonly used synonyms include "activity," "action," "performance," "responding," "response," and "reaction." Essentially, behavior is anything that a person says or does. Technically, behavior is any muscular, glandular, or electrical activity of an organism. Is the color of someone's eyes behavior? Is blinking behavior? Are the clothes someone is wearing behavior? Is dressing behavior? If you said no to the first and third questions and yes to the second and fourth, we are in agreement. One of the goals of this book is to encourage you to begin thinking and talking very specifically about behavior.

How about getting an "A" in a behavior modification course, or losing 10 pounds; are those behaviors? No. Those are *products of behavior*. The behavior that produces an "A" is studying effectively. The behaviors that lead to weight loss are resisting overeating and exercising more.

Walking, talking out loud, throwing a baseball, yelling at someone—all are overt (visible) behaviors that could be observed and recorded by an individual other than the one performing the behavior. As will be discussed in later chapters, the term *behavior* can also refer to *covert* (private, internal) activities that cannot be readily observed by others. All behavior is potentially observable. However, private or covert behaviors do *not* typically refer to behaviors done in private, such as undressing in one's bedroom. Nor do they usually refer to secretive actions, such as cheating on an exam. Rather, they refer to activities that occur "within one's skin" and that therefore require special instruments for others to observe. For example, just before stepping onto the ice at an important competition, a figure skater might think, "I hope I don't fall," and he or she is likely to feel nervous (increased heart rate, etc.). Thinking and feeling are private behaviors, and are discussed further in Chapters 15, 27 and 28. Both overt and covert behaviors can be influenced by techniques of behavior modification.

Sometimes we think in words, called *private self-talk,* as illustrated by the figure skater in the previous paragraph. At other times we think by imagining. If I were to ask you to close your eyes and imagine a clear, blue sky, with a few white fluffy clouds, you would be able to do so. Imagining and private self-talk, in addition to being called *covert behaviors,* are sometimes referred to as *cognitive behaviors.* (Techniques for dealing with cognitive behaviors—called cognitive behavior modification—are discussed in Chapter 27.)

Characteristics of behavior that can be measured are called *dimensions of behavior.* The *duration* of a behavior is the length of time that it lasts (e.g., Mary studied for one hour). The *frequency* of a behavior is the number of instances that occur in a given period of time (e.g., Frank planted five tomato plants in his garden in 30 minutes). The *intensity* or *force* of a behavior refers to the physical effort or energy involved in emitting the behavior (e.g., Mary has a strong grip when shaking hands). Strategies for measuring dimensions of behavior are discussed in Chapter 21.

While we have all learned to talk about behavior in various ways, we often do so in quite general terms. Terms such as "honest," "carefree," "hardworking," "unreliable," "independent," "selfish," "incompetent," "kind," "graceful," "unsociable," and "nervous" are summary labels for human actions, but they do not refer to specific behaviors. If, for example, you were to describe a man as nervous, others might know generally what you mean. But they would not know if you were referring to that person's tendency to chew his fingernails frequently, his constant fidgeting when sitting in a chair, the tendency for his left eye to twitch when talking to someone of the opposite sex, or some other behavior. In later chapters we discuss ways to measure specific dimensions of behavior.

Traditional helping specialists often use general summary terms such as *intelligence, attitudes,* and *creativity.* Behavior modifiers, however, generally try to talk more precisely about behavior. What do we mean when we say that a person is *intelligent?* To many people, intelligence is something that you are born with, a sort of "inherited brain power" or innate capacity for learning. But we never observe or directly measure any such thing. On an intelligence test, for example, we simply measure people's behavior—their answers to questions—as they take the test. The word *intelligent* is best used in its adjective form (e.g., "he is an *intelligent* speaker," "his speech is *intelligent*") or its adverb form (e.g., "she writes *intelligently*") to describe how people behave under certain conditions, such as taking a test, not as a noun for some "thing." Perhaps a person described as intelligent readily solves problems that others find difficult, performs well on most course examinations, reads many books, talks knowledgeably about many topics, or scores well on an intelligence test. Depending on who uses the word, *intelligence* can mean any or all of these—but whatever it means, it refers to ways of behaving. Therefore, in this book we avoid using the word *intelligence* as a noun.

What about an *attitude?* Suppose that Johnny's teacher, Ms. Smith, reports that he has a bad attitude toward school. What does Ms. Smith mean by this? Perhaps she means that Johnny frequently skips school, refuses to do his classwork when he does attend, and swears at the teacher. Whatever she means when she talks about Johnny's "bad attitude," it is clearly his behavior with which she is really concerned.

Creativity also refers to the kinds of behavior in which a person is likely to engage under certain circumstances (for a behavioral approach to creativity, see Marr, 2003). The creative individual frequently emits behaviors that are novel or unusual and that, at the same time, have desirable effects.

Other psychological terms, such as developmental disabilities (discussed further in Chapter 2), learning disabilities, autism, and so on, also are labels for certain ways of behaving. They do not refer to invisible mental abnormalities. How do psychologists and other helping specialists decide that someone has a developmental disability? They make the decision primarily because they might observe that the person, at a certain age,

    cannot tie shoelaces;

    is not toilet trained;

    eats only with fingers or a spoon;

performs on psychological tests in such a way that the combined answers yield an IQ score of 75 or less.

How do specialists decide that a school-age child has a learning disability? They make the decision on the basis of certain behaviors that they observe, such as:

attending to a task for only a few seconds or minutes (typically labeled a *short attention span*);

staring at an item for many minutes (typically labeled *perseveration*);

moving frequently from one position, location, or task to the next (often labeled *hyperactivity*);

confusing words while speaking, such as "thumb" for "tongue" (labeled *speech disability*);

inverting words while reading, such as "saw" for "was" (labeled a *reading disability* or *dyslexia).*

How do specialists diagnose a child as showing an autistic disorder? They make this decision on the basis of certain behaviors that they observe. For example, they might observe that a child

frequently mimics particular questions rather than answering with an appropriate statement (more generally, shows impaired communication);

when called, does not respond, or moves away from the person calling (more generally, shows impaired social behavior);

engages in various self-stimulatory behaviors, such as rocking back and forth, twirling objects with the fingers, or fluttering the hands in front of his or her eyes;

performs much below average on a variety of self-care tasks, such as dressing, grooming, and feeding.

Other summary labels commonly used to refer to psychological problems include attention-deficit/hyperactive disorder, anxiety, depression, low self-esteem, road rage, interpersonal difficulties, and sexual dysfunction. Why are summary terms or labels for behavior patterns so frequently used in psychology and in everyday life? First, they may be useful for quickly providing general information about how a labeled individual might perform. A 10-year-old child who has been labeled as having a severe developmental disability, for example, is not able to read even at the first-grade level. Second, the labels may imply that a particular treatment program will be helpful. Someone experiencing problems with frequent anger might be encouraged to take an anger-management program. Someone who is unassertive might benefit from an assertiveness training course. However, the use of summary labels also has disadvantages. One is that they may lead to *pseudo-explanations* of behavior (*pseudo* means false). For example, a child who inverts words while reading, such as "saw" for "was," might be labeled as *dyslexic*. If we ask why the child inverts words, and we are given the answer, "Because he is dyslexic," then the summary label for the behavior has been used as a pseudo-explanation for the behavior. (Another name for pseudo-explanation is circular reasoning.) A second disadvantage of labeling is that labels can negatively affect the way an individual might be treated. Teachers, for example, may be less likely to encourage children to persist in problem solving if the children have been labeled as *sexually abused* or *mentally retarded* (Bromfield, Bromfield, & Weiss, 1988; Bromfield, Weisz, & Messer, 1986). Another disadvantage of labeling is that it may direct our focus to an individual's problem behaviors rather than to his or her strengths. Suppose, for example, that a teenager consistently fails to make his bed, but reliably mows the lawn and places the garbage cans on the street on pickup days. If the parents describe their son as "lazy," that label may cause them to focus more on the problem behavior than to praise the positive behaviors.

In this book, we strongly stress the importance of defining all types of problems in terms of *behavioral deficits* (too little behavior of a particular type) or *behavioral excesses* (too much behavior of a particular type). We do so for several reasons. First, we want to help you to avoid the problems of using general summary labels discussed earlier. Second, regardless of the labels attached to an individual, it is *behavior* that causes concern—and behavior that must be treated to alleviate the problem. Certain behaviors that parents see and hear often cause them to seek professional help for their children. Certain behaviors teachers see and hear often prompt them to seek professional help for their students. Certain behaviors that can be seen or heard cause governments to set up institutions, clinics, community treatment centers, and special programs. And certain behaviors that you emit might cause you to go on a self-improvement program. Third, specific procedures are now available that can be used in school, in the workplace, and in home settings—in fact, just about anywhere that there is a need to establish more desirable behaviors. These techniques are referred to collectively as *behavior modification*.

WHAT IS BEHAVIOR MODIFICATION?

The most important characteristic of behavior modification is *its strong emphasis on defining problems in terms of behavior that can be measured in some way, and using changes in the behavioral measure of the problem as the best indicator of the extent to which the problem is being helped.*

Another characteristic of behavior modification is that *its treatment procedures and techniques are ways of altering an individual's current environment* to help that individual function more fully. The term **environment** refers to the people, objects, and events currently present in one's immediate surroundings that impinge on one's sense receptors and that can affect behavior. The people, objects, and events that make up a person's environment are called **stimuli** (plural of **stimulus**). For example, the teacher, chalkboard, other students, and the furniture in a classroom are all potential stimuli in a student's environment in a classroom setting. An individual's own behavior can also be a part of the environment influencing that individual's subsequent behavior. When hitting a forehand shot in tennis, for example, both the sight of the ball coming near and the behavior of completing your backswing provide stimuli for you to complete the forehand shot and hit the ball over the net. Things that a therapist might say to a client are also a part of that client's environment. But behavior modification is much more than just *talk therapy* or *verbal psychotherapy* (such as psychoanalysis or client-centered therapy). Although both behavior modifiers and "talk" therapists talk to their clients, their approaches to therapy differ in several important ways. One difference between behavior modifiers and "talk" therapists is that a behavior modifier is frequently actively involved in restructuring a client's daily environment to strengthen appropriate behavior, rather than spending a great deal of time discussing the client's past experiences. While knowledge of a client's past experiences might provide some useful information for designing a treatment program, knowledge of the current environmental variables that control a client's behavior is most useful for designing an effective behavioral treatment. Another difference between behavior modifiers and "talk" therapists is that a behavior modifier frequently gives homework assignments to clients in which they change their own everyday environments for therapeutic purposes. Such homework assignments are discussed in Chapter 26.

A third characteristic of behavior modification is that *its methods and rationales can be described precisely*. This makes it possible for behavior modifiers to read descriptions of procedures used by their colleagues, replicate them, and get essentially the same results. It also makes it easier to teach behavior modification procedures than has been the case with many other forms of psychological treatment.

As a consequence of the third characteristic, a fourth characteristic of behavior modification is that *the techniques of behavior modification are often applied by individuals in everyday life*. Although, as you will read in Chapters 2, 28, and 30, appropriately trained professionals and paraprofessionals use behavior modification in helping others, the precise description of behavior modification techniques makes it possible for individuals such as parents, teachers, coaches, and others to apply behavior modification to help individuals in everyday situations.

A fifth characteristic of behavior modification is that, to a large extent, *the techniques stem from basic and applied research in the science of learning in general, and the principles of operant and Pavlovian conditioning in particular* (e.g., see Pear, 2001). Therefore, in Part II we cover these principles in considerable detail and show how they are applicable to various types of behavior problems.

Two final characteristics are that *behavior modification emphasizes scientific demonstration that a particular intervention was responsible for a particular behavior change, and it places high value on accountability for everyone involved in behavior modification programs:* client, staff, administrators, consultants, and so on.[1]

Thus, **behavior modification** involves the systematic application of learning principles and techniques to assess and improve individuals' covert and overt behaviors in order to enhance their functioning.

BEHAVIORAL ASSESSMENT

In the preceding section, we said that the most important characteristic of behavior modification is its use of measures of behavior to judge whether or not an individual's behavior had been improved by a behavior modification program. Behaviors to be improved in a behavior modification program are frequently called **target behaviors.**

---

[1]We thank Rob Hawkins for bringing these last two points to our attention.

Note 1   **Behavioral assessment** involves the collection and analysis of information and data in order to (a) identify and describe target behaviors; (b) identify possible causes of the behavior; (c) guide the selection of an appropriate behavioral treatment; and (d) evaluate treatment outcome. One type of behavioral assessment that has become especially important is termed *functional analysis*. Essentially, this approach (discussed in Chapter 22) involves isolating through experimentation the causes of problem behavior and removing or reversing them. As the interest in behavior modification has expanded during the past four decades, so has the demand for guidelines for conducting behavioral assessments. For more information on behavioral assessment, refer to Chapters 20, 21, and 22 of this text, and the book by Bellack and Hersen (1998).

BEHAVIORAL MODIFICATION AND RELATED TERMS

Several terms are closely related to behavior modification. *Behavior analysis* refers to the scientific study of laws that govern the behavior of human beings and other animals. You might think of behavior analysis as the science on which behavior modification is based. *Applied behavior analysis* is behavior modification in which there is typically an attempt to analyze or clearly demonstrate controlling variables of the behavior of concern. Applied behavior analysis typically focuses on overt behaviors that are of social significance (e.g., littering, public education, parenting skills) or clinical significance (e.g., anger management, coping by the elderly), and includes a strong emphasis on the learning principles frequently referred to as operant conditioning (described in Chapters 3 through 13). The term *behavior therapy* is typically used to refer to behavior modification carried out on dysfunctional behavior. The term *behavior modification* encompasses both behavior therapy and applied behavior analysis, and that is the term that we generally use throughout this book. (The historical use of these and similar terms is discussed in Chapter 29.) Behavior modification includes all explicit applications of behavior principles to improve individual's covert and overt behaviors—whether or not in clinical settings and whether or not controlling variables have been explicitly demonstrated. Related terms that you may encounter include behavior modifier, behavior analyst, behavior manager, behavioral engineer, and performance manager. These terms refer to an individual who deliberately applies behavior principles to improve behavior, whether that individual is a teacher, parent, spouse, peer, roommate, supervisor, colleague, psychologist, social worker, or the person whose behavior is being modified.

SOME MISCONCEPTIONS ABOUT BEHAVIOR MODIFICATION

You probably encountered the term *behavior modification* before reading this book. Unfortunately, because there are a number of myths or misconceptions about this area, some of what you have heard is likely false. Consider the following statements.

Myth 1: Use of rewards by behavior modifiers to change behavior is bribery.
Myth 2: Behavior modification involves the use of drugs, psychosurgery, and electroconvulsive therapy.

Myth 3: Behavior modification only changes symptoms, it doesn't get at the underlying problems.

Myth 4: Behavior modification can be applied to deal with simple problems, such as toilet training children or overcoming fear of heights, but it is not applicable for changing complex problems such as low self-esteem or depression.

Myth 5: Behavior modifiers are cold and unfeeling and don't develop empathy with their clients.

Myth 6: Behavior modifiers deal only with observable behavior; they don't deal with thoughts and feelings of clients.

Myth 7: Behavior modification is outdated.

In various sections throughout this book you will encounter evidence to dispel these myths or misconceptions.

THE APPROACH OF THIS BOOK

The main purpose of this book is to describe behavior modification techniques in an enjoyable, readable, and practical manner. Since it has been written for people in various helping professions as well as for students, we intend to help readers learn not merely about behavior modification but also how to use it to overcome behavioral deficits and excesses.

"Wait a minute," you may say. "From many of your examples it sounds as if this book is intended primarily for people concerned with observable behavior of individuals with severe handicaps." In answer to such an observation, we wish to point out that the behavior modification procedures described in this volume can be used to change any individual's behavior. Even people who are normal or average in most respects usually have some behavior that they would like to improve. Behavior that someone would like to improve can be classified as either behavioral deficits or behavioral excesses, and can be overt or covert. Below are examples of each type.

Examples of behavioral deficits

1. A child does not pronounce words clearly and does not interact with other children.
2. A teenager does not complete homework assignments, help around the house, work in the yard, or discuss problems and difficulties with her parents.
3. An adult does not pay attention to traffic regulations while driving, thank others for courtesies and favors, or meet his or her spouse at agreed-upon times.
4. A basketball player, encouraged by the coach to visualize the ball going into the net just before a foul shot, is unable to do so.

Examples of behavioral excesses

1. A child frequently gets out of bed and throws tantrums at bedtime, throws food on the floor at mealtime, and plays with the controls for the television set.
2. A teenager frequently interrupts conversations between his parents and other adults, spends hours talking on the telephone in the evening, and uses abusive language.
3. An adult watches television continuously, frequently eats candies and other junk food between meals, smokes one cigarette after another, and bites his or her fingernails.
4. A golfer often thinks negatively (e.g., "If I miss this one, I'll lose!") and experiences considerable anxiety (i.e., heart pounding, palms sweating) just before important shots.

To identify a behavior as excessive or deficient, we must consider the context in which it occurs. For example, a child drawing on paper is showing appropriate behavior, but if the child repeatedly draws on the living room wall, most parents would regard that as a behavioral excess. A normal teenager might interact appropriately with members of the same sex, but be extremely embarrassed and have difficulty talking to members of the opposite sex (a behavioral deficit). Some behavioral excesses—for example, self-injurious behavior—are inappropriate no matter what the context. In most cases, however, the point at which a particular behavior is considered deficient or excessive is determined primarily by the practices in our culture or by the ethical views of concerned individuals. The relationship between cultural practices, ethics, and behavior modification is discussed in Chapter 30.

Note 2   To summarize, the behavior modification approach focuses primarily on behavior and involves current environmental (as opposed to medical, pharmacological, or surgical) manipulations to change behavior. Individuals who are labeled as persons with developmental disabilities, autism, schizophrenia, depression, or an anxiety disorder, for example, are individuals who show behavioral deficits or excesses. Similarly, individuals who are labeled lazy, unmotivated, selfish, incompetent, or uncoordinated are also individuals who show behavioral deficits or excesses. Behavior modification consists of a set of procedures that can be used to change behavior so that these individuals will be considered less of whatever label has been given them. Some traditional psychologists have shown an excessive concern for labeling and classifying individuals. Regardless of the label given, the individual's behavior is still there and is still being influenced by the individual's immediate environment. The mother in Figure 1–1, for example, is still concerned about what to do with her child and how to handle the problem. That is where behavior modification comes in.

After the overview in the next chapter, Part II (Chapters 3–16) describes the principles and procedures of behavior modification. In essence, principles are procedures that have a consistent effect and are so simple that they cannot be broken down into simpler procedures. Principles are like laws in science. Most procedures used in behavior modification are combinations of the principles of behavior modification. These principles are almost never used in isolation from other principles in practical applications, especially with highly verbal individuals. Therefore, to better illustrate the principles under discussion, we have selected relatively simple lead cases for the chapters in Part II. After illustrating the principles involved in such cases, we elaborate on how these principles are used with other types of problems. We also give numerous illustrations of these principles from normal behavior in everyday life. Later parts of the book show how highly complex programs are built from the principles and procedures introduced in Part II. In addition to these detailed programming strategies, ethical issues in their use are described. We hope that this book provides satisfactory answers to teachers, counselors, psychologists, students, teenagers, fathers, mothers, and others who say, "Thank you, Ms. or Mr. Expert, but what can I do about it?" (This is the question asked by the mother in Figure 1–1.) We hope also that the book will give introductory students of behavior modification an understanding of why the procedures are effective.

Figure 1–1 The experts "helping" mother with her child?

STUDY QUESTIONS

1. What is behavior, generally and technically? Give three synonyms for behavior.
2. Distinguish between behavior and products of behavior. Give an example of a behavior and a product of that behavior.
3. Distinguish between overt and covert behaviors. Give two examples of each.
4. What are cognitive behaviors? Give two examples.
5. Describe two dimensions of behavior. Give an example of each.
6. From a behavioral point of view, what is intelligence? creativity?
7. What are three disadvantages of using summary labels to refer to individuals or their actions?
8. What is a behavioral deficit? Give two examples.
9. What is a behavioral excess? Give two examples.
10. Why do behavior modifiers describe behavioral problems in terms of specific behavioral deficits or excesses?
11. What do behavior modifiers mean by the term *environment?* Give an example.
12. What are stimuli? Describe two examples.
13. Describe seven defining characteristics of behavior modification.

14. Define behavior modification.
15. Define behavioral assessment.
16. What is meant by the term *target behavior?* Give an example of a target behavior of yours that you would like to improve. Is your target behavior a behavioral deficit to increase or a behavioral excess to decrease?
17. List four myths or misconceptions about behavior modification.
18. Briefly distinguish between behavior analysis, behavior therapy, applied behavior analysis, and behavior modification.

APPLICATION EXERCISES

In most of the chapters of this book, we provide you with exercises to apply the concepts you learned in the chapters. Generally, we present two types of application exercises: (a) exercises that involve the behavior of others, and (b) self-modification exercises in which you apply the behavior modification concepts you have learned to your own behavior.

A. Exercise Involving Others

Consider someone other than yourself. From your point of view, identify:
1. two behavioral deficits for that person to overcome
2. two behavioral excesses to decrease

For each example, indicate whether you have described:
a. a specific behavior or a general summary label
b. an observable behavior or a covert behavior
c. a behavior or the outcome of a behavior

B. Self-Modification Exercise

Apply the above exercise to yourself.

NOTES AND EXTENDED DISCUSSION

1. Behavioral assessment emerged as an alternative to traditional psychodiagnostic assessment in the 1960s. Psychoanalytic approaches to abnormal behavior originated with Sigmund Freud and others who viewed abnormal behavior as a symptom of an underlying mental disturbance in a personality mechanism. A major purpose of traditional diagnostic assessment was to identify the type of mental disorder assumed to underlie abnormal behavior. To help therapists diagnose clients with different types of presumed mental illness, the American Psychiatric Association developed the *Diagnostic and Statistical Manual of Mental Disorders* (*DSM-I*, 1952). The manual was later revised as the *DSM-II* in 1968, the *DSM-III* in 1980, the *DSM-III-R* (*R* is for "revised") in 1987, the *DSM-IV* in 1994, and the *DSM-IV-TR* (*TR* is for "Text Revision") in 2000. Behavior modifiers made little use of the first two DSMs

because they did not agree with Freud's model of abnormal behavior on which the DSMs were based, and because there was little evidence that diagnoses based on that model were reliable or valid (Hersen, 1976). However, the *DSM-IV* improved considerably over the earlier manuals in several respects. First, it is based primarily on research rather than on Freud's theory. Second, individual disorders (e.g., obsessive-compulsive disorder, generalized anxiety disorder, major depression) are based on categories of problem behaviors. Third, it uses a multidimensional recording system that provides extra information for planning treatment, managing a case, and predicting outcomes. With the improvements in the *DSM-IV* (now the *DSM-IV-TR*), behavior modifiers in a variety of settings are increasingly likely to use it to classify clients. They do so in part because official diagnoses are usually required by clinics, hospitals, schools, and social service agencies before treatment can be offered, and because health insurance companies reimburse practitioners on the basis of the diagnoses in the *DSM-IV-TR*. However, it is important to remember that because a *DSM-IV-TR* diagnosis (such as autistic disorder) refers to an individual's behaviors, it is likely to result in the individual being labeled (e.g., autistic), which may lead to the disadvantages of labeling mentioned in this chapter. Moreover, in spite of the implication that all individuals with the same label (e.g., autistic) are the same, they are not. To avoid labeling, we should use what has come to be referred to as "people first language" when describing individuals with problems. For example, in the case of autism, we should describe the client as a child with autism rather than an autistic child. Moreover, in addition to obtaining a *DSM-IV-TR* diagnosis for an individual, we should always conduct detailed behavioral assessments in order to obtain the necessary information for designing the most effective, individualized treatment program.

2. Because of this emphasis on the environment, behaviorists are often accused of denying the importance of genetics in determining behavior. This mistaken impression may stem in part from the writings of John B. Watson (1913), who, dissatisfied with the introspective psychology of his day, argued that the correct subject matter of psychology was observable behavior and only observable behavior. Watson also advocated an extreme form of environmentalism, summarized in the following famous (or infamous) claim:

> Give me a dozen healthy infants, and my own specified world to bring them up in and I'll guarantee to take any one at random and train him to become any type of specialist I might select—doctor, lawyer, artist, merchant-chief, and, yes, even beggarman and thief, regardless of his talents, penchants, tendencies, abilities, vocations, and race of his ancestors. (Watson, 1930, p. 104).

However, Skinner (1974) pointed out that Watson himself admitted that this claim was exaggerated, and he did not disregard the importance of genetics. An appreciation by behavior modifiers of the importance of genetics was indicated by the publication of a miniseries on behavioral genetics in the journal *Behavior Therapy* (1986, Vol. 17, No. 4). Included in the miniseries were articles on cardiovascular stress and genetics, childhood obesity and genetics, smoking and genetics, and alcoholism and genetics (see also Turner, Cardon, & Hewitt, 1995). However, even though the influence of heredity may increase the susceptibility of an individual to certain behavioral problems such as obesity or alcoholism, an individual's environment still plays a major role in the development and maintenance of behaviors that lead to such problems.

Study Questions on Notes

1. What is the full title of the *DSM-IV-TR?* In two or three sentences, what is it?
2. Give five reasons why many behavior modifiers use the *DSM-IV-TR.*
3. What is a potential disadvantage of using the *DSM-IV-TR?*
4. What is meant by "people first language" when describing individuals with problems? Illustrate with an example.
5. Do behavior modifiers deny the importance of genetics? Discuss.

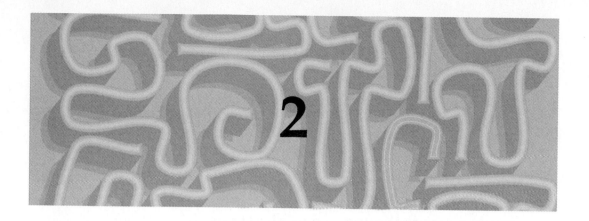

2

Areas of Application:
An Overview

The value of behavior modification techniques for improving a wide variety of behaviors has been amply demonstrated in thousands of research reports. Successful applications have been documented with populations ranging from persons with profound learning disabilities to the highly intelligent, with the very young and the very old, both in controlled institutional programs and in less controlled community settings. The behaviors have ranged from simple motor skills to complex intellectual problem solving. Applications are occurring with an ever-increasing frequency in such areas as education, social work, nursing, clinical psychology, psychiatry, community psychology, medicine, rehabilitation, business, industry, and sports. This chapter briefly describes major areas of application in which behavior modification has a solid foundation and a promising future.

PARENTING AND CHILD MANAGEMENT

Being a parent is a tremendously challenging job. In addition to meeting a child's basic needs, parents are totally responsible for their child's initial behavioral development, and they continue to share that responsibility with teachers and others as the child matures through the early school years, adolescence, and into adulthood. There are numerous applications of behavior modification to teach parents methods to improve their child-rearing practices. Behavioral techniques have been applied to help parents more effectively teach their children to walk, develop initial language skills, provide effective toilet training, and influence their children to do household chores (Kendall, 2000; Meadows, 1996). Parents have also been taught behavioral strategies for decreasing problem behaviors, such as nail biting, temper tantrums, aggressive behaviors, ignoring of rules, failure to comply with parents' requests, and frequent arguing (Christopherson & Mortweet, 2001; Schaefer & Briesmeister, 1998; Serketich & Dumas, 1996). Allen and Warzak (2000) provided a useful analysis of conditions that strengthen or weaken adherence by parents to effective behavioral programs with their children. Some child and adolescent behavior problems are complex enough that, in addition to helping parents work with their children, behaviorally oriented clinical psychologists treat the problems directly (Blum & Friman, 2000; Gimpel & Holland, 2003; Hersen & Last, 1999; Watson & Gresham, 1998).

EDUCATION: FROM PRESCHOOL TO UNIVERSITY

Since the early 1960s, behavior modification applications in classrooms have progressed on several fronts. Many applications in elementary school were designed to change student behaviors that were disruptive or incompatible with academic learning. Out-of-seat behavior, tantrums, aggressive behavior, excessive socializing—all have been successfully dealt with in classroom settings. Other applications have been concerned with modifying academic behavior directly, including oral reading, reading comprehension, spelling, handwriting, mathematics, English composition, creativity, and mastering science concepts. Considerable success has also been achieved in applications with individuals with special problems, such as learning-disabled and hyperactive children (Barkley, 1998).

Inroads have also been made in the use of behavior modification in physical education. The progress that has been made includes (a) development of reliable observations for monitoring the behavior of physical education teachers and students so as to provide usable information on "what's happening in the gym"; (b) increased acceptance of behavioral teaching skills as important components of teacher preparation programs; and (c) increased acceptance of behavioral strategies to help physical educators manage a variety of behavioral difficulties of students (Martin, 1992). Discussions of behavior modification in physical education can be found in Siedentop and Tannehill (2000) and Ward (2005).

An important innovation in behavioral approaches to teaching is the Personalized System of Instruction (PSI). PSI was developed by Fred S. Keller and his colleagues in the United States and Brazil in the 1960s as a behavior modification approach to university teaching (Keller, 1968). Since then it has spread to a wide variety of subject matters and levels of instruction (Keller & Sherman, 1982). The approach has a number of distinctive characteristics that make it possible for teachers to use principles of behavior modification effectively to improve classroom instruction. In particular, PSI (also known as the Keller plan):

1. identifies the target behaviors or learning requirements for a course in the form of study questions, such as the questions at the end of each chapter in this book;
2. requires students to study only a small amount of material before demonstrating mastery, such as the amount of material in one or two chapters that might be studied in a week or two;
3. has frequent tests (at least once every week or two) in which students demonstrate their knowledge of the answers to the study questions;

4. has mastery criteria so that students must demonstrate mastery at a particular level before going on to the next level;
5. is nonpunitive, in that students are not penalized for failing to demonstrate mastery on a test but simply restudy and try again;
6. uses a number of student assistants (called proctors) to score tests immediately and provide feedback to students concerning test performance;
7. incorporates a "go-at-your-own-pace" feature in which students are allowed to proceed through the course material at rates that suit their own particular abilities and time demands;

Note 1

8. uses lectures primarily for motivation and demonstration, rather than as a major means of presenting new information.

As originally conceived by Keller (1968), PSI courses can require a good deal of labor to administer, especially with large classes, because of the extensive record keeping that PSI requires. With the rise of computer technology, some instructors have automated much of the PSI procedure to make it more efficient. Moreover, some instructors have added electronic backup components, such as videotapes, interactive videodiscs, and computer-delivered tutorials, to increase the efficiency of PSI (Crosbie & Glenn, 1993; Crowell, Quintanar, & Grant, 1981; Hantula, Boyd, & Crowell, 1989; Rae, 1993). In addition, computers that are part of networks have built-in telecommunications capabilities (e.g., electronic mail) that enable students to write and submit tests for marking, and that allow instructors and proctors to mark tests and provide rapid feedback without the instructor, proctors, and students having to be at the same location or working on the course at the same time. This can be of great benefit to students who are unable to attend classes because of where they live, their job, or a disability. At the University of Manitoba, where it has been used for a number of years in several psychology courses, computer-aided PSI (called CAPSI) is popular with both on-campus and off-campus students (Kinsner & Pear, 1988; Pear & Crone-Todd, 1999; Pear & Kinsner, 1988; Pear & Novak, 1996). Studies have demonstrated measurable feedback accuracy by proctors and compliance with feedback by students in a CAPSI-taught course (Martin, Pear, & Martin, 2002a, b). In addition, students receive much more substantive feedback than would be possible in a course taught by traditional methods (Pear & Crone-Todd, 2002). CAPSI is now on the World Wide Web and is used at several universities. (For a review of CAPSI, see Pear and Martin, 2004.)

Excellent "how-to" descriptions of behavior modification techniques for teachers have been published by Alberto and Troutman (2004), Cipani (2004a), and Schloss and Schloss (2004). Discussion of behavior analysis and school psychology can be found in Ervin and Ehrhardt (2000) and Frederick, Deitz, Bryceland, and Hummel (2003). Discussions of behavioral approaches to college teaching, including PSI, can be found in Austin (2000b).

SEVERE PROBLEMS: DEVELOPMENTAL DISABILITIES, CHILDHOOD AUTISM, AND SCHIZOPHRENIA

Beginning in the 1960s, some of the most dramatic successes of behavior modification have occurred in applications to individuals with severe behavioral handicaps.

Developmental Disabilities

Although the term *developmental disability* has replaced the term *mental retardation* among most professionals who treat this type of problem, in 2002 the American Association on Mental Retardation (AAMR) decided to retain the earlier term. Their definition states:

> Mental retardation is a disability characterized by significant limitations both in intellectual functioning and in adaptive behavior as expressed in conceptual, social, and practical adaptive skills. This disability originates before age 18. (2002, p. 8)

In the AAMR definition, limited intellectual functioning is defined as an IQ score that is at least two standard deviations below the mean of an appropriate assessment instrument, which would be a score approximately 70 to 75 or below on some IQ tests. This includes approximately 2.3% of the population. In 1992, the AAMR proposed that the previously used categories of mild, moderate, severe, and profound mental retardation no longer be used. Instead, they proposed that individuals be classified according to the intensity and pattern of support that they require (intermittent, limited, extensive, or pervasive). Although researchers often still find the more traditional diagnostic categories of mild, moderate, severe, and profound mental retardation useful (Conyers, Martin, Martin, & Yu, 2002), the 2002 AAMR definition places a greater emphasis on assessing and improving an individual's adaptive behavior than did definitions prior to 1992. This changed emphasis was a result of several developments during the past four decades.

Before the 1960s, treatment and training programs for all levels of developmental disabilities were minimal, and were most limited for the severe and profound levels. Fortunately, three forces materialized that, collectively, revolutionized the education of persons with developmental disabilities. One force was represented by normalization advocates, such as Wolfensberger (1972), who argued that persons with developmental disabilities should be helped to lead the most normative lives possible, and that traditional large institutions were simply not normative. This led to a deinstitutionalization movement and the development of community living options for persons with developmental disabilities. The second force was represented by civil rights advocates and parents of persons with developmental disabilities, who secured the legal right of individuals with severe handicaps to receive an education. This meant that educational programs for persons with developmental disabilities had to be established. The third force came primarily through the efforts of behavior modifiers, who created the technology that made it possible to dramatically improve the behavior of persons with severe and profound developmental disabilities.

During the ensuing decades, many studies have demonstrated the applicability of behavioral techniques for teaching persons with developmental disabilities such behaviors as toileting, self-help skills (i.e., feeding, dressing, and personal hygiene), social skills, communication skills, vocational skills, leisure-time activities, and a variety of community survival behaviors. Reviews of the literature can be found in such sources as Carr, Coriaty, and Dozier (2000), Cuvo and Davis (2000), Konarski, Favell, and Favell (1997), and Williams (2004); see also issues of the *Journal of Applied Behavior Analysis*.

Childhood Autism

Children diagnosed with autism often show some behaviors similar to children diagnosed with developmental disabilities in that they score much below average on a variety of self-care tasks, such as dressing, grooming, and feeding. However, they are also likely to show some combination of impaired social behavior (e.g., not showing distress when their mother leaves the room), impaired communication (e.g., repeating words or phrases without indicating that the words convey any meaning), abnormal play behaviors, and repetitive self-stimulatory behaviors (e.g., spinning objects in front of their eyes).

Beginning in the 1960s and continuing to the present, Ivar Lovaas (1966) and others developed behavioral treatments for children with autism. Using behavior change techniques, Lovaas (1977) focused on strategies to teach social behaviors, eliminate self-stimulatory behaviors, and develop language skills. When his intensive treatment programs were applied to children with autism less than 30 months old, 50% of those children were able to enter a regular classroom at the normal school age (Lovaas, 1982), and the behavioral treatment produced long-lasting gains (McEachin, Smith, & Lovaas, 1993). While reviewers have raised important questions concerning experimental design limitations of the Lovaas study (e.g., Gresham & MacMillan, 1997), no alternative treatment for children with autism has been shown to be as successful as applied behavior analysis (Frea & Vittimberga, 2000; Ghezzi, Williams, & Carr, 1999; Lovaas, 1993). There are now an increasing number of government-funded programs providing behavior analysis training for children with autism. In Canada, for example, at the time of this writing, such programs are available in seven of the 10 provinces.

Schizophrenia

Beginning with a few case studies in the 1950s, major attention was directed toward schizophrenia by behavior therapists in the 1960s and early 1970s (Kazdin, 1978). During the late 1970s and early 1980s, however, interest in this area decreased and only a small number of articles on behavior modification were published (Bellack, 1986). There is, nevertheless, clear evidence of the success of behavior modification treatments with this population. Because inadequate social relationships are a prime contributor to the poor quality of life experienced by people with schizophrenia, social skills have been one of the behaviors targeted for change. Available research indicates considerable success in teaching positive social interactions, communication skills, assertiveness skills, and job-finding skills (Bellack & Hersen, 1993; Bellack & Muser, 1990; Bellack, Muser, Gingerich, & Agresta, 1997). Cognitive-behavioral techniques have also been used effectively to reduce or eliminate hallucinations or delusions in persons with schizophrenia (Bouchard, Vallieres, Roy, & Maziade, 1996). These and other studies strongly indicate that behavior therapy can make a significant contribution to the treatment, management, and rehabilitation of persons with schizophrenia (McKinney & Fiedler, 2004; Wong & Liberman, 1996).

CLINICAL BEHAVIOR THERAPY

Behavioral treatment of people who are treated by therapists in office settings has steadily increased since the 1970s. In Chapters 27 and 28, we provide a detailed discussion of the treatment of such clinical problems as anxiety disorders, obsessive-compulsive disorders, stress-related problems, depression, obesity, marital problems, sexual dysfunction, and habit disorders. More detailed discussion of these and other areas of clinical treatment can be found in Antony and Barlow (2004), Dougher (2000), Emmelkamp (2004), Hayes and Bissett (2000), and Hayes, Follette, and Linehan (2004).

How common is behavior therapy among practicing psychologists? By the early 1980s, surveys indicated that at least half of clinical child psychologists followed a behavioral orientation, and that behavior therapy had become one of the top two orientations (about on par with the psychodynamic orientation) for psychologists treating adults (O'Leary, 1984). While many behavioral psychologists are likely to qualify their orientation as "cognitive behavioral" rather than straight behavioral (cognitive behavior modification is discussed in Chapter 27), the behavioral approach in general continues to grow.

How effective is behavior therapy with clinical populations? Many studies have demonstrated that there are clear problem areas (e.g., phobias, obsessive-compulsive disorders) in which specific behavior therapy procedures are demonstrably superior to existing psychotherapeutic alternatives. In some cases, the treatment of choice may be a combination of behavior therapy and medical treatments (such as drugs). Behavioral treatments for clinical disorders are discussed further in Chapter 28.

SELF-MANAGEMENT OF PERSONAL PROBLEMS

Recall some of the problems described in Chapter 1. Sam had difficulty studying and finishing his term papers on time. Karen was not able to get started on that novel she wanted to write. And then there was Albert and his phobia of riding in airplanes. Many people would like to change something about themselves. How about you? Would you like to lose a few pounds? Get into an exercise program? Become more assertive? Are there skills you can learn to help you to modify your behavior? A great deal of progress has been made in the area referred to as self-management, self-control, self-adjustment, self-modification, or self-direction. Successful self-modification requires a set of skills that can be learned. These skills involve ways of rearranging your environment to control your subsequent behavior. Hundreds of successful self-modification projects directed at problems such as saving money, increasing exercise behavior, improving study habits, and controlling gambling have been reported in the psychological literature (Logue, 1995). Self-modification for personal adjustment is described in more detail in Chapter 26. Extensive discussion of this topic can be found in Watson and Tharp (2003).

MEDICAL AND HEALTH CARE

Traditionally, a person who suffered from chronic headaches, a respiratory disorder, or hypertension would see a physician. In the late 1960s, however, psychologists working with physicians began using behavior modification techniques to treat these and other medical problems such as seizure disorders, chronic pain, addictive disorders, and sleep disorders (Doleys, Meredith, & Ciminero, 1982). This launched *behavioral medicine,* a broad interdisciplinary field concerned with the links among health, illness, and behavior (Searight, 1998). Behavioral psychologists practicing behavioral medicine work in close consultation with physicians, nurses, dieticians, sociologists, and other specialists on problems that, until recently, have been considered to be of a purely medical nature. Within behavioral medicine, *health psychology* considers how psychological factors can influence or cause illness, and how people can be encouraged to practice healthy behavior so as to prevent health problems (Taylor, 2003). Health psychologists have applied behavioral principles in five major areas.

1. *Direct Treatment of Medical Problems.* Do you suffer from migraine headaches, backaches, or stomach problems? At one time it was thought that such problems were of purely a medical nature. But sometimes such problems have an environmental connection. Health psychologists are continuing the trend of the late 1960s of developing behavioral techniques to treat symptoms such as these directly (Taylor, 2003). One such technique is called *biofeedback,* which consists of providing immediate information to an individual about that person's physiological processes, such as heart rate, blood pressure, muscle tension, and brain waves. Such information helps the individual to gain control over the physiological process that is monitored. Biofeedback has been successfully used to treat a variety of health problems, including high blood pressure, seizures, chronic headaches, cardiac arrhythmia, accelerated heart rate, and anxiety (Schwartz & Andrasic, 1998; also see p. 135). Behavioral treatments are also being applied to ameliorate symptoms of other medical problems, such as Parkinson's disease (Mohr et al., 1996), and brain injury (Jacobs, 2000).

2. *Establishing Treatment Compliance.* Do you always keep your appointments with the dentist? Do you always take medication exactly as prescribed by your doctor? Many people do not. Because it is behavior, compliance with medical regimens is a natural for behavior modification (Taylor, 2003). Thus, an important part of health psychology is promoting treatment compliance.

3. *Promotion of Healthy Living.* Do you exercise at least three times per week? Do you eat healthy foods and minimize your consumption of saturated fat, cholesterol, and salt? Do you limit your consumption of alcohol, say, to no more than five drinks a week? Do you say no to nicotine and other addictive drugs? If you can answer yes to these questions, and if you can continue to answer yes as the years go by, then you can considerably lengthen your life span (see Figure 2–1). As indicated in Chapter 1, preventable behaviors such as tobacco use, poor diet, and physical inactivity are the underlying cause of half of the deaths in the United

Figure 2–1 Behavioral strategies have been used effectively to help people persist in physical fitness programs.

States (see the March 2004 issue of the *Journal of the American Medical Association* and the January 2003 issue of *Behavior Modification*). An important area of behavior modification involves the application of techniques to help people manage their own behavior to stay healthy, such as by eating well-balanced meals and getting adequate exercise (Taylor, 2003; Williamson, Champagne, Jackman, & Varnado, 1996).

4. *Management of Caregivers.* Health psychologists are concerned not only with the behavior of the client or patient, but also with the behavior of those who have an impact on the medical condition of the client. Thus, health psychologists deal with the behavior of the client's family, friends, and various medical staff. Changing the behavior of physicians, nurses, psychiatric nurses, occupational therapists, and other medical personnel to improve service provided to patients is receiving increased attention (see, e.g., Engelman, Altus, Mosier, & Mathews, 2003; Hrydowy & Martin, 1994).

5. *Stress Management.* Like death and taxes, stress is one of the things that you can be sure of encountering in life. Stressors are conditions or events (e.g., being stuck in traffic, lack of sleep, smog, pending examinations, debts, marital breakdown, and serious illness or death in the family) that present coping difficulties. Stress reactions are physiological and behavioral responses, such as fatigue, high blood pressure, and ulcers that are brought on by stressors. An important area of health psychology concerns the study of stressors, their effects on behavior, and the development of behavioral strategies for coping with stressors (e.g., Moller, Milinski, & Slater, 1998; Taylor, 2003). Some of these strategies are described in later chapters.

The broad interdisciplinary field of behavioral medicine and the subfield of health psychology have the potential to make a profound contribution to the efficiency and effectiveness of modern medicine and health care. For additional reading in this area, see issues of the *Journal of Behavioral Medicine,* and the books by Cummings, O'Donohue, and Ferguson (2003) and Taylor (2003).

GERONTOLOGY

Do you want to know what it's like to be old? Then "you should smear dirt on your glasses, stuff cotton in your ears, put on heavy shoes that are too big for you, and wear gloves, and then try to spend the day in a normal way" (Skinner & Vaughan, 1983, p. 38). As an increasing percentage of the population is elderly, more and more individuals must deal on a daily basis with the loss of skills and ability to function independently that occurs with old age or with chronic illness. Once again, behavior modification can make a positive contribution. For example, habitual ways of performing daily routines at home or at work may no longer be possible. New routines must be developed and learned. Anxiety or fear about the possibility of failing to cope also might have to be dealt with. Disruptive behaviors in nursing homes may have to be decreased. And new relationships might have to be developed with professional care staff. Behavioral techniques are being used increasingly to help the elderly and chronic-care patients to solve such problems (Coon & Thompson, 2002; Derenne & Baron, 2002; Dick-Siskin, 2002; Wetherall, 2002; Wisocki, 1999).

COMMUNITY BEHAVIORAL ANALYSIS

As you will read in Chapter 29, which gives a brief history of behavior modification, the bulk of the early (1950s) applications were done with individuals (such as persons with developmental disabilities and psychiatric patients) who experienced severe problems, and took place in institutional or highly controlled settings. By the 1970s, however, important behavior modification projects were occurring in such areas as controlling littering in public campgrounds, increasing recycling of returnable soft drink containers, helping community boards to problem solve, promoting energy conservation by increasing bus ridership, encouraging welfare recipients to attend self-help meetings, and helping college students live together in a cooperative housing project (for reviews of the early research in these areas, see Geller, Winett, & Everett, 1982; Martin & Osborne, 1980). The scope of behavior modification had clearly expanded from individual problems to community concerns. One of the early studies in this area defined behavioral community psychology as "applications to socially significant problems in unstructured community settings where the behavior of individuals is not considered deviant in the traditional sense" (Briscoe, Hoffman, & Bailey, 1975, p. 57).

Glenwick (1990) identified five trends in behavioral community applications. The first is greater involvement of the target populations in all aspects of the intervention process. If, for example, an overall goal in an AIDS treatment program is to increase glove wearing by nurses (see, e.g., DeVries, Burnette, & Redmon, 1991), then the nurses would be fully involved in selecting subgoals, choosing an intervention, and monitoring the results. Second, there is increased fostering of the target individual's personal control (vs. control by professionals). In the project with nurses, there might be an emphasis on self-control techniques (described in Chapter 26) to increase their glove wearing, rather than relying on their being told to do so by the head nurse. Third, there is increased inclusion of subjective assessments when evaluating treatment outcomes. Objectively, one might assess whether or not the nurses are wearing gloves more often. Subjectively, we would want to know how they feel about the overall program (subjective assessment is discussed further in Chapter 23). Fourth, there is increased emphasis on antecedent events (the intervention with the nurses might rely on posted reminders and the example of senior staff wearing their gloves) versus consequent events (such as praising the nurses for wearing their gloves). (Issues regarding antecedent and consequent events are discussed in Chapters 8, 17, 18, and 19.) Finally, there is greater interdisciplinary collaboration among professionals. For additional readings in community behavioral analysis, see issues of the *Journal of Applied Behavior Analysis*.

BUSINESS, INDUSTRY, AND GOVERNMENT

Behavior modification has also been applied to improve the performance of individuals in a wide variety of organizational settings. This general area has been referred to as *organizational behavior management* (OBM), which has been defined as the application of behavioral principles and methods to the study and control of individual or group behavior within organizational settings (Frederiksen & Lovett, 1980). Other labels used interchangeably with organizational behavior management include *performance management, industrial behavior modification, organizational behavior modification, organizational behavior technology,* and *organizational behavior analysis.* Like all areas of application in this overview, organizational behavior management is data oriented. It emphasizes specific activities of staff that characterize successful performances or produce successful results. It also emphasizes frequent feedback and rewards for employees who show desirable behaviors. Examples of the types of organizations involved range from small businesses to large corporations and from small community centers (note the overlap with behavioral community psychology) to large state hospitals. Thus, OBM is concerned with organizations both small and large, private and public.

One of the earliest studies in what was to become the field of OBM was carried out at the Emery Air Freight Company. According to an article titled "Conversations with B. F. Skinner" in the 1973 issue of *Organizational Dynamics,* the desired behavior—employees' placement of packages in special containers—was increased from 45% to 95% through the use of positive reinforcement in the form of praise from supervisors.

Other studies since then have used behavioral techniques to change behavior in ways that improve productivity, decrease tardiness and absenteeism, increase sales volume, create new business, improve worker safety, reduce theft by employees, reduce shoplifting, and improve management-employee relations. For additional reading in this area, see Austin (2000a), Johnson, Redmon, and

Mawhinney (2001), Poling, Dickinson, Austin, and Normand (2000), Reid and Parsons (2000), and issues of the *Journal of Organizational Behavior Management.*

SPORT PSYCHOLOGY

Since the early 1970s, there has been a growing desire on the part of coaches and athletes for more applied sport science research, particularly in the area of sport psychology. *Applied sport psychology* has been defined as the use of psychological knowledge to enhance athletic performance and the satisfaction of athletes and others associated with sports (Blimke, Gowan, Patterson, & Wood, 1984). Behavior modification has made a number of contributions to this area (Martin, 2003; Martin, Thomson, & Regehr, 2004).

Techniques for Improving Skills of Athletes   What is the most effective way to help an athlete learn new skills, eliminate bad habits, and combine simple skills into complex patterns of execution? Considerable research has examined behavior modification techniques for effectively improving athletes' skills (Martin & Tkachuk, 2000) and practical strategies for applying these techniques have been described (Martin, 2003).

Strategies for Motivating Practice and Endurance Training   How can a coach effectively improve attendance at practices, motivate athletes to get the most out of practice time, and organize practices so that there is little downtime? Techniques for solving these types of problems include goal-setting strategies, reinforcement (or reward) strategies, self-recording and self-monitoring by individual athletes, and team-building sessions (Martin, 2003). All of these motivational techniques are based on principles described in later chapters of this book and can readily be learned by coaches.

Changing the Behavior of Coaches   Coaches have a very difficult job. From a behavior modification perspective, a coach must effectively instruct, set goals, praise, reprimand, and perform other activities that, collectively, determine his or her effectiveness as a behavior modifier. Numerous research studies have been conducted in this area (Martin & Tkachuk, 2000).

"Sports Psyching" to Prepare for Competition   We have all heard expressions such as "The reason the team lost was that they were psyched-out," or "If you want to do your best, you have to get psyched-up." While we may have some general ideas as to what these kinds of phrases mean, knowing generally what they mean and learning how to teach psychological coping skills to athletes are two different things. A number of behavioral strategies have been described for helping athletes prepare for serious competition in sport (see recent issues of *The Sport Psychologist,* and books by Martin, 2003, and Martin, Toogood, & Tkachuk, 1997).

BEHAVIOR MODIFICATION WITH CULTURALLY DIVERSE INDIVIDUALS

Behavior modifiers have begun to pay more attention to issues of race, gender, ethnicity, and sexual orientation as variables that can influence the effectiveness of treatment (see, e.g., Hatch, Friedman, & Paradis, 1996; Iwamasa, 1999; Iwamasa & Smith,

1996; Paradis, Friedman, Hatch, & Ackerman, 1996; Purcell, Campos, & Perilla, 1996). It is helpful, for example, for therapists to know that many Asian American clients prefer to be told specifically what to do by the therapist (as opposed to a more nondirective approach) (Chen, 1995). On the other hand, with many Hispanic American clients, compliance with specific goal-directed suggestions is likely to be more effective if they are preceded by a period of familiarizing "small talk" (Tanaka-Matsumi & Higginbotham, 1994). As another example, Dr. Tawa Witko, a psychologist who, at the time of this writing, lived and practiced on a Lakota Sioux reservation near the Badlands in South Dakota, described the case of an individual on the reservation who had been diagnosed by a psychologist as schizophrenic because he heard voices, especially around ceremony times. Dr. Witko explained that if the therapist had dug deeper, she would have found that this phenomenon is common among Native Americans, has spiritual meaning, and does not on its own indicate mental illness (Winerman, 2004). Although such information can be helpful for therapists, we must also be sensitive to the dangers of overgeneralizing about any particular cultural group. (Cautions similar to those we made earlier about the dangers of labeling are relevant here.) As Iwamasa (1999) pointed out, for example, the Asian American population is comprised of over 30 different cultural and ethnic groups, and each has its own language, values, lifestyles, and patterns of adaptation to the United States. As another example, it might be appropriate to select increased eye contact as a target behavior for a social skills training program for some Native Americans, but doing so would be inappropriate for Navajos because, in their culture, prolonged eye contact is typically considered to be an aggressive behavior (Tanaka-Matsumi, Higginbotham, & Chang, 2002). Readers interested in behavioral treatment with culturally diverse clients are encouraged to examine the special issues on cultural diversity in *Cognitive and Behavioral Practice* (1996, Vol. 3, No. 1) and in *The Behavior Therapist* (1999, Vol. 22, No. 10).

CONCLUSION

The rise of behavior modification as a successful approach for dealing with a wide range of human problems has been remarkable. Books and journal articles describe behavioral procedures and research ranging from child rising to coping with old age and from work to play. It has been used both with persons with profound handicaps and with gifted students, for self-improvement, and to preserve
Note 2 the environment in which we live. Several thousand books have been published concerning basic, applied, and theoretical issues in behavior modification. At least 31 journals are predominantly behavioral in their orientation. Examples of applications in many of these areas are described and illustrated in the following chapters.

STUDY QUESTIONS

1. List five areas in which behavior modification is being applied.
2. List four behaviors of children that have been improved by the application of behavior modification by parents.

3. List four behaviors in education that have been modified with behavior modification.

4. What is PSI, and who was its founder? State eight characteristics of PSI.

5. Briefly describe how PSI has made use of computer technology. State two benefits of this use of computer technology.

6. Name and briefly describe the three forces that have revolutionized the education of persons with developmental disabilities since the 1960s.

7. List four behaviors in persons with developmental disabilities that have been modified by behavior modification.

8. List four behaviors in children with autism that have been modified by behavior modification.

9. List four behaviors in people with schizophrenia that have been modified by behavior modification.

10. List four behaviors in the area of self-management of personal problems that have been modified by behavior modification.

11. What is health psychology?

12. Describe five areas of application within health psychology.

13. List four behaviors of elderly persons that have been improved with behavior modification.

14. What is behavioral community psychology?

15. List five current trends in behavioral community applications.

16. List four behaviors in the area of behavioral community psychology that have been modified by behavior modification.

17. Define organizational behavior management.

18. List four behaviors in business, industry, or government that have been modified by behavior modification. (Be sure that you are referring to actual behaviors, and not just products of behavior.)

19. List four general areas of sport psychology in which behavior modification has been applied.

20. Describe how knowledge of a cultural characteristic might be helpful for behavior modifiers working with individuals from different cultures. Give an example.

NOTES AND EXTENDED DISCUSSION

1. Lecturing (in combination with two or three exams per semester) continues to be the overwhelming method of choice for teaching undergraduates in most universities (Terenzini & Pascarella, 1994). A number of studies have consistently demonstrated that PSI is more effective in enhancing learning of the subject matter than is the more traditional approach (Kulik, Kulik, & Bangert-Drowns, 1990). In fact, PSI has produced a statistically significant average learning advantage of 19 percentile points over traditional approaches (Pascarella & Terenzini, 1991). Course evaluations indicate that most students strongly praise such a system and identify frequent exams as being responsible for generating extensive and well-paced study (Michael, 1991).

2. Wyatt, Hawkins, and Davis (1986) critiqued the claim by some nonbehavioral psychologists that behaviorism—the philosophy behind behavior modification—is dead. They argued that it is very much alive and growing. Part of the evidence is the abundance of journals that are primarily behavioral in orientation, including the following: *Behavior Analysts for Social Action* (1980–), originally *Behaviorists for Social*

Action; Behavior and Social Issues (1991–); *Behaviour Change* (1984–), the official journal of the Australian Behavior Modification Association, which changed its name in 1995 to the Australian Association for Cognitive and Behavior Therapy; *Behavior Modification* (1977–); *Behavior Research and Therapy* (1963–); *Behavior Therapy* (1970–); *Behavioral and Cognitive Psychotherapy* (1973–), originally *Behavioral Psychotherapy; Behavioral Counselling Quarterly* (1981–); *Behavioral Interventions* (1986–); *Behavioral Processes* (1981–), originally *Behavior Analysis Newsletters; Behavioral Residential Treatment* (1986–); *Child and Family Behavior Therapy* (1979–), originally *Child Behavior Therapy; Education and Treatment of Children* (1969–), originally *School Applications of Learning Theory; Japanese Journal of Behavior Therapy* (1976–); *Journal of Applied Behavior Analysis* (1968–); *Journal of Behavior Therapy and Experimental Psychiatry* (1970–); *Journal of Behavioral Education* (1991–); *Journal of the Experimental Analysis of Behavior* (1958–); *Journal of Organizational Behavior Management* (1978–); *Journal of Psychopathology and Behavioral Assessment* (1979–), originally *Journal of Behavioral Assessment; Journal of Rational-Emotive and Cognitive Behavior Therapy* (1983–); *La Technologie du Comportment* (1977–); *Mexican Journal of Behavior Analysis* (1975–); *Research in Developmental Disabilities* (1987–) (in 1987, *Applied Research in Mental Retardation* [1980–86] and *Analysis and Intervention in Developmental Disabilities* [1981–1986] were collapsed into one journal); *Scandanavian Journal of Behavior Therapy* (1972–); *The Behavior Analyst* (1978–); *The Behavior Therapist* (1978–).

Study Questions on Notes

1.   Which is more effective for teaching undergraduates, the traditional lecturing approach or PSI? Justify your choice.
2.   What is behaviorism? Is it dead, sleeping, or very much alive? Justify your answer.

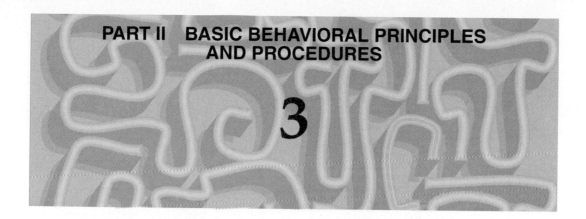

3

Getting a Behavior to Occur More Often with Positive Reinforcement

"Do you want to sit here, Mommy?"

REINFORCING DARREN'S COOPERATIVE BEHAVIOR[1]

Six-year-old Darren was extremely uncooperative with his parents. In the hope of learning how to deal more effectively with his excessive commanding behavior, Darren's parents took him to the Gatzert Child Developmental Clinic at the University of Washington. As his parents put it, Darren virtually "ran the show," deciding when he would go to bed, what foods he would eat, when his parents could play with him, and so on. To obtain direct observations of Darren's behavior, both cooperative and unco-operative, Dr. Robert Wahler asked Darren's mother to spend some time with Darren in a playroom at the clinic. The playroom was equipped with adjoining observation rooms for data recording. During the first two 20-minute sessions (called a baseline phase[2]), Darren's mother was instructed: "Just play with Darren as you might at home." Darren's commanding behavior was defined as any verbal or nonverbal instructions to his mother, such as pushing her into a chair or saying such things as "You go over there and I'll stay here," or "No, that's wrong. Do it this way." Cooperative behavior was defined as any noncommanding statements, actions, or questions, such as, "Do you want to sit here?" while pointing to a chair. To illustrate the consistency of Darren's

---

[1]This example is based on an article by Wahler, Winkel, Peterson, and Morrison (1965).
[2]A *baseline phase* (discussed further in Chapter 23) is a measure of behavior in the absence of a treatment program.

behavior, Figure 3–1 is a graph of the data collected in consecutive 10-minute intervals. As can be seen, Darren showed a very low rate of cooperative behavior during the baseline sessions. His commanding behavior (not shown in the figure), on the other hand, occurred at an extremely high rate. Following the baseline sessions, Darren's mother was asked to be very positive and supportive to any instances of cooperative behavior shown by Darren. At the same time, she was instructed to completely ignore his commanding behavior. Over the next two sessions, Darren's cooperative behavior steadily increased. (During the same time, his commanding behavior decreased to near zero.) Further experimentation was done by Dr. Wahler and his colleagues to demonstrate that Darren's improvement resulted from the positive consequences provided by his mother following instances of Darren's cooperative behavior (in conjunction with her ignoring of commanding behavior).

POSITIVE REINFORCEMENT

A **positive reinforcer** is an event that, when presented immediately following a behavior, causes the behavior to increase in frequency (or likelihood of occurrence). The term *positive reinforcer* is roughly synonymous with the word *reward*. Once an event has been determined to function as a positive reinforcer for a particular individual in a particular situation, that event can be used to strengthen other behaviors of that individual in other situations. In conjunction with the concept of positive reinforcer, the principle called **positive reinforcement** states that *if, in a given situation, somebody does something that is followed immediately by a positive reinforcer, then that person is more likely to do the same thing again when he or she next encounters a similar situation.*

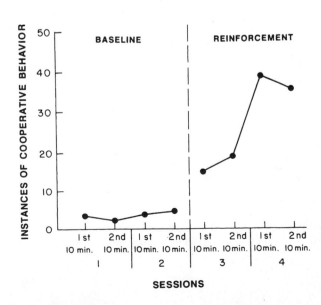

Figure 3–1   Darren's cooperative behavior. Each data point (dot) represents the total instances of Darren's cooperative behavior during a 10-minute interval within a session. Baseline refers to the observation phase prior to the reinforcement program. (Replotted from "Mothers as Behavior Therapists for Their Own Children," by R. G. Wahler, G. H. Winkel, R. F. Peterson, and D. C. Morrison, *Behavior Research and Therapy*, Vol. 3, 1965, Figure 1, p. 117. Copyright © 1965 with permission from Elsevier Science.)

Although everyone has a common sense notion of rewards, very few people are aware of just how frequently they are influenced by positive reinforcement during every day of their lives. Some examples of instances of positive reinforcement are shown in Table 3–1. (The terms *positive reinforcement* and *reinforcement* are often used interchangeably.)

The individuals in each of the examples in Table 3–1 were not consciously using the principle of reinforcement; they were just "doing what comes naturally." In each example, it might take several repetitions before there would be any really obvious increase in the reinforced response (that is, an increase that would be noticeable to a casual observer). Nevertheless, the effect is still there. Every time we do something, no matter what it is, there are consequences that "turn us on" or "turn us off" or don't affect us one way or the other. Think about some of your behaviors during the past hour. Were any of those behaviors followed immediately by reinforcing consequences? In some cases we may not be aware of these consequences and the effects they are having on our behavior.

Behaviors that operate on the environment to generate consequences, and are in turn influenced by those consequences, are called **operant behaviors** (or *operant responses*). Each of the responses listed in Table 3–1 is an example of operant behavior. Operant behaviors that are followed by reinforcers are strengthened, while operant behaviors that are followed by punishers (see Chapter 12) are weakened. A different type of behavior—reflexive behavior—is discussed in Chapters 14 and 15.

It is helpful to think about behavior in the same way that we think about other aspects of nature. What happens when you drop a shoe? It falls toward the earth. What happens to a lake when the temperature drops below $0°$ C? The water freezes. These are things that we all know about and that physicists have studied extensively and formulated into laws, such as the law of gravity. The principle of positive reinforcement is also a law. Scientific psychology has been studying this principle in great detail since the early part of the last century (e.g., Thorndike, 1911), and we know that it is an extremely important part of the learning process. We also know of a number of factors that determine the degree of influence the principle of reinforcement has on behavior. These factors have been formulated into guidelines to be followed when using positive reinforcement to strengthen desirable behavior.

FACTORS INFLUENCING THE EFFECTIVENESS OF POSITIVE REINFORCEMENT

1. Selecting the Behavior to Be Increased

The behaviors to be reinforced must first be identified specifically. If you start with a general behavior category (e.g., being more friendly), you should then identify specific behaviors (e.g., smiling) that characterize that category. By being specific in this way, you (a) help to ensure the reliability of detecting instances of the behavior and changes in its frequency, which is the yardstick by which one judges reinforcer effectiveness; and (b) increase the likelihood that the reinforcement program will be applied consistently.

TABLE 3–1   EXAMPLES OF INSTANCES OF REINFORCEMENT
OF DESIRABLE BEHAVIORS

Situation	Response	Immediate Consequences	Long-term effects
1. Mother is busy ironing in the kitchen.	Her 3-year-old daughter begins playing with baby brother.	Mother has just completed her ironing and sits down to play with daughter and baby brother for a brief period.	In the future, the daughter is more likely to play with baby brother when mother is ironing, because of the attention given when she began playing with her baby brother.
2. While you are waiting in a long line of cars for the light to change at a busy intersection, a car stops in the alley on your right.	You wave to the driver in the alley to pull into the line of traffic in front of you.	The driver nods and waves thanks to you and pulls into the line of traffic.	The pleasant feedback from the driver increases the likelihood that you will be courteous in similar situations in the future.
3. The students in a third-grade class have been given an assignment to complete.	Suzy, who is often quite disruptive, sits quietly at her desk and works on the assignment.	The teacher walks over to Suzy and pats her gently on the shoulder.	In the future, Suzy is more likely to work on the assignments given to her in class.
4. Father and child are shopping in a department store on a hot afternoon and both are very tired.	The child (uncharacteristically) follows father around the store quietly and without complaining.	Father turns to the child and says, "Let's go and buy an ice cream cone and sit down for a while."	On future shopping excursions, the child is more likely to follow father quietly.
5. A woman has just tasted a batch of soup she made, and it tasted very bland.	She adds a little Worcestershire sauce.	"It tastes very tangy, just like minestrone soup," she says to herself.	There is an increased likelihood that, in similar situations in the future, she will add Worcestershire sauce to her soup.
6. A husband and wife are undressing and getting ready for bed.	The husband picks up the wife's underwear and places it in the laundry hamper.	His wife pats him and murmurs her thanks.	On future evenings, the husband is more likely to put his wife's underwear in the laundry hamper.
7. One of the authors of this book is attempting to dictate some material into a tape recorder, but it is not working.	The author jiggles one of the wires attached to the microphone.	The tape recorder starts working.	The likelihood of wire jiggling will increase in similar situations in the future.

2. Choosing Reinforcers ("Different Strokes for Different Folks")

Some stimuli are positive reinforcers for virtually everyone. Food is a positive reinforcer for almost anyone who has not had anything to eat for several hours. Candy is a reinforcer for most children. On the other hand, different individuals are frequently turned on by different things. Consider the case of Dianne, a 6-year-old girl with a developmental disability who was in a project conducted by one of the authors. She was able to mimic a number of words, and we were trying to teach her to name pictures. Two reinforcers commonly used in the project were candy and bites of the child's supper, but neither of these proved effective with Dianne. She spat them out about as often as she ate them. After trying many other potential reinforcers, we finally discovered that allowing her to play with a toy purse for 15 seconds was very reinforcing. As a result, after many hours of training she is now speaking in phrases and complete sentences. For another child, listening to a music box for a few seconds turned out to be an effective reinforcer after other potential reinforcers failed. These stimuli might not have been reinforcing for everyone, but that is not important. The important thing is to use a reinforcer that is effective with the individual with whom you are working.

It is important to keep in mind that positive reinforcers are events that strengthen a response when they are introduced or added following the response. The removal of an event following a response may also strengthen that response, but this is not positive reinforcement. For example, a parent might nag a teenager to do the dishes. When the child complies, the nagging stops. Although the cessation of nagging when dishwashing occurs may strengthen the dishwashing response, it was the nagging's *removal* (not its introduction) following the response that strengthened it. (This process, which is referred to as *negative reinforcement* or *escape conditioning*, is discussed further in Chapter 13.)

Most positive reinforcers can be classified under five somewhat overlapping headings: *consumable, activity, manipulative, possessional*, and *social*. Consumable reinforcers are items that one can eat or drink (i.e., consume), such as candy, cookies, fruit, and soft drinks. Examples of activity reinforcers are the opportunities to watch television, look at a picture book, or even stare out of a window. Manipulative reinforcers include the opportunities to play with a favorite toy, color or paint, ride a bicycle, surf the Internet, or tinker with a tape recorder. Possessional reinforcers refer to the opportunities to sit in one's favorite chair, wear a favorite shirt or dress, have a private room, or enjoy some other item that one can possess (at least temporarily). Social reinforcement includes affectionate pats and hugs, praise, nods, smiles, and even a simple glance or other indication of social attention. Attention from others is a very strong reinforcer for almost everyone (see Figure 3–2).

In choosing effective reinforcers for an individual, it is often helpful to examine a list of reinforcers used by others (see Table 3–2) or to complete a reinforcer survey. An example of such a survey is shown in Figure 3–3.

A considerable amount of trial and error may be involved in finding an appropriate reinforcer for a particular individual. Another method is simply to

Figure 3–2   Praise is a powerful positive reinforcer for strengthening and maintaining valued behaviors in everyday life.

observe the individual in everyday activities and note those activities engaged in most often. This method makes use of a principle first formulated by David Premack (1959), which states that the opportunity to engage in a behavior that has a high probability of occurring can be used to reinforce a behavior that has a lower probability of occurring. For example, W. G. Johnson (1971) used this principle to help a depressed 17-year-old college student increase the frequency of positive self-statements. The student was asked to imagine a positive thought (a low-probability behavior) as prompted from a statement on an index card just before each instance of urinating (the high-probability behavior). After a few days, the student spontaneously thought the positive self-statements just before urinating, without the necessity of reviewing the index card. After two weeks of this procedure, the student reported that the positive thoughts were occurring at a high rate (and that the

TABLE 3–2   REINFORCERS FOR EMPLOYEES IN A VARIETY
OF WORK SETTINGS

SPECIAL-ATTENTION REINFORCERS	MONETARY REINFORCERS
Praise	Promotion
Praise in front of others	Paid days off
Special work assignments	Company stock
Reserved parking space	Company car
Choice of office	Pay for sick days not taken
Selection of own office furnishings	Pay for overtime accumulated
Invitation to higher-level meetings	Tickets to special events
Choice of work attire	Free raffle or lottery tickets
Social contacts with others	Extra furnishings for office
Solicitation of opinions and ideas	Gift certificates
Choice of work partner	Dinner for family at nice restaurant
Flexible job duties	Personalized license plate
	Personalized gifts
COMPANY-TIME REINFORCERS	Desk calculator or computer terminal
Time off for work-related activities	Business cards
Time off for personal business	Expense account
Extra break time	
Extra meal time	*PARTICIPATION REINFORCERS*
Choice of working hours or days off	Voice in policy decisions
	Help set standards
	More responsibility
	Opportunity to learn new skills

Note: From *Turning Around: The Behavioral Approach to Managing People* (p. 45), by Beverly Potter. All rights reserved. New York: AMACOM, a division of American Management Association. Copyright © 1980. Reprinted with permission.

depressive thoughts had completely disappeared). For a discussion of the limitations of the Premack principle, see Timberlake and Allison (1974) and Timberlake and Farmer-Dougan (1991).

It is often quite effective to allow an individual to choose among a number of available reinforcers (DeLeon & Iwata, 1996). Variety is not only the spice of life; it is also a valuable asset to a training program. For example, in a program for a person with developmental disabilities, a tray containing sliced fruits, peanuts, raisins, and diet drinks can be presented with the instruction to take one item. The advantage of this is that at least one reinforcer among the selection is likely to be strong. If the individual can read, the reinforcers can be listed in the form of a "reinforcer menu," and the preferred reinforcers can be chosen in the same way that one would order a meal at a restaurant. Matson and colleagues (1999) described a reinforcer menu that staff might use to select reinforcers for persons with severe and profound developmental disabilities.

No matter how you have selected a potential reinforcer for an individual, it is always the individual's performance that tells you whether or not you have selected an effective reinforcer. When you are not sure if a particular item is reinforcing, you can always conduct an experimental test that involves *going back to the definition of a reinforcer given at the beginning of this chapter*. Simply choose a behavior that the individual emits occasionally and that does not appear to be followed

This questionnaire is designed to help you find some specific activities, objects, events, or individuals that can be used as reinforcers in an improvement program. Read each question carefully and then fill in the appropriate blanks.

A Consumable reinforcers: What does this person like to eat or drink?
   1 What things does this person like to eat most?
      a regular meal-type foods _____
      b health foods—dried fruits, nuts, cereals, etc. _____
      _____
      c junk foods—popcorn, potato chips, etc. _____
      d sweets—candies, ice cream, cookies, etc. _____
   2 What things does this person like to drink most?
      a milk _____   c juices _____
      b soft drinks _____   d other _____

B Activity reinforcers: What things does this person like to do?
   1 Activities in the home or residence
      a hobbies _____
      b crafts _____
      c redecorating _____
      d preparing food or drinks _____
      e housework _____
      f odd jobs _____
      g other _____
   2 Activities in the yard or courtyard
      a sports _____
      b gardening _____
      c barbecue _____
      d yardwork _____
      e other _____
   3 Free activities in the neighborhood (window shopping, walking, jogging, cycling, driving, swinging, teeter-tottering, etc.) _____
      _____
   4 Free activities farther away from home (hiking, snow shoeing, swimming, camping, going to the beach, etc.) _____
      _____
   5 Activities you pay to do (films, plays, sports events, night clubs, pubs, etc.) _____
      _____
   6 Passive activities (watching TV, listening to the radio, records, or tapes; sitting, talking, bathing, etc.) _____
      _____

C Manipulative reinforcers: What kinds of games or toys interest this person?
   1 Toy cars and trucks _____
   2 Dolls _____
   3 Wind-up toys _____
   4 Balloons _____

(Continued)

Figure 3–3 A questionnaire to help an individual identify reinforcers.

    5 Whistle _____

    6 Jump rope _____

    7 Coloring books and crayons _____

    8 Painting kit _____

    9 Puzzles _____

  10 Other _____

D Possessional reinforcers: What kinds of things does this person like to possess?

    1 Brush _____

    2 Nail clippers _____

    3 Hair clips _____

    4 Comb _____

    5 Perfume _____

    6 Belt _____

    7 Gloves _____

    8 Shoelaces _____

    9 Other _____

E Social reinforcers: What kinds of verbal or physical stimulation does this person like to receive from others? (specify who)

    1 Verbal stimulation

       a "Good girl (boy)" _____

       b "Good work" _____

       c "Good job" _____

       d "That's fine" _____

       e "Keep up the good work" _____

       f other _____

    2 Physical contact

       a hugging _____

       b kissing _____

       c tickling _____

       d patty-cake _____

       e wrestling _____

       f bouncing on knee _____

       g other _____

Figure 3–3 *(Continued)*

by any reinforcer, record how often the behavior occurs without reinforcement over several trials, and then present the item immediate following the behavior for a few additional trials and see what happens. If the individual begins to emit that behavior more often, then your item is indeed a reinforcer. If the performance does not increase, then you do not have an effective reinforcer. In our experience, not using an effective reinforcer is a common error of training programs. For example, a teacher may claim that a particular reinforcement program that he is trying to use is failing. Upon examination, the reinforcer used may turn out not to be a reinforcer for the student. You can never really be sure that an item is a reinforcer for someone until it has been demonstrated to function as such for that person. In other words, an object or event *is defined as a reinforcer only by its effect on behavior.*

    If you deliberately use a tangible item to reinforce someone's behavior, will you undermine that person's "intrinsic motivation" to perform that behavior?

Some critics of behavior modification (e.g., Deci, Koestner, & Ryan, 1999) have suggested that you will. Some individuals (e.g., Kohn, 1993) have gone so far as to suggest that tangible rewards should never be given because, for example, if a parent gives a child money as a reinforcer for reading, then the child will be less likely to "read for reading's sake." However, a careful review of the experimental literature on this topic (Cameron, Banko, & Pierce, 2001), and two recent experiments (Flora & Flora, 1999; McGinnis, Friman, & Carlyon, 1999), clearly indicate that such a view is a myth. Moreover, the notion that extrinsic reinforcers undermine intrinsic interest flies in the face of common sense (Flora, 1990). If extrinsic reinforcers undermine intrinsic motivation, for example, then those fortunate people who genuinely enjoy their jobs should refuse to be paid (or demand only a minimal subsistence wage) for fear that their paychecks will destroy their enjoyment of their work. It is also worth noting that the extrinsic–intrinsic distinction between reinforcers may not even be valid: All reinforcers involve external (i.e., extrinsic) stimuli and all have internal (i.e., intrinsic) aspects.

3. Motivating Operations

Most reinforcers will not be effective unless the individual has been deprived of them for some period of time prior to their use. In general, the longer the deprivation period, the more effective the reinforcer will be. Sweets will usually not be reinforcing to a child who has just eaten a large bag of candy. Playing with a purse would not have been an effective reinforcer for Dianne had she been allowed to play with one prior to the training session. We use the term **deprivation** to indicate the time, prior to a training session, during which an individual does not experience the reinforcer. The term **satiation** refers to that condition in which the individual has experienced the reinforcer to such an extent that it is no longer reinforcing. "Enough's enough," as the saying goes.

Events or conditions—such as deprivation and satiation—that (a) temporarily alter the effectiveness of a reinforcer, and (b) alter the frequency of behavior reinforced by that reinforcer, are called **motivating operations (MOs)** (discussed further in Chapter 19). Thus, food deprivation not only establishes food as an effective reinforcer for the person who is food deprived, it also momentarily increases various behaviors that have been reinforced with food. As another example, feeding a child very salty food would be an MO. It would momentarily increase the effectiveness of water as a reinforcer for that child, and it would also evoke behavior (e.g., asking for a drink, turning on a tap) that had previously been followed by water. An MO might be thought of as a *motivational variable*—a variable that affects the likelihood and direction of behavior. Because it is genetically determined (i.e., not learned) that food deprivation increases the effectiveness of food as a reinforcer and salt ingestion increases the effectiveness of water as a reinforcer, these events are called *unconditioned motivating operations*. In Chapter 19, we will introduce you to the notion of conditioned MOs. In general terms, motivating operations might be thought of as motivators. In everyday life, people might say that depriving one of food motivates that individual to seek food. Similarly, they might say that giving an individual salted peanuts motivates the individual to find something to drink.

Two basic types of motivating operations are establishing and abolishing. Deprivation is an example of an **establishing operation** because it temporarily increases the effectiveness of a reinforcer. Satiation is an example of an **abolishing operation** because it temporarily decreases the effectiveness of a reinforcer.

4. Reinforcer Size

The size (or amount or magnitude) of a reinforcer is an important determinant of its effectiveness. Consider the following example. Staff at a large mental hospital discovered that only 60% of the female patients brushed their teeth. When the patients were given a token (which could be cashed in later for cigarettes, coffee, or snacks) for brushing their teeth, the percent who did so increased to 76%. When the patients were given five tokens for brushing their teeth, the percent who did so increased to 91% (Fisher, 1979). Now consider an everyday example. Many teenagers in a northern state like Minnesota would likely be unwilling to shovel snow from the driveway for 25¢, although many would eagerly do so for $10. As we will discuss further in Chapter 6, the optimum amount of a reinforcer to ensure its effectiveness will depend on other factors, such as the difficulty of the behavior and the availability of competing behaviors for alternative reinforcers. For now, keep in mind that the size of the reinforcer should be sufficient to strengthen the behavior that you want to increase. At the same time, if the goal is to conduct a number of trials during a session, such as in teaching basic language skills to a person with developmental disabilities, the reinforcer on each trial should be small enough so as to minimize satiation and maximize the number of reinforced trials per session.

5. Instructions: Make Use of Rules

Note 1 For a reinforcer to increase an individual's behavior, it is not necessary that that individual be able to talk about or indicate an understanding of why he or she was reinforced. After all, the principle has been shown to work quite effectively with animals that cannot speak a human-type language. Nevertheless, instructions should generally be used.

Instructional influences on behavior will be easier for you to understand after reading Chapters 8 and 17. For now, let's view instructions as specific rules or guidelines that indicate that specific behaviors will pay off in particular situations. For example, your instructor might suggest the rule, "If you learn the answers to all of the study questions in this book, you will receive an A in the course."

Instructions can facilitate behavioral change in several ways. First, specific instructions will speed up the learning process for individuals who understand them. For example, beginning tennis players practicing backhand shots showed little progress when simply told to "concentrate." However, they showed rapid improvement when told to vocalize the word "ready" when the ball machine was about to present the next ball, the word "ball" when they saw the ball fired from the machine, the word "bounce" as they watched the ball contact the surface of the court, and the word "hit" when they observed the ball contacting their racquet while swinging their backhand (Ziegler, 1987). Second, as indicated earlier (and discussed further in Chapter 17), instructions may influence an individual to work for delayed reinforcement. Getting an A in the course for which you are using this book, for example, is delayed several months from the beginning of the course. Daily rehearsing of the rule, "If I learn the answers to the questions at the end of each chapter, I'll likely get an A," may exert some influence over your study behavior. Third (as discussed further in Chapter 8), adding instructions to reinforcement programs may help to teach individuals (such as very young children or persons with developmental disabilities) to follow instructions.

Because bribery typically involves instructions and reinforcers, some critics have accused behavior modifiers of using bribery. Suppose that a gambler offered $500,000 to a famous baseball player if he would strike out during each at-bat in the World Series. Clearly, that fits the definition of *bribery*—a reward or a gift offered to induce one to commit an immoral or illegal act. Now suppose that a parent offers a child a token exchangeable for a portion of her allowance if the child completes assigned homework within a set period of time. Is that bribery? Of course not. It is the use of instructions about a reinforcement program to strengthen desirable behavior, not to commit an illegal or immoral act. Similarly, people at most jobs are told ahead of time how much they will be paid for their work, but that is not bribery. Obviously, critics who accuse behavior modifiers of using bribery fail to distinguish between the promise of reinforcers for desirable behaviors versus the promise of reinforcers for immoral or illegal deeds.

6. Reinforcer Immediacy

For maximum effectiveness, a reinforcer should be given immediately after the desired response. In the example in Table 3–1, where the husband picked up his wife's underthings and placed them in the laundry hamper, his wife immediately thanked him. If she had waited until the next morning to do so, her "thanks" wouldn't have had the same effect. In some cases, it may appear that a behavior is influenced by delayed reinforcement. Telling a child that if she cleans up her room in the morning her father will bring her a toy in the evening is sometimes effective. Moreover, people do work toward long-delayed goals, such as college degrees. However, it is a mistake to attribute such results just to the effects of the principle of positive reinforcement. It has been found with animals that a reinforcer is unlikely to have much direct effect on a behavior that precedes it by much longer than 30 seconds (Chung, 1965; Lattal & Metzger, 1994; Perin, 1943), and we have no reason to believe that humans are essentially different in this respect (Michael, 1986).

How is it, then, that a long-delayed reinforcer might be effective with humans? The answer is that there must be certain events that mediate or "bridge the gap" between the response and the long-delayed reinforcer (see Pear, 2001, pp. 246–249). Consider the case of Fernando. Fernando worked in a U.S.-owned factory located on the outskirts of Mexico City.[3] He was one of a group of 12 workers

---

[3]This example is based on the article by Hermann, deMontes, Dominiquez, Montes, and Hopkins (1973).

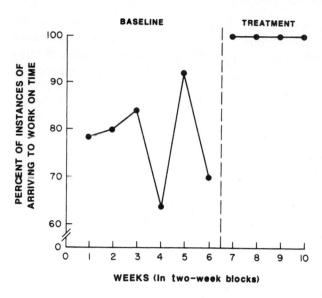

Figure 3–4 Fernando's instances of arriving at work on time. Each data point (dot) represents the percentage of total instances that Fernando arrived at work on time during a 2-week period. (Replotted from "Effects of Bonuses for Punctuality on the Tardiness of Industrial Workers," by J. A. Hermann, A. I. Montes, E. Dominguez, F. Montes, and B. L. Hopkins, 1973, *Journal of Applied Behavior Analysis*, Vol. 6, 1973, Figure 2, p. 568. Copyright © 1973. Reprinted by permission.)

who had a chronic problem—they were frequently late for work. Annual bonuses given by the factory to the 40 workers who had the best attendance records had no effect on Fernando. Likewise, disciplinary interviews and one-day suspensions without pay failed to increase the frequency with which he arrived on time. In fact, over a 12-week period while the latter condition was in effect, Fernando arrived on time less than 80% of the working days (see Figure 3–4, baseline phase). Jaime Hermann, with the support of managers at the factory, decided to implement a treatment program involving positive reinforcers. Jaime explained the procedure individually to Fernando and the other workers who participated in the program. Each day that Fernando punched in on time, he was immediately given a slip of paper indicating that he had earned approximately 2 pesos (which had considerable value for Fernando at the time the study was conducted). At the end of each week, Fernando exchanged his slips for cash. As can be seen in Figure 3–4, the program had an immediate effect. Fernando arrived at work on time every day during the first 8 weeks of the program. The program had a similar positive effect on the other 11 workers who had also frequently been late for work. Moreover, additional experimental phases demonstrated that the improvement was due to the treatment.

At first glance, Fernando's improvement may appear to represent a straightforward case of the effects of positive reinforcement. A closer analysis reveals the necessity for an alternative interpretation (Michael, 1986). The response that made it possible for Fernando to arrive on time was leaving for work a half-hour earlier in the morning, but that response preceded his receiving the slip of paper (indicating 2 pesos) by much longer than 30 seconds. Did some other variable affect Fernando's behavior? Perhaps just after awaking, Fernando said to himself, "I'm going to leave for work a half-hour early to make sure that I earn 2 extra pesos," and these self-statements may have influenced the critical behavior. Although the positive effects of the program were due to the treatment, the treatment was more complex than that of a positive reinforcer increasing the frequency of a response that immediately preceded it.

The **direct-acting effect** of the principle of positive reinforcement is the increased frequency of a response because of its immediate reinforcing conse-
quences. The **indirect-acting effect** of positive reinforcement is the strengthening of a response (such as Fernando leaving for work earlier) that is followed by a reinforcer (earning 2 pesos) even though the reinforcer is delayed. Delayed reinforcers may have an effect on behavior because of instructions about the behavior leading to the reinforcer, and because of self-statements (or "thoughts") that intervene between that behavior and the delayed reinforcer. On the way to work, for example, Fernando may have been making self-statements (i.e., "thinking") about how he would spend his extra pesos. (Other explanations of indirect-acting effects of positive reinforcement are presented in Chapter 17.)

The distinction between direct- and indirect-acting effects of reinforcement has important implications for practitioners. If you can't present a reinforcer immediately following the desired behavior, then provide instructions concerning the delay of reinforcement.

7. Contingent versus Noncontingent Reinforcement

When a behavior must occur before a reinforcer will be presented, we say that the reinforcer is *contingent* on that behavior. If a reinforcer is presented at a particular time, regardless of the preceding behavior, we say that the reinforcer is *noncontingent*. To illustrate the importance of this distinction, consider the following example.[4] Coach Keedwell watched her young swimmers swim a set during a regular practice at the Marlin Youth Swim Club. (A set is several lengths of a particular stroke to be swum within a specified time.) She had frequently tried to impress on them the importance of practicing their racing turns at each end of the pool and swimming the sets without stopping in the middle. Following the suggestion of one of the other coaches, she had even added a reward to her practices. During the last 10 minutes of each practice, the swimmers were allowed to participate in a fun activity of their choice (swimming relays, playing water polo, etc.). However, the results were still the same: The young swimmers continued to show a high frequency of improper turns and unscheduled stops during sets.

The mistake made by Coach Keedwell is common among novice behavior modifiers. Incorporating a noncontingent fun activity into practices might increase attendance, but it's not likely to have much effect on practice behaviors. Educators frequently make the same mistake as did Coach Keedwell. They assume that creating a pleasant environment will improve the learning of the students in that environment. However, reinforcers must be contingent on specific behaviors in order for those behaviors to improve. When this was pointed out to Coach Keedwell, she made the fun activity contingent on desirable practice behaviors. For the next few practices, the swimmers had to meet a goal of practicing a minimum number of racing turns at each end of the pool and swimming their sets without stopping in order to earn the reinforcer at the end of practice. As a result, the swimmers showed approximately 150% improvement. Thus, to maximize the effectiveness of

---

[4]This example is based on a study by Cracklen and Martin (1983).

a reinforcement program, be sure that the reinforcers are contingent on specific behaviors that you want to improve.

In addition to not increasing a desirable behavior, a noncontingent reinforcer may increase an undesirable behavior that it happens to follow. Suppose, for example, that, unbeknown to a parent, little Johnny is in his bedroom drawing on the walls with a crayon when the parent calls out, "Johnny, let's go get some ice cream." This accidental contingency might strengthen Johnny's tendency to draw on his walls. That is, behavior that is "accidently" followed by a reinforcer may be strengthened even if it did not actually produce the reinforcer. This is called **adventitious reinforcement,** and behavior strengthened in this way is called **superstitious behavior** (Skinner, 1948a). As another example, suppose that a man playing a slot machine tends to cross his fingers because, in the past, doing so was accidentally followed by winning a jackpot. Such behavior would be considered superstitious.

8. Weaning the Student from the Program and Changing to Natural Reinforcers

The factors described above influence the effectiveness of positive reinforcement while it is being applied in a program. But what happens to the behavior when the reinforcement program terminates and the individual returns to his or her everyday environment? Most behaviors in everyday life (i.e., the natural environment) are followed by reinforcers even though no one specifically or deliberately programmed the reinforcers to increase or maintain them. Reading signs is frequently reinforced by finding desired objects or directions. Eating is reinforced by the taste of food. Flipping on a light switch is reinforced by increased illumination. Turning on a water tap is reinforced by the flow of water. Verbal and social behaviors are reinforced by the reactions of other people. Unprogrammed reinforcers that occur in the normal course of everyday living are called **natural reinforcers,** and the settings in which they occur are called the **natural environment.** Such consequences may be manipulated deliberately by psychologists, teachers, and others in behavior modification programs, and in such cases they would be referred to as arbitrary, contrived, or programmed reinforcers.

After we have strengthened a behavior through proper use of positive reinforcement, it may then be possible for a reinforcer in the individual's natural environment to take over the maintenance of that behavior. For example, sometimes it is necessary to use reinforcers such as edibles to strengthen object naming in children with developmental disabilities. However, when the children leave the classroom and return to their homes, they often say the words that they have learned and receive a great deal of attention from their parents. Eventually, the edibles may no longer be needed to reinforce the children for saying the names of objects. This, of course, is the ultimate goal of any training program. The behavior modifier should always try to ensure that the behavior being established in a training program will be reinforced and maintained in the natural environment. One thing that you can count on is that if a behavior that has been strengthened in a reinforcement program is no longer reinforced at least occasionally (either by arbitrary or natural reinforcers), then that behavior will return to its original level. Because the problem of maintaining desirable behaviors is so important, it is discussed in much more detail in Chapters 6, 7, and 16.

PITFALLS OF POSITIVE REINFORCEMENT

How the Principle Can Work Against the Unwary

Those who are aware of the principle of positive reinforcement can use it to bring about desirable changes in behavior. The principle operates equally well for those who are not aware of it. Unfortunately, those who are not aware of it are apt to use it unknowingly to strengthen undesirable behavior. Table 3–3 presents some examples of how positive reinforcement may work against us in the long run.

In our experience, many undesirable behaviors are due to the social attention that such behavior evokes from aides, nurses, peers, teachers, parents, doctors, and others. This may be true even in cases where one would least expect it. Consider, for example, children who exhibit extreme social withdrawal. One behavioral characteristic of such children is that they avoid looking at someone who is talking to them. Frequently, they move away from adults. We might conclude that they don't want our attention. Actually, the withdrawn child's behavior probably gains him or her more social attention than would have been obtained by looking at the adult. In such cases it is only natural for adults to persist in attempting to get a child to look at them when they speak. Unfortunately, this behavior is likely to reinforce the child's withdrawal behavior. The tendency to shower attention is sometimes maintained by the theory that social interaction is needed to "bring the child out of his or her withdrawn state." In reality, an appropriate treatment might involve withholding social attention for withdrawal behavior and presenting it only when the child engages in some sort of social-interaction behavior—such as looking in the direction of the adult who is attempting the interaction. The hard work of one behavior modifier using appropriate behavior techniques can be greatly hindered, or completely undone, by others who reinforce the wrong behavior. For example, an aide who attempts to reinforce eye contact in a withdrawn child is probably not going to have much effect if other people who interact with the child consistently reinforce looking-away behavior. In Chapter 22 we discuss methods for assessing whether a problem behavior is being maintained by positive reinforcement and how to treat it if it is.

Other Pitfalls

Another pitfall is the tendency for novice behavior modifiers to assume that presenting reinforcers noncontingently will strengthen a specific behavior. For example, in the case of Coach Keedwell described earlier in this chapter, the coach assumed that providing a fun activity at the end of each swimming practice would strengthen desirable swimming behaviors. That didn't occur, however, because the fun activity was not contingent on specific practice behaviors.

Another pitfall is to mistakenly offer positive reinforcement as an overly simplistic explanation of a change in behavior. Suppose, for example, that a college student studies for three hours on Monday evening for an exam, writes the exam on Tuesday, and finds out on Thursday that she received an A. If we were to say that the college student studied for three hours because the student was reinforced by

TABLE 3–3   EXAMPLES OF POSITIVE REINFORCEMENT FOLLOWING UNDESIRABLE BEHAVIOR

Situation	Response	Immediate consequences	Long-term effects
1. A 3-year-old child who has been playing with her coloring book gets up and looks around the living room.	The child goes over to the TV remote and begins fiddling with the buttons.	Mother immediately comes over to her and says, "I guess you're tired of playing by yourself; let's go for a walk."	The chances of the child fiddling with the TV remote in the future increases because of the attention from mother.
2. While getting ready for work in the morning, a man cannot find his clean shirt.	He hollers loudly, "Where in the hell is my shirt?"	The wife immediately finds the husband's shirt.	In the future, the husband is more likely to holler and swear when he can't find his clothes.
3. A father is busy ironing, and his two young children are playing quietly.	One child hits his little brother over the head with a toy truck.	Father stops ironing and sits down to play with the children for a while.	The child is more likely to hit his little brother in the future to gain father's attention.
4. Mother and child are shopping in a department store.	Child begins to whine, "I want to go home; I want to go home; I want to go home."	Mother is embarrassed and leaves the store immediately with the child, before making her purchases.	Child is more likely to whine in a similar situation in the future.
5. Persons with severe developmental disabilities are eating their meal in the dining room at a group home.	One girl holds up her empty glass and grunts loudly, "Mmmm, mmmm, mmmm."	One of the staff members immediately comes and fills the glass with milk.	The girl is likely to hold up her glass and make similar noises in future situations when she wants milk.
6. Father is watching a Stanley Cup playoff hockey game on TV.	Two of the children are playing in the same room and are being extremely noisy.	Father gives them each some money so that they will go to the store and not interfere with his TV watching.	The children are more likely to play noisily when father is watching TV in similar situations in the future.
7. At a party, a husband becomes sullen when his wife is dancing flirtatiously with another man.	The husband shows signs of jealousy and angrily leaves the party.	The wife immediately follows him, and showers him with attention.	The husband is more likely to leave parties in similar situations in the future.

getting a good grade, that would be an overly simplistic explanation. When explaining a behavior, we should always look for immediate consequences that may have strengthened that behavior. With respect to the student's studying behavior, perhaps the night before the exam the student worried about failing, which caused the student to feel anxious. Perhaps the immediate consequence of studying was the removal of that anxiety (as discussed further in Chapters 13 and 17). Or perhaps immediately after studying the student thought about the likelihood of getting an A, which helped "bridge the gap" between the behavior and the reinforcer. As discussed in Chapter 26, reminding oneself of a delayed natural reinforcer for a behavior immediately after it occurs can strengthen that behavior. Remember, when you are attempting to explain the strengthening of a behavior by positive reinforcement, always look for an immediate consequence of that behavior. If a reinforcer is delayed (by more than 30 seconds) following a behavior, then offering positive reinforcement as an explanation of the increase in that behavior is overly simplistic.

GUIDELINES FOR THE EFFECTIVE APPLICATION OF POSITIVE REINFORCEMENT

These summary guidelines are offered to ensure the effective use of positive reinforcement.

1. *Selecting the behavior to be increased.* As indicated earlier in this chapter, the target behavior should be a specific behavior (such as smiling) rather than a general category (such as socializing). Also, if possible, select a behavior that will come under the control of natural reinforcers after it has been increased in frequency. Finally, as shown in Darren's case, to judge the effectiveness of your reinforcer accurately it is important to keep track of how often the behavior occurs prior to your program.

2. *Selecting a reinforcer.*
   a. If possible, complete the reinforcer survey presented in Figure 3–3 and select strong reinforcers that
      (1) are readily available.
      (2) can be presented immediately following the desired behavior.
      (3) can be used over and over again without causing rapid satiation.
      (4) do not require a great deal of time to consume (if it takes a half-hour to consume the reinforcer, this minimizes the training time).
   b. Use as many reinforcers as feasible, and, where appropriate, use a reinforcer tray or menu.

3. *Applying positive reinforcement.*
   a. Tell the individual about the plan before starting.
   b. Reinforce *immediately* following the desired behavior.
   c. Describe the desired behavior to the individual while the reinforcer is being given. (For example, say "You cleaned your room very nicely.")
   d. Use lots of praise and physical contact (if appropriate and if these are reinforcing to the individual) when dispensing reinforcers. However, to avoid satiation, vary the phrases you use as social reinforcers. Don't always say "Good for you." (Some sample phrases are "Very nice," "That's great," "Super," "Tremendous.")

4. *Weaning the student from the program* (discussed more fully in Chapter 16).
   a. If, during a dozen or so opportunities, a behavior has been occurring at a desirable rate, you might try to gradually eliminate tangible reinforcers (such as treats and toys) and maintain the behavior with social reinforcement.
   b. Look for other natural reinforcers in the environment that might also maintain the behavior once it has been increased in frequency.
   c. To ensure that the behavior is being reinforced occasionally and that the desired frequency is being maintained, plan periodic assessments of the behavior after the program has terminated.

STUDY QUESTIONS

1. What is a positive reinforcer?
2. What is the principle of positive reinforcement?
3. What is operant behavior? Describe an example, and indicate how the example fits the definition of operant behavior.
4. In what way is positive reinforcement like gravity?
5. Why is it necessary to be specific when selecting a behavior for a reinforcement program?
6. After dinner, a teenager begins washing dishes and the parent stops nagging the teenager to do so. Is that an example of positive reinforcement? Explain why or why not, in terms of the definition of positive reinforcement.
7. Describe the Premack principle. Give an example.
8. Using the definition of positive reinforcer, describe the steps to test if a particular item is a reinforcer for someone. Illustrate with an example.
9. What is a motivating operation? Describe two examples, one of which was not in this chapter.
10. Does extrinsic reinforcement undermine intrinsic motivation? Discuss.
11. What is a baseline? Give an example.
12. Distinguish between the direct-acting and indirect-acting effects of reinforcement.
13. Should you tell an individual with whom you are using reinforcement about the reinforcement program before putting it into effect? Why or why not?
14. If you instruct someone about a positive reinforcement program for his or her behavior, is that bribery? Why or why not?
15. When Coach Keedwell required young swimmers to show improved performance in order to earn a fun activity at the end of practice, their performance improved dramatically. Was this a direct-acting or an indirect-acting effect of reinforcement? Justify your choice.
16. Describe an example of contingent reinforcement.
17. Describe an example of noncontingent reinforcement.
18. What do we mean by the *natural environment?* by *natural reinforcers?*
19. Describe three behavioral episodes in this chapter that involved natural reinforcers. Justify your choices.
20. Briefly describe eight factors that influence the effectiveness of reinforcement.
21. Is it correct to conclude that a withdrawn child necessarily does not like attention from other people? Explain.
22. Using the definition of positive reinforcer, how might you conduct a test to determine if the social attention of a particular adult is or is not reinforcing for a withdrawn child?
23. Ideally, what four qualities should a reinforcer have (besides the necessary quality of functioning as a reinforcer)? (See p. 46.)

24. Describe two examples of positive reinforcement that you have encountered, one involving a desirable behavior and one involving an undesirable behavior. For each example, identify the situation, behavior, immediate consequence, and probable long-term effects (as shown in Tables 3–1 and 3–3). (The examples should not be from the text.)
25. What is adventitious reinforcement? What is superstitious behavior? Give an example of each.
26. Describe an example of a pitfall of positive reinforcement in which a person unknowingly applies it to strengthen undesirable behavior.
27. Consider this statement: "A college student was reinforced for studying for three hours on the weekend by getting a good grade on the test the following week." Why is this an overly simplistic explanation of the student's studying behavior?
28. What is plotted on the vertical axis in Figure 3–1?
29. What is plotted on the horizontal axis in Figure 3–1?

APPLICATION EXERCISES

A. Exercises Involving Others

1. During an hour that you spend with children, how many times do you dispense social approval (nods, smiles, or kind words)? How many times do you dispense social disapproval (frowns, harsh words, etc.)? Ideally, your social approval total at the end of the hour will be four or five times the social disapproval total. We encourage you to continue this exercise until you have achieved this ratio. Several studies have shown this ratio of reinforcers to reprimands to be beneficial (e.g., Madsen & Madsen, 1974; Stuart, 1971; also see Flora, 2000).
2. List 10 different phrases that you might use to express your enthusiastic approval to an individual. Practice varying these phrases until they come naturally to you.
3. Are you aware of how your gestures, expressions, posture, and body language in general affect those around you? Briefly describe five different examples of one or more of these behaviors that you might show when expressing your approval to an individual.

B. Self-Modification Exercises

1. Be aware of your own behavior for five 1-minute periods while behaving naturally. At the end of each minute, describe a situation, a specific behavior, and the immediate consequences of that behavior. Choose behaviors whose consequences seemed pleasant (rather than neutral or unpleasant).
2. Complete the reinforcer questionnaire (Figure 3–3) for yourself.
3. Assume that someone close to you (your husband, wife, friend, etc.) is going to reinforce one of your behaviors (such as making your bed daily, talking in conversation without swearing, or reading pages of this book). Select the two reinforcers from your completed questionnaire that best satisfy the guidelines given previously for *selecting a reinforcer* (p. 46). Indicate how the guidelines have been satisfied.

NOTES AND EXTENDED DISCUSSION

1. Although it may seem strange to think of people learning without understanding, or being reinforced for emitting a certain behavior without being aware of it, this is much easier to understand when we consider the following observations: First, from everyday experience as well as from basic experiments, it is obvious that animals can learn even though they are not able to verbalize an understanding or an awareness of their behavioral changes. Similarly, the behavior of persons with profound developmental disabilities who cannot speak has been shown to be strengthened by reinforcement (see Fuller, 1949). Finally, a number of experiments have demonstrated that normal adult humans can be influenced by reinforcement to show behavioral changes even if they are unable to verbalize them. For example, university students in an experiment were instructed to say words individually and not use sentences or phrases. When the experimenter nodded and said "Mmm-hmm" following particular types of words (such as plural nouns), the students showed an increased frequency of saying that particular type of word. And yet, when questioned after the experiment, the students were unaware (i.e., were unable to verbalize) that their behavior had been influenced (Greenspoon, 1951).

2. Michael (1986) identified three indicators that a behavior change is due to indirect-acting (vs. direct-acting) effects: (a) the critical response precedes the reinforcer by more than 30 seconds (such as in the case of Fernando, in which the critical response was leaving for work earlier than usual); (b) the behavior that is measured shows some increase in strength prior to the first occurrence of the consequence (such as Fernando arriving for work on time the very first morning of the program, before he had even received the 2-peso consequence); and (c) a single occurrence of a consequence produces a large change in behavior (such as Fernando maintaining 100% on-time arrivals from the onset of the treatment). In Chapter 17, we discuss in detail strategies that teachers can use to increase the chances of obtaining indirect-acting effects with procedures that involve positive reinforcers.

3. Suppose that you're trying to teach an individual with a profound developmental disability to open containers. In one condition, on each trial, you give a container to the client and ask the client to "open it"; if he or she does so, you hand an edible to the client as a reinforcer. In the second condition, everything is the same, except that the edible is hidden inside the container and will be discovered if the client opens it. Research indicates that individuals with profound developmental disabilities or autism learn better under the second condition (Koegel & Williams, 1980; Thompson & Iwata, 2000). The authors in these studies describe the first arrangement as an indirect reinforcement contingency, and the second arrangement as a direct reinforcement contingency. To avoid confusion with what we are here calling direct and indirect reinforcement contingencies, we suggest that an instance where a response reveals the reinforcer (such as opening the container revealing the edible hidden within it) be described as a *reinforcer discovery contingency.*

Study Questions on Notes

1. Discuss evidence that people's behavior can be modified without their being aware of it.

2. What are three clues for deciding if a behavior change is due to indirect-acting versus direct-acting effects?

3. How do some authors use the terms *direct* and *indirect contingencies of reinforcement*? What suggestions do the authors of this text make regarding that usage, and why?

4

Developing and Maintaining Behavior with Conditioned Reinforcement

"OK, team! Here's how you can earn an Eagle Effort award."

COACH DAWSON'S POINTS PROGRAM[1]

"Let's see a little concentration out there. You should hardly ever miss lay-ups in drills!" shouted Jim Dawson at basketball practice. Jim was coach of the Clinton Junior High basketball team in Columbus, Ohio. He was concerned about the players' performance during a series of drills that he used to open each practice. There was also an attitude problem. "Some of them just aren't team players," he thought to himself. "Some of them really have a bad attitude."

With the help of Daryl Siedentop of Ohio State University, he worked out a motivational system in which players could earn points for performance in lay-up drills, jump-shooting drills, and free-throw drills at daily practice. In addition, they could earn points by being a team player and encouraging their teammates by making supportive comments. Points were deducted if Coach Dawson saw a lack of hustle or a bad attitude. The points were recorded by student volunteers who served as managers for the team. All of this was explained to the players in detail. At the end of a practice, the coach praised players who earned a lot of points, as well as players who earned more points than in the previous practice. In addition, players who earned a sufficient number of points had their names posted in a conspicuous place on the "Eagle Effort" board in the hall leading to the gymnasium and were rewarded

[1]This example is based on a report by Siedentop (1978).

with an "Eagle Effort" award at a postseason banquet. Overall, the program was highly effective. Performance in lay-up drills improved from an average of 68% before the program to an average of 80%. Jump-shooting performance improved from 37% to 51%. Free-throw shooting at practices improved from 59% to 67%. However, the most dramatic improvement was in the team player category: The number of supportive comments increased rapidly, to such an extent that the managers could not monitor them all. In addition, while at first most of the comments were "pretty phony," over sessions they became increasingly sincere. By the end of the season the players were exhibiting positive attitude behaviors to a remarkable extent and, in Coach Dawson's words, "We were more together than I ever could have imagined."

UNCONDITIONED AND CONDITIONED REINFORCERS

We have inherited the capacity to be reinforced by some stimuli without prior learning. Such stimuli or events, which usually are important for our survival or biological functioning, are called **unconditioned reinforcers** (that is, stimuli that are reinforcing without being conditioned). (They are sometimes also called *primary* or *unlearned reinforcers*.) Examples include food for a hungry person, water for a thirsty person, warmth for someone who is cold, and sexual contact for someone who has been deprived of such contact. Other stimuli become reinforcers because of particular experiences. Specifically, stimuli that are not originally reinforcing can become reinforcers by being paired or associated with other reinforcers. Stimuli that

Note 1 become reinforcers in this way are called **conditioned reinforcers** because conditioning is needed to establish such stimuli as reinforcers. (They are sometimes also called *secondary* or *learned reinforcers*.) Examples of conditioned reinforcers include praise, a picture of a loved one, books that we like to read, our favorite television programs, and clothes that make us look good. When a stimulus becomes a reinforcer through association with other reinforcers, the other reinforcers are sometimes called **backup reinforcers.** Consider, for example, the type of training conducted with dolphins at Sea World. Early in training, the trainer pairs the sound from a hand-held clicker with the delivery of fish to a dolphin. A fish is a backup reinforcer, and after a number of pairings, the clicking sound becomes a conditioned reinforcer. Later, when teaching a dolphin to perform a trick, the sound of the clicker is presented as an immediate conditioned reinforcer, and the clicker sound continues to be intermittently paired with fish. Backup reinforcers can be either conditioned or unconditioned reinforcers.

The points that Coach Dawson used at basketball practices were not primary reinforcers for the players. We doubt that the players would have worked very hard, if at all, to get points for their own sake. The points became conditioned reinforcers because they were paired with backup reinforcers, including praise from Coach Dawson, the "Eagle Effort" award at the postseason banquet, and the posting of the players' names on the "Eagle Effort" board in the hall leading to the gymnasium. Previously, honors and praise were likely (perhaps in early childhood) paired with other reinforcers (e.g., mothers' hugs); in addition, they likely still are occasionally backed up by reinforcers in the natural environment.

Recall from Chapter 3 that positive reinforcers have a direct-acting effect on behaviors that immediately preceded them. However, the points in Coach

Dawson's program were not awarded until the end of the practice. Were there any immediate reinforcers contingent on improved performance? There are several possibilities.

Perhaps the players noticed managers recording points just after a correct behavior was performed, which may have served as a conditioned reinforcer. Or perhaps, as positive peer comments increased, these served as immediate conditioned reinforcers for improved performance. Third, immediately after performing well, a player might have thought, "I'm going to get lots of points after practice," which "bridged the gap" to reinforcement. Thus, even though the overall improvement might be attributed to the points program, and the points were conditioned positive reinforcers, the improved performance of the players in practice was not due to the direct-acting effect of those points as conditioned reinforcers.

Some conditioned reinforcers, called **tokens,** can be accumulated and exchanged for backup reinforcers. A behavior modification program in which individuals can earn tokens for specific behaviors and can cash in their tokens for backup reinforcers is called a **token system.** For example, a kindergarten teacher might implement a token system in which the children could earn gold stars for various behaviors, such as one star per child for playing cooperatively during recess, and one star per correct answer given in class. At the end of the day, the children might be allowed to cash in their stars for backup reinforcers, such as five stars to play a computer game or three stars per child for an extra five minutes of story time. Just about anything that can be accumulated can be used as the medium of exchange in a token system. In some token systems, individuals earn plastic discs (like poker chips), which they can retain until they are ready to cash them in for backup reinforcers. In other token systems, they are paid with "paper money," on which (to control use and facilitate record keeping) is written the amount earned, the individual's name, the name of the employee who paid him, the date, and the task the individual performed to earn the token. In still others, as in Coach Dawson's program, individuals receive points, which are recorded on a chart beside their names or in notebooks they keep with them. (Token reinforcement programs are discussed further in Chapter 25.)

Tokens constitute one type of conditioned reinforcer, but stimuli that cannot be accumulated can also be conditioned reinforcers. A common example, already mentioned, is praise. A mother who expresses pleasure at her child's good behavior is simultaneously disposed to smile at the child, hug her, play with her, and give her a treat or a toy. Praise is normally established as a conditioned reinforcer during childhood, but it continues to be maintained as one for adults. When people praise us, they are generally more likely to favor us in various ways than when they do not praise us.

The main advantage of using conditioned reinforcers in a behavior modification program is that they often can be delivered more immediately than the backup reinforcer can. Hence, they help to bridge delays between behavior and more powerful reinforcers.

Before closing this section, we mention briefly the principle of conditioned punishment, which is very similar to that of conditioned reinforcement. Just as a stimulus that is paired with reinforcement becomes reinforcing itself, so a stimulus that is paired with punishment becomes punishing itself. "No!" and "Stop that!" are examples of stimuli that become conditioned punishers because they are often followed by punishment if the individual continues to engage in the behavior that provoked them. Moreover, punishing tokens as well as reinforcing ones are possible. The demerit system used in the military is an example of a punishment token system. There are, however, problems with the use of punishment (see Chapter 12).

FACTORS INFLUENCING THE EFFECTIVENESS OF CONDITIONED REINFORCEMENT

1. The Strength of Backup Reinforcers

The reinforcing power of a conditioned reinforcer depends in part on the reinforcing power of the backup reinforcer(s) on which it is based. For example, suppose that Coach Dawson had used only praise as a backup reinforcer for those players who earned points. In that case, the points would have been effective reinforcers only for the players for whom the coach's praise was an effective reinforcer.

2. The Variety of Backup Reinforcers

A stimulus can become a conditioned reinforcer because of pairings with a single backup reinforcer. This is illustrated by the example of an ice cream vendor who rings a bell when entering a neighborhood. After a few pairings, the sound of the ice cream vendor's bell will be a conditioned reinforcer for the children in the neighborhood. A conditioned reinforcer that is paired with a single backup reinforcer is called a **simple conditioned reinforcer.** In contrast, a stimulus that is paired with many different kinds of backup reinforcers is referred to as a **generalized conditioned reinforcer.** Early in life, for example, parents feed their infants, wash them, play with them, and meet their needs in many other ways. Because it is thus paired with many kinds of reinforcers, adult attention becomes a powerful generalized conditioned reinforcer. Similarly, money is a powerful generalized reinforcer for us because of its pairings with food, clothing, shelter, transportation, entertainment, and other reinforcers (see Figure 4–1).

The reinforcing power of a conditioned reinforcer depends in part on the number of different backup reinforcers available for it. This factor is related to the preceding one in that, if there are many different backup reinforcers available, then at any given time at least one of them will probably be strong enough to maintain tokens at a high reinforcing strength for any individual in the program. Examples of the main types of conditioned reinforcers are given in Table 4–1.

3. The Schedule of Pairing with the Backup Reinforcer

Conditioned reinforcement is more effective if a backup reinforcer does not follow each occurrence of the conditioned reinforcer. For example, the players in Coach Dawson's program had to earn a certain number of points before they were given backup reinforcement.

Figure 4–1   Why is money a generalized conditioned reinforcer?

4. Extinction of the Conditioned Reinforcer

For a conditioned reinforcer to remain effective, it must continue to be associated with a suitable backup reinforcer, at least occasionally. Had Coach Dawson discontinued the backup reinforcers of praise and the "Eagle Effort" program, the players may eventually have stopped working for the points. Ceasing to provide backup reinforcement for a conditioned reinforcer is called extinction of a conditioned reinforcer and is similar to the procedure described in Chapter 5 for extinguishing a response.

TABLE 4–1   EXAMPLES OF CONDITIONED REINFORCERS

Examples of simple conditioned reinforcers	Examples of generalized conditioned reinforcers	Examples of unconditioned reinforcers
Air miles	Money	Food
Being told, "Your order is ready, " at a take-out restaurant	Points in Coach Dawson's program	Water
A subway token	Praise	Sex
A coupon for a free hamburger	A gift certificate for food and beverages at a restaurant	Warmth

PITFALLS OF CONDITIONED REINFORCEMENT

How the Principle Can Work Against the Unwary

People who are unfamiliar with the principle of conditioned reinforcement may unknowingly misapply it in various ways. One very common misapplication occurs when an adult scolds a child for behaving inappropriately, but (a) does not provide any type of "backup punisher" (see Chapter 12) along with the scolding, and (b) does not reinforce desired alternative behavior. The scolding, no doubt, is given in the expectation that it will be punishing, but often this is not the case. Indeed, the attention that accompanies such negative verbal stimuli may even be highly reinforcing, especially for individuals with developmental handicaps who often do not receive much attention from adults. In this way, scoldings and other negative verbal stimuli (such as "No!") can become conditioned reinforcers, and the individual will behave inappropriately to obtain them.

Indeed, even stimuli that are normally punishing can become conditioned reinforcers through association with powerful primary reinforcers. The classic example is the parent who spanks a child for misbehavior and then, "feeling guilty" from the ensuing piteous crying, immediately hugs the child and gives her ice cream or some other treat. The possible outcome of this unthinking procedure is that the child will develop a "liking for lickings"; that is, the spanking could become a conditioned reinforcer that would maintain, not eliminate, the misbehavior it follows.

Another Pitfall

Extinction of a conditioned reinforcer can be unknowingly applied with unfortunate results by those who are unfamiliar with this aspect of conditioned reinforcement. An example of this is a teacher who awards stars for good behavior but fails to use effective backup reinforcers. The result is that the stars eventually lose whatever reinforcing power they may have had when they were first introduced. Failure to use effective backup reinforcers can account for the lack of motivation **Note 2** students sometimes show on certain token systems.

GUIDELINES FOR THE EFFECTIVE USE OF CONDITIONED REINFORCEMENT

The following guidelines should be observed in applying conditioned reinforcement.

1. A conditioned reinforcer should be a stimulus that can be managed and administered easily in the situations in which you plan to use it. For example, points were ideally suited for the players in Coach Dawson's program.
2. As much as possible, use the same conditioned reinforcers that the individual will encounter in the natural environment. For example, it is desirable in training programs to transfer control from artificial-token systems to the monetary-token systems used in the natural environment or to naturally given praise and attention from others.

3. In the early stages of establishing a conditioned reinforcer, a backup reinforcer should be presented as quickly as possible after the presentation of the conditioned reinforcer. Later, the delay between the conditioned reinforcer and the backup reinforcer can be increased gradually if desired.

4. Use generalized conditioned reinforcers whenever possible; that is, use many different types of backup reinforcers, not just one. This way, at least one of the backup reinforcers will probably be strong enough at any given time to maintain the power of the conditioned reinforcer.

5. When the program involves more than one individual (as was the case in Coach Dawson's program), avoid destructive competition for conditioned and backup reinforcers. If one person receives reinforcement to the detriment of another, that may evoke aggressive behavior in the second individual or cause his desirable behavior to extinguish. This rule implies in particular that one should avoid making an issue out of the fact that one individual is earning more conditioned and backup reinforcement than another. Of course, people differ in their abilities, but the bad effects of these differences can be minimized by designing programs so that each individual earns a good deal of reinforcement for performing at his or her own level.

6. In addition to these rules, one should follow the same rules for conditioned reinforcers that apply to any positive reinforcer (Chapter 3). Additional details for establishing token economies are described in Chapter 25.

STUDY QUESTIONS

1. Explain what an unconditioned reinforcer is. Give two examples.
2. Explain what a conditioned reinforcer is. Give and explain two examples.
3. Explain what a backup reinforcer is. Give and explain two examples.
4. What were the backup reinforcers in Coach Dawson's program?
5. Can we attribute the improved performance of Coach Dawson's basketball players to the direct-acting effects of points as conditioned reinforcers? Why or why not?
6. If Coach Dawson had not paired praise and the "Eagle Effort" program with the points, the players may have continued to work because of a variety of natural reinforcers that had been paired with points during the players' experiences of growing up in Western society. What might these natural reinforcers have been?
7. Which of the seven categories of reinforcers in Figure 3–3 include primarily unconditioned reinforcers and which include primarily conditioned reinforcers? Defend your answer.
8. What are tokens? Explain in two or three sentences what a token system is.
9. Give two examples of stimuli that are conditioned reinforcers but not tokens. Explain why they are conditioned reinforcers.
10. Explain what a conditioned punisher is. Give and explain two examples.
11. Distinguish between a simple conditioned reinforcer and a generalized conditioned reinforcer. Explain why a generalized conditioned reinforcer is more effective than a simple conditioned reinforcer.
12. Is praise a generalized conditioned reinforcer? Defend your answer.
13. Were the points in Coach Dawson's program a generalized conditioned reinforcer? Defend your answer.
14. Explain what extinction of a conditioned reinforcer is.
15. How does the schedule of pairing a conditioned and backup reinforcer affect the strength of the conditioned reinforcer?

APPLICATION EXERCISES

A. Exercises Involving Others

1. What is the probable reinforcer and what behavior does it strengthen in each of the following situations? Are these reinforcers unconditioned or conditioned? Justify your choice in each case.
   (a) An individual walks through a park in autumn and admires the beautifully colored leaves on the trees.
   (b) A person finishes jogging 3 miles and experiences the runner's "high" (caused by the release of endorphins in the brain).
   (c) A teenager finishes mowing the lawn and is allowed to use the family car.
   (d) A thirsty child holds a glass of milk to her lips and drinks several swallows.
2. Observe four instances that are different from the above in which people are probably being reinforced, and answer the above for those instances.

B. Self-Modification Exercise

Identify a behavioral deficiency of yours that you would like to overcome. Next, describe the details of a plausible token system that might be applied by a friend or a relative to help you overcome your behavioral deficiency.

NOTES AND EXTENDED DISCUSSION

1. How is it that infants appear to learn new words when those words are not immediately followed by an observable form of reinforcement? A part of the answer lies with automatic conditioned reinforcement—a reinforcing effect produced by a response due to the resemblance of that response to a conditioned reinforcer (Skinner, 1957). Suppose, for example, that a parent says "say ma ma" to an infant while providing reinforcement (tickling, touching, clapping, etc.). After several such trials, the sounds "ma ma" will become a conditioned reinforcer. Later, when the infant is in the crib alone, the infant may begin saying "ma ma" because of the automatic conditioned reinforcement received from reproducing the same sound. More generally, vocal responses of infants may increase in frequency because the sounds that those vocal responses produce have become conditioned reinforcers and thus automatically strengthen their production responses. Recent studies have clearly confirmed this role of automatic conditioned reinforcement in early language acquisition (Smith, Michael, & Sundberg, 1996; Sundberg, Michael, Partington, & Sundberg, 1996). Automatic reinforcement appears to be important not only in language acquisition, but also in the strengthening of a variety of practical and artistic behaviors (Skinner, 1957; Vaughan & Michael, 1982).

2. Knowledge of conditioned reinforcement can also help us to understand behavior that has often been attributed to inner motivational states. For an industrious college student, for example, good grades are likely powerful conditioned reinforcers. In this person's childhood, a good report was probably followed by words of endearment, hugs, and special treats. Now that he or she is a young adult, the backup reinforcers that maintain grades may be more difficult to identify, but the good grades likely still occur and they are probably conditioned reinforcers (and may be combined with the schedule effects discussed in Chapter 6).

Study Questions on Notes

1. How is conditioned reinforcement involved in influencing babies to babble sounds in their native language, even when no adults are around to reinforce this behavior?

2. Describe how knowledge of conditioned reinforcement that can help us to understand behavior that is often attributed to inner motivational states.

Decreasing a Behavior
with Extinction

"Louise, let's get rid of your migraines."

LOUISE'S CASE[1]

When Louise was 13 years old she began complaining about headaches. Over the next few years she received inordinate amounts of parental, social, and professional attention for her headaches, including comments such as, "You poor dear, that must really hurt," "Let me give you a hug, that might make you feel better," and "I'm so sorry about your headaches—is there anything I can do to help?" In addition, Louise's complaints about headaches often led to her being allowed to stay home from school. These consequences may have reinforced the problem. At 26 years of age, Louise experienced debilitating headaches almost daily. These headaches had typical migraine characteristics—some visual effects (seeing "silver specks"), followed by throbbing pain over her temples, nausea, and occasional vomiting. Various treatments had been tried unsuccessfully, including medication, acupuncture, chiropractic, psychotherapy, and electroconvulsive shock. Demerol injections, which she received from her physician approximately three times per week, appeared to provide temporary relief.

Several medical examinations failed to identify an organic basis for Louise's headaches. Following extensive assessment by behavior therapist Dr. Peter Aubuchon, Louise agreed that her migraines may have been learned through reinforcement of them, and said she would try a behavioral treatment program. First, Louise understood that her physician would no longer provide Demerol. Second,

[1]This case is based on one reported by Aubuchon, Haber, and Adams (1985).

> Louise and her husband agreed that he would record her pain behaviors (which were identified as complaints, going to bed, and putting cold compresses on her head). Third, Louise's parents, husband, physician, and nurses at the clinic that she regularly visited all agreed to completely ignore all pain behaviors exhibited by Louise. Moreover, these same individuals provided praise and other reinforcers for "well" behaviors (such as exercising and performing domestic duties). To ensure her commitment to the program, Louise signed a statement (called a behavioral contract, discussed more in Chapter 26) outlining the treatment components. The results of this program are shown in Figure 5–1.

EXTINCTION

The principle of **extinction** states that (a) if, in a given situation, an individual emits a previously reinforced response and that response is not followed by a reinforcing consequence, then (b) that person is less likely to do the same thing again when he or she next encounters a similar situation. Stated differently, if a response has been increased in frequency through positive reinforcement, then completely ceasing to reinforce the response will cause it to decrease in frequency.

Note 1 Discussions with Louise had indicated that she received a lot of attention for showing overt symptoms of and talking about her headaches. It is possible that this attention was a positive reinforcer in maintaining the high frequency of her pain behaviors. In the program described, Louise's pain behaviors no longer received attention, and their frequency decreased to a very low level. Although extinction was an effective treatment for Louise, we don't mean to imply that all pain behaviors are maintained by attention from others. For an evaluation of other factors that may influence behaviors of patients with chronic pain, see Turk and Okifuji (1997).

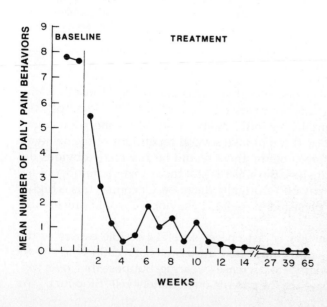

Figure 5–1   Mean number of Louise's daily pain behaviors as reported by her spouse. (Reprinted from *Journal of Behavior Therapy and Experimental Psychiatry, 16,* "Can migraine headaches be modified by operant pain techniques?" by P. Aubuchon, J. D. Haber, and H. E. Adams, p. 262. ©1985, with permission of Elsevier Science Ltd., The Boulevard, Langford Lane, Kidlington OX5 1GB, UK.)

TABLE 5–1   EXAMPLES OF EXTINCTION

Situation	Response	Immediate consequences	Long-term effects
1. A 4-year-old child is lying in bed at night while the parents are sitting in the living room talking to guests.	The child begins to make loud animal noises while lying in bed.	The parents and guests ignore the child and continue to talk quietly.	The child is less likely to make animal noises in future situations of that sort.
2. The next evening, the same child and parents are having dinner at the dining room table. The child has just finished the main course.	The child holds up her empty plate and yells, "Dessert! Dessert! Dessert!"	The parents continue talking and ignore the child's loud demands.	The behavior of demanding dessert is less likely to occur in similar situations in the future.
3. A husband and wife are standing in the kitchen just after the husband comes home from work.	The husband, continuing to stand in the kitchen, complains about the traffic.	The wife goes about preparing supper and does not pay attention to his comments about the traffic.	Unproductive complaining by the husband is less likely to occur in that situation in the future.
4. A child in a third-grade classroom has just finished an assignment and raised his hand.	The child begins to snap his fingers.	The teacher ignores the child and responds to those children who raised their hand and are not snapping their fingers.	The child is less likely to snap his fingers in similar situations in the future.
5. A 3-year-old child working on a plastic puzzle is attempting to put a piece in the wrong place.	The child rotates the piece to try to make it fit.	The piece still doesn't fit, no matter how many times it is rotated.	The likelihood of the child attempting to insert that piece in that position decreases.

As with positive reinforcement, very few of us are aware of just how frequently we are influenced by extinction every day of our lives. Some examples appear in Table 5–1. In each example, the individuals are simply doing what comes naturally in their daily activities. It might take several repetitions of the behavior occurring and not being reinforced before there would be any really obvious decrease in its frequency. Nevertheless, the effect is still there. Over a number of trials, behaviors that no longer "pay off" gradually decrease. Of course, this is highly desirable in general, for if we persisted in useless behavior we would quickly disappear as a species.

Keep in mind that extinction is just one of several possible causes of decreases in behavior. Suppose, for example, that the parents of a child who swears a lot decide to implement a program to decrease swearing. Suppose that, over several days, each time the child swears, the parents immediately yell "Stop that!". As a result, swearing is eliminated. In this case, swearing decreased because it was followed by a punisher (a reprimand). Now consider another possibility. Suppose that rather than reprimanding the child following instances of swearing, the parents said to the child, "You have just lost 25¢ of your weekly allowance," and that this procedure eliminated swearing. In this case the removal of the child's allowance contingent on swearing is referred to as *response-cost punishment* (both reprimands and response-cost punishment are discussed in Chapter 12). Behavior can also decrease because of forgetting. In forgetting, a behavior is weakened as a function of time following the last occurrence of the behavior. (For a behavioral interpretation of memory, see Palmer, 1991.) Extinction differs from all of these in that in extinction, behavior is weakened as a result of being emitted without being reinforced. Extinction, like the principle of positive reinforcement, has been studied extensively by experimental psychologists over many decades, and we are able to describe a number of factors that influence its effectiveness. These are discussed now.

FACTORS INFLUENCING THE EFFECTIVENESS OF EXTINCTION

1. Controlling Reinforcers for the Behavior That Is to Be Decreased

Consider the case of a 4-year-old girl, Susie, who has developed a great deal of whining behavior, especially in situations in which she wants something. Her mother has decided to ignore this behavior, in the hope that it will go away. On three occasions during an afternoon, Mother ignored the behavior until it ceased, and then, following a brief period of no whining, provided Susie with the item she desired. Things seemed to be progressing well until early evening, when Father came home. While Mother was in the kitchen, Susie approached her and in a whiny tone asked for some popcorn to eat while watching TV. Although Mother completely ignored Susie, Father entered the room and said, "Mother, can't you hear your child? Come here, Susie, I'll get your popcorn." We are sure that you can now predict the effect this episode will have on Susie's future whining behavior

Note 2 (not to mention Mother's anger toward Father).

Reinforcers presented by other people or by the physical environment can undo your good efforts at applying extinction. Unfortunately, it is often difficult to convince others of this if they are not familiar with the principles of positive reinforcement and extinction. For example, if several nursery school staff are ignoring a child's tantrumming behavior and another staff member enters and says, "Oh, I can get this child to stop crying—here, Tommy, have a candy," then Tommy is likely to stop crying at that moment. But in the long run his crying may increase in frequency because of that reinforced trial. Since Tommy did stop crying temporarily, however, it would probably be difficult to convince that staff member of the importance of extinction. In such cases, it is necessary either to control the behavior of individuals who might sabotage an extinction procedure or to carry out the procedure in their absence.

2. Extinction of a Behavior Combined with Positive Reinforcement for an Alternative Behavior

Extinction is most effective when combined with positive reinforcement for some alternative behavior (Lerman & Iwata, 1996). Thus, not only were Louise's pain behaviors ignored (extinction), alternative behaviors (exercising, performing domestic duties, etc.) were positively reinforced. The combination of the two procedures probably decreased the frequency of the undesirable behavior much faster (and possibly to a lower level) than would have been the case had the extinction procedure been used alone.

Suppose that you want to combine extinction of a child's inappropriate crying with positive reinforcement for a desirable alternative behavior. It is often impractical to reinforce a child every few seconds for engaging in some desirable behavior (such as playing quietly) in place of disruptive behavior. It is possible, however, to begin with short intervals of desirable behavior and gradually increase them to longer, more manageable intervals. For example, a child who is engaging in inappropriate crying could be ignored until he had stopped crying for a period of 10 seconds. At the end of the 10-second interval, he could be reinforced with praise. On subsequent trials, the teacher could require successively longer periods of silence—15 seconds, then 25, then a minute, and so on—before presenting reinforcement. It is important that the increase in the requirement be very gradual; otherwise, the undesirable behavior will not decrease very rapidly. Also, care must be taken not to present the reinforcer immediately after the crying ceases, as this would tend to reinforce the crying, thereby increasing rather than reducing it.

It is also important during the application of extinction to ensure that the reinforcers that you are withholding are the ones that were actually maintaining the undesirable behavior. Failure to do this, technically, would not meet the definition of extinction, and the undesirable behavior would not likely decrease, as shown in Figure 5–2.

Extinction is sometimes criticized on the grounds that it is cruel to deprive people of social attention during their time of need (this criticism usually assumes that an individual who is crying, whining, or showing various other behaviors that commonly evoke attention is in a time of need). In some cases, this might be a valid criticism. In many situations crying does indicate injury, emotional distress, and other forms of discomfort. We suggest that any behavior must be examined closely in terms of the desirability of decreasing it. If a decrease is desired, then extinction frequently is the right procedure.

3. The Setting in Which Extinction Is Carried Out

As indicated previously, one reason for changing the setting in which extinction is carried out is to minimize the possibility that other people will reinforce the behavior you are trying to decrease. There is another reason. It would probably be unwise, for example, for a mother to initiate extinction of her child's temper tantrums in a department store. The child is likely to display behavior in the department store such that the nasty looks from other shoppers and store clerks

Figure 5–2   An extreme example of why attempts to apply extinction often fail. The actual reinforcer for the behavior must always be withheld.

would decrease the chances of mother carrying through effectively. In other words, it is important to consider the setting in which extinction will be carried out to (a) minimize the influence of alternative reinforcers on the undesirable behavior to be extinguished and (b) maximize the chances of the behavior modifier persisting with the program.

4. Instructions: Make Use of Rules

Although it is not necessary that an individual be able to talk about or understand extinction, it will probably help to speed up the decrease in behavior if the person is initially told something like this: "Each time you do X, then Y [the reinforcing item] will no longer occur." Consider, for example, the third case described in Table 5–1. The husband, upon arriving home from work each day, complains excessively about the slow traffic. His wife would be adding instructional control to extinction if she said something like, "George, the traffic is the same each day, and it doesn't do any good complaining about it. I love to talk to you about other things. But each time that you come home and complain excessively about the traffic, I'm just going to ignore it." This should cause George's complaining to decrease rapidly, although it may take a few trials. But remember that this procedure is more complex than simple extinction. (Instructional control is discussed further in Chapter 17.)

5. Extinction May Be Quicker After Continuous Reinforcement

Let's take another look at the case concerning Susie's whining behavior. Before Mother decided to introduce extinction, what happened when Susie was whining? Sometimes nothing would happen because Mother would be busy with other things, such as talking on the telephone. But at other times (often after five or six instances of whining), Mother would attend to Susie and give her what she wanted. This is typical of many reinforcement situations in that Susie's whining was not reinforced following each instance. Rather, her whining was reinforced occasionally, following several instances of it. This type of situation is referred to as *intermittent reinforcement* and is discussed in detail in Chapters 6 and 7. It is necessary to mention intermittent reinforcement here because it can influence the effectiveness of extinction.

The influence of the reinforcement schedule on extinction can easily be imagined if you consider a little problem that you may have encountered. Suppose you are writing with a ballpoint pen that suddenly stops. What do you do? You probably shake it up and down a couple of times and try to write with it a few more times. If it still doesn't write, you throw it away and get another pen. Now suppose that you are writing with another ballpoint pen. This second pen occasionally skips. You shake it a few times and write some more, and then it misses some more. Each time you shake it, it writes a little more. Now comes the question: In which situation are you likely to persist longer in shaking and attempting to use the pen? Obviously, the second, because the pen occasionally quits but it usually writes again.

When a behavior has always been reinforced and then is never reinforced (such as when a pen quits suddenly), behavior extinguishes fairly quickly. When intermittent reinforcement has maintained a behavior (such as a pen writing after shaking it), that behavior is likely to extinguish more slowly (Kazdin & Polster, 1973), although this phenomenon is quite complex and depends (in part) on how you measure behavior during extinction (Lerman, Iwata, Shore, & Kahng, 1996; Nevin, 1988). Behavior that extinguishes slowly is said to be *resistant to extinction.*

Now let us take a look at Susie's whining. It will likely take longer for extinction to eliminate her whining completely if it sometimes pays off and sometimes does not than if it always paid off before being completely ignored. In other words, extinction is often quicker after *continuous reinforcement* (in which each response was reinforced) than after intermittent reinforcement (in which reponses were reinforced only occasionally). If you try to extinguish a behavior that has been reinforced intermittently, you must be prepared for extinction to take longer.

6. Behavior Being Extinguished May Get Worse Before It Gets Better

During extinction, behavior may increase before it begins to decrease. That is, things may get worse before they get better. An increase in responding during extinction is commonly referred to as an **extinction burst.** Suppose that a child in the classroom is constantly raising her hand and snapping her fingers to gain the teacher's attention. If the teacher were to keep track of the frequency of finger snapping for a while and then introduce extinction (that is, completely ignore the finger snapping), she would probably observe an increase in finger snapping during the first few minutes of extinction before the behavior gradually began to taper off. Why? Most of us have learned that if something is no longer paying off, a slight increase in the behavior may be sufficient to again bring the payoff. Well documented in basic research, extinction bursts have also been reported in applied research (Lerman & Iwata, 1995; Lerman, Iwata, & Wallace, 1999). Thus, extinction bursting is something that everyone who attempts to apply an extinction procedure should know. If a teacher decided to introduce extinction following finger snapping and then observed an increase in this behavior during the next few minutes, he might erroneously conclude that extinction wasn't working and give up in the middle of the program. The effect of this action would be to reinforce the behavior when it gets worse. The rule to follow here is this: If you introduce extinction, keep with it. Things usually get worse before they get better, but hang in there; doing so will pay off in the long run. Exceptions to this rule are situations where an extinction burst may be harmful. If you can anticipate that possibility, you might take preventive steps. For example, before implementing an extinction program to decrease head-banging of a young girl with developmental disabilities, Brian Iwata put a helmet on the girl during extinction sessions so that she would not harm herself during an extinction burst (Iwata, Pace, Cowdery, & Miltenberger, 1994). Alternatively, if you predict that an extinction burst might cause harm, then extinction should not be used. Other strategies for decreasing problem behaviors are described in later chapters.

7. Extinction May Produce Aggression That Interferes with the Program

Another difficulty of extinction is that the procedure may produce aggression. Again, we have all experienced this. Probably all of us have performed the act (or at least had the desire) of pounding and kicking a vending machine that took our money and did not deliver the merchandise. If we reconsider the finger-snapping example, we might see some mild aggression. If a teacher ignores a child's finger snapping, the child might start snapping her fingers louder and louder and perhaps banging on the desk and hollering "Hey!" This characteristic of extinction has been studied extensively in laboratory situations, and has also been reported in applied research (Lerman et al., 1999; Lerman & Iwata, 1996). In studies of extinction of self-injurious behavior, aggression was observed in nearly half of the cases in which extinction was the sole intervention. However, the prevalence of aggression was substantially lower when extinction was implemented as part of a treatment package that included positive reinforcement for an alternative desirable behavior. It is important to minimize aggression not only because it is undesirable but also because it could lead to giving up too soon. This might not only reinforce the undesirable behavior on an intermittent schedule but also reinforce aggression.

Another option would be to conduct an extinction program in a setting in which a certain amount of aggression can be tolerated. If parents decide to apply extinction to decrease a child's tantrumming, for example, they might do so at home after removing glass or other breakable objects. As another example, in an extinction program to decrease aggressive behaviors (scratching, hitting, kicking, and biting) of a boy with a severe developmental disability, Carr had teachers wear protective clothing that consisted of a thick corduroy coat and rubber gloves (Carr, Newson, & Binkoff, 1980).

8. Extinguished Behavior May Reappear
After a Delay

Another difficulty of extinction is that a behavior that has completely disappeared during an extinction session may reappear at the next opportunity after some time has passed. Let's reconsider the finger-snapping example. Suppose that the teacher initiated an extinction program for finger snapping when the student returned to school after lunch. During the first hour there were 10 instances of finger snapping and each instance was ignored by the teacher (and presumably by the other students). Let's suppose further that there were no instances of finger snapping during the remainder of the afternoon, and that the teacher assumed that finger snapping had been successfully extinguished. When the teacher returned to class the next morning, however, another five instances of finger snapping were observed during the first hour of school. This reappearance of an extinguished behavior following a rest is called **spontaneous recovery.** Typically, the amount of behavior that recovers spontaneously is less than the amount that occurred during the previous extinction session. After several additional extinction sessions, spontaneous recovery is usually not a problem. Although these characteristics of spontaneous recovery are well documented in basic research (Pear, 2001), it has not been formally studied in applied research and there are very few anecdotal (i.e., informal) reports of spontaneous recovery occurring in applications of extinction (Lerman & Iwata, 1996). If spontaneous recovery should occur, we recommend that the teacher be prepared to continue with the extinction program.

Note 3   To somewhat oversimplify the discussion in this chapter and Chapter 3, we suggest that if you want behavior to happen more often, reinforce it; if you want behavior to happen less often, ignore it. But beware: There is much more to positive reinforcement and extinction than first meets the eye. For maximal effectiveness in the application of positive reinforcement and extinction, one should be aware of their pitfalls as well as the guidelines for the effective application of the two principles.

PITFALLS OF EXTINCTION

As with the law of gravity, the principle of positive reinforcement, and other natural laws, the principle of extinction operates whether or not we are aware of it. Unfortunately, those who are not aware of extinction are apt to apply it unknowingly to the desirable behavior of friends, acquaintances, family, and others. Table 5–2 presents some examples of how extinction may, in the long run, work to decrease desirable behavior.

Even when some individuals are knowledgeably applying behavior modification in an effort to help behaviorally deficient individuals, their good work may be undone by others who are not knowledgeable about extinction. Suppose, for example, that a child in a program for persons with developmental disabilities has been reinforced by an aide for dressing himself. Suppose, further, that this aide has

TABLE 5–2 EXAMPLES OF UNDESIRABLE INSTANCES OF EXTINCTION

Situation	Response	Immediate consequences	Long-term effects
1. You ask a friend to call you on the telephone on a particular evening.	Your friend dials your number several times.	Each time the phone rings, you ignore it, and continue reading your novel.	Your friend is less likely to attempt to call you when requested to do so.
2. Two staff members are talking to each other in a special education classroom and a student approaches and stands nearby.	The student stands and waits patiently beside the two staff members for several minutes. Finally, the student interrupts.	The staff members continued talking while the student waited patiently, and stopped talking and listened after the student interrupted.	The response of standing beside the staff and waiting patiently is less likely to occur in the future, and the response of interrupting staff is more likely to occur in the future.
3. A man carrying several parcels is walking toward the exit door of a department store. A woman standing by the door sees the man coming.	The woman opens the door for the man.	The man rushes out without saying a word.	The chances of the woman opening the door in similar situations in the future are decreased.
4. A 3-month-old baby is lying quietly in the crib just before feeding time.	The baby begins making cooing sounds (which, might be interpreted by eager parents as "mama" or "dada").	The mother, busy preparing a bottle, ignores the child. When the child is picked up later, she is again quiet (or, more likely, crying).	The mother has just missed an opportunity to reinforce noise making that approximates speech. Instead, she reinforced lying quietly (or crying). Therefore, cooing is less likely to occur in the future.

been transferred or has gone on vacation and is replaced by an aide who is not familiar with the principles of positive reinforcement and extinction or with the particular program for the child. Confronted with a child who dresses himself and many children who do not, the new aide will quite likely spend a great deal of time helping the latter children but giving very little attention to the one child. It is a common human tendency to give plenty of attention to problems and to ignore situations in which things seem to be going well. It is easy to rationalize this selective attention. "After all," the aide may say, "why should I reinforce Johnny for doing something that he already knows how to do?" However, if the child's self-dressing behavior is to be maintained after it has been established, it must be reinforced at least occasionally. Strategies to maintain desirable behavior (and thereby prevent unwanted extinction) are described in Chapter 16.

GUIDELINES FOR THE EFFECTIVE APPLICATION OF EXTINCTION

The following rules are offered as a checklist for individuals who wish to utilize extinction to decrease a particular behavior. As with the guidelines for positive reinforcement in Chapter 3, assume that the user is a parent, teacher, or some other person who is working with individuals with behavior problems.

1. *Selecting the behavior to be decreased*
   a. In choosing the behavior, be specific. Don't expect a major character improvement to take place all at once. For example, do not try to extinguish all of Johnny's troublemaking behavior in a classroom. Rather, choose a particular behavior, such as Johnny's finger snapping.
   b. Remember that the behavior may get worse before it gets better and that aggressive behavior is sometimes produced during the extinction process. Therefore, make sure that the circumstances are such that you can follow through with your extinction procedure. For example, be very careful if the target behavior is destructive to the individual or others. Will it be harmful for you to persist in your extinction program if the behavior gets worse? You should also consider the setting in which the target behavior is likely to occur. It may be impractical to extinguish temper tantrums in a restaurant because of obvious social pressures that you may be unable to resist. If you are concerned with decreasing a particular behavior but you cannot apply extinction because of these considerations, do not despair. We will describe other procedures for decreasing behavior in Chapters 7, 12, 17, 18, and 22.
   c. Select a behavior for which you can control the reinforcers that are currently maintaining it.
2. *Preliminary considerations*
   a. If possible, keep track of how often the target behavior occurs prior to your extinction program. During this recording phase, do not attempt to withhold the reinforcer for the undesirable behavior.
   b. Try to identify what is currently reinforcing the undesirable behavior so that you can withhold the reinforcer during treatment. (If this is not possible, then, technically, the program does not have an extinction component.) The reinforcement

history of the undesirable behavior might provide some idea of just how long extinction will take.

   c. Identify some desirable alternative behavior in which the individual can engage.
   d. Identify effective reinforcers that can be used for desirable alternative behavior by the individual.
   e. Try to select a setting in which extinction can be carried out successfully.
   f. Be sure that all the relevant individuals know before the program starts just which behavior is being extinguished and which behavior is being reinforced. Be sure that all who will be coming in contact with the individual have been prompted to ignore the undesirable behavior and to reinforce the desirable alternative behavior.

3. *Implementing the plan*
   a. Tell the individual about the plan before starting.
   b. Regarding the positive reinforcement for the desirable alternative behavior, be sure that the rules in Chapter 3 for putting the plan into effect are followed.
   c. After initiating the program, be completely consistent in withholding reinforcement after all instances of the undesirable behavior and reinforcing the desirable alternative behavior.

4. *Weaning the student from the program* (discussed in more detail in Chapter 16)
   a. After the undesirable behavior has decreased to zero there may be occasional relapses, so be prepared.
   b. Three possible reasons for the failure of your extinction procedure are
      (1) the attention you are withholding following the undesirable behavior is not the reinforcer that was maintaining the behavior.
      (2) the undesirable behavior is receiving intermittent reinforcement from another source.
      (3) the desired alternative behavior has not been strengthened sufficiently.
      Examine these reasons carefully if it is taking a long time to complete the extinction procedure successfully.
   c. Regarding the reinforcement of the desirable alternative behavior, try to follow the rules in Chapter 3 for weaning the child from the program.

STUDY QUESTIONS

1. What are the two parts to the principle of extinction?
2. If you tell someone to stop eating candies and the person stops, is that an example of extinction? Explain why or why not, on the basis of the definition of extinction.
3. If a parent ignores the behavior of a child, is that an example of extinction? Explain why or why not, on the basis of the definition of extinction.
4. Suppose that, immediately after an instance of swearing, parents remove a portion of the child's weekly allowance and the result is that swearing decreases. Is this an example of extinction? Explain why or why not, on the basis of the definition of extinction.
5. Explain the difference, in terms of procedure and results, between extinction of a conditioned reinforcer and extinction of a positively reinforced behavior.
6. Why did the mother's attempt to extinguish the child's cookie eating fail (refer to Figure 5–2)?
7. Describe a particular behavior you would like to decrease in a child with whom you have contact. Would your extinction program require a special setting? Why or why not?

8. Why is it necessary to consider the setting as a factor influencing your extinction program?
9. If a behavior that was maintained by positive reinforcement is not reinforced at least once in a while, what will happen to it?
10. What is an extinction burst? Describe an example.
11. What is spontaneous recovery? Describe an example.
12. In a sentence each, describe eight general factors influencing the effectiveness of extinction.
13. If you were recording some observations of an undesirable behavior prior to introducing an extinction program, what five things would you be looking for?
14. What are three possible reasons for the failure of an extinction program?
15. Extinction should not be applied to certain behaviors or in certain situations. What types of behaviors and situations would these be? Give an example of a behavior to which extinction should not be applied. Give an example of a situation in which extinction should not be applied.
16. Describe two examples of extinction that you have encountered, one involving a desirable behavior and one involving an undesirable behavior. For each example, identify the situation, behavior, immediate consequence, and probable long-term effects, as is done in Tables 5–1 and 5–2. (Your examples should not be from the text.)
17. Briefly describe a pitfall of extinction. Give an example.
18. Examine Table 5–1. Which of those examples involve positive reinforcement for an alternative response? For those that do not, indicate how positive reinforcement for an alternative response might be introduced.

APPLICATION EXERCISES

A. Exercise Involving Others

Choose a situation in which you can sit and watch an adult interact with one or more children for approximately a half-hour. During this period, mark down the number of times that the adult pays attention to desirable behaviors of the children and the number of times the adult ignores specific desirable behaviors. This will give you some idea of how often we miss opportunities to reinforce desirable behaviors of those around us.

B. Self-Modification Exercises

1. Think of something you did today that did not pay off. Give a specific, complete description of the situation and behavior, following the examples in Table 5–1.
2. Select one of your behavioral excesses (perhaps one that you listed at the end of Chapter 1). Outline a complete extinction program that you (with a little help from your friends) might apply to decrease that behavior. Make sure that you select a behavior such that the reinforcer that maintains it can be withheld. Make sure that your plan follows the guidelines given for the effective application of extinction.

NOTES AND EXTENDED DISCUSSION

1. Louise's case raises some intriguing questions. Was it simply her reports of pain that decreased? Did her "feelings" of pain—the actual headaches—also decrease? Although there was no self-monitoring of headache frequency, Louise reported at a 12-month follow-up that she had experienced only two headaches over the previous several months. Her other behaviors tended to support this, in that she was able to perform a variety of activities (domestic chores, work, etc.) that she had not been able to do in the past, and she and her husband reported that their marital relationship had greatly improved. As discussed further in Chapters 15, 26, and 27, private behaviors are assumed to be affected by behavioral techniques in the same way as are public behaviors. Perhaps in Louise's case both public complaints about pain and private pain behavior were decreased as a function of the extinction procedure.

2. One of the greatest hazards faced by an extinction program is reinforcement from a well-intentioned person who does not understand the program or its rationale. This obstacle was encountered in one of the earliest reports on the application of extinction to a child's temper tantrums. C. D. Williams (1959) reported the case of a 21-month-old infant who screamed and cried if his parents left the bedroom after putting him to bed at night. A program was initiated in which the parent left the room after bedtime pleasantries and did not reenter it, no matter how much the infant screamed and raged. The first time the child was put to bed under this extinction procedure, he screamed for 45 minutes. By the tenth night, however, he no longer cried but rather smiled as the parent left the room. About a week later, however, when the parents were enjoying a much-needed evening out, he screamed and fussed after his aunt, the babysitter, had put him to bed. The aunt reinforced the behavior by returning to the bedroom and remaining there until he went to sleep. It was then necessary to extinguish the behavior a second time, which took almost as long as the first time. Ayllon and Michael (1959) observed the bad effect of unwanted reinforcement in extinction, which they called "bootleg reinforcement." A patient in a psychiatric hospital engaged in such annoying psychotic talk (of the type referred to as delusional) that other patients had on several occasions beaten her in an effort to keep her quiet. To decrease her psychotic talk, the doctors instructed the nurses to ignore it and to pay attention only to sensible talk. As a result, the proportion of her speech that was psychotic decreased from 0.91 to 0.25. Later, though, it increased to a high level, probably because of bootleg reinforcement from a social worker. This came to light when the patient remarked to one of the nurses, "Well, you're not listening to me. I'll have to go and see [the social worker] again, 'cause she told me that if she listens to my past she could help me."

3. An alternative to extinction for reducing undesirable behavior with persons with developmental disabilities is *noncontingent reinforcement*. For example, suppose that in a treatment center for children with developmental disabilities, Suzy appears to display frequent tantrums because tantrumming usually leads to adult attention. A noncontingent reinforcement program might involve giving Suzy adult attention once every 30 seconds regardless of the behavior that is occurring. In a number of studies, this type of treatment has proven to be effective in decreasing challenging behavior (for a review of such studies, see Tucker, Sigafoos, & Bushell, 1998). A potential criticism of this strategy to decrease behavior is that it might reduce the client's motivation to participate in teaching sessions (considering that a reinforcer is received frequently for essentially doing nothing). In addition, since it acts indiscriminately on any behavior that occurs at a high rate, it can also reduce desirable behavior.

Study Questions on Notes

1. Discuss whether the extinction program with Louise decreased her "feelings" of pain.
2. What is bootleg reinforcement? Give an example.
3. Describe how noncontingent reinforcement might be used to decrease challenging behavior. What is a potential limitation of this approach?

Developing Behavioral Persistence Through the Use of Intermittent Reinforcement

"Jan, let's see how many arithmetic problems you can do."

IMPROVING JAN'S WORK RATE IN MATH CLASS[1]

Jan, a 13-year-old girl of average intelligence, was enrolled in the seventh grade at Humboldt State College Elementary School. During math classes, Jan exhibited a great deal of nonattending behavior and made frequent errors on arithmetic problems. With the support of Jan's teacher, two behavior modifiers introduced a strategy for improving Jan's work rate. One of them worked with Jan every day during math class, where Jan received a worksheet containing arithmetic problems to solve. During the first two days, whenever Jan completed two problems correctly, the behavior modifier responded with, "Good work," or "Excellent job," or some similar positive reaction. During the next two days, the number of problems to be completed before praise was given was increased to four. Two days after that, Jan had to complete eight problems correctly before receiving praise. And during the final two days, no praise was given until Jan had completed 16 problems.

The praise schedule had a positive effect on Jan's work rate. From the beginning to the end of the study, her rate of correct problem solving tripled, with the highest work rate occurring when Jan was praised following each 16 problems solved. Moreover, by the end of the study, Jan was attending to the task 100% of the time.

---

[1]This case is based on a report by Kirby and Shields (1972).

SOME DEFINITIONS

The term **intermittent reinforcement** refers to the maintenance of a behavior by reinforcing it only occasionally (i.e., intermittently) rather than every time it occurs. Jan's work behavior was not reinforced after each work response. Instead, she was reinforced after a fixed number of responses had occurred. On this reinforcement schedule, Jan worked at a very steady rate. (*Note:* Response rate and response frequency are synonymous terms; although we tended to use the latter in the earlier chapters of this book, we now switch to the former.)

To talk about intermittent reinforcement, we must first define schedule of reinforcement. A **schedule of reinforcement** is a rule specifying which occurrences of a given behavior, if any, will be reinforced. The simplest schedule of reinforcement is **continuous reinforcement (crf).** Had Jan received reinforcement for each problem solved, we would say that she was on a continuous reinforcement schedule. Many behaviors in everyday life are reinforced on a continuous reinforcement schedule. Each time you turn the tap, your behavior is reinforced by water. Each time that you insert and turn the key in the front door of your home or apartment, your behavior is reinforced by the door opening.

The opposite of continuous reinforcement is called **extinction.** As we have seen in Chapter 5, on an extinction schedule no instance of a given behavior is reinforced. The effect is that the behavior eventually decreases to a very low level or ceases altogether.

Between these two extremes—continuous reinforcement and extinction—lies intermittent reinforcement. Many activities in the natural environment are not reinforced continuously. You may not always get a good grade after studying. You have to work for a week before you get your weekly paycheck. Experiments on the effects of various strategies for reinforcing behaviors have been studied under the topic of schedules of reinforcement. Any rule specifying a procedure for occasionally reinforcing a behavior is called an **intermittent reinforcement schedule.** There are an unlimited number of such schedules. Because each produces its own characteristic behavior pattern, different schedules are suitable for different types

Note 1   of applications. In addition, certain schedules are more practical than others (e.g., some are more time consuming or labor intensive than others).

While a behavior is being conditioned or learned, it is said to be in the *acquisition* phase. After it has become well learned, it is said to be in the *maintenance* phase. Usually, it's desirable to provide continuous reinforcement during acquisition, and then to switch to intermittent reinforcement during maintenance. Intermittent schedules have several advantages over continuous reinforcement for maintaining behavior: (a) The reinforcer remains effective longer because satiation takes place more slowly; (b) behavior that has been reinforced intermittently tends to take longer to extinguish (see Chapter 5); (c) individuals work more consistently on certain intermittent schedules; and (d) behavior that has been reinforced intermittently is more likely to persist after being transferred to reinforcers in the natural environment. In this chapter we discuss four types of intermittent schedules for increasing and maintaining behavior: ratio, simple interval, interval with limited hold, and duration. Each of these is subdivided into fixed and variable, giving eight basic schedules. (Basic research on these schedules is described in Pear, 2001.)

Before describing the basic schedules of reinforcement we will first distinguish between free-operant procedures and discrete-trials procedures. A *free-operant procedure* is one in which the individual is "free" to respond repeatedly, in the sense that there are no constraints on successive responses. In Jan's math class, for example, when Jan was given a worksheet containing a number of arithmetic problems to solve, Jan could have worked at various rates (e.g., one problem solved per minute, three problems per minute). In a *discrete-trials procedure,* a distinct stimulus is presented prior to an opportunity for a response to occur and be followed by reinforcement. Thus, if Jan's teacher presented a math problem and waited a brief time for Jan to solve it, following which another problem was presented to Jan, and so on, then this would be a discrete-trials procedure. You can see that in a discrete-trials procedure the rate of responding is limited to the rate at which successive stimuli at the beginning of each trial are presented. When we talk about the characteristic effects of schedules of reinforcement in this chapter, we are referring to free-operant procedures, unless otherwise specified.

RATIO SCHEDULES

The reinforcement schedules for Jan (in the case at the beginning of this chapter) were **fixed-ratio (FR) schedules.** In an FR schedule, reinforcement occurs each time a set number of responses of a particular type are emitted. Recall that early in her program, Jan had to complete two problems for each reinforcement, which is abbreviated FR 2. Later she had to solve four arithmetic problems for reinforcement, which is abbreviated FR 4. Finally, she had to make 16 responses, which is abbreviated FR 16. Note that the schedule was increased in steps. If Jan's arithmetic responses had been put on FR 16 immediately (i.e., without the intervening FR values), her behavior might have deteriorated and appeared as though it were on extinction. This deterioration of responding from increasing an FR schedule too rapidly is sometimes referred to as *ratio strain*. The optimal response requirement differs for different individuals and for different tasks. For example, Jan increased her response rate even when the FR was increased to 16. Other students may have shown a decrease before FR 16 was introduced. In general, the higher the ratio at which an individual is expected to perform, the more important it is to approach it gradually through exposure to lower ratios. The optimal ratio value that will maintain a high rate of response without producing ratio strain must be found by trial and error.

Note 2   FR schedules, when introduced gradually, produce a high steady rate until reinforcement, followed by a postreinforcement pause. The length of the postreinforcement pause depends on the value of the FR—the higher the value, the longer the pause. FR schedules also produce high resistance to extinction (see Chapter 5, p. 66).

There are many examples of FR schedules in everyday life. If a football coach were to say to the team, "Everybody do 20 push-ups before taking a break," that would be an FR 20. Another example is paying an industrial worker for a specified number of completed parts (called *piece-rate pay*).

In a **variable-ratio (VR) schedule,** the number of responses required to produce reinforcement changes unpredictably from one reinforcement to the next. The number of responses required for each reinforcement in a VR schedule varies around some mean value, and this value is specified in the designation of that particular VR schedule. Suppose, for example, that over a period of several months, a door-to-door salesperson averages one sale for every 10 houses called on. This does not mean that the salesperson makes a sale at exactly every 10th house. Sometimes a sale might have been made after calling on five houses. Sometimes sales might occur at two houses in a row. And sometimes the salesperson might call on a large number of houses before making a sale. Over several months, however, a mean of 10 house calls is required to produce reinforcement. A VR schedule that requires an average of 10 responses is abbreviated VR 10. VR, like FR, produces a high steady rate of responding. However, it also produces no (or at least a very small) postreinforcement pause. The salesperson can never predict exactly when a sale will occur and is likely to continue making house calls right after a sale. Three additional differences between the effects of VR and FR schedules are that the VR schedule can be increased somewhat more abruptly than an FR schedule without producing ratio strain, the values of VR that can maintain responding are somewhat higher than FR, and VR produces a higher resistance to extinction than FR schedules of the same value.

The natural environment contains many examples of VR schedules. Asking someone for a date is an example because even the most popular people often have to ask an unpredictable number of different people to obtain an acceptance. Slot machines are programmed on VR schedules, in that the gambler has no way of predicting how many times he or she must put in money to hit a payoff. Similarly, casting for fish is also reinforced on a VR schedule, in that one must cast an unpredictable number of times in order to get a bite.

Ratio schedules are used when one wants to generate a high rate of responding and can monitor each response (since it is necessary to count the responses in order to know when to deliver reinforcement on a ratio schedule). FR is more commonly used than VR in behavioral programs because it is simpler to administer.

Ratio schedules have also been studied in discrete-trials procedures, such as in a task designed to teach children with developmental disabilities to name pictures of objects. The procedure involves presenting a carefully designed sequence of trials in which the teacher sometimes speaks the name of the picture for the child to imitate and sometimes requires that the child name the picture correctly. Correct responses are reinforced with praise (e.g., "Good!") and a treat; and children make more correct responses and learn to name more pictures when correct responses are reinforced with a treat on a ratio schedule than when they are continuously reinforced with a treat. However, this is true only if the ratio schedule does not require too many correct responses per reinforcement. As the response requirement increases, performance improves at first but then begins to show ratio strain (see Stephens, Pear, Wray, & Jackson, 1975).

SIMPLE INTERVAL SCHEDULES

In a **fixed-interval (FI) schedule,** the first response after a fixed period of time following the previous reinforcement is reinforced (see Figure 6–1), and a new interval begins. All that is required for reinforcement to occur is that the individual

TIME PERIODS

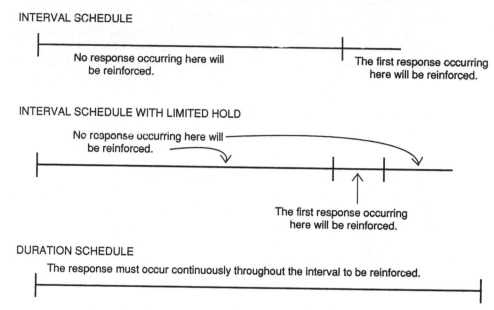

Figure 6–1 Diagrams illustrating the differences between the time-based schedules described in the text. In each diagram, the horizontal line represents a period of time.

engage in the behavior after reinforcement has become available because of the passage of time. The size of the FI schedule is the amount of time that must elapse before reinforcement becomes available (e.g., if one minute must elapse before the behavior can be reinforced, we call the schedule an FI one-minute schedule). Note from Figure 6–1 that although the passage of a certain amount of time is necessary for reinforcement to occur, a response must occur sometime after the specified time interval. Note also that there is no limit on how long after the end of the interval a response can occur in order to be reinforced. Finally, note that a response occurring before the specified interval is up has absolutely no effect on the occurrence of the reinforcer.

The typical effects of an FI schedule are illustrated in the following example. Suppose that two young children (approximately ages 4 and 5) play together each morning. Approximately two hours after breakfast, a parent has a midmorning snack prepared for them; and approximately two hours after that, lunch is prepared for them. Thus, the behavior of arriving at the kitchen is reinforced on an FI two-hour schedule. Within each two-hour period, as the time draws to a close, the children begin making more and more frequent trips to the kitchen, each time asking, "Is our food ready yet?" After eating, they run out and play, and there's a fairly lengthy passage of time before they start again to make trips to the kitchen. The children's behavior of going to the kitchen is characteristic of behavior reinforced on an FI schedule. That is, provided that the individuals who are so reinforced don't have access to clocks or others who will tell them the time, then

FI schedules produce (a) a rate of responding that increases gradually near the end of the interval until reinforcement and (b) a postreinforcement pause. Note that the term "pause" does not mean that no behavior occurs; it simply means that the behavior of interest does not occur. The length of the postreinforcement pause depends on the value of the FI—the higher the value (i.e., the more time between reinforcers), the longer the pause. Most of us, however, rely on clocks to tell us when to do things that are reinforced on an FI schedule. We usually wait until the reinforcer is available, then make one response and receive it. (But note that the behavior of glancing at a clock or watch follows the typical FI pattern. Can you see why?)

When judging whether or not a behavior is reinforced on a fixed-interval schedule, you should ask yourself two questions: (a) Does reinforcement require only one response after a fixed interval of time? (b) Does responding during the interval affect anything? If you can answer "yes" to the first question and "no" to the second question, then your example is an FI. Consider, for example, a college class in which students have a test on the same day of the week. The student's pattern of studying would likely resemble the characteristic pattern of responding on an FI schedule in that there would be little or no studying immediately after a test and studying would increase as the test day draws near. However, consider the two questions listed above. Can the students wait around until a week has passed, make "one" study response, and receive a good grade? No, a good grade is contingent on studying during the one-week interval. Does responding before the interval is up affect anything? Yes, it contributes to a good grade. Therefore, this is not an example of FI, although it may resemble it in some ways.

A job that pays by the hour is sometimes cited as an example of an FI schedule, but this is not correct, because hourly pay assumes that the individual works during the hour. An FI schedule, however, requires only one response at the end of the interval. Going to pick up one's paycheck is an example of behavior reinforced on an FI schedule in that the check is ready only after a certain period of time and going to the pay window earlier does not make it ready any sooner.

In a **variable-interval (VI) schedule,** the length of the interval changes unpredictably from one reinforcement to the next. The lengths of the intervals in a VI schedule vary around some mean value, and this value is specified in the designation of that particular VI schedule. For example, if a mean of 25 minutes is required before reinforcement becomes available, the schedule is abbreviated VI 25 minutes. VI produces a moderate steady rate of responding and no (or at most a very small) postreinforcement pause. Like the intermittent schedules discussed previously, VI produces a high resistance to extinction relative to continuous reinforcement. However, responding is lower during extinction after VI than it is after FR or VR.

Numerous examples of variable interval schedules can be found in the natural environment. Checking one's answering machine for messages or one's computer for email are examples of VI schedules, since messages may be left at unpredictable times.

Simple interval schedules are not often used in behavior modification programs for several reasons: (a) FI produces long postreinforcement pauses; (b) although VI does not produce postreinforcement pauses, it does generate lower response rates than ratio schedules do; and (c) simple interval schedules require continuous monitoring of behavior after the end of each interval until a response occurs.

INTERVAL SCHEDULES WITH LIMITED HOLD

When what is called a *limited hold* is added to an interval schedule, it can have a powerful effect on behavior. We'll explain how it works by describing an effective strategy for managing the behavior of kids on a family car trip. It's based on "The Timer Game."[2] When one of the authors' two boys (2½ years apart) were children, family car trips were trying, to say the least. With Mom and Dad in the front seat and the boys in the back seat, nonstop bickering between the boys seemed to be the rule of the day ("You're on my side," "Give me that," "Don't touch me," etc.). After several unpleasant car trips, Mom and Dad decided to try a variation of The Timer Game. First, they purchased a timer that could be set at values up to 25 minutes and that produced an audible "ding" when the set time ran out. Then, at the beginning of the car trip, they announced the new rules to the boys: "Here's the deal. Every time this timer goes 'ding,' if you are playing nicely, you can earn five extra minutes for watching late-night TV in the motel room (a powerful reinforcer for the boys in the days before there were DVDs in vehicles). But if you are bickering you lose those five minutes. We'll play the game until we get there." Thereafter, a parent set the timer at random intervals for the duration of the trip. The results seemed miraculous. From nonstop bickering, the boys switched to mainly cooperative play. Although it only required an instant of cooperative play to earn a reinforcer, the boys never knew when that opportunity might occur. The result: continuous cooperation. The reinforcement schedule applied in this case was a VI with a limited hold.

A *limited hold* is a finite time, after a reinforcer becomes available, that a response will produce it. A limited hold is essentially a deadline for meeting the response requirement of a schedule of reinforcement. That is, once a reinforcer is "set up," its availability is "held" only for a limited period (hence the term *limited hold*). For the boys in The Timer Game, following a VI, the limited hold was zero seconds because they had to be behaving at the instant the "ding" occurred in order to receive reinforcement. The addition of a limited hold to an interval schedule is indicated by writing the abbreviation for the schedule followed by "/LH" and the value of the limited hold. For example, if a limited hold of two seconds is added to an FI one-minute schedule, the resulting schedule is abbreviated FI 1 minute/LH 2 seconds.

Interval schedules with short limited holds produce effects similar to those produced by ratio schedules (including strain if large increases in interval size are introduced abruptly). For small FIs, FI/LH produces effects similar to those produced by FR schedules. VI/LH produces effects similar to those produced by VR schedules. Thus, interval schedules with short limited holds are sometimes used

---

[2]This procedure was developed on the basis of a study by Wolf, Hanley, King, Lachowicz, and Giles (1970).

when a teacher wants to produce ratiolike behavior but is unable to count each instance of the behavior (e.g., when the teacher can monitor the behavior only periodically or at irregular intervals).

In the natural environment, a good approximation of an FI/LH schedule is waiting for a bus. Buses usually run on a regular schedule (e.g., one every 20 minutes). An individual may arrive at the bus stop early, just before the bus is due, or as it is arriving—it makes no difference, for that person will still catch the bus. So far, this is just like a simple FI schedule. However, the bus will wait only a limited time—perhaps one minute. If the individual is not at the bus stop within this limited period of time, the bus goes on and the person must wait for the next one. A good approximation of behavior on a VI/LH schedule is telephoning a friend whose line is busy. Note that as long as the line is busy, we will not get through to our friend no matter how many times we dial, and we have no way of predicting how long the line will be busy. However, after finishing the call, our friend may leave or may receive another call. In each case, if we do not call during one of the limited periods in which the line is free and the friend is at home, we miss the reinforcement of talking to our friend and must wait another unpredictable period before we again have an opportunity to gain this particular reinforcement. Other examples of VI/LH in everyday life are shown in Figure 6–2.

Interval schedules with short limited holds are common in behavior modification projects. For example, a teacher faced with a classful of rambunctious young students might use a variation of The Timer Game, such as a VI 30 minutes/LH 0 seconds schedule to reinforce in-seat behavior. That is, if the children are working quietly at their seats whenever the timer rings after a variable 30-minute interval, they would receive some desirable item such as points that could be accumulated toward extra free time.

DURATION SCHEDULES

In a duration schedule, reinforcement occurs after the behavior has been engaged in for a continuous period of time. In a **fixed-duration (FD) schedule,** the period that the behavior must be engaged in is fixed from reinforcement to reinforcement. The value of the FD schedule is the amount of time that the behavior must be engaged in continuously before reinforcement occurs (e.g., if it is one minute, we call

Note 3   the schedule an FD one-minute schedule). In a **variable-duration (VD) schedule,** the interval of time that the behavior must be engaged in continuously changes unpredictably from reinforcement to reinforcement. The mean interval is specified in the designation of the VD schedule. For example, if the mean is one minute, the schedule is abbreviated VD one-minute. Both FD and VD schedules produce long periods of continuous behavior. The FD schedule, however, produces a postreinforcement pause, whereas the VD schedule does not (or, at most, a very short one).

The natural environment provides a number of examples of duration schedules. For instance, a worker who is paid by the hour might be considered to be on an FD schedule. Melting solder might also be an example of behavior on an FD schedule. To melt the solder, one must hold the tip of the soldering iron on the solder for a continuous fixed period of time. If the tip is removed, the solder cools

Response: Watching for one's luggage at an airport
Reinforcer: Getting the luggage

Contingency arrangement: After an unpredictable time, luggage appears on the conveyor.

Response: Stacking pieces on a pegboard
Reinforcer: Getting all the pieces stacked
Contingency arrangement: After a fixed number of responses, all the pieces will be stacked.

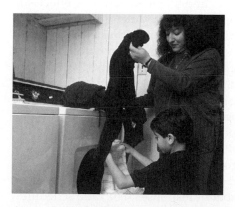

Response: Taking clothes out of dryer
Reinforcer: Clothes are dry

Contingency arrangement: After a fixed period of time, the first response will pay off.

Response: Watching TV
Reinforcer: Viewing an enjoyable scene
Contingency arrangement: Enjoyable scene occurs unpredictably, and lasts briefly.

Figure 6–2 Examples of people responding on intermittent reinforcement schedules.

quickly and the person has to start over again and apply heat for the same continuous period. An example of a VD schedule might be rubbing two sticks together to produce fire, since the amount of time this takes varies as a function of factors such as the size, shape, and dryness of the sticks. Another example of a VD schedule is waiting for traffic to clear before crossing a busy street.

In behavior modification programs, duration schedules are useful only when the target behavior can be measured continuously and reinforced on the basis of its duration. One should not assume that this is the case for any target behavior. Presenting reinforcement contingent on a child studying or practicing the piano for an hour may work. However, it may also only reinforce sitting at the desk or in front of the piano. This is particularly true of something like studying, for which it is difficult for the parent or teacher to observe whether the desired behavior is occurring (the child may be daydreaming or reading a comic book hidden in the text). Practicing the piano is easier to monitor, because the parent or teacher can hear whether the child is doing the lesson.

Eye contact is a behavior that is commonly reinforced on duration schedules in training programs for children with developmental disabilities and autism. Many such children do not make eye contact with others, and any attempt by an adult to initiate this behavior causes the child to quickly avert his eyes from the adult. Eye contact is important as a prerequisite to further social development.

OVERVIEW OF EIGHT BASIC SCHEDULES
FOR INCREASING AND MAINTAINING BEHAVIOR

Note 4 The eight schedules we discussed in this chapter and their characteristic effects are illustrated in Table 6–1. To summarize, the eight basic schedules are: ratio, simple interval, interval with limited hold, or duration schedules, and as either fixed or variable. *Ratio schedules* make reinforcement contingent on a certain number of responses being completed; *simple interval schedules* make reinforcement contingent on a response being made after a certain time period has elapsed; *interval schedules with limited hold* make reinforcement contingent on a response occurring within a limited period of time after reinforcement becomes available; and *duration schedules* make reinforcement contingent on a response being made for a certain continuous period of time.

Thus, the schedules in each of the categories listed along the side of Table 6–1 have certain requirements that must be met in order for reinforcement to occur. These requirements are based on either number of responses (i.e., ratio schedules) or time plus a response(s) (i.e., simple interval schedules, interval schedules with limited hold, and duration schedules).

CONCURRENT SCHEDULES OF REINFORCEMENT

In most situations, we have the option of performing more than just one type of behavior. At home during a particular evening, for example, a student might have the options of watching TV, surfing the Internet, doing homework, talking on the

TABLE 6–1 CHARACTERISTIC EFFECTS AND APPLICATIONS OF BASIC REINFORCEMENT SCHEDULES FOR INCREASING AND MAINTAINING BEHAVIOR

Schedule	Fixed	Variable	Application
Ratio	High steady rate; short postreinforcement pause; high R.T.E.*	High steady rate; no postreinforcement pause; high R.T.E.	To increase and maintain rate of specific responses that can be easily counted, such as solving addition or subtraction problems correctly, or correct repetitions of a sport skill.
Simple interval	Gradually increasing rate; long post-reinforcement pause; moderate R.T.E.	Moderate steady rate; no postreinforcement pause; moderately high R.T.E.	Not commonly used in behavioral programs.
Interval with limited hold	High steady rate (with small intervals); short postreinforcement pause; moderate R.T.E.	High steady rate; no postreinforcement pause; high R.T.E.	To increase and maintain duration or steady rate of behaviors such as on-task behavior of children in a classroom, cooperative behavior of children on a family car trip, or treading water by persons in a swimming class.
Duration	Continuous behavior; moderate R.T.E.	Continuous behavior; high R.T.E.	To increase and maintain behaviors that can be monitored continuously and that should persist throughout a period of time, such as practicing piano lessons.

*R.T.E. = resistance to extinction.

phone with a friend, and perhaps several other possibilities. Each of these different behaviors is likely to be reinforced on a different schedule. The schedules of reinforcement that are in effect at a particular time are called *concurrent schedules of reinforcement*. Which option is the student likely to engage in? In 1961, Herrnstein proposed the matching law, which states that the response rate or the time devoted to an activity in a concurrent schedule is proportional to the rate of reinforcement of that activity relative to the rates of reinforcement on the other concurrent activities. Research has indicated other factors that are likely to influence one's choice when several schedules are available. They are: (a) the types of schedules that are operating; (b) the immediacy of reinforcement; (c) the magnitude of reinforcement (e.g., studying for an exam worth 50% of the student's grade might be chosen over watching a boring TV show); and (d) the response effort involved in the different options (Friman & Poling, 1995; Mazur, 1991; Myerson & Hale, 1984; Neef, Mace, & Shade, 1993; Neef, Mace, Shea, & Shade, 1992; Neef, Shade, & Miller, 1994).

An understanding of the research on concurrent schedules is valuable when designing a behavior modification program. Suppose, for example, that you are attempting to decrease an undesirable behavior by reinforcing a desirable alternative behavior. You should ensure that the schedule of reinforcement for the desirable alternative behavior involves more immediate reinforcers, more frequent reinforcement, more powerful reinforcement, and a response of less effort than that which occurs for the undesirable behavior.

PITFALLS OF INTERMITTENT REINFORCEMENT

The most common pitfall of intermittent reinforcement often traps not only the unwary but also those with some knowledge of behavior modification. It involves what may be described as inconsistent use of extinction. For example, a parent may at first attempt to ignore a child's tantrums. But the child persists, and in despair the parent finally gives in to the child's obnoxious demands for attention, candy, or whatever. Thus, the child obtains reinforcement on a VR or VD schedule, and this leads to further persistent tantrumming in the future. Many times, parents and staff say that they had to give in to the child's demands because "extinction was not working." However, the resulting intermittent reinforcement produces behavior that will likely occur at a higher rate and be more resistant to extinction than behavior that has been continuously reinforced.

GUIDELINES FOR THE EFFECTIVE USE
OF INTERMITTENT REINFORCEMENT

To use intermittent schedules effectively in generating and maintaining desired behaviors, it is important to observe the following rules:

1. Choose a schedule that is appropriate to the behavior you wish to strengthen and maintain.

2. Choose a schedule that is convenient to administer.

3. Use appropriate instruments and materials to determine accurately and conveniently when the behavior should be reinforced. For example, if you are using a ratio schedule, make sure that you have a counter of some sort—be it a wrist counter (as used for keeping golf scores), a calculator, a string of beads, or simply pencil and paper. Similarly, if you are using an interval or duration schedule, make sure that you have an accurate timer appropriate to your schedule. If you are using a variable schedule, make sure that you have arranged to follow a sequence of random numbers that vary around the mean you have chosen.

4. The frequency of reinforcement should initially be high enough to maintain the desired behavior and should then be decreased gradually until the final desired amount of behavior per reinforcement is being maintained. (Recall that for Jan, the fixed ratio was at first very small and was then increased.) Always remain at each stage long enough to ensure that the behavior is strong. This is similar to the shaping procedure described in Chapter 10. If you increase the requirement too rapidly, the behavior will deteriorate and you will have to return to an earlier stage (possibly continuous reinforcement) to recapture it.

5. In language that he or she can understand, inform the individual of the schedule you are using. A number of studies (Pouthas, Droit, Jacquet, & Wearden, 1990; Shimoff, Matthews, & Catania, 1986; Wearden, 1988) indicate that people perform more efficiently if they have specific rules to follow regarding the schedule in effect (see discussion of rule-governed behavior in Chapter 17).

STUDY QUESTIONS

1. Define and give an example of each of the following:
   a. intermittent reinforcement
   b. schedule of reinforcement
   c. continuous reinforcement
2. Describe four advantages of intermittent over continuous reinforcement for maintaining behavior.
3. What is a free-operant procedure? Give an example.
4. What is a discrete-trials procedure? Give an example.
5. Name the schedules of reinforcement used to develop behavior persistence (i.e., the ones described in this chapter).
6. Explain what an FR schedule is. Describe the details of two examples of FR schedules in everyday life (at least one of which is not in the text). (By everyday life, we mean situations that occur commonly and that are not training programs, as defined in Question 13.) Do your examples involve a free-operant procedure or a discrete-trials procedure?
7. What are three characteristic effects of an FR schedule?
8. What is ratio strain?
9. Explain why FR would not be used to teach students to sit at their desks.
10. Explain what a VR schedule is. Describe the details of two examples of VR schedules in everyday life (at least one of which is not in the text). Do your examples involve a free-operant procedure or a discrete-trials procedure?

11. Describe how a VR schedule is similar to an FR schedule, procedurally. Describe how it is different, procedurally.
12. What are three characteristic effects of a VR schedule?
13. Describe two examples of how FR or VR might be applied in training programs. (By training program, we refer to any situation in which someone deliberately uses behavior principles to increase and maintain a behavior of someone else, such as parents to influence a behavior of a child, a teacher to influence a behavior of students, a coach to influence behavior of athletes, an employer to influence a behavior of employees, etc.) Do your examples involve a free-operant procedure or a discrete-trials procedure?
14. What is an FI schedule?
15. What are two questions to ask when judging whether or not a behavior is reinforced on an FI schedule? What answers to those questions would indicate that the behavior is reinforced on an FI schedule?
16. Suppose that a professor gives an exam to students every Friday. The studying behavior of the students would likely resemble the characteristic pattern of an FI schedule in that studying would gradually increase as Friday approaches, and the students would show a break in studying (similar to a lengthy postreinforcement pause) after each exam. But this is not really an example of an FI schedule for studying. Explain why.
17. What is a VI schedule?
18. Explain why simple interval schedules are not often used in training programs.
19. Explain what an FI/LH schedule is, and describe the details of an example from everyday life. (*Hint:* Think of behaviors that occur at certain fixed times, such as arriving for meals, plane departures, and cooking.)
20. Describe how an FI/LH schedule is similar to a simple FI schedule, procedurally. Describe how it differs, procedurally.
21. Explain what a VI/LH schedule is. Describe the details of two examples of a VI/LH schedule that occurs in everyday life (at least one of which is not in the text).
22. What are three characteristic effects of a VI/LH schedule?
23. Describe two examples of how VI/LH might be applied in training programs.
24. Explain what an FD schedule is. Describe the details of two examples of FD schedules that occur in everyday life (at least one of which is not in the text).
25. Suppose that each time that you put bread in a toaster and press the lever, it takes 30 seconds for your toast to be ready. Is this an example of an FD schedule? Why or why not? Would it be an FD schedule if (a) the catch that keeps the lever down doesn't work, or (b) the timer that releases it doesn't work? Explain in each case.
26. Explain why FD might not be a very good schedule for reinforcing study behavior.
27. Describe two examples of how FD might be applied in training programs.
28. Explain what a VD schedule is. Describe the details of an example of a VD schedule that occurs in everyday life.
29. If an individual has an option of engaging in two or more behaviors that are reinforced on different schedules by different reinforcers, what four factors, in combination, are likely to determine the response that will be made?
30. Describe how intermittent reinforcement works against those who are ignorant of its effects. Give an example.
31. For each of the photos in Figure 6–2, identify the schedule of reinforcement that appears to be operating. In each case, justify your choice of schedule.

APPLICATION EXERCISES

A. Exercise Involving Others

Assume that the following behaviors have been established:
1. dishwashing behavior of roommate or spouse
2. dusting behavior of son or daughter
3. doing mathematics assignments by a student

You are now faced with the task of maintaining them. Following the guidelines for the effective use of intermittent reinforcement, describe in detail the best schedules of reinforcement and how you might apply them for each of the above behaviors.

B. Self-Modification Exercise

Assume that you have been assigned a 200-page book to read during the next few days. Select an appropriate reinforcer for yourself, and identify the best schedule on which to dispense the reinforcer. Describe the reasons for your selections (characteristic effects, ease of application, etc.), and outline the mechanics of how you might implement the program and complete it successfully.

NOTES AND EXTENDED DISCUSSION

1. The effects of the various schedules of reinforcement have been worked out mainly with animals. The classic authoritative work on this topic, written by Ferster and Skinner (1957), deals mostly with pigeons pecking on a response key to obtain reinforcement in the form of access to grain for a few seconds. A number of experiments have been conducted to determine whether humans show the same patterns of responding that other animals do when exposed to basic schedules of reinforcement. In one common procedure, for example, a human volunteer presses a lever to produce points that can be exchanged for money or some other reinforcing item. In many cases, however, humans responding under these conditions do not show the behavior patterns described in this chapter. In particular, humans often do not show decreased response rates and pauses in responding where animals typically do (see Pear, 2001, pp. 74–75).

One possible reason for these differences between humans and animals has to do with the complex verbal behavior humans have typically been conditioned to emit and to respond to—that is, humans can verbalize rules (as described in Chapter 17) that may influence them to show different behavior patterns than animals show when exposed to various reinforcement schedules (Michael, 1987). Thus, humans may make statements to themselves about the schedule of reinforcement in effect and respond to those statements rather than to the actual schedule itself. For example, humans may tell themselves that the experimenter will be pleased if they respond at a high rate throughout the session—even though the schedule may be one that normally generates a low rate of responding—and this self-instruction may then produce a high rate. Evidence for this view comes from data indicating that the patterns shown by preverbal infants are similar to those shown by animals (Lowe, Beasty, & Bentall, 1983), and gradually become less similar as children become increasingly verbal (Bentall, Lowe, & Beasty, 1985). In addition, rate and patterns of responding on various schedules of reinforcement can be very much influenced by instructions (Otto, Torgrud, & Holborn, 1999), especially when the instructions are given by the experimenter rather than by a computer (Torgrud & Holborn, 1990).

2.   An analysis of records kept by novelist Irving Wallace suggests that novel writing follows a fixed-ratio pattern (Wallace & Pear, 1977). Wallace typically stopped writing immediately after completing each chapter of a book he was working on. After a brief pause of a day or so he resumed writing at a high rate, which he maintained until the next chapter was completed. In addition, longer pauses typically occurred after a draft of a manuscript was completed. Thus, one might reasonably argue that completed chapters and completed drafts of manuscripts are reinforcements for novel writing and that these reinforcements occur according to FR schedules. Of course, it should be recognized that novel writing is a complex behavior and that other factors are also involved.

3.   There is evidence that, when FR and FD both appear to be applicable, the former is preferable. Semb and Semb (1975) compared two methods of scheduling workbook assignments for elementary school children. In one method, which they called "fixed-page assignment," the children were instructed to work until they finished 15 pages. In the other method, "fixed-time assignment," they were instructed to work until the teacher told them to stop. The amount of time they were required to work was equal to the average amount of time they spent working during the fixed-page condition. In both methods, each child received free time if he or she answered correctly at least 18 of 20 randomly selected workbook frames; otherwise, the child had to redo the entire assignment. On the whole, the children completed more work and made more correct responses under the fixed-page condition than under the fixed-time condition.

4.   Schedules of reinforcement can help us understand behavior that has frequently been attributed to inner motivational states. For example, consider the pathological gambler. Because this individual is obviously acting against his or her own best interests, it is sometimes said that he or she has an inner motive of masochism—a need for self-punishment. However, it seems that (at least in many cases) the pathological gambler is a victim of an accidental adjustment to a high VR schedule. Perhaps when first introduced to gambling, this individual won several large sums in a row. Over time, however, the gambler won bets less frequently and now his or her gambling is being maintained at a high rate by very infrequent reinforcements. Similar adjustment to a high VR schedule with a low reinforcement rate can account for highly persistent desirable behavior as well—for example, that of the dedicated student, businessperson, or scientist.

Study Questions on Notes

1.   Who wrote the classic authoritative work on schedules of reinforcement, and what is the title of their book?

2. What may account for the failures to obtain the schedule effects in basic research with humans that are typically found in basic research with animals?

3. Describe how FR schedules may be involved in novel writing.

4. Might it be better to reinforce a child for dusting the living room furniture for a fixed period of time or for a fixed number of items dusted? Explain your answer.

5. Briefly describe how schedules of reinforcement can help us understand behavior that has frequently been attributed to inner motivational states.

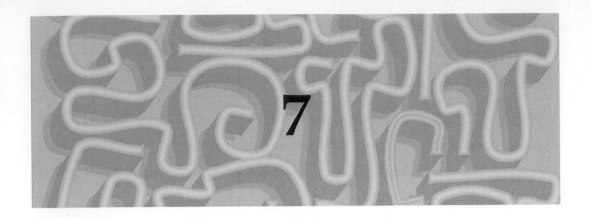

Types of Intermittent Reinforcement to Decrease Behavior

"Tommy, a little less talking out, please!"

DECREASING TOMMY'S TALKING OUT[1]

Tommy, an 11-year-old student with a developmental disability, was judged by his teacher to be the most disruptive student in his special education classroom. He frequently engaged in inappropriate talking and other vocalizations during class. The behavior was troublesome not so much because of its nature, but because of the high rate at which it occurred. A program was therefore undertaken, not to eliminate it, but rather to reduce it to a less bothersome level.

The undesirable behavior, "talking out," was given the following precise behavioral definition: "talking to the teacher or classmates without the teacher's permission; talking, singing, or humming to himself; and making statements not related to the on-going class discussion." A practice teacher located in the back of the room recorded Tommy's talk-outs during one 50-minute session per day. (A second trained observer also recorded Tommy's talk-outs, to ensure the accuracy of the observations.)

In phase 1 of the program, the behavior was recorded for 10 sessions. It was found that Tommy averaged about one talk-out every nine minutes (or about 0.11 per minute). In phase 2, Tommy was told the definition of a talk-out and instructed that he would be allowed five minutes of free play time at or near the end of the day if at the end of the 50-minute session he had made three or fewer talk-outs (i.e., less than about one every 17 minutes). At the end of each session, Tommy was told by the teacher whether he had met the requirement, but during the session he was never told the number of talk-outs recorded.

---

[1]This case is based on Deitz and Repp (1973).

> *This procedure was quite effective. During phase 2, which lasted 15 sessions, Tommy averaged about one talk-out every 54 minutes (0.02 per minute). Moreover, he never exceeded the upper limit of three per session.*
>
> *In the third and final phase, the reinforcement schedule was removed and Tommy was told that he would no longer receive free time for low rates of talk-outs. Over the eight sessions of this phase for which data were taken, his rate of talking out increased to an average of one every 33 minutes (0.03 per minute). Although this rate was higher than the rate during the treatment procedure (phase 2), it was still a great deal lower than the rate before the procedure was introduced (phase 1). Thus, the treatment had a beneficial effect even after it was terminated.*

THE SCHEDULES IN THIS CHAPTER

The schedules of reinforcement in the previous chapter are used to increase and maintain appropriate behavior. The schedules in this chapter, as illustrated by Tommy's case, are used to decrease and/or eliminate responding that is inappropriate (see O'Brien & Repp, 1990).

DIFFERENTIAL REINFORCEMENT OF LOW RATES

If reinforcement occurs only when responding is occurring at a low rate, responding will subsequently tend to occur at a low rate. This phenomenon is called **differential reinforcement of low rates** (DRL). One type of DRL, called **limited-responding DRL,** specifies a maximum allowable number of responses during a certain time interval in order for reinforcement to occur. This was the type of schedule used with Tommy. In that case, an interval was specified (50 minutes)

Note 1 and reinforcement occurred at the end of the interval if it contained fewer than a specified number of responses (three talk-outs).

In limited-responding DRL, the maximum allowable number of responses for reinforcement to occur can be specified for an entire session, or for separate intervals throughout a session. For example, it would have been possible to divide Tommy's 50-minute session into three intervals, each approximately 17 minutes long, and to give Tommy reinforcement at the end of each interval in which a limit of one talk-out occurred.

Limited-responding DRL is useful when two conditions hold: (a) some of the behavior is tolerable, but (b) less of it is better. In Tommy's case, the teacher believed that three talk-outs per session would not be too disruptive; no doubt she would have preferred none at all, but she did not wish to impose too stringent a requirement on Tommy. Therefore, Tommy would hear that he had earned his five minutes of free time by making three, two, one, or zero talk-outs during any given session.

A second type of DRL, called **spaced-responding DRL,** requires that a specified behavior does not occur during a specified interval, and after the interval has passed, that an instance of that behavior must then occur for reinforcement. In other words, instances of a specific behavior must be spaced out over time. Spaced-responding DRL is useful when the behavior you want to reduce is actually desirable, provided that it does not occur at too high a rate. For example, a student who always calls out the correct answer deprives classmates of the chance to respond to the teacher's questions. Naturally, we would not wish to eliminate this child's correct answering. We would hope, however, to reduce the calling-out behavior. We might do this by placing the behavior on the following type of DRL schedule: any target response that occurs after 15 minutes of the previous target response is immediately reinforced; any target response that occurs within 15 minutes of the previous target response is not reinforced. Note that a target response before the interval has passed causes the timing of the interval to start over again. This procedure is called a spaced-responding DRL 1-response/15-minute schedule. This type of schedule requires that responses be emitted in order for reinforcement to occur. On the limited-responding schedule used with Tommy, the individual need not respond at all to obtain reinforcement.

Another example of the use of spaced-responding DRL is the reinforcement of slow speech in a student who speaks too rapidly. The student would be asked questions such as "How are you?" or "Where do you live?" for which standard responses are reinforced—but only if they encompass a certain minimum time period whose length is determined by what the teacher regards as a normally acceptable rate of speech. Thus, the sequence of respond–wait–respond is reinforced (provided that the wait is long enough). As another example, Lennox, Miltenberger, and Donnelly (1987) used a spaced-responding DRL to decrease the eating rate of three individuals with profound developmental disabilities who ate their meals at such a rapid rate that it was considered unhealthy.

DIFFERENTIAL REINFORCEMENT OF ZERO RESPONDING

In Tommy's case, the teachers were willing to put up with a certain amount of talking out. But consider the case of Gerry, a 9-year-old boy of apparently normal intelligence who scratched or rubbed his skin so severely that he produced open sores all over his body. Because of this problem, he had spent most of his time in hospitals and had never attended school. A DRL procedure in such a case would not be acceptable. The procedure that was used is referred to as DRO (pronounced "dee-arr-oh"), which stands for **differential reinforcement of zero responding.** A DRO is a schedule in which a reinforcer is presented *only* if a specified response does *not* occur during a specified period of time. Note that a target response before the interval has passed causes the timing of the interval to start over again. Working with the nurses in the hospital, researchers (Cowdery, Iwata, & Pace, 1990) began with a schedule referred to as DRO 2 minutes. If scratching occurred during the two-minute interval, the interval started all over. However, if scratching did not occur (i.e., was at a zero rate), Gerry was given tokens that he could later exchange for access to TV, snacks, video games, and various play materials. Over several days the interval was increased to a DRO 4 minutes, a DRO 8 minutes, a DRO 15 minutes, and eventually to a DRO 30 minutes. Although the DRO was initially applied during relatively brief sessions, it was subsequently extended to the entire day. Eventually, after spending two years in the hospital, Gerry was discharged and his parents continued to use the procedure at home.

Technically, when Gerry was reinforced on a DRO 30 minutes he would have received a token for doing anything other than scratching. For this reason a DRO is sometimes referred to as **differential reinforcement of other responding.** Practically, however, we're sure that Gerry would not have been allowed to do "anything" other than scratching. If, for example, he began breaking windows instead of scratching, we're sure that the behavior modifiers would have intervened. DRO schedules have been used successfully to decrease a variety of target behaviors, such as inappropriate behaviors in classrooms (Repp, Deitz, & Deitz, 1976), bedtime thumbsucking in children (Knight & McKenzie, 1974), and self-injurious behavior of persons with developmental disabilities (Mazaleski, Iwata, Vollmer, Zarcone, & Smith, 1993).

If an undesirable behavior occurs often and for long intervals, it would be wise to begin with a DRO of short duration. For example, DRO 5 minutes might be used to eliminate tantrum behavior. This procedure could be carried out by resetting a stopwatch to zero each time a tantrum occurred and allowing it to "tick off" seconds when the tantrum stopped. Reinforcement would occur when a continuous five minutes had elapsed with no tantrumming. When the nonoccurrence of the behavior is under good control of this contingency, the schedule should be increased—for example, to DRO 10 minutes. The size of DRO should continue to be increased in this fashion until (a) the behavior is occurring very rarely or not at all and (b) a minimum amount of reinforcement is being given for its nonoccurrence.

DIFFERENTIAL REINFORCEMENT OF INCOMPATIBLE RESPONDING

When applying a DRO, some behavior is occurring when the reinforcer is received. Even though Gerry wasn't scratching, for example, he was doing something when the 30-minute interval passed and he was given a token. An alternative is to specify explicitly an incompatible response that is to be reinforced in eliminating a particular target response. By an incompatible response, we mean a response that cannot be emitted at the same time as the target response. For example, sitting and standing are incompatible behaviors. If we decide to decrease a target response by withholding reinforcers for it (if we know their source and block them) and by reinforcing an incompatible response, the schedule is referred to as DRI, which stands for **differential reinforcement of incompatible responding.** Suppose, for example, that you are a grade-school teacher who wants to eliminate the running-around-the-room behavior of one of your students with attention-deficit hyperactivity disorder (ADHD). One possibility would be to put the behavior on a DRO schedule; however, it might be replaced by an incompatible behavior that is also undesirable—such as, for example, lying on the floor. To avoid this, you might use DRI, instead of DRO, by specifying the incompatible behavior that is to be reinforced. You might, for example, reinforce sitting quietly. An even better choice would be completing school work, since this behavior is more useful to the child. As another example, Allen and Stokes (1987) applied DRI successfully to strengthen the incompatible behavior of being still and quiet

TABLE 7–1   EXAMPLES OF INCOMPATIBLE BEHAVIORS
FOR TARGET BEHAVIORS

Target Behaviors to Decrease	Incompatible Behaviors to Increase
Driving after excessive alcohol drinking	Taking a taxi or asking a friend to drive
Biting fingernails	Keeping hands below shoulders
Swearing	Talking without swearing
Arriving late to classes	Arriving to classes on time

while children were being treated in a dentist's chair. Other examples of potential incompatible behaviors for target behaviors are presented in Table 7–1.

DIFFERENTIAL REINFORCEMENT OF ALTERNATIVE BEHAVIOR

An alternative to DRI is the **differential reinforcement of alternative behavior** (DRA), which is a procedure that involves extinction of a problem behavior combined with reinforcing a behavior that is topographically dissimilar to, but not necessarily incompatible with, the problem behavior (Vollmer & Iwata, 1992; Vollmer, Roane, Ringdahl, & Marcus, 1999). Consider, for example, the case of Kyle, a four-year-old boy with severe developmental disabilities. During training sessions, Kyle was frequently aggressive and attempted to hit, scratch, or kick the therapist. To decrease this behavior, Vollmer et al. implemented a DRA. During training sessions, compliance with performing various requested tasks was reinforced and aggressive behavior was ignored. Note that this was a DRA instead of a DRI in that Kyle was physically able to be compliant and still show aggression. The DRA nevertheless was effective in decreasing his aggression as well as increasing his compliance.

The use of DRA to eliminate an undesirable behavior is essentially what we recommended in Chapter 5 when we stated: "Extinction is most effective when combined with positive reinforcement for some desirable alternative behavior." In fact, DRA (and the other schedules discussed in this chapter) will likely be very effective if you use the reinforcer that was maintaining the undesirable behavior; techniques for identifying that reinforcer are described in Chapter 22. The choice of schedule for reinforcing the alternative behavior should be based on considerations discussed in Chapter 6.

PITFALLS OF SCHEDULES FOR DECREASING BEHAVIOR

Pitfalls of DRO and DRI are similar to the pitfalls already discussed for reinforcement (Chapter 3), extinction (Chapter 5), and schedules of intermittent reinforcement to increase behavior (Chapter 6). One interesting pitfall that is unique to

DRL should be described here. Understanding it may help us to appreciate how underachievers are frequently generated in our society.

Consider what happens when a child starts performing well in school—by giving correct answers to questions, for example. At first, the teacher is quite impressed and enthusiastically reinforces the behavior. However, as the rate of the behavior increases, the teacher gradually becomes less impressed. This is "obviously a bright child," and so one expects a high rate of good behavior from her. Thus, the reinforcement gradually decreases, perhaps to zero, as the rate of the behavior increases. Eventually, the child learns that she obtains more reinforcement if she performs at a low rate, because the teacher is more impressed with good behavior when it occurs infrequently than when it occurs frequently. Many kids breeze through school showing only occasional "flashes of brilliance" instead of developing to their full potential. To avoid this type of inadvertent DRL schedule, teachers should define precisely the behavior they want to maintain at a high rate. They should then make sure that they reinforce this behavior on an appropriate schedule, whether or not they happen to be impressed with it on any particular occasion.

GUIDELINES FOR THE EFFECTIVE USE OF INTERMITTENT SCHEDULES TO DECREASE BEHAVIOR

1. Decide which type of schedule should be used to reduce the target behavior. Use limited-responding DRL if some of the target behavior is tolerable, but the less the better. Use spaced-responding DRL if the behavior is desirable as long as it does not occur too rapidly or too frequently. Use DRO if the behavior should be eliminated and there is no danger that the DRO procedure might result in the reinforcement of an undesirable alternative behavior. Use DRI or DRA if the behavior should be eliminated and there is a danger that DRO would strengthen undesirable alternative behavior.
2. Decide what reinforcer to use. In general, the procedure will be most effective if the reinforcer is the one maintaining the behavior that you want to reduce and if the reinforcer can be withheld for that behavior (see Chapter 22).
3. Having chosen which schedule to use and a reinforcer, proceed as follows.
   a. If a limited-responding DRL schedule is to be used:
      (1) Record as baseline data the number of target responses per session for several sessions or more to obtain an initial value for the DRL schedule that will ensure frequent reinforcement.
      (2) Gradually decrease the responses allowed on the DRL in such a way that reinforcement occurs frequently enough throughout the procedure to ensure adequate progress by the student.
      (3) Gradually increase the size of the interval to decrease response rate below that obtained with (2).
   b. If a spaced-responding DRL schedule is to be used:
      (1) Record baseline data over several sessions or more, determine the average time between responses, and use this average as the starting value of the DRL schedule.
      (2) Gradually increase the value of the DRL schedule in such a way that reinforcement occurs frequently enough throughout the procedure to ensure adequate progress by the student.

   c. If DRO is to be used:
      (1) Record baseline data over several sessions or more to obtain an initial interval for the DRO.
      (2) Use DRO starting values that are approximately equal to the mean value between instances of the target behaviors during baseline.
      (3) Gradually increase the size of the interval in such a way that reinforcement occurs frequently enough to ensure adequate progress by the student.
   d. If DRI is to be used:
      (1) Choose an appropriate behavior to be strengthened that is incompatible with the behavior to be eliminated.
      (2) Take baseline data of the appropriate behavior over several sessions or more to determine how frequently the appropriate behavior should be reinforced to raise it to a level at which it will replace the inappropriate behavior.
      (3) Select a suitable schedule of reinforcement for increasing the appropriate behavior (see Chapter 6).
      (4) While strengthening the incompatible behavior, apply the guidelines for the extinction of the problem behavior, as described in Chapter 5.
      (5) Gradually increase the schedule requirement for the appropriate behavior in such a manner that it continues to replace the inappropriate behavior as the reinforcement frequency decreases.
   e. If DRA is to be used:
      (1) Follow all of the guidelines listed above for DRI, except that the behavior to be strengthened does not have to be incompatible with the behavior to be eliminated.
  4. If possible, inform the individual, in a manner that he or she is able to understand, of the procedure that you are using.

STUDY QUESTIONS

   1. Describe briefly, point by point, how Tommy's talking out in class was reduced.
   2. Explain, in general, what a DRL schedule is. Give an example of a DRL schedule that occurs in everyday life.
   3. Distinguish between limited-responding DRL and spaced-responding DRL.
   4. How is a spaced-responding DRL different from an FI schedule, procedurally?
   5. How is a spaced-responding DRL different from an FD schedule, procedurally?
   6. Describe in some detail two examples (at least one of which is not in the text) of how DRL would be useful in treating a behavioral problem.
   7. Explain what a DRO schedule is. Give an example of a DRO schedule that occurs in everyday life.
   8. Describe in some detail two examples (at least one of which is not in the text) of how DRO might be useful in treating a behavioral problem.
   9. What does the "O" in DRO stand for? Explain your answer.
  10. Explain what a DRI schedule is. Give an example.
  11. What is the difference between DRI and DRA?
  12. What happens if the frequency of reinforcement on DRL, DRO, DRI, or DRA is too low or is decreased too rapidly?
  13. Describe how DRL works to the disadvantage of people who are ignorant of its effects. Give an example.
  14. Explain how DRL, DRO, DRI, and DRA differ from the intermittent-reinforcement schedules discussed in Chapter 6.

APPLICATION EXERCISES

A. Exercises Involving Others

1. For each of the two types of DRL schedules cited in Study Question 3, describe a possible application in training programs with children with developmental disabilities. Describe in detail how you would program and administer DRL in these situations.
2. Describe two possible applications of DRO in programs of early-childhood education. Describe in detail how you would program and administer DRO in these situations.

B. Self-Modification Exercise

Describe in some detail how you might use one of the schedules in this chapter to reduce one of your own behaviors that you would like to occur less frequently.

NOTE AND EXTENDED DISCUSSION

1. One might think that the five minutes of free play that occurred near the end of the day functioned as a reinforcer for decreasing Tommy's talk-outs much earlier in the day. Recall from Chapter 3, however, that the direct effects of reinforcement operate only over very short intervals. Therefore, Tommy's improvement cannot be attributed to the direct effect of the free play near the end of the day as a reinforcer for the behavior of working quietly in the classroom. Rather, when Tommy was working quietly, the immediate consequence was probably praise and attention from the teacher, who might have said, "You're doing great, Tommy; keep it up and you'll earn another five minutes of free play. Just think of how much fun you're going to have." The praise may have been a reinforcer for Tommy's improved performance. In addition, Tommy might have spent much of the day telling himself how much fun he was going to have during his extra play time. This rehearsal of a rule (as discussed earlier and will be further explained in Chapter 17) may have helped to bridge the time gap between the occurrence of desirable behavior during the 50-minute session and the extra play time that occurred on a much-delayed basis.

Study Question on Note

1. What might account for the effectiveness of the delayed reinforcement contingency applied to Tommy's talk-outs?

Doing the Right Thing
at the Right Time and Place:
Stimulus Discrimination and
Stimulus Generalization

"Now, children, please work at your desks."

LEARNING TO FOLLOW TEACHER'S INSTRUCTIONS[1]

The teacher in a regular third-grade class in an Auckland suburban elementary school had a problem. When she was giving instructions to the class she wanted the children to listen attentively from their seats. At other times she wanted them to work quietly on their own. But 9 of the 34 children posed special problems of inattention and poor in-seat behavior. These youngsters frequently argued, shouted, hit and kicked other youngsters, banged furniture, and left the classroom without permission. They did listen attentively and work quietly occasionally, but not often and usually not when the teacher wanted them to. This was clearly a situation in which the desired behavior (listening attentively or working quietly) was in the children's repertoire (i.e., they could do it), but it did not occur at the desired times.

On several mornings, observers recorded the on-task behavior of the nine problem children during teacher instruction, when they were to remain silently in their seats and attend to the teacher, and during work periods, when they were to write a story, draw a picture, or perform other activities prescribed by the teacher. The problem children were typically on-task less than 50% of the time. The teacher then introduced a procedure for getting the desired behavior to occur at the desired time during an oral and written language lesson from 9:30 to 10:20 every morning. She made a large chart, on one side of which was printed in red letters:

---

[1]This example is based on a study by Glynn and Thomas (1974).

> *LOOK AT THE TEACHER*
> *STAY IN YOUR SEAT*
> *BE QUIET*
>
> *On the other side, in green letters, was*
>
> *WORK AT YOUR PLACE*
> *WRITE IN YOUR BOOKS*
> *READ INSTRUCTIONS ON THE BLACKBOARD*
>
> *At various times one side of the chart or the other was showing. The children were each given a 10-by-12-inch card with several rows of squares on it, one row for each day of the week, and the definitions of on-task behaviors during teacher instruction and during work periods were explained to them. The children were told that a "beep" would sound several times throughout the lesson, and they were to mark themselves on-task by placing a checkmark in one of the squares if they were "doing what the chart says" when a beep occurred. The beeps occurred an average of once every two minutes. The children were also told that, at the end of the lesson they would be able to cash in each checkmark for one minute of free play time in a nearby room that contained a variety of games and toys. The program was introduced for all of the children in the class, although data were taken only on the nine problem children. In very short order the sign telling them what to do exerted strong control over their behavior, influencing them to perform the desired behavior at the desired times. The program increased the on-task behavior of the nine problem children to approximately 91%.*

STIMULUS DISCRIMINATION LEARNING AND STIMULUS CONTROL

As we have seen in previous chapters, behavior is strongly affected by its consequences. Behavior that is reinforced increases. Behavior that is not reinforced decreases. However, any behavior is valuable only if it occurs at the right times and in appropriate situations. For instance, at an intersection it is desirable to stop the car when the light is red, not when the light is green. Executing a perfect double back flip will earn you valuable points in a gymnastics routine, but it probably won't have the same effect in your first corporate-level job interview. As we acquire new behaviors we also learn to produce those behaviors at the right time and place. How do we learn to do this successfully?

To understand the process we must first recognize that there are always other people, places, or things that are around when behavior is reinforced or extinguished. For example, when Johnny is playing outside with his friends, swearing is likely to be reinforced by laughter and attention. When Johnny is sitting at the dinner table at Grandpa and Grandma's on Sunday, his swearing is not likely to be reinforced, and may even be punished. After several such experiences, the people and things that were around during reinforcement and extinction come to cue the behavior. Swearing by Johnny becomes highly probable in the presence of the kids on the street and very improbable in his grandparents' house.

Any situation in which behavior occurs can be analyzed in terms of three sets of events: (a) the stimuli that exist just prior to the occurrence of the behavior, called *antecedent stimuli* (such as the presence of friends or the dinner table at Grandma and Grandpa's house just before Johnny swore), (b) the behavior itself (Johnny's swearing), and (c) the consequences of the behavior (either approval from Johnny's friends or disapproval from Grandma and Grandpa). Recall from Chapter 1 that **stimuli** are the people, objects, and events currently present in one's immediate surroundings that can be detected by one's sense receptors. Chairs, books, lights, pens, people, trees, shoes, and other visible objects are all potential stimuli, as are all types of sounds, smells, tastes, and physical contacts with the body. Any stimulus can be an antecedent or a consequence of a behavior. Identifying the antecedents and consequences of a behavior is sometimes referred to as an *ABC (antecedents, behavior, and consequences) assessment.*

When a behavior is reinforced in the presence of a particular stimulus and not others, that stimulus begins to exert control over the occurrence of that behavior. For example, at the end of the program at the Auckland elementary school, when the children saw the sign in big red letters saying LOOK AT THE TEACHER (etc.), they listened carefully to what the teacher had to say, because doing so was reinforced in the presence of that stimulus. We say that the stimulus exerted control over the behavior. When a particular behavior is more likely to occur in the presence of a particular stimulus and not others, we say that the behavior is under the control of that stimulus.

We use the term **stimulus control** to refer to the degree of correlation between a stimulus and a subsequent response. *Good* or *effective stimulus control* refers to a strong correlation between the occurrence of a particular stimulus and a particular response; that is, when the stimulus occurs, the response is likely to follow. For example, suppose that you have just put money into a vending machine and you are looking for your favorite candy bar. You see the name of that bar beside a particular button and you press that button. The sign exerted good stimulus control over your button-pressing behavior. Similarly, at the end of the program in the lead example for this chapter, the sign LOOK AT THE TEACHER (etc.) exerted good stimulus control over the children's behavior of paying attention.

While some stimuli are consistent predictors that a particular behavior will be reinforced, other stimuli are consistent predictors that a particular behavior will not be reinforced. An OUT OF ORDER sign on a vending machine is a cue that the behavior of inserting money into the machine will not be reinforced. The appearance of an empty cup is a cue that raising the cup to your lips will not result in a drink. Through experience, we learn to refrain from performing certain behaviors in the presence of certain stimuli because we have learned that those behaviors will go unreinforced. Thus, good stimulus control also exists when a particular stimulus controls the absence of a particular behavior as a result of that behavior having gone unreinforced in the presence of that stimulus.

The process by which we learn to emit a specific behavior in the presence of some stimuli and not in the presence of other stimuli is called *stimulus discrimination learning*. The procedure of teaching a stimulus discrimination, called *stimulus discrimination training*, involves reinforcement of a behavior in the presence of a specific stimulus and extinction of that behavior in the presence of a different stimulus. Such stimuli are called *controlling stimuli*. There are two types of controlling stimuli, as described below.

TYPES OF CONTROLLING STIMULI: S^{D}s AND S$^\Delta$s

One type of controlling stimulus is an S^D (pronounced "ess-dee") or discriminative stimulus. If a response has been reinforced only in the presence of a particular stimulus, that stimulus is referred to as an S^D. Loosely speaking, an S^D is a cue that a particular response will pay off. If a response has been extinguished only in the presence of a particular stimulus, that stimulus is referred to as an S$^\Delta$ (pronounced "ess-delta"). An S^D might be called a stimulus for reinforcement and an S$^\Delta$ might be called a stimulus for extinction. Thus, an S$^\Delta$ is a cue that a particular response will *not* pay off.

In our example of Johnny's swearing, the stimulus of the other kids is an S^D for the response of swearing because that response has been reinforced by their laughter and attention. The stimulus of Grandpa and Grandma is an S$^\Delta$ for the response of swearing because it was not reinforced in their presence. This can be diagrammed as follows:

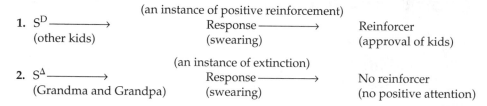

1. S^D ⟶   (an instance of positive reinforcement)   Response ⟶   Reinforcer
　　(other kids)　　　　　　　　　　　　　　　(swearing)　　　　　　　(approval of kids)

2. S$^\Delta$ ⟶   (an instance of extinction)   Response ⟶   No reinforcer
　　(Grandma and Grandpa)　　　　　　　　　(swearing)　　　　　　　(no positive attention)

A stimulus can simultaneously be an S^D for one response and an S$^\Delta$ for another; that is, in the presence of a particular stimulus, one response may be reinforced while another may not be reinforced (e.g., see Figure 8–1). For instance, if you are eating dinner with friends and someone asks you, "Please pass the pepper," that statement is an S^D for your response of passing the pepper, and it is an S$^\Delta$ for you to pass the salt. As another example, when the teacher in the Auckland classroom presented the sign LOOK AT THE TEACHER (etc.), that stimulus was an S^D for the children's on-task behavior (staying in their seats and attending to the teacher), and it was an S$^\Delta$ for their off-task behavior (writing in their books, running around the room, etc.). This may be diagrammed as follows:

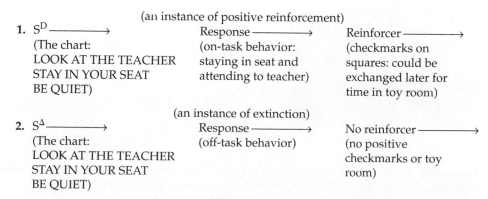

1. S^D ⟶   (an instance of positive reinforcement)
　　(The chart:　　　　　　　Response ⟶　　　　Reinforcer ⟶
　　LOOK AT THE TEACHER　　(on-task behavior:　　(checkmarks on
　　STAY IN YOUR SEAT　　　staying in seat and　　squares: could be
　　BE QUIET)　　　　　　　attending to teacher)　exchanged later for
　　　　　　　　　　　　　　　　　　　　　　　　time in toy room)

2. S$^\Delta$ ⟶   (an instance of extinction)
　　(The chart:　　　　　　　Response ⟶　　　　No reinforcer ⟶
　　LOOK AT THE TEACHER　　(off-task behavior)　　(no positive
　　STAY IN YOUR SEAT　　　　　　　　　　　　checkmarks or toy
　　BE QUIET)　　　　　　　　　　　　　　　　room)

A phrase that is frequently used in connection with these types of diagrams is *contingency of reinforcement.* According to Skinner (1969, p. 7), an "adequate

The sign is an S^Δ for inserting money, and an S^D to seek out a different machine (one that is not out of order).

The sign is in an S^D for a female to enter and "go" to the bathroom, and an S^Δ for a male to enter.

The sign is an S^D for driving in the direction of the arrow, and an S^Δ for driving in a direction against that signified by the arrow.

Figure 8–1   Many stimuli are simultaneously an S^D for one response and an S^Δ for a different response, although such stimuli do not always control the appropriate responses.
Source: 8-1c, "You May Not Tie An Alligator to a Fire Hydrant: 101 Dumb Laws"

formulation of the interaction between an [individual] and [his or her] environment must always specify three things: (1) the occasion upon which a response occurs, (2) the response itself, and (3) the reinforcing consequences. The interrelationships among them are the 'contingencies of reinforcement.'" Thus, all the reinforcement schedules (including extinction) discussed earlier in combination with the contexts in which they occur are contingencies of reinforcement, as is any arrangement among stimulus, response, and consequences. Earlier in this chapter we described ABC (antecedent, behavior, consequence) assessment. We can now see that performing an ABC assessment is the same as identifying the contingencies of reinforcement controlling a behavior.

Stimulus discrimination training refers to the *procedure* of reinforcing a response in the presence of an S^D and extinguishing that response in the presence of an S^Δ. After sufficient training, the effects can be described as: (1) *stimulus control*—a high correlation between a stimulus and a response; or (2) a *stimulus discrimination*—the response occurs to the S^D and not to the S^Δ. Note that there are two different ways of talking about the same result. It is also important to note than an S^D does not automatically elicit the response to it in a reflexive one-to-one manner. We therefore do not use the word "elicit" in talking about the control an S^D exerts over behavior. Instead we speak of an S^D *controlling* or *evoking* a response. We may also say that the response is *emitted* in the presence of the S^D.

STIMULUS GENERALIZATION

Stimulus generalization occurs when behavior becomes more probable in the presence of one stimulus or situation as a result of having been reinforced in the presence of another stimulus or situation. In other words, instead of discriminating between two stimuli and responding differentially to them, an individual responds in the same way to two different stimuli. Thus, stimulus generalization is the opposite of stimulus discrimination. There are several reasons for the occurrence of stimulus generalization.

Unlearned Stimulus Generalization due to Considerable Physical Similarity We (along with other animals) have evolved such that we are likely to perform a behavior in a new situation if that situation is similar to the one in which we learned the behavior. Consider a case that is familiar to many parents: an infant learns to say "doggie" to a large, hairy, four-legged creature with floppy ears and a friendly bark. Later, the infant sees a different kind of large dog and says "doggie." It is fortunate that we have evolved in this way. Imagine what life would be like if you could not perform a newly learned skill in a new situation that was somewhat different from the circumstances under which you originally learned the skill. You would have to "relearn" how to make coffee in each new kitchen with somewhat different appliances; when skiing, you would learn to stop safely on one slope and have to be taught to stop safely on each new slope; you would learn to dance to one song but be unable to do so when a similar song was played. Fortunately, we have evolved such that the more physically similar two stimuli are, the more stimulus generalization will occur between them.

Learned Stimulus Generalization Involving Minimal Physical Similarity   Suppose that a child learns to say "dog" to a large German shepherd. Would the child also spontaneously say "dog" to a tiny Chihuahua? Probably not. Although the dogs have some limited physical similarity, they are very different in many respects. Stimulus generalization is not likely to occur in the latter case until the child has learned the stimulus class "dog." A **stimulus common-element class** is a set of stimuli, all of which have some physical characteristic(s) in common. Many behavior modifiers refer to such a set of stimuli as simply a stimulus class. We use the term *stimulus common-element class* to distinguish it from a *stimulus equivalence class,* discussed later.

Another word for stimulus class is *concept.* For some concepts, their respective members have many physical characteristics in common. For example, cars have four wheels, glass windows, a steering wheel, and so forth. When a child learns to say the word "car" when seeing a particular car, the child is likely to show unlearned stimulus generalization and be able to identify other cars. For other concepts, however, their members have only limited physical characteristics in common, and some learning is likely required for stimulus generalization to occur. To teach a child the concept "red," you might reinforce the response "red" to many different red-colored objects, and extinguish that response to objects that are not red. Eventually, the child would learn to recognize a red pencil and a red automobile as both being "red," even though the pencil and the automobile are very different in other respects. As another example, to teach the concept of wetness, you would reinforce the response "wet" to many different wet objects and extinguish that response (and reinforce the response "dry") to dry objects.

When an individual emits an appropriate response to all the members of a stimulus common-element class and does not emit that response to stimuli that do not belong to the class, we say that the individual generalizes to all members within a stimulus common-element class or concept (e.g., recognizes red objects as red), and discriminates between stimulus common-element classes (e.g., between red objects and blue objects). When an individual responds in this way, such as to the concept "red," we say that the individual is showing *conceptual behavior.*

It is important to note that verbal behavior is not necessarily involved in conceptual behavior. Pigeons, although completely nonverbal, can readily learn a surprising range of concepts. By presenting slides to them and reinforcing pecks at slides that are exemplars of a particular concept while withholding reinforcement for pecks at slides that are not exemplars of that concept, researchers have taught pigeons concepts such as "person," "tree," and some number concepts such as "16 versus 20" (Herrnstein & deVilliers, 1980; Herrnstein & Loveland, 1964; Herrnstein, Loveland, & Cable, 1976; Honig & Stewart, 1988; Lubow, 1974; Vaughan & Herrnstein, 1987). The proof that the pigeons have learned a concept (such as "fish") is that they respond correctly to new exemplars (e.g., types of fish that they have never seen before).

Learned Stimulus Generalization due to Stimulus Equivalence Classes   Suppose that you are shown a carrot, a pencil, a pea, a calculator, and a carton of milk, and you are asked to identify the food items. Obviously, you will be able to do so. You would be showing conceptual behavior with respect to the concept food. Yet there is nothing physically similar about a carrot, a pea, and a carton of milk. We have learned that these items belong to a **stimulus equivalence class,** commonly called an **equivalence class,** a set of completely dissimilar stimuli in which all members of the class control the same response, namely, the word "food." Behavioral researchers have typically studied the formation of equivalence classes, during matching-to-sample training. Consider the following experiment for teaching the equivalence class "three" to a 3-year-old child. In Phase I, the child is given a number of trials with Training Panel 1 in Figure 8–2. Across trials, the positions of "∴," "IV," and "7" are randomly alternated. Using appropriate prompting and reinforcement, the child is taught to match "3" to "∴." Then, Phase II proceeds similarly, but with Training Panel 2, and the child is taught to match "∴." to "III." Now comes a test to see whether the child has learned the equivalence class. The child is shown the Test Panel, and asked to match "III" to 4, 6, or 3. In such an experi-

Note 1 ment, the child will likely match "III" to "3." The "III" and the "3" have become members of an equivalence class, even though those two stimuli were never previously paired. The members of this equivalence class are functionally equivalent in the sense that they all control the same behavior.

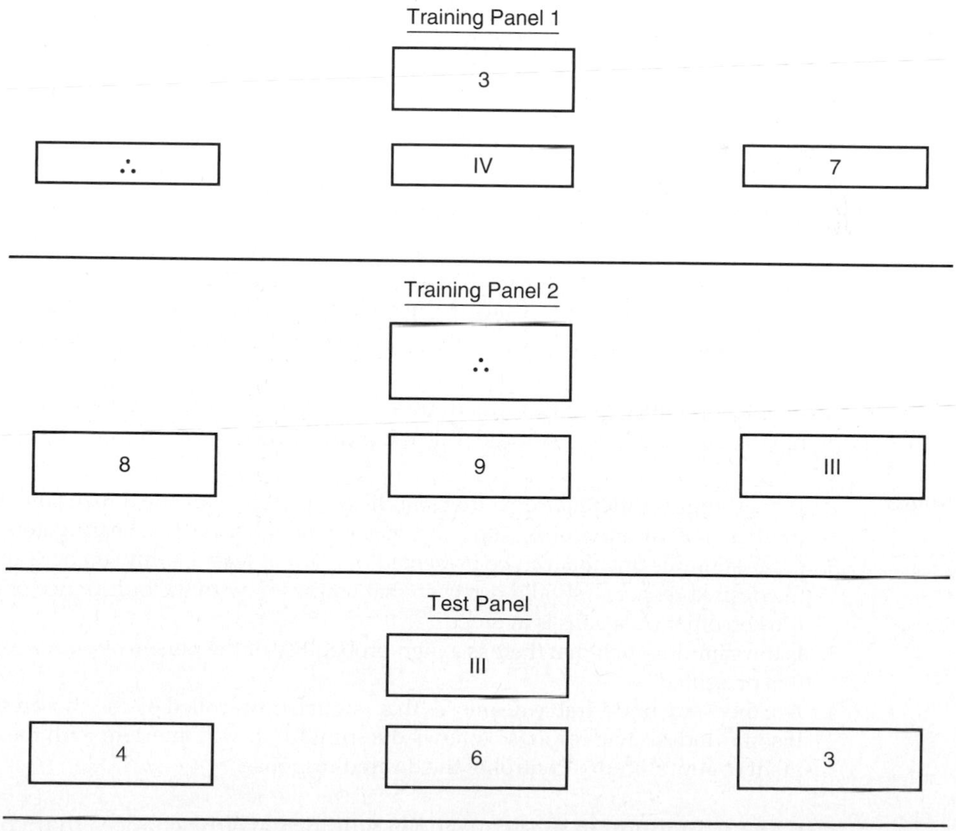

Training Panel 1

3

| ∴ | | IV | | 7 |

Training Panel 2

∴

| 8 | | 9 | | III |

Test Panel

III

| 4 | | 6 | | 3 |

Figure 8–2   Visual displays in a stimulus equivalence experiment.

As we grow up, we acquire many equivalence classes in which all members of a class control the same response, but in which the members of the class are physically very different. When a new behavior becomes conditioned to one member of an equivalence class, that behavior is likely to be controlled by other members of the class without explicit training. In everyday speech we would say that **Note 2** the members of an equivalence class "mean" the same thing (as when we learn the different representations of "3," the different words for "drinking utensil," that tomatoes and mushrooms are both "vegetables," etc.). Each of these equivalence classes (vegetables, drinking utensils, etc.) are also referred to as concepts. Thus, you can see that some concepts are based on stimulus common-element classes, and others are based on stimulus equivalence classes.

In summary, if a response that has been reinforced to one stimulus occurs to a different stimulus (due to unlearned generalization, the learning of a stimulus common-element class, or the learning of an equivalence class), we say that stimulus generalization has occurred. However, not all instances of stimulus generalization are favorable. For example, a child might learn to say "doggie" to a hairy four-legged creature, and later say "doggie" when seeing a cat. In these (and thousands of other) instances, it is necessary to teach discriminations, as described in the next section. (Strategies for improving generalization are discussed further in Chapter 16.)

FACTORS DETERMINING THE EFFECTIVENESS OF STIMULUS DISCRIMINATION TRAINING

1. Choosing Distinct Signals

If it is important to develop stimulus control of a particular behavior, it is often desirable to identify controlling S^Ds that are very distinctive. For example, the teacher in the Auckland school (described at the beginning of this chapter) used large, red letters for the sign that prompted the students to listen and look at the teacher, and large, green letters for the sign that prompted the students to work at their desks.

When considering a stimulus to be set up as an S^D for the behavior of another person, you might ask yourself the following questions.

Note 3
1. Is the stimulus different from other stimuli along more than one dimension? That is, is it different in location, size, color, and sensory modality (vision, hearing, touch, etc.)?
2. Is the stimulus one that can be presented only (or at least mainly) on occasions when the desired response should occur, so that confusion with the occurrence of the stimulus on other occasions is avoided?
3. Is the stimulus such that there is a high probability of the person attending to it when it is presented?
4. Are there any undesirable responses that might be controlled by the chosen stimulus? If some undesirable response follows the stimulus, it will interfere with the development of new stimulus control of the desired response.

Careful attention to these questions will increase the chances that your stimulus discrimination training will be effective.

2. Minimizing the Opportunities for Error

Consider the example of a child learning to pick up a phone when it rings, but not when it doesn't ring. The response of picking up the phone if it has not been ringing is a response to an S^Δ. This is typically referred to as an *error*. Stimulus control can be developed most effectively when the behavior modifier minimizes the possibility of errors. For example, a parent who is teaching a child to answer the phone appropriately might move the phone out of reach if it is not ringing and add verbal prompts of this sort: "Now remember, we don't pick up telephones when they are not ringing. We only answer them just after they've begun to ring." Then, as soon as the phone rings (perhaps a phone call from a friend, made specifically for training purposes), the parent might immediately place the phone in front of the child and say, "The phone is ringing. Now you should answer it."

At this point you might be thinking, "But often we want to teach people to respond to subtle cues. Why should we then maximize distinctive signals?" Let us simply reply that choosing distinctive cues and minimizing errors will lead to more rapid stimulus control than might otherwise occur. In Chapter 9, we discuss techniques for gradually introducing discriminations involving very subtle cues. For the moment, it is important to keep in mind that efforts to choose distinctive signals and to minimize errors will lead to the development of effective stimulus control more quickly and with less frustration than attempting to develop discriminations that involve subtle cues.

3. Maximizing the Number of Trials

In general, it is well accepted that a number of reinforced trials are necessary for the development of consistent behaviors in persons with developmental disabilities and other behaviorally deficient individuals. What many people forget is that this is often true for all of us when we are acquiring new discriminations. Suppose, for example, that, after a few months of marriage, one of the partners presents subtle cues that he or she is not "in the mood" for lovemaking. What that partner must realize is that the other person may not learn to respond to subtle cues, or even obvious cues, with just one or two trials. After a number of instances of reinforcement for correct responding to the S^Ds and extinction for responses to the S^Δs, those S^Ds and S^Δs will likely control the response on subsequent trials.

4. Make Use of Rules: Describe the Contingencies

The development of stimulus control often involves trial and error—several trials of positive reinforcement for a behavior in the presence of an S^D and several trials of that behavior going unreinforced in the presence of an S^Δ. Johnny's swearing, for example, came under the control of the other kids as S^Ds (and came not to occur in the presence of Grandma and Grandpa as S^Δs) through trial and error. However, the children in the classroom example at the start of this chapter did not take a few trials to show evidence of stimulus control. During the very first session after the teacher explained the new set of classroom rules, the children showed an immediate increase in on-task behavior in the presence of the appropriate signs (LOOK AT THE TEACHER, etc.), and they immediately earned reinforcement for doing so.

Johnny's swearing likely illustrates what is called *contingency-shaped behavior.* This is behavior that is developed by the direct-acting effects of reinforcement in the absence of statements to or by an individual specifying the contingency. No one told Johnny, "Swear and we'll laugh and give you attention!" In contrast, the behavior of the children in the classroom in the example at the beginning of this chapter illustrates what is called rule-governed behavior. A *rule* describes a contingency of reinforcement—stimuli, behavior, and consequences. *Rule-governed behavior* is behavior that is controlled by the statement of a rule. When you wish to develop good stimulus control over a particular behavior, you should always provide the individual with a rule or set of rules stating what behaviors in what situations will lead to what consequences. Because of our complex conditioning histories for following instructions, the addition of a set of rules to a stimulus discrimination program may lead to instantaneous stimulus control.

One way to look at the difference between contingency-shaped behavior and rule-governed behavior is to ask yourself if an animal could do it. Johnny's dog, for example, would probably not snarl at Grandma and Grandpa's house if its snarling was never reinforced there. But Johnny's dog could not verbalize, either overtly or covertly, "I'd better not snarl at Johnny's grandparents' house because they don't reward me for that behavior there." In our example of Johnny's swearing, we are assuming that he doesn't verbalize the contingency operating on his swearing any more than his dog verbalizes the contingency operating on his snarling. In the classroom example, in contrast, the children verbalized the rules they were given, which, in turn, exerted immediate control over their behavior; hence, their behavior was rule governed. (Use of rules is discussed further in Chapter 17.)

PITFALLS OF STIMULUS DISCRIMINATION TRAINING

Any effective method can be misapplied, and stimulus discrimination training is no exception. One of the authors observed an example of this with a 7-year-old boy with developmental disabilities who banged his head against hard surfaces unless an adult was holding his hand. As soon as the adult dropped the child's hand and moved away, the child would immediately dive to the floor and begin banging his head hard enough to cause considerable bleeding. This behavior occurred only when the child was standing on a hard floor or on concrete. It did not occur when he was standing on a rug or on grass. The reason for this is easy to see. No one would come running to give him attention if he banged his head on a soft carpet or on grass, since he did not injure himself when he did that. Of course, the staff had no choice but to give him attention when he banged his head on hard surfaces. The staff had thus inadvertently taught the boy the discrimination on the next page.

1. S^D $\longrightarrow$ Response $\longrightarrow$ Reinforcer
      (hard surface)   (banging head)   (attention from staff)
2. S^Δ $\longrightarrow$ Response $\longrightarrow$ No reinforcer
      (soft surface)   (banging head)   (no attention from staff)

There are numerous examples of situations in which people inadvertently teach others to respond inappropriately to particular cues. If they were aware of what they were doing, they would not teach those discriminations. Behavioral episodes of the following sort are common in many households with young children. Terry, a 3-year-old boy, is playing with the remote control for the TV set. Mother says quietly, "Terry, please leave that alone." Terry continues to fiddle with the remote control. A few minutes later, Mother hollers a little louder and a little less politely, "Terry, put that down." Terry continues to fiddle with the remote, rapidly changing channels, which is a natural reinforcer for Terry. A minute or two later Mother says, this time loudly and with a threatening look, "Terry, for the last time, leave the remote alone and get away from the TV set before I get really mad!" Terry finally moves away from the TV set and Mother says, "Now, that's better, Terry. Mommy likes it when you do what I tell you; why didn't you do that in the first place?" It is probably obvious to you that Mother has just reinforced Terry for responding to her third-level threats. The discrimination Terry is learning is that of waiting until Mother is really angry and threatening before attending to her requests.

If you feel that you have to tell an individual something many times before he or she responds, or that nobody listens to you, or that others are not doing the right thing at the right time and place, you should closely examine your interactions with these individuals for instances of misapplication of stimulus discrimination training.

GUIDELINES FOR EFFECTIVE STIMULUS DISCRIMINATION TRAINING

1. *Choose distinct signals.* Specify the S^Ds and at least one S^Δ. (In other words, specify conditions under which the behavior should and should not occur.)
2. *Select an appropriate reinforcer.* See Figure 3–3.
3. *Develop the discrimination.*
    a. Arrange for several reinforced responses in the presence of the S^D.
        (1) Specify clearly in a rule the S^D–desirable response–reinforcer sequence. Help identify the cues that indicate that the behavior will be reinforced versus the cues that indicate that the behavior will not be reinforced, and use instructions when appropriate to teach the student to act in a particular way under one set of circumstances but not under another.
        (2) Keep verbal cues constant initially.
        (3) Post the rules in a conspicuous place, and review them regularly.
        (4) Recognize that stimulus control over the behavior will not develop if the individual is not attending to the cues; therefore, use prompts (discussed further in Chapter 9) to emphasize the cues.
        (5) To teach the individual to act at a specific time, present prompts for correct performance just before the action is to occur.
    b. When the S^Δ is presented, make the change from the S^D very obvious and follow the rules for extinction for the behavior of concern. Stimuli that can acquire

control over behavior include such things as geographic location of training place; physical characteristics and location of furniture, equipment, and people in the training room; time of day of training; and sequence of events that precede and accompany training. A change in any of these may disrupt stimulus control.

4. *Weaning the individual from the program* (discussed in more detail in Chapter 16).
   a. If the behavior occurs in the right place at the right time at a desirable rate during a dozen or so of the opportunities (for the behavior), and if it is not occurring in the presence of the S^Δ situations, it might be possible to gradually eliminate contrived reinforcers and maintain the behavior with natural reinforcers.
   b. Look for other natural reinforcers in the environment that might maintain the behavior once it is occurring in the presence of S^Ds and not in the presence of S^Δs.
   c. After the program is terminated, plan periodic assessments of the behavior in order to ensure that it is occasionally being reinforced, and that the desired frequency of the behavior is being maintained in the presence of the S^Ds.

STUDY QUESTIONS

1. What is a stimulus?
2. What is meant by good stimulus control? Describe an example.
3. Define and give an example of an S^D. Identify the response in the example.
4. Define and give an example of an S^Δ. Identify the response in the example.
5. What is the difference between a stimulus and a discriminative stimulus?
6. Distinguish between stimulus discrimination training and stimulus control.
7. Describe an example (not from the text) of a stimulus that is an S^D for one behavior and an S^Δ for a different behavior.
8. What is an ABC assessment?
9. Identify examples of S^Ds and S^Δs as follows: two S^Ds from Table 3–1, two S^Ds from Table 3–3, two S^Δs from Table 5–1, and two S^Δs from Table 5–2.
10. Define stimulus generalization and give an example.
11. What do we mean by stimulus common-element class? by conceptual behavior? Describe an example of each.
12. Describe how you might teach the concept "honest" to a child. Would your program teach a child to be honest? Why or why not?
13. Explain the difference between stimulus generalization and stimulus discrimination.
14. What do we mean by equivalence class? Describe an example.
15. What is a primary distinction between stimulus generalization involving stimulus common-element classes and stimulus generalization involving stimulus equivalence classes?
16. When you are considering the selection of a stimulus to be set up as an S^D, what questions might you ask yourself about that stimulus? (See p. 108.)
17. For each of the questions that you asked yourself in Question 16, provide an example from your own experience.
18. What do we mean by an error in stimulus discrimination training?
19. What are "contingencies of reinforcement"? Explain.
20. With examples, distinguish between rule-governed and contingency-shaped behavior.
21. Was the children's high on-task behavior to the posted rule in the Auckland classroom likely rule governed or contingency shaped? Justify your choice.
22. Describe an example of how ignorance of stimulus discrimination training may lead parents or other caregivers to develop an undesirable behavior in a child or adult in their care.

APPLICATION EXERCISES

A. Exercises Involving Others

1. Identify five situations in which you presented an S^D that controlled the behavior of some other person. Clearly identify the general situation, the controlling S^D, the behavior controlled, and the reinforcers.
2. Describe five situations in which you presented an S^Δ to some other person. Clearly identify the general situation, the S^Δ, the behavior for which your stimulus was an S^Δ, and the consequences. Indicate whether or not the S^Δ controlled the behavior appropriately.

B. Self-Modification Exercises

1. Describe a recent situation in which you generalized in a desirable way. Clearly identify the behavior, the situation in which the behavior was initially reinforced (the training situation), and the situation to which the behavior generalized (target situation).
2. Describe a recent situation in which you generalized in an undesirable way (in other words the outcome was undesirable). Again, identify the behavior, training situation, and target situation.
3. Choose an excessive behavior of yours that you might like to decrease. Carefully monitor those situations in which the behavior occurs and does not occur over a two- or three-day period. Clearly identify the controlling S^Ds, and, if possible, some controlling S^Δs for the behavior. Such information will prove to be extremely helpful if you decide to set up a self-control program after completing this book.
4. On the basis of the material you have read thus far in this book, describe in detail how you might set up a program to control your study behavior so as to improve your learning of the discriminations that are necessary in mastering the remainder of the material in this book. (*Hint:* Consider stimulus control, reinforcement, extinction, incompatible behaviors, and schedules of reinforcement.)

NOTES AND EXTENDED DISCUSSION

1. Technically, stimulus equivalence requires the demonstration of three relationships; reflexivity, symmetry, and transitivity (Dymond & Rehfeldt, 2000; Sidman, 1994). Reflexivity simply involves recognizing instances of a stimulus. In other words, a child is able to match 3 to 3, ∴ to ∴, and III to III. Now consider the top panel in Figure 8–2. Suppose that, after training, the child has learned to correctly press the panel "∴" when shown "3." We then place "∴" in the top panel and "3" is then randomly placed with the other two choices. If the child, when now shown "∴," chooses "3," the child has demonstrated symmetry. Transitivity is the type of relationship successfully demonstrated when the child passes the test in the fourth panel shown in

Figure 8–2. In other words, as a result of learning to match A to B and B to C, an individual now matches C to A without specific training to do so.

2.   Since Skinner (1957) published a behavioral account of language, psycholinguists have argued that operant conditioning is inadequate to explain a child's acquisition of his or her native language (Brown, 1973; Chomsky, 1959; Pinker, 1994). Their argument is based largely on the view that children learn more about language than is directly trained or directly reinforced. However, through automatic conditioned reinforcement (described in Note 1 of Chapter 4), infants are able to emit vocal behaviors that have not been directly reinforced. And through stimulus equivalence training, children can learn that physically different sounds can "mean" the same thing as other sounds, provided that they are members of the same equivalence class. Such factors can explain the acquisition of syntax and grammar, and provide empirical support for Skinner's behavioral view of language development (Stromer, Mackay, & Remington, 1996).

3.   Some forms of stimulus control are more complex than a single stimulus (such as a green light or a sign in a window) controlling a single response (such as crossing a street or going into a shop to buy something). One complex type of stimulus control, called contextual control, is that in which the general setting or context may alter the manner in which an individual responds to particular stimuli. For example, when you drive in Great Britain, the highway dividing line is an S^D to steer to the left of it, whereas when you drive in Canada, it is an S^D to steer to the right of it. In this example, the country in which you are driving is the context that determines how a particular stimulus controls your behavior. Knowledge of contextual control can be important in designing effective behavioral treatments. For example, Haring and Kennedy (1990) found that a procedure was effective in reducing the self-stimulating behavior of a girl with autism in the classroom but was not effective in a recreational setting; and, conversely, a procedure that was effective in reducing her self-stimulatory behavior when she was doing leisure activities was not effective in reducing it when she was performing classroom tasks.

Study Questions on Notes

1.   Using examples, explain what is meant by reflexivity, symmetry, and transitivity.
2.   How have studies of stimulus equivalence provided support for a behavioral view of language development?
3.   What is meant by the term *contextual control*? Illustrate with an example.
4.   Just before starting to cross a street, a pedestrian visiting Canada from England observed that the street was clear to his right, stepped into the street, and was struck by a car. Explain how lack of contextual control was involved in this accident.

Developing Appropriate Behavior with Fading

"Peter, what's your name?"

TEACHING PETER HIS NAME[1]

Peter, diagnosed with autism, possessed an extensive vocal mimicking repertoire (he could repeat many of the words other people said) but had little other verbal behavior. He would imitate many words, even when it was not appropriate. For example, when asked, "What's your name?," he would reply "Name." Sometimes he would repeat the entire question, "What's your name?" This was a problem of stimulus control in that questions (stimuli) evoked mimicking responses rather than appropriate answers.

A university student named Veronica taught Peter to respond appropriately to the question, "What's your name?" as follows. First, Veronica identified an effective reinforcer. Since Peter had been taught to work for plastic chips that could be exchanged for treats such as candy and popcorn, Veronica decided to use the chips as reinforcers.

Peter sat at a small table in a quiet room, and Veronica sat across from him. In a very soft whisper, Veronica asked, "What's your name?" Then very loudly and quickly, before Peter could respond, she shouted, "PETER!" Of course, Peter mimicked the word "Peter," and Veronica reinforced this with "Good boy!" and a chip. You may wonder how this could represent any progress, since the boy was still only mimicking the student. However, over several trials Veronica began asking the question "What's your name?" more loudly and supplying the answer "Peter" more quietly. On each trial, she continued to reinforce the correct response—"Peter." Eventually, Veronica asked loudly "What's your name?" and simply mouthed the word "Peter." Nevertheless, the boy responded with the correct answer, "Peter." Over several trials Veronica ceased even mouthing the correct answer, but Peter still responded correctly to the question "What's your name?"

---

[1]This case is taken from Martin, England, Kaprowy, Kilgour, and Pilek (1968).

FADING

Fading is the gradual change over successive trials of a stimulus that controls a response so that the response eventually occurs to a partially changed or completely new stimulus (Deitz & Malone, 1985). In the case described, Peter would at first say his name only when it was said to him. Through a fading process, the stimulus control over the response "Peter" was gradually transferred from the stimulus "Peter" to the stimulus "What's your name?" (At this point one might ask whether Peter knew that he was saying his own name. But this is a vague question, so let's try to phrase it more behaviorally. Would Peter have consistently responded correctly when asked other questions involving his name; for example, would he have consistently answered "Peter" when shown his reflection in the mirror and asked "Who's that?" Probably not. However, teaching him to answer "What's your name?" was an appropriate and important start to teaching him to answer other questions involving his name and to his knowing that he was saying his name.)

Fading is involved in many everyday situations in which one person teaches a behavior to another person. Parents are likely to fade out their help and support when teaching a child to walk or ride a bicycle. A dance instructor might use less and less hand pressure to guide a student through new dance steps. And as a teenager progresses in drivers' education, the driving instructor is likely to provide fewer and fewer verbal hints to attend to various traffic regulations.

In any situation in which a stimulus exerts strong control over a response, fading can be a very useful procedure for transferring the control of that response to some other stimulus. The discovery and development of fading techniques have led to some changes in educators' views regarding the learning process. At one time it was believed that people had to make mistakes while learning in order to know what not to do. However, errorless transfer of a discrimination can occur, and it has at least three advantages over procedures involving trial and error. First, errors consume valuable time. Second, if an error occurs once, it tends to occur many times, even though it is being extinguished. (Remember from Chapter 5 that during extinction, "things may get worse before they get better.") Third, the nonreinforcement that occurs when errors are being extinguished often produces emotional side effects such as tantrums, aggressive behavior, and attempts to escape from the situation.

We have used fading procedures in many learning situations in our programs with persons with developmental disabilities and autism, and with very young children. In teaching students to name an item of clothing—a shirt, for example—teachers might proceed according to the following steps.

1. Point to your shirt and say "shirt." Keep doing this until the student consistently mimics "shirt" a number of times, and immediately reinforce each correct response. (This assumes that you have a student who is able to mimic this particular word. It also assumes that the student has been trained to look at any item you point to.)
2. When the student consistently mimics "shirt," present the stimulus that you want to control the response, and at the same time gradually fade out saying "shirt." That is, you might say, "What's this? Shirt" while pointing to the shirt. In response, the student usually mimics "shirt." Over several trials, gradually decrease the intensity of

saying "shirt" to zero, so that the student eventually responds with the answer "shirt" to the stimulus of someone pointing at a shirt and asking "What's this?" Again, each appropriate response is to be reinforced.

Fading can also be used to teach tracing, copying, and drawing circles, lines, squares, triangles, numerals, and letters of the alphabet. To teach a student to trace a circle, the teacher might begin with a large number of sheets with a heavily dotted circle on each of them. The teacher places a pencil in the student's hand, says "Trace the circle," and then guides his hand so that the pencil traces the circle by connecting the dots. Immediately after this, of course, the student receives a reinforcer. After several such trials, the teacher fades out the pressure of her hand as a cue controlling the student's tracing by

1. lightly holding the student's hand for several trials;
2. touching her fingertips to the back of the student's hand for several trials;
3. pointing to the item to be traced;
4. finally, simply giving the instruction, "Trace the circle." (Steps 1, 2, and 3 are always accompanied by this instruction.)

Once the teacher has taught the student to trace, she or he can teach the student to draw or copy by fading out the dotted cues that guide the tracing. For example, the teacher might use a sheet on which there are several dotted circles. The circles progress from a heavily dotted circle on the left to a circle with very few dots on the right. The teacher points to the most heavily dotted circle and instructs the student, "Trace the circle here." The desired response is reinforced, and the procedure is repeated for each of the more lightly dotted circles. On subsequent steps, the dots can be faded out completely so that the student will draw a circle in the absence of dots. It is then a simple matter to fade in the instruction "Draw a circle" to this newly acquired response. The instruction "Copy a circle," said while the teacher points to a circle, can also be faded in and come to control the response. Teaching the student to copy many different figures in this fashion will eventually enable him to copy adequately figures that he has had little experience copying.

DIMENSIONS OF STIMULI FOR FADING

As illustrated by the above examples, fading occurs along dimensions of stimuli, such as the loudness of the question that Veronica presented to Peter, or the pressure of a teacher's hand that guides a student's printing, or the clarity of dots that a student might be expected to trace. In general, a *dimension* is any characteristic that can be measured on some continuum. Thus far, we have talked of fading across very specific stimulus dimensions, but fading can also occur across changes in a general situation or setting. For example, in one of the authors' programs with children with autism, we wanted to have a group of children respond appropriately in a classroom setting (Martin et al., 1968). However, they were very disruptive, especially in a group situation. Therefore, we could not at first place them in a classroom setting. We decided first to obtain the desired behavior from each child in an individual situation and then fade in the classroom setting.

Our initial training sessions were conducted in a small room in which there were several chairs and tablet-arm desks. Two or three teachers (university students) worked individually with two or three students on a one-to-one basis. The procedures involved eliminating tantrums through extinction and reinforcing sitting attentively, appropriate verbal behavior, drawing, copying, and other desirable behaviors. Each child's desk was placed against the wall in such a fashion making it difficult for him to leave the situation.

Within one week, the children learned to sit quietly, attend to the teacher, and imitate words in verbal training. Stimulus control was established between the general training situation and the children's attentiveness. But our goal at that time was to teach the children to function appropriately in a regular classroom situation with one teacher at the front of the class. If we had switched immediately to this situation after the first week, however, much inattentiveness and disruptive behavior would no doubt have occurred. Therefore, over a period of four weeks, we gradually changed from one small room with three students and three teachers to a standard-sized classroom with seven students and one teacher. This fading occurred along two stimulus dimensions.

One dimension was the physical structure of the room. We moved the children from the small room to the regular large classroom. However, we did so by first placing the three tablet-arm desks against the wall of the regular classroom, just as we had done in the small room. The three chairs that the teachers sat in were also moved to the regular classroom. The rest of the classroom was empty. Over several days, the tablet-arm desks were gradually moved away from the wall and toward the center of the room until, finally, the three desks were side by side. Additional desks and furnishings were added one at a time until the children were finally sitting in desks in a normally furnished classroom.

The second dimension was the number of children per teacher. Fading along this dimension was carried out at the same time that fading along the first dimension took place. At first, one teacher worked with one student for several sessions. The teacher then worked with two students, alternating questions between them for several sessions. In this fashion, the student–teacher ratio was increased gradually until only one teacher worked with as many as seven children in a classroom situation.

FACTORS INFLUENCING THE EFFECTIVENESS OF FADING

1. Choosing the Final Desired Stimulus

The *final desired stimulus* (i.e., the stimulus we want to evoke or produce the behavior at the end of the fading procedure) should be chosen carefully. It is important to select the final desired stimulus so that the occurrence of the response to that particular stimulus is likely to be maintained in the natural environment. Some fading programs make the error of stopping with a stimulus that does not include some aspect of the situation that the student will frequently encounter in the natural environment. Consider Peter's case. It would have been easy for Veronica to stop training at the second to last step, at which Veronica asked loudly, "What's your name?" and then mouthed the word "Peter." However, when others approached Peter in his natural environment and asked "What's your name?" they would not likely mouth "Peter." Therefore, Veronica conducted the last step of the program, in which Peter responded correctly to the question "What's your name?" completely on his own.

2. Choosing the Starting Stimulus: A Prompt

At the beginning of a fading program, it is important to select a starting stimulus that reliably evokes the desired behavior. In the task of teaching Peter his name, Veronica knew that Peter would mimic the last word of a question when that word was spoken loudly. Therefore, the starting stimulus with Peter was the question "What's your name?" said very softly and followed quickly by the shouted word, "Peter!" The shouted word "Peter" prompted him to give the correct answer. A **prompt** is a stimulus (such as saying "Peter") introduced to increase the likelihood of the desired behavior, but that is not the final desired stimulus to control that behavior.

Teacher Behaviors as Prompts   It is helpful to distinguish between several types of teacher behaviors that can be used as prompts. *Physical prompts* (also called *physical guidance*) consist of the teacher touching the learner to guide him or her appropriately. Parents frequently use physical guidance to help their children learn new behavior, such as holding their hand while teaching them to walk. As other examples, beginning dancers, martial arts students, and novice golfers often find a "guiding hand" to be helpful. *Gestural prompts* are certain motions that the teacher makes, such as pointing to the correct cue or making motions directed toward the learner without touching him or her. A teacher might, for example, put his finger to his lips as a prompt for children to be quiet in the library, or extend his hand palm outward to prompt walking slowly in the hall. *Modeling prompts* occur when the teacher demonstrates the correct behavior (modeling is discussed further in Chapter 18). A swimming coach might model the correct arm movements for the freestyle stroke for young swimmers. A golfing instructor might model the correct way to grip a golf club for a group of beginning golfers. *Verbal prompts* are verbal hints or cues. A driving instructor might use verbal prompts by telling a student driver to "check over your left shoulder before pulling out." Parents frequently use verbal prompts when teaching their children how to dress themselves (e.g., "Now pull the sweater over your head.").

Note 1

Environmental Alterations as Prompts   *Environmental prompts* consist of alterations of the physical environment in a manner that will evoke the desired behavior. Someone attempting to eat healthy, for example, might put a bowl of fresh fruit in easy reach while keeping junk food out of sight in a difficult-to-reach cupboard. A student might, as another example, ensure that her study area contains only objects and material related to studying.

Extra-Stimulus versus Within-Stimulus Prompts   Teacher-behavior prompts and environmental prompts can be further subdivided into extra-stimulus prompts and within-stimulus prompts. An *extra-stimulus prompt* is something that is added to the environment to make a correct response more likely. Suppose, for example, that a parent wanted to teach a child to place a knife, fork, and spoon appropriately when setting a table for dinner. One option would be for the parent to point to the appropriate location of each utensil as it was named and placed. Pointing would be an extra-stimulus teacher-behavior prompt, and it would be faded over trials. Alternatively, the parent might draw a knife, fork, and a spoon in their appropriate location on a placemat, and require the child to place the utensils appropriately. The line drawings would be an extra-stimulus environmental prompt, and they could gradually be erased over trials. A *within-stimulus prompt* is an alteration of the characteristics of the S^D or the S^Δ to make them more noticeable and therefore easier to discriminate. In the table-setting example, training might be initiated with a normal fork and knife in their normal positions, with a large wooden spoon as the training item. This would be a within-stimulus environmental prompt. The initial focus would be on teaching the child to place the spoon in the correct position. Over trials, the size of the spoon could be faded back to normal. This process could then be repeated with the knife and the fork until the child sets the table correctly. A within-stimulus prompt could also involve teacher behavior. If a teacher, for example, was trying to teach a child to respond appropriately to two words that sound similar, such as pen and pencil (both include the "pen" sound), the teacher might initially exaggerate differences in the sounds of the words when asking for either a pen ("PEN!") or a pencil ("pen-CIL!") and then gradually fade the sounds to their normal pitch and loudness. The different types of prompts are listed in Table 9–1. Several studies have indicated that within-stimulus prompt fading is more effective than extra-stimulus prompt fading with children with developmental disabilities and autism (Schreibman, 1975; Witt & Wacker, 1981; Wolfe & Cuvo, 1978).

A behavior modifier may provide any or all of these types of prompts to ensure the correct response. For example, suppose that a teacher wishes to develop appropriate stimulus control by the instruction "Touch your head" over the response of a student touching her head. The teacher might initiate training by saying "Touch your head. Raise your hand and put it on your head like this" while touching his own head. In this example, "Raise your hand and put it on your head

TABLE 9–1   TYPES OF PROMPTS

Teacher-Behavior Prompts
Physical guidance—physically assisting the learner *Gestures*—pointing or motioning *Modeling*—demonstrating the correct behavior *Verbal*—words as hints or cues, instructions

Environmental Prompts
Environmental—rearranging the physical surroundings

Extra-Stimulus versus Within-Stimulus Prompts
Extra-stimulus—adding another stimulus to make a correct response more likely *Within-stimulus*—making the S^D or the S^Δ more noticeable and easier to discriminate

like this" is a verbal prompt and the teacher's action of putting his hand on his head is a modeling prompt. Selecting several kinds of prompts that, together, reliably produce the desired response will minimize errors and maximize the success of the fading program.

3. Choosing the Fading Steps

Note 2 When the desired response is occurring reliably to the prompts given at the onset of the training program, they can then be gradually removed over trials. The steps through which prompts are to be eliminated should be carefully chosen. Unfortunately, effective use of fading is, like shaping (see Chapter 10), still somewhat of an art. It is very important to monitor the student's performance closely to determine the speed at which fading should be carried out. Fading should be neither too fast not too slow. If the student begins to make errors, the prompts may have been faded too quickly or through too few fading steps. It is then necessary to backtrack until the behavior is again well established before continuing with fading. However, if too many steps are introduced or too many prompts are provided over a number of trials, the student might become overly dependent on the prompts. Consider the example of teaching a child to touch his head when asked to do so. If the teacher spends a great many trials providing the prompt of touching her own head, the child may become dependent on it and attend much less to the instruction "Touch your head."

PITFALLS OF FADING

Just as other behavior principles and procedures can be applied unknowingly by those who are not familiar with them, so can fading be misused. However, it appears to be more difficult to misuse fading inadvertently because the necessary gradual change in cues rarely occurs by chance.

The case of the child who banged his head on hard surfaces (described in Chapter 8) might be an example of the effects of the misuse of fading. In Chapter 10 we point out that shaping might produce such behavior. It is also possible that fading is responsible for it. Suppose that the child began attracting attention initially by hitting his head on soft surfaces, such as grass. At first, this behavior may have caused adults to come running to see if the child had injured himself. When they eventually learned that no injury resulted from this behavior, they ceased providing him with attention. The child may then have progressed to hitting his head with the same force but on slightly harder surfaces, such as carpeted floors. For a while, this perhaps increased the amount of attention elicited from adults, but this amount of attention may eventually have decreased when the adults learned that the child did not injure himself in this way. Only when the child graduated to hitting his head on surfaces such as hard floors and even concrete, which caused real and serious self-injury, did the adults give him continued attention. Note that throughout this example there was a gradual change in the stimulus (the type of floor surface) evoking the undesired behavior; eventually, the behavior was evoked by the most undesirable stimulus possible. Thus, this example fits the technical definition of fading.

GUIDELINES FOR THE EFFECTIVE APPLICATION OF FADING

1. *Choose the final desired stimulus.* Specify very clearly the stimuli in the presence of which the target behavior should eventually occur.
2. *Select an appropriate reinforcer* (see Chapter 3).
3. *Choose the starting stimulus and fading steps.*
   a. Specify clearly the conditions under which the desired behavior now occurs—that is, what people, words, physical guidance, and so forth, are necessary, at present, to evoke the desired behavior.
   b. Specify specific prompts that will evoke the desired behavior.
   c. Specify clearly the dimensions (such as color, people, and room size) that you will fade to reach the desired stimulus control.
   d. Outline the specific fading steps to be followed and the rules for moving from one step to the next.
4. *Put the plan into effect.*
   a. Present the starting stimulus and reinforce the correct behavior.
   b. Across trials, the fading of cues should be so gradual that there are as few errors as possible. However, if an error occurs, move back to the previous step for several trials and provide additional prompts.
   c. When the desired stimulus control is obtained, review the guidelines in previous chapters for weaning the learner from the program (a topic that is discussed in more detail in Chapter 16).

STUDY QUESTIONS

1. Define fading and give an example of it.
2. Why is it advantageous to establish stimulus control without errors?
3. Identify three stimulus dimensions along which fading occurred in the examples cited in the first two sections of this chapter.
4. Describe an example from this chapter in which the training situation remained constant but a specific stimulus dimension was faded.
5. Describe an example from this chapter in which the general training situation was faded.
6. Describe how you might use fading to teach your pet to perform a trick.
7. Assume that you have an 18-month-old child who will imitate the word "chip." Describe in detail how you might use fading to teach your child to correctly identify a chip (i.e., a potato chip) when you point to it and ask "What's that?"
8. What do we mean by *final desired stimulus*? Give an example.
9. What do we mean by *starting stimulus*? Give an example.
10. Define *prompt.* Describe an example that is not from the text.
11. Define the four major categories of teacher-behavior prompts. Give an example of each.
12. Define *environmental prompt,* and describe an example that is not from the text.
13. Define *within-stimulus prompt,* and describe an example that is not from the text. Does your example involve a teacher-behavior prompt or an environmental prompt?
14. Define *extra-stimulus prompt,* and describe an example that is not from the text. Does your example involve a teacher-behavior prompt or an environmental prompt?
15. How many reinforced trials should occur at any given fading step before the stimuli of that particular step are changed? (*Hint:* What suggestions were made in the examples in this chapter?)

APPLICATION EXERCISES

A. Exercises Involving Others

1. Suppose that a 2- or 3-year-old child has reached the stage at which he is beginning to wander away from his front yard. The child has already learned some speech, and you wish to teach him to answer the question "Where do you live?" Outline a fading program with which you could teach the answer to this question; indicate what you would use as a reinforcer, the number of trials you would have at each fading step, and so forth.

2. Assume that you must teach a child with severe developmental disabilities, or a very young normal child, to eat with a spoon. Name and describe the categories of prompts that you would use. Describe how each of the prompts would be faded.

B. Self-Modification Exercise

Suppose that you detest certain vegetables from the cabbage family—such as broccoli—but research studies have convinced you that you can reduce your chances of heart disease and cancer by eating more of these vegetables. Outline a fading program that you could use to increase the amount of broccoli (and other such vegetables) that you eat. (*Hint:* Your program should not—at least in the long run—increase your fat intake, as that would defeat its purpose.)

NOTES AND EXTENDED DISCUSSION

1. The use of physical guidance raises a potential ethical issue. Suppose that, in a program for persons with developmental disabilities, a teacher decides to use physical guidance . Suppose further that an individual client resists being guided. Physical guidance in that instance would therefore be viewed as somewhat intrusive or restrictive. However, as indicated in the discussion of ethical guidelines in Chapter 30, it is generally agreed that behavior modifiers should use the least intrusive and restrictive interventions possible. Thus, the teacher applying physical guidance in this instance should ensure that doing so meets the ethical guidelines and accreditation standards of that particular agency. This issue is discussed further in Chapter 30.

2. There are four methods of removing prompts gradually: (a) decreasing assistance; (b) increasing assistance; (c) graduated guidance; and (d) time delay. Decreasing assistance, in which a starting stimulus that evokes the response is gradually removed or changed until the response is evoked by the final desired stimulus, is the method that is illustrated by all the examples of this chapter. Increasing assistance takes the opposite approach. The teacher begins with the final desired stimulus, and introduces prompts only if the student fails to respond appropriately to the final desired stimulus. The level of the prompts is gradually increased during a trial in which the student failed to respond at the preceding level until eventually the student responds to the prompt. Graduated guidance is similar to the method of decreasing assistance, except that the teacher's physical guidance is gradually adjusted from moment to moment within a trial as needed, and then faded across trials. For example, the teacher may grasp the student's hand firmly at the beginning of the trial and gradually reduce the force on the student's hand as the trial progresses. With time delay, the final desired stimulus and the starting stimulus are presented together at first; then, rather than changing the starting stimulus, the time interval between the final desired stimulus and the starting stimulus is gradually increased until eventually the individual is responding only to the final desired stimulus. Many studies have indicated little or no difference in the effectiveness of these different prompt-removal methods (for a review, see Demchak, 1990).

Study Questions on Notes

1. Describe a plausible example in which use of physical guidance in a teaching program might require ethical approval. Why would ethical approval be required?

2. Which of the prompt-removal procedures fit the definition of fading given at the beginning of this chapter, and which do not? Explain.

10

Getting a New Behavior to Occur: An Application of Shaping

"Frank, did you do your jogging?"

IMPROVING FRANK'S EXERCISING[1]

After taking an early retirement at the age of 55, Frank decided to make some changes in his life. But he wasn't sure where to start. Knowing that he needed to change some of his long-standing habits, he enrolled in a behavior modification course at the local community college. Next, on the advice of his doctor, he resolved to begin a regular exercise program. Frank had been a "couch potato" all his life. He typically came home from work, grabbed a can of beer, and parked himself in front of the television set. Frank launched his exercise program with a pledge to his wife that he would jog a quarter of a mile each day. But after a couple of attempts, he returned to his couch-potato routine. He had expected too much too soon. He then decided to try a procedure called shaping that he had studied in his behavior modification course. The following three stages summarize that procedure.

1. Specify the final desired behavior. Frank's goal was to jog a quarter of a mile each day. However, for a chronic nonexerciser, this was more than could be expected.
2. Identify a response that could be used as a starting point in working toward the final desired behavior. Frank decided that, at the very least, he would put on his sneakers and walk around the outside of the house once (approximately 30 yards). Although this was a long way from a quarter of a mile, it was at least a start.

_____

[1]This case is based on one described by Watson and Tharp (1997).

> *3. Reinforce the starting response; then make closer and closer approximations until eventually the desired response occurs. Frank decided to use the opportunity to drink a beer as a reinforcer. He explained his program to his wife and asked her to remind him that he had to complete his exercise before he could have a beer. After the first approximation had occurred on several successive afternoons, Frank increased the requirement to walking around the house twice (approximately 60 yards). A few days later, the distance was increased to walking around the house four times (approximately 120 yards), then six times (180 yards), then farther and farther until the distance was approximately a quarter of a mile, and then finally to jogging that distance. By reinforcing successive approximations to his goal, Frank reached the point where he jogged a quarter of a mile regularly. (The application of behavior modification techniques to improve self-control is discussed further in Chapter 26.)*

SHAPING

In the previous two chapters we described how stimulus discrimination training and fading could be used to establish appropriate stimulus control over a behavior, provided that that behavior occurred at least occasionally. But what if a desired behavior never occurs? In that case, it is not possible to increase its frequency simply by waiting until it occurs and then reinforcing it. However, a procedure called *shaping* can be used to establish a behavior the individual never performs. The behavior modifier begins by reinforcing a response that occurs with greater than zero frequency and at least remotely resembles the final desired response. (Frank, for example, was first reinforced for walking once around his house because this behavior occurred occasionally and remotely approximated the nonexistent behavior for him of jogging a quarter of a mile.) When this initial response is occurring at a high frequency, the behavior modifier stops reinforcing it and begins reinforcing a slightly closer approximation of the final desired response. Thus, the final desired response is eventually established by reinforcing successive approximations to it. For this reason, shaping is sometimes referred to as "the method of successive approximations." **Shaping** can be defined as the development of a new behavior by the successive reinforcement of closer approximations and the extinguishing of preceding approximations of the behavior.

The behaviors that an individual acquires during a lifetime develop from a variety of sources and influences. Sometimes a new behavior develops when an individual performs some initial behavior and the environment (either the physical environment or other people) then reinforces slight variations in that behavior across a number of trials. Eventually that initial behavior may be shaped so that the final form no longer resembles it. For example, most parents use shaping in teaching their children to talk. When an infant first begins to babble, some of the sounds remotely approximate words in the parents' native language. When this happens the parents usually reinforce the behavior with hugs, caresses, kisses, and smiles. The sounds "mmm" and "daa" typically receive exceptionally large doses of reinforcement from English-speaking parents. Eventually "ma-ma" and "da-da" occur and are strongly reinforced, and the more primitive "mmm" and "daa" are subjected to extinction. At a later stage, reinforcement is given after the child says "mommy" and "daddy," and "ma-ma" and "da-da" are extinguished.

The same process occurs with other words. First, the child passes through a stage in which very remote approximations of words in the parents' native language are reinforced. Then the child enters a stage in which "baby talk" (i.e., closer approximations of actual words) is reinforced. Finally, the child is required by the parents and others to pronounce words in accordance with the practices of the verbal community before reinforcement is given. For example, if a child says "wa-wa" at an early stage, she is given a glass of water, and if she is thirsty that reinforces the response. At a later stage "watah" rather than "wa-wa" is reinforced with water. Finally, the child is required to say "water" before water reinforcement will be given.

Of course, this description greatly oversimplifies the way in which a child learns to talk. However, it serves to illustrate the importance of shaping in the process by which normal children gradually progress from babbling to baby talk and finally to speaking in accordance with prevailing social conventions. Other processes that play important roles in speech development are discussed elsewhere in this text; for example automatic reinforcement in Chapter 4, stimulus equivalence in Chapter 8, and fading in Chapter 9.

There are five aspects or dimensions of behavior that can be shaped: topography, frequency, duration, latency, and intensity (or force). *Topography* refers to the spatial configuration or form of a particular response (i.e., the specific movements involved). Printing a word and writing the same word are examples of the same response made with two different topographies. Topography shaping occurs, for example, when teaching a child to switch from a printing response to a writing response, shaping a child's saying, "Mommy" instead of "Mama," learning to ice skate with longer and longer strides rather than short choppy steps, and shaping the proper finger movements for eating with chopsticks. An example of an early study involving topography shaping involved teaching a child to wear his glasses by reinforcing successive approximations of touching them, picking them up, putting the glasses up to his face, and finally wearing them (Wolf, Risley, & Mees, 1964).

We sometimes refer to the frequency or duration of a particular behavior as the *amount* of that behavior. The *frequency* of a behavior is the number of instances that occur in a given period of time. Examples of frequency shaping include increasing the number of steps (the distance) that Frank walked in his exercise program, and increasing the number of repetitions that a golfer practices a particular golf shot. The frequency of a response may also be reduced by shaping, as in a behavior modification program in which a patient with multiple sclerosis learned through shaping to gradually increase the time between (and hence decrease the frequency of) bathroom visits (O'Neill & Gardner, 1983). The *duration* of a response is the length of time that it lasts. Examples of duration shaping include lengthening the time spent studying before taking a break, and gradually adjusting the duration of stirring of pancake batter until it achieves just the right consistency.

Latency refers to the time between the occurrence of a stimulus and the response evoked by that stimulus. A common term for latency is reaction time. On the popular TV quiz show *Jeopardy!*, the time from the presentation of the host's verbal stimulus until a contestant presses a button is the contestant's latency of responding to that particular stimulus. In a race, the time between the firing of the starter's pistol and the runner leaving the blocks is the latency of the runner's response to the firing of the starting pistol. Latency shaping might enable the runner to react more quickly to the sound of the gun.

The *intensity* or force of a response refers to the physical effect the response has (or potentially has) on the environment. For an example of shaping force, consider a young farm boy whose job it is to pump water out of a well with an old-fashioned hand pump. When the pump was first installed, it was freshly oiled, the boy applied a certain amount of force to the handle; it moved up and down very easily; and water was produced. Let us suppose, however, that with lack of regular oiling, the pump has gradually acquired a little rust. Each day the boy probably applies the approximate amount of force he applied the previous day. When that force is no longer reinforced by the production of water, because the addition of the small amount of rust has made the pump handle more difficult to move, the boy will likely apply a little more force and find that it pays off. Over several months, the boy's behavior is gradually shaped so that he presses very hard on the first trial, a terminal behavior quite different from the initial behavior. Other examples of intensity shaping include learning to shake hands with a firmer grip and learning to apply the right amount of force when scratching to relieve an itch without damaging one's skin. An example of intensity shaping in a behavior modification program involved teaching a socially withdrawn girl whose speech was barely audible to speak louder and louder until she was speaking at normal voice volume (Jackson & Wallace, 1974). See Table 10–1 for a summary of the dimensions of behavior.

Note 1   Shaping is so common in everyday life that often people aren't even aware of it. Sometimes the shaping procedure is applied systematically (as in Frank's case), sometimes nonsystematically (such as when parents shape correct pronunciation of words spoken by their children), and sometimes shaping occurs from consequences in the natural environment (you gradually perfect your method for flipping pancakes).

Care should be taken to avoid confusing shaping with fading. Both are procedures of gradual change. However, as described in Chapter 9, fading involves reinforcement of a specific response in the presence of slight changes in a stimulus so that the stimulus gradually comes to resemble the stimulus that you wish to

TABLE 10–1   DIMENSIONS OF BEHAVIOR THAT CAN BE SHAPED

Dimension	Definition	Example
Topography (form)	Physical movements involved in the behavior	Extent of follow through on a tennis serve
Amount: frequency	Number of instances of the behavior in a given time	Number of dishes washed in 5 minutes
Amount: duration	Continuous amount of time behavior lasts	Length of time treading water
Latency	Time between the controlling stimulus and the behavior	Time between the question "What time is it?" and the response of looking at your watch
Intensity (force)	Amount of energy expended on the behavior	Force of a punch in boxing

control that particular response. Shaping, on the other hand, involves reinforcement of slight changes in a behavior so that it gradually comes to resemble the target behavior. Thus, *fading involves the gradual change of a stimulus while the response stays about the same; shaping involves the gradual change of a response while the stimulus stays about the same.*

FACTORS INFLUENCING THE EFFECTIVENESS OF SHAPING

1. Specifying the Final Desired Behavior

The first stage in shaping is to identify clearly the final desired behavior, which is often referred to as the *terminal behavior*. In Frank's case, the final desired behavior was jogging a quarter of a mile each day. With a definition as specific as this, there was very little possibility that Frank or his wife would develop different expectations regarding Frank's performance. If different people working with the individual expect different things, or if one person is not consistent from one training session or situation to the next, then progress is likely to be retarded. A precise statement of the final desired behavior increases the chances for consistent reinforcement of successive approximations of that behavior. The final desired behavior should be stated in such a way that all the relevant characteristics of the behavior (its topography, amount, latency, and intensity) are identified. In addition, the conditions under which the behavior is or is not to occur should be stated, and any other guidelines that appear to be necessary for consistency should be provided.

2. Choosing a Starting Behavior

Because the final desired or terminal behavior does not occur initially, and because it is necessary to reinforce some behavior that approximates it, you must identify a starting point. This should be a behavior that occurs often enough to be reinforced within the session time, and it should approximate the final desired behavior. For example, Frank's behavior of walking around the house once (approximately 60 yards) is something that he did periodically. This was the closest approximation that he regularly made with respect to the goal of jogging a quarter of a mile.

In a shaping program it is crucial to know not only where you are going (the terminal behavior), but also the level at which the individual is currently performing. The purpose of the shaping program is to get from one to the other by reinforcing successive approximations from the starting point to the final desired behavior, even though they might be very dissimilar. For example, in a classic study, Isaacs, Thomas, and Goldiamond (1960) applied shaping to redevelop verbal behavior in a catatonic schizophrenic man who had been mute for 19 years. Using chewing gum as a reinforcer, the experimenter took the patient through the shaping steps of eye movement toward the gum, facial movement, mouth movements, lip movements, vocalizations, word utterance, and, finally, understandable speech.

3. Choosing the Shaping Steps

Before initiating the shaping program, it is helpful to outline the successive approximations through which the person will be moved in the attempt to approximate the final desired behavior. For example, suppose that the final desired behavior in a shaping program for a child is saying "daddy." It has been determined that the child says "daa," and this response is set as the starting behavior. Let us suppose that we decide to go from the initial behavior of "daa" through the following steps: "da-da," "dad," "dad-ee," and "daddy." To begin, reinforcement is given on a number of occasions for emitting the initial behavior ("daa"). When this behavior is occurring repetitively, the trainer moves to step 2 ("da-da") and reinforces that approximation for several trials. This step-by-step procedure continues until the child finally says "daddy."

Note 2
How many successive approximations should there be? In other words, what is a reasonable step size? Unfortunately, there are no specific guidelines for identifying the ideal step size. In attempting to specify the behavioral steps from the initial behavior to the terminal behavior, the behavior modifier might imagine what steps she herself would go through. Also, it is sometimes helpful to observe learners who can already perform the terminal behavior and to ask them to perform the initial and subsequent approximations. Whatever guidelines or guesses are used, it is important to try to stick to them and yet be flexible if the trainee does not proceed quickly enough or is learning more quickly than had been expected. Some guidelines for moving through the behavioral program are offered in the following section.

4. Moving Along at the Correct Pace

How many times should each approximation be reinforced before proceeding to the next approximation? Again, there are no specific guidelines for answering this question. However, there are several rules of thumb to follow in reinforcing successive approximations of a final desired response:

    a. Reinforce an approximation at least several times before proceeding to the next step. In other words, avoid underreinforcement of a shaping step. Trying to go to a new step before the previous approximation has been well established can result in losing the previous approximation through extinction without achieving the new approximation.

    b. Avoid reinforcing too many times at any shaping step. Item *a* cautions against going too fast. It is also important not to progress too slowly. If one approximation is reinforced for so long that it becomes extremely strong, new approximations are less likely to appear.

    c. If you lose a behavior because you are moving too fast or taking too large a step, return to an earlier approximation where you can pick up the behavior again. You also may need to insert an extra step or two.

These guidelines may not seem very helpful. On the one hand, it is advisable not to move too fast from one approximation to another; on the other hand, it is advisable not to move too slowly. If we could accompany these guidelines with a mathematical formula for calculating the exact size of the steps that should be taken in any situation and exactly how many reinforcements should be given at each step, the guidelines would be much more useful. Unfortunately, the experiments necessary for providing this information have not yet been carried out. The teacher must observe the behavior carefully and be prepared to make changes in the procedure—changing the size of, slowing down, speeding up, or retracing steps—whenever the behavior does not seem to be developing properly. Shaping requires a good deal of practice and skill if it is to be performed with maximum effectiveness.

PITFALLS OF SHAPING

As with other behavior principles and procedures, shaping can be accidentally
Note 3 applied with unfortunate results by people who are not knowledgeable about it. An example of this can be seen in Figure 10–1. A harmful behavior

Figure 10–1 A misapplication of shaping.

that might never have occurred without shaping is gradually developed as a result of it.

Another example of the misuse of shaping, one that is sometimes observed in children with developmental disabilities, leads to self-destructive behavior. Recall the case of the child who banged his head on hard surfaces, which was given in Chapters 8 and 9 as a possible example of pitfalls of stimulus discrimination training and fading, respectively. It could also be an example of a pitfall of shaping. Suppose that because of an unusual and unfortunate family situation, a small child receives very little social attention when he performs appropriate behavior. Perhaps one day the child accidentally falls and strikes his head lightly against a hard floor. Even if the child is not injured seriously, a parent may come running quickly and make a big fuss over the incident. Because of this reinforcement, and because anything else the child does that is appropriate seldom evokes attention, he is likely to repeat the response of striking his head lightly against the floor. The first few times this occurs, the parent may continue to reinforce the response. Eventually, however, seeing that the child is not really hurting himself, the parent may stop reinforcing it. Since the behavior has now been placed on extinction, the *intensity* of the behavior may increase (see Chapter 5). That is, the child may begin to hit his head more forcefully, and the slightly louder thud will cause the parent to come running again. If this shaping process continues, the child will eventually hit his head with sufficient force to cause physical injury. It is extremely difficult, if not impossible, to use extinction to eliminate such violently self-destructive behavior. It would have been best never to have let the behavior develop to the point where the child's parents were forced to continue reinforcing it and increasing its strength.

Many undesirable behaviors commonly seen in special needs children—for example, violent temper tantrums, constant fidgeting, injuring other children, voluntary vomiting—are often products of shaping. It is quite possible that these behaviors can be eliminated by a combination of extinction of the undesirable behavior and positive reinforcement for desirable behavior. Unfortunately, this is often difficult to do, because (a) the behavior is sometimes so harmful that it cannot be allowed to occur even once during the period in which extinction is to take place, and (b) adults who are ignorant of behavior principles sometimes unknowingly foil the efforts of those who are conscientiously attempting to apply these principles.

In Chapter 22 we describe how to diagnose and treat problem behaviors that may have been developed inadvertently through shaping. As in medicine, however, the best "cure" is prevention. Ideally, all persons responsible for the care of other persons will be so thoroughly versed in behavior principles that they will refrain from shaping undesirable behavior.

Another Pitfall   Another kind of pitfall is the unknowing failure of a person to apply shaping when it should be applied. Some parents, for example, are simply not very responsive to their child's babbling behavior. Perhaps they expect too much from the child right from the beginning and are not inclined to reinforce extremely remote approximations of normal speech. (Some parents, for example, seem to expect their tiny new genius to say "Father!" right off the bat and are not at all impressed when the child says "da-da.") Or perhaps their personal problems interfere with their devoting the necessary attention to the child. The opposite type of problem also exists. Instead of not giving enough reinforcement for the right behavior, some parents give their children plenty of reinforcement noncontingently. Perhaps they are so overly concerned about the child's well-being that they provide the child with all kinds of reinforcement without the child ever having to say or do anything for it. In other words, although shaping is a process that most parents apply more or less appropriately (probably without even being fully aware that they are doing so, in most instances), there are some parents for whom this is not true. Thus, many variables can prevent a physically normal child from receiving the shaping that is necessary to establish normal behaviors. If a child has not learned to talk by a certain age, he or she may be labeled as developmentally disabled or autistic. It is quite possible that there are individuals with developmental disabilities whose deficiency exists not because of any genetic or physical defect, but simply because they were never exposed to effective shaping procedures.

GUIDELINES FOR THE EFFECTIVE APPLICATION OF SHAPING

1. *Select the terminal behavior.*
   a. Choose a specific behavior (such as working quietly at a desk for 10 minutes) rather than a general category of behavior (for example, "good" classroom behavior). Shaping is appropriate for changing amount, latency, and intensity of behavior, as well as for developing new behavior of a different topography (form). If your terminal behavior is a complex sequence of activities (such as making a bed) that you have broken down into sequential steps, and if your program amounts to linking the steps together in a particular order, then your program is not best described as shaping, nor is it best developed through a shaping program. Rather, it should be developed by chaining (see Chapter 11).
   b. If possible, select a behavior that will come under the control of natural reinforcers after it has been shaped.
2. *Select an appropriate reinforcer.* See Figure 3–3 and the "Guidelines for the Effective Application of Positive Reinforcement," p. 46.
3. *The initial plan.*
   a. List successive approximations to the terminal behavior, beginning with the starting behavior. To choose the starting behavior, find a behavior already in the learner's repertoire that resembles the terminal behavior most closely and that occurs at least once during an observation period.
   b. Your initial steps or successive approximations are usually "educated guesses." During your program, you can modify these according to the learner's performance.
4. *Implementing the plan.*
   a. Tell the learner about the plan before starting.
   b. Begin reinforcing immediately following each occurrence of the starting behavior.
   c. Never move to a new approximation until the learner has mastered the previous one.

    d. If you are not sure when to move the learner to a new approximation, utilize the following rule. Move to the next step when the learner performs the current step correctly in six out of ten trials (usually with one or two trials less perfect than desired and one or two trials in which the behavior is better than the current step).

    e. Do not reinforce too many times at any one step, and avoid underreinforcement at any one step.

    f. If the learner stops working, you may have moved up the steps too quickly, the steps may not be the right size, or the reinforcer may be ineffective.

      (1) First, check the effectiveness of your reinforcer.

      (2) If the learner becomes inattentive or shows signs of boredom, the steps may be too small.

      (3) Inattention or boredom may also mean you have progressed too rapidly. If so, return to the previous step for a few more trials and then try the present step again.

      (4) If the learner continues to have difficulty, despite retraining at previous steps, add more steps at the point of difficulty.

STUDY QUESTIONS

1. Identify the three basic stages in any shaping procedure, as presented at the start of this chapter, and describe them with an example (either the case of Frank or an example of your own).
2. Explain how shaping involves successive applications of the principles of positive reinforcement and extinction.
3. Why bother with shaping? Why not just learn about the use of straightforward positive reinforcement to increase a behavior?
4. Define shaping.
5. What is another name for shaping?
6. In terms of the three stages in a shaping procedure, describe how parents might shape their child to say a particular word.
7. List five dimensions of behavior that can be shaped. Give two examples of each.
8. Distinguish between shaping and fading.
9. How do you know you have enough successive approximations or shaping steps of the right size?
10. Why is it necessary to avoid underreinforcement at any shaping step?
11. Why is it necessary to avoid reinforcing too many times at any shaping step?
12. Give an example of how shaping might be accidentally used to develop an undesirable behavior. Describe some of the shaping steps in your example.
13. Give an example of how the failure to apply shaping might have an undesirable result.
14. Give an example from your own experience of a terminal behavior that might best be developed through a procedure other than shaping (see p. 133). Explain why shaping would probably not be effective in developing that behavior.
15. How do you know if you are allowing enough reinforced trials to occur at each of the approximations?
16. What do behavior modifiers mean by terminal behavior in a shaping program? Give an example.
17. Why do we refer to positive reinforcement and extinction as principles, and to shaping as a procedure (*Hint:* See Chapter 1, p. 10.)

APPLICATION EXERCISES

A. Exercise Involving Others

Think of a normal child, one between the ages of 2 and 7, with whom you have had contact (for example, a sister, brother, or neighbor). Specify a realistic behavior of that child that you might try to develop by utilizing a shaping procedure. Identify the starting point you would choose, the reinforcer, and the successive approximations you would go through.

B. Self-Modification Exercises

1. Take a close look at many of your own skills—for example, personal interaction, lovemaking, and studying. Identify two specific skills that were probably shaped by others, either knowingly or unknowingly. Identify two specific behaviors that were probably shaped by the natural environment. For each example, identify the reinforcer and at least three approximations that you likely performed during the shaping process.
2. Select one of your behavioral deficits, perhaps one that you listed at the end of Chapter 2. Outline a complete shaping program that you (with a little help from your friends) might use to overcome that deficit. Make sure that your plan follows the above guidelines for the effective application of shaping.

NOTES AND EXTENDED DISCUSSION

1. Shaping appears to be useful in modifying not only external behavior but also internal behavior. For example, R. W. Scott and colleagues (1973) demonstrated that shaping could be used to modify heart rate. In this study, the device monitoring heart rate was hooked up to the video portion of a TV set that the individual watched. Although the sound portion of the TV was on continuously, the video portion appeared only when the individual's heart rate changed by a few beats per minute from its previous level. When the subject's heart rate remained at a new level for three consecutive sessions, the video portion was used to reinforce a further change in heart rate. In one case involving a psychiatric patient suffering from chronic anxiety and manifesting a moderately elevated heart rate, the investigators shaped several decreases in the individual's heart rate. Interestingly, when the individual's heart rate had been decreased to a lower level, reports from his ward indicated that "he seemed less 'tense' and 'anxious'" and that "he made fewer requests for medication."

In other studies, information about a person's physiological processes, such as heart rate or muscle tension, is displayed on a screen or in some way made immediately available to the individual. Such techniques, which are referred to as **biofeedback,** enable individuals to gain control over the physiological processes being monitored. Clinical applications of biofeedback have used it successfully to reduce epileptic seizures by helping individuals learn to control electrical brain activity associated with their seizures, to reduce blood pressure, thereby enabling hypertensive patients to use less medication, and to reduce chronic headaches, accelerated heart rate, and anxiety (Schwartz & Andrasic, 1998).

2. How fast should you move from one step to the next? How large should step size be? One reason there are no specific answers to these questions is the difficulty of measuring specific step sizes and consistently reinforcing responses that satisfy a given step size. Human judgment is simply not fast enough or accurate enough to ensure that any given shaping procedure is being applied consistently in order to make comparisons between it and other consistently applied shaping procedures. This is particularly true when topography is the aspect of behavior that is being shaped. Computers, however, are both accurate and fast and may therefore be useful in answering fundamental questions concerning which shaping procedures are most effective (Midgley, Lea, & Kirby, 1989; Pear & Legris, 1987). For example, using two video cameras that were connected to a microcomputer which was programmed to detect the position of a pigeon's head within a test chamber, Pear and Legris (1987) demonstrated that a computer can shape where the pigeon moves its head.

In addition to providing a methodology for studying shaping, these studies suggest that computers may be able to shape at least some kinds of behavior as effectively as humans. For example, a device that shapes movements may help a person regain the use of a limb that has been paralyzed from a stroke or accident. Such a device would have the advantage over a human shaper in its precision, its ability to provide extremely rapid and systematic feedback, and its patience (i.e., computers are nonjudgmental and untiring).

3. Rasey and Iversen (1993) provided a good laboratory demonstration of a potential maladaptive effect of shaping. They reinforced rats with food for extending their noses over the edge of a platform on which they were standing. Over trials the rats were required to extend their noses farther and farther over the edge before receiving reinforcement. Eventually, each rat extended its nose so far over the edge that it actually fell off the platform. A net under the platform kept the rat from being injured; however, this experiment demonstrates that animals (and thus, probably humans as well) can be shaped to engage in behavior that is harmful to them.

Study Questions on Notes

1. Describe how Scott and colleagues used shaping to decrease the heart rate of a man suffering from chronic anxiety.
2. What is biofeedback?
3. Describe how computer technology might be used to shape specific limb movements in a paralyzed person.
4. Describe how computer technology might be used to study shaping more accurately than can be done with the usual shaping procedures.
5. Describe an experiment demonstrating that maladaptive behavior can be shaped.

Getting a New Sequence
of Behaviors to Occur
with Behavioral Chaining

"Steve, your preputt routine is inconsistent."

TEACHING STEVE TO FOLLOW A CONSISTENT PREPUTT ROUTINE[1]

Steve was a young professional golfer on the Canadian PGA Tour who, although playing well, had not yet won a professional tournament, due in part to inconsistent putting. Steve knew that professional golfers have a more consistent preputt routine than skilled amateur golfers, and that skilled amateur golfers have a more consistent preputt routine than less skilled amateur golfers. Upon reflection, Steve realized that his own preputt routine was not as consistent as it might be. He did not always check the slope of the putting green from both sides of the ball before putting. If it was an especially important putt, he tended to stand over the ball for a longer period of time than usual before stroking it toward the hole. Other inconsistencies also occurred from one instance of putting to the next during a competitive round. He concluded that his inconsistent preputt routine could be contributing to inconsistent putting.

The first step to establishing a consistent sequence of responses during his preputt routine was to list the specific steps that he wanted to follow on each occasion. They were as follows:

1. *When approaching the ball, forget about the score and think only about the putt at hand.*
2. *Go behind the hole, look back at the ball, and check the slope of the green in order to estimate the speed and path of the putt.*
3. *Move behind the ball, look toward the hole, and recheck the slope.*

---

[1]This example is based on a consultation with G. Martin (1999).

4. *While standing behind the ball, pick a spot to aim at, take two practice strokes, and visualize the ball rolling in the hole.*
5. *Move beside the ball, set the putter down behind the ball, and adjust it so that it is aiming at the desired spot.*
6. *Adjust your feet so that they are parallel to the putting line, grip the putter in the usual way, and say, "Stroke it smooth."*
7. *Look at the hole, look at the ball, look at the spot, look at the ball, and stroke the putt.*

The training procedure carried out by Steve involved 10 trials. On each trial he performed all seven steps of the preputt routine while practicing a short putt on the practice green. The reason that he practiced the preputt routine on short putts was that he wanted each sequence to be followed by the reinforcer of making the putt. On each trial, a friend checked off the steps on a checklist as they were performed. If he missed a step, he was prompted by his friend to perform it before continuing to the next step. After completing the 10 trials, Steve and his friend played a practice round of golf during which his friend prompted him to complete the preputt routine on every putt. Subsequently, during tournament rounds Steve asked his caddy to remind him frequently to follow his preputt routine. Three weeks later Steve won his first tour event. While there were no doubt a number of contributing factors, Steve felt that one of them was his improved putting due to a more consistent preputt routine.

BEHAVIORAL CHAINING

A **behavioral chain** is a sequence of discriminative stimuli (S^Ds) and responses (Rs) in which each response except the last produces the S^D for the next response, and the last response is typically followed by a reinforcer. In addition to being a cue for the next response, each S^D (after the first) in a behavioral chain is a conditioned reinforcer for the previous response. What Steve had acquired in learning to follow a consistent preputt routine was such a sequence of stimuli and responses. The first stimulus (S^D_1) for the entire sequence was the feedback from walking toward his ball on the putting green. The response (R_1) to that stimulus was "I'm going to focus just on this putt." The completion of that statement was the cue (S^D_2) to go behind the hole, look back at the ball, and check the slope of the green in order to estimate the speed and path of the putt (R_2). The resulting visual stimuli (and perhaps certain internal stimuli we might call "an image of the putt and speed of the ball") was the cue (S^D_3) for the next response (R_3), walking behind the ball and looking toward the hole to observe the slope of the green from that angle. In this way, each response produced the cue for the next response until the entire chain was completed, and Steve experienced the reinforcer of making the putt. The reason for calling this procedure a stimulus response chain can be seen by writing it out as follows:

$$S^D_1 \rightarrow R_1 \rightarrow S^D_2 \rightarrow R_2 \rightarrow S^D_3 \rightarrow R_3 \ldots S^D_7 \rightarrow R_7 \rightarrow S^+$$

The stimulus–response connections are the "links" that hold the chain together. As the saying goes, "A chain is only as strong as its weakest link." Similarly, if any response is so weak that it fails to be evoked by the S^D preceding it, the next S^D will not be produced and the rest of the chain will not occur. The chain will be broken at the point of its weakest link. The only way in which to repair the chain is to strengthen the weak stimulus–response connection by means of an effective training procedure.

The symbol S$^+$ at the far right of the diagram symbolizes the positive reinforcer that follows the last response in the chain. It designates the "oil" that one must apply regularly to keep the chain rust-free and strong. The reinforcer at the end of a chain maintains the stimuli in the chain as effective S^{D}s for the responses that follow them and effective conditioned reinforcers for the responses that precede them.

Many behavioral sequences that you perform in everyday life are behavioral chains. Playing a particular song on a musical instrument, brushing your teeth, lacing and tying your shoes, and making a sandwich are all behavioral chains. However, not all behavioral sequences are behavioral chains. Studying for an exam, writing an exam, and attending the next class to get your grade represent a general sequence of behavior that you experience in each of your courses. But this general sequence consists of a variety of activities (reading, memorizing, writing, etc.), with many breaks in the action (studying, then sleeping, then going to class, etc.). It is not made up of a consistent series of stimuli and responses in which each stimulus (except the last) is a conditioned reinforcer for the previous response and an S^D for the next response.

METHODS FOR TEACHING A BEHAVIORAL CHAIN

There are three major methods of teaching a behavioral chain. One method is called **total-task presentation.** With this method, the learner attempts all the steps from the beginning to the end of the chain on each trial and continues with total task trials until all steps are mastered. Prompting is provided at each step as needed and a reinforcer follows correct completion of the last step. This was the strategy used to teach Steve to follow a consistent preputt routine. As another example, Horner and Keilitz (1975) used total task presentation to teach adolescents with developmental disabilities to brush their teeth.

A second major method of teaching a behavioral chain is called **backward chaining.** This method gradually constructs the chain in a reverse order from that in which the chain is performed. That is, the last step is established first, then the next-to-last step is taught and linked to the last step, then the third-from-last step is taught and linked to the last two steps, and so on, progressing backward toward the beginning of the chain. Backward chaining has been used in numerous programs, including teaching various dressing, grooming, work, and verbal behaviors to individuals with developmental disabilities (e.g., Martin, England, & England, 1971). To teach Craig, a boy with a developmental disability, to put on a pair of slacks, for example, we broke the task down into the seven steps illustrated in Figure 11–1. We then conducted a baseline assessment to determine the type of prompt needed for Craig to perform each step correctly. Next we began training, starting with the last step. The trainer helped Craig put on the slacks except for the response at step 7. Several training trials were then conducted to teach Craig the response at step 7. As you can see in Figure 11–1, over several trials prompts were faded until Craig could do up the zipper by himself. When Craig had learned this, the teacher then started him from step 6 and taught him to finish from there. When Craig could perform the last two steps without errors, training trials began at step 5. With the slacks down around his ankles, he was taught to pull them all the way up (step 5), which was the S^D for him to perform step 6. Performing step 6 provided the

TASK	Putting on slacks		Scoring System									
CLIENT	Craig		3 = without prompts									
REINFORCERS	praise & edible		2 = verbal prompt 1 = gestural/imitative prompts 0 = physical guidance									

S^Ds	Responses	Baseline	Training Trials									
1. "Put on your slacks."	Taking slacks from dresser drawer	2										
2. Slacks in hands	Hold slacks upright with front facing away from client	1										
3. Slacks held upright	Put one leg in slacks	1										
4. One leg in slacks	Put other leg in slacks	1										
5. Both legs in slacks	Pull slacks all the way up	2									2	3
6. Slacks all the way up	Do up the snap	0					0	1	2	3	3	3
7. Snap done up	Do up the zipper	0	0	1	2	3	3	3	3	3	3	3

Figure 11–1 A simple task analysis and data sheet for teaching a person with a developmental disability to put on slacks.

S^D to perform step 7. On each trial, Craig completed all the steps learned previously. Training proceeded in this way, with one step added at a time, until Craig could perform all seven steps. Throughout training, individual steps performed correctly were reinforced with praise, and the completion of step 7 on each trial was followed by an edible reinforcer.

Students of behavior modification often find backward chaining strange when they first read about it, apparently because they think that it teaches an individual to perform the chain backward, as the name suggests. Naturally, this is not true. There is a very good theoretical rationale for using backward chaining. Consider the above example of teaching a boy with developmental disabilities to put on a pair of slacks. By starting with step 7, the response of "doing up the zipper" was reinforced in the presence of the snap done up. Therefore, the sight of the snap done up became an S^D for step 7, doing up the zipper. On the basis of the principle of conditioned reinforcement, the sight of the snap done up also became a conditioned reinforcer for whatever preceded it. After several trials at step 7, the trainer went on to step 6. The behavior of doing up the snap produced the stimulus, sight of the snap done up. The sight of the snap done up had become a conditioned reinforcer, and it immediately followed performing step 6. Thus, when one uses backward chaining, the reinforcement of the last step in the presence of the appropriate stimulus, over trials, establishes that stimulus as a discriminative stimulus for the last step and as a conditioned reinforcer for the next-to-last step. When the step before the last is added, the S^D in that step also becomes a conditioned reinforcer, and so on. Thus, the power of the positive reinforcer that is presented at the end of the chain is transferred up the line to each S^D as it is added to the chain. In this way, backward chaining has a theoretical advantage of always having a built-in conditioned reinforcer to strengthen each new response that is added to the sequence.

The third major method of teaching a behavioral chain is called **forward chaining.** With this method, the initial step of the sequence is taught first, then the first and second steps are taught and linked together, then the first three steps, and so on until the entire chain is acquired. For example, Mahoney, Van Wagenen, and Meyerson (1971) used forward chaining to toilet train both normal and developmentally disabled children. The components of the chain included walking to the toilet, lowering the pants, sitting on or standing facing the toilet (as appropriate), eliminating, and pulling up the pants. Training began with the first step, and after a step was mastered, the next step was introduced. Each step was reinforced until the next step was introduced.

Note 1

At least partly because backward chaining resembles a reversal of the natural order of things, forward chaining and total-task presentation are used more often in everyday situations outside the behavior modification setting. Among the many examples that can be cited to illustrate forward chaining, consider the way in which a child might be taught to pronounce a word such as "milk." He might be first taught to say "mm," then "mi," then "mil," and finally "milk."

The three major chaining formats are diagramed in Figure 11–2 and outlined in Table 11–1. Which is most effective? Bellamy, Horner, and Inman (1979) concluded

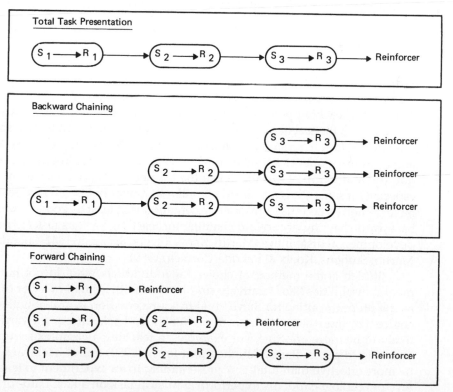

Figure 11–2   A diagram of the three major chaining formats.

TABLE 11–1   AN OUTLINE OF THE THREE MAJOR CHAINING METHODS

For All Methods
• Do a task analysis.

Total-Task Presentation
• The learner attempts every step on each trial, so that all unmastered steps are taught concurrently. • The trainer provides prompts and praise for all unmastered steps. • A reinforcer is presented following the last step. • Training continues in this way until all steps are mastered.

Forward Chaining
• Starting with the first step, the step must be mastered before proceeding to the next step. • The trainer provides prompts and a reinforcer for the step that is being taught. • On each trial, all previously mastered steps are required, up to the step that is being taught. • In this way, one step is learned at a time, progressing forward to the last step.

Backward Chaining
• Starting with the last step, the step must be mastered before proceeding to the next-to-last step. • The trainer provides prompts for the step that is being taught. • On each trial, all previously mastered steps are required, and the last step is followed by a reinforcer. • In this way, one step is learned at a time, progressing backwards to the first step.

that total-task presentation has several practical advantages over the other chaining formats for teaching persons with developmental disabilities. Total-task presentation requires the teacher to spend less time in partial assembly or disassembly to prepare the task for training; it appears to focus on teaching response topography and response sequence simultaneously and, therefore, should produce results more quickly; and it appears to maximize the learner's independence early in training, especially if some steps are already familiar to him or her. Moreover, several studies have demonstrated that total-task presentation is at least as good as, or better than, backward chaining or forward chaining for teaching various tasks to persons with developmental disabilities (Martin, Koop, Turner, & Hanel, 1981; Spooner, 1984; Yu, Martin, Suthons, Koop, & Pallotta-Cornick, 1980).

Which is the method of choice for individuals who do not have developmental disabilities? For relatively simple tasks with a small number of steps, such as the preputt routine for Steve, total-task presentation is probably the method of choice. For more complex tasks, however, either backward or forward chaining is likely to be more effective. For example, in teaching a complex sequence of dive bombing to pilots, Bailey, Hughes, and Jones (1980) found backward chaining to be more effective than total-task presentation. In an experiment to teach introductory psychology students to perform a musical task on a keyboard for which they were scored for both melodic and timing errors, backward chaining and forward chaining were both more effective than total-task presentation, and forward chaining was more effective than backward chaining on most measures (Ash & Holding, 1990). Also, there may be practical reasons for using backward chaining to teach certain tasks. When giving driving instructions, for example, it is highly advisable to teach the use of the brake before teaching the use of the accelerator (for obvious reasons).

CHAINING COMPARED WITH FADING AND SHAPING

Behavioral chaining, fading, and shaping are sometimes called *gradual change* procedures because they each involve progressing gradually through a series of steps to produce a new behavior, new stimulus control over a behavior, or a new sequence of stimulus–response steps. It is important to keep clear the distinctions among the three gradual change procedures.

In shaping, the steps consist of reinforcing closer and closer approximations to the final desired response (see Chapter 10). In fading, the steps consist of reinforcing the final desired response in the presence of closer and closer approximations to the final desired stimulus for that response (see Chapter 9). In chaining, the steps usually consist of reinforcing more and more of the specific stimulus–response links that comprise the chain. An exception to this is the method of total-task presentation; in this case all the links are taught right from the beginning of training, and shaping or fading may be used to develop the responses or to bring them under the control of their appropriate stimuli. Because shaping or fading is used, the procedure is still a gradual change procedure. Table 11–2 summarizes some of the similarities and differences of the three procedures as they are typically applied.

FACTORS INFLUENCING THE EFFECTIVENESS OF BEHAVIORAL CHAINING

1. Do a Task Analysis: Identify the Components of the Final Sequence

The behavioral sequence you wish to develop must be broken down into individual components, and the proper order of the sequence must be kept. The process of breaking a task down into smaller steps or component responses to facilitate training is referred to as **task analysis.** Examples of task analyses for teaching complex skills include apartment-upkeep skills (Williams & Cuvo, 1986), menstrual care skills (Richman, Reiss, Bauman, & Bailey, 1984), tennis skills (Buzas & Ayllon, 1981), play execution of the offensive backfield on a youth football team (Komaki & Barnett, 1977), leisure skills (Schleien, Wehman, & Kiernan, 1981), and pedestrian skills for walking safely through traffic (Page, Iwata, & Neef, 1976).

As with the selection of shaping steps (discussed in Chapter 10) the selection of chaining steps or components is somewhat subjective. The components should be simple enough to be learned without great difficulty. If you wanted to teach a

TABLE 11–2   SIMILARITIES AND DIFFERENCES AMONG SHAPING, FADING, AND CHAINING

	Shaping	Fading	Chaining
Terminal behavior	1. New behavior along some physical dimension such as topography, amount, or intensity.	1. New stimulus control of a particular behavior.	1. New sequence of responses, with a "clear-cut" stimulus signaling the end of each response and the start of the next.
	2. The final behavior consists of only the last shaping step.	2. The final stimulus control consists of only the last fading step.	2. The final behavior consists of all the chaining steps.
General training procedures	1. Often involves an unstructured environment in which the student has the opportunity to emit a variety of behaviors.	1. Typically involves a structured environment since the stimuli present must be controlled precisely.	1. Typically involves a semistructured or structured teaching environment.
	2. Proceeds in a forward fashion in terms of the "natural order" of behavior.	2. Proceeds in a forward fashion in terms of the "natural order" of behavior.	2. May proceed in a forward or backward fashion in terms of the "natural order" of behavior.
Other procedural considerations	1. Often involves instructional control; may involve some physical prompting at successive steps, but usually minimally. May also involve some fading at successive steps, but this is unusual.	1. May involve some shaping, although this is unusual.	1. Frequently involves verbal and physical prompts, physical guidance, fading, and perhaps shaping at successive steps.
	2. Involves successive application of reinforcement and extinction.	2. Involves successive application of reinforcement; if extinction has to be used, fading has not proceeded optimally.	2. Typically involves fewer extinction trials than in shaping, because of the strong stimulus control established by prompting and fading at successive steps.

child with severe developmental disability to brush her teeth, it would be a mistake to consider the task in terms of the three gross steps of putting toothpaste on the brush, brushing, and rinsing. For the child to master the chain, each of these steps would have to be subdivided into even smaller steps. The components should also be selected so that there is a clear-cut stimulus or set of stimuli signaling the completion of each component. This will facilitate the development of those stimuli as conditioned reinforcers for the preceding responses and as S^Ds for the subsequent responses throughout the chain. For example, in utilizing chaining to teach a child appropriate hand-washing behavior, you might select putting water in the sink as one of the components. It would be important to specify a particular level of water in the sink, and perhaps even make a mark (at least temporarily) at that level to provide a very clear stimulus that terminates the end of this particular component (which you might define as "holding the water taps on until the water level reaches the desired level").

After completing your task analysis, review each of the controlling stimuli for each of the responses in the sequence. Ideally, each controlling stimulus should be clearly distinctive from the other controlling stimuli. If similar stimuli control different responses, there is a greater chance for error and confusion by the client. If, in your task analysis, two of the controlling stimuli are quite similar and there appears to be nothing you can do about it, then consider artificially coding one of the stimuli in some way to make acquisition of the chain easier.

2. Consider Strategies for Independent Use of Prompts by Learners

As was the case with Steve, many individuals can use prompts independently to guide the mastery of a chain of behaviors. For learners able to read, a *written task analysis* might effectively prompt them to appropriately complete behavior chains (see, e.g., Cuvo, Davis, O'Reilly, Mooney, & Crowley, 1992). If they are unable to read, a series of *picture prompts* might guide clients through behavior chains. For example, Thierman and Martin (1989) prepared a picture-prompt album to guide adults with severe developmental disabilities to complete behavior chains that improved the quality of their household cleaning. The clients were taught to look at the picture of an appropriate step, perform that step, and then transfer a self-monitoring adhesive dot to indicate that the step had been completed. The strategy proved to be quite effective. Another strategy that involves independent use of prompts to guide completion of behavioral chains involves reciting *self-instructions*. Individuals with developmental disabilities have been taught to recite self-instructions in order to prompt correct completion of vocational tasks (Salend, Ellis, & Reynolds, 1989), completion of math problems correctly (Albion & Salzburg, 1982), and sorting letters into boxes correctly (Whitman, Spence, & Maxwell, 1987).

3. Consider Conducting a Preliminary Modeling Trial

In some cases, such as with persons with developmental disabilities or children, it may be desirable to model the entire sequence while verbally describing the performance of each step. (Guidelines for modeling are described in Chapter 18.) If only one sample of the training task is available, the task must be disassembled after the modeling trial and components rearranged for the learner to perform the task. Otherwise, the learner can be trained using alternative samples of the task.

4. Begin Training the Behavioral Chain

Give the learner an initial request to begin work and to complete the step(s) of the task. The step or steps to begin with will depend on whether you use total-task presentation, backward chaining, or forward chaining. If at any step the learner stops responding or appears distracted, you should first provide a pacing prompt such as "What's next?" or "Carry on." If the learner performs a response incorrectly or fails to begin responding at any step within a reasonable period of time, you should proceed with error correction. Provide the necessary instruction or physical guidance to help the learner perform that step correctly. After an error is corrected, go on to the next step.

5. Consider Using Ample Social and Other Reinforcers

Sometimes a natural reinforcer that follows completion of a chain will be sufficient to maintain it. This was the case with Steve, described at the beginning of this chapter. When teaching behavioral chains to persons with developmental disabilities or children, however, it is often desirable to immediately praise the correct completion of each step during early training trials (see, e.g., Koop, Martin, Yu, & Suthons, 1980). In addition, it is often desirable to provide a reinforcer (such as an edible) contingent upon successful completion of the last step in the chain. As the client becomes more skillful in performing the steps, praise and other reinforcers can be gradually eliminated. Additional strategies for maintaining behavioral chains that have been mastered are described in Chapter 16.

6. Decrease Extra Assistance at Individual Steps as Quickly as Possible

Depending on the details of the task analysis, it may be necessary to provide some additional instruction or physical assistance in correcting errors. Across successive trials, this extra assistance should be faded as quickly as possible. It is important not to provide assistance to the point where you create a dependency in your client. That is, be careful not to reinforce the client for making errors or for waiting for your help at particular steps.

PITFALLS OF BEHAVIORAL CHAINING

Chains that contain a response member that is not necessary for reinforcement are called *adventitious chains,* and the process that produces them is called *adventitious chaining*. Adventitious chaining is a form of adventitious reinforcement as described in Chapter 3 (p. 43). An **adventitious chain** has some components that are functional in producing the reinforcer, and at least one component (called a *superstitious component*) that is not. Special care often needs to be taken to avoid undesirable adventitious chaining. Just as relatively simple undesirable responses are often established inadvertently through the thoughtless administration of positive reinforcement, so also are chains with one or more undesirable components. Probably the most common kind of undesirable chaining occurs when an inappropriate response precedes one or more appropriate responses that are reinforced; both the inappropriate and appropriate responses are thereby strengthened. An example of this type of chaining is the distracting habit exhibited by some speakers of prefacing each remark with "uh." A similar though somewhat more serious example is the making of bizarre facial expressions prior to each utterance.

Some seemingly sound behavior modification procedures can promote undesirable chaining if the behavior modifier is not careful. This was illustrated in a project by Olenick and Pear (1980) to teach names of pictures to children with developmental disabilities. The children were given a question trial in which they were shown a picture to be named and were asked, "What's this?" Correct responses were reinforced. If the children made an error, they were then given an imitation trial in which the teacher presented the question and then immediately modeled the answer (e.g., "What's this? Cat."). Olenick and Pear observed that some children made a large number of errors even when it appeared that they could name the pictures appropriately. The researchers suggested that for these youngsters, a chain had developed in which errors on question trials were reinforced by imitation trials because an easier response (imitation) was reinforced on these trials. Olenick and Pear solved this problem by lowering the reinforcement rate for correct responses on imitation trials, while maintaining a high reinforcement rate for correct responses on question trials.

Self-control problems that plague many people provide several other examples of undesirable behavioral chains. Consider the problem of overeating. Although there are undoubtedly a variety of possible reasons for overeating, one of the more frequent causes may be the inadvertent development of undesirable behavioral chains. For example, it has been observed that some overweight people eat very rapidly. An examination of the behavioral sequence involved suggests the following chain: loading food onto the utensil, placing food in the mouth, reloading utensil while chewing the food, simultaneously swallowing the food while raising the next load of food to the mouth, and so forth. This behavioral chain can be broken successfully by extending the chain and introducing delays. A more desirable chain might be the following: loading food onto the utensil, placing food in the mouth, putting down the utensil, chewing the food, swallowing, waiting three seconds, reloading the utensil, and so on. In other words, in the undesirable chain the person gets ready to consume the next mouthful before even finishing the present one. A more desirable chain separates these components and introduces brief delays.

Another undesirable behavioral chain that is manifested by some overweight people consists of watching TV until a commercial comes on, going to the kitchen during the commercial, getting a snack, and returning to the TV program (which, along with the good taste of the food, reinforces getting the snack). There are a variety of procedures for solving such self-control problems, and these are discussed more fully in Chapter 26. The point to remember here is that undesirable behaviors are frequently components of unintentionally developed behavioral chains.

GUIDELINES FOR THE EFFECTIVE
USE OF BEHAVIORAL CHAINING

One should observe the following rules when teaching behavioral chains.

1. Do a task analysis. Identify the units of the chain that are simple enough to be learned without great difficulty by the learner.
2. Consider strategies (e.g., pictures) for independent use of prompts by learners.
3. If necessary, do a preliminary modeling trial.
4. Teach the units in the proper sequence. Otherwise, poor stimulus control will develop in that when one step is completed it will not necessarily be a discriminative stimulus for the next step, but rather may control some other step (as when a young child learns to count incorrectly, for example, 1, 2, 4, 3).
5. To expedite learning, use a fading procedure to decrease extra help that may be needed by a client to perform some of the steps.
6. If you are using backward or forward chaining, make sure that on each trial the student performs the entire set of components learned up to that point.
7. Early in training, use ample reinforcement for correct performance of individual steps. Gradually decrease this reinforcement as the learner becomes more skillful.
8. Make sure that the reinforcement provided at the end of the chain conforms to the guidelines for the effective application of positive reinforcement given in Chapter 3. The more effective this terminal reinforcement, the more stable the chain of responses. This does not mean, however, that once a chain is developed it must be reinforced each time it occurs in order to be maintained. After a chain has been taught, it can be viewed as a single response, which could, if desired, be put on any intermittent reinforcement schedule.

STUDY QUESTIONS

1. Briefly describe the chaining procedure used to teach Steve to perform a consistent preputt routine.
2. Describe or define a behavioral chain, and give an example other than the examples in this chapter.
3. Why do you suppose a behavioral chain is called a chain?
4. In a chain, a given stimulus is both an S^D and a conditioned reinforcer. How can this be? Explain with an example.
5. Using examples, distinguish between a behavioral sequence that is a chain and one that is not a chain.
6. In the behavioral chain of driving a car, accelerating, and changing gears (assume that you have a four-speed transmission), how is the chain of the driver who has a tachometer (and uses it) different from the chain of the driver who does not have a tachometer?
7. Name and describe briefly three major chaining methods.
8. Describe how each of the three major chaining methods might be used to teach bed making.
9. Which of the major chaining methods do the authors recommend for teaching persons with developmental disabilities, and why?
10. Distinguish among the types of terminal behavior typically established by shaping, fading, and chaining.
11. Suppose that you wanted to teach a teenager to change a tire on a car. Would you use shaping or chaining? Justify your choice.

12. What is meant by the term *task analysis*? Describe a plausible task analysis appropriate for teaching a 3-year-old child the behavior of tying a knot in a shoelace.
13. Briefly describe three strategies to help individuals use prompts independently to guide the mastery of a chain of behaviors.
14. How is an adventitious chain similar to, and how does it differ from, superstitious behavior? (See p. 43 and p. 146.)
15. Describe an example of an adventitious chain that is not from this chapter. Clearly identify the superstitious component.
16. Give an example of a pitfall of chaining. Explain how this pitfall can be avoided.

APPLICATION EXERCISES

A. Exercises Involving Others

1. Describe how you might use behavioral chaining to teach a child to lace his or her shoes.
2. Describe how you might use behavioral chaining to teach a child to tie a knot.
3. Describe how you might use behavioral chaining to teach a child to tie a bow.
4. Try out your chaining programs in Application Exercises 1 through 3 and see how they work.

B. Self-Modification Exercise

Identify a behavioral deficit of yours that might be amenable to a chaining procedure. Describe in detail how you might use the guidelines for the effective use of chaining to overcome this deficit.

NOTE AND EXTENDED DISCUSSION

1. In a variation on forward chaining referred to as the *pure-part method*, different parts of a chain are taught separately and then all are combined to form a whole. Suppose that you wished to teach someone to swim using a front crawl stroke. With appropriate guidance and flotation devices, the student might first be taught the proper arm stroke, then the proper kick, and then proper head turning and breathing. Finally, all three parts would be put together into one entire or whole sequence. Weld and Evans (1990) found little difference between pure-part learning and total-task presentation for teaching adolescents with severe or moderate developmental disabilities to prepare a bag lunch and to make a greeting card.

Study Question on Note

1. Describe the pure-part method of chaining. How does it differ from standard forward chaining?

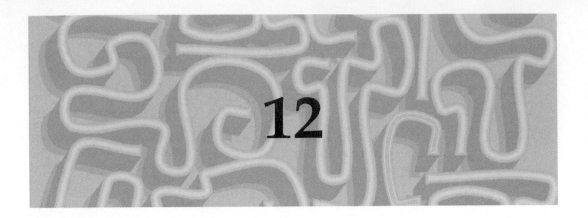

12

Eliminating Inappropriate Behavior Through Punishment

"Ben, don't be so aggressive."

ELIMINATING BEN'S AGGRESSIVENESS[1]

Ben was a 7-year-old boy enrolled in a public school program for severely disturbed children. He had been diagnosed as a child with developmental delay, and the staff in the school had noticed an increase in Ben's frequency of hitting other children and/or the staff. In fact, during baseline observations over approximately three weeks, the frequency of Ben's hits averaged about 30 per day. Something had to be done.

Although painful consequences (presented as punishers) have been demonstrated to reduce undesirable behaviors, such consequences have been found to be unacceptable in a number of situations, including many public school classrooms. Therefore, the staff decided to examine whether making exercise contingent on Ben's hitting might decrease it.

A number of precautions were taken to ensure that the contingent exercise would in no way be detrimental to Ben's health. The procedures were explained thoroughly to the parents, and parental consent was obtained for Ben's participation in the program. The procedures were also reviewed and approved by the ethical review board of the school district in which the program was carried out. The program was conducted at Ben's school throughout the school day. On the day that the contingent exercise was introduced, Ben's first hit was followed by the nearest adult saying, "Ben, no hitting. Stand up and sit down 10 times." The adult then held Ben's hand and lifted it over his head to prompt standing up and then pulled his upper body

[1]This example is based on an article by Luce, Delquadri, and Hall (1980).

forward to prompt sitting down, at the same time saying "Stand up, sit down" each time. Although Ben showed some verbal resistance to the exercise on a few occasions, the staff reported that physical prompting was necessary only on the first few training trials. On subsequent days, only verbal reminders were necessary to prompt the exercise task. From an average of approximately 30 hits per day during baseline, Ben's hits dropped to a frequency of 11 on the first day of the program, 10 on the second day, one on the third day, and either zero or one thereafter.

After two weeks of the procedure, the staff stopped applying the contingent exercise program to see what would happen to Ben's hits. The frequency of hits remained low for four days, but then they began to increase over the next four days. The staff reinstituted the contingent exercise program and observed an immediate drop in the frequency of hitting to near zero. The program continued formally for another two months, and the staff recorded one hit on each of three days during that entire time. Ben could run about and interact with other children and no longer showed the distressful aggressiveness characteristic of his past behavior.

THE PRINCIPLE OF PUNISHMENT

A **punisher** is an event that, when presented immediately following a behavior, causes the behavior to decrease in frequency. Punishers are sometimes referred to as **aversive stimuli,** or simply **aversives.** Once an event has been determined to function as a punisher for a particular behavior of an individual in a particular situation, that event can be used to decrease other behaviors of that individual in other situations. Associated with the concept of a punisher is the principle of **punishment:** *If, in a given situation, somebody does something that is immediately followed by a punisher, then that person is less likely to do the same thing again when he or she next encounters a similar situation.* In Ben's case, contingent exercise was a punisher for his aggressive hitting behavior.

Note that the meaning of punishment for behavior modifiers is quite specific, and differs from the meaning of the word "punishment" for most laypersons in our general culture. Consider, for example, sending a person to jail as "punishment" for committing a crime. First, going to jail is *not* likely to be an *immediate* consequence of committing the crime. Second, many individuals believe that "punishment" should involve *retribution* (as in saying that the "punishment" must fit the crime, and that more serious crimes deserve more severe sentences). Third, in the general culture, "punishment" is applied, in part, as a *deterrent* to potential "wrong-doers." For behavior modifiers, however, "punishment" is simply a technical word referring to the application of an immediate consequence following a behavior of an individual that has the effect of decreasing the likelihood of future instances of that behavior in that individual. When we use the term *punishment* in this chapter and elsewhere in this book, therefore, please think of it in that sense.

Like positive reinforcement, punishment affects our learning throughout life. The immediate consequences of touching a hot stove teach us not to do that again. As infants, the bruises from a few falls helped to teach us better balance while learning to walk. A frown from your date after you burp loudly in a restaurant would likely decrease the likelihood of your doing so on future dates. And we have all had our behavior affected by revoked privileges or reprimands from teachers, and an unlimited array of social "put-downs" from peers. However, it is important to recognize that there is some controversy within the field of behavior modification regarding the use of punishment. We return to this issue later in this chapter, after discussing the different types of punishment and the factors that influence the effects of punishment in suppressing behavior.

TYPES OF PUNISHERS

Many kinds of events, when delivered as immediate consequences for behavior, fit our definition of punisher given above. Most of these events can be classified into the following categories (see Van Houten, 1983): (a) pain-inducing punishers, (b) reprimands, (c) time-outs, and (d) response cost. Although there is some overlap among these categories, they provide a convenient way in which to organize punishment procedures. We now consider each category in turn.

Pain-Inducing Punishers

Pain-inducing punishers, also referred to as *physical punishers*, include all punishers immediately following a behavior that activate pain receptors or other sense receptors that typically evoke feelings of discomfort. Examples include spankings, pinches, electric shock, ammonia vapor, cold baths, very loud or harsh sounds, prolonged tickling, and hair tugging. Such stimuli or events are called **unconditioned punishers** (that is, stimuli that are punishing without any prior training or conditioning).

Application of punishers is not pleasant; nevertheless, there are cases in which individuals have benefited greatly from the procedure. A dramatic example is what may have been the life-saving treatment of a 6-month-old baby (Sajwaj, Libet, & Agras, 1974). Sandra was admitted to a hospital because of a failure to gain weight that was associated with the constant bringing up of food (ruminating). She was underweight and undernourished, and death was a distinct possibility. Preliminary observations indicated that a few minutes after being given milk, Sandra would begin ruminating and would continue for about 20 to 40 minutes until she had apparently lost all the milk she had consumed. Sajwaj and colleagues decided to administer lemon juice as a punisher. During treatment, Sandra's mouth was filled with lemon juice immediately after staff members detected the vigorous tongue movements that reliably preceded her rumination. After 16 feedings with lemon juice punishment, the rumination had decreased to a very low level. To ensure that the improvement was due to the treatment program, Sajwaj and coworkers suspended the use of lemon juice for two feedings. The result was a dramatic increase in rumination. Following additional treatment, Sandra was discharged to foster parents, who maintained the treatment until it was no longer necessary.

Reprimands

Reprimands are strong negative verbal stimuli (e.g., "No! That was bad!") immediately contingent on behavior. They also usually include a fixed stare and, sometimes, a firm grasp. In Chapter 4 we noted that a stimulus paired with punishment becomes itself a punisher. Such a stimulus is called a **conditioned punisher.** It is likely that the verbal component of a reprimand is a conditioned punisher. It is also possible that other components, such as the firm grasp, are unconditioned punishers. In some cases, the effectiveness of reprimands has been increased by pairing them with other punishers. For example, Dorsey, Iwata, Ong, and McSween (1980) paired reprimands with a water-mist spray to suppress self-injurious behavior in individuals with developmental disabilities. This caused the reprimands to become effective not only in the original setting but also in a setting where the mist had not been used.

Time-outs

Time-outs involve transferring an individual from a more reinforcing to a less reinforcing situation immediately following a particular behavior (Van Houten, 1983, p. 28). They can be viewed as time-out from the opportunity to earn reinforcers. There are two types of time-outs: exclusionary and nonexclusionary. An **exclusionary time-out** consists of removing the learner for a short time (e.g., five minutes) from the situation in which reinforcement is occurring. Often a special room, called a *time-out room*, is used for this purpose. The time-out room is bare of anything that might serve as a reinforcer and may be padded to prevent self-injury. The period in the time-out room should not be very long; about five minutes is usually quite effective (Brantner & Doherty, 1983; Fabiano et al., 2004). Also, ethical considerations (Do the ends justify the means? See Chapter 30.) and practical considerations (such as avoiding lengthy time-outs that take the individual away from a learning environment) must also be considered in selecting a particular time-out duration. A **nonexclusionary time-out** consists of introducing into the situation a stimulus associated with less reinforcement. An example of this was reported by Foxx and Shapiro (1978). Children in a classroom wore a ribbon that was removed for a short time when a child was disruptive. When not wearing the ribbon, the child was not allowed to participate in classroom activities and was ignored by the teacher.

Response Cost

Response cost involves the removal of a specified amount of reinforcer immediately following a particular behavior (Reynolds & Kelley, 1997). Response cost is sometimes used in behavior modification programs in which learners earn tokens as reinforcers (Kazdin, 1977a). Working in a classroom setting, for example, Sullivan and O'Leary (1990) showed that loss of tokens (each of which could be exchanged for one minute of recess) for off-task behavior successfully decreased it. Note that response cost differs from a time-out in that there is no change in the prevailing reinforcement contingencies when it is administered. Response cost is also not to be confused with extinction. In an extinction procedure, a reinforcer is withheld following a previously reinforced response. In response cost, a reinforcer is taken away following an undesirable response.

Examples of response cost in everyday life are library fines, traffic tickets, and charges for overdrawn bank accounts. However, these punishers are not typically applied immediately following the offending behavior. Just as we distinguished between the direct-acting effect and the indirect-acting effect of positive reinforcement in Chapter 3, we make a similar distinction with respect to punishment. The *direct-acting effect* of punishment is the decreased frequency of a response because of its immediate punishing consequences (within 30 seconds). The *indirect-acting effect* of punishment is the weakening of a response that is followed by a punisher even though the punisher is delayed. Suppose, for example, that a person speeds through an intersection, is caught by photo radar, and receives a ticket in the mail a week later. Although that person's future speeding may be reduced by that procedure, it involves much more than the principle of punishment. Delayed punishers may have an effect on behavior because of instructions about the behavior leading to the punisher, because of self-statements (or "thoughts") that intervene between that behavior and the delayed punisher, or because of immediate conditioned punishers that intervene between the behavior and the backup punisher. It is a mistake to offer punishment as an overly simplistic explanation of a decrease in behavior when the punisher does not follow the behavior immediately. Explanations of the indirect-acting effect of punishment are discussed further in Chapter 17.

We turn now to a discussion of factors influencing the effectiveness of punishment (for a review of research on this topic, see Lerman & Vorndran, 2002).

FACTORS INFLUENCING THE EFFECTIVENESS OF PUNISHMENT

1. Maximizing the Conditions for a Desirable Alternative Response

To decrease an undesirable response, it is maximally effective to concurrently in-
Note 1 crease some desirable alternative response that will compete with the undesirable be-
havior to be eliminated. You should attempt to identify powerful S^Ds that control the desirable behavior and present these to increase the likelihood that the behavior will occur. To maintain the desirable behavior, you should also have effective positive reinforcers that can be presented on an effective schedule. Because the staff members in Ben's case were concerned with examining contingent exercise as a punisher by itself, they did not incorporate a specific positive reinforcement contingency for a desirable alternative to Ben's hitting. They might easily have done so, however.

When consulted by individuals who are thinking about applying a punishment procedure to decrease an undesirable behavior, we always recommend that they first design effective positive reinforcement and stimulus control programs for desirable alternative behaviors (Figure 12–1). Thus, if you are considering developing and using a punishment program to decrease undesirable behavior, we strongly urge you first to review and apply the information in the earlier chapters concerning positive reinforcement and stimulus control. It may turn out that punishment is unnecessary once you sufficiently strengthen a desirable alternative

Figure 12–1   An example of the reinforcement of a desirable alternative behavior.

behavior. You should also familiarize yourself with the arguments against the use of punishment, which are summarized later in this chapter.

2. Minimizing the Cause of the Response to Be Punished

To maximize the opportunity for the desirable alternative behavior to occur, anyone attempting a punishment program should first minimize the causes of the undesirable behavior. This implies two things. First, one should try to identify the current stimulus control of the undesirable behavior. Second, one should try to identify existing reinforcers that are maintaining the undesirable behavior. If the behavior is occurring, it is likely that occasional reinforcers are maintaining it. Identifying the antecedents and consequences for a behavior is referred to as a functional assessment, and is discussed in more detail in Chapter 22. In Ben's case, the teachers were unable to identify S^Ds that consistently evoked hitting, nor could they identify maintaining reinforcement contingencies.

It is important to emphasize that punishment may often not be necessary. Minimizing the causes of the undesirable behavior while maximizing the conditions for a desirable alternative behavior may cause the latter to compete so strongly with the former that it is greatly reduced or completely suppressed without the use of punishment.

3. Selecting a Punisher

If punishment is to be used, it is important to be sure that the punisher is effective. In general, the more intense or strong the punishing stimulus, the more effective it will be in decreasing the undesirable behavior. However, the intensity of the punisher that is needed to be effective will depend on your success in minimizing the causes of the undesirable behavior while maximizing the conditions for a desirable

Note 2

alternative behavior. Even a mild punisher, such as a reprimand, can be effective if the reinforcer for the undesirable behavior is withheld following instances of the behavior, and if a desirable alternative behavior is reinforced with a strong reinforcer. It is also important to keep in mind that some stimuli may seem to be punishing when in fact they are not. For example, a parent may say "No! Naughty boy! Stop that!" to a child who is engaging in an undesirable behavior. The child may immediately cease the undesirable behavior and perform some other, desired behavior that will continue to receive the attention of the adult. The adult might then conclude that the reprimand was an effective punisher. However, if the adult were to keep track of the frequency of that undesirable behavior in the future, he or she might find that the verbal reprimand was not a punisher, but in fact a reinforcer. The child may have stopped temporarily because, having obtained the attention of the adult, he can perform other behavior that will maintain the adult's attention, at least for a short time. In other words, the verbal reprimand may function as an S^D for subsequent desirable behaviors of the child, regardless of the effects of the verbal reprimand as a punisher or a reinforcer on the preceding undesirable behavior. Several studies indicate that verbal reprimands can function as positive reinforcers and that the long-term frequency of the undesirable behavior that evoked the reprimand is therefore likely to increase (e.g., Madsen, Becker, Thomas, Koser, & Plager, 1970). This is not to say that verbal reprimands or threats are never punishing. Situations in which they are effective, however, seem to be those in which they are consistently backed up by another punisher, the causes of the undesirable behavior have been minimized, and the conditions for a desirable alternative behavior have been maximized (Van Houten & Doleys, 1983).

The punisher should be one that can be presented in a manner such that it is in no way paired with positive reinforcement. This requirement often presents difficulties in situations in which the punisher is delivered by an adult and the individual being punished receives very little adult attention. If a child has received a lot of loving attention from an adult during a period of time prior to the occurrence of the undesired behavior, and the adult immediately presents a strong verbal reprimand following the undesirable behavior, then the verbal reprimand is likely to be punishing. However, if that reprimand is the only adult attention that has been received by the child for an extended period of time, then such attention may in fact be reinforcing.

Contingent exercise turned out to be a very suitable punisher for Ben. It was highly effective, could be presented immediately following the undesirable behavior, and could be presented in a manner such that it was in no way paired with positive reinforcement. The care and attention that the staff gave to choosing the actual exercise task obviously paid off. The staff chose the task because it could be prompted by a voice command from a staff member; Ben frequently performed the behavior in various play situations; it could be carried out in a variety of settings; and it appeared to tire Ben quickly without causing any unnecessary strain.

Rather than selecting just one punisher, it may be more effective to select several that are varied over successive instances of the undesirable behavior. For example, Charlop, Burgio, Iwata, and Ivancic (1988) applied either a reprimand, physical restriction, a time-out, or a loud noise as a punisher following aggression and self-stimulation by children with developmental disabilities. In some sessions, only one of the punishers was applied. In other sessions, the four punishers were varied. The children showed less aggression and self-stimulation during sessions when the teacher varied the punishers.

4. Adding Antecedents (Including Rules) for Punishment

You will recall from Chapter 8 that an S^D is a stimulus in the presence of which a response will be reinforced. Similarly, an S^{Dp} is a stimulus in the presence of which a response will be punished.[2] When many of us were children, for example, we learned that asking our parents for treats when they were in a bad mood usually led to a reprimand. The parental behaviors characteristic of "being in a bad mood" constituted an S^{Dp}. Although there is very little research on the effects of S^{Dp}s, there is some (e.g., O'Donnell, Crosbie, Williams, & Saunders, 2000). Research has shown that if in the presence of an S^{Dp} a punisher is consistently applied following a response, then that response is less likely to occur when the S^{Dp} is encountered.

Note 3

As we described for positive reinforcement and extinction, adding rules to a punishment program will probably help to decrease the undesirable behavior and increase the desirable alternative behavior more quickly (e.g., see Bierman, Miller, & Stabb, 1987). Also, as stressed in Chapter 3, it is very important that emphasis be placed on the behavior, not the behaver. It is the behavior that is undesirable, not the individual. Appropriate use of rules is discussed further in Chapter 17.

5. Delivering the Punisher

Punishment is most effective when the punisher is presented *immediately* following every instance of the undesirable behavior. If the punisher is delayed, a more desirable behavior may occur prior to the punisher and this behavior may be suppressed to a much greater extent than the undesirable behavior. The classic example of this is the mother who asks her husband after he returns home from work to punish their child, who has misbehaved earlier in the day. This request is doubly disastrous. First, the child receives the punisher even though she may now be engaging in good behavior. Second, the father is punished for coming home from work. We do not mean to imply that delayed punishment is completely ineffective. As we point out in our discussion of rule-governed behavior in Chapter 17, must humans are adept at bridging rather large time gaps between their behavior and its consequences. Even so, immediate punishment is more effective than delayed punishment.

Occasional punishment is not as effective as punishment that follows every instance of the undesirable behavior (see, e.g., Kircher, Pear, & Martin, 1971). This implies that if the behavior modifier is unable to detect most instances of the behavior to be punished, he or she should have serious doubts about the value of implementing a punishment procedure.

The delivery of the punisher should in no way be paired with positive reinforcement. As already mentioned, such a pairing weakens the punisher. In addition, the person administering the punisher should remain calm when doing so. Anger

---

[2]We acknowledge Jennifer O'Donnell (2001) for introducing the symbol S^{Dp}.

and frustration on the part of the person administering the punisher may reinforce the undesirable behavior or inappropriately alter the consistency or intensity of the punisher. A calm, matter-of-fact approach helps ensure that a punishment program will be followed consistently and appropriately.

SHOULD PUNISHMENT BE USED?

The use of punishment has always been highly controversial, even before the advent of behavior modification, but the controversy intensified during the 1980s (Meyer & Evans, 1989; Repp & Singh, 1990). A number of organizations concerned with helping people have formulated official statements against at least some uses of punishment. For example, the Practice Directorates of the American Psychological Association and the National Association of School Psychologists have provided testimony to the United States Congress in support of an amendment banning the use of corporal (that is, physical and pain-inducing) punishment for emotionally disturbed children ("P.D. Supports Ban on Corporal Punishment," 1990). In 1990, the American Association on Mental Retardation adopted a policy statement condemning "aversive procedures which cause physical damage, pain, or illness" and "procedures which are dehumanizing—social degradation, verbal abuse and excessive reactions" (p. 5).

There are some who argue that nonaversive methods for eliminating unacceptable behavior are always at least as effective as punishment and that, therefore, there is never any justification for using pain-inducing punishment (see Guess, Helmstetter, Turnbull, & Knowlton, 1986. No humane person would think it is ethical to induce pain if nonaversive methods that are equally effective are available. It appears, however, that there are some extremely harmful behaviors that, in some cases, can be suppressed only with pain-inducing punishment. For example, there are individuals with developmental disabilities or autism who repeatedly engage in severe self-injurious behavior—damaging their vision by gouging their eyes, damaging their hearing by clapping their hands against their ears, causing tissue damage and bleeding by banging their heads on hard objects or tearing at their flesh, becoming malnourished by inducing vomiting after eating—that places them in great danger of disabling or killing themselves. A number of studies in the literature demonstrate that these behaviors can be suppressed by pain-inducing punishment (see, e.g., Favell et al., 1982; Linscheid, Iwata, Ricketts, Williams, & Griffin, 1990; Linscheid, Pejeau, Cohen, & Footo-Lenz, 1994). Once the self-injurious behavior is suppressed, positive reinforcement is then used to maintain desirable alternative behavior, but this cannot be done until the self-injurious behavior has been controlled. The only alternative to using pain-inducing punishment, in some cases, appears to be restraint—for example, tying heavily padded mittens to the individual's hands, or even tying the individual to a wheelchair or bed—but this effectively prevents the person from learning desirable behavior to replace the undesirable behavior.

Several authors have described methods, such as an approach called *gentle teaching* (McGee, Menolascino, Hobbs, & Menousek, 1987), that they claim can effectively replace all forms of aversive control. For the most part, the methods described are based on the behavior principles discussed in Chapters 3 through 11 of this text. Although these authors provide many good examples of alternatives that should be tried before resorting to aversive methods, it is not clear that the methods they propose can effectively replace aversive methods in all cases. Moreover, several authors (e.g., Bailey, 1992; Jones & McCaughey, 1992) have identified several important limitations of this approach. What is clear is that the decision to use or not use pain-inducing punishment in a particular case requires considerable professional training and expertise and should not be made by unqualified individuals. Treatment of severe behavior problems, which are the only type for which pain-inducing punishment should be considered, is best left to the appropriate professionals who are members of accredited professional organizations (Griffith & Spreat, 1989).

Although much controversy centers on pain-inducing punishment, other forms of punishment have also been criticized. Few would argue that all forms of punishment can be eliminated. It is extremely difficult, however, to specify the exact degree of punishment that is appropriate in a given situation. Regarding time-outs, Meyer and Evans (1989, p. 102) state: "The time-out area need not be incredibly comfortable and desirable, but also should not be extremely unpleasant." Clearly, this recommendation leaves a great deal of room for subjectivity in selecting a time-out area. Meyer and Evans also oppose the use of exercise as a punisher—such as that used with Ben—although they regard exercise as beneficial if used to "calm" an individual following inappropriate behavior (p. 137). Unfortunately, it is very difficult—perhaps even impossible—to distinguish between these two functions of exercise, because requiring someone to exercise for the purpose of "calming" may also punish behavior that it follows (according to the technical definition of punishment given at the beginning of this chapter). It appears that what Meyer and Evans are actually concerned with is that if punishment has to be used, it must never be used in a humiliating or degrading manner. We certainly concur in this. Regardless of the nature of a person's disability, or the inappropriateness of his or her behavior, that person should always be treated in a manner that shows respect for him or her as a human being.

Even though its use is highly controversial, it is clear that punishment can have a number of potentially harmful effects. These may be summarized as follows.

1. *Aggressive behavior.* Punishment tends to elicit aggressive behavior. Experiments with animals show that painful stimuli cause them to attack other animals—even though these other animals had nothing to do with inflicting these stimuli (Azrin, 1967). Some research (Berkowitz, 1988, 1989) suggests that this finding also applies to humans. Thus we should not be surprised to observe individuals who have just been punished attacking other individuals.

2. *Emotional behavior.* Punishment can produce other undesirable emotional side effects, such as crying and general fearfulness. Not only are these side effects unpleasant for all concerned, they frequently interfere with desirable behavior—especially if it is of a complex nature.

3. *Escape and avoidance behavior.* Punishment may cause the situation and people associated with the aversive stimulus to become conditioned punishers. For example, if, when teaching a child to read, you punish the child whenever he or she makes a mistake, anything associated with this situation—such as printed words, books, the person who delivers the punishment, the type of room in which the punishment occurs—will tend to become punishing. The child may attempt to escape or avoid these stimuli (see Chapter 13). Thus, instead of helping the individual to learn, punishment may drive him or her away from everything having to do with the learning situation.

The punisher need not be particularly strong to have the undesirable effects mentioned in points 1 through 3. For example, a teacher we know used a time-out chair as a punisher for students in her first-grade class. For some unknown reason— perhaps it had something to do with the fact that the chair was black and the teacher told rowdy children to go sit in the "black chair"—the chair became frightening to the students. Years later, former students who come back to visit her still mention how fearful they had been of the "black chair," even though nothing bad ever happened to them when they sat there. When the teacher discovered the problem with the chair, she changed her procedure. The chair is no longer black and she now calls it the "calming-down chair," and she periodically demonstrates its benign qualities to her students by sitting in it herself when she feels the need to calm down!

4. *No new behavior.* Punishment does not establish any new desirable behavior; it only suppresses old behavior. In other words, punishment does not teach an individual what to do; at best it only teaches what not to do. For example, the main defining characteristic of persons with developmental disabilities is that they lack behavior that the majority of people have. The primary emphasis for these individuals, then, should be on establishing new behavior rather than on merely eliminating old behavior. Reinforcement is required to accomplish this task.

5. *Modeling of punishment.* Children often model or imitate adults. If adults apply punishment to children, the children are apt to do the same to others. Thus, in punishing children we may inadvertently be providing a model for them to follow in presenting aversive stimuli toward others (Bandura, 1965, 1969). For example, children who were taught a game in which they were fined for incorrect behavior fined other children to whom they taught the game (Gelfand et al., 1974).

6. *Continued use of punishment.* Because punishment results in quick suppression of undesirable behavior, it can tempt the user to rely heavily on it and neglect the use of positive reinforcement for desirable behavior. However, the undesirable behavior may return after only a temporary suppression, or some other undesirable behavior could occur. The person administering punishment may then resort to progressively heavier doses, thereby creating a vicious circle with disastrous effects.

BEHAVIOR MODIFIERS AND PUNISHMENT PROGRAMS

Now let's reconsider the question, should punishment be used? Before doing so, we reemphasize a point made earlier in this chapter that we are not talking about the concept of punishment as it is thought of by laypersons. That is, we are *not* talking about punishment of an individual as a deterrent to others, as retribution, or as a delayed consequence for misbehavior. Rather, we are talking about consistently presenting an immediate punisher following a problem behavior, and doing so in full consideration of the factors influencing the effectiveness of punishment as discussed previously. Nevertheless, because punishers are so easy to abuse, and because their application can have a number of potentially harmful side effects, we recommend that punishment (as viewed behaviorally) be used only as a last resort. We recommend that behavior modifiers consider designing punishment programs, whether in schools, agencies for persons with developmental disabilities, or other settings, only when:

- Clear steps are taken to maximize the conditions for a desirable alternative response and to minimize the causes of the response to be punished.

Note 4
- The behavior is very maladaptive and it is in the client's best interest to bring about rapid behavior change.
- The client (or his or her parent or guardian) provides informed consent (see Chapter 30).
- The intervention meets ethical standards (see Chapter 30).
- Punishment is applied according to clear guidelines (see pp. 162).
- The program includes safeguards to protect the client (see Chapter 30).

PITFALLS OF PUNISHMENT

There are many instances in which punishment is applied by people who are not aware that they are doing so. A common example is criticizing or ridiculing a person for inadequate behavior. Criticism and ridicule are generally punishing, and they will likely suppress future instances of that behavior and tend to drive the individual away from the person administering them. Yet the inadequate behavior that is criticized and ridiculed may be an approximation of more adequate behavior. Suppressing it could destroy the individual's opportunity to obtain the more desired behavior through the use of shaping. In everyday language, the individual becomes discouraged and gives up in his or her attempt to develop adequate behavior. In addition, because he or she will attempt to escape from and avoid the person administering the criticism and ridicule (see Chapter 13), that person will have lost a great deal of potential reinforcing effectiveness.

Another example of someone's applying punishment without being aware of it is the person who says "That was good, but. . . ." Suppose that a teenager helps a parent with the dishes and the parent replies, "Thanks for helping, but next time don't be so slow." We are sure that, based on the foregoing discussion, you can describe a much more effective and pleasant way for the parent to react.

Punishment should be applied only in conjunction with positive reinforcement for a desirable alternative behavior, and only under the conditions described in the previous subsections.

GUIDELINES FOR THE EFFECTIVE APPLICATION
OF PUNISHMENT

The rules for the effective use of punishment are probably violated more than those for other principles. Therefore, if you propose a punishment procedure (even one involving a mild punisher), you owe it to yourself and the person whose behavior is to be punished to do an effective job. The conditions under which the program should be applied must be stated clearly, written down, and followed.

1. *Select a response.* Punishment is most effective with a specific behavior (such as jumping on the arm of the chair) rather than a general category of behavior (such as wrecking furniture).
2. *Maximize the conditions for a desirable (nonpunished) alternative response.*
   a. Select a desirable alternative behavior that competes with the behavior to be punished such that the alternative behavior can be reinforced. If possible, select a behavior that will be maintained by the natural environment after the termination of your reinforcement program.
   b. Provide strong prompts to increase the likelihood that the desirable alternative behavior will occur.
   c. Reinforce the desirable behavior with a powerful reinforcer on an appropriate schedule.
3. *Minimize the causes of the response to be punished.*
   a. Try to identify and eliminate many or all of the S^Ds for the undesirable behavior, at least early in the training program.
   b. Try to eliminate any possible reinforcement for the undesirable behavior.
4. *Select an effective punisher.*
   a. Choose an effective punisher that can be presented immediately following the undesirable behavior.
   b. The punisher should be one that will in no way be paired with positive reinforcement following the undesirable behavior.
   c. Select a punisher that can be presented following every instance of the undesirable behavior.
5. *Present clear S^{Dp}s.*
   a. Tell the learner about the plan before starting.
   b. Give a clear "warning" or "reminder" (e.g., "Wait for mommy before crossing").
6. *Deliver the punisher.*
   a. Present the punisher *immediately* following every instance of the response to be decreased.
   b. Administer the punisher in a calm and matter-of-fact manner.
   c. Take care not to pair punishment of the undesirable behavior with reinforcement for that behavior.
7. *Take data.* In all programs involving punishment, careful data should be taken on the effects of the program.

STUDY QUESTIONS

1. Describe how Ben's aggressive behavior was eliminated.
2. How was stimulus control an important part of the punishment contingency for Ben?
3. What is a punisher? State the principle of punishment.
4. How is the meaning of the term *punishment* for behavior modifiers different from the meaning of that term for most laypersons?
5. Describe four different types of punishers and illustrate each with an example.
6. Under which of the four categories of punishment would you put the type of punishment used with Ben? Justify your choice.
7. Define conditioned punisher and illustrate with an example.
8. Distinguish between an exclusionary and nonexclusionary time-out.

9. Distinguish between the direct-acting and indirect-acting effect of punishment. Give an example of each.
10. What are three reasons that might account for the effectiveness of a delayed punisher in decreasing a behavior?
11. If you do a good job of attending to the first two factors influencing the effectiveness of punishment, you may not have to apply punishment. Discuss.
12. What steps might you follow to experimentally determine if a verbal reprimand was a punisher for a particular child?
13. What is a common example of response-contingent withdrawal of positive reinforcement that is applied as punishment by parents to their children?
14. Procedurally, describe the differences between extinction, response cost, and exclusionary time-out.
15. Compare S^D to S^{Dp}. Give an example of each.
16. In the subsection "Delivering the Punisher," we suggested that if the behavior modifier is unable to detect most instances of a behavior to be punished, then he or she should have serious doubts about the value of implementing a punishment procedure.
    a. From the information in this chapter, what reasons can you cite to support this suggestion?
    b. What alternative means of managing the situation are available to the teacher?
17. What are three guidelines in regard to delivering punishment? (See Guidelines section.)
18. In view of the controversy regarding the use of punishment, do you agree with the way punishment was used with Ben? Defend your answer.
19. Cite six potentially harmful side effects of the application of punishment.
20. Describe an example illustrating how punishment is applied by people who are not aware that they are doing so.

APPLICATION EXERCISES

A. Exercises Involving Others

1. Consider the behavior of speeding (driving a car in excess of the speed limit) in our culture.
   • Briefly outline the current reinforcement and punishment contingencies with respect to speeding.
   • Compare the current punishment contingencies for speeding with the guidelines for the effective application of punishment procedures. Identify those guidelines that were ignored by the lawmakers and law enforcers.
2. Consider the behavior of littering the highways in your area. Answer the questions for this behavior that you answered for speeding in Application Exercise 1.

B. Self-Modification Exercise

Choose a behavior of yours that you would like to decrease. With the help of a friend, describe in detail a punishment program that would likely decrease that behavior. (Make the program as realistic as possible, but do not apply it.) Your punishment program should be consistent with all the guidelines for the effective application of punishment.

NOTES AND EXTENDED DISCUSSION

1. C. R. Johnson, Hunt, and Siebert (1994) combined reinforcement with punishment to treat pica, which is the ingestion of inedible objects or non-nutritive substances. Commonly seen among individuals with severe and profound developmental disabilities, this serious disorder has been associated with lead poisoning, intestinal blockage, intestinal perforation, and intestinal parasites. Items commonly ingested include cigarettes and cigarette butts, plastic objects, hair, paint chips, dirt and sand, and bits of paper. The client, a 15-year-old with profound developmental disabilities, was taught to eat only items that were placed on a bright yellow plastic placemat. The client received praise from the staff at the institution as well as the natural reinforcement (good taste) for eating the items on the placemat. Items that were not on the placemat that were ingested were followed by a consequence that was punishing for the client (his face was washed with a cool damp cloth for 15 seconds). The procedure eliminated the pica.

2. For example, Thompson, Iwata, Connors, and Roscoe (1999) evaluated the effects of reprimands and brief manual restraint as mild punishers contingent on the self-injurious behavior of four individuals who had been diagnosed with developmental disabilities. In all cases, the mild punishers produced greater response suppression when access to a reinforcer for desirable alternative behavior (manipulation of leisure materials) was available.

3. Beginning students of behavior analysis often confuse an S^{Dp} with an SD^{Δ}. Suppose, for example, that each time that a child swore, the parents deducted 25 cents from the child's allowance, and that as a result of this contingency, swearing decreased. In this example, the sight of the parents would be an S^{Dp} for swearing. If, on the other hand, the parents simply ignored the child when he swore (i.e., withheld their attention as a reinforcer), and the swearing decreased, then sight of the parents would be an S^{Δ} for swearing. In both scenarios, swearing would be eliminated in the presence of the parents. However, the causes of the behavior change are different.

4. Should parents use punishment? Many professional behavior modifiers have been hesitant to speak out on this issue because of the way that the media has misreported their comments. The issue of spankings by parents, for example, has made headlines in many newspapers, including the *New York Times* and *USA Today*. We hasten to point out, however, that discussion of use of punishment by parents need not imply corporal punishment (e.g., spankings; for a review of corporal punishment by parents, see Gershoff, 2002). Rather, punishment can involve time-out, response cost, or reprimands. Also, we want to reemphasize that any discussion of punishment should be done with full consideration of the behavioral approach to punishment used in this chapter. In that sense, there are situations where application of punishment by parents would likely be in the best interests of their children, such as in the case of a child who frequently runs on to a busy street, or sticks metal objects into electrical outlets, or eats paint chips off walls. However, before applying punishment, parents should become knowledgeable concerning the factors that influence the effectiveness of punishment. An excellent source for parents is the book by Cipani (2004b) that describes myths about punishment, basic principles of punishment, and guidelines for responsible use of punishment by parents.

Study Questions on Notes

1. What is pica? What factors influencing the effectiveness of punishment did Johnson et al. (1994) incorporate into their treatment program for pica?
2. What did Thompson et al. find with respect to the effectiveness of reprimands as a punisher when a reinforcer for alternative behavior was and was not available?
3. Give an example of an S^{Dp}.
4. Give an example of an S^{Δ}.
5. Do you think parents should use punishment? Discuss.

13

Establishing a Desirable Behavior by Using Escape and Avoidance Conditioning

CURING JASON'S SLOUCHING[1]

Jason was a model employee. An attendant at the Anna State Hospital, he was hardworking, punctual, and well liked by the patients. Unfortunately, Jason constantly slouched while he worked. At first glance, slouching might not seem like a serious problem. But slouching by staff presented an inappropriate role model for the psychiatric patients at the hospital. Poor posture by such individuals frequently discourages social acceptability when they return to the community. Moreover, many medical authorities believe that good posture benefits health.

Fortunately for Jason, some psychologists at the hospital were conducting research on behavioral engineering—the use of apparatus to manage contingencies to change behavior. Jason agreed to wear a specially designed shoulder harness that held an elastic cord across his back. The elastic cord was wired to a small tone generator and a clicker. When Jason wore a shirt and sweater over the harness, it was completely concealed from view.

Here's how the apparatus worked: When Jason slouched, the elastic cord stretched and caused a click sound. Three seconds later, a loud tone sounded and remained on until Jason stopped slouching. Thus, by exhibiting good posture after the tone came on, Jason would escape the sound of the tone. And if he continued to display good posture he would avoid the tone altogether. The results were dramatic. Before Jason wore the apparatus, he slouched almost 60% of the time, but

---

[1]This case is based on Azrin, Ruben, O'Brien, Ayllon, and Roll (1968).

when he wore the apparatus, he slouched only 1% of the time. When Jason re-moved the apparatus, his slouching did recover somewhat (to approximately 11%), but the clear demonstration of the effects of the apparatus gave him hope that he could cure his slouching habit.

ESCAPE CONDITIONING

Three behavioral principles were used in Jason's case: escape conditioning, avoidance conditioning, and punishment. The principle of **escape conditioning** states that there are certain stimuli whose removal immediately after the occurrence of a response will increase the likelihood of that response. In the escape procedure used with Jason, the removal of the loud tone following the response of showing good posture increased the probability that Jason would show good posture each time the tone was presented.

Escape conditioning is similar to aversive punishment in that both involve the use of an aversive stimulus (or punisher). While escape conditioning and punishment are therefore similar, they differ procedurally in terms of both the antecedents and the consequences of behavior. With regard to antecedents, in escape conditioning, the aversive stimulus (the loud tone in Jason's case) must be present prior to an escape response, whereas the aversive stimulus is not present prior to a response that is punished. With regard to consequences, in escape conditioning the aversive stimulus is removed immediately following a response, whereas in punishment the aversive stimulus (or punisher) is presented immediately following a response. In terms of results, with the punishment procedure the likelihood of the target response is *decreased*, whereas in the escape conditioning procedure the likelihood of the target response is *increased*.

Another name for escape conditioning is **negative reinforcement** (Skinner, 1953). The term *reinforcement* indicates that it is analogous to positive reinforcement, in that both strengthen responses. The term *negative* indicates that the strengthening effect occurs because the response leads to the removal (i.e., the taking away or subtraction) of an aversive stimulus.

Escape conditioning is common in everyday living. In the presence of a bright light, we have learned to escape the intensity of the light by closing our eyes or squinting. When a room is too cold, we escape the chill by putting on an extra sweater (see Figure 13–1). When it is too hot, we escape the heat by turning on a fan or air conditioner. If a street crew is repairing the street outside your room, you might close the window to escape the noise. Other examples of escape conditioning are presented in Table 13–1.

AVOIDANCE CONDITIONING

Escape conditioning has the disadvantage that the aversive stimulus must be present for the desired response to occur. In the escape procedure used with Jason, the loud tone was on before Jason showed good posture. Therefore, escape conditioning is generally not a final contingency for maintaining behavior, but rather is

Figure 13–1   Dressing warmly in the winter is strengthened by escape conditioning.

preparatory training for avoidance conditioning. Thus, Jason was influenced by avoidance conditioning after he had demonstrated escape behavior.

The principle of **avoidance conditioning** states that a behavior will increase in frequency if it prevents an aversive stimulus from occurring. During the avoidance procedure used with Jason, good posture prevented the tone from occurring. Note that both escape conditioning and avoidance conditioning involve the use of an aversive stimulus. And with both, the likelihood of a behavior is increased. However, an escape response removes an aversive stimulus that has already been presented, while an avoidance response prevents an aversive stimulus from occurring at all.

The click of the apparatus when Jason slouched was a **warning stimulus** (also called *conditioned aversive stimulus*)—it signaled the occurrence of the tone three seconds later. Jason quickly learned to show good posture at the sound of the click in order to avoid the backup aversive stimulus, the loud tone. This type of avoidance **Note 1** conditioning, which includes a warning signal that enables the individual to discriminate a forthcoming aversive stimulus, is called *discriminated avoidance conditioning*.

Because the sound of the click became a conditioned punisher (through pairings with the backup aversive stimulus), the procedure used with Jason also included a punishment component. If Jason showed poor posture, then the sound of a click, a conditioned punisher, would occur. Thus, when Jason began wearing the apparatus, good posture was strengthened through escape conditioning, and maintained through avoidance conditioning, and poor posture was immediately punished. It's no wonder that the results were so dramatic.

TABLE 13–1   EXAMPLES OF ESCAPE CONDITIONING

Aversive Situation	Escape Responses by Individual	Removal of Aversive Situation	Long-Term Effect
1. A child sees an adult with a bag of candies. The child begins to scream,"Candy, candy, candy."	To terminate the screaming, the adult gives the screaming child a candy.	The child stops screaming.	In the future, the adult is more likely "to give in to" the screaming child because of escape conditioning (and the child is more likely to scream when she sees a bag of candy, because of the positive reinforcement she gains for doing so).
2. A teacher presents prompts every 30 seconds to a child with developmental disabilities.	The child begins to tantrum.	The teacher gives the child a break from the training program.	The child is more likely to tantrum when presented with frequent prompts from the teacher.
3. A nonverbal child has had shoes put on her that are too tight and are pinching her toes.	The child makes loud noises in the presence of an adult and points to her toes.	The adult removes the shoes (and perhaps puts on larger shoes).	The child is more likely to make loud noises and point to her sore feet (or other areas of pain) more quickly in similar situations in the future.
4. A jogger experiences a sensation of sore lips while jogging on a windy day.	The jogger puts lip balm on his lips.	The sensation of soreness ceases.	The jogger is more likely to use lip balm to sooth sore lips.
5. A staff member in a zoo encounters a pile of smelly dung on the floor of a monkey cage.	The staff member walks away without cleaning it up.	The staff member escapes the aversive smell (and avoids having to clean up the dung).	In the future, the staff member will likely walk away from dung on the floor of the monkey cage.

Avoidance conditioning is also common in everyday living. In too many classrooms, unfortunately, children learn to give the right answers primarily to avoid ridicule and to avoid poor grades. Our legal system is based largely on avoidance conditioning. We pay our taxes to avoid going to jail. We put money in parking meters to avoid getting a ticket. We pay our parking fines in order to avoid a court summons. Other examples of avoidance conditioning are presented in Table 13–2.

Behavioral theoreticians have debated among themselves the theoretical explanation for avoidance responding. The increase in positively reinforced responses and escape responses, and the decrease in punished responses, are all explained by their immediate stimulus consequences. However, the consequence of an

TABLE 13–2   EXAMPLES OF AVOIDANCE CONDITIONING

Situation	Warning Stimulus	Avoidance Response	Immediate Consequences	Aversive Consequences Avoided
1. You are walking down the aisle of a shopping mall.	Someone whom you dislike comes out of a store some distance away.	You immediately enter the nearest store.	You no longer see the person whom you dislike.	You avoid an unpleasant confrontation.
2. A child playing in her front yard sees the neighbor's dog (the dog had previously scared the child by barking loudly).	The child feels anxious.	The child goes into her house.	The child feels less anxious.	The child avoids hearing loud barking.
3. One of the authors is about to leave his office to go home.	He remembers that his son is practicing his drumming at home.	He phones home to ask his son to stop practicing.	Thoughts of encountering loud drumming cease.	He avoids experiencing extremely loud drumming when he enters his house.

avoidance response is the nonoccurrence of a stimulus. How can the nonoccurrence of something be a cause of behavior? Since theoreticians tend to dislike paradoxes such as this, behavioral theoreticians have asked themselves the following question. Are there immediate stimulus consequences that perhaps are easily overlooked by the casual observer but that might nevertheless maintain avoidance responses?

There appear to be several possibilities. One possibility in discriminated avoidance conditioning is that the avoidance response is strengthened because it immediately terminates the warning stimulus. For example, recall that in Jason's case the loud tone was the backup aversive stimulus. Because the clicking sound was paired with the tone, the click became an aversive stimulus. When Jason showed good posture in the presence of the click, the immediate result was that the clicking noise ceased. Although Jason's good posture was an avoidance response with respect to the tone, we might view it as an escape response with respect to the click. This type of explanation might enable us to account for the first example of avoidance conditioning in Table 13–2.

A second possible explanation of avoidance conditioning in some cases is illustrated by the second example in Table 13–2. The sight of the dog caused the child to feel anxious. Immediately following the avoidance response, she felt less anxious. The possibility that avoidance responses occur because they enable us to escape from anxiety is discussed further in Chapter 15.

How do we explain the avoidance response in the third example in Table 13–2? Perhaps thoughts of experiencing his son's loud drumming were aversive, and these thoughts ceased following the phone call. (Or perhaps the explanation may involve rule-governed control over behavior, discussed further in Chapter 17.) While such explanations are plausible, they are clearly speculative. You can see why behavior modifiers are puzzled about how to explain avoidance responding in terms of immediate stimulus consequences.

PITFALLS OF ESCAPE AND AVOIDANCE CONDITIONING

There are many ways in which people unknowingly apply escape and avoidance conditioning with the result that undesirable behaviors are strengthened. For example, numerous studies have demonstrated that teachers of persons with developmental disabilities often unknowingly maintain problem behavior of such persons through escape conditioning. This is illustrated by Example 2 in Table 13–1 (and demonstrated by Lalli et al., 1999). Problem behaviors by persons with developmental disabilities frequently enable them to escape teaching situations, work situations, and performance of household chores. Observations of family interactions by Snyder, Schrepferman, and St. Peter (1997) indicated that parents of children labeled as antisocial frequently strengthened aggressive behavior in their children by "backing off" or "giving in" when the aggressive behavior occurred. Parents may inadvertently establish inappropriate verbal behavior with a child who desperately promises, "I'll be good; I won't do it again," to escape or avoid punishment for some infraction of parental authority. When such pleas are successful, the pleading behavior is strengthened and thus increased in frequency under similar circumstances, but the undesirable behavior the parent meant to decrease may have been affected very little or not at all. Verbal behavior having little relation to reality may be increased, while the undesirable target response may persist in strength.

Another example sometimes can be seen when prisoners learn to make the "right" verbal statements to obtain early parole. Parole boards often have difficulty determining when it is only the verbal behavior of prisoners that has been modified, not their antisocial behaviors (e.g., assaults, property destruction). Apologies, confessions, and the "guilty look" characteristic of transgressors in all walks of life can be traced to similar contingencies. Lying or misrepresenting the facts is a way of avoiding punishment, if one can get away with it. (Other examples of undesirable behavior maintained by escape conditioning are presented in Chapter 22.)

A second pitfall of escape and avoidance is the inadvertent establishment of conditioned aversive stimuli, to which an individual then responds in such a way as to escape or avoid them. For example, if a coach hollers at, criticizes, and ridicules athletes, the athletes may show improved skills primarily to avoid or escape the wrath of the coach, but they are also likely to avoid the coach, (who has become a conditioned aversive stimulus), off the athletic field. And if the coaching tactics become too aversive, some team members might quit the sport entirely. As another example, some teachers, by their excessive use of punishment, transform themselves, their classrooms, and the learning materials they use into conditioned aversive stimuli. All too frequently, this situation produces individuals who avoid teachers, school, and books and who therefore fail to advance academically. Clearly, this is a most unfortunate consequence of escape and avoidance conditioning.

A final pitfall of escape conditioning is that in many situations it maintains undesirable behaviors of the teacher and other caregivers. This can easily be seen in the first example in Table 13–1.

GUIDELINES FOR THE EFFECTIVE APPLICATION OF ESCAPE AND AVOIDANCE CONDITIONING

The following rules should be observed by any person who applies escape and avoidance conditioning:

1. Given a choice between maintaining behavior on an escape or an avoidance procedure, the latter is to be preferred. There are two reasons for this. First, in escape conditioning the backup aversive stimulus must be present prior to the target response, whereas in avoidance conditioning the backup aversive stimulus occurs only when the target response fails to occur. Second, in escape conditioning the target response does not occur when the backup aversive stimulus is not present, whereas in avoidance conditioning responding decreases very slowly when the backup aversive stimulus may no longer be forthcoming.

2. The target behavior should be established by escape conditioning before it is put on an avoidance procedure. In the case at the beginning of this chapter, Jason learned how to escape the loud noise prior to learning how to avoid it.

3. During avoidance conditioning, a warning stimulus should signal the impending aversive stimulus. This enhances conditioning by providing a warning that failure to respond will result in aversive stimulation. An example from the natural environment is the printed word "VIOLATION" on a parking meter, which indicates that the motorist may receive a parking ticket if he or she does not put a coin in the meter. The clicker served a similar function for Jason, indicating that the tone would occur three seconds later unless he showed good posture. And if Jason showed good posture during the three seconds, he could avoid the loud tone. (Similarly, putting a coin in a parking meter removes the "VIOLATION" sign and prevents a ticket.)

4. Escape and avoidance conditioning, like punishment, should be used cautiously. Because these procedures involve aversive stimuli, they can result in harmful side effects, such as aggression, fearfulness, and a tendency to avoid or escape any person or thing associated with the procedure.

5. Positive reinforcement for the target response should be used in conjunction with escape and avoidance conditioning. Not only will it help to strengthen the desired behavior, it will also tend to counteract the undesirable side effects mentioned. The procedure used with Jason would probably have worked even better if positive reinforcement for good posture had been added to it. (This was not done because the experimenters were interested in the escape and avoidance procedure by itself.)

6. As with all the procedures described in this text, the individual concerned should be told—to the best of his or her understanding—about the contingencies

in effect. Again, as with all these procedures, however, instructions are not necessary for escape and avoidance conditioning to work.

STUDY QUESTIONS

1. Define escape conditioning, and describe an example that is not in the text.
2. How is escape conditioning similar to punishment? In what two ways do they differ, procedurally? How do their effects differ?
3. Procedurally, in what two ways is escape conditioning different from positive reinforcement? How are their effects similar?
4. Procedurally, what are two differences between escape conditioning and avoidance conditioning?
5. How are conditioned positive reinforcers and conditioned punishers similar and how are they different?
6. Give another name for warning stimulus.
7. Describe two examples of escape conditioning in everyday life.
8. Describe two examples of avoidance conditioning in everyday life.
9. How is a warning stimulus like an S^D? How are they different?
10. How is a warning stimulus different than an S^{Dp} (Chapter 12)?
11. Explain, with an example of your own, why individuals frequently reinforce the undesirable behavior of other individuals. (*Hint:* See the first example in Table 13–1.) Clearly identify the behavior principles involved.
12. Explain how escape conditioning might maintain an adult's behavior of responding inappropriately to a child's extreme social withdrawal.
13. Describe three types of immediate consequences that might maintain avoidance responses.
14. Briefly describe three examples of how the principles of escape or avoidance conditioning can work against those who are unaware of them.

APPLICATION EXERCISES

A. Exercise Involving Others

Successful avoidance behavior means that an individual has been conditioned to respond (probably to a warning signal) in such a way as to avoid the occurrence of a backup aversive stimulus. This means that the avoidance behavior might persist even if (for whatever reasons) the environment has changed such that the backup aversive stimulus will no longer be presented regardless of the individual's behavior. Describe an example you have observed in someone other than yourself that illustrates this effect.

B. Self-Modification Exercise

Construct a chart similar to Table 13–1 in which you present five examples of escape conditioning that have influenced your behavior. Present each example in terms of the categories of aversive situation, escape responses, removal of aversive stimulus, and probable long-term effects on the escape response.

NOTE AND EXTENDED DISCUSSION

1. Not all types of avoidance conditioning involve a warning stimulus. One type that does not is known as Sidman avoidance (after Murray Sidman, who studied this type of avoidance extensively with lower organisms; e.g., Sidman, 1953). In a typical Sidman avoidance conditioning experiment with a laboratory rat, a brief electric shock is presented every 30 seconds without a preceding warning stimulus. If the rat makes a designated response, the shock will be postponed for 30 seconds. Under these conditions, the rat will learn to make the appropriate avoidance response on a regular basis and will be relatively shock free. Sidman avoidance conditioning is also referred to as nondiscriminated, noncued, or free-operant avoidance conditioning. Sidman avoidance has been demonstrated with humans (Hefferline, Keenan, & Harford, 1959) and appears to underlie some everyday examples of preventive behaviors. Consider, for example, that when the roads are muddy, drivers use lots of windshield washer fluid. To avoid running out of fluid, many of them regularly refill the container, even though in many cars there is no warning stimulus that the container (hidden under the hood) is near empty. (However, in Chapter 17, you will see that this type of example might also be explained as rule-governed behavior.)

Study Questions on Note

1. What is Sidman avoidance conditioning?
2. Explain how applying sunscreen or insect repellent is an example of Sidman avoidance. Give another example from everyday life. (*Hint:* Some common computer applications have built-in timers that fit the definition of Sidman avoidance conditioning.)

Procedures Based
on Principles
of Respondent Conditioning

"I hate that word!"

MAKING WORDS "UNPLEASANT"[1]

Sue was a student in first-year psychology at Arizona State University. As a participant in an experiment, she had been asked to memorize a list of words that were presented to her, one word at a time. Sitting as comfortably as one can be with electrical wires attached to one's ankle, and wearing headphones, Sue read the words as they were presented: "chair", "smile", "small", "large" (ZAP! CLANG! Sue was startled by the feeling of a mild electric shock to her ankle, and the sound of a loud "clang" through the headphones). Sue continued to memorize the words on the list. The word "large" appeared several times, and each time it was paired with the mild shock and the loud sound. During the experiment the shock and the sound caused Sue to feel anxious (as measured by her galvanic skin response [GSR], an increase in the electrical conductivity of the skin that occurs during a sweat gland reaction). As a result of pairing the word "large" with the mild shock and the loud sound, hearing the word "large" by itself now caused Sue to feel anxious. Afterward, when Sue was asked to rate the pleasantness of the meaning of the words, she rated "large" as much more unpleasant than the other words.

(Note: During a debriefing session, Sue learned the purposes of the experiment. She also discovered that saying the word "large" many times without pairing it with the mild shock and the loud tone caused that word to gradually lose its unpleasantness.)

---

[1]This example is based on an experiment by Staats, Staats, and Crawford (1962).

OPERANT VERSUS RESPONDENT BEHAVIOR

The principles and procedures described in the previous pages of this book are mainly those of **operant conditioning.** This term was coined by Skinner (1938) to refer to the fact that behavior that operates on the environment can be modified by its consequences. As we have seen, consequences that cause a behavior to increase are called reinforcers, and those that cause it to decrease are called punishers. Behaviors that operate on the environment to generate consequences, and are in turn controlled by those consequences, are called **operant behaviors.** Examples include putting gas in your car, asking for directions, writing an exam, turning on a TV set, and making breakfast.

Although operant principles have widespread applicability, some behavior does not seem to fit the model of operant conditioning. Some of our behaviors, like Sue's anxious feelings to the mild shock and loud "clang," seem to be reflexive (i.e., elicited by prior stimuli quite apart from the consequences of the behaviors). Examples include salivating when smelling dinner cooking, feeling frightened when watching a scary movie, blushing when told that your fly or blouse is undone, and becoming sexually aroused when watching X-rated movies. These are called **respondent behaviors** (a term coined by Skinner), and a different set of principles seems to apply to them. In this chapter we briefly describe these principles and how they differ from those of operant conditioning. In addition, we highlight some of the applications of these principles. Respondent conditioning is also called *Pavlovian conditioning* (after Ivan Pavlov, the Russian physiologist who studied it), and we use these terms interchangeably in the text.

PRINCIPLE OF RESPONDENT CONDITIONING

The respondent conditioning principle is based on the fact that certain stimuli automatically elicit certain responses apart from any prior learning or conditioning experience. These "automatic" stimulus–response relationships are called *unconditioned reflexes.* Examples of such reflexes are shown in Figure 14–1.

The reflexes in Figure 14–1 are unconditioned because the stimuli elicit the responses without prior conditioning (in other words, they are "hard wired" or inborn). A stimulus that elicits a response without prior learning or conditioning is called an **unconditioned stimulus (US).** A response elicited by such a stimulus is called an **unconditioned response (UR).** In the experiment with Sue, the mild shock and loud sound were USs, and Sue's GSR response to the shock was a UR.

Respondent Conditioning   For each of the responses in Figure 14–1, there are stimuli that do not elicit them. In that sense, such stimuli are considered neutral. For example, assume that a particular stimulus (such as the sound of classical music) is neutral in the sense that it does not elicit a particular response (salivation) in a particular individual. The principle of **respondent conditioning** states that if that stimulus (the sound of classical music) is followed closely in time by a US (food in the mouth), which elicits a UR (salivation), then the previously neutral stimulus (sound of classical music) will also tend to elicit the response of salivation

UNCONDITIONED REFLEX

Unconditioned Stimulus ·······························>	Unconditioned Response
Digestive system	
Food ··>	salivation
Bad food ···>	sickness, nausea
Object in esophagus ·······························>	vomiting
Reproductive system	
Genital stimulation ·······························>	vaginal lubrication, penile erection, orgasm
Nipple stimulation ·································>	milk release (in lactating women)
Circulatory system	
High temperature ··································>	sweating, flushing
Sudden loud noise ·································>	blanching, pounding heart
Respiratory system	
Irritation in nose ···································>	sneeze
Throat clogged ·····································>	cough
Allergens ···>	asthma attack
Muscular system	
Low temperature ··································>	shivering
Blows or burns ·····································>	withdrawal
Tap on patellar tendon ·························>	knee jerk
Light to eye ···>	pupil constriction
Novel stimulation ·································>	reflexive orienting
Infant reflexes	
Stroking the cheek ·······························>	head turning
Object touches lips ·······························>	sucking
Food in mouth ·····································>	swallowing
Object in the hand ·······························>	grasping
Held vertically, feet touching ground ······>	stepping

Figure 14–1   A partial list of unconditioned reflexes. *Source:* John D. Baldwin and Janice I. Baldwin, *Behavior Principles in Everyday Life*, 2nd ed. 1986, p. 44. Reprinted by permission of Prentice Hall, Inc., Upper Saddle River, NJ.

in the future. Of course, it may take more than just one pairing of classical music with food before the sound of classical music would elicit any noticeable amount of salivation. Figure 14–2 illustrates respondent conditioning.

  If a salivation response was in fact conditioned to the sound of classical music, the stimulus–response relationship would be referred to as a *conditioned reflex.* The stimulus in a conditioned reflex is called a **conditioned stimulus** (CS; e.g., the sound of the classical music), and the response in a conditioned reflex is referred to as a **conditioned response** (CR; e.g., salivation to the classical music). In the experiment with Sue, the word "large" became a CS eliciting a GSR response as a CR. You can see how respondent conditioning might explain your reactions to certain words (such as cancer) or even to a single letter (such as "F" on an exam). As indicated by Sue's rating of the word "large" as unpleasant, such pairings

Respondent Conditioning

Procedure: Pair neutral stimulus and unconditioned stimulus.

Many
pairings
{
NS (sound of classical music)

US (food in mouth) ⟶ UR (salivation)

Result: Neutral stimulus acquires ability to elicit response.

CS (sound of classic music) ⟶ CR (salivation)

Note: NS = neutral stimulus
US = unconditioned stimulus
UR = unconditioned response
CS = conditioned stimulus
CR = conditioned response

Figure 14–2   Model for respondent conditioning.

contribute to the meaning of words on a personal level (Staats, 1996; Tyron & Cicero, 1989).

Factors Influencing Respondent Conditioning   There are several variables that influence the development of a conditioned reflex. First, *the greater the number of pairings of a CS with a US, the greater is the ability of the CS to elicit the CR*, until a maximum strength of the conditioned reflex has been reached. If a child is scared several times by the loud barking of a dog, the sight of the dog will elicit a stronger fear than if the child had been scared by the dog only once.

Second, *stronger conditioning occurs if the CS precedes the US by about half a second, rather than by a longer time or rather than following the US*. Conditioning in the latter case is difficult to attain. (An exception to this rule is something called *conditioned taste aversion*, which is discussed later in this chapter.) If a child sees a dog, and then is immediately frightened by the dog's loud barking, sight of the dog is likely to become a CS with fear as a CR. However, if the child hears loud barking of a dog hidden from view and a few seconds later sees a dog trot around the corner of a building, the fear caused by the loud barking is not likely to be transferred to the sight of the dog.

Third, *a CS acquires greater ability to elicit a CR if the CS is always paired with a given US than if it is only occasionally paired with the US*. If a couple, for example, consistently lights a candle in the bedroom just before having sex and not at other times, then the candlelight is likely to become a CS eliciting sexual arousal. On the other hand, if they light a candle in the bedroom every night but have sex there only one or two nights each week, then the candlelight will be a weaker CS for sexual arousal.

Fourth, *when several neutral stimuli precede a US, the stimulus that is most consistently associated with the US is the one most likely to become a strong CS*. A child may experience thunderstorms in which dark clouds and lightning are usually followed by loud claps of thunder, which cause fear. On other occasions, the child sees dark clouds but there is no lightning or thunder. The child will acquire a stronger fear of lightning than of the dark clouds because lightning is more consistently paired with thunder.

Fifth, *respondent conditioning will develop more quickly and strongly when the CS or US or both are intense rather than weak* (Lutz, 1994; Polenchar, Romano, Steinmetz, & Patterson, 1984). A child will acquire a stronger fear of lightning if the lightning is exceptionally bright and the thunder is exceptionally loud than if either or both are relatively weak.

HIGHER-ORDER CONDITIONING

Suppose that someone is conditioned to salivate to the sound of classical music by following a brief presentation of classical music with food a great many times. Classical music will become a CS for salivation. Now let's suppose that, over several trials, just before presenting the classical music by itself, we turn on a yellow light. The light is a neutral stimulus for salivation, and is never paired with food. However, after a number of pairings of the light with the music (an established CS for the response of salivation), the light itself will come to elicit salivation. This procedure is known as **higher-order conditioning.** The pairing of the music with the food is referred to as conditioning of the *first order*. Pairing the light with the music is referred to as conditioning of the *second order*. Although third-order conditioning has been reported (Pavlov, 1927), higher-order conditioning beyond the second order appears to be difficult. The model for higher-order conditioning is presented in Figure 14–3.

Let's see how higher-order conditioning might apply in everyday life. Suppose that a child experiences painful stimuli several times, such as from touching a hot stove on one occasion and a sharp thorn on another. Each painful stimulus can be considered a US causing fear as a UR. Let's suppose further that, each time just before each painful experience, a parent yelled, "Watch out! You'll hurt

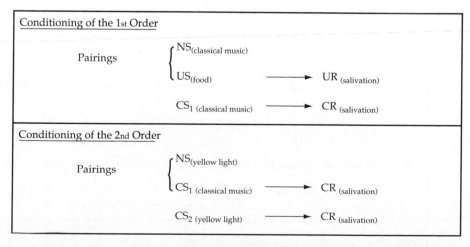

Figure 14–3 Model for higher-order conditioning.

yourself!" This warning from the parent is likely to become a CS eliciting fear. Suppose, also, that the parent later utters the same warning when the child climbs on a ladder, stands on a chair, or climbs onto the kitchen counter. Pairings of the warning with these other activities might influence the child to develop a general fear of heights through higher-order conditioning. The conditioning stages were as follows: First, the warnings were followed by painful stimuli; second, being in high places was followed by warnings. Result: Being in a high place now elicits a response (fear) similar to that elicited by painful stimuli.

RESPONDENT EXTINCTION

Once respondent conditioning occurs, does it stay with us forever? Not necessarily. It may be reversed through the principle of *respondent extinction*, which involves presenting a CS while withholding the US. After a number of such presentations, the CS gradually loses its capability of eliciting the CR. Let's suppose that a child reaches out to touch a large dog just as the dog barks very loudly, scaring the child. As a function of the pairing of the loud bark with the sight of the big dog, the sight of the dog alone now elicits crying and trembling. This is a Pavlovian conditioned response that we label fear. Now let's suppose that the parent takes the child to a dog show. Although there are lots of large dogs around, they have been trained to walk and sit quietly while on display. Repeated contact with these dogs (without pairings with barking) will help the child overcome fear of the sight of dogs. That is, the sight of dogs loses its capability of functioning as a CS to elicit the fear reaction as a CR. Many of the fears that we acquire during childhood—fears of the dentist, the dark, thunder and lightning, and so on—undergo respondent extinction as we grow older, as a function of repeated exposure to these things in the absence of dire consequences. Figure 14–4 illustrates respondent extinction. And luckily for Sue, after encountering the word "large" several times without further pairings with the shock and tone, it gradually lost its ability to elicit anxiety.

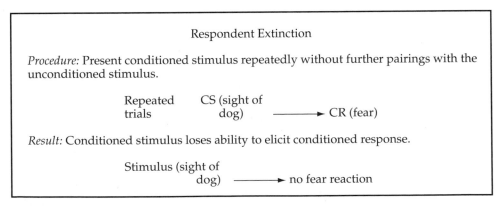

Figure 14–4   Model for respondent extinction.

Respondent extinction is the reason that higher-order conditioning is difficult to obtain beyond the second order. In the example cited in Figure 14–2, when conditioning of the second order is attempted, CS_1, classical music, is no longer paired with food, the US. Thus, the classical music is undergoing extinction as a CS and the salivation elicited by the classical music is weaker than the salivation originally elicited by food.

COUNTERCONDITIONING

Recall from Chapter 5 that operant extinction proceeds more quickly and effectively if an alternative response is reinforced. A similar rule holds for respondent extinction: A conditioned response may be eliminated more effectively if a new response is conditioned to the conditioned stimulus at the same time that the former conditioned response is being extinguished. This process is called **counterconditioning.** Stated technically, a CS will lose its ability to elicit a CR if that CS is paired with a stimulus that elicits a response that is incompatible with the CR. To illustrate this process, let's reconsider the example of a child who acquired a fear of the sight of dogs. Let's suppose that the child likes playing with a friend who has become a CS eliciting feelings of happiness as a CR, and let's suppose that the friend has a friendly dog who doesn't bark loudly. As the child plays with his or her friend and the friend's dog, some of the positive emotions elicited by the friend will become conditioned to the friend's dog. These positive conditioned emotional responses will help counteract the negative conditioned emotional responses previously elicited by dogs and thus more quickly and more effectively eliminate those responses. Figure 14–5 illustrates counterconditioning.

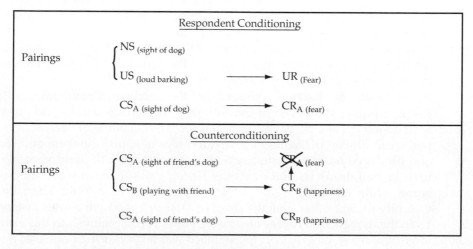

Figure 14–5   A diagram of counterconditioning.

COMMON RESPONDENTLY CONDITIONED RESPONSES

Through evolution, humans are born with numerous unconditioned reflexes, such as those listed in Figure 14–1. Such reflexes are important to our reproduction, survival, and day-to-day biological functioning. We have also evolved to be capable of Pavlovian conditioning. The fact that reflexive responses can be conditioned to previously neutral stimuli is biologically adaptive. Our capability of being conditioned to salivate at the sight of food, for example, prepares us to digest our food more rapidly than would occur if Pavlovian conditioning were not possible. Let's consider in more detail some major categories of conditioned reflexes.

Digestive System   The salivation reflex is only one of the digestive reflexes that are susceptible to Pavlovian conditioning. A student experiences butterflies in the stomach before giving a talk in class. After experiencing chemotherapy, some patients feel nauseous while waiting in the treatment room for therapy to begin. An extremely frightening experience, such as being threatened by a knife-wielding intruder, can cause anxiety defecation.

Circulatory System   Increased heart rate and blood flow are involved in many conditioned reflexes. Feeling embarrassed in a social setting, overhearing risqué topics discussed, experiencing socially inappropriate thoughts—all have become CSs, causing blushing in many individuals as blood flows to the outer layers of the skin. The circulatory system is involved in the startle reflex, such as when you are all alone in a house and an unexpected noise causes your heart to pound. The circulatory system is also involved in sexual stimulation, such as when nude photographs elicit increased heart rate and increased blood flow to the genital areas, causing penile or clitoral erection.

Respiratory System   Pavlovian conditioning has also been implicated in influencing coughing, sneezing, and asthma attacks—reflexes of the respiratory system. Suppose a person's aunt, who visits rarely, happens to visit when that person suffers a serious asthma attack. The aunt might become a CS for the coughing and wheezing characteristic of an asthmatic reaction. Dekker and Groen (1956) reported that asthmatic responses have been elicited by such CSs as the sight of horses, caged birds, goldfish, and police vans.

Other Systems   Other organ systems of the body—such as the urinary and reproductive systems—are also susceptible to Pavlovian conditioning. And of course, the nervous system is involved in all conditioning.

A Variation of Factors Influencing Respondent Conditioning: Biological Preparedness   When one of the authors was 16 years old, he had an encounter with lemon gin at a party. Except for the occasional bottle of beer, he was an inexperienced drinker of alcohol. The first few sips of lemon gin were quite enjoyable, and produced no immediate reaction of drunkenness. In approximately 15 minutes, he had drunk several ounces of lemon gin, similar to what one might consume while enjoying a soft drink. Approximately an hour later, he became violently ill. Since that time the smell or taste of lemon gin causes instant nausea. Even the thought of it causes his stomach to start complaining. In this example, the large amount of lemon gin in the stomach was a US causing nausea as a UR. Even though the smell and taste of lemon gin were paired with the reflexive responses of nausea and vomiting just once, and even though there was a long delay between the previously neutral stimuli (the taste and smell of lemon gin) and the experience of nausea, Pavlovian conditioning occurred. The taste and smell of lemon gin became a CS for the sickness reflex, and a *conditioned taste aversion*, in this case, a dislike for lemon gin, was established. Note that the phenomenon of conditioned taste aversion is an exception to the rule that respondent conditioning is ineffective if there is more than about one-half second between the CS and the US. Evolution has apparently provided for a longer delay in this case because of the time toxic substances take to have an effect on the body.

Seligman (1971) coined the term *biological preparedness* to refer to the predisposition of members of a species to be more readily conditioned to some stimuli as CSs than to others. In the case of taste aversion, for example, having evolved the strong tendency for taste to be conditioned to nausea greatly decreases the chances that one will repeatedly consume food that causes illness (and perhaps death).

Taste aversion is a conditioned reflex of the digestive system. As an example of biological preparedness pertaining to the circulatory system, humans will more quickly learn fears to stimuli that may have posed a threat to survival, such as snakes and insects, than to stimuli that were likely nonthreatening in our ancestors' history, such as pictures of flowers (Ohman, Dimberg, & Ost, 1984).

RESPONDENT AND OPERANT CONDITIONING COMPARED

Respondent and operant conditioning procedures appear to influence two different kinds of behaviors. Nevertheless, there are a number of parallels between the procedures. Let's examine some of those differences and parallels.

Responses   Respondent behaviors are reflexive in that they occur automatically to prior stimuli, and are typically referred to as involuntary. Few people, for example, are able to blush or salivate on command. Operant behavior, in contrast, is controlled by consequences, and is sometimes referred to as voluntary. When asked to do so, for example, physically intact people can readily stand up, sit down, talk, whisper, and so on. Reflexive responses usually involve smooth muscles and glands that are important in the functioning of internal bodily processes, such as relaxation before sleeping or arousal when exposed to a threatening situation. Operant behavior usually involves skeletal muscles and is generally important in enabling us to interact with the external environment.

Reinforcement   Pavlovian conditioning consists of pairing an NS with a US (or with a CS in the case of higher-order conditioning,) *before* the response. The result of Pavlovian reinforcement is that the NS (now called a CS) acquires the capability of eliciting the response (now called a CR). Operant conditioning consists of the presentation of a positive reinforcer (or the removal of an aversive stimulus) immediately *following* a response. The result is that the operant behavior increases in frequency.

Extinction   Pavlovian extinction involves the presentation of a CS without further pairings with the US. The result is that the CS loses the capability of eliciting the CR. Operant extinction involves withholding a reinforcer following a previously reinforced response. The result is that the response decreases in frequency.

CSs and S^Ds   Note that CSs are like S^Ds in that both produce responses that have been conditioned to them. The conditioning procedures that establish them differ, however. In addition, the ways in which CSs and S^Ds produce their responses seem to differ. Responses produced by CSs frequently seem to be more automatic or consistent. To capture this difference, standard behavioral terminology refers to CSs as *eliciting* the responses conditioned to them, whereas S^Ds are said to *evoke* the responses conditioned to them. In addition, operant behavior is sometimes said to be emitted by an individual, whereas respondent behavior is *elicited* by a stimulus. Throughout the text, we have been consistent in the use of the terms *elicit, evoke,* and *emit*.

APPLICATIONS OF RESPONDENT CONDITIONING

Note 1   Applications of respondent conditioning and extinction have involved controlling allergies, immune system function, reactions to drugs, sexual arousal, nausea, blood pressure, thoughts, and emotions (especially fear and anxiety). In Chapter 28 we discuss applications of respondent principles to treat phobias. In this section we illustrate its application to several other types of problems.

Aversion Therapy

Certain kinds of positive reinforcers can be very troublesome. People who find fattening foods overly reinforcing tend to eat too many and become overweight. Similarly, people who find cigarettes, alcohol, and other harmful commodities overly reinforcing tend to indulge in them to the detriment of their health and well-being. People who obtain sexual reinforcement in socially unacceptable ways—for instance, by seducing children—tend to endanger others, by exposing them to harmful experiences, and themselves by risking imprisonment and other social sanctions.

Aversion therapy was developed largely as an attempt to counteract the power of troublesome reinforcers (those that tend to be overindulged in or that harm others). Before describing some of the methods of aversion therapy, we should caution the reader that their safe and effective use requires special expertise. These procedures, as the label *aversion therapy* implies, involve the use of aversive stimulation. As we have seen in Chapter 12, there are serious dangers in the use of aversive stimulation. It should therefore be used only by qualified experts who know when and how it is most likely to be effective, and how to guard against potentially harmful side effects.

Basically, aversion therapy involves the repeated pairing (i.e., over a number of trials) of a troublesome reinforcer with an aversive event. The rationale of aversion therapy is counterconditioning; that is, it is assumed that the undesirable reinforcer should then become less reinforcing, because it will come to elicit a response similar to that elicited by the aversive stimulus.

For example, in the treatment of alcoholism, a person may be given a drug that will make him or her nauseous. Just before the drug takes effect, he or she is given a sip of an alcoholic beverage. Thus, the sight, smell, and taste of the drink is followed immediately by nausea. This pairing of alcohol with nausea is repeated over a number of sessions. Eventually, alcohol itself should tend to elicit nausea, which may cause the individual to avoid alcohol. How well the therapy works in any given case depends, at least in part, on other factors. These include whether the client continues taking the drug after leaving the hospital, and on operant processes operating in the natural environment, such as whether the client receives social reinforcement for his or her subsequent choosing of nonalcoholic over alcoholic beverages at parties, restaurants, and bars.

In a study in which alcoholics experienced the pairing of alcohol drinking with disulfiram (Antabuse) medication, less than 1% of the clients continued to take the drug after release from a hospital (Lubetkin, Rivers, & Rosenberg, 1971). In another study, only 7% of the patients continued to take disulfiram after one year (Ludwig, Levine, & Stark, 1970). An aversion-conditioning component involving disulfiram, however, proved to be a valuable addition to a program for treating alcoholics that included a multiple-component behavior therapy program with procedures directed toward job finding, marital counseling, social and recreational programming, and a buddy system (Azrin, 1976; Azrin, Sisson, Meyers, & Godley, 1982). Similar results have also been obtained for cigarette smoking. The aversion-conditioning procedure in this case involved requiring subjects to smoke one cigarette after another rapidly, until nausea occurred. In this way, the smell and flavor of cigarettes was paired with an aversive stimulus (nausea). This procedure, called *rapid-smoking aversion therapy*, caused short-term cessation of smoking but did not show successful long-term effects (Danaher, 1977). When the rapid-smoking aversion procedure was added to a behavioral counseling program for quitting smoking, however, both short-term and long-term results were better than with the behavior counseling program alone (Tiffany, Martin, & Baker, 1986).

Symbolic representations (such as pictures) of the troublesome reinforcers, rather than the actual reinforcers themselves, are commonly used in aversion therapy. This is largely a matter of convenience. Slides, videotapes, or computer disks containing pictures of a wide variety of troublesome reinforcers can easily be stored in the therapist's office. Moreover, it is relatively easy to make new stimuli appropriate to individual cases. These stimuli can then be presented at specified intervals and for specified durations and can be associated with the onset or termination of the aversive stimulus in a precisely controlled manner. In addition, their use precludes various problems that would arise if the actual undesirable reinforcers were used during therapy. To give an extreme example, one obviously would not use real children in treating a child molester. It is generally acceptable, however, to use pictures of children in various poses, but therapists should consult the laws of the jurisdiction in which they are working before using this type of procedure.

Although aversion therapy appears to be a valuable addition to multiple-component programs for treating various problems such as excessive alcohol drinking and cigarette smoking, it is not widely used. As indicated by Wilson (1991), its limited use stems from ethical concerns about the use of aversive stimulation in treatment, the expense typically associated with the continual supervision the treatment requires of a therapist or in a hospital, and the fact that there is a fairly high dropout rate from treatments by clients using aversion therapy.

Treatment of Chronic Constipation

An example of respondent conditioning of a desirable response is the treatment for chronic constipation developed by Quarti and Renaud (1964). Defecation, the desired response in cases of constipation, can be elicited by administering a laxative. However, reliance on such drugs to achieve regularity is not the healthiest solution because of the undesirable side effects that often result. Quarti and Renaud had their clients administer to themselves a distinctive electrical stimulus—a mild, nonpainful electric current—immediately prior to defecating. Defecation was initially elicited by a laxative, and then the amount of the drug was gradually decreased until defecation was elicited by the electrical stimulus alone. Then, by applying the electrical stimulus at the same time each day, several of the clients were eventually able to get rid of the electrical stimulus, because the natural environment stimuli characteristically present at that time each day acquired control over the behavior of defecating. Thus, these clients achieved regularity without the continued use of artificial stimulation (also see Rovetto, 1979).

Treatment of Nocturnal Enuresis (Bed-Wetting)

Note 2   Another example of respondent conditioning of a desirable response is the bell-pad treatment for nocturnal enuresis (Scott, Barclay, & Houts, 1992). One possible explanation for nocturnal enuresis (bed-wetting), a problem that is rather common in young children, is that pressure on the child's bladder when he or she is asleep and has to urinate does not provide sufficient stimulation to awaken him or her. A device that seems to be effective for many enuretic children consists of a bell connected to a special pad under the bottom sheet on the child's bed. The apparatus is wired so that the bell sounds (US) and awakens (UR) the child as soon as the first drop of urine makes contact with the pad. Eventually, in many cases, the child will awaken before he urinates—apparently because the response of waking up has been conditioned to the stimulus of pressure on the bladder. When that happens, the operant responses of getting up, walking to the bathroom, and urinating in the toilet should be positively reinforced by the child's parents.

STUDY QUESTIONS

1. To what fundamental fact of behavior does the term *operant conditioning* refer? Give five examples of operant behavior and explain why they are examples of it.
2. Give five examples of unconditioned reflexes. Describe both the stimulus and the response.
3. State the principle of respondent conditioning. Clearly describe and diagram two examples of respondent conditioning (one of which is not in the text). What is another name for respondent conditioning?

4. Define and give an example of the following: unconditioned stimulus, unconditioned response, conditioned stimulus, and conditioned response.
5. In a sentence each, briefly describe five variables that influence the development of a conditioned reflex.
6. Diagram an example of higher-order conditioning.
7. State the principle and describe an example of respondent extinction.
8. Describe the process of counterconditioning. Describe an example of counterconditioning that is not in the text.
9. Describe three examples of conditioned reflexes of yours, one for each of these categories: digestion, circulation, respiration.
10. Describe an example of a conditioned taste aversion.
11. Why do you suppose that we have evolved so that we are susceptible to conditioned taste aversion?
12. What is biological preparedness? Give an example.
13. Discuss whether all stimuli are equally capable of becoming CSs.
14. Describe three differences between operant responses and respondent responses.
15. Describe the procedures and results of both operant and respondent reinforcement.
16. Describe the procedures and results of both operant and respondent extinction.
17. In what way are CSs and S^{D}s similar? In what two ways are they different?
18. For what general type of problem is aversion therapy used? Give three examples of such problems (one of which is not in the text).
19. Describe the basic procedure and rationale of aversion therapy. Give an example of aversion therapy.
20. Why should aversion therapy be used only by competent professional practitioners?
21. Briefly describe a respondent conditioning procedure for treating constipation. Identify the US, UR, CS, and CR.
22. Describe the respondent conditioning component of a procedure for treating nocturnal enuresis. Identify the US, UR, CS, and CR.

APPLICATION EXERCISES

A. Exercise Involving Others

Interview a relative, friend, or acquaintance regarding something that elicits feelings of fear or nausea in that person, but does not do so in most people. Determine whether that person can recall events that may have led to this unusual reaction. Are these events consistent with the description of respondent conditioning in this chapter? Discuss.

B. Self-Modification Exercise

Cut a fresh lemon into four wedges. Each day, over a period of four days, squeeze the juice from one wedge into the same distinctive cup. Drink the juice (unsweetened) from the cup, and store the remaining wedges in the fridge for the next day's trial. Over the trials, note and describe any reactions you have that could be due to respondent conditioning as described in this chapter.

NOTES AND EXTENDED DISCUSSION

1. Pavlovian conditioning procedures may affect the functioning of our immune system. Ader and Cohen (1982) found with rats that pairing saccharine with an immune-suppressive drug established saccharine as a conditioned stimulus that elicits immune suppression. Other studies have also demonstrated classical conditioning of various aspects of immune responses in other species (Ader & Cohen, 1993; Maier, Watkins, & Fleshner, 1994; Turkkan, 1989). For an example with humans, consider the problem that chemotherapy for cancer involves chemical agents that are immuno-suppressive. When repeated chemotherapy was done in the same room in the same hospital setting for women suffering from ovarian cancer, the women eventually displayed immunosuppression after simply being brought to that room of the hospital prior to chemotherapy (Bovjberg et al., 1990). This exciting area of research on the effects of conditioning processes on the functioning of the body's immune system is called psychoimmunology or psychoneuroimmunology (Daruna, 2004).

2. In a case study with a 15-year-old female resident of Boys' Town, Friman and Vollmer (1995) demonstrated that a urine alarm may also be used effectively with diurnal enuresis (daytime wetting). The moisture-sensitive part of the alarm system was attached to the girl's underwear and the alarm was attached unobtrusively to her outer clothing. Although the procedure was successful almost immediately, it appears that its success was based on escape and avoidance rather than respondent conditioning. This was indicated in part by the fact that whenever the alarm sounded, the child seemed embarrassed and quickly left for the bathroom. Thus, her reduced wetting may have been under the control of aversive social stimuli that occurred when the alarm sounded.

Study Questions on Notes

1. Describe the field of psychoimmunology. What is its potential applied importance?
2. Discuss how different behavior principles may be responsible for the success of a urine alarm with nocturnal and diurnal enuresis.

15

Respondent and Operant Conditioning Together

"I have to finish my term paper!"

RESPONDING TO MEET DEADLINES

    Rick was a student in a second-year psychology course at the University of Manitoba. At the beginning of the course, students had been assigned a paper that was due by mid-term. Like many students, Rick liked to "party." A week before the paper was due, Rick still hadn't started to work on it. Five days before the due date, he started to get a little concerned. But when his friends asked him to go to a bar, he thought, "What the heck, I've got five days left." At the bar he told his friends, "Don't call me for the next four days. I have to finish a major paper." Although Rick started on his paper the next day, the deadline was fast approaching. As each day passed, he felt increasingly nervous about the likelihood of finishing it on time. Fortunately, after three late nights in a row, the paper was finished. Rick felt a huge weight lifted from his shoulders.

OPERANT–RESPONDENT INTERACTIONS

In Chapters 3 through 13 we talked about principles of operant conditioning. In Chapter 14 we talked about principles of respondent conditioning. This may have given you the impression that the two types of conditioning occur sequentially. However, any given experience is likely to include both respondent and operant conditioning occurring concurrently. Let's consider Rick's case. Like all of us, Rick probably had a history of being punished for failing to meet deadlines. Punishment elicits feelings of anxiety, a respondent reaction. As a consequence of prior pairings of deadlines with punishment, the approaching deadline for Rick was likely a CS eliciting anxiety as a CR. The closer to the deadline, the stronger would be the association of missing the deadline with punishment, and the stronger would be the anxiety as a conditioned response. What about working on the term paper? The relevant responses (looking up references, reading background material, taking notes, etc.) are operant responses. As such responses occurred, and as Rick began to see that he would meet the deadline, the anxiety decreased. Thus, thinking about the deadline likely caused Rick to feel anxious, a reflexive response, and responding to meet the deadline, an operant response, was maintained by escape conditioning (the anxiety decreased). While there were undoubtedly other factors influencing Rick's behavior in this instance, the above analysis illustrates how both operant and respondent conditioning may have occurred concurrently.

Here is another example of a behavioral sequence that involves both respondent and operant conditioning. A small child runs to pet a large dog. Never having had any reason to fear dogs, the child shows no fear now. Suppose, however, that the dog playfully jumps and knocks the child down. Quite naturally, the child will begin crying because of the pain and surprise of this rough treatment. With respect to this behavioral sequence, illustrated in Figure 15–1, let's first consider how it is an instance of respondent conditioning. A stimulus (sight of dog) that was previously not a CS for a particular response (crying and other types of fear behavior) has come to be one because it was paired with a US (suddenly being knocked down) that did elicit that response.

Now let's consider how that behavioral sequence involved an instance of operant conditioning. The operant response of the child approaching the dog was followed by a punisher (the child was knocked down). Consistent with the principle of punishment, the child is less likely to approach large dogs in the future. Moreover, the sight of a large dog nearby is likely to be a conditioned punisher (because of a pairing with being knocked down).

A result of this operant and respondent conditioning interaction is that it will likely cause the child to escape or avoid large dogs in the future. That is, if the child sees a large dog nearby, it will likely be a CS eliciting anxiety. If the child runs away, the anxiety is likely to decrease. Thus, running away from large dogs is likely to be maintained by escape conditioning in that the child will escape both the sight of the dog close by (a conditioned aversive stimulus) and the feelings of anxiety.

Operant and respondent conditioning also both occur in behavioral sequences involving positive reinforcers. As you can see in the behavioral sequence illustrated in Figure 15–2, the sound of the bell will become both a CS for a respondent response and an S^D for an operant response.

In the lead cases in Chapters 3 through 13, we focused on operant behavior. In the lead cases in Chapters 14 and 15, we focused on respondent behavior. However, each of the individuals in those cases likely experienced both respondent and operant conditioning in those situations. Although we, as behavior modifiers, chose to focus on one or the other, we should not lose sight of the fact that both are involved in most situations, and complete behavioral explanations sometimes necessitate consideration of both (see Pear & Eldridge, 1984). One area in which it is necessary to consider both respondent and operant conditioning is in the study of emotions.

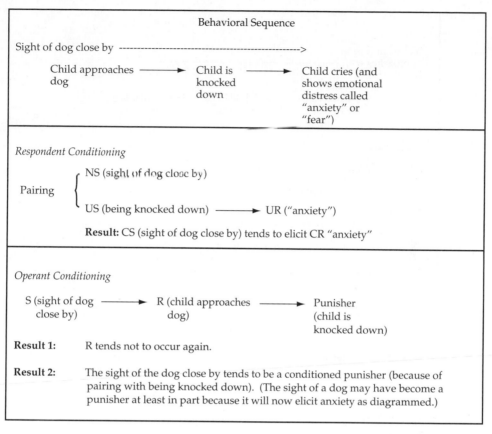

Figure 15–1 A behavioral sequence that involves both respondent and operant conditioning, and that leads to the development of a stimulus as a conditioned punisher.

RESPONDENT AND OPERANT COMPONENTS OF EMOTIONS

Emotions play an important role in our daily lives. To fully understand this important topic, we examine the role of respondent and operant conditioning in four areas: (a) the reaction that one feels during the experience of an emotion (such as the "queasiness" in the pit of one's stomach just before an important job interview); (b) the way that one learns to outwardly express or disguise an emotion (such as clasping one's hands tightly to hide nervousness); (c) how one becomes aware of and describes one's emotions (for example, "I'm nervous" as opposed to "I'm angry"); and (d) some causes of emotions.

The Respondent Component: Our Feelings

The respondent component of emotions involves primarily the three major classes of respondents discussed in Chapter 14—reflexes of the digestive system, the

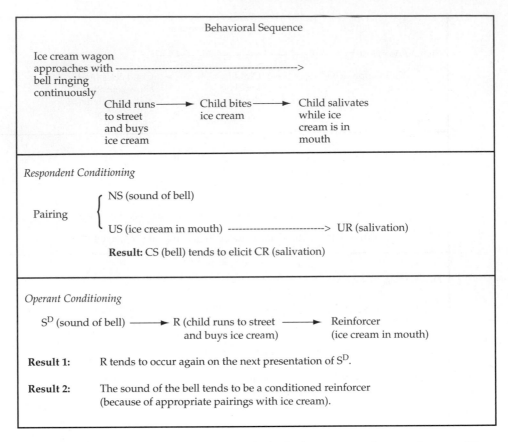

Figure 15–2   A behavioral sequence that includes both operant and respondent conditioning, and that leads to the development of a stimulus as a conditioned reinforcer.

circulatory system, and the respiratory system. These reflexes are controlled by the part of our nervous system referred to as the autonomic nervous system. What happens inside you, for example, in a moment of great fear? Your body is physically aroused—mobilized for action. Your adrenal glands secrete adrenalin into your bloodstream for extra energy. Your heart rate increases dramatically (circulatory system). At the same time, you breathe more rapidly (respiratory system), providing an increased supply of oxygen to the blood. This oxygen surges through your body with the increased heart rate, supplying more oxygen to your muscles. You may begin to sweat, which acts as a cooling mechanism in preparation for increased energy output of the body. At the same time that these changes are occurring, you may get a "queasy" feeling in your stomach (digestive system). Blood vessels to the stomach and intestines constrict and the process of digestion is interrupted, diverting blood from your internal organs to your muscles. Your mouth becomes dry as the action of the salivary glands is impeded. You might even temporarily lose bowel or bladder control (a reaction that for our primitive ancestors lightened their bodies in preparation for flight and tended to deter their pursuers).

These internal reactions of the body mobilize one's resources for fighting or flee-ing. They clearly had survival value in our evolutionary history, but they may not always be useful in modern society (e.g., when called upon to make a speech or to answer a question in class).

Autonomic responses occur as unconditioned reactions to stimuli, and such responses can be visible as blushing, trembling, and crying. In studies of newborn infants, loss of support, loud sounds, or a push are unconditioned stimuli that elicit the unconditioned responses of a sudden catching of breath, a clutching or grasping response, puckering of lips, and crying that we label as fear. Hampering an infant's movements elicits crying, screaming, and body stiffening that we label as anger. And tickling, gentle rocking, and patting appear to be unconditioned stimuli for the responses of smiling, gurgling, and cooing, labeled as joy. Cross-cultural evidence suggests that these reflexive reactions may be universal (Ekman, 1972). We learn to describe these physiological components of our emotions as our *feelings*.

Although the exact number of inherited emotional reflexes must await fur-ther research, there is no doubt about the importance of respondent conditioning for attaching physiological components of emotions to new stimuli. Nearly every organ and gland controlled by the autonomic nervous system is susceptible to re-spondent conditioning (Airapetyantz & Bykov, 1966). When experimenters have demonstrated respondent conditioning of emotions with humans, they have often relied on the visible signs of the physiological changes to demonstrate that learn-ing has occurred. Consider a classic experiment by John B. Watson and Rosalie Rayner (1920). They were interested in demonstrating that fears could be learned through Pavlovian procedures. They conducted their experiment with a normal 11-month-old infant called Albert in the report. He was in a hospital where the study was done because his mother was a nurse there. During preliminary obser-vations, it was demonstrated that Albert was not afraid of a variety of items that were placed near him when he was happily playing on a rug on the floor. The ex-perimenters also demonstrated that the noise from striking a steel box with a ham-mer would elicit a fear reaction. They introduced a white rat (of which Albert had previously shown no fear) and while Albert was watching the rat closely, one of the experimenters banged the bar with the hammer just behind Albert's head. The loud noise caused startle, crying, and other fearful behavior in Albert. After a total of seven pairings of the loud noises within the sight of the rat over two separate sessions approximately one week apart, Albert showed a very strong fear reaction to the rat. Whenever the rat appeared, Albert cried, trembled, and showed the fa-cial expression for fear. When other items were introduced, for which Albert had previously shown no fear, Albert's fear had spread to these items as well. In par-ticular, this fear was transferred to a rabbit, a dog, a seal fur coat, and a piece of cot-ton. Unfortunately, Albert left the hospital before Watson and Rayner had a chance to decondition the fear. However, Mary Cover Jones (1924) followed up some of Watson's suggestions and demonstrated that fear reactions in infants could be eliminated with respondent extinction. It would be considered unethical today to subject infants to aversive stimuli for experimental purposes. Procedural ques-tions about the Watson and Rayner study have also been raised (Harris, 1979). Nevertheless, the finding that fears are influenced by reflexive learning is well established.

The feelings associated with other emotions are also influenced by respondent conditioning. At a family reunion, for example, family members experience many happy moments. A few weeks later, when viewing the photos taken at the reunion, the pictures will likely be conditioned stimuli eliciting "happy" feelings. But there is more to emotions than the autonomic responses that we feel. Let's see how operant conditioning is also involved.

Operant Components: Our Actions, Descriptions, and Awareness

When you experience an emotion-causing event, your body responds with an immediate physiological reaction and accompanying facial expression. Then what happens? That depends on your operant learning experiences. In a situation that causes anger, for example, one person might clench her fists and swear (see Figure 15–3). Another person in that same situation might breathe heavily and walk away. Albert initially showed the respondent components of fear by crying and trembling (as well as the internal reaction mentioned earlier in this chapter). However, he also showed operant fear responses. When the white rat was presented, Albert crawled away as fast as he could. Because the operant component of

Figure 15–3   Withholding reinforcers following a previously reinforced response can cause anger. What are some operant and respondent components of anger?

emotions depends on each individual's learning history, these secondary displays of emotion vary from person to person and from culture to culture. Fans at a sporting event in North America, for example, are likely to show their displeasure toward unsportsmanlike play by booing, while fans in Europe express their displeasure by whistling. We learn to display our emotions in ways that have been modeled and operantly reinforced in the past.

Operant conditioning is also involved when we are taught to describe and be aware of our emotions. As we grow up, people around us teach us to label our emotions. Depending on our behavior, moms and dads ask questions such as, "Why are you so angry?" or "Aren't you having fun?" or "How are you feeling?" From such experiences, we learn about "being angry," "feeling happy," and "feeling sad." By age 9, most children have learned to recognize a large number of emotional expressions in themselves and others (Izard, 1991). Nevertheless, many emotions are not easily described or defined. We can account for this difficulty to some extent by considering the multiple sources of control over the naming of behavior that we describe as emotional. Suppose you see a girl's brother grab her toy train followed by the girl running after him screaming. You might conclude that the girl is angry. The next day, when coming out of your house, you see the same girl screaming and running after her brother. You might again conclude that she is angry. However, in the second instance the children are simply enjoying a game of tag. Thus, when labeling emotions, we don't always have access to the emotion-causing events, the inner feelings, and the relevant operant behaviors. This contributes to inconsistencies in the way that we talk about emotions.

Some Causes of Emotions

Presentation and withdrawal of reinforcers and presentation and withdrawal of aversive stimuli constitute four major causes of emotions. Presentation of reinforcers produces the emotion called *happiness*. Getting an "A" on an exam, receiving a compliment, cashing your paycheck, and watching a funny movie all involve the presentation of positive reinforcers. Withholding or withdrawal of reinforcers produces the emotion called *anger*. All of us have experienced such anger-causing events as a vending machine that takes your money but fails to produce the goods, being kept waiting in the doctor's office, a pen that stops writing in the middle of a quiz, and having a ticket line close just before you get to the window to buy a ticket. The presentation of aversive stimuli produce the emotion called *anxiety*. Approaching scary-looking strangers in a dark alley, seeing a car drive directly toward you at a high speed, or hearing a dog bark right behind you are all likely to cause you to feel anxious. Finally, withdrawal of aversive stimuli produces an emotion that is called *relief*. For example, when a woman receives the results from a test of a lump on her breast, or a man learns about the results of an assessment of an enlarged prostate, and learns that the problem is not cancer, the individual is likely to feel relief. Each of these causes of emotions is likely to occur on a continuum from very mild to very strong. Presentation of reinforcers, for example, can cause emotions ranging from mild pleasure to happiness to ecstasy. Withdrawal of reinforcers can cause emotions ranging from mild annoyance to anger to rage.

Presentation of aversive events can cause mild apprehension, anxiety, or stark terror. And the effects of withdrawal of aversive stimuli might range from mild relief to an emotional collapse. Other emotions might represent a mixture of some of these basic emotions (see, e.g., Martin & Osborne, 1993).

To summarize, many of our emotions are caused by either the presentation or withdrawal of reinforcers or aversive stimuli. Our emotions have three important characteristics: (a) the autonomic reaction that you feel during the experience of an emotion (typically accompanied by visible signs, such as frowns or smiles), which is influenced by respondent conditioning; (b) the way that you learn to express an emotion overtly (such as shouting, jumping up and down), which is influenced by operant conditioning; and (c) the way that you become aware of and describe your emotions, which is also influenced by operant conditioning. In Chapters 27 and 28 we'll discuss examples of how respondent and operant conditioning have been used to change troublesome emotions.

RESPONDENT AND OPERANT COMPONENTS OF THINKING

Like emotions, much of what we call "thinking" in everyday language involves both respondent and operant conditioning.

A Respondent Component: Our Imagery

Try the following exercise. Close your eyes and imagine that you are sitting on a lawn chair in your backyard on a warm summer day. You look up and see the clear blue sky. Imagine a few white fluffy clouds drifting slowly along. Chances are that you will be able to form a clear image of the blue sky and the white fluffy clouds—so clear that you can almost see the colors. Thus, one type of thinking appears to consist of imagining in response to words—imagining so vividly that it can sometimes seem almost like the real thing. This probably comes about through respondent or Pavlovian conditioning. If you actually look at a clear blue sky, the color elicits activity in the visual system much as food elicited salivation in Pavlov's dogs. As you grew up, you experienced many trials in which the words "blue sky" were paired with actually looking at and seeing a blue sky. As a consequence, when you close your eyes and imagine that you are looking at a blue sky (with white fluffy clouds), the words likely elicit activity in your visual part of the brain so that **Note 1** you experience the behavior of "seeing" the actual scene. This has been referred to as conditioned seeing (Skinner, 1953). In a broader sense, we might think of conditioned sensing. That is, just as we acquire conditioned seeing through experience, we also acquire conditioned hearing, conditioned smelling, and conditioned feeling. Consider the example described by Martin and Osborne (1993) in which an individual experienced numerous passionate sexual encounters with a partner who consistently used a very distinctive perfume. Then one day someone walked past that individual in a department store wearing that same perfume. The individual immediately imagined seeing the partner (conditioned seeing), felt "tingly" all over (conditioned feeling), and even imagined that he heard the partner's voice (conditioned hearing). This sort of thing is also a part of what goes on during fantasy. To experience a fantasy or to read or listen to a story is, in some sense, to be there. It's as though you can see what the people in the story see, feel what they feel, and hear what they hear. We are able to do this because of many instances of conditioned sensing. Our long histories of associating words with actual sights, sounds, smells, and feelings enable us to experience the scenes that an author's words describe. The internal actions that occur when we're thinking are real—we're really seeing, or feeling, or hearing when we respond to the words (Malott & Whaley, 1983; Pear, 2001).

An Operant Component: Our Self-Talk

Imaging (conditioned seeing) and other types of conditioned sensing constitute one type of thinking. Another type of thinking is self-directed verbal behavior, or self-talk. As we indicated in earlier chapters, our verbal behavior is taught to us by others through operant conditioning. We learn to speak because of effective consequences for doing so. As children, we learn to ask for such things as our favorite foods and the opportunity to watch our favorite cartoons, and we learn to say things that please Mom and Dad, aunts and uncles, and others. Much of our thinking is verbal behavior. We learn to think out loud as children because it helps us to perform tasks more efficiently (Roberts, 1979). When children first start attending school, they often say rules out loud to themselves to adjust to difficult tasks (Roberts & Tharp, 1980). When they are about 5 or 6 years old, however, they also begin to engage in subvocal speech in the sense that their self-talk begins to occur below the spoken level (Vygotsky, 1978).

  We learn to talk silently to ourselves at a very early age largely because we encounter punishers when we think out loud (Skinner, 1957). For example, teachers in school require children to think to themselves because thinking out loud disturbs the other students. As another example, naturally distressed reactions from others teach us to keep certain thoughts to ourselves. When you go to a party and are being introduced to the hostess, your first reaction might be, "Wow, is that an ugly dress!" But you probably won't say it out loud; instead you will just "say it to yourself" or "think" it. (Other reasons for silent self-talk is that it requires less effort and can occur more rapidly than overt self-talk.)

PRIVATE THOUGHTS AND FEELINGS: MORE RESPONDENT–OPERANT INTERACTIONS

Much of what we call "thinking" and "feeling" in everyday life goes on at a level that is not observable by others. As indicated in Chapter 1, we refer to such activity as covert, or private. Although private behavior is more difficult to "get at," behavior modifiers assume that in other respects it is the same as public behavior; that is, that the principles and procedures of operant and respondent conditioning apply to private behavior.

Often, an instance of what we would refer to as private behavior includes both respondent and operant components of thinking and emotions. To illustrate, consider the following example (described by Martin & Osborne, 1993). One of the authors grew up on a farm just outside of a small town. He attended school in the town and it was very important to him to be accepted by the town children. One of the town kids, Wilf, frequently teased him about being a "farmer." "Hey, gang," Wilf would say, "Here comes Garry the farmer. Hey, Garry, do you have cow dung on your boots?" Now imagine that it's Saturday afternoon and Garry and his family are getting ready to go to town. Garry will be going to the Saturday afternoon matinee at the Roxy Theatre with the rest of the gang (a big deal because they didn't yet have TV on the farm). Garry says to himself, "I wonder if Wilf will be there" (operant thinking). Garry can picture Wilf clearly (conditioned seeing) and can imagine Wilf teasing him about being a farmer (both operant thinking and conditioned hearing). Thoughts of the aversive experience elicit unpleasant feelings (a reflexively learned response). Garry reacts by paying special attention to his appearance in the hope that appearing "citified" will give Wilf nothing to say.

Consider some additional examples of private behavior that involve respondent and operant components of thinking and emotions. Imagine a lineman in football preparing to go after the opposing quarterback just before the ball is snapped. The lineman thinks "I'm all over him! I'll tear his head off! This guy is history!" That kind of self-talk (operant thinking) is likely to help the lineman feel aggressive (a respondent emotion). Or consider a sprinter who thinks "explode" while waiting in the blocks for the starter's pistol to sound; or a figure skater who says to herself during her program, "Graceful, feel the music" to help create the proper mood for the music and the choreography. In such instances the operant self-talk serves as a CS to elicit certain feelings—the respondent component of emotions.

You can see that, contrary to the impression given by many introductory psychology texts, behavior modifiers do not ignore what goes on inside a person. Although it is true that the great majority of studies in behavior modification have been concerned with observable behavior, many behavior modifiers have taken an interest in dealing with private behavior. As illustrated by the work of Joseph Cautela and his colleagues, thinking and feeling as private behaviors are a proper subject matter for behavior modifiers and can be readily dealt with in terms of operant and respondent conditioning principles (e.g., Cautela & Kearney, 1993). In Chapters 27 and 28, we'll describe behavioral strategies for overcoming troublesome thoughts and feelings.

STUDY QUESTIONS

1. Explain how respondent conditioning and operant conditioning can interact to cause an individual to escape or avoid a particular stimulus. Use diagrams and examples to clarify your explanation.
2. Describe several physiological activities that we experience in a moment of great fear.
3. Describe unconditioned reflexes that appear to characterize the emotions of fear, anger, and joy.

4. In the experiment with Albert, what was the US? the UR? the CS? the CR?
5. Cross-cultural studies of emotions suggest that emotions are both universal and culture specific. How can we explain this apparent contradiction?
6. In a sentence each, summarize three important characteristics that make up our emotions.
7. Describe an example of respondent thinking that is not in the text.
8. Describe an example of operant thinking that is not in the text.
9. When behavior modifiers speak of private behavior, to what are they referring?
10. What basic assumption do the authors of this text make about public and private behavior?
11. Describe a behavior not described in the text that illustrates how operant thinking might function as a CS to elicit the respondent component of an emotion.
12. Discuss whether behavior modifiers deny the existence and importance of thoughts and feelings.

APPLICATION EXERCISES

A. Exercise Involving Others

Pick an emotion (e.g., anger), and observe the operant displays of that emotion in two people you know. Are their operant components of that emotion similar or different?

B. Self-Modification Exercise

Consider an emotion that you frequently experience. Describe how experiencing that emotion includes both respondent and operant responses.

NOTE AND EXTENDED DISCUSSION

1. A number of behavioral techniques rely on imagery. In Chapter 28, we describe how Wolpe used imagery in systematic desensitization. Another procedure involving imagery is called covert sensitization (Cautela, 1966), which is essentially a form of aversion therapy (see Chapter 14) in which a troublesome reinforcer is paired repeatedly with an aversive stimulus. You will recall that aversion therapy is based on counterconditioning—it is assumed that the troublesome reinforcer will become less reinforcing because it will come to elicit a response similar to that elicited by the aversive stimulus. In covert sensitization, the client imagines both the troublesome reinforcer and the aversive stimulus. This procedure is so named because the pairing of the stimuli occurs only in the client's imagination (in other words, it is covert) and the anticipated result of this covert pairing process is that the undesirable reinforcer becomes aversive (i.e., the client becomes sensitized to it).

   The procedure has been used with clients who wish to give up smoking (as described by Irey, 1972). During a particular trial, the client might be instructed to vividly imagine lighting a cigarette after dinner in a restaurant, inhaling, and then suddenly becoming so violently ill that he vomits all over his hands, his clothes, the tablecloth, and the other people at the table. He continues to vomit and then, when his stomach is empty, to gag while the other people in the restaurant stare at him in disgust. In short, the scene is made extremely realistic and aversive. When the maximum degree of aversiveness is felt, the client is instructed to imagine turning away from his cigarette and immediately beginning to feel better. The scene concludes with the client washing up in the bathroom, without his cigarettes, and feeling tremendous relief. Research on covert sensitization can be found in Cautela and Kearney (1993).

Study Questions on Note

1. What is the rationale of covert sensitization?
2. Describe in some detail a plausible example of covert sensitization.

16

Transferring Behavior to New Settings and Making It Last: Generality of Behavioral Change

"Hi, there. I have a nice surprise for you in my car."

TEACHING STAN TO PROTECT HIMSELF[1]

During recess time, 4-year-old Stan was playing with a toy near the edge of his preschool playground, unaware that a stranger was observing him intently from a distance. No teacher was in sight. Gradually, the stranger approached until he was standing beside Stan.

"Hi, there," said the stranger, "What's your name?"

"Stan," the boy replied.

"Nice day, isn't it, Stan?"

The stranger engaged Stan in small talk for a few minutes. Then, casting his eyes around the school yard, the stranger casually asked, "Stan, how would you like to go for a walk with me?"

The stranger seemed friendly and Stan was used to taking directions from adults. He stood up and approached the stranger. Just then, a teacher appeared and the stranger quickly moved away.

An attempted child abduction? Not exactly. The stranger was actually an assistant in an experiment designed to study a method of teaching self-protection to young children, and Stan was being tested to determine his suitability for the experiment. He and two other children (Patti and John), who also appeared susceptible to lures often used by child molesters, were included in the experiment. The children were tested several times to verify that they would go with a stranger who approached

---

[1]This case is based on an experiment by Poche, Brouwer, and Swearingen (1981).

them using any of several kinds of lures (e.g., "Your teacher said it was all right for you to come with me" and "I have a nice surprise in my car. Would you like to come and see it?"). Then training began. Two adult trainers acted out a scene in which one trainer approached the other and used one of the lures. The other trainer responded with "No, I have to go ask my teacher," and ran toward the school building. The child was then instructed to respond in the same way as the second trainer to the lure of the first trainer and, contingent on doing so, was provided with social reinforcement (e.g., praise) that was occasionally followed with material and activity reinforcement (e.g., stickers, playing on the swings).

Responses were trained to one lure per day. When a child consistently responded correctly to the first lure, responding was trained to a second lure, and then to a third lure. In addition to the lures being varied in this manner, the exact location of each session on the school grounds was also varied by approximately 75 feet. After training was completed, each child was tested in a community setting to determine if the response established during training would be performed in a novel setting. All three children responded correctly to the lures in that setting. After 12 weeks, Stan and Patti were tested again in the community setting. Stan continued to respond perfectly, whereas Patti made the correct verbal response but stayed in the vicinity of the stranger.

GENERALITY

We say that training produces *generality* when the trained behavior transfers from the training situation to the natural environment, when training leads to the development of new behavior that has not been specifically trained, or when the trained behavior is maintained in the natural environment over time. Before examining strategies for programming for generality of behavior change in these three ways, it will be helpful to review stimulus generalization (which we introduced in Chapter 8) and response generalization.

Stimulus Generalization

Stimulus generalization occurs when behavior becomes more probable in the presence of one stimulus or situation as a result of having been reinforced in the presence of another stimulus or situation. As discussed in Chapter 8, there are several reasons for the occurrence of stimulus generalization. First, the more physically similar two stimuli are, the more stimulus generalization will occur between them (e.g., two similar-looking berries). This is an inherited (i.e., unlearned) characteristic. Second, stimulus generalization might occur from one stimulus to another because we have learned that the two stimuli are members of a stimulus common-element class—a set of stimuli that have some physical characteristic in common (e.g., a house with green shutters and a girl with green socks). Third, stimulus generalization might occur from one stimulus to another because we have learned that the stimuli are members of an equivalence class—a set of completely dissimilar stimuli that an individual has been trained to match together (e.g., the words "mutt," "pooch," and a picture of a dog). Such stimuli are functionally equivalent in the sense that they control the same response. Both stimulus common-element classes and stimulus equivalence classes are called *concepts*.

The first sentence in the paragraph above describes stimulus generalization of operant conditioning. Respondent stimulus generalization happens when a respondent CR occurs to a new stimulus, and is discussed later in this chapter.

Response Generalization

Not to be confused with stimulus generalization is the phenomenon called **response generalization.** This occurs when a behavior becomes more probable in the presence of a stimulus or situation as a result of another behavior having been strengthened in the presence of that stimulus or situation. Like stimulus generalization, response generalization occurs for several reasons.

Unlearned Response Generalization Due to Considerable Physical Similarity of Responses   The more physically similar two responses are, the more unlearned response generalization will occur between them. If, for example, you learn a forehand shot in racquetball, chances are that you would be able to perform a forehand shot in squash or tennis. The responses involved are very similar. Similarly, you will probably find roller blading relatively easy to learn if you have first learned to ice skate, because the responses involved in the two activities are similar.

Learned Response Generalization Based on Minimal Physical Similarity of Responses   Just as there are large classes of stimuli that share a common characteristic while differing in many other characteristics, there are also widely different responses that share a common characteristic. Learned response generalization can occur within such response classes. For example, a child who has learned to add "s" to the ends of words pertaining to more than one object or event may show response generalization even when it is grammatically incorrect (e.g., saying "foots" instead of "feet" while looking at a picture of two feet). In Stan's case, if a stranger tried to lure Stan and he said, "No, I have to ask my mother [instead of my teacher]," this would be an example of learned response generalization because the two sentences are different but have a common grammatical structure and share some of the same words.

Learned Response Generalization Due to Functionally Equivalent Responses   Different responses that produce the same consequences are called *functionally equivalent responses.* You might show response generalization because you have learned functionally equivalent responses to a stimulus. If you are asked to start a fire, for example, you might obtain and strike a match, flip a cigarette lighter, place a stick in an existing fire to start a new fire, or perhaps even rub two sticks together. As another example, a child who learns to "be honest" might tell the truth, return valued articles left or dropped by others, and refrain from copying another student's answers. All of these responses are functionally equivalent in the sense that they are likely to bring praise from various members of the child's community.

An important application of functionally equivalent responses in applied settings is termed *behavioral momentum.* As a result of some responses being emitted and reinforced, the probability of other functionally equivalent responses momentarily increases. Consider, for example, the problem of overcoming noncompliance with children. Compliance to instructions can include a variety of functionally equivalent responses. Thus, to increase the probability that a child will follow instructions that he or she normally does not follow, it is often effective first to give

Note 1

the child instructions that he or she is likely to follow, and to reinforce compliance with those instructions. If the instructions that the child is less likely to follow are then given soon after this, the chances are greatly increased that he or she will follow them (Mace & Belfiore, 1990; Mace et al., 1988; Singer, Singer, & Horner, 1987).

FACTORS INFLUENCING THE EFFECTIVENESS OF PROGRAMMING GENERALITY OF OPERANT BEHAVIOR

In discussing generality, we distinguish two situations: (a) the *training* situation and (b) the *target* situation—a situation in which we want generality to occur. The target situation is usually, but not necessarily, the natural environment. Because programming for generality is somewhat different for operant and respondent behavior, we shall consider each separately. *Programming for generality* of operant behavior change includes strategies of programming for stimulus generalization, response generalization, and behavior maintenance.

Programming Operant Stimulus Generalization

Note 2 The initial occurrence of stimulus generalization depends critically on the physical similarity between the training and target situations. The more similar they are, the more stimulus generalization (and hence the less discrimination) there will be between them.

Train in the Target Situation   Thus, the first effort of the behavior modifier attempting to program stimulus generalization should be to make the final stages of the training situation similar to the target situation in as many ways as possible. Other things being equal, the best way in which to do this is to train in the target situation itself. Suppose, for example, that a parent would like to teach a child to count out the correct amount of change for purchasing a bag of candy. The ideal place to do this would be in a store that sells candy. (Of course, some preliminary training in a more controlled setting might be necessary.)

Vary the Training Conditions   This might be done by conducting training sessions with relatively little control over the stimuli in the presence of which correct responses are reinforced. If behaviors are brought under the control of a greater variety of stimuli during training, then there is an increased probability of some of those stimuli being present in the target situation. Thus, in the lead case for this chapter, no attempt was made to control background stimuli, such as playground and traffic noise, as might be done in more basic research.

Program Common Stimuli   A third tactic is to program common stimuli deliberately by developing the behavior to specific stimuli that are present in both the training and target settings. For example, Walker and Buckley (1972) described a program in which social and academic classroom behaviors were taught to children in a remedial classroom. Stimulus generalization to the regular academic classroom was ensured by using the same academic materials (i.e., common stimuli) in both classrooms.

A useful strategy for programming common stimuli is to bring the desired behavior under the control of instructions or rules that the student can rehearse in novel situations (Guevremont, Osnes, & Stokes, 1986; Stokes & Osnes, 1986). Stan might have been taught the rule, "If someone approaches me in the schoolyard whom I don't know, I should run into the school building." Rehearsal of an appropriate rule in novel settings might lead to desired behavior, even though the stimuli in the novel settings are physically dissimilar to the stimuli that were present during training. For example, if Stan is in his yard and a stranger approaches him, he might run into his house as a result of saying the rule. (Rule control over behavior is discussed further in Chapter 17.)

Train Sufficient Stimulus Exemplars   A fourth tactic, which Stokes and Baer (1977) considered to be one of the most valuable areas for programming generality, is called *training sufficient stimulus exemplars*. With this technique, the probability of appropriate generalization to new stimuli and situations is increased because of the large number and variety of stimuli and situations to which training has occurred. Thus, in the lead case for this chapter training occurred in several different places in the schoolyard and with several different lures.

Horner and colleagues described a variation of training sufficient stimulus exemplars that they referred to as *general case programming* (Horner, Sprague, & Wilcox, 1982). With this approach, the teacher begins by identifying the range of relevant stimulus situations to which a learner will be expected to respond, and the response variations that might be required. Then, during training, the learner's behavior and acceptable variations are brought under the control of samples of the range of relevant stimuli. Sprague and Horner (1984) used this approach to teach adolescents with developmental disabilities to use vending machines by introducing them to a variety of different machines and the responses needed to use them. This approach was very effective in producing generalization in that the learners were subsequently able to operate any available vending machine with which they came in contact.

Programming Operant Response Generalization

It appears that there has been less concern in the literature for programming response generalization than there has been for programming stimulus generalization. This may be because there is a great emphasis in our educational system on teaching students the "correct" answers to questions. Variations on correct answers (that may show response generalization) are either not accepted or are followed by reinforcers of an inferior quality (such as a "B" instead of an "A" as a grade on a mathematics exam). Nevertheless, there are some strategies for programming response generalization, two of which are described now.

Train Sufficient Response Exemplars   A strategy for programming response generalization is similar to that of training sufficient stimulus exemplars to establish stimulus generalization. This is referred to as *training sufficient response exemplars*
Note 3 (Stokes & Baer, 1977). Guess, Sailor, Rutherford, and Baer (1968) taught a girl with a developmental disability to use plural nouns correctly in speech with this technique. With prompting and reinforcement, they first taught the girl to name objects correctly in the singular and the plural when presented with one object (e.g., cup) and two objects (e.g., cups). They continued in this way until, after a number of exemplars of the correct singular and plural labels had been taught, the girl appropriately

named new objects in the plural even though only the singular labels for these objects had been taught. Thus, the girl showed response generalization.

Vary the Acceptable Responses During Training   Another strategy is to vary the responses that are acceptable during training. For example, in developing creativity, Goetz and Baer (1973) reinforced children during block building in a nursery school setting for any response that was different from prior block-building responses. This tactic led to an increase in the creative block building demonstrated by the children.

Programming Operant Behavior Maintenance

It is one thing to program stimulus generalization to a new setting or response generalization for new behaviors. It's another thing for a therapeutic behavioral change to last in those new settings or with those new behaviors. Maintenance depends critically on whether the behavior will continue to be reinforced. There are four general approaches to the problem of achieving behavior maintenance.

Behavioral Trapping: Allow Natural Contingencies of Reinforcement to Take Effect   In a **behavioral trap,** reinforcers in the natural environment maintain a behavior that was initially developed by programmed reinforcers (Baer & Wolf, 1970; Kohler & Greenwood, 1986). Making use of a behavioral trap can be a very effective way to program generality. This approach requires the behavior modifier to realistically identify contingencies in the natural environment and then to tailor the target behavior so that it will be trapped (i.e., maintained) by those contingencies. Talking is an obvious example of behavior that is heavily reinforced in most social environments. After speech has been established in a training situation, it may continue unabated in the natural environment because of the natural contingencies of reinforcement for it there. Indeed, it often seems necessary only to establish vocal imitation and a few object-naming responses for the natural contingencies of reinforcement to take over and develop functional speech behavior. As another example, behavioral trapping might be involved in overcoming a child's shyness. Playing with other children is a behavior that might gradually be shaped in a shy child. Once this behavior is strongly established, however, the behavior modifier probably will not have to worry about reinforcing it further. The other children will take care of that themselves in the course of their play, for, indeed, that is what social play is all about. Another example of behavioral trapping is shown in Figure 16–1.

Change the Behavior of People in the Natural Environment   A second approach to the problem of achieving lasting generality is usually more difficult than the first. It involves actually changing the behavior of people in the target situation so that they will maintain the behavior of the learner that has generalized from the training situation. In following this approach, it is necessary to work with people in the target situation—ward staff, parents, teachers, neighbors, and others who have contact with the target behavior. The behavior modifier must teach these individuals how to reinforce the learner's behavior (if it is desirable) or how to extinguish it (if it is undesirable). The behavior modifier must also occasionally reinforce the appropriate behavior of these individuals—at least until it comes into contact with the improved target behavior of the learner, which will then, ideally, reinforce their continued application of the appropriate procedures.

Figure 16–1   An example of behavioral trapping.

As an example of this second approach, consider the case of a child living at home who has shown a very high frequency of tantrumming. Possibly this is her sole means of gaining attention and other reinforcers from her parents. There is little doubt that more desirable behaviors could be established in a training situation, but such behaviors would not be maintained in the home situation unless the contingencies operating there were changed. A behavior modifier called in on this case might therefore adopt the following plan. In a training situation designed to teach the child to play with toys rather than to tantrum, the behavior modifier would first adjust the desired behavior to an appropriate schedule—for instance, VI/LH with infrequent reinforcement (because it will not be practical for the parents to give extremely frequent reinforcement in the home environment). Having accomplished this, the behavior modifier would then show the mother how to keep accurate records of the child's desirable and undesirable behavior. Next, the mother, with the help and prompting of the behavior modifier, would frequently reinforce the child for playing with her toys in the living room. Gradually the mother would decrease the frequency of reinforcement to have more time for activities that did not involve the child. She could use a kitchen timer, or similar device, to remind herself to reinforce the child. Throughout this procedure, the behavior modifier would frequently reinforce the mother for appropriately managing and recording the child's behavior. Then the behavior modifier would fade out of the situation by visiting less and less frequently to check the mother's records. However, if the program deteriorated, he or she would temporarily stop the fading process and spend enough time in the training situation to correct matters. Ideally, the mother's behavior of appropriately reinforcing the target behavior would eventually be maintained by the child's good play behavior and her decreased whining, crying, and tantrumming.

Use Intermittent Schedules of Reinforcement in the Target Situation   After a behavior has generalized to a target situation, it may be desirable to reinforce the behavior deliberately in the target situation on an intermittent schedule for at least a few reinforced trials. The intermittent schedule should make that behavior more persistent in the target situation and thereby increase the probability of the behavior lasting until it can come under the control of natural reinforcers.

Give the Control to the Individual   An area within behavior modification has been concerned with helping individuals to apply behavior modification to themselves. This area, which has been referred to as self-management, self-modification, or behavioral self-control, has produced many books containing easy-to-follow "how-to" procedures that help individuals to manage their own behavior, and is discussed more fully in Chapter 26. Concerning the problem of maintaining behavior in target situations, giving the control to the individual might occur in one of two major ways. First, it might be possible to teach an individual to assess and record instances of his or her own generalized behavior and apply a specific reinforcement procedure to that behavior, as suggested in Chapter 26. Second, as suggested by Stokes and Baer (1977), it might be possible to teach an individual a means of *recruiting a natural community of reinforcement* to maintain generalized responding. For example, in a study by Hildebrand, Martin, Furer, and Hazen (1990), workers with developmental disabilities in a sheltered workshop usually showed very low productivity. On the few occasions when they worked at a high rate, they received little feedback from staff. Hildebrand and colleagues taught the workers to meet a productivity goal and then to call staff members' attention to their good work. This led to increased feedback for the workers from the staff, and helped to maintain a higher level of productivity by the workers.

PROGRAMMING GENERALITY OF RESPONDENT BEHAVIOR

As indicated previously, programming for generality of operant behavior often involves strategies to bring about stimulus generalization, response generalization, and behavior maintenance. When dealing with respondent behavior, sometime

Figure 16–2   An example of a failure to program stimulus generalization of a respondent behavior.

stimulus generalization is important. When extinguishing a phobia, for example, one would not want to decrease the fear to only one specific stimulus (see Figure 16–2). For most treatments involving respondent conditioning, however, we are typically concerned only with maintenance of the conditioned reflex over time. To help you to understand why this is so, let's review a couple of examples of respondent conditioning from Chapter 14. In that chapter, the results of a respondent conditioning program for constipation was a conditioned reflex in which a particular time of day became a CS causing an adult to experience a bowel movement as a CR. In each case, it was desirable that the adults experienced a bowel movement upon arising in the morning. Would they have wanted stimulus generalization to occur such that bowel movements were elicited at other times during the day? No, that would have been very inconvenient. Was it important to program response generalization so that a wide variety of bowel movements were elicited by the CS of a specific time of day? No, that would not have been adaptive.

Let's consider another example from Chapter 14 in which, after conditioning, pressure on a child's bladder in the middle of the night became a CS causing awakening as a CR (so that the child could subsequently go to the bathroom to urinate rather than wetting the bed). Would it have been desirable for stimulus generalization to occur so that only a slight amount of pressure would cause awakening? No—the amount of pressure just before having to urinate was the ideal CS, and that's what was trained. Was it necessary to have response generalization of awakening? Not really, the normal waking-up response served quite nicely. As these examples illustrate, programming stimulus and response generalization is typically not of concern in behavior management programs involving conditioned reflexes.

It is important, however, that conditioned reflexes be maintained over time. If a CS is presented without further pairings with a US, the CS will lose its ability to elicit the CR. Thus, in programs involving respondent conditioning, it is sometimes necessary to periodically pair the CS with the US so that the CS will continue to elicit the desired response over time.

PITFALLS OF GENERALITY

All the components of generality have potential pitfalls as well as positive aspects. Consider stimulus generalization. Without stimulus generalization, learning would be of very limited value. No matter how perfectly a person learned something, he or she would have to learn it all over again every time the situation changed even slightly. (Just imagine how annoying it would be to learn to dance to a piece of music only to discover that you had to learn to dance all over again when a new song was played.) However, stimulus generalization has its disadvantages too, in that a behavior learned in a situation in which it is appropriate may then emerge inconveniently in a situation in which it is inappropriate.

A conspicuous example of the stimulus generalization of a desirable behavior to an inappropriate situation that can often be seen among individuals with developmental disabilities involves greetings and displays of affection. Of course, it is highly desirable for these behaviors to occur under appropriate circumstances; but when an individual walks up to and hugs a total stranger, the results can be less than favorable for a number of obvious reasons. The solution to this problem is to teach the individual to discriminate between situations in which different forms of greetings and expressions of affection are appropriate and situations in which they are inappropriate.

Another example of inappropriate stimulus generalization of a desirable behavior may be the destructive competitiveness demonstrated frequently by some individuals and occasionally by all of us. Such behavior may stem in part from the strong reinforcement given in our culture for winning in sports and for achieving high grades in our educational system. As a wise person once remarked, "It may be true that wars have been won on the playing fields of Eton, but they have also been started there."

The opposite type of problem is the stimulus generalization of an undesirable behavior from the situation in which it developed to a new situation for which it is also undesirable. Suppose that an overly protective grandparent, while supervising a grandchild who is learning how to walk, provides a great deal of attention each time the child falls (presumably out of a concern that the child might be injured). As a result, falling increases in frequency. When the child is returned to the parents, the excessive falling might generalize to their presence as well.

A different pitfall is a lack of desirable stimulus generalization. This can be seen in the typical study habits of students. Frequently, students cram for exams the night before an examination. They memorize certain verbal chains in response to certain prompts and questions. What they frequently fail to consider is the importance of bringing their knowledge of the material under broader stimulus control than just one or two questions; that is, they do not program for generalization. A great many people have had the same experience with learning a second language. One of the authors was among the many who took a second language during four years of high school. At the end of that time, he was clearly incapable of speaking the language. He had a certain repertoire for answering questions on French exams, translating English articles into French, and translating French articles into English, but this repertoire had not been brought under the stimulus control of a typical conversational setting.

Another example of lack of desirable stimulus generalization occurs in the interaction between parents and their children. In various social situations, such as restaurants, parents frequently do not present the same stimuli to their children, or provide the same contingencies of reinforcement, that they present at mealtimes in the home situation. Consequently, the children frequently do not generalize their table manners and good behaviors that occur at home to the restaurant or other social settings. It is not uncommon to hear a parent lament, "I thought I taught you how to be a good child, and now look at you." We hope that after reading this book and performing the study questions and study exercises, the same parents will do a much better job of programming stimulus generalization. (If not, you will probably hear us lament, "I thought I taught you how to be a good behavior modifier, and now look at you.")

The pitfalls just listed indicate how stimulus generalization can work to the disadvantage of those who are ignorant of it. There are also many pitfalls for programming maintenance of behavior change. These were described at the end of Chapters 6 and 7 concerning schedules of reinforcement.

GUIDELINES FOR PROGRAMMING GENERALITY OF OPERANT BEHAVIOR

To ensure stimulus and response generalization from the training situation to the natural environment, and to ensure behavior maintenance, the behavior modifier should observe the following rules as closely as possible:

1. Choose target behaviors that are clearly useful to the learner, because these are the behaviors that are most likely to be reinforced in the natural environment.
2. Teach the target behavior in a situation that is as similar as possible to the environment in which you want the behavior to occur.
3. Vary the training conditions so as to maximally sample relevant stimulus dimensions for transfer to other situations and to reinforce various forms of the desirable behavior.
4. Establish the target behavior successively in as many situations as is feasible, starting with the easiest and progressing to the most difficult.
5. Program common stimuli (such as rules) that might facilitate transfer to novel environments.
6. Vary the acceptable responses in the training settings.
7. Gradually reduce the frequency of reinforcement in the training situation until it is less than that occurring in the natural environment.
8. When changing to a new situation, increase the frequency of reinforcement in that situation to offset the tendency of the learner to discriminate the new situation from the training situation.
9. Ensure sufficient reinforcement for maintaining the target behavior in the natural environment. This rule requires especially close attention in the early stages of transferring the target behavior from the training situation to the natural environment. Add reinforcement as necessary, including reinforcement to those (such as parents and teachers) who are responsible for maintaining the target behavior in the natural environment, and then decrease this reinforcement slowly enough to prevent the target behavior from deteriorating.

STUDY QUESTIONS

1. Define stimulus generalization and give an example.
2. Distinguish between unlearned stimulus generalization and learned stimulus generalization involving a stimulus common-element class. Give an example of each.
3. What is a primary distinction between stimulus generalization involving a stimulus common-element class and stimulus generalization involving an equivalence class?
4. Define or describe unlearned response generalization due to physical similarity of responses, and give an example.
5. Define or describe learned response generalization based on minimal physical similarity of responses, and give an example.
6. Define or describe learned response generalization due to functionally equivalent responses, and give an example.
7. List the three aspects of programming for behavioral generality. Describe an example of each aspect.

8. Briefly describe how behavioral generality was demonstrated in the experiment to teach self-protection skills to children.
9. Explain the difference between stimulus generalization and stimulus discrimination. Describe examples illustrating the difference.
10. Briefly describe four tactics for programming operant stimulus generalization. Give an example of each.
11. Which of the strategies for programming operant stimulus generalization appear to capitalize on stimulus generalization due to physical similarity? Justify your choices.
12. How might the teaching of a rule facilitate operant stimulus generalization? State the general factor for programming for generalization that seems to be operating, and illustrate with an example.
13. Describe the generalization strategy referred to as general case programming. Give an example.
14. Briefly describe two tactics for programming operant response generalization. Give an example of each.
15. Briefly describe four tactics for programming operant behavior maintenance in a target situation. Give an example of each.
16. Briefly explain why considerations regarding generality of respondent behavior differ from those regarding operant behavior.
17. Give two examples of a pitfall of stimulus generalization, one of which involves generalization of a desirable behavior to an inappropriate situation and the other of which involves generalization of an undesirable behavior.
18. Give an example of a pitfall of response generalization.
19. Give an example of a pitfall of behavior maintenance.

APPLICATION EXERCISES

A. Exercise Involving Others

Choose one of the cases described in the previous chapters in which there was no effort to program generality. Outline a specific plausible program for producing generality in that case.

B. Self-Modification Exercises

1. Describe a recent situation in which you generalized in a desirable way. Clearly identify the behavior, the training situation (where the behavior was initially reinforced), and the test situation (to which the behavior generalized).
2. Describe a recent situation in which you generalized in an undesirable way (in other words, the outcome was undesirable). Again, identify the behavior, training stituation, and test situation.
3. Consider the behavior deficit for which you outlined a shaping program at the end of Chapter 10. Assuming that your shaping program will be successful, discuss what you might do to program generality. (See the factors influencing the effectiveness of generality that were discussed in this chapter.)

NOTES AND EXTENDED DISCUSSION

1. The term *behavioral momentum* also refers to the fact that the more reinforcement that occurs in a given situation in which a response is reinforced, the more resistant to disruption that response will be in that situation (see, e.g., Mace, McCurdy, & Quigley, 1990). There are at least two practical implications of this fact: (a) As we pointed out in Chapter 6, a response that has been intermittently reinforced will take longer to be decreased by extinction than will a response that has been continuously reinforced. However, a response that has been continuously reinforced will probably be more resistant to other forms of disruption (Nevin, 1992); (b) One way to decrease a response is to present reinforcement noncontingently (i.e., independent of responding) (Tucker, Sigafoos, & Bushell, 1998). However, this method of decreasing a response results in more reinforcement in the situation, thus (in theory, at least) making the response more resistant to disruption.

2. An example of this occurred in a study by Welch and Pear (1980) in which objects, pictures of the objects, and photographs of the objects were compared as training stimuli for naming responses in four children with severe developmental disabilities in a special training room. It was found that three of the four children displayed considerably more generalization to the objects in their natural environment when they were trained with the objects rather than the pictures or photographs of the objects. The fourth child, who was also the most proficient linguistically, displayed substantial generalization regardless of the type of training stimulus used. A follow-up study by Salmon, Pear, and Kuhn (1986) indicates that training with objects also produces more generalization to untrained objects in the same stimulus class than does training with pictures. The results suggest that parents and teachers of children with severe developmental disabilities should use objects as training stimuli as much as possible whenever generalization to those objects is desired.

3. This instance of response generalization (as is true with the examples given on p. 203) is somewhat more complex than our straightforward definition given at the beginning of this chapter. It does appear, in this example, that the reinforcement of a specific response has increased the probability of similar responses. The new form of the response (the plural for a new object), however, is also occurring to a new stimulus (the plurality of the new object itself). Thus, stimulus generalization is also involved. For a discussion of difficulties in defining response generalization, see the *Journal of Organizational Behavior Management*, 2001, *21*(4).

Study Questions on Notes

1. What rule for programming stimulus generalization is exemplified by the study in which object and picture names were taught to children with developmental disabilities? Explain.
2. Describe the two ways in which the term behavioral momentum has been used in the behavioral literature.
3. Explain at least one practical implication of behavioral momentum with regard to response disruption.

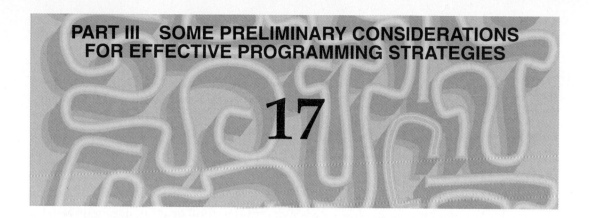

Capitalizing on Existing Stimulus Control: Rules and Goals

Suppose that a sport psychologist is talking to a young figure skater a few minutes before she will skate her program in an important competition. Showing signs of extreme nervousness, the skater expresses her concerns: "I hope I don't fall on my double axel. I hope I don't come in last. What if I don't skate well?" How can the sport psychologist help the skater? Given the assumption that her negative self-talk is what is causing the skater to feel anxious and that this anxiety might interfere with her skating well, it would seem desirable to design a program to develop more confident self-talk. But there's no time to go through a number of shaping steps to do this. Respondent extinction might be used to decrease feelings of excessive nervousness, but that, too, requires more time than is available in the few minutes before she is to perform. An alternative solution is for the psychologist to present stimuli that, because of the skater's conditioning history, already control the desired behavior. For example, the psychologist might ask the skater to repeat self-talk that is likely to elicit feelings of confidence, such as "I've landed all of my jumps in practice and I can land them all here. I'll focus on the things that I do when I'm skating well, and I'll take it one step at a time. I'll smile, have fun, and play to the judges." The psychologist might also encourage the skater to practice a relaxation technique called *deep center breathing,* in which she breathes low down in her abdomen, and quietly says, "r-e-l-a-x" each time she exhales. In other words, because of our various learning experiences over many years and because our behavior of responding to certain stimuli has been reinforced, those stimuli (people,

215

places, words, smells, sounds, etc.) are likely to exert control over our behavior when they are introduced. Before designing a behavior modification program, it's important to ask, "Can I capitalize on existing forms of stimulus control?" Treatment packages that do so fall into the categories of rules, goals, modeling, physical guidance, and situational inducement. We discuss the first two categories in this chapter and the others in the next chapter.

RULES

As described in Chapter 8, a **rule** is a description (oral or written) of a three-term contingency of reinforcement (antecedents–behavior–consequences). Speaking loosely, it is a statement that a specific behavior will pay off in a particular situation. When we were infants, rules were meaningless to us. As we grew older, however, we learned that following rules often led to rewards (e.g., "If you eat all your vegetables, you can have dessert.") or enabled us to avoid punishers (e.g., "If you don't be quiet, I'll send you to your room."). Thus, a rule can function as an S^D—a cue that emitting the behavior specified by the rule will lead to the reinforcer identified in the rule, or a cue that not following the rule will lead to a punisher (Skinner, 1969; Vaughan, 1989). (As described in Chapter 19, rules can also function as motivating operations.)

Sometimes rules clearly identify reinforcers or punishers associated with following the rules, as illustrated in the above examples. In other cases, consequences are implied. When a parent says to a child in an excited voice, "Wow! Would you look at that!", looking in the indicated direction will likely enable the child to see something interesting. Reinforcers are also implied for rules stated in the form of advice. For example, the advice, "You should get a good education," typically implies that doing so will lead to a well-paying job. On the other hand, rules given in the form of a *command* or a *threat* imply that noncompliance will be punished. For example, the command, "Don't touch that vase," implies that touching it will lead to unpleasantness (such as a reprimand).

Rules that do not identify all three aspects of a contingency of reinforcement might be referred to as *partial rules*. The examples of the partial rules in the preceding paragraph focused on the behavior. Other partial rules identify the antecedent (e.g., "school zone"), while the behavior ("drive slowly") and the consequences ("to avoid a speeding ticket") are implied. In other instances, partial rules identify the consequences (e.g., "98% payout"), while the antecedents ("at our casino") and the behavior ("put money in our slot machines") are implied. Because of our various learning experiences, partial rules also control our behavior.

Contingency-Shaped Versus Rule-Governed Behavior

Suppose that little Bobby whispers something funny to his sister while attending church with their parents. Bobby's sister ignores him (and his mom gives his hand a firm squeeze), and in the future, Bobby is less likely to whisper funny comments in church. Now suppose that Bobby whispers funny comments to his teammates on the pee-wee hockey team while his coach is trying to explain how to execute a play. Bobby's teammates laugh, and his whispering is strengthened in that setting. In these examples, we would refer to Bobby's whispering as *contingency-shaped behavior*—behavior that has been strengthened (or weakened) in settings by the direct-acting effects of consequences in those settings. Now let's suppose that Bobby's coach, wanting to decrease Bobby's disruptive whispering, says to Bobby at the start of a practice, "If you listen carefully and don't whisper when I'm talking to the team, we'll have an extra five minutes of scrimmage at the end of practice." During the practice, Bobby frequently repeats the rule, makes it through the practice without whispering, and he and the team earn the reinforcer. In this example, listening attentively to the coach without whispering would be referred to as *rule-governed behavior*—behavior that is controlled by the statement of a rule.

Contingency-shaped behavior involves immediate consequences and is typically strengthened gradually through trial and error. Bobby's whispering, for example, initially came under the control of his teammates at hockey practice as S^Ds through several trials involving immediate reinforcement for whispering. His whispering gradually decreased in the presence of his sister and parents at church as S^Δs as a result of several trials of extinction in their presence. Rule-governed behavior, on the other hand, often involves delayed consequences, and frequently leads to immediate behavior change. When Bobby's coach gave him a rule concerning not whispering at practices, Bobby's behavior improved immediately. It did not take a few trials to show evidence of stimulus control, even though the reinforcer for following the rule was delayed until the end of practice.

Knowledge of rule-governed behavior enables us to more fully explain some applications we presented earlier that involved indirect-acting effects of reinforcers. You may recall the case of Fernando in Chapter 3. When Fernando was told that he would be given a slip of paper that could be exchanged for 2 pesos immediately contingent upon arriving to work on time, he was never again late for work through the duration of the study. This was not an example of the direct-acting effects of reinforcement, because the reinforcer of 2 pesos occurred well after the behavior of leaving earlier for work. Instead, it was likely Fernando's rehearsal of a rule (e.g., "If I leave earlier, I will arrive on time and I can earn 2 extra pesos") that controlled the rule-following behavior of leaving a half-hour earlier in the morning. You might also remember the example in Chapter 4 of Coach Dawson's point program at basketball practices. Because they were not awarded to the players until the end of a practice, points were delayed considerably following various behaviors (such as improved shooting percentages) that had occurred earlier in that practice. Thus, the improved performance was not due to the direct-acting effects of the points as conditioned reinforcers. The players likely verbally rehearsed rules during practices, such as "If I make more jump shots, I'll earn more points," and such self-statements may have exerted rule-governed control over the improved performance.

Often, behavior that might seem to be strengthened by the direct-acting effects of reinforcement may result, at least partly, from the existence of rule-governed behavior. For example, the child who has just cleaned her room and is told, "Good girl for cleaning your room," may tend to engage in this behavior more frequently. The stimulus "Good girl for cleaning your room" seems to be acting as a reinforcer in this instance. But the child has also been given a rule—namely, "If I clean my room, I'll be a good girl" (and Mom and Dad will be nicer to me, etc.)—which tends to exert rule-governed control over the room-cleaning behavior in the future, quite apart from the reinforcing effect of praise. (This is one reason why we would not use "Good girl for cleaning your room" as a reinforcer for the child doing her homework!)

When Rules Are Especially Helpful

We have argued in several chapters that behavior modification programs should always include instruction in the form of rules, even with individuals with limited verbal skills. And in Chapter 30, we discuss ethical reasons why behavior modification programs should be clearly explained to all clients. However, there are some specific situations with verbal people when including rules in a behavior modification program is especially effective (Baldwin & Baldwin, 1998; Skinner, 1969, 1974).

When Rapid Behavior Change Is Desirable   Correct use of rules can often produce behavior change much more rapidly than shaping, chaining, or trial-and-error experiences with reinforcement and extinction. In the example of the sport psychologist attempting to help the figure skater, the skater was essentially given a rule (i.e., "If I focus on the things that I think about when I'm skating well at a practice, then I'll land all the elements in my program, just like I do at practice."). Rehearsing the rule might have helped the skater to focus on the cues that normally enable her to land her jumps, rather than worrying about falling. The rule might also have functioned as a conditioned stimulus to elicit the relaxed feelings that were typically experienced at practices (and which may be a part of the contextual stimuli that control good skating).

When Consequences Are Delayed   Suppose that a parent wants to encourage a child to study for an hour or so each evening during the week. A suitable reinforcer might be allowing the child to stay up late on the weekend to watch a movie. However, movie watching on Friday night is long delayed from studying for an hour on Monday. By adding the rule, "If you study for an hour each night this week, you can watch the late movie on Friday night," the parent has increased the chances of the delayed reinforcer having an indirect-acting effect on the desired behavior.

When Natural Reinforcers Are Highly Intermittent   Suppose that the salespeople in a department store are working on a commission. During the post-Christmas season in recessionary times, sales are very slow. The salespeople are immediately reinforced when they make a sale (by the fact that the sale gives them more money), but they must approach a great many customers before a sale is made. In other words, the schedule of reinforcement is very lean, so that ratio strain may occur. The store manager might increase the persistence of the salespeople by encouraging them to rehearse the rule, "Be persistent! The very next customer might mean a sale."

When Behavior Will Lead to Immediate and Severe Punishment   Rules can help people learn appropriate behavior when learning "the hard way" can be extremely costly. For example, surprising though it may seem, some students are genuinely unaware that copying parts of a textbook word for word on a term paper without acknowledging the source is unacceptable. All students should be taught, long before they ever reach college, the rule: "Copying from a source without giving credit is plagiarism and can lead to serious academic penalty."

Why Rules Control Our Behavior

It's easy to understand why people would learn to follow rules that describe direct-acting consequences. Following the rule "Try this new flavor of ice cream, you'll love it" will be reinforced immediately by the taste of the ice cream. Failure to follow the rule "Move back from the campfire or you'll burn yourself" will likely lead to a fairly immediate punisher. *But why do we follow rules that identify very delayed consequences?* There are several possibilities. First, although the reinforcer identified in a rule might be delayed for an individual, other people might provide other immediate consequences if the individual follows (or does not follow) the rule. In the example of the parent who provides the rule, "If you study for an hour each night this week, you can watch the late movie on Friday night," the parent might also say, immediately after an instance of studying on Monday night, "Good for you. Keep it up and you'll be able to stay up late on Friday."

Second, an individual might follow a rule and then immediately make reinforcing statements to himself or herself. In the case of Fernando, after complying with the rule of leaving a half-hour earlier for work in the morning, he might have speculated about what he might buy with the extra pesos that he would earn. (Self-reinforcement is discussed further in Chapter 26.) Alternatively, failure to comply with a rule might lead to immediate self-punishment.

A third possibility is that our operant–respondent interactions (see Chapter 15) give us a reinforcement history such that following rules is automatically strengthened and failure to follow rules is automatically punished. Suppose you give yourself the rule, "I better start studying my behavior modification text now or I'll fail the exam tomorrow." Perhaps because of your history of being punished for failing to meet deadlines, such a statement may increase the aversiveness of stimuli associated with not studying for the exam, which would elicit some anxiety. When you comply with the rule your anxiety decreases and your rule following is maintained by escape conditioning. In everyday language, rehearsal of the deadline causes you to feel anxious and responding to the rule to meet the deadline then makes you feel a lot better (Malott, 1989). Of course, whether or not such automatic consequences will continue to influence your rule following will depend on the extent to which you continue to experience punishment for noncompliance with rules and failure to meet deadlines.

Although we have given many examples illustrating how rules generally enhance the development and maintenance of behavior, it is important to realize that there are exceptions to this generalization. Rules introduce extra stimuli and responses that, in some circumstances, can have the net effect of interfering with contingency-shaped behavior. A person trying to verbalize and follow rules may, in these circumstances, become somewhat like the proverbial centipede that got itself tied in knots trying to think about how it walked!

Effective and Ineffective Rules

We have said that a rule is a cue that behaving as specified in the rule will lead to a reinforcer or escape from or avoidance of an aversive stimulus. But all rules are not created equal. Many people, for example, might follow the rule, "Try this new flavor of ice cream; it's delicious." Fewer, unfortunately, are likely to follow the rule, "Always wear safety gear when rollerblading, in order to avoid serious injury from an accident." Let's look at five conditions that affect the likelihood of rule-following behavior.

Specific Versus Vague Descriptions of Behavior   A rule that describes behavior specifically is more likely to be followed than a rule that describes a behavior vaguely. Telling young figure skaters, for example, that they will become better skaters if they work hard at practices is less effective than telling them, "If you try to complete at least 60 jumps and spins during each 45-minute practice, you will become a better skater than if you complete fewer than that number."

Specific Versus Vague Descriptions of Circumstances   A rule that describes specific circumstances in which the behavior should occur is more likely to be followed than a rule that describes the circumstances vaguely or not at all. Telling a young child, for example, "Remember to say 'please'" is less effective than telling the child, "Remember to say 'please' when asking for something." Saying "Be good" is less effective (by itself) than saying, for example, "Do what Grandma tells you."

Probable Versus Improbable Consequences   Rules are likely to be followed if they identify behavior for which the consequences are highly probable, even though the consequences may be delayed. If a parent tells her teenage child, "If you mow the lawn on Monday, I'll give you $10 on Saturday," and assuming that that parent always follows up on such rules, then it is highly likely that the teenager will mow the lawn on Monday. If the teenager does so, receiving the $10 the following Saturday is a certainty. Conversely, rules are likely to be ineffective if they describe low-probability outcomes for behavior, even if those outcomes are immediate when they occur (Malott, 1989, 1992). To illustrate this point, most people know that wearing a lifejacket when canoeing could save their lives. And most people know that wearing a helmet when rollerblading could prevent brain damage from a serious accident. So why do many people go canoeing without a lifejacket or rollerblading without a helmet? One reason (that does not necessarily involve rules) may be that desirable safety behavior in such instances leads to fairly immediate punishers (e.g., the lifejacket and the helmet are hot and uncomfortable). Another reason is that such rules (i.e., to wear a lifejacket while canoeing and a helmet while rollerblading) involve low-probability consequences. Many people have gone canoeing without ever upsetting the canoe. And the rollerblader knows (depending on his or her skill) that an accident sufficient to cause brain damage is unlikely. We are not suggesting that rules should not be used in such situations. The rollerblader might be encouraged to rehearse, before rollerblading, "If I wear my safety gear, I can avoid the possibility of serious injury." However, for a rule to be effective when it describes improbable consequences, it may need to be supplemented by other behavior management strategies, such as modeling (see Chapter 18), self-monitoring (see Chapter 26), or behavioral contracting (see Chapter 26).

Figure 17–1   Why are some rules (such as "resisting extra dessert") so difficult to follow?

Sizeable Consequences Versus Small but Cumulatively Significant Consequences
Rules that describe sizeable consequences are likely to be effective. In the example
cited above involving $10 for mowing the lawn, $10 was a sizeable consequence for
that teenager. However, a rule is less likely to be effective if the consequence is quite
small following each instance of rule following. Suppose, for example, an individual
resolves, "I'm going to stop eating desserts" and "I'm going to exercise three times a
week." Why are such rules often ineffective? One reason (that does not necessarily
involve rules) is that there are direct-acting consequences that support behavior that
is incompatible with following the rule. Eating a dessert is immediately reinforced
by the delicious taste. And exercising often involves fairly immediate punishers
(getting hot, sweaty, and tired). Another reason that such rules are ineffective is that
the supportive consequences of a single instance of following such a rule are too
small to be noticeable, and are only cumulatively significant (Malott, 1989, 1992).
(Other possibilities are discussed in Chapter 26.) That is, it's not the excess weight
from the single extra dessert that's a problem; it's the increased weight that occurs
when you have the extra dessert on many occasions (see Figure 17–1). Likewise, a single instance of exercising won't produce observable benefits. It's the accumulation of
the benefits of exercising on many occasions that is eventually noticeable. Rules
that describe immediate, small consequences that are harmful or beneficial only
after they have accumulated (and therefore only after a long delay) are likely to
be ineffective unless complemented by some of the self-management strategies
described in Chapter 26.
Deadlines Versus No Deadlines   Suppose that a preschool teacher says to a child,
"If you put all the toys away, I'll bring you a treat next week." Is the child likely to
put the books away for such a delayed reinforcer? What if the teacher says to the
child, "If you put all the toys away *right now*, I'll bring you a treat next week."

Would specifying "right now" make a difference? Surprisingly, it would. Braam and Malott (1990) found that with 4-year-old children, rules to perform behavior with no deadline and a one-week delay of the reinforcer were relatively ineffective, while rules to perform behavior *with a deadline* and a one-week delay of a reinforcer were quite effective. Very early in life we learn that meeting deadlines is likely to be reinforced and failing to meet deadlines leads to unpleasantness.

Note 1   To summarize, *rules that describe **specific circumstances** and **deadlines** for specific behavior that will lead to **sizeable** and **probable outcomes** are often effective, even when the outcomes are delayed. Conversely, rules that describe behavior and the circumstances for it vaguely, that do not identify a deadline for the behavior, and that lead to small or improbable consequences for the behavior are often ineffective.*

Guidelines for Using Rules Effectively

Here are some general guidelines for the effective use of rules.

1. The rules should be within the understanding of the individual to whom they are applied.
2. Rules should clearly identify:
   a. the circumstances in which the behavior should occur;
   b. the specific behavior in which the individual is to engage;
   c. a deadline for performing the behavior;
   d. the specific consequences involved in complying with the rule; and/or
   e. the specific consequences for not complying with the rule.
3. Rules should describe probable and sizeable outcomes, rather than improbable and small outcomes. (Rules that describe improbable and/or small consequences may need to be supplemented by some of the procedures described in Chapter 26.)
4. Complex rules should be broken into easy-to-follow steps.
5. Rules should be delivered in a pleasant, courteous manner.
6. Fading of rules should be used as necessary to allow other stimuli that are present to take control of the behavior.

GOALS

In industrial and organizational settings, goal-setting programs have led to improved performance in such areas as truck loading, safety behavior, customer service, and typing (Locke & Latham, 1990). In sports, goal-setting programs have led to improvements in such areas as laps completed in running, foul shots in basketball, serves in tennis, and accuracy in archery (Gould, 1998). In general, a *goal* describes a level of performance toward which an individual or group should work.

In everyday language, goals are considered to be motivational (discussed further in Chapter 19). They are seen as committing one to the effort and dedication that is necessary to achieve success; they give one a sense of purpose and help to keep one on target. From a behavioral perspective, however, a goal might be considered as a rule. For example, if a basketball player says, "I'll go to the gym and practice shooting foul shots until I can make 10 in a row," that player has identified the circumstances (at the gym), the behavior (practicing foul shots), and the reinforcer (making 10 in a row, plus the implied reinforcer of scoring a higher percentage of foul shots in games). And like the use of rules, goal setting is often applied to influence individuals to improve performance where reinforcers are delayed (a bonus in a work setting is received well after the work has been completed) or are immediate but highly intermittent (the basketball player might initially make only one out of every 30 foul shots).

Although goal setting might be viewed as use of rules, the circumstances in which one might apply goal setting are often somewhat different than those described at the beginning of this chapter. We previously suggested that it is possible to capitalize on stimulus control by using rules to bring about instant behavior change. The sport psychologist, for example, was concerned with helping the figure skater "on the spot." Goal setting, in contrast, is often used to influence individuals to work toward some objective over a period of time or during a number of practice opportunities. We wouldn't expect the basketball player to immediately meet the goal of making 10 foul shots in a row. Nevertheless, setting a practice goal in that type of situation is likely to lead to faster performance improvement than if the player just practiced shooting foul shots without a particular goal in mind.

Effective and Ineffective Goal Setting

The efficacy of goal setting as a performance improvement strategy is well established, provided that a number of conditions are met (Gould, 1998). We may distinguish two types of goals: behavior and the products or outcomes of behavior. Examples of the former would be eating a healthier diet and exercising more. An example of the latter would be losing 10 pounds.

Specific Goals Are More Effective Than Vague Goals Rather than a goal of "having a better relationship," a couple might agree to spend a half-hour of quality time together (such as going for a walk), telling each other on a daily basis at least three things that they appreciate about their relationship, and sharing equally the responsibility of how to spend their money. It would be more effective for an individual considering dieting to say that he wants to lose 10 pounds rather than saying that he wants to "lose some weight." As another example, saying that you want to save a specific percentage of your take-home pay might be more effective than the goal of "wanting to save some money."

Goals with Respect to Learning of Specific Skills Should Include Mastery Criteria A *mastery criterion* is a specific guideline for performing a skill such that if the guideline is met, the skill is likely to be mastered. This means that if an individual has met a mastery criterion for a skill, he or she has learned the skill well enough so that, if asked to do it sometime later, the skill would likely be performed correctly. Examples of mastery criteria for learning athletic skills might include making six 4-foot putts in a row in golf, hitting 10 backhands in a row down the line in tennis, making 10 foul shots in a row in basketball, or hitting five curveballs in a row out of the infield in baseball. An example of a mastery criterion for an academic skill might be reciting the Periodic Table or a Shakespearian sonnet five times in a row without making a mistake.

Goals Should Identify the Circumstances Under Which the Desirable Behavior Should Occur   A goal for a wrestler to "practice take-downs" is somewhat vague. A goal to "practice arm-drag take-downs until three in a row occur" adds a quantity dimension but still does not indicate the circumstances under which the behavior should occur. A goal to "practice arm-drag take-downs until three in a row occur on an opponent offering moderate resistance" identifies the circumstances surrounding the performance. Similarly, a goal to give a talk to an audience of 30 strangers is different from a goal to give the same talk to two friends.

Realistic, Challenging Goals Are More Effective Than "Do Your Best" Goals   The phrase "Just do your best" is often spoken by coaches to young athletes just before a competition, by parents to their children who are about to perform in a concert, by teachers to students before tests are presented, and by employers to employees doing their jobs. A number of studies, however, have demonstrated that "do your best" goals are not nearly as effective as are specific goals for improving performance. Perhaps "do your best" goals are ineffective because they are vague. Or perhaps individuals who are instructed to simply "do their best" set relatively easy goals, and, as suggested by Locke and Latham (1990), difficult or challenging goals may produce better performance. From a behavioral perspective, we might assume that a behavior modifier who identifies a specific goal for a learner is more likely to consistently provide backup reinforcers for meeting the goal than when the goal for the learner is simply to "do your best." The reason for this is that the behavior modifier and the learner might disagree as to whether or not the learner did his or her best. After all, the judgment of whether a goal is easy or difficult is somewhat subjective, given that our information about someone's physiological and behavioral capabilities is always incomplete. The accuracy of that judgment might be maximized, however, by considering the individual's current level of performance and the range of performance on similar tasks by others of similar ability.

Public Goals Are More Effective Than Private Goals   Consider the following experiment with three groups of students who were all given the same booklet of material to study. The first group of students participated in a public goal-setting program. Each student set a goal concerning the amount he or she would study and the score that the student hoped to receive on a test to be given at the end of the program. These students announced their goals to other members of their group. The second group of students practiced private goal setting. They were treated the same as the first group except that they kept their goals to themselves. The third group of students was not asked to set any goals. They were a control group who were simply given the material to study for the same amount of time as the first group, with the knowledge that they would receive a test at the end of the experiment. The results: the public goal-setting group scored an average of 17 percentage points higher on the test than either of the other two groups, who performed about the same (Hayes et al., 1985). Similar results on the effects of public goals versus private goals were found by Seigts, Meertens, and Kok (1997). Hayes and colleagues theorized that setting a public goal results in a public standard against which performance can be evaluated, and that it implies social consequences for achieving or not achieving the goal(s).

Although goals that someone else knows about may be more likely to be met than private goals that nobody knows about, the public component must be practiced with some caution. Suppose that you recommend goal setting as a part of a behavior modification program to help someone exercise consistently. If you recommend that the exerciser share the goals with another person, that person should be someone who is likely to prompt the exerciser with gentle reminders when goals are not met, and who will offer encouragement when progress is satisfactory. That person should not be someone who will send the exerciser on a heavy guilt trip for not meeting the goals. (This issue is discussed further in Chapter 30.)

Goal Setting Is More Effective if Deadlines Are Included   We all have a history of being reinforced for meeting various deadlines and for encountering aversiveness when deadlines are not met. Capitalizing on this history increases the effectiveness of goal setting. Suppose that you set a goal for yourself during the coming year of emailing friends and relatives more often. You are more likely to meet that goal if you resolve that by February 1, you'll have emailed specific individuals, by March 1 you'll have emailed so many more, and so on.

Goal Setting Plus Feedback Is More Effective Than Goal Setting Alone   Goals are more likely to be met if feedback indicates degree of progress toward the goal. One way of providing feedback is to chart the progress being made. As discussed in Chapter 20, individuals who chart their progress toward a goal are likely to find improvements in the chart to be reinforcing. Another way of providing feedback is to break long-term goals into a number of short-term goals. Suppose that a couple decides to repaint their entire house, inside and out. Short-term goals might include painting the bedroom by the end of February, then the living room by a certain date, and then the kitchen, and so on.

Goal Setting Is Most Effective When Individuals Are Committed to the Goals
Goals are likely to be effective only if there is a continuing commitment to them by the individuals involved. By commitment, we mean statements or actions by the learner that indicate the goal is important, that he or she will work toward it, and that he or she recognize the benefits of doing so. One way of gaining commitment is to have the learner participate in the goal-setting process. Research indicates that self-selected goals are at least as effective as those that are externally imposed (Fellner & Sulzer-Azaroff, 1984).

Guidelines for Goal Setting

Many individuals attempt to capitalize on goal setting with their annual New Year's resolutions. However, there are clearly some ways of setting goals that are more effective than others for influencing behavior. If, for example, goals are quite vague or are a "do your best" resolution, with no deadlines or timelines for meeting them, and without a feedback mechanism for monitoring progress, then they are not likely to have much effect on behavior. If, on the other hand, you practice goal setting according to the following guidelines, then your goals are likely to be a useful tactic to modify behavior.

1. Set goals that are specific, realistic, and challenging.
2. Identify the specific behaviors and the circumstances in which they should occur in order to meet the goals.

3. Be clear about the specific consequences that might occur for meeting or not meeting the goal.
4. Break long-term goals into several short-term goals.
5. If the goal is complex, devise an action plan for meeting it.
6. Set deadlines for goal attainment.
7. Ensure that individuals involved are committed to the goals.
8. Encourage the learner to share the goals with a friendly supporter.
9. Design a system for monitoring progress toward goals.
10. Provide positive feedback as progress toward goals is achieved.

STUDY QUESTIONS

1. What basic procedures discussed in Chapters 3 through 15 of this text might be used to
   a. increase an infrequent behavior?
   b. decrease an excessive behavior?
   c. develop a behavior or behavioral sequence that never occurs?
   d. get a desired behavior to occur in the presence of appropriate stimuli?
2. Define a rule and give an example.
3. A teacher of a second-grade class complains to you, "When I tell the children to stay at their desks and work, they never listen to me." Describe the contingencies that are likely operating with respect to that rule given by the teacher to the kids in the class.
4. Describe an example of a partial rule that is not in this chapter. What aspects of the three-term contingency does your partial rule identify? What are the missing parts that are implied by the partial rule?
5. Define contingency-shaped behavior and give an example.
6. Define rule-governed behavior and give an example.
7. Describe two common differences between rule-governed and contingency-shaped behavior.
8. Give two examples of direct-acting and two examples of indirect-acting reinforcers on your behavior.
9. Using examples, briefly describe four situations in which the addition of rules to a behavior modification program might be especially helpful.
10. Describe, using examples, three explanations for why we might follow rules that identify very delayed consequences.
11. Explain (in terms of contextual stimulus control, as described in Note 3 of Chapter 8) why the tone of voice of someone giving you instructions might determine whether or not you will follow the instructions.
12. How might we explain the behavior of someone who fails to wear a helmet when riding a bicycle even though that person knows that wearing a helmet could prevent brain damage from an accident?
13. How might we account for the relative ineffectiveness of such rules as "I need to go on a diet" or "I'll floss my teeth after every meal"?
14. In a couple of sentences, distinguish between rules that are often effective versus rules that are often ineffective in controlling behavior.
15. In general, what do we mean by a goal? Describe an example.
16. Is goal setting different from using rules? Discuss.
17. Briefly list six conditions that summarize effective versus ineffective goal setting as a behavior modification strategy.

18. From a behavioral perspective, why might realistic, challenging goals be more effective than "do your best" goals?

19. From a behavioral perspective, why might public goals be more effective than private goals?

APPLICATION EXERCISES

A. Exercises Involving Others

1. Choose a behavior that a parent might want to change in a child, such that there is no obvious immediate, natural reinforcer for that behavior. Describe how the parent, following the guidelines for using rules effectively, might capitalize on rule-governed behavior to bring about a desired outcome.

2. Consider a practice setting for a youth sport with which you are familiar. Describe how a coach might use goal setting to influence desirable practice behavior of an athlete in that setting. Indicate how the coach has followed the guidelines for goal setting.

B. Self-Modification Exercises

1. Consider the guidelines for using rules effectively. Now consider a behavior of yours that you have not emitted but that you would like to perform, or a behavior of yours that someone else would like you to emit, but that has not been occurring. Describe how rules might be used effectively to influence you to emit that behavior. (Identify a rule with respect to that behavior, and structure the contingencies according to the guidelines for using rules effectively.)

2. Identify a behavior of yours that was probably contingency shaped. It might be something like riding a bicycle, balancing on one foot, eating with a knife and fork or chopsticks, whistling a short tune, or flipping flapjacks. Devise a measure (e.g., number of errors) of how well you perform the behavior, and using the measure, record your performance of the behavior on several trials. Next write out a set of rules for performing the behavior, and again perform and record the behavior on several occasions, carefully following the rules. According to your measure, how did the addition of rules affect your performance? Interpret your finding.

NOTE AND EXTENDED DISCUSSION

1. Do you suffer from insomnia? Many people do. For persons who suffer from insomnia, one option is to treat the problem with drugs. Another option is sometimes referred to as behavioral sleep therapy, and it relies on rule-governed control over behavior (Smith et al., 2002). Behavioral sleep therapy includes the following rules: (1) Exercise regularly, but not in the late evening; (2) relax before bedtime; (3) don't consume caffeine or alcohol late in the evening; (4) go to bed only when you are feeling sleepy; (5) if sleep has not occurred within 10 minutes, leave the bedroom and read a book until you feel sleepy; (6) avoid nonsleep activities in bed; (7) get up at the same time each morning, regardless of the time that you go to bed. In a review of 21 studies of a total of 470 participants with insomnia, behavioral sleep therapy was more effective than pharmacological treatment on all measures. This shows that behavior therapy should be a first-line treatment for chronic insomnia.

Study Question on Note

1. List five rules that are a part of behavioral sleep therapy.

18

Capitalizing on Existing Stimulus Control: Modeling, Guidance, and Situational Inducement

As we indicated in the previous chapter, behavior modification programs should include instruction in the form of rules that can be followed easily. Sometimes, however, it is good to *model* the desired behavior in addition to telling a person what is expected. And if "show-and-tell" (i.e., modeling and instructing) are not enough, you may need to *physically guide* the learner through the desired actions on a few trials, and/or *rearrange the environment* to make a desired behavior more likely to occur. This chapter describes these additional strategies for capitalizing on existing forms of stimulus control.

MODELING

Modeling is a procedure whereby a sample of a given behavior is presented to an individual to induce that individual to engage in a similar behavior. As is true for rules, modeling can be quite powerful. You may convince yourself of this by performing the following simple experiments:

1. For an entire day, speak only in a whisper, and note how often people around you also whisper (this is a good experiment to try when you have laryngitis).
2. Yawn conspicuously in the presence of other people, and note their frequency of yawning.
3. Stand looking at the sky for an hour, and note how many people stop and also look at the sky.

In each case, compare the data obtained with data obtained under comparable circumstances when the behavior is not being modeled.

As with rules, modeling is in such common use by the general public that few people (other than behavior modifiers) think of it as a behavior modification procedure. Parents, for example, use it rather unsystematically, but quite effectively in many cases, to teach politeness, caring, language, and many other behaviors to their children (sometimes unintentionally). When a dog walks by a parent and a 2-year-old child, the parent might say, "Look at the doggie. Can you say 'doggie'?" Or when teaching a child how to make a sandwich, a parent might say "Do it this way" while modeling the desired behavior. Modeling affects the behavior of individuals of all ages, not just young children. When teenagers first enter high school they see how the older kids dress and talk, and the younger students are soon dressing the same way and using the same expressions. Neither of the authors can ever remember the day for garbage pickup with the rotating schedule in their neighborhood. We simply imitate the behavior of our neighbors, who always have their garbage placed at the curb at the appropriate time on the scheduled day. All of us in our daily lives have frequent opportunities to observe the actions of others, and we frequently imitate their behaviors.

Note 1   What determines whether or not we will imitate the behavior of a model? Although there are several possible explanations, clearly our history of being reinforced (or punished) for imitating others is an important factor. And because each of us has had different experiences, we expect that the specific factors that determine which modeled behaviors might serve as cues for imitation vary somewhat from person to person. Nevertheless, there are several factors that are likely to influence the effectiveness of modeling as a behavior modification technique for most people (Bandura, 1986).

Arrange for Peers to Be Models   People are more likely to imitate someone who is similar to them in various ways (age, socioeconomic status, physical appearance, etc.) than someone who is quite different from them. Friends and peers are more likely to be imitated than are strangers or individuals outside one's peer group. This is especially true for children. Thus, whenever possible, use peers as models in your behavior modification programs. Consider the case of an extremely withdrawn nursery school child who almost never interacts with other children. This behavior problem could be treated with shaping. A method that can perhaps produce faster results, however, is to have the child observe several instances of another child joining in the activities of a group of children. The group should be responding to the model in a reinforcing manner (e.g., by offering her play material, talking to her, and smiling). To ensure that the modeling occurs under opportune circumstances and in a suitable fashion, it may be necessary to instruct certain children to perform as models and to instruct the children in the group to behave in a conspicuously reinforcing manner to the models. It is sometimes convenient and effective to videotape a number of such episodes for viewing by socially withdrawn children (see O'Connor, 1969). The presentation of modeling scenes through film, videotape, and other media is called *symbolic modeling*. Studies show that this type of modeling can sometimes be as effective as the real thing.

Show the Behavior and Its Effects   Suppose that you want to improve your debating skills. Are you more likely to imitate the discussion strategies of friends who consistently get their points across, or friends who consistently lose arguments? Clearly, the perceived competence of the model in obtaining desired consequences is a factor that determines the effectiveness of modeling as a behavior modification technique. Even with children, peers who are more proficient at obtaining consequences for various behaviors are more likely to be imitated than are those who are less proficient (Schunk, 1987). To capitalize on this factor when using modeling in your behavior modification program, arrange for the learner to observe the model, emit the desired behavior, and receive a reinforcer.

Studies in social psychology have indicated that high-status and highly prestigious persons are more likely to be imitated than individuals of lower status or prestige. This might be interpreted as a subcategory of the competence factor. A popular teenager is likely to be imitated by peers because he or she is frequently observed receiving positive consequences for various behaviors.

Use Multiple Models   Sarah, a 35-year-old real estate salesperson and part-time student, drank beer regularly with six other women at a small local tavern on Friday afternoons. All of them were taking a course on behavior modification, but Sarah was unaware that her own drinking behavior was being studied. During several sessions of baseline, she invariably drank about 72 ounces of beer in an hour. During the first experimental phase, one of the other women modeled a drinking rate of half that. Sarah's drinking was not affected. Similarly, her drinking was unaffected when two of the other women modeled drinking rates exactly half of hers. However, when four other women modeled drinking rates that were half of Sarah's, her drinking rate was also cut in half (DeRicco & Niemann, 1980). Clearly, the number of persons modeling a particular behavior is a factor in determining whether or not that behavior will be imitated.

Combine Modeling with Rules   With verbal people, modeling is likely to be most effective when combined with rules and other behavioral strategies.

The following excerpt from a therapy session illustrates this (Masters, Burrish, Hollon, & Rimm, 1987, pp. 100–101). The client being treated was a male college student who had difficulty asking out a date. In the excerpt, the client is rehearsing asking out a date. Note how the therapist combines instruction and shaping with modeling.

Client: By the way (*pause*) I don't suppose you want to go out Saturday night?

Therapist: Up to actually asking for the date, you were very good. However, if I were the woman, I think I might have been a bit offended when you said, "By the way." It's like your asking her out is pretty casual. Also, the way you phrased the question, you are kind of suggesting to her that she doesn't want to go out with you. Pretend for the moment I'm you. Now, how does this sound: "There's a movie at the Varsity Theater this Saturday that I want to see. If you don't have other plans, I'd very much like you to go with me."

Client: That sounded good. Like you were sure of yourself and liked the woman too.

Therapist: Why don't you try it?

Client: You know that movie at the Varsity? Well, I'd like to go, and I'd like you to go with me on Saturday, if you don't have anything better to do.

> *Therapist:*   Well, that certainly was better. Your tone of voice was especially good. But the last line, "if you don't have anything better to do," sounded like you don't think you have much to offer. Why not run through it one more time?
>
> *Client:*   I'd like to see the show at the Varsity, Saturday, and, if you haven't made other plans, I'd like you to go with me.
>
> *Therapist:*   Much better. Excellent, in fact. You were confident, forceful, and sincere.

This example also illustrates a technique referred to as **behavioral rehearsal** or **role rehearsal,** in which a client practices particular behaviors (i.e., plays a role) in a practice setting to increase the likelihood that those behaviors will occur appropriately in the real world. In the above example, the client rehearsed asking for a date. A combination of instructions, modeling, behavioral rehearsal, and consequence management has been used to enhance performance in a variety of areas, such as social skills training (Huang & Cuvo, 1997), assertion training (Schroeder & Black, 1985), and anger management training (Larkin & Zayfert, 1996).

Guidelines for Using Modeling

Here are some general guidelines for the effective use of modeling.

1. If possible, select models who are friends or peers of the client and who are seen as competent individuals with status or prestige.
2. If possible, use more than one model.
3. The complexity of the modeled behavior should be suitable for the behavioral level of the learner.
4. Combine rules with modeling.
5. Have the learner watch the model perform the behavior and be reinforced (preferably by natural reinforcers).
6. If possible, design the training so that correct imitation of the modeled behavior will lead to a natural reinforcer for the learner. If this is not possible, arrange for reinforcement for correct imitation of the modeled behavior.
7. If the behavior is quite complex, then the modeling episode should be sequenced from very easy to more difficult approximations for the learner.
8. To enhance stimulus generalization, the modeling scenes should be as realistic as possible.
9. Use fading as necessary so that stimuli other than the model can take control over the desired behavior.

PHYSICAL GUIDANCE

Physical guidance is the application of physical contact to induce an individual to go through the motions of the desired behavior. Some familiar examples are a dance instructor leading a pupil through a new dance step, a golf instructor grasping the novice's arms and moving them through the proper swing, and a parent holding a child's hand while teaching her to cross the street safely. Guidance is always only one component of a teaching procedure. Both the dance instructor and the golf instructor will also use instruction (they will tell the student what to do and give pointers), modeling (they will demonstrate the appropriate physical postures and motions), and reinforcement for correct responses or approximations to them (such as "Excellent!" or "Much better!"). Likewise, the parent teaching her child to cross the street safely will use rules (e.g., by saying, "Look both ways") and modeling (by looking both ways in an exaggerated manner).

Some uses of guidance in behavior modification programs were given in Chapter 9—for example, using guidance and fading to teach a child to touch his head upon request. Guidance is generally used as an aide in teaching individuals to follow instructions or imitate a modeled behavior, so that instruction and/or modeling can then be used (without guidance) to establish other behaviors. For example, in one procedure for teaching instruction following, a child is placed in a chair opposite the teacher. At the beginning of a trial the teacher says, "Johnny, stand up," and then lifts the child onto his feet. Reinforcement is then presented immediately, as though the child himself had performed the response. Next, the teacher says, "Johnny, sit down," and, grasping the child's shoulders, the teacher gently but firmly presses him down on the chair. Again, immediate reinforcement is presented. The process is repeated over trials while guidance is faded out (see Kazdin & Erickson, 1975.) After this set of instructions is learned, the behavior modifier teaches another set (such as "Come here" and "Go there") using a similar procedure. Less and less guidance may be required to teach successive instruction following until eventually even fairly complex instruction following can be taught with little or no guidance.

As in teaching instruction following, the teacher who uses guidance to teach model imitation to a child starts with a few simple imitations (such as touching one's head, clapping one's hands, tapping the table, standing up, and sitting down) and adds new imitations as the previous ones are learned. Each time, the teacher says "Do this" while modeling the response and guiding the child to perform the response. Correct responses are reinforced and guidance is faded out over trials. This facilitates the development of **generalized imitation**, whereby an individual, after learning to imitate a number of behaviors (perhaps with some shaping, fading, guidance, and reinforcement), learns to imitate a new response on the first trial without reinforcement (Baer, Peterson, & Sherman, 1967).

Another common application of guidance is in helping individuals to overcome fears. Helping a person who is terrified of water might involve gradually leading her by the hand into the shallow end of a swimming pool and supporting her while she floats. The least fear-provoking aspects of a situation should be introduced first, and the more fear-provoking aspects later in a very gradual manner. One should never try to force an individual to do more than she feels comfortable doing. The more fearful the person is, the more gradual the process should be. In the case of a very fearful individual, one may have to spend many sessions simply sitting with her on the edge of the pool. (Use of modeling and other procedures to help a client overcome extreme fears is discussed further in Chapter 28.)

Guidelines for Using Physical Guidance

Some general guidelines for the effective use of guidance are as follows.

1. Make sure that the learner is comfortable and relaxed while being touched and guided. Some initial relaxation training may be necessary to accomplish this. Also, as indicated in Chapter 9, if the learner resists being guided, then, by definition, physical guidance would be considered a restrictive procedure, and it may be necessary to obtain ethical review and approval for you to proceed. In addition, one should obtain permission from a client before touching him or her.
2. Determine the stimuli that you want to control the behavior so that they can be conspicuously present during guidance.
3. Consider using rules or cue words during guidance so that they may eventually control the behavior. When teaching a novice right-handed golfer the proper shoulder turn during a golf swing, for example, the instructor might say the cue words, "Left shoulder to chin, right shoulder to chin," while guiding the novice through the backswing and the downswing.
4. Reinforcement should be given immediately after the successful completion of the guided response.
5. Guidance should be sequenced gradually from very easy to more difficult behavior for the learner.
6. Use fading as necessary so that other stimuli can take control over the behavior.

SITUATIONAL INDUCEMENT

Largely because of our similar histories of reinforcement and punishment, there are numerous situations and occasions in our society that control similar behavior in many of us. The interiors of certain public buildings, such as churches, museums, and libraries, tend to suppress loud talking. Parties tend to evoke socializing and jovial, carefree behavior. Catchy melodies prompt humming and singing, and strident march music tends to incite participation in a foot-stamping parade. Laugh tracks in TV situation comedies induce many people to continue watching these sitcoms. The assorted stimuli associated with Christmas induce cheerfulness, friendliness, and gift buying.

The term *situational inducement* refers to influencing a behavior by using situations and occasions that already exert control over the behavior. Such techniques, like others we have discussed, no doubt predate recorded history. Ceremonious gatherings involving singing and dancing probably served to strengthen a sense of community in ancient tribes, just as they do today in almost all cultures. Monasteries and convents have been used for centuries to promote asexual religious behavior by providing an environment conducive to reading religious texts and meditating and by restricting opportunities for the sexes to interact.

Supermarkets and department stores use many situational features to induce buying. Among these are the attention-evoking manner in which the products are displayed and pictures showing the products in an attractive way. Fine restaurants provide a relaxing atmosphere to induce leisurely enjoyment of a full-course meal.

If the restaurant becomes crowded and people are waiting for tables, fast music may be played to induce rapid eating.

Examples of situational inducement can also be found in the home. Many people prominently display items such as interesting *objets d'art,* a fancy computer or home entertainment system, and even unusual pets, that they have acquired partly to stimulate conversation when guests arrive. If a guest seems about to mishandle one of these conversation pieces, the host may use situational inducement by handing the potential offender a drink.

Situational inducement has been used in a number of imaginative and effective ways in behavior modification programs to help increase or decrease target behaviors, or to bring them under appropriate stimulus control. Examples can be discussed conveniently under four somewhat overlapping categories: (a) rearranging the existing surroundings, (b) moving the activity to a new location, (c) relocating people, and (d) changing the time of the activity.

Rearranging the Surroundings

An interesting example in the first category occurred in a case reported by the pioneering behaviorist Israel Goldiamond (1965). Goldiamond was consulted by a married couple who were having a problem in their relationship.[1] When the couple were together in the house, the husband could not refrain from screaming at his wife over her once having gone to bed with his best friend. One of the goals that was decided upon, therefore, was to replace screaming with civilized conversational behavior. Goldiamond reasoned that the husband's screaming had probably come under the control of the S^Ds in the home environment and that one way in which to weaken the behavior in that situation would be to change those S^Ds. He therefore instructed the couple to rearrange the rooms and furniture in the house to make it appear considerably different. The wife went one step further and bought herself a new outfit. Goldiamond then provided for the reinforcement of civilized conversation in the presence of these new cues that were not associated so strongly with screaming (how he did this is explained more fully in the next section). It was important to do this as quickly as possible, because if screaming occurred too often in the presence of the new S^Ds, it would become conditioned to them just as it had been conditioned to the old S^Ds.

Another example of rearranging the surroundings is altering the furniture and other items in one's room to promote better and more persistent studying behavior. One might, for example, improve the lighting, clear one's desk of irrelevant material, move the bed as far as possible from the desk, and have the desk facing away from the bed. Better yet, if possible, one should not even have the bed in the same room as the desk because the bed is an S^D for sleeping. To prevent nonstudy behaviors from being conditioned to the new stimuli, one should engage only in studying behavior in the rearranged environment (see Goldiamond, 1965).

Letter writing to people who don't use email is a behavior that is difficult to maintain because it involves a long delay of reinforcement (it takes at least several

---

[1]For additional discussion of behavior therapy for couples, see Chapter 28.

days to get a return letter). One way in which to strengthen your tendency to write, however, is to place before you a picture of the person to whom you are writing. This is another example of rearranging stimuli to control behavior.

Moving the Activity to a New Location

The second category of situational inducement is illustrated by another part of the procedure Goldiamond used in the case of the husband who screamed at his wife. The spouses were instructed that, immediately after rearranging the furniture in their home, they were to go to a place that would induce civilized conversation. It was hoped that this behavior would continue until they returned home, and would then come under the control of the new S^Ds in the home.

To quote from Goldiamond's report (1965, p. 856),

> Since it was impossible for [the husband] to converse in a civilized manner with his wife, we discussed a program of going to one evening spot on Monday, another on Tuesday, and another on Wednesday.
>
> "Oh," he said, "you want us to be together. We'll go bowling on Thursday."
>
> "On the contrary," I said, "I am interested in your subjecting yourself to an environment where civilized chit-chat is maintained. Such is not the case at a bowling alley."
>
> I also asked if there was any topic of conversation which once started would maintain itself. He commented on his mother-in-law's crazy ideas about farming. He was then given an index card and instructed to write "farm" on it and to attach some money to that card. The money was to be used to pay the waitress on Thursday, at which point he was to start the "farm" discussion which hopefully would continue into the taxi and home.

Changing the location of the activity is one approach to problems relating to studying (see Figure 18–1). The student using this approach should select a special place that is conducive to studying and that has distinctive stimuli that are not associated with any behavior other than studying. A reserved carrel in a university library is ideal for this purpose, although any other well-lit, quiet area with adequate working space would be suitable. Depending on the extent of appropriate study behavior in the student's repertoire, it may be necessary to combine relocating the activity with some of the basic procedures discussed in Part II of this text. For severe deficiencies, behavior incorporating good study skills should first be shaped and then placed on either a low-duration or a low-ratio schedule in the special studying area. The value of the schedule should then be increased gradually so that the behavior will eventually be maintained at the desired level. Appropriate reinforcement (such as coffee with a friend) should be arranged to occur immediately after the schedule requirement has been met. Should one experience a tendency to daydream or to engage in other nonstudy behavior while in the studying area, one should do a little more productive studying and then leave immediately so that daydreaming does not become conditioned to the stimuli in the studying area. Similarly, the husband in the case reported by Goldiamond was instructed to go to the garage and sit on a specially designated "sulking" stool whenever he was in the house and felt a tendency to sulk—this being a behavior that was threatening the recently strengthened conversational behavior after screaming had been eliminated.

Figure 18–1 An example of situational inducement.

Relocating People

The third category of situational inducement, relocating people, was not illustrated in Goldiamond's case study. The procedures used in that case were effective; therefore, a separation of the spouses was not necessary. Although relocating the participants is generally a measure of last resort when dealing with individuals who wish to maintain their respective relationships, it is sometimes the most practical tactic in other circumstances. If you just cannot get along with Sam Jones, and there is no particular reason for you to associate with him anyway, then why try to change his behavior or yours to make the two of you more compatible? Both of you will probably be happier respecting each other from a distance. Relocating people can also be used to bring about the opposite effect, that is, to bring people together. For example, getting dates is a problem for many college students. To deal with this problem, therapists often recommend that clients increase their contact with the opposite sex.

Teachers of small children often change seating arrangements to relocate pupils whose close proximity leads to various types of disruptions. This is usually much easier than designing and carrying out reinforcement or punishment programs to eliminate undesirable interactions, and the end result may be just as effective, or more so.

Changing the Time of the Activity

The final category of situational inducement involves taking advantage of the fact that certain stimuli and behavioral tendencies change predictably with the passage of time. For example, two sexual partners may find that sexual activity is better for them in the morning than at night, when one of them is "too tired." Changing the time of an activity has been used effectively in weight-control programs. People who cook for their families sometimes put on excess weight by "nibbling" while preparing meals and then sitting down for a full-course dinner. Rather than foregoing dinner with one's family, a partial solution to this problem is to do the preparation, except for the actual cooking, shortly after having eaten the previous meal, while the tendency to eat is still relatively weak (see LeBow, 1981, 1989).

Guidelines for Using Situational Inducement

Situational inducement covers a broad set of procedures. Its use, therefore, is considerably less straightforward than is that of the other methods discussed in this chapter. In short, a good deal of imagination is typically required if it is to be used effectively. We suggest the following guidelines.

1. Clearly identify the desired behavior to be strengthened, and, if appropriate, the undesirable behavior to be decreased.
2. Next, brainstorm all possible environmental arrangements in the presence of which the desired behavior has occurred in the past or is likely to occur. Remember, situations and controlling stimuli can be anything—people, places, times, days, events, objects, and so on.
3. From the list of stimuli that have controlled the target behavior in the past, identify those that could be easily introduced to control the target behavior.
4. Arrange for the learner to be exposed to the stimuli that control the target behavior in the desired way and to avoid locations and arrangements that do not have this control.
5. Make sure that undesirable behavior never occurs in the presence of situations introduced to strengthen desirable behavior.
6. When the desirable behavior occurs in the presence of the new arrangement, be sure that it is reinforced.
7. Use fading to bring the behavior under desired stimulus control.

STUDY QUESTIONS

1. List four strategies that you might follow to influence the effectiveness of modeling as a behavior modification technique.
2. Describe two recent situations in which you were influenced by modeling to emit a behavior. For each instance, describe whether or not the four factors that influence the effectiveness of modeling were present.
3. What is meant by symbolic modeling? Describe how this might explain how a city-dwelling child might learn to fear snakes.
4. Describe the results of the study of modeling of alcohol drinking by DeRicco and Niemann.
5. Describe the specific steps you might go through in using modeling to overcome the extreme withdrawal behavior of a nursery school child who never interacts with other children. Identify the basic principles and procedures being applied in your program.
6. In the dialogue between the client and the therapist concerning the client's difficulty in asking for dates, briefly describe
   a. how modeling was involved.
   b. how instructions were involved.
   c. how shaping was involved.
7. Define or describe behavior rehearsal, and give an example.
8. What is meant by physical guidance? How does it differ from gestural prompting (see p. 119).
9. Identify a behavior that you were influenced to perform as a result of physical guidance. Describe how physical guidance was involved.
10. What is generalized imitation? Describe an example.
11. What do we mean by the term *situational inducement*? Which term given previously in this book has essentially the same meaning (see p. 119)?
12. Describe each of the four proposed categories of situational inducement.
13. Give an example from your own experience of each of the four categories of situational inducement.
14. For each of the following examples, identify the category of situational inducement in which it might best be placed and indicate why.
    a. On Saturday afternoon, an exercise buff can't seem to "get up the energy" to lift weights. To increase the likelihood of weight lifting, she places the weights in the center of the den (where she usually exercises), turns on the TV to the Saturday afternoon wrestling matches, and opens her *Muscle Beach* magazine to the centerfold showing her favorite bodybuilder.
    b. It is said that Victor Hugo, a famous writer, controlled his work habits in his study by having his servant take his clothes away and not bring them back until the end of the day (Wallace, 1971, pp. 68–69).
    c. To stop drinking, an alcoholic surrounds himself with members of Alcoholics Anonymous and stops seeing his old drinking buddies.
    d. Another exercise buff has decided to jog a mile every night before going to bed. Alas, "the road to hell [or perhaps to heart attack] is paved with good intentions." Late nights, good TV, wine with dinner, and other delights take their toll. Three months later, our "exercise buff" is still overweight and out of shape because of many missed jogging nights. He therefore changes the routine and begins jogging each day immediately upon arriving home and before eating dinner.
    e. After many interruptions while working on this book at the university, the authors began working at one of their homes.

15. According to the proposed guidelines for the use of rules, modeling, and physical guidance,
    a. What behavior principle is used with all three procedures?
    b. What two other behavioral procedures are likely to be used with all three procedures?

APPLICATION EXERCISES

A. Exercise Involving Others

Outline a program that a parent might follow to teach a 2-year-old child to respond consistently to the instruction, "Please bring me your shoes." Indicate how your program might use rules, modeling and guidance, and how it follows the guidelines for the effective application of each.

B. Self-Modification Exercise

Select two of your behaviors from the following list:
1. Doing the dishes or putting them in the dishwasher immediately after a meal
2. Getting up when the alarm sounds
3. Feeling happy
4. Cleaning up your bedroom twice per week
5. Doing some exercises daily
6. Increasing your studying

Describe how you might influence each behavior by combining at least four of the following tactics: rules, modeling, guidance, rearranging the existing surroundings, moving the activity to a new location, relocating people, and changing the time of the activity. Make your suggestions highly plausible in regard to the situation.

NOTE AND EXTENDED DISCUSSION

1. Historically, learning by imitation has been given an important place in a number of different psychological theories, not just behavioristic ones. In Freudian (psychoanalytic) theory, a male child typically develops certain "male" behavior patterns through identification with his father, whereas a female child develops female behavior patterns through identification with her mother. Thus, the absence of a strong male figure with whom to identify could (in Freudian theory) lead to feminine traits—even homosexuality—in a boy who identifies excessively with his mother. Gestalt psychologists considered imitative learning to be innate in higher species and attempted to show, for example, that chimpanzees could learn to solve problems by watching other chimpanzees solve them. Bandura (1977) defined observational learning (also called vicarious learning) as the increase or decrease of an observer's behavior that is similar to that of a model, as a result of watching the model's behavior be reinforced or punished. Bandura believes that this type of learning can occur without external reinforcement for the observer, although he agrees that external reinforcement may be necessary to influence the observer to perform the behavior. If so, then it seems that we would have to add observational learning as a basic type of learning. Many behavioral psychologists, however, believe that the behavioral learning principles described in Chapters 3 through 15 of this book can account for behavior acquired through observation.

There are several processes by which observational or imitative behavior might be learned. First, an individual is frequently reinforced when he or she performs the same actions that another individual performs; hence, other people's actions tend to become S^Ds for engaging in similar actions. For example, a child who watches someone open a door to go outside receives the reinforcement of going outside when he or she performs the same action. Second, to the extent that other people are reinforcing to us, their actions acquire conditioned reinforcing properties; hence, we receive conditioned reinforcement when we perform the same actions. A third possibility is that once we have learned to imitate simple responses, we can then imitate more complex behaviors, provided that these are composed of the simpler responses. For example, once an individual has learned to imitate "al," "li," "ga," and "tor" as single syllables, or as units of various words, she can then imitate the word "alligator" the first time she hears it (Skinner, 1957). A fourth possibility is that imitative behavior is not just a set of separate stimulus–response relationships but is itself an operant class of responses. In other words, it is possible that, once a person is reinforced for imitating some behaviors, he or she will then tend to imitate other behaviors, even if they contain no elements in common with the imitative behaviors that were reinforced. As indicated earlier in this chapter, this is referred to as generalized imitation. (For more detailed interpretations of vicarious or imitative learning from a contemporary behavioral approach, see Masia and Chase, 1997; Pear, 2001, pp. 95–100).

Study Questions on Note

1. How did Bandura define observational learning? What is another name for observational learning?
2. Describe four processes by which imitative behavior might be learned, and give an example of each.

19

Motivation and Behavior Modification

In the previous two chapters, we discussed considerations for influencing behavior by manipulating antecedent conditions, including rules, goals, modeling, and situational inducement. In this chapter, we focus on antecedent conditions called motivational variables, which temporarily alter the effectiveness of consequences as reinforcers or punishers, and which temporarily influence the occurrence of behavior influenced by such consequences.

A TRADITIONAL VIEW OF MOTIVATION

Consider the behavior of Susie and Jack, two children in third grade at an elementary school. Susie consistently completes homework assignments, works hard during various classroom activities, listens attentively to the teacher, and is polite with the other children. According to Susie's teacher, "Susie is a good student *because* she's highly motivated." Jack, on the other hand, is the opposite of Susie. Jack rarely completes homework assignments, fools around while the teacher is talking, and doesn't appear to apply himself. Jack's teacher feels that Jack is lacking motivation. As illustrated by these examples, many people conceptualize motivation as some "thing" within us that causes our actions. Consistent with this traditional view, *Webster's Unabridged Dictionary* defines *motive* as "some inner drive that causes a person to act in a certain way." And many introductory psychology texts describe motivation as the study of inner drives, needs, and wants that cause our actions.

A conceptual limitation of the traditional view of motivation is that it involves circular reasoning. The causal "thing" (drive, motive, etc.) is usually inferred from the very behavior that it is supposed to explain (e.g., Why does Susie work hard? Because she is highly motivated. How do we know she's highly motivated? Because she works hard.). There are also several practical limitations to conceptualizing motivation as an internal cause of behavior. First, the suggestion that the causes of behavior lie within us might influence some to ignore the principles for changing behavior described in earlier chapters, and the enormous amount of data demonstrating that application of those principles can effectively modify behavior. Second, it may influence some to blame individuals for inferior performances (e.g., "Jack just isn't motivated"), rather than trying to help such individuals to improve their performance. Third, it may influence some to blame themselves for failures to emit various behaviors (e.g., "I just can't get motivated to go on a diet"), rather than examining potential self-management strategies (see Chapter 26) for improving their performance.

A BEHAVIORAL VIEW OF MOTIVATION

It's one thing for a person to *know how* to emit a behavior; it's another thing for that person to *want* to emit that behavior. In traditional psychology, the "processes of wanting" have been addressed by theories of motivation (Michael, 1993). However, rather than hypothesizing internal drives or motives, behavioral psychologists define a motivating operation as a type of antecedent environmental manipulation. Specifically, **motivating operations (MOs)** are events or operations that (a) temporarily alter the effectiveness of consequences as reinforcers or punishers (a value-altering effect), and (b) influence behaviors that normally lead to those reinforcers or punishers (a behavior-altering effect) (Laraway, Snycerski, Michael, & Poling, 2003). Let's first examine MOs involving reinforcers, and let's look at the value-altering effect. Consider, for example, the unconditioned reinforcer of food. When we are deprived of food, food becomes a powerful reinforcer for us. Just after eating a big meal, however, food temporarily loses its effectiveness as a reinforcer. Thus, deprivation and satiation of food are MOs. You can see from these examples that there are two main types of MOs: **motivating establishing operations (MEOs)** and **motivating abolishing operations (MAOs).** An MEO increases the effectiveness of a consequence as a reinforcer. Food deprivation is an MEO. An MAO decreases the effectiveness of a consequence as a reinforcer. Food satiation is an MAO.

Note 1

MOs also have a behavior-altering effect. Once again, we'll look at MOs involving reinforcers. The behavior-altering effect of MEOs is an increase in the frequency of behavior that led to the reinforcer affected by the MEO. Thus, deprivation of food leads to various food-seeking behaviors. The behavior-altering effect of MAOs is a decrease in the frequency of behavior that led to the reinforcer affected by the MAO. Thus, satiation of food leads to a decrease in various food-seeking behaviors.

Note 2

Thus far, our discussion of MOs has focused on reinforcers. However, MOs also affect punishers. Consider, for example, the punisher of time-out discussed in

Chapter 12. Suppose that, at Little League baseball practices of the Fargo Pirates, contingent upon misbehavior (swearing, throwing bats, etc.), Coach Jackson typically requires a player to sit in the dugout alone for five minutes or so as a time-out punisher. Suppose also that at one particular practice, Coach Jackson announced that players could earn points for performing well (catching the ball, getting a hit, etc.), and that the five players with the most points would each be awarded a ticket to attend a major league baseball game in Minneapolis. When the points program was in effect, all of the players likely wanted to increase their opportunities to earn points, which they were less likely to do if they were sitting in the dugout for misbehavior. The announcement of the points program was therefore an MEO that increased the effectiveness of the time-out punisher (a value-altering effect) and decreased the likelihood of misbehavior that lead to that punisher (a behavior-altering effect). Coincidentally, the announcement of the points program was also an MEO because it established points as effective conditioned reinforcers, and increased the likelihood of behaviors that produced points.

Unconditioned Versus Conditioned Motivating Operations

Michael (1993) distinguished between unconditioned and conditioned motivating operations. With *unconditioned motivating operations* (UMOs), the value-altering effect is innate. Thus, deprivation of food is an unconditioned MEO (UMEO) because it increases the effectiveness of food as a reinforcer without prior learning. Satiation is an unconditioned MAO (UMAO) because it decreases the effectiveness of food as a reinforcer without prior learning. The behavior-altering effect of UMOs, however, is learned. For example, when someone is hungry, the behaviors of looking in the refrigerator or going to a fast-food outlet are learned behaviors. **Note 3** Other UMEOs include deprivation of water, sleep, activity, oxygen, and sexual stimulation (and satiation of each of these are UMAOs); temperatures that are too hot or too cold; and the onset of painful stimulation (which establishes the reduction of that stimulation as a negative reinforcer).

Some MOs alter the effectiveness of consequences as reinforcers or punishers (the value-altering effect), because of prior learning. Such MOs are called *conditioned motivating operations* (CMOs). Consider, for example, Coach Dawson's points program with the basketball players described at the beginning of Chapter 4. Coach Dawson's explanation of the program was an MEO because it established the points as reinforcers, and it increased the likelihood of desirable practice behaviors to earn those reinforcers. However, his explanation of the program would be described as a conditioned MEO (CMEO)—because it altered the effectiveness of points as conditioned reinforcers because of prior learning. Consider another example of a CMEO. Martin (2003) described the strategy that a young competitive golfer used to motivate himself to practice putting. The golfer used imagery to create pressure games. When practicing putting, for example, the golfer would frequently imagine that he was leading the tournament on the final day of the U.S. Open. For each of 18 practice putts, he would pretend that he needed the putt to maintain the lead. In this example, by using the imaginary pressure game the golfer was administering a CMEO to himself. The pressure game increased the conditioned reinforcing value of making a putt, and increased the likelihood of focusing appropriately to make the putt.

Consider another example described by Martin (2003). Suppose that the coach of a high school football team initiates a new set of drills to open practices at the beginning of a season. Initially the players perform the drills enthusiastically, presumably in part because of some of the natural reinforcers for doing so (the drills are novel, challenging, etc.). After several weeks of performing the same drills, however, the coach notices that the players have begun to delay the start of the drills, terminate the drills more quickly than they should, and are not nearly as enthusiastic. Presumably, the repetitive nature of the drills, day in and day out, had abolished the effectiveness of natural conditioned reinforcers for performing them, and functioned as an MO to motivate escape and avoidance behaviors that were incompatible with productively completing the drills. An obvious solution is for the coach to introduce more variety in the opening drills. Posting a new schedule listing different types of drills would function as a CMEO in that it would temporarily increase the extent to which aspects of the drills are conditioned reinforcers, and would influence behaviors that increase drill completion.

As indicated previously, the value-altering effect of a UMO is innate, while the behavior-altering effect is learned. With conditioned CMOs, both the value-altering and the behavior-altering effects are due to learning. As Sundberg (2004) has pointed out, many of the topics discussed under motivation in introductory psychology books, such as "acquired drives" or "social motives," involve CMOs.

CMEOs and S^Ds

When considering stimulus control over behavior, students sometimes confuse the concept of discriminative stimulus or S^D and the concept of CMEO. Knowledge of both is important in order to be able to reliably and effectively use either as antecedent variables to influence behavior. An S^D is a stimulus that has been correlated with the availability of a reinforcer for a particular behavior (with the implication that the reinforcer does not follow that behavior in the absence of the S^D). In order to influence an individual's behavior by presenting an S^D, that individual must have been deprived of the reinforcer that was associated with responding to that S^D. In everyday language, an S^D is a cue that tells you what to do to get what you already want. Suppose that a family is camping on a cold fall evening. A parent might say to a shivering child, "Move your sleeping bag closer to the campfire and you'll feel warmer." This statement would be an S^D for the child to move the sleeping bag closer to the campfire. A CMEO is a motivator that momentarily increases the value of a conditioned reinforcer and increases the likelihood of behavior that has led to that reinforcer in the past. In everyday language, a CMEO is a cue that changes what you want and tells you what to do to get whatever it is that you now want. Suppose a parent says to his teenage daughter, "Each time that you mow the lawn, you can earn 3 points, and each time that you trim the hedges you can earn 2 points. When you accumulate 20 points, you can use the family car for a weekend." In this example, the rule given by the parent would be more accurately described as a CMEO than as an S^D. The rule established points as conditioned reinforcers for the daughter, and it told her how to earn them.

CMAOs and S^Δs

The distinction between S^Δ and CMAO is analogous to the distinction between S^D and CMEO. An S^Δ is a stimulus in the presence of which a response has not been reinforced (with the implication that the response has been reinforced in the presence of some other stimulus). It is also assumed that the individual has been deprived of that particular reinforcer. In everyday language, an S^Δ is a cue that tells you that emitting a particular behavior will not lead to a reinforcer that you want. Suppose that parents have, while shopping with their child in the past, typically purchased candy when the child screamed, "I want candy." Suppose further that, at the beginning of a shopping excursion, the parents tell their child, "We will no longer buy you candy when you scream," and that they stick to that rule. This instruction would be considered an S^Δ for further screaming. A CMAO is a motivator that momentarily decreases the value of a conditioned reinforcer, and decreases the likelihood of behavior that has led to that reinforcer in the past. In everyday language, a CMAO influences someone to no longer want a particular consequence, and decreases behavior that led to that consequence. Suppose, for example, that Charlie, a "movie buff," shopped at a particular grocery store, even though prices were a little on the high side, primarily because purchases were accompanied by coupons that could be saved and cashed in for movie tickets. Suppose further that the store announced that in the future the coupons could be exchanged for country-western CDs but not for movie tickets. Charlie, who was not a country-western fan, began to shop at another store. In this example, the announcement that coupons could be exchanged for CDs but not for movies would be a CMAO. It decreased the value of the coupons for Charlie, and decreased behavior that had led to those coupons.

To summarize the difference between CMOs and discriminative stimuli, Michael (1993) stated the difference as follows: "Discriminative variables (i.e., S^Ds and S^Δs) are related to the *differential availability* of an effective form of reinforcement given a particular type of behavior; motivative variables (i.e., CMEOs and CMAOs) are related to the differential *reinforcing effectiveness* of environmental events" (p. 193).

SOME APPLICATIONS OF MOTIVATING OPERATIONS

Teaching Mands to Children with Autism

In recent years, considerable success has been achieved in a number of language intervention programs for children with autism and other developmental disabilities by combining intensive behavioral interventions with Skinner's (1957) analysis of verbal behavior (Sundberg & Michael, 2001; Sundberg & Partington, 1998). Skinner was interested in studying the verbal behavior of individual speakers rather than the grammatical practices of a verbal community. He defined verbal behavior as behavior that is reinforced through the mediation of another person, where the person providing the reinforcement was specifically trained to provide such reinforcment. Verbal behavior is contrasted with nonverbal behavior, which is behavior that is reinforced through contact with the physical environment. Skinner distinguished among several types of basic verbal responses, three of which were echoics, tacts, and mands. An *echoic* is a vocal imitative response that is typically reinforced by a social reinforcer. For example, during language training with a child, a parent might say, "Say 'water,' and the child might mimic "Water" and be praised. A *tact* is a naming response that is typically reinforced by a social reinforcer. If the parent were to point to a glass of water and ask "What's that?" and the child replied "Water," the child would likely be praised. A *mand* is a verbal response that is under the control of a motivating operation, and is reinforced by the corresponding reinforcer (or removal of the corresponding aversive stimulus). In everyday language, a *mand* is a request (or demand) for something that a person "wants," and the person is typically reinforced by receiving whatever that is. If a child is thirsty, for example, a child might approach a parent and say "Water." As another example, if you are trying to listen to and watch a TV show while children are playing noisily, you might mand that they "Be quiet!" and you would be reinforced through the reduction of the aversive noise. With this approach to language, the same spoken word (e.g., "water") can be considered a different verbal response (e.g., an echoic, a tact, or a mand), depending on its controlling variables.

Observations suggest that mands are the first type of verbal behavior acquired by a child (Bijou & Baer, 1965; Skinner, 1957), and MOs have been used effectively in mand training programs with children with autism and developmental disabilities (Sundberg & Michael, 2001). Structured mand training typically begins by teaching a child to mand for a reinforcer that has high motivational value (such as a specific food or a favorite toy). Suppose, for example, that a child really enjoys orange juice, and consumes it whenever it is offered. To teach the child to mand for juice, the parent might give the child a sip of juice on the first trial. Next, in full view of the child, the parent might hide the juice under the table and ask the child, "What do you want? Say 'Juice.'" If the child responds correctly, the child would be given another sip of juice. You probably have discerned that, at this point, the child is showing echoic behavior. On subsequent trials, however, while hiding the juice, the parent would simply say, "What do you want?" and **Note 4** would reinforce asking for "Juice." After a certain amount of this type of training, the child is likely to generalize to situations where the parent is in the kitchen preparing a meal or doing other things, and would likely mand "Juice" when motivated for juice. Additional strategies for using MOs for mand training are described by Sundberg and Partington (1998) and Sundberg (2004).

Motivating Seat Belt Use Among Senior Drivers

Pleasant Oaks is a residential senior community in Virginia. The seniors living there have an enjoyable lifestyle, including frequent car trips to nearby Charlottesville. Many of those at Pleasant Oaks were acutely aware that automobile accidents are the leading cause of accidental death among individuals between the ages of 65 and 74. And although injuries, hospitalizations, and deaths are significantly fewer among drivers who wear safety belts, 30% of the drivers and passengers entering and leaving Pleasant Oaks did not buckle up. Brian, Amanda, and Daniel Cox decided to implement a simple procedure to try to encourage more residents of Pleasant Oaks to wear their seat belts. On stop signs located at the exits of the community scattered around Pleasant Oaks, the researchers placed a positive health-related message, "BUCKLE UP, STAY SAFE" on permanent, aluminum vinyl-lettered signs. Because feeling safe is an important concern for seniors, the Coxes hypothesized that the sign would function as a CMEO to increase the reinforcing value of having a seat belt fastened, and increase the behavior of buckling up. And they were right. Following installation of the signs, the percentage of seniors who buckled up increased from 70% to 94%. Six months after installation of the signs, 88% of the seniors continued to use seat belts appropriately (Cox, Cox, & Cox, 2000).

Decreasing Self-Injurious Behavior Maintained by Attention

Brenda was a 42-year-old woman with profound developmental disabilities who lived in a public residential facility for persons with developmental disabilities. She had a long history of self-injurious behavior (SIB), including severe head-banging and head-hitting. Observations indicated that her SIB was maintained by reactions of concern by well-meaning staff. After an instance of SIB, for example, a staff member might say, "Brenda, don't do that, you'll hurt yourself." To treat Brenda's SIB, Timothy Vollmer and colleagues introduced a program that included an MAO for staff attention. During treatment sessions a schedule of noncontingent reinforcement was arranged in which attention was initially provided every 10 seconds. This satiated Brenda on attention, and her SIB that had been previously reinforced by attention immediately dropped to a very low level. Extinction was also a part of the treatment in that, on the few occasions that SIB occurred, it was no longer followed by attention. Over several sessions, the frequency of noncontingent attention was gradually decreased from its initial rate of six instances per minute to a final rate of one instance every five minutes. SIB remained at a very low level. Similar results were obtained with two other individuals (Vollmer, Iwata, Zarcone, Smith, & Mazaleski, 1993).

MOTIVATING OPERATIONS AND BEHAVIOR MODIFICATION

In previous chapters we discussed strategies for influencing behavior by manipulating discriminative stimuli and consequences. In this chapter, we have discussed antecedent variables—MOs—that temporarily alter the effectiveness of consequences as reinforcers or punishers and that temporarily alter the occurrence of behavior influenced by such consequences. In general, MOs might be thought of as motivators. Consideration of MOs in the design of behavior modification programs is likely to enhance their effectiveness.

STUDY QUESTIONS

1. How do many people who are not behaviorists or behavior modifiers conceptualize motivation? Illustrate with an example.
2. What is a conceptual limitation of the traditional view of motivation? Illustrate with an example.
3. Describe three practical limitations to conceptualizing motivation as an internal cause of behavior.
4. If by "motivating someone to do something" we mean nothing more than influencing them to behave in a certain way, what strategies have been presented in the book thus far to accomplish that task?
5. Define motivating operation. Describe an example that illustrates both aspects of the definition.
6. In what two ways are motivating establishing operations and motivating abolishing operations different?
7. What is an unconditioned motivating operation? Illustrate with an example.
8. What is a conditioned motivating operation? Illustrate with an example.
9. Suppose that a football team has been practicing for an hour in the hot sun without water. The coach says to one of the players, "Here are the keys to my car. Bring the jug of ice water from the trunk." Would this request be classified as an S^D or a CMEO for getting the water? Justify your choice.
10. Suppose the coach in the previous question forgot to say anything about the keys and did not give the player the keys, even though the car was locked. Would the coach's request be an S^D or an CMEO for asking for the keys? Justify your choice.
11. Define *echoic*, and describe an example that is not in the book.
12. Define *tact*, and describe an example that is not in the book.
13. Define *mand*, and describe an example that is not in the book.
14. Using an example, describe how a motivating operation might be incorporated into mand training with a child.
15. Suppose that a pianist, practicing a piece, sets a goal for herself: "Before I can stop practicing, I have to play this piece through 10 times in a row without making a mistake." Is that goal best conceptualized as an S^D or a CMEO? Justify your choice.

APPLICATION EXERCISE

Self-Modification Exercise

Suppose that you want to increase the frequency of your studying. To master the answers to the study questions in this book, you might post the date of the final exam for the course and cross off each day as it passes. You might arrange to study with a friend on a regular basis. You might sign a contract with your roommate or a relative that stipulates that they will give you certain reinforcers only if you meet certain study objectives. You might rearrange your study environment to present cues for studying and to eliminate cues for incompatible behaviors (such as watching TV). Pick three such strategies (or three others that you might think of) and briefly describe each of them. For each of the strategies, indicate whether they involve presentation of S^Ds, S^As, CMEOs, or CMAOs. In each case, justify your choice.

NOTES AND EXTENDED DISCUSSION

1. As described in Chapter 29, two major texts in the history of applied behavior analysis in the 1950s were *Principles of Psychology* (Keller & Schoenfeld, 1950) and *Science and Human Behavior* (Skinner, 1953). Both texts discussed a behavioral approach to the topic of motivation, and considered variables such as deprivation and satiation. Keller and Schoenfeld introduced the term *establishing operation* to refer to such variables. By the 1970s, however, the topic of motivation was no longer emphasized in behavior modification texts (e.g., Fantino & Logan, 1979; Martin & Pear, 1978; Powers & Osborne, 1976; Whaley & Malott,1971). Beginning in the 1980s, Jack Michael argued in a series of papers (1982, 1988, 1993, 2000) that behaviorally oriented psychologists needed to give more weight to the topic of motivation. Michael adopted Keller and Schoenfeld's term, establishing operation, and defined it essentially as we have defined motivating operation. Because establishing operations as defined by Michael included *increasing* (i.e., establishing) the effectiveness of reinforcers as well as *decreasing* (i.e., abolishing) the effectiveness of reinforcers, Michael and colleagues (Laraway et al., 2003) proposed changing the term *establishing operation* to *motivating operation,* and that motivating operations be analyzed as establishing or abolishing operations. Those are the terms that we have adopted in this book. For a detailed discussion of the history of the treatment of motivation in applied behavior analysis, see Sundberg (2004). For a discussion of the application of motivating operations in organizational behavior management, see Agnew (1998) and Olsen, Laraway, and Austin (2001). For a discussion of the role of motivating operations in the treatment and prevention of problem behavior, see McGill (1999) and a special section of the *Journal of Applied Behavior Analysis* (Winter 2000).

2. As Poling (2001) has pointed out, it is important to keep in mind that a given MO is likely to affect many behaviors, and a given behavior is likely to be affected by many MOs. Consider, for example, the MEO of food deprivation. Not only does food deprivation increase the reinforcing value of food and lead to various food seeking behaviors, it increases the reinforcing value of a broad range of abused drugs and could lead to increased drug use, and it increases the reinforcing value of water and thus increases water intake (Poling, 2001). Thus, in order for the MO concept to be maximally useful as a behavior management tool, researchers must examine ways for isolating MOs that affect important behaviors in predictable ways.

3. Ingestion or injection of drugs also functions as a motivating operation (Pear, 2001). Amphetamines, for example, function as a UMAO to decrease the reinforcing effectiveness of food; aphrodisiacs function as a UMEO to increase the reinforcing effectiveness of sexual stimulation. In this book, however, we focus on motivational variables that are located in the individual's external environment.

4. If you are familiar with Skinner's (1957) analysis of verbal behavior, you will recognize that, during mand training, at the point where the parent asks "What do you want?" and the child replies "Juice," the child's response might be considered to be, in part, an intraverbal. An *intraverbal* is a verbal response under the control of a preceding verbal stimulus, and there is no point-to-point correspondence between the stimulus and the response. Thus, if someone asks Sally, "What's your name?" and the child correctly replies, "Sally," then the child's response is an intraverbal. An echoic is also a verbal response under the control of a preceding verbal stimulus, but there is point-to-point correspondence between the stimulus and the response. Thus, if a child's name is Sally, and a parent says, "Say Sally," and the child responds by saying, "Sally," then the child's response would be an echoic. The aforementioned child's response of "Juice" is, however, at least in part a mand because it is under the control of a specific deprivation state. Thus there can be overlap among the different categories of verbal behavior.

Study Questions on Notes

1. What psychologist influenced a renewed emphasis on the concept of motivation by behaviorally oriented psychologists in the 1980s?
2. Describe an example illustrating that a given MO may affect the value of more than one reinforcer, and may influence the occurrence of many behaviors.
3. Describe an example that illustrates how a drug might function as an MO.
4. Distinguish between an echoic and an intraverbal. Illustrate each with an example that is not in the text.

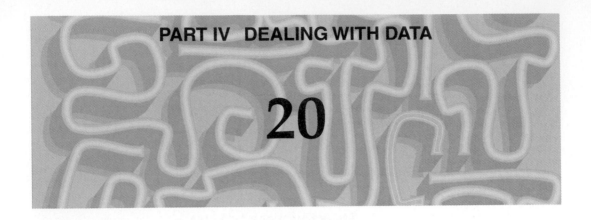

20

Behavioral Assessment: Initial Considerations

Throughout this book, numerous examples illustrate the effectiveness of behavior modification procedures. Many of these examples are accompanied by graphs showing the changes (increases or decreases) that occurred in behavior when particular procedures were applied. Some of the graphs also include follow-up observations indicating that the improvements were maintained after the programs had terminated. The graphs were presented not just to make it easier for you to understand the material; precise records of behavior are an inseparable part of behavior modification procedures. Indeed, some people have gone so far as to say that the major contribution of behavior modification has been the insistence on accurately recording specific behaviors and making decisions on the basis of recorded data rather than merely on the basis of subjective impressions.

As indicated in Chapter 1, the behaviors to be improved in a behavior modification program are frequently called **target behaviors. Behavioral assessment** involves the collection and analysis of information and data in order to identify and describe target behavior, identify possible causes of the behavior, select appropriate treatment strategies to modify the behavior, and evaluate treatment outcome.

MINIMAL PHASES OF A PROGRAM

A successful behavior modification program typically involves four phases during which the target behavior is identified, defined, and recorded: (a) a screening or intake phase, for clarifying the problem and determining who should treat it; (b) a baseline, or preprogram assessment phase; (c) a treatment phase; and (d) a follow-up phase. In this section we give a brief overview of these phases. In subsequent sections and chapters we discuss them in greater detail.

Screening or Intake Phase

The initial interactions between a client and a practitioner or an agency are often referred to as the *intake,* and a client is typically asked to complete an *intake form.* Such a form requests general information such as the client's name, address, date of birth, marital status, and so forth, and also asks the client to state the reason for seeking service from that agency or practitioner.

As expressed by Hawkins (1979), a question commonly asked when a client or student first appears at the door of a clinic or educational institution is, "Does this case belong here?" One function of the screening phase is to determine whether a particular agency or behavior modifier is the appropriate one to deal with a potential client's behavior. If not, the results of this phase should indicate which agency or practitioner should deal with the client. A second function is to inform the client about the agency or practitioner's policies and procedures related to service provision. A third function of this phase is to screen for the presence of a crisis condition (e.g., child abuse, suicide risk, etc.) that might require immediate intervention. For some therapists, a fourth function of the screening phase is to gather sufficient information (through client interview and psychological tests) to diagnose the client according to the standardized categories of mental disorder, as listed in the *Diagnostic and Statistical Manual of Mental Disorders, 4th ed., Text Revision* (American Psychiatric Association, 2000), also known as the *DSM-IV-TR.* As indicated in Note 1 of Chapter 1, such diagnoses may be required by clinics, hospitals, schools, and other agencies before treatment can be offered, and by health insurance companies before treatment can be paid for. While a *DSM-IV-TR* diagnosis might also be helpful for comprehensive treatment planning for a client, we must remember that a *DSM-IV-TR* diagnosis and a behavioral assessment provide very different information. A fifth function of the intake phase is to provide information as to which behavior(s) should be baselined. For example, a center for children with learning difficulties might screen a child to determine whether his or her academic skills are unusual enough to require some sort of program that is not ordinarily provided by the school. To achieve this initial assessment, the agency might use a number of different preliminary indicators, ranging from teachers' reports to the child's IQ score (although these indicators would, of course, be interpreted by behavior modifiers simply as crude measures of behavior rather than as measures of underlying traits). Behavior modifiers may make use of traditional tests, such as intelligence tests, in their screening and intake assessments—although they typically don't interpret them in the traditional manner. Behavior modifiers also use other assessment devices to aid in pinpointing specific behaviors of interest, as described later in this and the next chapter.

Baseline Phase

During the **baseline** phase, the behavior modifier assesses the target behavior to determine its level prior to the introduction of the program or treatment, and analyzes the individual's current environment to identify possible controlling variables of the behavior to be changed. Assessment of possible controlling variables of the target behavior is referred to as a functional assessment, and is discussed further in Chapter 22.

The need for a baseline phase follows from the importance that behavior modifiers place on directly measuring the behavior of concern and using changes in the measure as the best indicator that the problem is being helped (see Chapter 1). If a child is having difficulty in school, for example, the behavior modifier would be considerably more interested in a baseline of specific behavioral excesses or deficits that constitute the problem (e.g., reading deficiency, inattentive behavior, excessive fighting with other children) than in the child's score on an intelligence test (although the behavior modifier would probably not be disinterested in the latter information).

Treatment Phase

After making a precise baseline assessment, a behavior modifier will design a program to bring about the desired behavior change. In educational settings, such a program is typically referred to as a *training* or *teaching program*. In community and clinical settings, the program is referred to more often as an *intervention strategy* or a *therapy program*.

Behavior modification programs typically provide for frequent observation and monitoring of the behavior of interest during training or treatment. In some cases, the difference between behavior modification and other approaches on this point is primarily a matter of degree. Traditional educational practices typically involve periodic assessment during the teaching program for the purpose of monitoring the performance of the students. Certain clinical treatment programs involve assessment of the clients at various intervals. Moreover, some programs that have been labeled behavior modification have consisted primarily of before-and-after measures and have lacked precise, ongoing recording during treatment. Nevertheless, many behavior modifiers have emphasized and practiced, to a degree rarely found in other approaches, frequent monitoring of the behavior throughout the application of the specific treatment or intervention strategies. In addition, behavior modifiers strongly emphasize changing the program if the measurements taken indicate that the desired change in behavior is not occurring within a reasonable period of time.

Follow-up Phase

Finally, the *follow-up phase* is carried out to determine whether the improvements achieved during treatment are maintained after the termination of the program. Considering that a problem has not really been solved if the improvement is not permanent, behavior modifiers agree that programs should include a follow-up phase to assess the persistence of the desirable behavior change.

In many cases, such as behavioral programs involving one or two behaviors and a small number of individuals, it is both possible and desirable to gather reliable follow-up information. In some cases, this might consist of precise observation or assessment in the natural environment or under circumstances in which the behavior is expected to occur. In other cases, however, precise follow-up observations simply are not possible. Consider a behavior modification program set up for an entire classroom and conducted for many months. At the end of the program, the children may go on to another class, graduate to another program, leave the school, or in some other way become unavailable for follow-up observation. Under these circumstances it would be impossible to do anything other than conduct pre- and posttests that sample a few of the behaviors developed by the behavior modification program.

SOURCES OF INFORMATION FOR BASELINE ASSESSMENT

Defining target behaviors clearly, completely, and in measurable terms is an important prerequisite to the design and implementation of behavior modification programs. Behavioral assessment procedures for collecting information to define and monitor target behaviors fall into three categories: indirect, direct, and experimental.

Indirect Assessment Procedures

In many situations in which a behavior modification program might be applied, the behavior modifier (e.g., a nurse, a teacher, a parent, a coach) can directly observe the behavior of interest. However, suppose that you are a behavior therapist who, like other professional therapists, sees clients in your office at regularly scheduled appointment times. It would be impractical for you to observe your clients regularly in the situations in which the target behaviors occur. Moreover, what if some of your clients wanted to change some of their thoughts and feelings that others couldn't observe? (As discussed in Chapters 15 and 27, thoughts and feelings are regarded by behavior modifiers as private or covert behaviors.) In such situations, behavior therapists have made considerable use of indirect assessment procedures. The more common among these are interviews with the client and significant others, questionnaires, role playing, obtaining information from consulting professionals, and client self-monitoring. Indirect assessment procedures have the advantages of being convenient, not requiring an inordinate amount of time, and potentially providing information about covert behaviors. However, they suffer from the disadvantages that those providing information may not remember relevant observations accurately, or they might have particular biases that would influence them to provide inaccurate data.

Interviews with the Client and Significant Others   Observation of an initial interview across a random sample of behavior therapists and therapists of other orientations is likely to show numerous commonalities. Because many clients are anxious

TABLE 20–1   EXAMPLES OF QUESTIONS TYPICALLY ASKED BY A
BEHAVIOR THERAPIST DURING AN INTAKE INTERVIEW

1. What seems to be the problem?
2. Can you describe what you typically say or do when you experience the problem?
3. How often does the problem occur?
4. For how long has the problem been occurring?
5. In what situations does the problem typically occur? In other words, what
   sets it off?
6. What tends to occur immediately after you experience the problem?
7. What are you typically thinking and feeling when the problem occurs?
8. How have you tried to deal with the problem thus far?

when first meeting a therapist, the therapist typically does much of the initial talking. The therapist might begin by describing briefly the types of problems with
which he or she typically works. The therapist might then ask a number of simple
questions concerning the background of the client, or might ask the client to complete a simple demographic referral form. The therapist might next invite the client
to describe, in general terms, what the problem is (see Table 20–1). During initial
interviews, behavior therapists and traditional therapists are likely to use similar
techniques, such as being a good listener, asking open-ended questions, requesting
clarification, and expressing concern for and acknowledging the validity of the
client's feelings and problems, to help the client feel at ease and to gain information
about the problem.

In interviewing the client and significant others (the client's spouse, parents,
or anyone else directly concerned with the client's welfare), behavior therapists
attempt to establish and maintain rapport (i.e., a relationship of mutual trust) with
the client and any significant others included, just as do traditionally oriented
therapists. This relationship can be facilitated by the therapist being especially
attentive to the client's description of the problem while refraining from expressing personal values that may unduly influence the client, showing empathy by
communicating some understanding of the client's feelings, and emphasizing the
confidentiality of the client–therapist relationship (Sarwer & Sayers, 1998).

Some behavior therapists deliberately keep the discussion during the initial interview at a general level. Others lead the discussion more directly to the
presenting problem. Although there are individual differences among behavior
therapists in this respect, it is probably accurate to say that they are likely to focus
discussion on the specific behaviors that characterize the problem or problems of
a client relatively soon in the therapeutic relationship. This can be done by asking
a number of questions about a problem and its controlling variables (see, e.g.,
Sarwer & Sayers, 1998). At some point in the interviewing process, the behavior
therapist will help the client to identify major problem areas; select one or two
problem areas for initial treatment focus; translate the problem areas into specific
behavioral deficits or excesses; attempt to identify controlling variables of the
problem behavior; and identify some specific behavioral objectives for treatment.
Specific behavioral questionnaires and role playing are often used to facilitate this
process.

Questionnaires   A well-designed questionnaire can provide information that may be useful in assessing a client's problem and developing a behavioral program tailored to the client. There are a large number of such questionnaires; for example, Fischer and Corcoran (1994) published a collection of more than 300 questionnaires to help assess and treat a wide range of problems of clients. Several types of questionnaires are popular with behavior therapists.

Life history questionnaires provide demographic data such as marital status, vocational status, and religious affiliation, and background data such as sexual, health, and educational histories. Two notable examples of such questionnaires are Cautela's *Behavioral Analysis History Questionnaire* (1977) and Wolpe's *Life History Questionnaire* (1982).

Self-report problem checklists have the client indicate which problem(s) applies to him or her from a detailed list of problems. Such questionnaires are particularly useful in helping the therapist completely specify the problem or problems for which the client is seeking therapy (Jensen & Haynes, 1986). An example is the *Behavior Self-Rating Checklist* (Upper, Cautela, & Brook, 1975). Another example is the behavioral checklist shown in Figure 20–1, which was developed by the first **Note 1** author for sport psychology consulting with figure skaters.

Survey schedules provide the therapist with information needed to conduct a particular therapeutic technique with the client. The questionnaire shown in Figure 3–3 provides information useful in applying positive reinforcement procedures. Other types of survey schedules are designed to provide information preparatory to using other behavioral procedures. Different types of survey schedules can be found in Cautela (1977, 1981).

Third-party behavioral checklists or *rating scales* permit significant others and professionals involved with the client to assess subjectively the frequency and/or quality of certain behaviors. An example of such a checklist for use with individuals with developmental disabilities is the *Objective Behavioral Assessment of the Severely and Moderately Mentally Handicapped* (OBA); Hardy, Martin, Yu, Leader, & Quinn, 1981). The OBA enables third-party informants who are familiar with the behavior of the client to rate whether the client can perform a variety of tasks such as putting on a shirt or tying shoelaces. Incidentally, the OBA can also be used as a direct observation instrument.

Role Playing   If it is not feasible for the therapist to observe the client in the actual situation in which the problem occurs, an alternative is to re-create that situation (or at least certain crucial aspects of it) in the therapist's office. That, essentially, is the rationale behind role playing, in which the client and therapist enact interpersonal interactions related to the client's problem. For example, the client may enact himself or herself being interviewed for a job, with the therapist playing the role of the interviewer. Not only is role playing frequently used in conjunction with behavioral interviews in assessing a problem, it is also often used in treating it (see, e.g., pp. 231–232).

Information from Consulting Professionals   If other professionals (e.g., physicians, physiotherapists, teachers, nurses, social workers) have been dealing with the client in any way related to the problem, relevant information should be obtained from them. A client's problem might be related to some medical factor about which his or her physician could provide important information for dealing

Name _____   Date _____

Would you say you need help or need to improve:	Check here if not sure	Definitely No	To Some Extent		Definitely Yes

Regarding Free Skating Practices, to:

	Check here if not sure	Definitely No	To Some Extent			Definitely Yes
1. Set specific goals for every practice?	_____	1	2	3	4	5
2. Arrive at every practice totally committed to do your best?	_____	1	2	3	4	5
3. Consistently be stretched and warmed up <u>before</u> stepping on the ice at practice?	_____	1	2	3	4	5
4. Be more focused when doing your jumps and spins? (Answer "yes" if you often just do the jumps or spins in a haphazard way without trying to do your best.)	_____	1	2	3	4	5
5. Stay positive and not get down on yourself when you're having a bad practice?	_____	1	2	3	4	5
6. Make better use of <u>full</u> practice time?	_____	1	2	3	4	5
7. Overcome fear of doing difficult jumps?	_____	1	2	3	4	5
8. Improve consistency of jumps you can already land?	_____	1	2	3	4	5
9. Feel more confident about your ability to do difficult jumps?	_____	1	2	3	4	5
10. Not worry about what other skaters are doing?	_____	1	2	3	4	5
11. Figure out how to monitor progress on a new jump that you are learning, so that you don't get discouraged when progress seems slow?	_____	1	2	3	4	5
12. Do more <u>complete</u> program run-throughs (where you try everything in your program)?	_____	1	2	3	4	5
13. Keep track of your % landed during program run-throughs?	_____	1	2	3	4	5
14. Make better use of videotaped feedback when learning a new jump?	_____	1	2	3	4	5
15. Push harder while stroking, in order to get in better shape?	_____	1	2	3	4	5
16. Keep a written record of your progress in meeting your goal?	_____	1	2	3	4	5

Figure 20–1   A questionnaire to assess areas in need of help during a seasonal sport psychology program for figure skaters.

with the problem. Before such steps are taken, however, appropriate permission should always be obtained from the client.

   Client Self-Monitoring   Self-monitoring—the direct observation by the client of his or her own behavior—may be the next best thing to direct observation by the therapist. We mention it under indirect assessment procedures, however, because the therapist does not observe the behavior directly. Thus, as with the other indirect assessment procedures, the therapist cannot have as much confidence in the

Would you say you need help or need to improve:	Check here if not sure	Definitely No	To Some Extent	Definitely Yes
Regarding Free Skating at a Competition, to:				
1. Stay confident at practices when you see what the other skaters are doing?	____	1	2	3	4	5
2. At practices, forget about other skaters and just focus on your own skating?	____	1	2	3	4	5
3. Avoid putting extra pressure on yourself when you see what other skaters are doing at practices?	____	1	2	3	4	5
4. Learn how <u>not</u> to worry about other skaters?	____	1	2	3	4	5
5. Learn how <u>not</u> to worry about where you will place?	____	1	2	3	4	5
6. Have a better time management plan for the entire competition so you are well organized, eat healthy, and get lots of rest?	____	1	2	3	4	5
7. Skate as well during a competition as during the last 2 or 3 weeks before the competition (in other words, to skate up to your potential)?	____	1	2	3	4	5
8. Stay loose (not too tense) during the last ½-hour or so before the 6' warmup?	____	1	2	3	4	5
9. Stay loose (not too tense) during the 6' warmup?	____	1	2	3	4	5
10. Stay loose (not too tense) after the 6' warmup while waiting for your turn?	____	1	2	3	4	5
11. Stay loose (not too tense) when you go on the ice for your turn?	____	1	2	3	4	5
12. Feel confident about your skating while stretching before the 6' warmup?	____	1	2	3	4	5
13. Not be psyched out by other skaters?	____	1	2	3	4	5
14. Feel confident about your skating during the 6' warmup?	____	1	2	3	4	5
15. Feel confident about your skating after the 6' warmup, while waiting for your turn to skate?	____	1	2	3	4	5
16. Take it one element at a time during your program (& not get ahead of yourself or think only about difficult elements)?	____	1	2	3	4	5
17. Concentrate on easy elements as well as hard ones?	____	1	2	3	4	5
18. Stay positive and skate well for the rest of your program, even if you fall?	____	1	2	3	4	5

Figure 20–1 (*Continued*)

observations as would be the case if she or some other trained observer had made them.

Except for covert behavior, the characteristics of behavior that might be self-monitored are the same as those that would be observed directly by a trained observer and are described in Chapter 21. Self-monitoring might also aid the discovery of the causes of the problem behavior, as discussed in Chapter 22. Additional examples of self-monitoring are provided in Chapter 26.

Direct Assessment Procedures

In each of the case histories at the beginning of Chapters 3 through 14, specific behaviors of a client were precisely defined and directly observed by other individuals. This defines a direct assessment procedure. The main advantage of direct assessment procedures over indirect assessment procedures is that the former are likely to be more accurate. Disadvantages of direct assessment procedures are that they tend to be time consuming, they require that observers be appropriately trained, and they cannot be used to monitor covert behaviors. Chapter 21 is devoted to discussion of direct assessment procedures.

Experimental Assessment Procedures

Experimental assessment procedures are used to clearly reveal the antecedent and consequent events that control and maintain problem behavior. Such procedures are referred to as *experimental functional analyses* (or more simply as *functional analyses*) in that they attempt to demonstrate that the occurrence of a behavior is a function of certain controlling variables. Such procedures are discussed in detail in Chapter 22.

Computer-Assisted Data Collection

Increasingly, computers are being used to facilitate data collection in behavioral assessment (Haynes, 1998). Hand-held computers have also been used to facilitate client self-monitoring. For example, in a study by Taylor, Fried, and Kenardy (1990), clients used hand-held computers to record panic and anxiety symptoms, cognitive factors, and settings. In a study by Agras, Taylor, Feldman, Losch, and Burnett (1990), obese clients used hand-held computers to monitor their weight, caloric intake, exercise, daily goals, and goal attainment. Computers can greatly simplify and increase the cost effectiveness of the collection and analysis of direct observation and self-monitoring data (Farrell, 1991). Examples of computerized observation systems for direct assessment procedures were described by Bush and Ciocco (1992), Hile (1991), and Richard and Bobicz (2003). For a summary of 15 computerized systems for collecting observational data, see Kahng and Iwata (1998).

DATA! DATA! DATA! WHY BOTHER?

There are a number of reasons for recording accurate data during the baseline and throughout a program. First, an accurate behavioral assessment provides a description of the problem that will help the behavior modifier to decide whether he or she is the appropriate one to design a treatment program. Considerations relevant to this are described in more detail in Chapter 24.

Sometimes an accurate baseline will indicate that what someone thought to be a problem is actually not a problem. For example, a teacher may say, "I don't know what to do with Johnny; he's always hitting the other kids." But after taking a baseline, the teacher may discover that the behavior actually occurs so rarely that it does not merit a special program. Both of the authors have experienced this phenomenon more than once. Others have too, as illustrated by the following example from Greenspoon (1976, p. 177).

> The reliance on casual observation led a woman to complain to a psychologist that her husband rarely talked to her during mealtime. She said that his failure to talk to her was becoming an increasing source of annoyance to her and she wanted to do something about it. The psychologist suggested that she prepare a chart and record on the chart the number of times that he initiated a conversation or responded to the verbal behavior that she emitted. She agreed to the suggestions. At the end of a week, she called back to inform the psychologist that she was surprised and pleased to report that she had been in error. It turned out that her husband both initiated conversation and responded to her verbal emissions at a very high rate.

A second reason for assessing and recording behavior carefully is that the initial assessment process often helps the behavior modifier to identify the best treatment strategy. For example, determining whether a behavioral excess of an individual is reinforced by the attention of others, or whether it enables the individual to escape from the demands of an unpleasant task, or whether it is controlled by some other variable, can be helpful for discovering potential reinforcers and designing an effective intervention program. As indicated previously, using information from a baseline to analyze the causes of behavior is referred to as a functional assessment and is discussed further in Chapter 22.

A third reason for recording accurate data during the baseline and throughout a program is that accurate baseline and program data provide a means for clearly determining whether the program has produced, or is producing, the desired change in behavior. Sometimes people claim that they do not need to record data to know whether a desirable change in behavior has occurred. No doubt this is often true. A mother obviously needs no data sheet or graphs to tell her that her child is completely toilet trained. There is ample evidence (or, it is hoped, lack of it) in the child's pants. But not all cases are so clear-cut—at least not immediately. Suppose that a child is acquiring toileting behavior very slowly. The parent may think that the program is not working and abandon it prematurely. With accurate data, this type of mistake can be avoided. This point is well illustrated by the following case.[1] Dr. Lynn Caldwell was consulted by a woman whose 6-year-old son was, in her words, "driving me up a wall with his constant slamming of the kitchen door every time he goes out of the kitchen." Dr. Caldwell asked the mother to obtain a baseline of the target behavior by tallying each instance of it on a sheet of paper attached to the refrigerator. Over a three-day period, the total number of

---

[1]This case was described by Lynn Caldwell at the first Manitoba Behavior Change Conference, Portage la Prairie, Manitoba, Canada, 1971.

door slams was 123. Dr. Caldwell then instructed the mother to provide approval each time the boy went through the door without slamming it. However, she was to administer a brief time-out whenever he slammed the door (he was to go back and remain for three minutes in whichever room he had just left, and the mother was to ignore him during that time) and then require him to proceed through the door without slamming it. After applying this procedure for three days, the mother brought the tally sheet to Dr. Caldwell. "This behavior modification stuff doesn't work," she complained, pointing to the large number of tally marks on the data sheet. "He's just as bad as he ever was." When the tally marks were counted, however, there were only 87 of them over the three days of treatment, compared with the 123 that were entered over the three days of baseline. Encouraged by this observation, the mother continued the program, and the behavior quickly dropped to an acceptable level of about five per day (after which the satisfied mother did not make further contact with Dr. Caldwell).

Without accurate data, one might also make the opposite type of error. One might conclude that a procedure is working and continue it when in fact it is ineffective and should be abandoned or modified. For example, Harris, Wolf, and Baer (1964) described the case of a boy in a laboratory preschool who had the annoying habit of pinching adults. His teachers decided to use a behavior modification procedure to encourage him to pat rather than pinch. After the procedure had been in effect for some time, the teachers agreed that they had succeeded in reducing pinching by substituting patting. When they looked at the data recorded by an outside observer, however, they saw clearly that, although patting was considerably above the level it had been during the baseline recordings, pinching had not decreased from its baseline level. Perhaps concentrating on the procedure or the patting so diverted the teachers that they had failed to notice the pinching as much as they had before introducing the procedure. In any case, had it not been for the recorded data, the teachers probably would have wasted a great deal more time and effort than they did on an ineffective procedure.

A fourth reason for accurately recording behavior is that publicly posted results—preferably in the form of a graph or a chart—can prompt and reinforce behavior modifiers for carrying out a program. Staff in training centers for persons with developmental disabilities, for example, often become more conscientious in applying procedures when up-to-date charts or graphs clearly showing the effects of the procedures are posted conspicuously (e.g., see Hrydowy & Martin, 1994). Parents and teachers alike may find that their efforts to modify children's behavior are strengthened by graphic representation of the improved behavior.

A fifth reason for recording and graphing behavior is that the displayed data may lead to improvements by the learner apart from any further treatment program. This is an example of a phenomenon known as *reactivity* (Tyron, 1998): when people know that their behavior is being observed (either by others or by self-recording), their observed behaviors may change. For example, students who graph their own study behavior (e.g., by recording the daily number of paragraphs or pages studied, or the amount of time spent studying) may find

Figure 20–2 Monitoring and charting performance can serve at least five functions. Can you name them?

increases in the graph to be reinforcing (see Figure 20–2). Data that are presented appropriately can be reinforcing even to young children. For example, an occupational therapist at a school for children with handicaps once consulted one of the authors concerning a 7-year-old girl who each morning took an excessive amount of time taking off her outside garments and hanging them up. It appeared that the teachers could not be persuaded to stop attending to the child when she was in the coatroom. The author suggested that the therapist somehow attempt to influence the child with a graph of the amount of time she spent in the coatroom each morning. The procedure that the therapist devised proved to be as effective as it was ingenious.[2]

A large chart was hung on the wall. The chart was colored green so as to represent grass, and a carrot patch was depicted near the bottom of it. Days were indicated along the bottom of the chart and the amount of time in the coatroom was indicated along the side. Each day, a circle was marked on the chart

---

[2]We are grateful to Nancy Staisey for providing us with the details of this procedure.

to indicate the amount of time spent in the coatroom in the morning, and a small paper rabbit was attached to the most recent circle. Using simple language, the therapist explained the procedure to the child and concluded by saying, "Now let's see if you can get the bunny down to eat the carrots." When the rabbit was down to the level of the carrots, the child was encouraged to keep him there. "Remember, the longer the bunny stays in the carrot patch, the more he can eat." A follow-up showed that the improved behavior persisted over a period of one year.

Behavior modifiers were not the first to discover the usefulness of recording one's behavior to help modify that behavior. As with many other supposedly "new" psychological discoveries, the real credit should perhaps go to the writers of great literature. For example, novelist Ernest Hemingway used self-recording to help maintain his literary output. One of his interviewers reported the following (Plimpton, 1965, p. 219).

> He keeps track of his daily progress—"so as not to kid myself"—on a large chart made out of the side of a cardboard packing case and set up against the wall under the nose of a mounted gazelle head. The numbers on the chart showing the daily output of words differ from 450, 575, 462, 1250, back to 512, the higher figures on days Hemingway puts in extra work so he won't feel guilty spending the following day fishing on the gulf stream.

Well-known author Irving Wallace used self-recording even before he was aware that others had done the same. In a book touching on his writing methods (1971, pp. 65–66), he made the following comment.

> I kept a work chart when I wrote my first book—which remains unpublished—at the age of nineteen. I maintained work charts while writing my first four published books. These charts showed the date I started each chapter, the date I finished it, and number of pages written in that period. With my fifth book, I started keeping a more detailed chart which also showed how many pages I had written by the end of every working day. I am not sure why I started keeping such records. I suspect that it was because, as a free-lance writer, entirely on my own, without employer or deadline, I wanted to create disciplines for myself, ones that were guilt-making when ignored. A chart on the wall served as such a discipline, its figures scolding me or encouraging me.

BEHAVIORAL ASSESSMENT COMPARED TO TRADITIONAL ASSESSMENT

As indicated in Chapter 2, a major purpose of traditional psychodiagnostic assessment is to identify the type of mental disorder presumed to underlie abnormal behavior. Behavioral assessment began to emerge during the 1960s and 1970s in response to criticisms made by behaviorally oriented psychologists against underlying assumptions of traditional psychodiagnostic assessment approaches (Nelson, 1983). Some differences in the aims, assumptions, and applications of the behavioral and traditional approaches to assessment were described by Barrios and Hartmann (1986), and are summarized in Table 20–2.

TABLE 20–2   SOME DIFFERENCES BETWEEN BEHAVIORAL AND TRADITIONAL APPROACHES TO ASSESSMENT

Behavioral Approach	Traditional Approach
Basic Assumptions	
—Performance on a checklist is a sample of a person's response to specific stimuli —Covert behaviors (thoughts and feelings) are like overt behaviors (in terms of their controlling variables), and are not accorded special status —Behavior is a function of past environmental experiences and current setting events (including environmental, social, and health/physical fitness variables)	—Test performance is viewed as a sign of an enduring, intrapsychic trait, or person variable —Covert behaviors (e.g., cognitions) are viewed as fundamentally different from overt behaviors
Goals of Assessment	
—To identify behavioral excesses or deficits —To identify causes of current problem behaviors —To provide information that can be used directly for the design of interventions —To evaluate the effects of interventions	—To diagnose or classify individuals —To identify intrapsychic or trait causes of behavior —To provide information that *may* aid in the design of interventions —To obtain information helpful for prognosis
Methods of Assessment	
—Preference for direct observation of specific behaviors —Some indirect assessment of specific behaviors to be changed	—Direct assessment is impossible (by definition) —Indirect assessment of intrapsychic factors, underlying states, or traits based on performance on standardized tests
Frequency of Assessment	
—Preference for continuous assessment before, during, and after application of interventions	—Typically pre- and posttreatment assessments based on standardized tests

STUDY QUESTIONS

1. What is meant by the term *target behavior*? Illustrate with an example from an earlier chapter.
2. Define behavioral assessment.
3. Briefly describe the minimal phases of a behavior modification program.
4. What is a prebaseline phase often called, and what functions does it serve?

5. What is the difference between a training program, a therapy program, and an intervention strategy?

6. What is an important prerequisite to the design and implementation of a behavior modification program?

7. Briefly distinguish between direct and indirect assessment procedures.

8. Describe two circumstances that might lead one to use indirect assessment procedures.

9. Briefly describe the advantages and disadvantages of indirect assessment procedures.

10. Briefly describe the advantages and disadvantages of direct assessment procedures.

11. List and describe briefly the five main types of indirect assessment procedures.

12. List and describe briefly four types of questionnaires used in behavioral assessments.

13. Give five reasons for collecting accurate data during a baseline and throughout a program.

14. What error is exemplified by the case of Dr. Caldwell and the door slammer's mother? Explain how accurately recorded data counteracted this error.

15. What error is exemplified by the case of the boy who went around pinching adults? Explain how accurately recorded data counteracted this error.

16. Briefly describe the details of the clever graphing system devised for the child who got the rabbit to the carrot patch.

17. What is meant by reactivity in behavioral assessment? Illustrate with an example.

18. Briefly describe how self-recording was used by Ernest Hemingway and Irving Wallace to help them maintain their writing behavior.

19. How does a behavioral approach differ from a traditional approach to assessment in terms of a basic assumption about performance on a test or a checklist?

20. Describe two differences in the goals of a behavioral approach to assessment compared to a traditional approach.

21. Describe a difference between the method of a behavioral approach compared to a traditional approach to assessment.

NOTE AND EXTENDED DISCUSSION

1. Martin, Toogood, and Tkachuk (1997) developed a manual of self-report problem checklists for sport psychology consulting. For example, the sport psychology checklist for basketball players asks such questions as: "Would you say that, just before or during a game, you need to improve at tuning out negative thoughts, staying relaxed, and not getting too nervous?" and "Do you need to improve at identifying and reacting to your opponents' weaknesses and making adjustments as the game progresses?" The manual includes self-report problem checklists for 21 sports. Each checklist contains 20 items to identify areas in which an athlete may need to improve before or during competitions, 5 items to identify areas in which an athlete may need to improve concerning postcompetition evaluations, and 17 items to identify areas in which an athlete may need to improve at practices. These behavioral checklists are not like traditional psychological tests such as the Wexler Adult Intelligence Scale (Wexler, 1981) or the 16-Personality Factor Inventory (Cattell, Eber, & Tatsuoka, 1970). Behavioral checklists do not have norms, and they are not designed to measure character or personality traits. Rather, such behavioral assessment tools provide information necessary to design effective interventions for remediating deficits or excesses in specific situations with individual athletes. While formal research on these tools has been limited, those checklists that have been formally researched have shown high test–retest reliability and high face validity (Leslie-Toogood & Martin, 2003; Lines, Schwartzman, Tkachuk, Leslie-Toogood, & Martin, 1999). Feedback from athletes and sport psychology consultants who have used various checklists in the manual mentioned above has been uniformly positive concerning their value in obtaining useful behavioral assessment information.

Study Questions on Note

1. What is the major purpose of sport-specific behavioral checklists?
2. What are two differences between behavioral checklists and traditional psychological tests?

Direct Behavioral
Assessment: What
to Record and How

Suppose that you have chosen a particular behavior to be modified. How do you directly measure, assess, or evaluate that behavior? As mentioned in Chapter 20, behavior modifiers generally prefer direct to indirect measurement of behavior whenever direct measurement is feasible. In measuring behavior directly, there are six general characteristics to consider: topography, amount, intensity, stimulus control, latency, and quality.

CHARACTERISTICS OF BEHAVIOR TO BE RECORDED

Topography

As indicated in Chapter 10, *topography* refers to the form of a particular response (i.e., a description of the specific movements involved). Suppose that a teacher wanted to shape arm raising by a child with developmental disabilities as a means of obtaining attention in a classroom. The teacher might identify the levels of arm raising described in Table 21–1 and proceed with a shaping program from step 1 through step 6.

Picture prompts are sometimes useful for helping observers to identify variations in the topography of a response. One of the authors developed detailed checklists with picture prompts for evaluating swimming strokes of young competitive swimmers. Figure 21–1 shows the checklist for the backstroke.

TABLE 21–1   LEVELS OF ARM RAISING FROM POOR QUALITY TO GOOD QUALITY

1. While sitting at a table and resting both arms on the table,	the student raises an arm so that the hand and forearm are 2 inches off the table.
2. While sitting at a table and resting both arms on the table,	the student raises an arm so that it is approximately at the student's chin level.
3. While sitting at a table and resting both arms on the table,	the student raises an arm so that it is approximately at the student's eye level.
4. While sitting at a table and resting both arms on the table,	the student raises an arm so that his hand is slightly above his head.
5. While sitting at a table and resting both arms on the table,	the student raises an arm so that it is pointing upward with his hand six inches above his head, but the elbow is still bent.
6. While sitting at a table and resting both arms on the table,	the student raises an arm so that it is pointing straight above his head.

Amount

Two common measures of the overall amount of a given behavior are its frequency and its duration.

Frequency   *Frequency* refers to the number of instances of the behavior that occur in a given period of time. (The term *rate* is often used interchangeably with frequency.) If you were interested, for example, in improving the practice performance of young figure skaters, you might examine the frequency with which they performed various jumps and spins during practices. That was the approach taken by Michelle Hume, a figure skating coach at the St. Anne's Figure Skating

Note 1   Club in Manitoba (Hume et al., 1985). Coach Hume first defined jumps and spins in such a way that student observers at figure skating practices could decide when either of those responses occurred. A *jump* was defined as any occasion when a skater jumped in the air so that both skates left the ice, a minimum of one complete revolution occurred in the air, and the skater landed on one foot, facing backward, without falling. A *spin* was defined as spinning on one skate for a minimum of three revolutions while maintaining a balanced, stationary position. Now that the observers knew what behaviors to look for, Ms. Hume's next step was to take a baseline of how many jumps and spins individual skaters performed during several practices. The observers used the data sheet shown in Figure 21–2.

In many situations an individual doesn't have a helper or the time to take data with paper and pencil. Fortunately, there are other ways of measuring quantity that require minimal time. One such method is to use a counter, such as the relatively inexpensive wristwatch type used by golfers to record their score. With these counters you can count up to 99 simply by pressing a button for each instance of the behavior. Another easy recording technique is to transfer items, such as beads, from one pocket to another. At the end of the session, or at the end of the day, depending on the particular behavior being recorded, the number of beads in the second pocket is counted and recorded. You could also use an electronic calculator. Press "+1" each time an instance of the behavior occurs and the calculator keeps track of the total. Hand-held computers have been used to record more than

Hands: Fingers together
Arms: Roll shoulder into your ear
(Recovery) Arm comes over straight
           Arm comes over close to ear
           Little finger enters water first

Arms: Lower arm bends to almost 90 degrees under shoulder
(Pull) As arm straightens underwater, snap wrist at thigh and down

Legs: Leg action begins at the hips
        Knees move up and down very little
        Knees don't break the surface
        Toes point down at bottom of kick
        Toes just break surface at top of kick

Body: Hips kept high in the water
       Hips kept as flat as possible
Head: Tilted up slightly, ears in water
       Head kept stationary, don't rock

Figure 21–1 Checklist for the backstroke.

one behavior or the behavior of more than one individual, along with the times at which each instance of behavior occurs (Paggeot, Kvale, Mace, & Sharkey, 1988; Repp, Karsh, Felce, & Ludewig, 1989). Adequate ways of counting instances of behavior (or responses) that require little of the observer's time can almost always be found. For a detailed guide to this and other topics relating to measuring and

Date: January 3				Observer: Bill K.
Student: Kathy		Observation		
	Instances	Total	Time	Additional Comments
Jumps:	//// //// //// //// //// //// //// //	37	25 min	Kathy spent 5 minutes chatting with other skaters
Spins:	//// //// ////	15	20 min	

Figure 21–2 A sample data sheet for recording jumps and spins at figure skating practices.

graphing behavioral outcomes, and letting the results influence clinical decisions, see Hawkins, Mathews, and Hamdan (1999).

The baseline performance of one of the figure skaters in Coach Hume's program can be seen in Figure 21–3. This type of graph is called a *frequency graph*. Each data point represents the total number of elements (jumps plus spins) completed by a skater during a practice session. Following baseline, a big chart was prepared for each skater that contained a checklist of all of the jumps and spins that the skaters should be practicing, and the charts were posted at the side of the rink. Coach Hume explained to the skaters: "Each practice session, I want you to do the

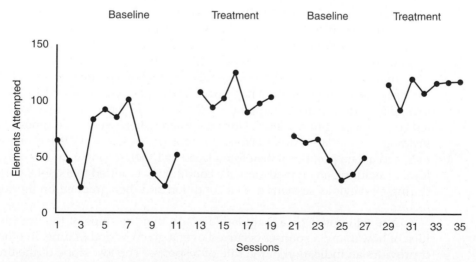

Figure 21–3 Frequency graph of the number of elements (jumps and spins) per session performed by a figure skater during baseline and treatment (self-recording).

first three elements on your chart, and then record them here. Then practice the next three elements and record them. Continue in this way until you've practiced all the elements. Then go through the whole routine again until the end of practice. At the end of practice, I will check your charts to see how you are doing." As can be seen in Figure 21–3, the self-charting program combined with positive feedback from Coach Hume at the end of each practice was very effective in improving the number of jumps and spins performed. Interestingly, when the chart was removed, performance decreased to near baseline levels. When the treatment (i.e., self-charting and coach feedback) was reintroduced, performance once again improved.

Sometimes a frequency graph is not the most informative way to present data. Consider, for example, a study by Mulaire-Cloutier, Vause, Martin, and Yu (2000). They examined the effects of giving persons with severe developmental disabilities a choice versus no choice of work tasks. The participants in the study were given three sessions per day. During the first session each participant was given a choice of which of two tasks to work on. The task chosen was called the preferred task for each participant, and the task not chosen was called the less preferred task. In the remaining two sessions each day, the participants were randomly given either the preferred task or the less preferred task to work on, without a choice. Because the participants were nonverbal and could not describe how they felt about the work sessions, one of the dependent measures was happiness indicators, which consisted of behaviors such as smiling, laughing, and yelling while smiling. A frequency graph of the happiness indicators displayed by one of the participants in the three conditions is shown in Figure 21–4A. As you can see in that graph, because of the small, somewhat inconsistent effects of the three conditions, it's difficult to recognize differences caused by those conditions.

But now examine Figure 21–4B. This figure is based on the same data as Figure 21–4A. However, Figure 21–4B is a *cumulative graph* in that each of the responses for a condition during a session cumulate or are added to the total responses of all previous sessions for that condition. Consider, for example, the happiness indicators during the no-choice, less preferred task (the bottom line). During the first three sessions there were 0 happiness indicators, and the cumulative total of 0 was therefore plotted corresponding to sessions 1, 2, and 3. During the fourth session there were 3 happiness indicators, yielding a cumulative total of 3 plotted for session 4. During the fifth session there were 2 happiness indicators, which, added to the previous total of 3, made a total of 5 happiness indicators, and that cumulative total was plotted corresponding to session 5. During session 6 there were 5 happiness indicators, yielding a cumulative total across the first six sessions of 10 happiness indicators, and a data point was therefore placed at 10 for session 6. In this way, the performance during any one session of a condition was added to the total performance during all previous sessions of that condition and then graphed on the cumulative record.

You will notice on a cumulative graph that the slope of the line gives us an idea of how many responses occurred over a given period of time. In other words, it provides an indication of the rate of response. The low slope of the line during the no-choice, less preferred condition indicates a very low rate of happiness indicators. The highest slope during the choice condition indicates the highest rate of

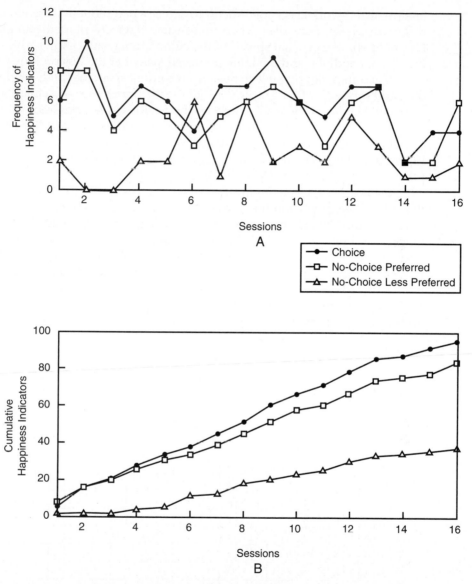

Figure 21–4 A frequency graph **(A)** and a cumulative graph **(B)** of the same data.

happiness indicators. Another feature of a cumulative graph should be noted: The line can never decrease. If a participant is not performing at all, such as during the first three sessions of the no-choice, less preferred condition, there are no responses cumulating with what is already there, and the line is flat.

A cumulative graph is usually preferred over a frequency graph when comparing two or more behaviors or conditions concurrently, and when the differences are small within each session. You can see that differences in the frequency of happiness indicators between the choice, no-choice preferred, and no-choice, less preferred work tasks are difficult to detect when plotted as frequency graphs in Figure 21–4A. However, when those same data are plotted cumulatively in Figure 21–4B, the gradual spread of the cumulative results shows a clear effect of the choice condition and the more preferred task over the less preferred task.

It is sometimes possible to design a recording sheet that both records the raw data and serves as a final graph. Consider the fictitious case of a child, Jackie, who frequently swore at the teacher and teacher's aides in the classroom. To treat this problem, suppose that the following program was devised: Each time the teacher or teacher's aides observed an instance of swearing, during a baseline, they were to ignore Jackie, go to a chart on the front desk, and place an X in the appropriate place. The chart is shown in Figure 21–5.

As you can see from Figure 21–5, the instances of swearing were recorded up the side of the graph and the days of the program were recorded across the bottom. Each time an instance of swearing occurred, the staff would simply add an X for the appropriate day to the number of Xs that were already on the chart for that particular day. The graph shows clearly that ignoring Jackie's swearing had no effect. This might happen if swearing was being reinforced by other students rather than by the teacher and teacher aides. The graph also shows that when Jackie was placed on a treatment program in which she received reinforcement at the end of each 15-minute period in which swearing did not occur, swearing decreased to 0.

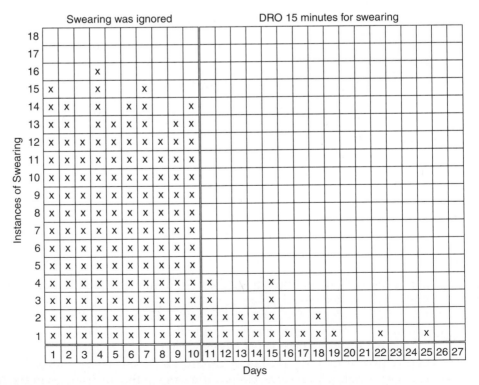

Figure 21–5 Jackie's swearing behavior. Each X represents one swear word.

(*Note:* These data are hypothetical and are presented simply to illustrate the plotting procedure.) This type of graph is especially useful for those who do not have the time to rechart their behavior tallies from their data sheet to a graph.

Each instance of a behavior that is recorded in terms of frequency, such as jumping or spinning as defined for the figure skaters, is a separate, individually distinct behavior that is easy to tally in a given period of time. Behavior modifiers have recorded the frequency of such behaviors as saying a particular word, swearing, throwing objects, completing arithmetic problems, chewing mouthfuls of food, taking puffs on a cigarette, and exhibiting nervous twitches. Each of these behaviors has characteristics such that successive occurrences of the given behavior are relatively brief and the amount of time that it takes to perform the behavior is about the same from one occasion to the next.

Duration   While frequency or rate is a common measure of the amount of behavior, the relative duration of a behavior (or, more precisely, the sum of its durations divided by total time) is also sometimes important in measuring amount. The *relative duration* of behavior is the length of time that it occurs within some period. In dealing with a behavior such as temper tantrumming, you may be more concerned with its duration than with its frequency. In fact, frequency can be quite ambiguous when trying to apply it to something like temper tantrums (Pear, 2004). What should we count as a separate response? Each cry, scream, or kick on the floor? Or should we count each episode of tantrumming as a separate response? It's usually difficult to answer these questions. We can generally avoid these types of questions, however, by focusing on the duration of tantrumming. Other examples of behaviors for which duration of responding may be more appropriate than frequency of responding are listening attentively, sitting in one's seat in a classroom, watching television, talking on the telephone, and taking coffee breaks.

If you are concerned simply with keeping track of the relative duration of some activity over successive sessions, or days, then you might easily tabulate and present these data for effective visual display on a combined data sheet/graph. For example, an individual concerned with monitoring his or her TV watching might prepare a chart showing cumulative minutes of TV watching up the side and days across the bottom. The slope of this graph would indicate relative duration of the person's TV watching, just as the slope of a cumulative frequency graph indicates response rate. Stopwatches or clocks are usually used to record time.

Intensity

Sometimes we are concerned with measuring the intensity or force of a response. Assessments of intensity often utilize instrumentation. For example, when voice loudness is the behavior of concern, decibel level can be measured by a device called a *voice meter*. To measure the strength of grip pressure (such as during a handshake), a device called a *dynamometer* can be used. Measures of force are common in the skills involved in various sports. Machines are now available that assess how hard a pitcher can throw a baseball or a hockey player can shoot a hockey puck. With these types of devices the speed of an object is used to infer the force with which it was propelled.

Stimulus Control

We often wish to assess a behavior in terms of the conditions under which it might be observed to occur. As we pointed out in Chapter 8, the term *stimulus control* is used to indicate that a certain behavior occurs in the presence of certain stimuli (and not others). Hardy and colleagues (1981) designed a detailed system called the Objective Behavioral Assessment of the Severely and Moderately Mentally Handicapped (OBA). The OBA assesses the stimulus control of basic self-care skills, social and advanced self-care skills, sheltered domestic skills, prevocational motor dexterity skills, and sheltered work performance of persons with severe and moderate developmental disabilities. In this test, the learner is instructed to perform a particular behavior—for example, "Please put on your socks." The behavior is then scored as shown in Table 21–2.

Hardy and colleagues (1981) identified specific behaviors that are taught in many training programs with persons with severe and moderate developmental disabilities. Those target behaviors were then specified in the OBA; instructions were prepared for the tester; and definitions of the different types of prompts were standardized so that the behaviors could all be assessed on the basis of the rating system in Table 21–2. This testing system for identifying the conditions under which the behavior will occur is very useful for placement and evaluation of students in individualized training programs.

In many cases, behavior modification programs concerned with the development of preverbal and verbal skills are typically preceded by behavior assessments of the stimulus control of the student's verbal behavior. Tests are available that determine the conditions under which the students will emit appropriate requesting behavior, echoic behavior, or object identification (i.e., mands, echoics, or tacts, as described in Chapter 19, also see Marion et al., 2003). For that matter, any test in which a student is given instructions, some paper, **Note 2** and a pencil and is asked to answer the questions is a test of the stimulus control of behavior. Are the correct answers under the control of the questions? In many training programs, the critical measure of behavior is whether the student identifies some pictorial or printed stimulus correctly. In such cases, the student's identification response is said to be controlled by the stimulus that the student is identifying.

TABLE 21–2   SCORING STUDENT BEHAVIOR FROM THE OBA

Test item	Score
The test item was performed appropriately in all respects without further prompting or guidance of any kind after a specific instruction was presented.	3
The test item was performed appropriately only after the instruction and a verbal prompt were provided by the tester.	2
The test item was performed appropriately only after the instruction and a prescriptive verbal prompt (similar to the verbal prompt except that it provides much more detail) were given concurrently with modeling of the desired behavior.	1
The test item was not performed appropriately to the preceding level of prompting.	0

Latency

Another characteristic of behavior with which we are sometimes concerned is its latency—the time between the occurrence of a stimulus and the beginning of a response. For example, a child in a classroom might work effectively once she gets started. The problem is that she shows a very long latency; that is, after the teacher asks her to do something, she fools around "forever" before starting. Like duration, latency is usually assessed with stopwatches or clocks.

Quality

Concern about the quality of a behavior is frequently encountered in everyday life. Teachers might describe the quality of a child's handwriting as "good," "average," or "poor." In judgmental sports such as diving, gymnastics, and figure skating, the athletes receive points based on the quality of their performances. And in our own lives we regularly make resolutions to do various activities "better." But quality is not a characteristic additional to those mentioned previously. Rather it is a refinement of one or more of them. Sometimes differences in judgments of quality are based on topography, such as when a figure skating jump that is landed on one foot is considered better than one that lands on two feet. With respect to frequency and stimulus control, many general evaluations of whether a person is good or poor at some task relate to how many times they tend to emit some behavior in a given period of time appropriately. For example, the person who is a good student is most likely someone who shows a high frequency of studying and answering test questions correctly. A child who is said to be "good" shows a high frequency of "minding" (i.e., following the instruction of) his or her parents and teachers. In terms of latency, a runner who leaves the blocks very quickly after the firing of the starter's pistol might be considered to have a "good" start, while a runner who shows a longer latency had a "poor" start. Thus, quality of response is essentially an arbitrary designation of one or more of the above-mentioned characteristics of behavior that is identified as having some functional value.

STRATEGIES FOR RECORDING BEHAVIOR

For any given target behavior, one could attempt to record that behavior whenever the individual has an opportunity to emit it. In most cases, this method is far too ambitious for our time and resources. One alternative is to designate a specific segment of time, such as a one-hour training session, an afternoon, a mealtime, or a recess time, and attempt to record every instance of the target behavior throughout that interval. Recording every instance of a behavior during a specified time segment is called *continuous recording*.

An alternative strategy is *interval recording*. Here, a specific block of time is selected (such as a 30-minute observation period). This time is then divided into equal intervals of relatively short duration (e.g., intervals of 10 seconds). The target behavior is recorded as occurring or not occurring during each interval. There are two types of interval recording procedures. The most frequently used procedure is called *partial-interval recording*. With this procedure, the target behavior is recorded a maximum of once per interval throughout the observation period, regardless of how many times the behavior might occur during each interval and regardless of the duration of the behavior. An observer might use a tape recorder that plays a prerecorded beep (or some such signal) every 10 seconds. Let us suppose that the behavior of concern is an appropriately defined social-interaction response. If the response occurs once during a 10-second interval, a tally is made on the data sheet (for a sample data sheet, see Figure 21–6). If several responses or continuous social interaction occurs during the 10-second interval, the observer still makes only one tally. As soon as the beep is heard, indicating the start of the next 10-second interval, the behavior is again recorded either 1 or 0 depending on its occurrence. Alternatively, the second type of interval recording, *a whole-interval recording* procedure, can be used. With this approach, the target behavior is recorded during an interval only if it persists throughout the entire interval. Behavior recorded with either a partial-interval recording or a whole-interval recording procedure is typically graphed in terms of the percentage of observation intervals in which the behavior is recorded as occurring.

Another behavior recording technique that is often used is time sampling (see, e.g., Powell, Martindale, & Kulp, 1975). In *time-sampling recording*, a behavior is scored as occurring or not occurring during very brief observation intervals that are separated from each other by a much longer period of time. For example, a parent of a preschool child might be concerned about the frequency of the child's sitting and rocking back and forth (a self-stimulation behavior). It might be useful to have records of this behavior whenever it occurs and for as long as it occurs throughout the child's waking hours, but in general this is not realistic. An alternative is for the parent to seek out the child once every hour and make a note of whether or not the child shows any sitting and rocking behavior during a 15-second observation interval. Each observation interval is separated from the next by approximately one hour. This type of observational technique enables one observer

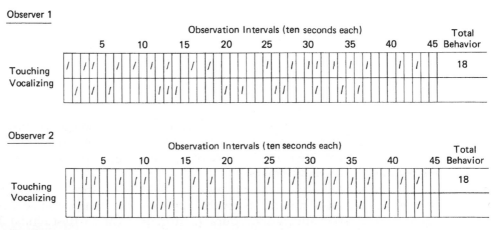

Figure 21–6   Sample data sheet for interval recording.

DATE _____

Time	Behavior			Location			Comments
	Sitting	Standing	Rocking	Kitchen	Living Room	Bedroom	
8:00 AM							
9:00							
10:00							
11:00							
12:00 PM							
1:00							
2:00							
3:00							
4:00							
5:00							
6:00							
7:00							
8:00							
9:00 PM							

Figure 21–7 A time-sampling data sheet for recording behavior of a child who frequently sits and rocks.

to record one or more behaviors of one or more students, even though the observer has many other commitments during the day. An example of a data sheet for time sampling appears in Figure 21–7. A variation of time sampling is referred to as *momentary time sampling*. With this approach, a behavior is recorded as occurring or not occurring at specific points in time, such as every hour on the hour.

Often a recording procedure with features of both interval recording and time-sampling recording is used. An observer might watch the learner for a specified interval (say, 10 seconds) and then record the behavior during the next 10 seconds. This strategy of *observe* (for 10 seconds) and *record* (for 10 seconds) would continue over a given period of time (for instance, a half-hour). In this way, one observer may record the behavior of several students. In such a case, the observer might watch one student for 10 seconds and then record a behavior as occurring or not occurring, watch another student for 10 seconds and record a behavior as occurring or not occurring, and so forth, until all the students have been observed once. All of the students would then be observed a second time, a third time, and so forth, throughout the observation period. Such a procedure would likely be referred to as an interval-recording procedure, although, strictly speaking, it could also be described as time sampling with a very brief time between observation intervals.

ASSESSING THE ACCURACY OF OBSERVATIONS

Hawkins and Dotson (1975) identified three sources of error that can affect the accuracy of observations. First, the *response definition* might be vague, subjective, or incomplete, so that the observer has problems in making accurate observations.

Second, the *observational situation* might be such that it is difficult for an observer to detect the behavior because of distractions or other obstructions to the observing process, or because the behavior is too subtle or complex to be observed accurately in that situation. Third, the *observer* might be poorly trained, unmotivated, biased, or generally incompetent. We might add two other possible sources of error: poorly designed *data sheets* and cumbersome *recording procedures*. Because any one or combination of these sources of error might be present in any behavior modification project, behavior modifiers frequently conduct **interobserver reliability (IOR)** estimates. Two independent observers might record observations of the same behavior of the same individual during a given session. They are careful not to influence or signal each other while they are recording or to peek at each other's observations. The question is, given their best efforts while using the available behavior definitions and recording procedures, and considering their training, how closely will their scores compare? There are several ways of evaluating this, but two IOR procedures are more common than the others.

One IOR procedure can be illustrated as follows. Let us return to our example of the observer who is recording the number of elements (jumps plus spins) of figure skaters, as defined earlier in this chapter. Let us suppose that we bring in a second observer, who stands on the opposite side of the ice rink from the first observer and watches the skaters. The second observer is familiar with the definitions of jumps and spins and uses a data recording sheet identical to that used by our first observer. At the end of the session, our first observer recorded 20 elements. Let us suppose that our second observer recorded 22 elements. This can be converted to an IOR estimate by dividing the smaller number by the larger number and multiplying by 100%: IOR equals 20 divided by 22 times 100% equals 91%. Now it is important to ask what this IOR score means. It means that the two observers agreed quite closely (almost 100%) on the total *number* of elements. It does not mean that they agreed on 20 specific elements, with the second observer counting 2 extra to make 22. It is quite possible that one observer recorded an element that the second observer missed. The second observer could then have counted an element that the first observer missed. This could have gone on throughout the session, in which case the two observers would have disagreed completely on specific individual responses. Nevertheless, their close agreement on the total gives us confidence that the actual total was close to the number that each observer tallied, in spite of the possible disagreements on individual cases. This approach of counting two totals and then dividing the smaller by the larger and multiplying by 100% is quite common when two observers are counting the frequency of a particular response over a period of time.

The other common IOR procedure is used with interval recording. Recall that in interval-recording procedures, one and only one response can be recorded during each brief period of time (usually 5 or 10 seconds) over an extended observation period. If we have two independent observers recording the same behavior, and each is using an interval-recording procedure, then the question is: How do their successive intervals compare with regard to those that contain a response versus those that do not? Let us suppose that two observers are recording two types of social interaction for one child. The behaviors are defined as touching another child and vocalizing in the direction of the other child. Their interval scores are shown in Figure 21–6.

As you can see, the first observer counted 18 instances of touching, as did the second observer. However, the two observers agreed on only 16 of these 18 in-
Note 3 stances. Each counted two instances that the other missed, yielding a total of four disagreements. If we used the procedure described above we would obtain an IOR of 100%. However, in the second procedure the IOR is obtained by dividing the number of intervals on which the two observers agree that the behavior occurred by the total number of intervals on which either recorded a behavior (agreements divided by agreements plus disagreements on the occurrence of a behavior) and multiplying by 100%. Thus, in this instance the second procedure would yield an IOR of 80%.

Typically, by convention in behavior modification studies, IOR scores between 80% and 100% are considered acceptable. Potential variation in computational procedures, however, renders the final IOR value potentially misleading when considered by itself. We suggest that readers of behavior modification literature consider the response definitions, observer-training procedures, recording system, method of calculating IOR, and the final IOR value as a total package when judging the reliability of reported data. Defects in any of these might make the results suspect.

STUDY QUESTIONS

1. What is meant by the topography of a response? Describe an example.
2. What are two measures of the amount of behavior? Define and give an example of each.
3. Describe three ways of keeping track of the number of times a certain response occurs during a day.
4. Prepare a cumulative graph of the following instances of a behavior that were observed during successive sessions: 3, 7, 19, 0, 0, 0, 27, 12, 12, 6.
5. Describe at least four ways in which a cumulative graph of a set of data differs from a frequency graph of the same data.
6. On a cumulative graph, what can you infer from the following?
   a. a steep slope
   b. a low slope
   c. a flat line
7. What two characteristics do behaviors recorded in terms of frequency usually show?
8. What do we mean by the relative duration of a behavior? Give and explain an example in which relative duration might be more appropriate than frequency.
9. What is another word for the intensity of a response? Describe an example in which it would be important to measure the intensity of a behavior.
10. What do we mean by the latency of a response? Give an example.
11. What behavioral characteristic does the OBA assess? Explain your answer.
12. What behavioral characteristics do we use to assess the quality of a response? Discuss using examples.
13. Describe with an example the continuous-recording system.
14. Describe with an example the partial-interval recording system.
15. Describe with an example the time-sampling recording system.
16. When would one likely select an interval-recording system over a continuous-recording system?

17. Describe five sources of error in recording observations.
18. In a sentence or two, what do we mean by interobserver reliability? (Describe it in words, and don't give the procedures for calculating IORs).
19. Using the procedure described in the text for computing IORs with interval data, compute an IOR for the data of vocalizing, as recorded by observers 1 and 2 (Figure 21–6). Show all your computations.
20. According to convention, what is an acceptable IOR in a research program? What does "by convention" mean?

APPLICATION EXERCISES

A. Exercise Involving Others

Select a behavioral deficit or excess that was modified successfully (e.g., Peter's tantrums), as described in one of the other chapters. For that behavior:
1. Design a plausible data sheet, including a column for sessions and a column for the instances of behavior per session.
2. Prepare a summary of some representative data (real or hypothesized), and write it in your data sheet.
3. Graph your data in a frequency graph.
4. Graph your data in a cumulative graph.

B. Self-Modification Exercise

Select one of your own behavioral excesses or deficits. For that behavior, answer questions 1 to 4 in the previous exercise.

NOTES AND EXTENDED DISCUSSION

1. When the observational method affects the behaviors being observed, we say that the observation is *obtrusive*. To record observations *unobtrusively* means that the observations should not cause those being observed to deviate from their typical behavior. In other words, we don't want our observations to influence the behavior we are observing. There are several ways to ensure that your observations are unobtrusive. One possibility is to observe the behavior from behind a one-way window, as illustrated in the case of Darren in Chapter 3. Another possibility is to inconspicuously observe individuals from a distance. This strategy was used to study the drinking habits of patrons in bars in a mid-sized U.S. city (Sommer, 1977). Another method is to have a confederate make observations while working side by side with a client in a normal work setting (Rae, Martin, & Smyk, 1990). Other alternatives include videotaping with a hidden camera and evaluating products of the behavior of the client (such as items littered in a public campground; Osborne & Powers, 1980). However, such tactics raise a moral question: Is it ethical to observe individuals without their consent? The American Psychological Association (APA, 2000) has developed a set of ethical guidelines governing all types of experiments of psychological researchers. Among the factors these guidelines stipulate for making observations for experimental purposes are whether there is formal consent from the person being observed or from his or her guardian, whether the observations will aid in carrying out a therapeutic program for the person being observed, whether the confidentiality of the observations will be maintained, and whether specific individuals or groups can be identified from any reports stemming from the observations. Anyone contemplating recording the behavior of another person should consult the ethical guidelines of his or her professional organization and the applicable laws pertaining to privacy and confidentiality. (See also Chapter 30 of this text.)

2. Another assessment instrument that evaluates stimulus control is the Assessment of Basic Learning Abilities (ABLA) test developed by pioneering behaviorists Nancy Kerr and Lee Meyerson. The ABLA assesses the ease or difficulty with which persons with profound, severe, or moderate developmental disabilities are able to learn tasks ranging from a simple imitation task to relatively complex discriminations involving visual and auditory cues. Level 3, for example, is a two-choice visual discrimination in which a client is required to place a piece of foam into a yellow can that randomly alternates in position with a red box. Level 4 is a visual–visual identity discrimination in which a client is randomly given a red cube or a yellow cylinder and must place the cube in a red box and the cylinder in a yellow can that randomly alternate in left–right positions. Level 6, as another example, is a two-choice auditory–visual discrimination. A tester randomly says either "Red box" or "Yellow can," and a correct response involves a client placing a piece of foam in the container that is identified when the two containers are randomly alternated in front of the client. During the assessment of each ABLA level, correct responses are reinforced and incorrect responses are followed by an error-correction procedure. Testing at a level continues until a client meets a pass criterion of eight consecutive correct responses, or a failure criterion of eight cumulative errors. Research on the ABLA test indicates that the six levels are hierarchically ordered in difficulty, and that the ABLA test is a valuable tool for teachers and rehabilitation workers for selecting and sequencing training and work tasks for persons with profound, severe, and moderate developmental disabilities (Martin & Yu, 2000; Martin, Yu, & Vause, 2004). If a client passes ABLA level 4, for example, then that client will be able to readily learn socially useful identity matching tasks, such as sorting socks into pairs or restocking a salad bar at a fast-food restaurant.

3. The procedure that we have suggested for computing IOR during interval recording is that of dividing the number of intervals on which observers agree that a behavior occurred by the total number of intervals on which either recorded a behavior (agreements plus disagreements on a behavior) and multiplying by 100%. Some researchers, however, include in their measure of agreements those agreements that no behavior occurred—in other words, agreements on blank intervals. When very few behaviors have been recorded, however, this can greatly inflate a reliability score. For example, consider the 45 observation intervals given in Figure 21–6. Let us suppose that observer 1 recorded an instance of touching during interval 5 and that observer 2 recorded an instance of touching during interval 6. No other instances of touching were recorded. In such a case, the two observers would disagree completely on the occurrence of the behavior and the IOR would be zero if it is computed as suggested in the text. However, if agreements on blank intervals are included, the IOR equals 43 agreements divided by 43 agreements plus 2 disagreement times 100%, which equals 95.6%. Because of this distortion, many researchers do not count agreements on blank intervals. In other words, intervals in which neither observer scores a behavior are ignored. An acceptable exception to this would be when one is concerned with decreasing a behavior and it is important to have agreement that the behavior did not occur. These points and other comments on the complexity of computing IOR are discussed in more detail by Poling, Methot, and LeSage (1995).

Study Questions on Notes

1. What is the difference between obtrusive and unobtrusive observations?
2. When is it especially misleading to include agreement on blank intervals in computing the IOR? Give an example.
3. When might it be acceptable to include agreement on blank intervals in your computation of an IOR? Why would this be acceptable?
4. What information does the ABLA test provide?

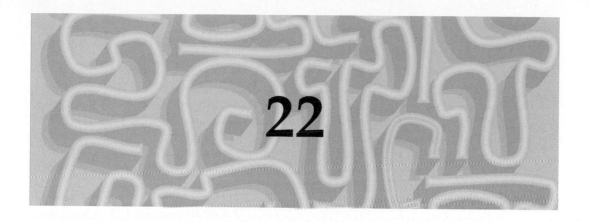

22

Functional Assessment
of the Causes
# of Problem Behavior

Throughout Part II of this book, especially in the "pitfalls" sections, we repeatedly pointed out how misapplication of behavior principles by those who are unaware of them can cause problem behavior. Increasingly, behavior analysts are utilizing an understanding of the causes of problem behaviors in order to treat them more effectively.

A functional assessment of the causes of problem behaviors involves asking (a) what are the antecedents (i.e., the S^Ds [see Chapter 8], or the eliciting stimuli [see Chapter 14], or the motivating operations [see Chapter 19]) of the behavior, and (b) what are the immediate consequences (i.e., the positive or negative reinforcement) of the behavior? More specifically, we ask: Is the behavior being controlled or elicited by particular stimuli? Is it being reinforced? Does the behavior lead to escape from aversive events? From the client's point of view, what function does the behavior serve? The answers to such questions have important implications for planning effective treatment.

APPROACHES TO FUNCTIONAL ASSESSMENT

Let us now consider procedures—broadly termed functional assessment—for identifying variables that are controlling specific problem behaviors, and examples of how such knowledge can help in designing a treatment program. In general, you will see that the information presented here follows quite logically from the basic principles and procedures discussed in the earlier chapters of this book.

285

Questionnaire Assessment

One way to discover antecedents and consequences that control problem behavior is to do a questionnaire analysis in which people familiar with the client are asked a series of relevant questions. For example, Matson and Vollmer (1995) devised a questionnaire called *Questions About Behavioral Function* to help staff determine whether problem behavior of persons with developmental disabilities was maintained by attention from others, escape from aversive conditions, sensory feedback, or tangible reinforcers. Kearney and Silverman (1990) developed a similar questionnaire, called the *School Refusal Assessment Scale*, to assess variables responsible for children refusing to attend school. Sobell, Toneatto, and Sobell (1994) reviewed questionnaires for identifying antecedents and consequences of excessive alcohol drinking. As with other indirect assessment procedures (see Chapter 20), such measures may not always be reliable (Iwata, Kahng, Wallace, & Lindberg, 2000; Sturmey, 1994).

Observational Assessment

Another way to discover controlling variables of a problem behavior is to do an observational or a descriptive assessment in which one carefully observes and describes the antecedents and immediate consequences of the behavior in its natural settings. (For examples, see Table 3–3 in Chapter 3.) From these descriptions, one forms hypotheses about the antecedent stimuli, motivational variables, and consequences controlling the problem behavior. Then one devises and implements a treatment plan based on these hypotheses. If the treatment is successful, the descriptive analysis is validated. (For additional discussion and examples of observational assessment, see Iwata et al., 2000.)

Functional Analysis

A third way to discover controlling variables is to directly assess their effects on the problem behavior, which is referred to as an *experimental functional assessment* or a *functional analysis*. Consider the case of Susie, a 5-year-old child with developmental disabilities who had been referred for therapy because of a high frequency of self-injurious behavior, including banging her head and slapping her face. Was this a way for Susie to get attention (positive reinforcement, see Chapter 3) from well-meaning adults who, following an instance of self-abuse, would run to Susie saying, "Don't do that! You'll hurt yourself"? Was it a way for Susie to escape from having to perform various tasks (negative reinforcement, see Chapter 13) in nursery school (i.e., when Susie was abusive, the teachers likely backed off from asking her to do those tasks)? Or were the injurious behaviors self-reinforcing (perhaps the tingling sensation in her skin felt good afterward)? To assess these possibilities experimentally, Iwata, Pace, Kalsher, Cowdery, and Cataldo (1990) studied Susie's self-abusive behavior over several sessions in a therapy room. In an "attention" condition, the therapist approached Susie and voiced concern following instances of self-abuse (e.g., "Oh Susie, what's wrong?"). In a "demand" condition, the therapist presented various educational tasks to Susie at a rate of one every 30 seconds. In other sessions, Susie was either left alone in an empty therapy room or was observed when the therapy room contained a number of toys and games. These conditions were compared in what is called an *alternating-treatments* or *multielement* research design (see Chapter 23). Across several sessions, the results were clear: Susie was frequently self-abusive in the demand condition but was rarely self-abusive in the other two conditions.

Armed with this functional analysis, the therapist designed a treatment program in which the self-injurious escape behavior was extinguished by continuing the demand when Susie engaged in self-abuse. Instead of backing off following instances of self-abuse, Susie was physically guided to complete the various educational activities as they were presented. By the fifth session, self-abuse had decreased to near zero and Susie was more compliant in performing the various tasks. Because the treatment was successful, we may infer that the therapist had correctly identified the cause of the behavior through the experimental functional analysis. In other words, the success of the treatment validated the results of the functional analysis. (For additional discussion and examples of functional analyses, see Iwata et al., 2000.)

There has been some confusion in the literature concerning the terms *functional assessment* and *functional analysis.* Some writers have used the terms interchangeably. Others (e.g., Cone, 1997; Horner, 1994) have distinguished between the terms, as we have in this book. That is, a **functional assessment** refers to a variety of approaches for attempting to identify antecedents and consequences for behavior, while a **functional analysis** refers to the systematic manipulation of environmental events to experimentally test their role as antecedents or as consequences in controlling and maintaining specific problem behaviors.

In a review of 277 published studies of functional analyses of problem behavior, 253 (91%) were with persons with developmental disabilities and 25 (9%) were with typically developing children (Hanley, Iwata, and McCord, 2003). Examples of the latter studies include finger sucking by children in their home (Ellingson, Miltenberger, Stricker, Garlinghouse, Roberts, & Galensky, 2000), disruptive classroom behavior of students with emotional problems (DePaepe, Shores, Jack, & Denny, 1996), reluctant speech of an elementary school student (Mace & West, 1986), inappropriate classroom behavior of an elementary school student (Lewis & Sugai, 1996), and the emotional problems of an 11-year-old boy in the fifth grade (Kern, Childs, Dunlap, Clarke, & Falk, 1994). For a description of step-by-step procedures to guide school practitioners in conducting functional analyses of problem behaviors of children in schools, and using the analyses to plan effective interventions, see Watson and Steege (2003).

Although functional analyses can provide convincing demonstrations of the controlling variables of problem behaviors, they do have some limitations (Cone, 1997; Sturmey, 1995). First, many behavior problems (e.g. those that occur in community settings) occur at frequencies of less than one per day (Whitaker, 1993). Functional analyses for such low-frequency behaviors require a great deal of time before sufficient data can be obtained to draw valid conclusions. Second, they cannot be applied to extremely dangerous behaviors, such as suicide threats (Sturmey, 1995). Third, because they require scheduling a number of observational sessions, the expense and personnel requirements may be prohibitive. For example, in a summary of 152 functional analyses, it was reported that the length of assessments ranged from 8 to 66 sessions (2 to 16.5 hours) (Iwata et al., 1994). In an attempt to minimize this limitation, several researchers have compared standard functional analyses to ones involving fewer and shorter sessions for each condition. The results suggest that valid conclusions can usually be drawn from only one or two repetitions of selected test and control conditions, and with a session length usually limited to five minutes (see, e.g., Northup et al., 1991; Tincani, Gastrogiavanni, & Axelrod, 1999).

We now take a detailed look at some major categories of causes of problem behaviors and examples of the general type of treatment that may be indicated in each category.

MAJOR CAUSES OF PROBLEM BEHAVIORS

Problem Behaviors Maintained by Attention from Others (Social Positive Reinforcement)

As we have seen in the "pitfalls" sections of earlier chapters, behavioral excesses often are developed and maintained by the social attention they evoke. Indicators that the behavior is maintained by attention include: (a) whether attention reliably follows the behavior; (b) whether the individual looks at or approaches a caregiver just before engaging in the behavior; and (c) whether the individual smiles just before engaging in the behavior. All three of these occurring together are a strong indication that the behavior is maintained by attention. (Attention from others can also function as an S^D for problem behavior, as illustrated by Bergen, Holborn, & Scott-Huyghebart, 2002).

If a causal analysis indicates that the behavior is maintained by attention, treatment involving social reinforcement would be recommended. For example, one might devise a treatment using attention when the individual is not engaging in the problem behavior (DRO, see Chapter 7) or is engaging in some behavior that is incompatible with it (DRI, see Chapter 7). The goal of such a program would be to eliminate the undesirable behavior. Another alternative is to get the behavior to occur when it is more appropriate (i.e., bring it under appropriate stimulus control, see Chapter 8) and then to decrease it to the point that it is acceptable. This strategy is illustrated by the following case.

A Case of Pestering   Lori was an attractive girl in a treatment center for children with developmental disabilities.[1] She was small for her age and had an irresistible appeal. Perhaps in part because of these characteristics, staff attention had gradually shaped extreme persistence in her approach to the staff, to the point that she had become a chronic pest. The following sequence was typical. While Bonnie, the nurse in charge of the ward, sat working in her office, Lori peeked in and said,

---

[1]This example is based on an unpublished case report by G. Martin at Cedar Cottage, The Manitoba Developmental Centre, Portage la Prairie, Manitoba, Canada 1971.

"Hi." "Hi, Lori, I'm busy now but I'll talk to you later," said Bonnie. "You busy now?" said Lori. There was no response from Bonnie, who was trying to work and to ignore Lori's pestering. "You work hard?" asked Lori. (No response from Bonnie.) "Hi," said Lori. (No response from Bonnie.) "You don't love me?" said Lori with a sad look. "Of course I love you, Lori," said Bonnie, unable to resist any longer. Although the staff attempted to ignore Lori's excessive pestering, it was almost impossible to do so consistently. An observational analysis indicated that the antecedent for Lori's pestering consisted of a staff member in Lori's vicinity (within approximately 10–15 feet), and that the behavior was being maintained by a schedule of intermittent positive social reinforcement.

Since total elimination of the behavior would have been extremely difficult, and probably not even desirable, the staff designed a procedure for eliminating the behavior only partially—that is, eliminating it only when it was most disruptive. Because pestering appeared to be a function of social attention from staff, they decided to use this reinforcer in the program. Each staff member pinned a 2 × 4-inch card to his or her shirt or dress. The card was red on one side and green on the other. On the first morning of the procedure, a staff member walked quickly toward Lori, before she had a chance to begin pestering, and said quickly and firmly, "Hi, Lori. See my card [while pointing to the card]? I can't talk to you because I'm busy and the card is red. I'll see you later." The staff member then quickly turned and walked away, leaving Lori standing in a state of stunned silence. Within a few seconds, the staff member returned with the green side of the card showing. Smiling pleasantly, she said, "Hi, Lori. See my card? It's on the green side and I'm not busy, so now I can talk to you." The staff member then proceeded to engage Lori in a brief conversation. When there was a pause in the conversation, the staff member suddenly assumed a business-like attitude, turned the card to the red side, and said, "I can't talk to you now, Lori. My card will be red for awhile. I'll see you later." The staff member then quickly walked away before Lori had a chance to respond.

During the first few days of the procedure, the green side was usually showing, and Lori's soliciting social interaction with a staff member was reinforced. At times when the staff had their cards turned to the red side, they consistently ignored Lori's attention-seeking behavior. Over several days, the staff introduced the red side for longer and longer periods of time. Lori quickly learned to discriminate whether or not a nearby staff member was available for conversation, and she responded appropriately. After two weeks, the staff managed their red and green cards individually. Moreover, over time, Lori appeared to learn more subtle discriminations, such as distinguishing between staff behaviors when they were busy versus when they were relaxing or socializing. And if the staff were busy, she would refrain from pestering.

Problem Behaviors Maintained by Self-Stimulation (Internal Sensory Positive Reinforcement)

Behaviors are often reinforced by some form of sensory stimulation from our bodies. For example, massaging one's scalp produces an enjoyable tingling sensation. Unfortunately, for persons with autism and developmental disabilities, this type of consequence might also maintain extreme self-stimulatory behaviors such as body rocking, hand flipping, gazing at lights, and even self-injurious behaviors such as slapping or scratching one's face. Reinforcers for such behaviors might consist of sensory or perceptual feedback including vestibular sensations, visual patterns, repetitive sounds, and tactile or kinesthetic sensations (Guess & Carr, 1991; Lovaas, Newsom, & Hickman, 1987). An indicator that the behavior is being maintained by the internal reinforcing effect of self-stimulation would be that the behavior continues unabated at a steady rate although it has no apparent effect on other individuals or the external environment. If it appears that stereotypic or self-injurious behavior is maintained by sensory reinforcement, then an important component of treatment might be the enrichment of the individual's environment so as to reduce his or her deprivation of sensory stimulation. Alternatively, extinction of a self-stimulatory behavior by altering the sensory consequences that the behavior produces might be effective, as illustrated by the following case.

A Case of Face Scratching   This case, described by Rincover and Devaney (1982), illustrates a functional analysis and treatment of a problem behavior maintained by sensory stimulation. Sarah was a 4½-year-old child with a developmental disability who severely scratched her face with her nails. Although her nails were cut so short that it was impossible for them to tear her skin, her scratching still resulted in worsening skin irritations and abrasions. Observations during daily five-hour classes in a treatment center for persons with developmental disabilities indicated that the scratching occurred frequently during the day. She scratched when smiling, when upset, when interacting with others, when alone, and whether or not demands were placed on her. Clearly, the behavior appeared to be motivated by sensory rather than social reinforcement. The treatment therefore consisted of extinction of scratching by eliminating the tactile sensations that the scratching had produced. Each day her hands were covered with thin rubber (dishwashing) gloves that did not prevent her from scratching, but did eliminate the sensory stimulation (and prevented her from damaging her skin). The result was an immediate and substantial decrease in the rate of scratching. Within four days, scratching was eliminated. During follow-up sessions the gloves were removed, first for just 10 minutes a day, then for longer and longer intervals until finally they were no longer needed.

Problem Behaviors Maintained by Environmental Consequences (External Sensory Positive Reinforcement)

Some problem behavior might be maintained by reinforcing sights and sounds from the nonsocial external environment. A child who throws toys, for example, might enjoy the loud noise when they land. Flushing items down the toilet repeatedly or letting taps run to overflow a sink might be maintained by the sights produced. For an indicator that a particular problem behavior is being reinforced by nonsocial external sensory stimulation, note whether the individual continues the behavior undiminished even though it appears to have no social consequences over numerous occasions. If a functional assessment indicates that the behavior is maintained by external sensory reinforcement, then a component of the treatment program might involve sensory reinforcement of a desirable alternative behavior, as illustrated in the following case.

A Case of Flushing Jewelry Down the Toilet   This case, treated by one of the authors, involved a child with developmental disabilities who was living at home. It illustrates a problem behavior that may have been maintained by social attention, by sensory stimulation from the nonsocial external environment, or by both. Occasionally during the day, and always just when the mother was busy in the kitchen, the child would go to the mother's bedroom, take a piece of jewelry out of the jewelry box, carry it to the bathroom, and flush it down the toilet. She would then come and tell her mother what she had done. For the purposes of assessment and treatment, the mother had replaced her jewelry with "junk" jewelry. An observational assessment suggested two possible explanations of the problem behavior. First, the appearance of the jewelry swirling around the toilet bowl before disappearing might have functioned as a sensory reinforcer. Second, the entire sequence of activities may have been a behavioral chain that was reinforced by mother's attention when the child told her what she had done. The treatment procedure that was used took both possibilities into account. The girl was given several prompted trials during which, when mother and daughter were both in the kitchen, the mother took the daughter by the hand, went into the bedroom, prompted the daughter to take a piece of jewelry out of the box, and guided the daughter to bring the jewelry into the kitchen and drop it in a jar on the kitchen table, which produced an audible tinkling sound. Thus, the sound of the jewelry as it dropped into the jar may have served as a sensory reinforcer to replace the sight of the jewelry disappearing down the toilet. In addition, the new sequence (or behavioral chain) was highly reinforced with praise and sometimes a treat from mom. Just in case mother's attention was the variable maintaining the original sequence, her attention was now contingent upon a new sequence.

After several guided trials, the mother was able to initiate the new chain by instructing the child while they were both in the kitchen. During the first two days of treatment, the child was not given an opportunity to go into the bedroom on her own. On the start of the third day, the child was instructed that any time she wanted to, when mom was in the kitchen, she could get some jewelry, place it in the jar in the kitchen, and receive praise from mom. To enhance the likelihood of this new sequence, the mother took a photograph of the daughter putting the jewelry into the jar on the kitchen table and placed the picture beside the jewelry box in the bedroom. During the next three weeks, the daughter continued periodically to bring jewelry to the kitchen and to receive praise and sometimes treats for doing so. Not once did she flush jewelry down the toilet. Eventually, the girl stopped playing with mother's jewelry altogether.

Problem Behaviors Maintained by Escape from Demands (Social Negative Reinforcement)

Note 1   Many of our behaviors are maintained by escape from aversive stimuli (see Chapter 13), such as squinting in the presence of bright light or covering your ears to escape a loud sound. Escape from aversive stimuli (escape conditioning or negative reinforcement) can also cause problem behaviors. For some individuals, for example, requests by others may be aversive. The problem behavior may be a way of escaping from the demands being placed on that individual. For example, when requested to answer difficult questions, some children may engage in tantrums that are strengthened by the withdrawal of the request. A strong indicator that a problem behavior is in this category is that the individual engages in the behavior only when certain types of requests are made of him or her. If your functional assessment supports this type of interpretation, it might be possible to persist with requests (demands) until compliance (rather than the problematic escape behavior) occurs. As illustrated in the case of Susie's self-abusive behavior earlier in this chapter, removing the escape function of a behavioral excess will cause that behavior to decrease. Alternatively, with nonverbal persons, you might teach the individual some other way of communicating (such as by finger tapping or hand raising) that the task is aversive. In this way, the behavioral excess can be replaced by an adaptive response that produces the same or similar function as that which was produced by the problem behavior (Mace, Lalli, Lalli, & Shey, 1993). In other situations, you might design a treatment program in which the level of difficulty of the requested behavior starts low and is gradually increased, as illustrated by the following case.

A Case of Unwanted "Tarzan" Noises   Edward was an 8-year-old child with a mild developmental disability who was in a special education class.[2] His teacher, Ms. Millan, reported to one of the authors that Edward consistently (three or four times a day) made loud "Tarzan" noises in class. A questionnaire assessment with Ms. Millan indicated that Edward made the Tarzan noises whenever he was asked questions for which he did not know the answer. Rather than giving wrong answers, Edward would burst out with his Tarzan imitation. Needless to say, the Tarzan noises disrupted the class. (Ms. Millan reported that one of the other boys climbed on a desk and jumped up and down while scratching himself underneath the armpits and making noises like Cheetah the Chimp.) It appeared that Edward's outbursts enabled him to escape from questions that he found difficult. Therefore, the program Ms. Millan implemented at first eliminated such questions. Each day, she spent some time with Edward individually regarding the work to be done for the next day. During these sessions, she quizzed Edward on his knowledge of the subject matter. Although he would occasionally make mistakes, he did not make Tarzan noises. Because only he and Ms. Millan were present during those sessions, the behavior was apparently under the stimulus control of the presence of the other class members.

During class, over the next two weeks, Ms. Millan asked Edward questions to which he knew the answers and gave him a great deal of approval for correct answers. Then, over the next two weeks, she began asking slightly more difficult questions, each of which was prefaced with a strong prompt such as "Now, Edward, here's a question that's a little difficult. But I'm sure you can answer it, and if you can't we'll figure out the answer together, won't we, class?" Thus, if

---

[2]The details of this case were provided by a student in a behavior modification course for resource teachers taught by G. Martin at the Winnipeg School Division, Winnipeg, Manitoba, Canada January–March 1973.

Edward did give a wrong answer, he was immediately engaged with the teacher and the rest of the class in an attempt to figure out the answer. This gave Edward the opportunity to receive the attention of the class for desirable behavior rather than for the undesirable Tarzan noises. The entire project required approximately a month of careful attention from Ms. Millan. Thereafter, Edward required no special attention. To maintain his good behavior, Ms. Millan made sure that she periodically asked Edward questions to which he knew the answers.

Elicited (Respondent) Problem Behaviors

Some problem behavior appears to be elicited (i.e., respondent—see Chapter 14) rather than controlled by its consequences (i.e., operant). For example, aggression can be elicited by aversive stimuli (Chapter 12) or by the withholding of a reinforcer following a previously reinforced response (i.e., extinction, see Chapter 5). And emotions have elicited components (see Chapter 15). If a previously neutral stimulus has occurred in close association with an aversive event, for example, that stimulus might come to elicit troublesome anxiety. Several behavioral checklists have been published for conducting questionnaire assessments of the conditioned stimuli (CSs) that elicit the respondent components of emotions. Examples include the *Fear Survey Schedule* (Cautela, Kastenbaum, & Wincze, 1972) and the *Fear Survey for Children* (Morris & Kratochwill, 1983). A descriptive functional assessment or a functional analysis could also be conducted to determine the specific stimuli, circumstances, or thoughts that might elicit respondent components of emotions (Emmelkamp, Bouman, & Scholing, 1992). The two main indicators that a problem behavior is elicited are that it consistently occurs in a certain situation or in the presence of certain stimuli and that it is never followed by any clearly identifiable reinforcing consequence. Another indicator, as suggested by the term elicited, is that the behavior seems to be involuntary (i.e., the person seems unable to inhibit it). If a problem behavior appears to be elicited, the treatment might include establishing one or more responses that compete with it so that their occurrence precludes the occurrence of the undesirable response (i.e., counterconditioning, see Chapter 14), as illustrated in the following example.

A Respondent Conditioning Approach to Reducing Anger Responses   Joel was a 26-year-old individual with a mild developmental disability who had recently been dismissed from a dishwashing position due to angry outbursts toward coworkers and supervisors. A questionnaire assessment with Joel's mother and staff members of the Association for Retarded Citizens (with whom Joel was associated), and observational assessments with Joel himself, led to the identification of three categories of CSs for respondent components of emotions. The CSs included "jokes" (humorous anecdotes told to Joel), "criticism" (especially about deficiencies in Joel's conduct or appearance), and "heterosexual talk" (discussions of dating, marriage, etc.). Within each category, a hierarchy of provoking events was established, ranging from those that caused the least anger to those that caused the most anger. The respondent components of emotions included rapid breathing, facial expression associated with anger, and trembling. Operant components of emotion were also monitored, including talking loudly and avoiding eye contact with the person whose comments were eliciting Joel's anger. Treatment focused primarily on counterconditioning. Joel was first taught how to relax using a process called progressive muscle relaxation (described further in Chapter 28). Then, while in a state of relaxation, a CS for anger from one of the categories was presented. For example, a "joke-related" situation was described to Joel and he was asked to imagine it while remaining relaxed. Across several sessions, more and more of the CSs for anger were introduced, gradually proceeding up each of the hierarchies from situations that caused the least anger to those that caused the most anger. (As described in Chapter 28, this procedure is referred to as systematic desensitization.) In addition to the clinic-based procedures, Joel was requested, while at home, to listen to a tape recording that induced muscle relaxation, and to practice relaxation exercises when CSs for anger were encountered in everyday life. Overall, the program was very successful. Anger-related responses decreased to a very low level during training sessions and generalized to natural settings for each of the categories (Schloss, Smith, Santora, & Bryant, 1989).

MEDICAL CAUSES OF PROBLEM BEHAVIORS

Often, the controlling variables with which behavior modifiers are concerned lie in the individual's external environment. Sometimes, however, a behavior that appears problematic may have a medical cause. For example, a nonverbal individual may bang his or her head against hard objects to reduce pain from an internal source, such as an ear infection (internal negative reinforcement). A medical cause may be indicated if the problem emerges suddenly and does not seem to be related to any changes in the individual's environment.

In order to encourage behavior modifiers to gather all possible information about the causes of problem behaviors, Jon Bailey and David Pyles have developed the concept of *behavioral diagnostics* (Bailey & Pyles, 1989; Pyles & Bailey, 1990).With this approach to behavioral assessment, the therapist diagnoses the problem after examining antecedents, consequences, and medical and nutritional variables as potential causes of problem behaviors. Based on the diagnosis, the therapist develops a treatment plan, tests the plan under controlled conditions, and if the results are successful, puts the treatment plan in place including necessary training of persons who will conduct the program.

With the behavioral diagnostic model, examples of data that might be collected during the diagnosis phase include: health/medical variables (such as menstrual cycles or constipation), nutrition variables (such as caloric intake or food allergies), medications, and, of course, the kinds of antecedents and consequences of behavior illustrated in this chapter. The concept of behavioral diagnostics is broader than that of a functional assessment, and may enhance the acceptability of behavioral procedures among medical personnel (who have a long history of emphasizing diagnosis prior to treatment). Consistent with this broader view, variables that influence problem behavior of many individuals are listed in Table 22–1. Variables that commonly act as antecedents or consequences for problem behavior with persons with developmental disabilities are listed by Demchak and Bossert (1996).

TABLE 22–1   FACTORS TO CONSIDER IN ASSESSING CAUSES
OF PROBLEM BEHAVIOR

General Setting

Low overall level of reinforcement
Conditions that cause discomfort (e.g., hot, noisy, crowded)
Presence or absence of particular people

Organismic Variables

State of health (e.g., flu, headache, allergies)
Motivational state (e.g., hungry, thirsty)
Emotional state (e.g., angry, jealous)
Temporary, bodily states (e.g., fatigue, menstrual cramps)

Task Variables

Too difficult
Improper pace (too fast, too slow)
Lack of variety
Lack of choice
Lack of perceived importance

Specific Antecedents

Sudden change in immediate surroundings
Introduction of new tasks
Excessive demands
Unclear instructions
Removal of visible reinforcers
Witholding of reinforcers following previously reinforced responses
Presentation of aversive stimuli
Being told to wait
Seeing someone else be reinforced

Specific Consequences: Problem behavior leads to

Escape from demands
Attention from others
Sympathy
Getting one's way
Tangible reinforcers
Internal sensory feedback
External sensory feedback

If there is any chance that a behavior problem has a medical cause, a physician should be consulted prior to treating the problem. This is not to say that behavioral techniques cannot be effective if the problem has a medical cause; on the contrary, often they can. For example, hyperactivity is often treated by a combination of behavioral and medical procedures (Barkley, 1998). Such treatment, however, should be carried out in consultation with a physician (see Chapter 2 for a discussion of behavioral approaches to medical problems).

GUIDELINES FOR CONDUCTING
A FUNCTIONAL ASSESSMENT

Several manuals have been published that provide practical guidance for conducting a functional assessment. Four of these manuals were reviewed by Dunlap and Kincaid (2001). The following is a summary of important guidelines for conducting a functional assessment.

1. Define the problem behavior in behavioral terms.
2. Identify antecedent events that consistently precede the problem behavior.
3. Identify consequences that immediately (although possibly intermittently) follow the problem behavior.
4. As suggested by behavioral diagnostics, consider health/medical/personal variables that might contribute to the problem.
5. Based on guidelines 2, 3, and 4, form hypotheses about the consequent events that maintain the problem behavior, the antecedent events that elicit it or evoke it, and/or the health/medical/personal variables that exacerbate it.
6. Take data on the behavior, its antecedents and consequences in its natural setting, and health/medical/personal variables to determine which of the hypotheses in guideline 5 are likely to be correct.
7. If possible, do a functional analysis by directly testing the hypotheses developed in guideline 5.
8. Incorporating the principles discussed in Part II of this text, and following the guidelines for designing treatment programs in Chapter 24, develop and carry out a treatment program based on the hypothesis that is most likely to be correct, as determined by guidelines 6 and 7.
9. If the treatment is successful, accept the causal analysis as confirmed. If it is not successful, redo the functional analysis, or attempt a solution still based on the principles in Part II of the book, and follow the guidelines in Chapter 24.

STUDY QUESTIONS

1. Briefly describe three ways of discovering controlling variables of problem behavior.
2. How does a functional analysis (as the term is used in this book) differ from other types of functional assessment?
3. Briefly describe how a functional analysis indicated that Susie's self-abusiveness was likely maintained because it enabled her to escape from demanding adults. How did the treatment condition confirm the functional analysis?
4. Describe three limitations of functional analyses.
5. In a sentence or two each, outline six possible causes of problem behaviors.
6. What are three indicators that a problem behavior is probably maintained by the social attention that follows it?
7. Describe how Rincover and Devaney applied extinction to a problem that appeared to be maintained by internal sensory positive reinforcement.
8. What is an indicator that a problem behavior is being reinforced by nonsocial external sensory stimulation? Give an example illustrating this indicator.
9. What were two plausible explanations of the behavior of the child with developmental disabilities of flushing jewelry down the toilet? How did the treatment procedure take both possibilities into account?

10. What is a strong indicator that a problem behavior is being maintained as a way of escaping from demands? Give an example illustrating this indicator.
11. Suppose that a nonverbal child screams loudly as a way of escaping from demands by adults in various training settings. Describe two alternative strategies that the adults might follow to deal with the problem behavior.
12. What are the two main indicators that a problem behavior is elicited by prior stimuli (vs. being maintained by reinforcing consequences)? Give an example illustrating this indicator.
13. Describe the main components in the treatment of Joel's anger.
14. What is behavioral diagnostics? In what sense is this term broader than functional assessment?

APPLICATION EXERCISES

A. Exercise Involving Others

Identify a behavioral excess of someone you know well (but do not identify that person). Try to identify the stimulus control and maintaining consequences for that behavior. Based on your functional assessment, what do you think would be the best treatment procedure to decrease or eliminate that behavior?

B. Self-Modification Exercise

Identify one of your own behavioral excesses. Try to identify the stimulus control and maintaining consequences for that behavior. Based on your functional assessment, what do you think would be the best treatment procedure to decrease or eliminate that behavior?

NOTE AND EXTENDED DISCUSSION

1. Some problem behaviors might be maintained by nonsocial negative reinforcement (i.e., they enable the individual to escape from aversive nonsocial stimulation). A nonverbal child might repeatedly remove her shoes because they squeeze her toes too tightly. Or an individual who was used to loose-fitting clothes and accepts a job that requires formal attire might frequently loosen his top button and tie (knowingly or unknowingly). Of course, it is debatable as to whether such behaviors are undesirable. For the nonverbal child, removing her shoes may be a way of communicating that they are too tight. And some might argue that buttoned-up collars and ties are unnecessary in any environment.

Study Question on Note

1. Describe an example that is not in the text of how nonsocial negative reinforcement could produce undesirable behavior.

Doing Research
in Behavior Modification

A minimal behavior modification program has four phases: a *screening phase*, for clarifying the problem and determining who should treat it; a *baseline phase*, for determining the initial level of the behavior prior to the program; a *treatment phase*, in which the intervention strategy is initiated; and a *follow-up phase*, for evaluating the persistence of the desirable behavioral changes following termination of the program. Many behavior modification projects go beyond these minimal phases, however, and demonstrate convincingly that it was indeed the treatment that caused a particular change in behavior. The value of such demonstrations might be illustrated best with a hypothetical example.

Our example involves a second-grade student's frequency of successfully completing addition and subtraction problems in daily half-hour math classes. The student, Billy, was performing at a much lower level than were any of the other students and was showing a great deal of disruptive behavior during the class. The teacher, Ms. Johnson, reasoned that an increase in Billy's performance at solving the assigned math problems might make it more pleasurable for Billy to work at the problems and might thereby decrease his disruptive interactions with those around him. During a one-week baseline, Ms. Johnson assigned a certain number of problems to the class and recorded the number that Billy completed successfully during each half-hour period. Billy averaged successful completion of seven math problems per half-hour, less than half the class average of 16 problems per half-hour. Ms. Johnson next introduced a reinforcement program. She told Billy that for each math problem he completed successfully, he could add one extra minute of time to his physical education class on Friday afternoon, an activity that

Billy enjoyed. Billy's performance improved during the first week of the program. During the second week, he exceeded the class average of 16 correct math problems per half-hour class.

Can the teacher attribute the improvement in Billy's performance to the treatment? Our initial tendency might be to say "yes," because the performance is much better now than it was during the original baseline. Consider, however, that the improvement may have been the result of other factors. For example, a bad cold could have depressed Billy's baseline performance, and the recovery from his cold caused his improved mathematical performance after the program was introduced. Or a new student, who set a good example for Billy to model, may have been seated near him during the treatment phase but not during the baseline. Or perhaps the problems assigned during the treatment phase were easier than those assigned during baseline. Or perhaps something that the teacher could not possibly have been aware of was responsible for his improved performance.

In any program in which a treatment phase is introduced for the purpose of modifying some behavior, it is quite possible for an uncontrolled or interfering variable or condition to occur concurrently with the treatment, such that the change in the behavior is due to the uncontrolled variable rather than the treatment itself. A behavior modification research project attempts to demonstrate convincingly that it was the treatment, rather than some uncontrolled variables, that was responsible for the change in the behavior in question.

THE REVERSAL-REPLICATION (ABAB) RESEARCH DESIGN

Let us suppose that Ms. Johnson, being scientifically inclined, is aware of the possibility of uncontrolled variable affecting her results with Billy and would like to demonstrate convincingly that it was indeed her program that was responsible for his improvement. (Besides satisfying her curiosity, there are several practical reasons why she might have wanted such a demonstration. It would indicate whether she should try a similar procedure with another problem Billy might have, whether she should try similar procedures with other students in her class, and whether she should recommend similar procedures to other teachers.) Therefore, at the end of the second week of the reinforcement program, she eliminated the reinforcement and returned to the baseline condition. Let us suppose that the hypothetical results of this manipulation by the teacher are those shown in Figure 23–1.

Note 1   By the end of the second week of return to the baseline conditions (which is called a *reversal*), Billy was performing at a level approximately that of his original baseline. Ms. Johnson then reintroduced the treatment phase, just as it had been before, and, as can be seen in Figure 23–1, Billy again improved his performance. Ms. Johnson had replicated both the original baseline and the original treatment effects. If some uncontrolled variable was operating, one must hypothesize that it was occurring mysteriously at exactly the same time the treatment program was operative and was not occurring when the treatment program was removed. This becomes much less plausible with each successful replication of the effect. We now have much more confidence that it was indeed the teacher's procedure that produced the desired behavioral change. Thus, Ms. Johnson demonstrated a cause–effect

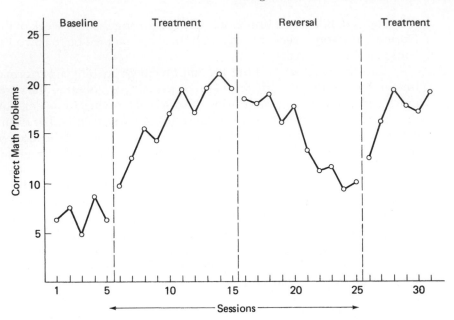

Figure 23–1 Hypothetical data showing a reversal-replication (ABAB) design for Billie.

relationship between a particular behavior and her treatment program. In research terminology, correctly completing math problems was the **dependent variable** and Ms. Johnson's program for Billy was the **independent variable.**

The type of experimental strategy that Ms. Johnson employed is called a **reversal-replication** research design. It is so named because it includes a reversal to baseline conditions followed by a replication of the treatment phase (and, it is hoped, of the effect). The baseline condition is often abbreviated "A," and the treatment condition "B." Hence, this research design is also called an **ABAB** design. It has also been called a *withdrawal* design for the reason that during the B phases the treatment is withdrawn (Poling et al., 1995). For an application of this design, see Ivancic, Barrett, Simonow, and Kimberly (1997).

Although the reversal-replication design appears simple at first glance, beginning students doing behavior modification research quickly encounter several questions that are not easy to answer. Assuming that problems of response definition, observer accuracy, and data recording (discussed in Chapter 21) have been solved, the first question is this: How long should the baseline phase last? The difficulties of answering this question might be appreciated best by viewing Figure 23–2. Which of the baselines in this figure do you consider to be the most adequate? If you selected baselines 4 and 5, we agree. Baseline 4 is acceptable because the pattern of behavior appears stable and predictable. Baseline 5 is acceptable because the trend observed is in a direction opposite to the effect predicted for the independent variable acting on the dependent variable. Ideally, then, a baseline phase should continue until the pattern of performance is stable or until it shows a trend in the direction opposite to that predicted when the independent variable is introduced.

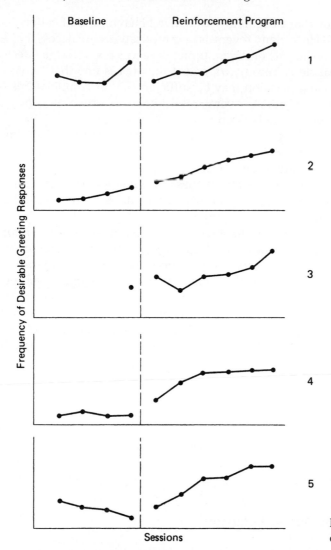

Figure 23-2 Hypothetical data for five children.

Other considerations, however, may lead one to shorten or lengthen a baseline in an applied research project. First, there are scientific considerations related to the newness of the independent and dependent variables being studied. One might be more comfortable conducting a shorter baseline in a new study of behavior that has already been well researched than in a study of a less explored area. Second, practical considerations might limit the length of baseline observations. The available time of the experimenter, the availability of observers, restrictions on students for completing projects on time, and any of a number of other factors might lead one to limit or extend the baseline for nonscientific reasons. Finally, ethical considerations often affect baseline length. For example, if one is attempting to manage the self-abusive behavior of a child with a developmental disability, an extended baseline phase is ethically unacceptable.

Another question that a beginning student in behavior modification research will encounter is this: How many reversals and replications are necessary? Again, there is no easy answer to this question. If one observes a very large effect when the independent variable is introduced, and if the area is one that has been explored before, then one replication may be sufficient. Other combinations of factors might lead one to conduct several replications in order to convincingly demonstrate a cause–effect relationship.

Although a reversal-replication design is a common behavior modification research strategy, it does have limitations that make it inappropriate in certain situations. First, it may be undesirable to reverse to baseline conditions following a treatment phase. When treating abusiveness of a child with a developmental disability, for example, it would be ethically unacceptable to reverse to baseline immediately following a successful treatment.

Second, it may be impossible to obtain a reversal due to behavioral trapping. In Chapter 16 we described how a shy child might be taught to interact with his peers; once the teacher's reinforcement produces the desirable interaction, the child's behavior might be "trapped" and maintained by attention from his peers after the withdrawal of the teacher's attention. Other behaviors might be trapped by the individual's physical rather than social environment. Once a golf pro has taught a novice golfer to hit a golf ball over 200 yards, it is unlikely that the golfer will return to his original, unorthodox swing, which produced a 150-yard drive.

MULTIPLE-BASELINE DESIGNS

Not only may it sometime be impossible to return a behavior to baseline, it is usually undesirable to reverse an improvement in behavior—even for a short time. Multiple-baseline designs are used to demonstrate the effectiveness of a particular treatment without reversing to baseline conditions.

A Multiple Baseline Across Behaviors

Let us suppose that Ms. Johnson was concerned with demonstrating the effects of her reinforcement procedure on Billy's academic performance, but she did not want to do a reversal and risk losing the improvement shown by Billy. She might have accomplished her demonstration of treatment control over improved performance by constructing a **multiple-baseline-across-behaviors** design. Her first step would have been to baseline two or more behaviors concurrently. Specifically, she might have recorded Billy's performance in solving math problems during math class, his performance in spelling correctly during English class, and his sentence writing during creative writing class. These baselines might have been those shown in Figure 23–3. The multiple-baseline-across-behaviors design calls for the introduction of the treatment sequentially across two or more behaviors. The extra minute of physical education class per correct problem might have been introduced in the math class while the baseline condition was continued during spelling and writing classes. If the results were those shown in Figure 23–3, the

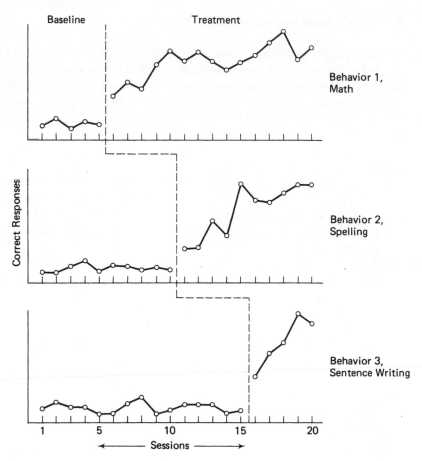

Figure 23–3 Hypothetical data illustrating a multiple-baseline-across-behaviors design for Billy.

teacher might next have introduced the treatment for the second behavior by allowing an extra minute of physical education class for each word spelled correctly.

Finally, the teacher might have introduced the treatment for the third behavior—sentence writing. If performance was as indicated in Figure 23–3, then it clearly indicated that the behavior changed only when the treatment was introduced. This example provides a good demonstration of the control of the treatment over several behaviors. For another example of application of this design, see Gena, Krantz, McClannahan, and Poulson (1996).

The application of this design assumes that the behaviors are relatively independent. If Ms. Johnson had applied the treatment program to one behavior while the other two behaviors were kept at baseline conditions, and if an improvement had been observed in all three behaviors concurrently, then she could not have confidently attributed the improvement to the treatment itself. An example of such response generalization was reported by Nordquist (1971). Other limitations are that it may not be possible to find two or more suitable behaviors or sufficient observers to gather the necessary data on several behaviors.

A Multiple Baseline Across Situations

Another variety of multiple-baseline design studies the effects of a treatment on a single behavior that occurs in several situations. For example, Allen (1973) was concerned with decreasing bizarre verbalizations of Mike, an 8-year-old boy diagnosed as being "minimally brain damaged." While attending a sleep-away summer camp, Mike fantasized for hours about his pet penguins, whom he called "Tug Tug" and "Junior Polka Dot." These verbalizations interfered with Mike's interactions with both his peers and the camp counselors. During an initial baseline phase, data were collected on the verbalizations in four situations: during trail walks in the evening, in the dining hall, in Mike's cabin, and during education classes. The treatment, an extinction program in which verbalizations were ignored, was then introduced in the first situation (trail walking), while the remaining three situations continued on baseline. Following the successful reduction of the verbalizations during trail walking, treatment was introduced to the second situation, the dining hall, and the remaining two situations continued on baseline. Eventually, the treatment was introduced sequentially across the remaining two situations. The daily number of bizarre verbalizations decreased to near zero in each situation following the introduction of treatment to that situation.

A potential problem with a **multiple-baseline-across-situations** design is that, when the treatment is applied to the behavior in the first situation, it may cause subsequent improvement in all situations (i.e., stimulus generalization across situations). When this happens, the experimenter is not able to conclude that the improvement was necessarily the result of the treatment. Other potential limitations are that the behavior may occur in only one situation, or there may not be sufficient observers to gather the necessary data.

A Multiple Baseline Across People

Yet another multiple-baseline design demonstrates the effectiveness of a treatment by applying it sequentially to individuals. For example, Fawcett and Miller (1975) used a **multiple-baseline-across-people** design to demonstrate the effectiveness of a combination of procedures (called a *treatment package*) designed to improve public speaking. The public speaking skills of three individuals were recorded during initial public speaking sessions. The first individual was then given the treatment package while the others continued on baseline. Exposure to the treatment package improved the public speaking behaviors of the first individual. The treatment package was introduced sequentially to the second person, and then to the third person, and each time it led to an improvement in public speaking behaviors. This demonstration of improvement in individuals who receive treatment sequentially across time is a convincing demonstration of the effectiveness of a treatment program. For an application of this design, see Wanlin, Hrycaiko, Martin, and Mahon (1997).

A potential problem with the multiple-baseline-across-people design is that the first individual might explain the treatment or model the desirable behavior to the other individuals, causing them to improve in the absence of treatment (see, e.g.,

Kazdin, 1973). Also, it is not always possible to find two or more individuals who can be multiply baselined, nor the additional observers to gather the necessary data.

THE CHANGING-CRITERION DESIGN

Another way to demonstrate the control a particular treatment has on behavior is to introduce successive changes in the behavioral criterion for application of the treatment. This is called the **changing-criterion design.** If the behavior changes in a consistent direction each time a change is made in the criterion for application of the treatment, then we can conclude that the treatment was responsible for the change in behavior.

DeLuca and Holborn (1992) used a changing-criterion design to demonstrate the effects of a token reinforcement system on exercising by 11-year-old boys with or without obesity. First, during a baseline phase consisting of several 30-minute exercise sessions, they assessed each boy's pedaling rate on a stationary bicycle. Next, they set a criterion for reinforcement for each boy that was approximately 15% above his average baseline rate of pedaling. In this second phase, when a boy met criterion, he earned points (signaled by a bell ringing and a light going on) that could be exchanged later for backup reinforcers. When a boy's performance had stabilized at this new higher level of pedaling in Phase 2, Phase 3 was initiated. In Phase 3, the criterion for reinforcement was changed to approximately 15% above the average rate of performance in Phase 2. Similarly, each subsequent phase increased the criterion for reinforcement to 15% higher than the average pedaling rate of the preceding phase. As can be seen in Figure 23–4, which shows the data for one of the boys, performance improved with each subsequent change in the criterion for reinforcement. This pattern was demonstrated for both the three boys with obesity and

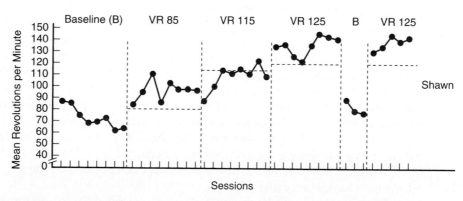

Figure 23–4 Mean number of revolutions per minute pedaled on a stationary bicycle by a boy. After a baseline phase, token reinforcement was given at increasingly larger levels of variable ratio (VR) reinforcement (that is, the mean response requirement became increasingly larger). *(Source:* Figure 1 in "Effects of a Variable Ratio Reinforcement Schedule with Changing Criteria on Exercise in Obese and Non-Obese Boys" by R. V. DeLuca and S. W. Holborn, *Journal of Applied Behavior Analysis,* 25, 1992. Copyright ©1992. Reprinted by permission of Dr. Rayleen DeLuca, University of Manitoba.)

the three boys without obesity. To further demonstrate the experimental control of the reinforcement program, as indicated in Figure 23–4, a reversal to baseline phase was included in this study. Although the reversal provided confirming information, such reversals are not a defining feature of the changing-criterion design.

ALTERNATING-TREATMENTS (OR MULTIELEMENT) DESIGN

The preceding research designs are ideally suited for demonstrating that a particular treatment was indeed responsible for a specific behavioral change. However, what if one wanted to compare the effects of different treatments for a single behavior of a single individual? Multiple-baseline designs are not well suited for this purpose. An alternative design for such a concern is the **alternating-treatments design** (Barlow & Hersen, 1984). As the name suggests, this design involves alternating two or more treatment conditions considerably more rapidly than would be done in a reversal-replication design. For example, Wolko, Hrycaiko, and Martin (1993) were concerned with comparing three treatments for improving the frequency of completed skills by young gymnasts during practice on the balance beam. One treatment was the standard coaching typically applied by the gymnastics coach. The second condition was standard coaching plus public goal setting, monitoring, and coach feedback. In this condition, the coach posted written goals for a gymnast, the gymnast recorded her practice performance and placed it on a graph in the gymnasium, and the gymnast received feedback from the coach at the end of each practice. The third condition was standard coaching and private self-management. Private self-management involved a gymnast setting her own goals and keeping track of her performance in a private notebook. The three conditions were randomly alternated across practices. The results with one of the gymnasts can be seen plotted as three cumulative graphs in Figure 23–5. As can be seen for this gymnast, standard coaching plus private self-management was consistently more effective than standard coaching plus public self-management and standard coaching alone (the baseline condition). For another example of the alternating-treatments design, see Daly, Martens, Kilmer, and Massie (1996).

A potential problem with the alternating-treatments design is that the treatments may interact; that is, one of the treatments may produce an effect either because of contrast to the other treatments in alternating sessions, or because of stimulus generalization across treatments. And in many studies using an alternating treatment design, interactions have occurred (e.g., Hains & Baer, 1989). In other words, if just one of the treatments had been applied to the gymnasts, the effects may have been different.

As suggested by Sidman (1960, p. 326), it is possible to use the alternating treatments design to study topographically different forms of behavior. An example of this was described by Ming and Martin (1996).

Another name for the alternating-treatments design is *multielement design*. This term is particularly appropriate when the conditions being compared are not actually therapeutic treatments. Consider the functional analysis performed on Susie's self-injuring behavior, as described in Chapter 22. In this example, you will

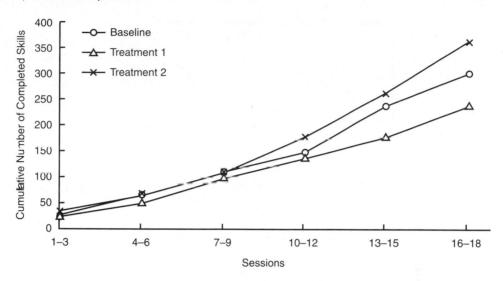

Figure 23–5   Frequency of completed beam skills for a gymnast under conditions of standard coaching (Baseline), standard coaching plus public self-management (Treatment 1), versus standard coaching plus private self-management (Treatment 2). Each condition was in effect for six sessions, with the conditions randomly alternated across a total of 18 sessions. (*Source:* Adapted from data presented by Wolko, Hrycaiko, and Martin, 1993.)

recall, several conditions were alternated: an attention condition, a demand condition, an alone condition with toys and games, and an alone condition in an empty room. These conditions were not being compared in order to determine which one was an effective treatment, but rather to help determine the cause of the behavior in order to design an effective treatment.

DATA ANALYSIS AND INTERPRETATION

Note 2   Researchers who employ the behavior modification research designs described in this chapter typically analyze their data without using control groups and statistical techniques that are more common in other areas of psychology. In general, this is because behavior modifiers are interested in understanding and improving the behavior of individuals, not group averages (see Sidman, 1960, for justification and elaboration of this approach). The evaluation of the effect of a particular treatment is typically made on the basis of two major sets of criteria: scientific and practical. Scientific criteria are the guidelines used by a researcher to evaluate whether or not there has been a convincing demonstration that the treatment was responsible for producing a reliable effect on the dependent variable. This judgment is commonly made by visually inspecting the graph of the results. Problems in deciding whether or not a treatment produced a reliable effect on a dependent variable might best be appreciated by examining Figure 23–6. Most observers of the five graphs would probably agree that there is a clear, large effect in graph 1, a reliable, though small effect in graph 2, and questionable effects in the remaining graphs.

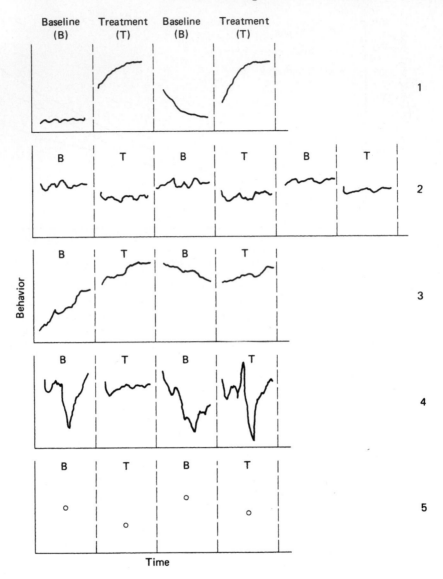

Figure 23–6   Some hypothetical data.

There are seven commonly used guidelines for inspecting data to judge whether or not the treatment had an effect on the dependent variable. There is greater confidence that an effect has been observed the greater the number of times that it is replicated, the fewer the overlapping points between baseline and treatment phases, the sooner the effect is observed following the introduction of the treatment, the larger the effect is in comparison to baseline, the more precisely the treatment procedures are specified, the more reliable the response measures, and the more consistent the findings with existing data and accepted behavioral theory. (For discussion of a problem of visual inspection of data, see Fisch, 1998. For a description of a visual aid and a staff training program for improving the reliabiity and validity of visual in-spection of single-case designs, see Fisher, Kelley, and Lomas, 2003.)

Judging whether or not a significant effect has occurred from a scientific point of view is one thing; evaluating the practical importance of behavior change to the client, other significant individuals in the client's life, and society in general is something else again. In evaluating the practical impact of the treatment, we must consider more than the scientific guidelines for judging the treatment's effect on behavior. That is, if graph 2 in Figure 23–6 were a graph of self-abusive behavior, the reliable cause–effect relationship demonstrated therein might be of little clinical significance. If the individual is still extremely self-abusive, as indicated by the per-formance during treatment phases, then the people responsible for caring for that child would not be satisfied. Judgments about the practical importance of behavioral change are referred to as judgments of clinical effectiveness or social importance.

A concept related to practical importance is that of social validity. Wolf (1978) has suggested that behavior modifiers need to socially validate their work on at least three levels: (a) They must examine the extent to which target behaviors iden-tified for treatment programs are really the most important for the client and soci-ety; (b) they must be concerned with the acceptability to the client of the particular procedures used, especially when alternative procedures can accomplish approxi-mately the same results; and (c) they must ensure that the consumers (the clients or their caregivers) are satisfied with the results. One social validation procedure involves subjective evaluation in which clients or other significant individuals are asked about their satisfaction with the goals, procedures, and results. Another so-cial validation procedure is to conduct preference tests with clients and to deter-mine which of two or more alternatives they prefer. In a third procedure, the goals as well as the results of treatment are validated socially by comparing results with clients to the average performance of some comparison group, such as normal peers. These strategies are discussed in more detail by Kazdin (1977b) and Wolf (1978). Social validation helps to ensure that behavior modifiers do the best job that they can in helping individuals function fully in society. Other strategies to ensure accountability of treatment specialists are discussed in Chapter 30.

STUDY QUESTIONS

1. Briefly describe the minimal components of a behavior modification program.
2. In two or three sentences, distinguish between a minimal behavior modification pro-gram and behavior modification research.
3. In two or three sentences, explain why we cannot necessarily claim that a change in be-havior during a minimal behavior modification program was due to the treatment.
4. Describe briefly, with reference to an example, the four components of the reversal-replication design. What is another name for this design?
5. Ideally, how long should the baseline phase of the reversal-replication design continue?
6. In a sentence or two each, describe why baselines 1, 2, and 3 from Figure 23–2 are in-adequate.
7. What scientific, practical, and ethical considerations might lead one to lengthen or shorten a baseline?

8. How many reversals and replications are necessary in a reversal-replication design?
9. Identify two limitations of the reversal-replication design, and give an example of each.
10. State an advantage of a multiple-baseline design over a reversal design.
11. Describe briefly, with reference to an example, a multiple-baseline-across-behaviors design.
12. When is a multiple-baseline-across-behaviors design inappropriate?
13. Describe briefly, with reference to an example, a multiple-baseline-across-situations design.
14. When is a multiple-baseline-across-situations design inappropriate?
15. Describe briefly, with reference to an example, a multiple-baseline-across-people design.
16. When is a multiple-baseline-across-people design inappropriate?
17. Describe briefly, with reference to an example, the changing-criterion design.
18. Describe briefly, with reference to an example, an alternating-treatments design. What is another name for this design? Explain when that name might be preferred and why?
19. Briefly describe a potential problem with the alternating-treatments design.
20. In a sentence or two each, what are the scientific and practical criteria for evaluating the effects of a particular treatment? Be sure to distinguish between the two in your answer.
21. For graphs 3, 4, and 5 in Figure 23–6, describe why it is difficult to draw conclusions about the effects of the treatments.
22. What seven criteria would give you maximum confidence that the treatment in an ABAB design had produced a significant effect on the dependent variable?
23. What are the three levels of social validation and why are they important?

APPLICATION EXERCISES

A. Exercise Involving Others

Suppose that you are teaching some students about doing research that utilizes reversal and multiple-baseline designs. Your students must do a research project in which they select a dependent variable and then evaluate the effects of some treatment on that dependent variable. Your task as teacher is to analyze the material in this chapter to prepare a guide that will help the students to select the appropriate research design. Your guide should take the form of a series of questions that they might ask, the answers to which would lead to a particular design. For example, if (a) and (b), then choose a reversal design; but if (c), (d), and (e), then choose a multiple-baseline design; and so forth.

B. Self-Modification Exercise

As described in Chapter 20, self-recording without any additional behavioral procedures sometimes causes **reactivity**—that is, the self-recording alone leads to behavioral change. Let us suppose you have decided to describe a self-recording procedure and then to investigate that as a treatment in a self-modification program. Describe a plausible multiple-baseline design that would enable you to assess self-recording as an effective self-control treatment.

NOTES AND EXTENDED DISCUSSION

1. Two considerations in evaluating a possible cause–effect relationship are internal validity and external validity. A finding is internally valid if the independent variable did, in fact, cause observed changes in the dependent variable. A finding is externally valid to the extent that it can be generalized to other behaviors, individuals, settings, or treatments.

2. The research designs described in this chapter are referred to as single-case, single-subject, or within-subject research designs. In most of these designs, an individual serves as his or her own control in the sense that performance of that individual in the absence of treatment is compared to that individual's performance during treatment. More common designs in many areas of psychology are control-group or between-subjects research designs. A control-group design typically involves at least two groups, one that receives the treatment and one that does not. The average performance of the two groups is then compared according to appropriate statistical procedures. Single-case designs are more popular than control-group designs among behavior modifiers for a number of reasons (Hrycaiko & Martin, 1996). First, they focus on repeated measurement of an individual's performance across a number of sessions, and therefore provide potentially valuable information on individual variation in performance. Group designs, with their emphasis on the average performance of groups, typically gather data at a single point in time, rather than continuously monitoring individuals over time. Second, researchers using single-case designs typically need to locate only a few individuals with the same performance problem in order to evaluate an intervention. With group designs, it is often difficult to locate enough individuals with the same performance problem to form the different groups. Third, because all individuals in a single-case design receive the intervention at one time or another, an applied researcher is not faced with resistance from clients (or their significant others) to participate in a no-treatment control group. Fourth, because single-case designs rely on a replication logic rather than the sampling logic of the group designs (Smith, 1988), they are not hampered by some of the statistical assumptions required of group designs. Group designs, for example, assume that the dependent variable is distributed in the population in some fashion (usually normally) and that the samples are randomly selected from that population. Often, however, these assumptions are either not assessed or not met. For these and other reasons, behavior modifiers favor single-case designs. For an excellent, practical, easy-to-read book on single-case designs, see Bailey and Burch (2002).For a review of research using single-case designs in sport psychology, see Martin, Thompson, and Regehr (2004). For a discussion of some common misunderstandings about single-case designs, see Hrycaiko and Martin (1996). For a discussion of reasons for using between-subjects designs, see Poling, Methot, and LeSage (1995). For a discussion of the pros and cons of using statistical inference procedures in behavior analysis research, see *The Behavior Analyst,* 2000, Vol. 22, No. 2.

Study Questions on Notes

1. What do we mean by internal validity? external validity?
2. List four reasons why many behavior modifiers prefer single-case designs to group designs.

24

Planning, Applying, and Evaluating a Treatment Program

This chapter provides *general* guidelines that should be followed when designing a behavioral program. The client might be a person with autism or developmental disabilities, a psychiatric patient, a predelinquent or delinquent child or teenager, a typically developing child or teenager at home, a typically developing child or teenager in a classroom or community setting, or perhaps a normal adult. The situation is one in which you, the behavior modifier, or a mediator (parent, teacher, or some other person) would be largely responsible for carrying out the program.

A PROBLEM HAS BEEN REFERRED:
SHOULD YOU DESIGN A PROGRAM?

Behavioral problems have a variety of causes, exist in a variety of different forms, and differ widely in degree of complexity and severity. The fact that a problem has been referred is not always sufficient reason for proceeding with program design and implementation. To decide where to begin or, indeed, if to begin at all, it is helpful to try to answer the following questions. (It is usually possible to obtain answers to these questions during the screening and intake phase of behavioral assessment described in Chapter 20.)

1. *Was the problem referred primarily for the benefit of the client?* If the problem was referred by others, then you must determine whether the accomplishment of the goal will be for the benefit of the client. If its accomplishment is for the benefit

of others, it should at least be neutral for the client. One must be careful about one's ethics, and some referrals might simply stop here.

2. *Can the problem and the goal be specified such that you are dealing with a specific behavior or set of behaviors that can be counted, timed, or measured in some way?* Many referrals are vague, subjective, and general, such as, "Johnny is hyperactive," "My child is driving me up a wall," "I'm really an unorganized person," "I don't want Teddy to be so darn stubborn." If the problem is initially vague (e.g., if it is merely labeled "aggression"), you must specify a component behavior(s) (e.g., kicking furniture) that can be measured or assessed objectively. In such cases, however, it is extremely important to ask whether dealing with the component(s) will solve the general problem in the eyes of the referring agent or agencies. If it is impossible to agree with the agent on the component behaviors that define the problem, then you should probably stop here. If you do achieve agreement, it should be specified in writing, because people are sometimes forgetful and may later believe that you did not deal with the problem that they referred to you.

3. *Is the problem important to the client or to others?* There are several questions that one might ask to evaluate the importance of the problem. If the problem is an undesirable behavior, does it usually lead to much immediate aversiveness for the client or others? Will solving the problem lead to much more positive reinforcement for the client or others? Will solving the problem be likely to stimulate other desirable behaviors, directly or indirectly? If the answer to some of these questions is no, then you might reconsider your involvement with that particular problem.

Note 1   **4.** *Have you eliminated the possibility that there are complications involved in this problem that would necessitate referring it to another specialist?* (In other words, are you the appropriate person to deal with this problem?) It should be obvious that if there is any chance that the problem has serious medical complications (e.g., excessive weight gain or loss) or serious psychological complications (e.g., the danger of suicide), or a *DSM-IV-TR* diagnosis (see Note 1 of Chapter 1) that you are not qualified to treat or have not previously treated, the appropriate type of specialist should be consulted. You should then treat the problem, if at all, only in a manner that is consistent with the recommendation of that specialist.

5. *Is the problem one that would appear to be easily manageable?* To answer this question, you might consider the following: If the problem is to decrease an undesirable behavior, has the behavior been occurring for a short time, under narrow stimulus control, and with few instances of intermittent reinforcement? A problem with these characteristics is likely to be much easier to solve than an undesirable behavior that has been occurring for a long time, under the control of many situations, and with a history of intermittent reinforcement. Moreover, you should be able to identify desirable behavior that can replace the undesirable behavior. If the problem is to teach a new behavior, you should assess whether the client has the prerequisite skills. If there is more than one problem, you should rank-order them according to their priorities for service, and begin with the problem assigned the highest priority.

6. *If the goal is reached, might it be easily generalized and maintained?* To answer this question, you should consider the following: Can the problem and the improved behavior be managed in the natural environment? If not, can a special training setting be developed that can easily be faded into the natural environment? You should also consider whether there are natural contingencies that will likely maintain the behavioral objective after it has been achieved, if you can change the people in the natural environment so that they will help maintain the desired behavior, or if it is possible for the client to learn a self-control program (discussed in Chapter 26) so that the improved behavior will persist.

Note 2   7. *Can you identify significant individuals (such as relatives, friends, and teachers) in the client's natural environment who might help to record observations and manage controlling stimuli and reinforcers?* When designing programs for children, for example, parents can often successfully implement and maintain the program. In contrast, it makes little sense to accept a referral concerned with the development of a language-training program that will require approximately two hours of concentrated effort per day if you have only about one hour each week to spend on the project, or if it is a single-parent family and the parent works full time during the day and has four other children who occupy his or her attention in the evening.

8. *If there are individuals who might hinder the program, can you identify ways of minimizing their potential interference?* It makes little sense for you to design a program if people are going to sabotage it.

9. *On the basis of your tentative answers to these eight questions, do your training qualifications, daily schedule, and available time seem adequate for you to participate in the program?* You should only accept those referrals for which you have appropriate training and adequate time to carry out an effective program.

When a behavior modifier first enters a group home for persons with developmental disabilities, the home of a family with a child with problems, the classroom of a second-grade teacher, or other settings where interventions are requested, the behavioral problems and the number and complexity of potentially disruptive influences are often staggering. For obvious reasons, it is better to start simply so as to succeed in a small way rather than to attempt too much and risk failing gloriously. A careful evaluation of the initial referral in terms of these questions and considerations can often contribute greatly to the initial success of the behavioral program.

SELECTING AND IMPLEMENTING AN ASSESSMENT PROCEDURE

Let us suppose that you have decided to proceed with designing and implementing a program for a person with a behavioral handicap who has been referred to you. You might then proceed through the following steps.

1. For reliable baselining, define the handicap in precise behavioral terms.
2. Select an appropriate baseline procedure (see Chapters 20, 21, and 22) that will enable you to
   a. monitor the problem behavior.
   b. identify its current stimulus control.

      c. identify the maintaining consequences of the problem behavior.

      d. monitor relevant medical/health/personal variables.

      e. identify an alternative desirable behavior.

3. Design recording procedures that will enable you to log the amount of time devoted to the project by the professionals working on it (such as teachers and behavior modifiers). This will help you to do a cost–effectiveness analysis.

4. Ensure that the observers have received appropriate training in identifying critical aspects of the behavior, applying the recording procedures, and graphing data.

5. If the baseline is likely to be prolonged, select a procedure for increasing and maintaining the strength of the record-keeping behavior of the data recorders.

6. Select a procedure for ensuring the reliability of the baseline observations (see Chapter 21).

7. After beginning to collect baseline data, analyze those data carefully to select an appropriate intervention strategy and decide when to terminate the baseline phase and begin the intervention

We reviewed the guidelines for behavioral assessment in Chapters 20, 21, and 22, and will not repeat them here. However, there are some additional considerations that a behavior modifier should review before and during assessment procedures.

What daily times can the mediator(s) schedule for this project? If, for example, a teacher has about 10 minutes each day just before lunchtime to devote to the project, it is senseless to design time-sampling data sheets that require her to assess behavior throughout the day. It is also senseless to gather data on a wide variety of behaviors that the teacher will never have time to examine.

Will others in the situation help or hinder your data collection? There is no sense in designing a baseline procedure to record the duration of a child's tantrumming in a home situation if a grandparent, an aunt, a brother, or other relatives are going to give the child a candy to stop tantrums because "they can't stand seeing the poor little child upset." On the other hand, friends and relatives can often be extremely helpful, either by recording data directly or by reminding others to do so. If the help of others is to be utilized, posting data sheets and a summary of the recording procedures where everyone involved in the project can see them (such as in a conspicuous place in the kitchen) may be a desirable practice.

Will the surroundings help or hinder your assessment? Let us suppose that you wish to take a baseline on the frequency and timing of a child's marking on walls throughout the day. If the house has many rooms and the child wanders through them, it may be difficult to immediately detect instances of the behavior. Or suppose that someone wishes to take a baseline of smoking behavior but during the baseline spends some time in the house of a friend who doesn't smoke and doesn't have ashtrays around. Obviously this is not ideal for assessment procedures. If you wish to assess the basic self-dressing skills of a child with a severe developmental disability by presenting clothing items with appropriate instructions and the child's favorite TV program is blaring in the background, then your assessment is not likely to be accurate.

What is the frequency of the existing behavior? Is it a behavior that occurs frequently throughout the day in many situations, such as thumb sucking, fingernail biting, whining, or pestering? Or is it one that occurs once every two or three weeks, such as occasional but severe tantrums, stealing, or running away from home? In some cases, your answers to these questions might influence you to withdraw from the project. A problem behavior that occurs rarely can be extremely difficult to treat if you have limited time available for the project. Certainly the frequency of the behavior will dictate the type of recording procedure to be selected, as described in Chapter 21.

How rapidly should the behavior change? Does the behavior require immediate attention because of its inherent danger (as, for example, in the case of self-abuse)? Or is the behavior one whose immediate change would be extremely convenient for those concerned (for instance, parents who want to toilet-train their child just before going on vacation)? If the behavior is one that has been occurring for many months, and if another few days or weeks more or less can be tolerated, then you might be more diligent in the design of a detailed data-recording system to reliably assess baseline levels of performance. Examples of this latter type of behavior might include smoking, excessive TV watching, and inadequate housecleaning.

STRATEGIES OF PROGRAM DESIGN AND IMPLEMENTATION

Some behavior modifiers appear to be extremely skillful at designing effective programs "off the top of their heads"—that is, identifying the program details critical to their success and designing programs that show quick, desirable results. There is probably no set of guidelines that will immediately turn you into that kind of behavior modifier. Nor are there any rigid sets of guidelines to which you should adhere for every program you design. Many behaviors can be managed successfully with a minor rearrangement of existing contingencies; others require much creativity. The following guidelines will help you to design an effective program in most instances.

1. Define the goal, and identify the target behaviors and their desired amount and stimulus control. Then answer these questions.
   a. Is the description precise?
   b. On what grounds was the goal chosen, and how is that in the client's best interest?
   c. Has the client been given all possible information about the goal?
   d. Have steps been taken to increase the client's commitment to accomplish the goal? (Commitment was discussed in Chapter 17, and is discussed later in this chapter.)
   e. What are potential side effects of accomplishing the goal, for both the client and others?
   f. Do the answers to these questions suggest that you should proceed? If so, then continue.
2. Identify individuals (friends, relatives, teachers, and others) who might help to manage controlling stimuli and reinforcers. Also, identify individuals who might hinder the program.
3. Examine the possibility of capitalizing on antecedent control. Can you use:
   a. rules?
   b. goal setting?
   c. modeling?

     d. physical guidance?

     e. situational inducement (rearrange the surroundings, move the activity to a new location, relocate people, or change the time of the activity)?

     f. motivating operations?

4. If you are developing a new behavior, will you use shaping, fading, or chaining? What motivation establishing operation (MEO) will you use?

5. If you are changing the stimulus control of an existing behavior, can you select the controlling S^Ds such that they:

     a. are different from other stimuli on more than one dimension?

     b. are encountered mainly in situations in which the desired stimulus control should occur?

     c. evoke attending behavior?

     d. do not evoke undesirable behavior?

6. If you are decreasing a behavioral excess:

     a. Can you remove S^Ds for the problem behavior?

     b. Can you withhold reinforcers that are maintaining the problem behavior, or present motivation abolishing operations (MAOs) for those reinforcers (see Chapter 19)?

     c. Can you apply DRL to reduce the rate of the behavior to a low, but acceptable rate?

     d. Can you apply DRO, DRI, or DRA (note that each of these may incorporate extinction of the problem behavior, given that you can identify and withhold maintaining reinforcers for it)?

     e. Should punishment be used? Remember that punishment is only acceptable (if at all) as a last resort and under appropriate professional supervision with appropriate ethical approval.

7. Specify the details of the reinforcement system by answering these questions.

     a. How will reinforcers be selected? (See Chapter 3.)

     b. What reinforcers will be used? Can you use the same reinforcers currently maintaining a problem behavior? (See Chapter 22.)

     c. How will reinforcer effectiveness be continually monitored, and by whom?

     d. How will reinforcers be stored and dispensed, and by whom?

     e. If a token system is used, what are the details of its implementation (see Chapter 25)?

8. Specify the training setting. What environmental rearrangement will be necessary to maximize the desired behavior, minimize errors and competing behavior, and maximize proper recording and stimulus management by the mediators (those directly carrying out the program)?

9. Describe how you will program generality of behavior change (Chapter 16) by:

     a. Programing stimulus generalization. Can you

       i) train in the test situation?

       ii) vary the training conditions?

       iii) program common stimuli?

       iv) train sufficient stimulus exemplars?

       v) establish a stimulus equivalence class?

     b. Programing response generalization. Can you:

       i) train sufficient response exemplars?

       ii) vary the acceptable responses during training?

       iii) use behavioral momentum to increase low probability responses within a response class?

     c. Programing behavior maintenance (generality over time). Can you:

       i) use natural contingencies of reinforcement?

       ii) train the people in the natural environment?

       iii) use schedules of reinforcement in the training environment?

       iv) give the control to the individual?

10. Specify the details of the daily recording and graphing procedures.
11. Collect the necessary materials (such as reinforcers, data sheets, graphs, and curriculum materials).
12. Make checklists of rules and responsibilities for all participants in the program (staff, teachers, parents, peers, students, the client, and others) (see Figure 24–1).
13. Specify the dates for data and program reviews and identify those who will attend.
14. Identify some contingencies that will reinforce the behavior modifiers and mediators (in addition to feedback related to the data and program reviews).
15. Review the potential cost of the program as designed (cost of materials, teacher time, professional consulting time, etc.), and judge its merit against its cost. Reprogram as necessary or desired on the basis of this review.
16. Sign a behavioral contract.
17. Implement the program.

If you have followed all these guidelines, the program is ready to go. However, step 16, signing a behavioral contract, requires some additional discussion. Behavioral contracting was described initially as a strategy for scheduling the exchange of reinforcers between two or more individuals, such as between a teacher and students (Homme, Csanyi, Gonzales, & Rechs, 1969) or between parents and children (Dardig & Heward, 1976; DeRisi & Butz, 1975; Miller & Kelley, 1994). Such contracts typically provide a clear statement of what behaviors of what individuals will produce what reinforcers and who will deliver those reinforcers. Treatment contracts between therapists and clients are also recommended, however, as a strategy for ensuring that the therapist is responsible or accountable to

Figure 24–1 Behavior modification places high value on accountability for everyone involved in behavior modification programs.

the client (Sulzer-Azaroff & Reese, 1982). In general, a *treatment contract* is a written agreement between the client and the behavior modifier that indicates, in some detail, how the behavior modifier will help the client overcome a behavioral problem. Richard Stuart (1975) developed a client–therapist treatment contract that clearly outlines the objectives and methods of treatment, the framework of the service to be provided, and contingencies for remuneration that may be forthcoming to the therapist. When the agreement is signed, both the client and the therapist have secured basic protections of their rights. We recommend that behavior modifiers prepare such a written agreement with the appropriate individual(s) prior to implementing a program.

The implementation of your program also requires a great deal of consideration. This might be done in two parts. First, you must be certain that those carrying out the program—the mediators—understand and agree with their roles and responsibilities. This might involve a detailed discussion-and-review session with the mediators. It may also involve some modeling and demonstration on your part, perhaps some role playing on the part of the mediators (depending on the complexity of the programs), and finally some monitoring and on-the-spot feedback when the program is actually implemented. This ensures that parents, teachers, or others are encouraged to follow the program and receive reinforcement for doing so (see, e.g., Hrydowy & Martin, 1994). The second aspect of program implementation is introducing it to the client in a manner that will enhance his or her *commitment* to the program. It is very important that the initial contact of the client with the program be highly reinforcing, so that the probability of further contacts is increased. Questions to consider include: Does the client fully understand and agree with the goals of the program? Is the client aware of how the program will benefit him or her? Has the mediator spent sufficient time with the client and interacted in such a way to gain his or her trust and confidence (see Chapter 20)? Has the program been designed so that the client is likely to experience some success quickly? Will the client come in contact with reinforcers early in the program? A positive answer to such questions greatly increases the chances that the program will be successful.

PROGRAM MAINTENANCE AND EVALUATION

Is your program having a satisfactory effect? This is not always an easy question to answer. It is also not always easy to decide, by some criterion or other, what to do if the program is not having a satisfactory effect. We suggest reviewing the following guidelines to assess a program that has been implemented.

1. Monitor your data to determine whether the recorded behaviors are changing in the desired direction.
2. Consult the people who must deal with the behavioral handicap, and determine whether they are satisfied with the progress.
3. Consult the behavioral journals, professional behavior modifiers, or others with experience in using similar procedures on similar problems to determine if your results are reasonable in terms of the amount of behavior change during the period the program has been in effect.

4. If, on the basis of guidelines 1, 2, and 3, the results are satisfactory, proceed directly to guideline 8.

5. If, on the basis of guideline 1, 2, or 3, your results are unsatisfactory, answer the following questions and make the appropriate adjustment for any yes answer.
   a. Have the reinforcers that are being used lost their appeal?
   b. Are competing responses being reinforced?
   c. Are the procedures being applied incorrectly?
   d. Is there outside interference that is disrupting the program?
   e. Are there any subjective variables—staff or client negative attitudes, teacher or client lack of enthusiasm, and so forth—that might be adversely affecting the program?

6. If none of the answers to these four questions is yes, check to see if additional programming steps need to be added or removed. The data may show excessive error rates, which would suggest the need for additional programming steps. Or they may show very high rates of correct responses, which might indicate that the program is too easy and that a certain amount of boredom is occurring. Add, remove, or modify steps as necessary.

7. If the results are now satisfactory, proceed to guideline 8; otherwise consult with a colleague, or consider redesigning a major aspect of the program or redoing a functional analysis to identify the antecedents and consequences controlling the target behavior.

8. Decide how you will provide appropriate program maintenance until the behavioral objective is reached (see Chapter 16).

9. Following attainment of the behavioral goal, outline an appropriate arrangement for assessing performance during follow-up observations and assessing social validity (see Chapter 23).

10. After successful follow-up observations have been obtained, determine the costs for the behavior changes that occurred (called a *cost–effectiveness analysis*).

11. Where possible and appropriate, analyze your data and communicate your procedures and results to other behavior modifiers and interested professionals (be sure to conceal the client's identity to maintain confidentiality.)

STUDY QUESTIONS

1. What is the purpose of this chapter, and how does it relate to the other chapters in the book?

2. Assume that you are a professional behavior modifier. List at least four possible conditions under which you would not treat a behavioral problem that has been referred to you.

3. What does a behavior modifier do when given a vague problem (such as "aggression") to work on? Illustrate with an example.

4. How does a behavior modifier evaluate the importance of a problem?

5. How does a behavior modifier evaluate the ease with which a problem might be solved?

6. How does a behavior modifier evaluate the ease with which the desired behavioral change might be generalized to, and maintained in, the natural environment?

7. What are some considerations that a behavior modifier should review before and during assessment procedures?

8. You are about to design a treatment program. After defining the target behavior and identifying its desired level of occurrence and stimulus control, what five questions should you answer before proceeding to the design?
9. If you are thinking of capitalizing on antecedent control, what six categories should you consider?
10. If you are decreasing a behavioral excess, what five questions should you ask?
11. What questions should you ask to specify the details of a reinforcement system?
12. What factors should you consider in programming for generality?
13. What strategy is recommended to ensure accountability of the therapist?
14. How can you increase the client's commitment to the program?
15. After a program has been implemented, what three things should be done to determine whether it is producing satisfactory results? (See guidelines 1, 2, and 3.)
16. If a program is producing satisfactory results, what two things should be done prior to successfully terminating the program? (See guidelines 8 and 9.)
17. Describe in detail the steps that should be followed if a program is not producing satisfactory results (See guidelines 5, 6, and 7).

APPLICATION EXERCISE

A. Exercise Involving Others

Suppose that you are a behavior modifier. The mother of a "normal" 4-year-old child asks for your help in designing a program to overcome the child's extreme disobedience. Construct realistic but hypothetical details of the behavior problem and take it through all steps in each of the following stages of programming:
1. Deciding whether you should design a program to treat the problem
2. Selecting and implementing an assessment procedure
3. Developing strategies of program design and implementation
4. Establishing program maintenance and evaluation

(Note: The problem will have to be fairly complex for you to take it through all the steps in each of these stages.)

NOTES AND EXTENDED DISCUSSION

1. Whether you are the appropriate person to deal with a particular problem may be influenced, in part, by whether you live in an urban or a rural setting. Rodrigue, Banko, Sears, and Evans (1996) identified a number of difficulties associated with providing behavior therapy services in rural areas. While rural regions have a disproportionate number of at-risk populations that are costly to serve (e.g., elderly people, children, minorities, poor persons), they typically do not offer the full array of needed mental health services and are characterized by lower availability of and accessibility to specialized services. In other words, while you may not be the ideal person to treat the problem, you may be the best person available. Before accepting the responsibility of designing a program in such a case, however, you should consult the ethical guidelines for human services of your professional organization. (See also Chapter 30 of this book.)

2.   Even if significant others are not necessary to implement a program, their availability can be extremely valuable for programming generality. Consider the problem of developing effective behavioral weight-loss programs for children (see LeBow, 1991). Israel, Stolmaker, and Adrian (1985) introduced two groups of overweight children (from 8 to 12 years of age) to an eight-week intensive, multicomponent, behavioral weight-reduction program. The parents of one group were also presented with a short course on behavioral child-management skills. At the end of the eight-week treatment program, both groups of children had lost approximately the same amount of weight. After a one-year follow-up, however, maintenance of improved weight status was superior for the children whose parents had been introduced to the behavioral child-management procedures.

Study Questions on Notes

1.   What impact might the geographic setting have on your decision, as a behavior modifier, to accept a referral?
2.   How did Israel and colleagues demonstrate that utilizing significant others in a program can enhance generality?

25

Token Economies

Recall from Chapter 4 that a conditioned reinforcer is a stimulus that was not originally reinforcing but acquires reinforcing power from being paired appropriately with other reinforcers. Some conditioned reinforcers, such as praise, are quite brief. The stimulus is gone almost as soon as it is presented. Other conditioned reinforcers, such as money, endure and can be accumulated until they are exchanged for backup reinforcers, such as food. Conditioned reinforcers of the latter type are called **tokens.** A program in which a group of individuals can earn tokens for a variety of desirable behaviors, and can exchange tokens earned for backup reinforcers, is called a **token economy.**

There are two major advantages to using token reinforcers. First, they can be given immediately after a desirable behavior occurs and cashed in at a later time for a backup reinforcer. Thus they can be used to "bridge" long delays between the target response and the backup reinforcer, which is especially important when it is impractical or impossible to deliver the backup reinforcer immediately after the behavior. Second, tokens that are paired with many different backup reinforcers are generalized conditioned reinforcers and therefore do not depend on a specific motivating operation for their strength. This makes it easier to administer consistent and effective reinforcers when dealing with a group of individuals who may be in different motivational states.

Token economies have been used in psychiatric wards, in institutions and classrooms for persons with developmental disabilities, in classrooms for children and teenagers with attention-deficit hyperactivity disorder (ADHD), in normal classroom settings ranging from preschool to college and university classes, in homes for predelinquents (i.e., juveniles who have engaged in antisocial behaviors), in prisons, in the military, in wards for the treatment of persons with drug addiction or alcoholism, in nursing homes, in convalescent centers, in normal family homes to control children's behavior and to treat marital discord, and in various work settings to increase safety behavior, decrease absenteeism, and enhance on-the-job performance (Kazdin, 1977a, 1985). A token economy has also been used in a behaviorally managed experimental community of 30 college students (Johnson, Welch, Miller, & Altus, 1991; Thomas & Miller, 1980).

Although developed primarily in institutional settings, the techniques used in token economies have been extended to various community settings to decrease littering, increase recycling of wastes, increase energy conservation, increase use of mass transportation, decrease noise pollution, increase racial integration, increase behaviors involved in gaining employment, and increase self-help behaviors in people who are disadvantaged by the economic system.

In this chapter we cannot do justice to the extremely wide range of behaviors and situations to which the techniques of token economies apply. What we intend
Note 1   to do, however, is to describe typical steps in the use of token economies in various settings. For more specific details on establishing a token economy in a particular setting, the reader is referred to any of the excellent handbooks that are available for that purpose in several areas of application.

INITIAL STEPS IN SETTING UP A TOKEN ECONOMY

Deciding on the Target Behaviors

The target behaviors will be determined largely by the type of individuals with whom you are working, by the short-range and long-range objectives you wish to accomplish with those individuals, and by specific behavioral problems you are encountering that interfere with the realization of those objectives. For example, if you are the classroom teacher of a group of rambunctious first graders, your objectives will likely include teaching reading, writing, counting, addition, subtraction, and constructive social interaction. Your target behaviors will include those that are involved in these skills or are prerequisite to them, and they must be defined clearly enough so that the students know what behaviors are expected of them and so that you can reinforce those behaviors reliably when they occur. Thus, at least one of your target behaviors might be "sitting quietly when the teacher gives out instructions." A more advanced target behavior might be "correctly completing problems in a workbook."

The more homogeneous the group with which you are dealing, the easier it is to standardize the rules concerning which specific responses will be reinforced with what specific number of tokens. From this perspective, at least, it is fortunate that many groups for whom token economies are appropriate are composed of individuals who are at roughly the same behavioral level (e.g., individuals with severe developmental disabilities or college students enrolled in a Personalized System of Instruction (PSI) course; see Chapter 2). Even with very homogeneous groups, however, it will probably be necessary to have some specific reinforcement rules for certain individuals, according to their respective behavioral needs. This necessity for individualizing programs adds to the complexity of administering a token economy, but the resulting difficulties are not serious if a staff member is not required to handle too many radically different individual programs at once. Assigning special cases to special treatment groups may be one efficient way in which to solve the problem of individualization in certain types of settings.

Taking Baselines

Just as is done before initiating other procedures, baseline data on the specific target behaviors should be obtained before initiating a token economy. It may be that your clients are already performing at a satisfactory level and that the potential benefits to be gained from setting up a token economy do not justify the time, effort, and cost involved in doing so. After the program has been started, comparing the data with the baseline data will enable you to determine the effectiveness of the program.

Selecting Backup Reinforcers

The methods for selecting backup reinforcers are essentially the same as the methods for selecting reinforcers (described in Chapter 3). Keep in mind, however, that a token system will generally increase the variety of practical reinforcers that you can use, because they need not be limited to those that can be delivered immediately following a desired response.

In considering reinforcers that are normally available, take extreme caution to avoid the serious ethical problems that can arise. Various legislatures have enacted laws affirming the rights of mentally ill patients and residents of treatment centers to have access to meals, comfortable beds, TV, and so on. Furthermore, a number of court decisions have upheld these civil rights. Therefore, never plan a program that might involve depriving individuals of something that legally and morally belongs to them.

After establishing what your backup reinforcers are going to be and how you are going to obtain them, you should next consider the general method of dispensing them. A store or commissary is an essential feature of most token economies. In a small token economy, such as a classroom, the store can be quite simple, say, a box located on the teacher's desk or another table in the room. In a larger token economy, the store is typically much larger, perhaps occupying one or more rooms. Regardless of the size of the store, a definite method of keeping records of purchases must be devised so that an adequate inventory (especially of items in high demand) can be maintained at all times, within the limit of your budget.

Selecting the Type of Tokens to Use

Tokens can take on any of the forms that money has assumed. These include personal "checks," entries in a "bank book," marks on a chart on the wall or in notebooks carried by clients, stickers, stars, or stamps pasted in booklets—all these and numerous other possibilities may suit the needs of your particular token economy, depending mainly on the type of client involved.

Figure 25–1 Tokens should not be easily counterfeited.

In general, tokens should be attractive, lightweight, portable, durable, easy to handle, and, of course, not easily counterfeited (Figure 25–1). If automatic dispensers of backup reinforcement are used, you should ensure that your tokens will operate those devices. You should also ensure that you have an adequate number of tokens for your clients. For example, Stainback, Payne, Stainback, and Payne (1973) suggest that you should have on hand about 100 tokens per child when starting a token economy in a classroom.

You should also acquire the necessary accessories for handling and storing tokens. For example, schoolchildren may need boxes, bags, or purses in which to store the tokens they have earned.

Identifying Available Help

Help from other individuals may not be essential in a small token economy, such as a classroom, but is certainly to be desired especially in the initial stages of the program. In a large token economy, such as a psychiatric facility, such help is essential.

Note 2 There are a number of sources from which help may be obtained: (a) people already assigned to work with the clients (e.g., teachers' aides, nurses' aides, teaching assistants); (b) volunteers (e.g., homemakers, retired couples, senior citizens, members of civic organizations and community action groups); (c) behaviorally advanced individuals within the institution (e.g., conscientious fifth graders assigned to help manage a token economy for first graders); and (d) members of the token economy itself. In some cases, clients have been taught to deliver tokens to themselves contingent on appropriate behavior.

Note 3 After the token economy begins to function smoothly, more and more of its members will gradually become able to assume more and more responsibility in helping to achieve its goals. For example, at **Achievement Place,** a group home for predelinquent boys (see Fixsen & Blase, 1993), some of the youths supervise others in carrying out routine household tasks. The supervisor, or "manager," as he is called, has the authority to both administer and remove tokens for his peers' performances. Of the several methods that were studied for selecting managers, democratic elections proved to be best in terms of the performances of the youths and their effectiveness in accomplishing their tasks (Phillips, Phillips, Wolf, & Fixsen, 1973; Wolf, Braukmann, & Ramp, 1987). In another experiment at Achievement Place, some youths served with remarkable effectiveness (and earned tokens for doing so), despite their having very little adult supervision and no specific training, as therapists for others who had speech problems (Bailey, Timbers, Phillips, & Wolf, 1971).

In some courses that use PSI (including CAPSI—e.g., see Pear & Crone-Todd, 1999; Pear & Martin, 2004), students who are among the first to master an assignment have served to evaluate the performance of other students on that assignment and to give them immediate feedback concerning their performance. Another method used in college and university classes is to give the students a test near the beginning of the term on the first several sections of the course material. Those students who demonstrate on this test that they can readily master the course material are each put in charge of a small group of students, whom they help to tutor and supervise throughout the remainder of the course (Johnson & Ruskin, 1977).

In deciding how you are going to obtain workers who will help to manage your token economy, you will need to consider how their helping behavior is to be reinforced. Your approval is, of course, a potential reinforcer that should be used generously. Permission to continue working in the token economy and to work at desired jobs are additional reinforcers at your disposal.

Choosing the Locations

No special locations are essential for a token economy, which is nice since the designer of a token economy often has little or no choice in its location. Some locations are better than others, however, depending on the type of token economy under consideration. For example, college instructors using token economies (i.e., PSI courses) often arrange to have their courses scheduled in lecture halls or very large classrooms designed originally for at least twice as many students as the number anticipated to attend class at any given time. Movable desks are generally preferred over stationary ones because they enable students to work easily in small groups. Classrooms with token economies are often very noisy places and give the initial impression of mass confusion to a casual observer. Surprising as it may seem, however, almost all students soon adjust quite well to the noise, so that it does not prevent them from working with great efficiency. Of course, the Internet has provided a virtual-classroom location for academic token economies in which students may be in almost any physical environment of their choosing (e.g., Pear & Crone-Todd, 1999; Pear & Martin, 2004).

SPECIFIC IMPLEMENTATION PROCEDURES

Before and during the implementation of a token economy there are, as with any other new program, a number of specific procedures to be decided on and implemented. These can be categorized as follows.

Keeping Data   Here we are concerned with what sort of data sheets should be used, who is to record the data, and when the data are to be recorded.

The Reinforcing Agent   It is important to decide who is going to administer reinforcement, and for what behaviors. For example, Ayllon and Azrin (1968) recommended that, when several managers dispense tokens to several clients (such as in a psychiatric ward), only one person should be assigned to reinforce a particular response at a particular time. Otherwise, "no one individual can be held responsible for failure to administer the reinforcement procedures properly, since any deviation, omission, or modification is easily attributed to the behavior of some other employee" (p. 136).

In addition, care should be taken to ensure that tokens are always delivered in a positive and conspicuous manner immediately following a desired response. Friendly, smiling approval should be administered along with the token, and the client should be told (at least in the initial stages) why he or she is receiving the token.

Number or Frequency of Tokens to Pay   There are several important considerations concerning the amount of tokens to give for a particular behavior. One consideration is the stage of the economy, that is, how accustomed the clients are to receiving tokens. Stainback and colleagues (1973) recommended that from 25 to 75 tokens per child is not excessive on the first day of a token economy in a classroom. They recommended further that the number be decreased gradually from 15 to 30 each day. Other considerations are the therapeutic value of the behavior being reinforced and the likelihood that the client will engage in it without tokens. As an example of the latter consideration, the number of tokens that college students at the University of Kansas Experimental Living Project could earn for doing chores in their residence was related to the amount of time required to perform the chore (Johnson, Welch, Miller, & Altus, 1991).

Managing the Backup Reinforcers   Here we have to consider how frequently backup reinforcers will be available to be purchased (that is, how frequently "store time" should be scheduled). In the beginning, the frequency should probably be quite high, then decreased gradually. For schoolchildren, Stainback, Payne,

Stainback, and Payne (1973) recommended that store time be held once or twice per day for the first three or four days and then decreased gradually in frequency until it is held only once each week (Friday afternoon) by the third week of the token economy.

It is also necessary to decide how many tokens each backup reinforcer will cost. In addition to the monetary cost, which is the most obvious consideration in assigning token values to backup reinforcers, two other factors should be considered. One is supply and demand. That is, charge more for items whose demand exceeds the supply and less for items whose supply exceeds the demand. This will help to maintain an adequate supply of effective reinforcers and promote optimal utilization of the reinforcing power of each backup reinforcer. The other factor to consider is the therapeutic value of the backup reinforcer. A client should be charged very little for a backup reinforcer that is beneficial to him or her. This will help to induce the client to partake of the reinforcer. For example, a client whose social skills need improving may be charged only a few tokens for admission to a party because of the valuable behavior that participating in this event may help to develop.

Possible Punishment Contingencies   The use of tokens provides the possibility of using fines as punishment for inappropriate behavior (see, e.g., Lippman & Motta, 1993; Sullivan & O'Leary, 1990). This type of punishment may be preferable, from an ethical point of view, to physical punishment and timeout. As with all forms of punishment, it should be used sparingly and only for clearly defined behaviors (see Chapter 12).

If fines are used in a token economy, it may be necessary to add training contingencies that teach clients how to accept fines in a relatively nonemotional, nonaggressive manner. Such contingencies were described by Phillips, Phillips, Fixsen, and Wolf (1973) for their token economy with predelinquent youths. In that economy, the contingencies related to fines probably helped to teach youths an important social skill: how to accept reprimands from law enforcers in society.

Supervision of Staff   The managers of a token economy, no less than the clients, are subject to the laws of behavior. They must receive frequent reinforcement for appropriate behavior, and their inappropriate behavior must be corrected if the token economy is to function effectively. Their duties must therefore be specified clearly, and they must be supervised in the performance of those duties.

Continuous supervision is generally impractical. Therefore, time sampling should be used. The director of the economy should start with frequent supervision and then gradually reduce its frequency. A desirable schedule of staff supervision and reinforcement might be a VI/LH to maintain a high, steady rate of appropriate staff performance (see Ayllon & Azrin, 1968, p. 151).

Handling Potential Problems   In the design of a token economy, as with any complex procedure, it is wise to plan for potential problems. Some of the problems that are likely to arise are (a) confusion, especially during the first few days after the initiation of the economy; (b) staff shortages; (c) attempts by clients to get tokens they have not earned or backup reinforcers for which they do not have enough tokens; (d) clients playing with tokens and manipulating them in distracting ways; and (e) failure to purchase backup reinforcers. All these and other problems that may arise can almost always be managed by careful planning beforehand.

PREPARING A MANUAL

The final stage to complete before implementing the token economy is to prepare a manual or written set of rules describing exactly how the economy is to run. This manual should explain in detail what behaviors are to be reinforced, how they are to be reinforced with tokens and backup reinforcers, the times at which reinforcement is to be available, what data are to be recorded, how and when they are to be recorded, and the responsibilities and duties of every staff member. Each rule should be reasonable and acceptable to clients and staff. Every staff member should receive a copy of the manual or a clear and accurate version of those portions of it pertaining to his or her specific duties and responsibilities. If feasible, each client should be given a clear and accurate version of those portions of the manual pertaining to him or her. If the client is not able to read fluently but can understand the spoken language, a clear explanation of the relevant portions of the manual should be provided.

The manual should include definite procedures for evaluating whether or not the rules are being followed adequately and procedures for ensuring that they are. Methods for arbitrating disputes concerning the rules should be included in the manual, and the participation of clients in the arbitration procedures should be provided to the greatest extent that is practical and consistent with the goals of the token economy. Effecting such client participation is a step toward developing the behaviors involved in individual initiative, self-government, and other skills that are highly prized in the natural environment. Toward this end, it is desirable at some stage in the token economy to have the clients themselves participate in constructively revising the rules and designing new ones for running the economy. The rules should also be capable of modification when there is evidence that a change is desirable. Sudden and drastic changes, however, can generate undesirable emotional behavior in clients. Moreover, clients may become disinclined to follow the rules when they are changed frequently or arbitrarily. So that rule modifications may occur in the smoothest manner possible, it is advisable to have the manual itself specify the basis on which it will be revised. Advance notification of impending rule changes should be given to all concerned, and revisions and additions to the manual should be explained, discussed, justified, put in writing, and disseminated prior to being put into effect.

PROGRAMMING GENERALITY
TO THE NATURAL ENVIRONMENT

Token economies are sometimes regarded as ways in which to manage problem behavior in institutional settings. They do serve this function, but this observation should not let us neglect their more important function of helping clients to adjust to the natural environment beyond the institution. Kazdin (1985) has summarized a large amount of data indicating that token economies are effective with diverse populations, and that the gains achieved with token economies are often maintained for at least several years following the termination of the program. However, because social reinforcement, not tokens, prevails in the natural environment, a token economy should be designed so that social reinforcement gradually replaces token reinforcement.

There are two general ways of weaning a client from tokens. One is to eliminate them gradually. The second is to decrease their value gradually. The first alternative can be accomplished by gradually making the schedule of token delivery more and more intermittent, by gradually decreasing the number of behaviors that earn tokens, or by gradually increasing the delay between the target behavior and token delivery. The second alternative can be accomplished by gradually decreasing the amount of backup reinforcement that a given number of tokens can purchase or by gradually increasing the delay between token acquisition and the purchase of backup reinforcers. At present, we cannot say which method or combination of methods produces the best results. In addition, all the considerations involved in programming generality (discussed in Chapter 16) should be reviewed.

Gradually transferring control to the clients themselves so that they plan and administer their own reinforcements is another step in preparing clients for the natural environment. An individual who can evaluate his or her own behavior, decide rationally what changes need to be made in it, and program effectively for these changes is clearly in a good position to cope with almost any environment. Methods for establishing these skills are discussed in Chapter 26.

ETHICAL CONSIDERATIONS

Token economies involve the systematic application of behavior modification techniques on a relatively large scale. The possibilities of abusing the techniques, even unintentionally, are thereby magnified. Precautions should be taken to avoid such abuse. One such precaution is to make the system completely open to public scrutiny, provided that such openness is subject to the approval of clients or their advocates. Ethical considerations involving all behavior modification programs are discussed extensively in Chapter 30.

A SUMMARY OF CONSIDERATIONS IN DESIGNING A TOKEN ECONOMY

1. Review some appropriate literature.
2. Identify your target behaviors.
   a. List short-range and long-range objectives.
   b. Arrange your objectives in order of priority.
   c. Select those objectives that are most important for the clients and that are prerequisites for later objectives.
   d. Identify several of the priority objectives on which to start, emphasizing those that can be accomplished quickly.
   e. Pinpoint a number of target behaviors for each of the starting objectives.
3. Take a baseline of your target behaviors.
4. Select your backup reinforcers.
   a. Use reinforcers that are usually effective with the population of interest.
   b. Use the Premack principle (see Chapter 3).

c. Collect verbal information from the clients concerning their reinforcers.
d. Give the clients catalogs that will help them to identify reinforcers.
e. Ask clients what they like to do when they have free time away from work or other demands.
f. Identify natural reinforcers that might be programmed.
g. Consider ethics and legalities regarding the reinforcers on your list.
h. Design an appropriate store to keep, display, and dispense your backup reinforcers.

5. Select the most appropriate type of token for your client. (They should be attractive, lightweight, portable, durable, easy to handle, and difficult to counterfeit.)
6. Identify those who are available to help manage the programs:
    a. Existing staff
    b. Volunteers
    c. University students
    d. Residents of the institution
    e. Members of the token economy themselves
7. Obtain an appropriate location and necessary equipment.
    a. Accept the location with the greater space.
    b. Equipment and furnishings should be easily movable.
    c. Rearrange the setting so that behaviors of the clients can be detected most easily and reinforced immediately.
8. Decide on specific implementation procedures.
    a. Design appropriate data sheets and determine who will take data and how and when it will be recorded.
    b. Decide who is going to administer reinforcement, how it will be administered, and for what behaviors.
    c. Decide on the number of tokens that can be earned per behavior per client per day.
    d. Establish "store" procedures and determine the token value of backup reinforcers.
    e. Be wary of punishment contingencies. Use them sparingly, only for clearly defined behaviors, and only when it is ethically justifiable to do so.
    f. Ensure that staff duties are clearly defined and that a desirable schedule of staff supervision and reinforcement is implemented.
    g. Plan for potential problems.
9. Prepare a token economy manual for the clients and the staff.
10. Institute your token economy.
11. Plan strategies for obtaining generality to the natural environment.
12. Monitor and practice relevant ethical guidelines at each step.

STUDY QUESTIONS

1. What is a token economy?
2. What are two major advantages to using token reinforcers?
3. List at least five settings in which token economies have been used.
4. List at least five behaviors that token economies have been designed to develop.
5. List and briefly describe six initial steps in setting up a token economy.
6. What is the store of a token economy? Give examples.
7. What six characteristics should a token have?
8. How is PSI like other token economies, and how does it differ from them?
9. Identify three sources of potential volunteer help in managing a token economy.

10. What do you think are some advantages in having the members of the token economy themselves function as the main source of help?

11. Before and during implementation of a token economy, what eight specific procedures must be decided on and implemented?

12. What are some of the advantages and disadvantages of assigning only one person to reinforce a particular response at a particular time in a token economy in an institutional ward?

13. How should tokens be delivered?

14. How many tokens should you have for each student in the group?

15. According to Stainback and others, how often should store time be held during the first few days of a token economy?

16. For a token economy program involving a number of staff, describe a plausible VI/LH schedule of staff supervision (think of a variation of the Timer Game from Chapter 6).

17. Why would a VI/LH schedule be preferred over an FI/LH schedule for staff supervision?

18. Describe two general methods of weaning clients from tokens when transferring behavior to the natural environment.

19. If one decides to effect a gradual decrease in the number of behaviors that earn tokens, what general guidelines might be followed in deciding which behaviors no longer require token reinforcement? That is, where do you start and on which behaviors do you start?

20. What is one precaution to help ensure high ethical standards for a token economy?

APPLICATION EXERCISES

A. Exercises Involving Others

1. For a group of individuals of your choosing (for instance, in an elementary school classroom, a university class, or training program for persons with developmental disabilities), identify five plausible goals for a token economy.

2. Define precisely the target behaviors related to each of the five goals listed in Exercise 1.

3. Describe a number of things you might do to identify backup reinforcers for the group of individuals you chose in Exercise 1.

NOTES AND EXTENDED DISCUSSION

1. Much of the material in this chapter is covered in greater detail in the following major works on token economies: Ayllon and Azrin (1968), which deals with token economies in mental hospitals; Stainback et al. (1973), which deals with token economies in elementary school classrooms; M. W. Welch and Gist (1974), which deals primarily with token economies in sheltered workshops; Ayllon and others

(1979), which describes token programs in prisons; and Kazdin (1977a), which presents a comprehensive review of token-economy research. For more information on token systems for children and teens with ADHD, see Barkley (1996). For more information on the use of token-economy procedures in college and high school courses, in which systems incorporating these procedures are sometimes called Personalized System of Instruction (PSI), see Keller and Sherman (1982) and Chapter 2 of this book.

2. Rae, Martin, and Sanyk (1990) designed a program to pay tokens to clients with developmental disabilities in a sheltered workshop for improved on-task performance. The tokens could be redeemed for items in the workshop cafeteria. However, the workshop had insufficient staff to reliably keep track of those clients who were on-task and those who were not. A solution was to teach the workers to self-monitor their own on-task performance. A pencil and a sheet with squares on it were placed in front of each worker. The workers were taught that when a buzzer sounded, they should mark an X on one of the squares if they were on-task. The buzzer was set to go off at six random times during a half-day. When a worker earned six Xs, he or she could exchange them for a token. The total program proved to be effective for increasing the on-task behavior of the workers on a variety of workshop tasks.

3. Achievement Place is a group home in which a very effective program was developed for predelinquent youth—individuals from 10 to 16 years of age who had been referred by the courts for committing minor crimes, such as petty theft and fighting, and who were typically from difficult home environments. The program uses a Teaching Family Model (TFM) in which six to eight adolescents live with a married couple in a large, domestic home. Major features of the program include:
   a. A token economy in which participants earn points for appropriate social behaviors, academic performance, and daily-living skills, and exchange them for privileges such as snacks, television, hobbies, games, allowance, and permission to participate in activities away from the home.
   b. A self-government system in which the youth participate in the development of daily-living rules and the management of the program.
   c. An emphasis on normalization.
   d. Ongoing evaluation of the performance of the participants.
Developed in the early 1970s, there are now approximately 22 certified "Achievement Places" or TFMs in the United States, including Boystown, and as many as 100 programs that use a modified version of TFM (Friman, 2000). Although further research is needed to develop strategies for long-term maintenance of gains achieved by youth who participate in TFM programs, they continue to be one of the most effective approaches for the treatment of predelinquent youth (Braukmann & Wolf, 1987; Friman, 2000).

Study Questions on Notes

1. Describe a token program in which clients in a sheltered workshop administered tokens to themselves.
2. Describe the key features of the Teaching Family Model. Identify the type of client for which it is used, and give the names of two places where it is used.

Helping an Individual to Develop Self-Control[1]

Al and Mary have just finished having doughnuts and coffee in the campus cafeteria. "I think I'll have another doughnut," said Al. "They look so delicious! I just don't have the willpower to resist. Besides," he added, while patting his protruding midsection, "one more won't make any difference."

Many problems of self-control involve self-restraint—learning to decrease excessive behaviors that have immediate gratification—such as excessive smoking, eating, drinking, and TV watching. Other problems of self-control require behavioral change in the opposite direction—responses that need to be increased—such as studying, exercising, being assertive, and performing household chores. Many people speak as though there is some magical force within us—called *willpower*—that is responsible for overcoming such problems. People probably believe this, in part, because others are always saying things like, "If you had more willpower you could get rid of that bad habit," or "If you had more willpower you could improve yourself and get some better habits." Most of us have heard such advice many times. Unfortunately, it's usually not very helpful advice, because the person offering it almost always neglects to tell us how we can get more of this so-called willpower. It is more useful to look at how problems of self-control stem from differences between effective versus ineffective consequences of a behavior. From such a starting point, we proceed to a model for self-control. Finally, we describe

---

[1]Material in this chapter was described by Martin and Osborne (1993) and is paraphrased with permission.

how most successful self-control (also called **self-management** or **self-modification**) programs proceed through five basic steps.

CAUSES OF SELF-CONTROL PROBLEMS

> "I just *can't* resist having an extra dessert."
>
> "I *really* should get into an exercise program. I wish I weren't so lazy."
>
> "My term paper is due, I have a big midterm, and I have to finish writing up that lab assignment. What am I doing here at this bar? Why aren't I home studying?"

Do any of these sound familiar? If you're like most people, you've probably heard yourself say such things many times. These are the sorts of times when we are tempted to talk about not having enough willpower. Let's see how such situations can be explained by examining how immediately significant, delayed, cumulatively significant, and improbable consequences affect (or fail to affect) behavior.

Problems of Behavioral Excesses

One type of self-control problem consists of behavioral excesses—doing too much of something. Examples are overeating, excessive TV watching, drinking too much coffee, and so on. All such behavioral excesses lead to immediate reinforcers (good taste of food, enjoyable scenes on TV, etc.). And even though they might also lead to negative consequences, the latter are often ineffective. Let's see why.

Immediate Reinforcers Versus Delayed Punishers for a Behavior   Suppose that a teenager wants to go out with friends, but there is still homework to be done. When the parents ask about the homework, the teenager lies and is allowed to leave with his friends. Lying is immediately reinforced. The lie is not discovered until later, and the consequent punishment (e.g., being grounded, failing the assignment) is long delayed from the instance of lying. If a behavior leads to immediate reinforcers but delayed punishers, the immediate reinforcers often win out. Many problems of self-control stem from this fact (Brigham, 1989b). The immediate backslapping and laughter of friends after someone "chugs" a pitcher of beer may override the delayed punishing consequences of a hangover. The immediate reinforcing consequences from sexual behavior with a best friend's spouse or partner may override the delayed hurt and emotional anguish when the friend finds out and is no longer a friend.

Immediate Reinforcers Versus Cumulatively Significant Punishers for a Behavior Consider the problem of eating too many sweets. Eating an extra dessert is immediately reinforced by the good taste. And although the negative effects (excess cholesterol, etc.) of the extra dessert are immediate, they are too small to be noticed. Rather, it is the accumulation of extra desserts on many occasions that causes a health problem. As another example, consider the problem of smoking. The immediate consequences of smoking (nicotine effects, etc.) are positive for smokers. And although there are immediate negative effects (additional tar deposited on the smoker's lungs), the harmful outcomes from a single cigarette are too small to counteract the enjoyment of smoking. Rather, it is the accumulation of the effects of hundreds of cigarettes that results in shortness of breath, sore throat, coughing, and possible lung cancer. Thus, for many self-control problems, the immediate reinforcement for consumption of harmful substances (nicotine, cholesterol, etc.) wins out over the unnoticeable immediate negative effects that are only cumulatively significant (Malott, 1989).

Immediate Reinforcers (for Problem Behavior) Versus Delayed Reinforcers (for Alternative Desirable Behaviors)   Let's suppose it's a Thursday evening in the middle of your term. Your roommate just rented a movie that you would like to watch. But you also have an exam the next day. Do you watch the movie (and all those enjoyable scenes) or do you study for three hours (and receive a higher grade a week or two later)? Unfortunately, many students choose the movie. Consider the case of a worker who receives a large Christmas bonus from the company. Will the worker blow the Christmas bonus on a highly pleasurable ski trip, or invest it in a tax-free retirement fund? Which would you choose if you were the worker? For self-control problems involving a choice between two alternative behaviors, both of which result in positive outcomes, the one that produces the immediate reinforcer frequently wins out (Brigham, 1989b).

Problems of Behavioral Deficiencies

Another type of self-control problem consists of responses that need to be increased—such as flossing your teeth, taking good lecture notes, and exercising regularly. Such behaviors usually lead to small, immediate punishers. And even though there may be positive outcomes if the behaviors occur, or major negative outcomes if the behaviors don't occur, both of these outcomes are often ineffective. Let's see why.

Immediate Small Punishers for a Behavior Versus Reinforcers That Are Cumulatively Significant   For nonexercisers, an initial exercising session can be quite unpleasant (time consuming, tiring, stressful, etc.). And even though an instance of exercising may have immediate benefits (increased blood circulation, better removal of waste products, etc.), such outcomes are too small to be noticed. Rather, it is the accumulation of the benefits of exercising on many occasions that is eventually noticeable. Many people fail to follow desirable health practices (exercising, taking prescribed medications, etc.) because doing so leads to immediate small punishers, whereas the positive effects, though immediate, are too small to be effective until they have accumulated over many trials (Malott, 1989).

Immediate Small Punisher for Behavior Versus Immediate but Highly Improbable Major Punisher if the Behavior Does Not Occur   Most people know that wearing eye protection when playing racquetball can prevent serious eye damage and that wearing a helmet when riding a bicycle could prevent brain damage from a serious accident. Why, then, are there many people who do not wear goggles when playing racquetball or helmets when riding bicycles? First, such behaviors usually lead to immediate mild punishers (the goggles and the helmet may be hot and uncomfortable).

Second, although the major punishers for not performing the behavior would be immediate, they are highly improbable.

Immediate Small Punisher for a Behavior Versus a Delayed Major Punisher if the Behavior Does Not Occur   Why do many people fail to floss their teeth or put off going for a dental checkup or fail to take good lecture notes? In this type of self-control problem, there are immediate weak punishers contingent upon performing. The dental floss hurts your gums or your fingers. The sound of the dentist's drill is unpleasant. Your fingers get tired while taking good lecture notes. And while the delayed consequences (such as a major toothache or a poor grade) can be much more aversive, they occur long after many missed flossing opportunities or cancelled dental appointments or missed lecture notes. Unfortunately, in such situations, the immediate consequences often win out.

A MODEL FOR SELF-CONTROL

An effective model of self-control must deal satisfactorily with the causes of self-control problems described in the preceding section. The model that we describe here has two parts. The first part requires clear specification of the problem as a behavior to be controlled. The second part requires that you apply behavioral techniques (i.e., emit controlling behavior) to manage the problem. In that sense, this model of self-control consists of doing one thing (applying techniques of behavioral change or behavior modification) to increase the chances of doing some other thing (i.e., behaving in a way that solves the problem). An individual must behave in some way that arranges the environment to manage his or her own subsequent behavior. This means emitting a *controlling behavior* to effect a change in a *behavior to be controlled* (Skinner, 1953) (see Figure 26–1).

In the examples in the previous chapters, the behavior to be controlled was emitted by one person, and the controlling behaviors (providing prompts and applying consequences) were emitted by one or more other persons. In instances of self-control, however, the behavior to be controlled and the

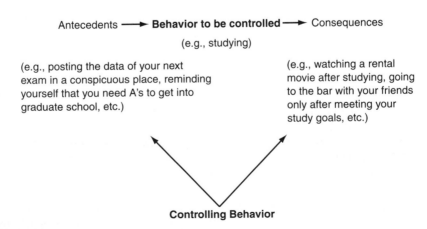

Figure 26–1   A model for self-control.

controlling behaviors are emitted by the same person. This raises the problem of *controlling the controlling behavior*. That is, because self-control implies that some behavior of a person controls other behavior of that person, the question arises as to what is to control the controlling behavior. We assume that the society in which we live teaches us various controlling behaviors (see Skinner, 1953, p. 240). You may have been taught, for example, to emit such controlling behaviors as setting goals for studying, giving yourself reminders for meeting those goals, and keeping track of your progress in doing so. If your efforts at emitting such behaviors are successful, and your behaviors to be controlled do in fact occur (e.g., your studying improves), then society provides maintaining contingencies for your efforts (e.g., successful studying leads to better grades, getting the kind of job that you want, being able to talk intelligently with other people, and so forth).

Let us now turn to self-control strategies that have been successful for many individuals.

STEPS IN A SELF-CONTROL PROGRAM

Let us assume that you have decided to use behavior modification to treat one of your self-control problems. We describe how to do so through the following steps: (a) specify the problem and set goals, (b) make a commitment to change, (c) take data and assess the causes of the problem, (d) design and implement a treatment plan, and (e) prevent relapse. In our discussion we are assuming that *you* are the client; the "you" below could be anyone who wants to change some aspect of his or her own behavior.

1. Specify the Problem and Set Goals

What is it that you would like to change? How will you know if you have succeeded? To answer these questions, you need to try to specify the problem and set some goals in quantitative terms. For Al (in the example beginning this chapter), this was relatively easy: His goal was to lose 30 pounds. Stated more precisely, he wanted to use about 1,000 calories more each day than he consumed to give a weight loss of about 2 pounds each week. Many problems of self-control can be easily specified in quantitative terms. It's relatively easy, for example, to set specific goals in the areas of weight control and exercise. In contrast, other self-improvement goals are more difficult to measure. These might include "having a more positive attitude toward school," "becoming less tense," or "improving a relationship." Mager (1972) refers to such vague abstractions as "fuzzies." A fuzzy is an acceptable starting point for identifying a self-control goal, however, you must then "unfuzzify" the abstraction by identifying the performance(s) that would cause you to agree that your goal has been achieved. Mager outlined a number of useful steps for this process.

   a. Write out the goal.
   b. Make a list of the things that you should say or do that clearly indicate that you've met the goal. That is, what would you take as evidence that your goal has been achieved?

   c. Given a number of people with the same goal, how would you decide who had met
      the goal and who had not?
   d. If your goal is an outcome (rather than something that you do) such as achieving a
      certain weight, accumulating a certain amount of money, or having a clean room,
      then make a list of specific behaviors that will help you to achieve that outcome.

2. Make a Commitment to Change

Note 1 Commitment to change refers to your statements or actions that indicate that it is
important to change your behavior, that you will work toward doing so, and that
you recognize the benefits of doing so. Perri and Richards (1977) demonstrated
that both a commitment to change and knowledge of change techniques were important for successful accomplishment of self-modification projects by undergraduate psychology students. In problem areas such as eating, smoking, studying, or
dating, successful self-managers had both a stronger commitment to change and
used more behavior change techniques than did unsuccessful self-managers (Perri
& Richards, 1977).

   A high probability of success in changing your behaviour requires actions to
keep your commitment strong. First, make a list of all of the benefits for changing
your behavior. Write them out and post them in a conspicuous place. Second,
make your commitment to change public (Hayes et al., 1985; Seigts et al., 1997).
Increasing the number of people who can remind you to stick to your program increases your chances of success (Passman, 1977). Third, rearrange your environment to provide frequent reminders of your commitment and your goal
(Graziano, 1975). You could write your goals on 3 × 5 cards and leave them in conspicuous places, such as taped to the door of your fridge or on the dashboard of
your car. Or you might creatively use photographs to remind you of your goal.
Also, make sure those reminders are associated with the positive benefits of reaching your goal. Fourth, invest considerable time and energy in planning your project initially (Watson & Tharp, 2003). Prepare a list of statements related to your
investment in your project so that you can use those statements to help strengthen
and maintain your commitment (e.g., "I've put so much into it, it would be a
shame to quit now"). Fifth, because you will undoubtedly encounter temptations
to quit your project, plan ahead for various ways to deal with any temptations
(Watson & Tharp, 2003).

3. Take Data and Analyze Causes

The next step is to take data on the occurrence of the problem behavior—when,
where, and how often it occurs. This is especially important when the goal is to
decrease excessive behaviors. As indicated in Chapter 20, there are a number of
reasons for keeping track of the problem behavior, not the least of which is to provide a reference point for evaluating progress. For many self-control projects, a
3 × 5 card and a pencil can be used to tally instances of the problem as they occur throughout the day. There are a number of techniques for increasing the

strength of record keeping. If the problem behavior is smoking, you should record each cigarette before it is smoked, so that the behavior will reinforce recording it. You might set up external reinforcers that are controlled by other people. You might give control of your spending money to someone who can monitor your behavior continuously for extended periods of time and who could return your money contingent upon consistent data taking. You might also get other people to reinforce your recording behavior by (a) telling friends about your self-modification project, (b) keeping your recording chart or graph in an obvious place to increase the likelihood of feedback from friends, and (c) keeping your friends informed on how the project and results are progressing. Contingencies mediated by other people are important sources of maintenance for your controlling behaviors.

In some cases (as pointed out in Chapter 20), recording and graphing the behavior may be all that's needed to bring about improvement. A convincing demonstration of this effect was made by Maletsky (1974). Three of the five cases that he studied were completed successfully, even though Maletsky was careful not to introduce any treatment other than the counting and graphing of unwanted behaviors. The first case concerned repetitive scratching that resulted in unsightly lesions on the arms and legs of a 52-year-old woman. The woman had been suffering with this problem for 30 years. The second case concerned a 9-year-old boy's repetitive hand raising in class. (Often he didn't know the answers to the teacher's questions.) The third case involved the out-of-seat behavior in school of a hyperactive 11-year-old girl. In all three cases, the behavior decreased over a six-week period as a result of daily counting and graphing. In some cases, it might even be possible to count each thought, desire, or urge to emit a behavior before the behavior occurs. McFall (1970) reported a study in which recording each urge to have a cigarette was sufficient to decrease not only the likelihood of subsequently taking a cigarette, but also the number of urges. Additional examples of beneficial effects of self-monitoring can be found in Cone (1999), Latner and Wilson (2002), and Wood, Murdock, and Cronin (2002).

When recording the frequency of the problem during these initial observations, you should take a close look at the antecedents that might be S^Ds or $S^\triangle$s for the problem behavior, and at the immediate consequences that might be maintaining the problem. From this exercise often comes suggestions for successful programming strategies.

Recall Al at the beginning of the chapter. When he began examining the circumstances in which he typically snacked, Al made a surprising finding. The great majority of instances of eating were followed immediately by some other reinforcing event.

A bite of a doughnut, then a sip of coffee;

Another potato chip while watching TV—his favorite basketball player just scores another basket;

Another candy to munch on while in his car—the stoplight turns green and Al drives away;

And so on.

Al ate while drinking coffee, while drinking beer, while talking to friends, while talking on the phone, while riding in a car . . . in other words, while coming into contact with a wide variety of reinforcing events in the natural environment. As we indicated in earlier chapters, the effects of reinforcers are automatic and do not depend on an individual's awareness. Moreover, aspects of the different settings became cues for Al's excessive eating. No wonder Al had trouble dieting.

Thus, during preliminary observations, it's important to analyze antecedents for the undesired behavior, immediate consequences that might maintain the undesired behavior to be eliminated, and the immediate consequences (or lack of them) of the behavior that you wish to develop. This information can be very useful in the next step of your program.

4. Design and Implement a Program

Throughout your life, in the presence of certain *antecedents* certain *behaviors* have had certain *consequences*. Each of these three variables provides a fertile area for selecting self-control techniques.

Manage the Antecedents   As indicated in Chapters 17, 18, and 19, it is helpful to think of major classes of antecedents that control our behavior, such as instructions, modeling, guidance, our immediate surroundings, other people, the time of day, and motivating operations.

Instructions.   Meichenbaum (1977) suggested that almost every self-modification program should include some self-instructions. Self-instructions have been used in formal self-management projects to increase exercise and study behavior (Cohen, DeJames, Nocera, & Ramberger, 1980), reduce fears (Arrick, Voss, & Rimm, 1981), reduce nail biting (Harris & McReynolds, 1977), and improve a variety of other behaviors (Watson & Tharp, 2003). Before planning instructions for your self-control program, we encourage you to review the guidelines for using rules and goals in Chapter 17. Also, self-instructional strategies are discussed further in Chapter 27.

Modeling.   Modeled behavior is another class of stimulus events that is useful in self-control programs. For example, do you want to improve your skills at introducing yourself to another person at social gatherings? Find someone who's good at it, observe that person's behavior, and try to imitate it. A procedure called *participant modeling* (described more fully in chapter 28) is an especially effective method for reducing fears. With this procedure, the fearful person observes a model interacting with the fear-inducing stimulus and then imitates the model.

Physical guidance.   In Chapter 18 we described how behavior modifiers use physical contact to induce an individual to go through the motions of the desired behavior. In his classic analysis of self-control, Skinner (1953) described how individuals also use physical restraint to control their own behavior. You might, for example, keep your hands in your pockets to avoid nail biting, cover your eyes to avoid looking at someone during an embarrassing moment, press your finger under your nose to suppress a sneeze, put your hand over your mouth to suppress a laugh on a solemn occasion, bite your tongue to avoid making a rude comment, or clasp your hands to avoid striking someone in a moment of anger.

The immediate surroundings.   Do you have trouble studying at home? Try going to the library, where studying is a high-probability behavior (Brigham, 1982). Many people have a particular behavior they would like to decrease. That behavior occurs in particular situations. An alternative desirable behavior occurs in other situations. A useful strategy is to rearrange the environment to present cues for the desirable alternative behaviors (see Chapter 18).

Other people.   As we said above, modeling is one way of providing strong prompts for you to engage in some behavior. Another strategy is simply to change the people around you. You've learned to behave in one way with some people and in another way with others. For example, you're likely to talk without swearing when in conversation with Grandma and Grandpa, but are more likely to swear when shooting the breeze with the gang. In some cases, your self-adjustment program will consist of minimizing contact with certain people. Marlatt and Parks (1982) have indicated that people with addictive behaviors are more likely to relapse if they hang out with others engaging in those behaviors.

The time of day.   We've all learned to do certain things at certain times. Sometimes our problems are related to that fact. Sometimes it's possible to achieve successful self-control by changing the time of the activity. For example, many students are most alert in the morning. Yet they spend their free time during the mornings having coffee with friends and socializing, and leave their studying to the evening when they are less alert. Successful self-control of studying for such students might be accomplished by moving studying to mornings and socializing to evenings.

Motivating operations.   You will recall from Chapter 19 that motivating operations are events that affect the strength of consequences as reinforcers or punishers, and that influence behaviors affected by those consequences. In self-control programs, a strategy for increasing desirable behavior is to introduce an MEO for reinforcers that influence that behavior. For example, when one of the authors and his wife were visiting Brazil in the early years of their marriage, he took a picture of his wife jogging on the beach in Rio de Janeiro. In later years, when his wife looked at an enlargement of the photo posted on the closet door in their bedroom, it motivated her to continue her jogging program in order to maintain her slim figure. Also, in self-control programs, MAOs can be used to decrease the likelihood of undesirable behavior. A strategy used by Al, in the example beginning this chapter, to decrease his doughnut consumption when having coffee with Mary in the campus cafeteria was to eat a couple of carrots before going to the cafeteria. This functioned as an MAO for food, and decreased the likelihood of his purchasing doughnuts with his coffee.

Manage the Behavior   If the behavior of concern is relatively simple, such as swearing, you're likely to focus more on antecedents and consequences. If the behavior is complex, you need to spend some time focusing on the behavior itself. If your goal is to acquire some complex skills, it's helpful to consider task analysis and mastery criteria. *Mastery criteria* are performance requirements for practicing a skill such that if the criteria are met, the behavior has been learned. Consider, for example, learning to play golf. Simek and O'Brien (1981) task-analyzed a golf game into 22 components. They arranged these in a behavioral progression for instructional purposes and identified mastery criteria for each component (see Table 26–1). Then they taught a group of novices by starting with 10-inch putts

TABLE 26–1   A BEHAVIORAL PROGRESSION AND MASTERY CRITERIA
FOR LEARNING GOLF

	Complete Golf Chain and Mastery Criterion	
Step	Shot	Mastery Criterion
1.	10-inch putt	4 putts consecutively holed
2.	16-inch putt	4 putts consecutively holed
3.	2-foot putt	4 putts consecutively holed
4.	3-foot putt	4 putts consecutively holed
5.	4-foot putt some break	2 holed, 2 out of 4 within 6 inches
6.	6-foot putt	4 consecutively within 6 inches
7.	10-foot putt	4 consecutively within 12 inches
8.	15-foot putt	4 consecutively within 15 inches
9.	20-foot putt	4 consecutively within 18 inches
10.	30-foot putt	4 consecutively within 24 inches
11.	35-foot chip, 5 feet off green, 7-iron	4 out of 6 within 6 feet
12.	35-foot chip, 15 feet off green, wedge	4 out of 6 within 6 feet
13.	65-foot chip	4 out of 6 within 6 feet
14.	25-yard pitch	4 out of 6 within 10 feet
15.	35-yard pitch	4 out of 6 within 15 feet
16.	50-yard pitch	4 out of 6 within 15 feet
17.	75-yard shot	4 out of 6 within 30 feet
18.	100-yard shot	4 out of 6 within 40 feet
19.	125-yard shot	4 out of 6 within 45 feet
20.	150-yard shot	4 out of 6 within 54 feet
21.	175-yard shot	4 out of 6 within 66 feet
22.	200-yard shot (if within your range)	4 out of 5 within 90 feet

Source: From Total Golf: A Behavioral Approach to Lowering Your Score and Getting More Out of Your Game (p. 2),
by T. C. Simek and R. M. O'Brien, 1981. Huntington, NY: B-Mod Associates. Copyright 1981 by T. C. Simek and
R. M. O'Brien. Reprinted with permission.

rather than by first teaching them to swing a club, as is often done by golf pros.
Why? For two reasons. First, it seemed like the simplest response—and the general
rule is to start with the simple and proceed to the complex. Second, it incorporated
a powerful natural reinforcer for performing the response correctly—namely, hitting the ball into the hole (note that this is similar to the argument for using backward chaining; see Chapter 11). Gradually, as mastery criteria for simple responses
were met, the length of the shot was increased to longer putts, then to short chip
shots, to longer chip shots, to short pitch shots, to longer pitch shots, to middle
iron shots, eventually to hitting fairway woods, and finally a driver. "But how well
did they score when put on a golf course?" one might ask. In a study with 12
novice golfers, six of the golfers completed the behavioral progression and mastery criteria in eight lessons. The other six golfers received eight lessons of traditional instruction from a golfer who had taught golf for several years. All 12 then
played a complete, 18-hole round of golf. The behavioral progression group
"whipped" the traditional group handily, beating them by an average of 17
strokes.

  Shaping is another procedure for focusing on the behavior, and it is useful for
self-improvement projects in which your ultimate goal involves a large behavioral
change from your starting point. Important rules of thumb to keep in mind include

starting small, meeting mastery criteria before moving up a step, and keeping progressive steps small. Studies of dieters, for example, have reported that those who set small, gradual shaping steps for reducing calories were more likely to develop self-control of binge eating (Gormally, Black, Daston, & Rardin, 1982; Hawkins & Clement, 1980).

Another manipulation that requires you to focus on the behavior is consideration of the energy expenditure needed to perform the behavior, generally referred to as *effort*. One strategy for decreasing a problem behavior is to arrange conditions so that it requires more effort to perform the behavior. Susan, for example, typically studies in a carrel in the library. Frequently, she interrupts her studying to call her friends using her cell phone. With her cell phone clearly visible in the study carrel, there is very little effort involved in picking it up and dialing. Leaving her cell phone in a locker at the entrance to the library, however, would greatly increase the effort involved in making a call, and would likely decrease the instances of doing so. Altering response requirements to decrease the effort needed to emit a behavior can be used to increase desirable behavior. David, for example, decided that his daily water consumption was too low, and he set a goal of going to a water fountain at least four times a day at the university where he was a student. However, doing so required considerable effort, and he rarely met his goal. He therefore decided to purchase a bottle of water and keep it with him throughout the day, which required much less effort. His water consumption increased considerably. Although these examples involve manipulating response effort, note that they might also be described as managing antecedents by manipulating the immediate surroundings.

Manage the Consequences   One strategy for manipulating consequent events is to eliminate certain reinforcers that may inadvertently strengthen a particularly undesirable behavior in a particular situation. When Al analyzed his eating problem, he noticed that, in addition to the taste of food itself, other reinforcers (TV, pleasant conversation, etc.) were usually associated with eating. A major feature of Al's dieting control program, therefore, should be to disassociate eating from these other activities. Recommendations by LeBow (1981) to accomplish this include: (a) develop an eating place in the home that is to be used only for that purpose, and eating only there when at home; (b) using the same eating utensils and placemats at each meal; (c) eating only at designated times; and (d) keeping food out of every room but the kitchen.

A second way of manipulating consequences is by self-recording and self-graphing the target behavior (see, e.g., Watson & Tharp, 2003). Seeing a line that shows gradual improvement can serve as a prompt to think a variety of positive thoughts about your progress. It can also serve as a prompt for extra social attention from others for sticking to a self-control program.

A third way of manipulating consequences involves arranging for specific reinforcers to be earned by you for showing improvement or even for just sticking to the program (see Watson & Tharp, 2003). This is especially important if your desired behavior will lead to small but cumulatively significant or highly improbable reinforcers, or if failure to perform your desired behavior will lead to small but cumulatively significant or highly improbable punishers. Three ways of arranging for reinforcers to be earned in a self-control program include: asking others to manage them for you, reminding yourself of delayed natural reinforcers, and managing reinforcers yourself. (This last way may seem the most obvious, given that we are talking about *self*-control; however, there is a problem with it, as we shall see.)

Asking others to manage reinforcers for you is an effective reinforcement strategy in self-control programs (Watson & Tharp, 2003). For example, Mary decided to initiate a jogging program. She also decided that she would receive money immediately after jogging. Also, if she jogged every day, she could select and engage in one of several possible social activities with her husband. If she met her goals, Mary's husband dispensed the reinforcers. The program was quite successful (Kau & Fischer, 1974).

The second reinforcement strategy—reminding yourself of delayed natural consequences for a behavior immediately after it occurs—may be illustrated by the problem of shopping for Christmas presents. Suppose that an individual sets a goal for her or himself of buying Christmas presents early during the year, rather than waiting until the last minute. There are sizable natural consequences for doing so. Presents can be bought on sale, saving a significant amount of money. The Christmas rush can be avoided, minimizing the stress and hassles that typically accompany Christmas shopping. And there is also the expressions of joy that the presents will bring. However, all of these consequences are long delayed after the behavior of shopping early. A solution, therefore, is to increase their saliency right after the behavior to be controlled. Immediately after a gift is purchased during a fall sale, for example, our shopper might write on a 3×5 card the amount saved, and post it in a conspicuous place. He or she might look at a photograph of the person for whom he bought the present, and imagine how happy that person will feel when the present is opened on Christmas morning. The shopper might also make a list of fun activities he or she will enjoy doing during the Christmas rush.

The third reinforcement strategy recommended for self-control programs is for individuals to manage consequences for their own behavior (Watson & Tharp, 2003). Suppose, for example, that you decide to allow yourself to surf the Internet only after studying for an exam. This seems like an example of self-reinforcement. However, in such circumstances, you can always access the reinforcer without emitting the desired behavior, as illustrated in Figure 26–2. What would prevent you from doing so? We suspect that in this and other such examples of self-reinforcement, there are other contingencies operating. Perhaps, just before studying, you worried about the likelihood of failing the exam, and studying enabled you to escape from such worrying. Perhaps, immediately after studying, you thought about the likelihood of getting an "A." Or perhaps there were other factors influencing your studying. Thus, while it is certainly possible for an individual to give themselves a reinforcer only after emitting some behavior, it is not clear that that contingency alone is responsible for the improved behavior.

Some guidelines for incorporating reinforcers into your program include: (a) make it possible for you to earn specific reinforcers on a daily basis; (b) set up bonuses that can be earned for progress on a weekly basis; (c) vary the reinforcers from one day to the next and one week to the next so as to prevent boredom with

Figure 26–2   Does self-reinforcement work?

the entire system; (d) if possible and desirable, have other individuals dispense the reinforcers to you for meeting your goals; and (e) tell others about your progress.

Recall the Premack principle from Chapter 3. The Premack principle states that any activity that you are more likely to perform can be used to reinforce a behavior that you are less likely to perform. This strategy can also be used in self-control programs. High-frequency behaviors used in documented cases of self-improvement have involved making telephone calls (Todd, 1972), urinating (Johnson, 1971), opening daily mail at the office (Spinelli & Packard, 1975), and sitting on a particular chair (Horan & Johnson, 1971).

5. Prevent Relapse and Make Your Gains Last

Let's suppose you've made good progress on your self-control program: You've lost those 20 pounds, or you haven't had a cigarette in three months, or your studying has paid off and you got an "A" on your last two exams. Now the question is: Will it last? Will you be able to maintain your gains over the long run? Unfortunately, relapses are common in self-control programs (Marlatt & Parks, 1982). By **relapse,** we mean going back to the unwanted behavior at approximately the same rate that you were at before you started your program. Just as the three variables of *situations, behaviors,* and *consequences* were valuable areas to consider when designing your program, they also provide a useful framework for analyzing causes of relapses and how to prevent them.

Causes of Relapse in Situations   A strategy in preventing relapses is to recognize their possible causes and to take steps to minimize them. Let's look at some examples involving situations.

Avoidable setback situations.   A common cause of relapses in self-control programs is a failure to anticipate setback situations—when one is at risk for returning to earlier unwanted behavior patterns. Some setback situations can simply be avoided until you are better able to cope with them. For example, Carla decided to quit smoking. Initially she believed that she couldn't resist the temptation to smoke while playing poker with her friends on Friday nights. Her strategy was simply not to play poker for the first month of the program. Fred decided to go on a diet, to eat more healthfully, and to consume fewer calories. But he knew that he couldn't resist the banana splits at the ice cream store beside the supermarket where he usually bought groceries. His solution: He changed the place where he shopped so that he didn't have to walk by the ice cream store and resist his favorite dessert. If you can successfully avoid setback situations until after you have achieved some success with your self-control program, you may then be better able to cope with situations that provide strong cues for the problem behavior.

Unavoidable setback situations.   Some setback situations simply can't be avoided. A strategy to prevent relapse is to anticipate unavoidable setback situations and to take steps to cope with them. Consider John's case. John had faithfully followed his exercise program for a month and a half, but he was about to embark on a motorhome trip. He knew that the complete change in routine and the duties each night around the campground were not conducive to exercising. His solution was to obtain his traveling companions' approval to stop traveling each night half an hour early. While the others relaxed in the motorhome, John exercised. They then all shared in the campground duties. The more that you can recognize unavoidable setback situations before they are encountered, the better are your chances for planning coping strategies.

Overreaction to occasional setbacks.   Janice, after two weeks of sticking faithfully to her schedule for studying, rented five movies and watched them for 10 hours straight. Fred, following a month of successful dieting, had a triple-topping sundae at the ice cream parlor three days in a row. Very few people achieve successful self-control without experiencing an occasional setback. However, temporary setbacks are not a problem provided that you get right back into your program. If you suffer a setback, don't dwell on it. Instead, use a review of the many occasions when you have stuck to your program as a prompt to set new goals and to make a renewed commitment to stick with it.

Counterproductive self-talk.   When people attempt to change, they are bound to encounter stumbling blocks. In such situations, counterproductive self-talk can exacerbate the problem and may lead to a relapse. People who have difficulty dieting may say things to themselves like, "I'm too hungry to wait until dinner. I'll have a snack to tide myself over." That type of self-talk is a cue to eat.

What kinds of self-talk in your self-control program might lead to a relapse? For each example that you can think of, identify desirable alternative self-talk that might have the opposite effect. Dieters, for example, might tell themselves things like, "I feel hungry, but I'm not starving. I'll just focus on something to take my mind off food."

Causes of Relapse in the Specification of the Response   Sometimes relapses occur because individuals do not pay sufficient attention to the response component of their self-control program. Let's look at some examples.

A *fuzzy target behavior*.   Tracy wanted to improve her golf skills. After a month of regular practice at the driving range, however, she wasn't sure if she was improving. The problem was that "wanting to improve" was too vague. She had not specified her target behavior precisely enough. If Tracy's goal had been to hit five drives in a row over 175 yards, or to hit three 7-irons in a row within 30 feet of the 100-yard marker, or to make four 3-foot putts in a row, then she would have been able to evaluate her progress more easily (Martin & Ingram, 2001). As we described earlier, a fuzzy goal is an acceptable starting point, but you must then "unfuzzify" your target behavior by phrasing it in a way such that you and others can easily recognize it when it occurs.

A *long-term target behavior*.   Suppose that you set a long-term goal for yourself of obtaining an "A" in a particular course. Your goal is clear, but it's a long way away. For such projects, you should set short-term goals that provide specific progress checks along the way. With respect to your goal of obtaining an "A," you might set a short-term goal of studying the material for that course for a minimum of one hour every day. Another short-term goal might be to complete a certain number of study questions each day. Daily short-term goals should be precisely stated and realistic and should move you in the direction of your long-term goal.

Trying too much too soon.   Some self-control projects never get off the ground because they are too ambitious. Wanting to eat more healthfully, exercise more, floss your teeth regularly, manage your money more wisely, and get better grades are admirable goals, but trying to improve in all areas at once is a formula for failure. If you've identified several areas to improve, prioritize them in order of their personal value to you. From the top two or three priority areas, select one to work on. Starting small increases your likelihood of success.

Causes of Relapse in Consequences   Recall our model of self-control. It involves emitting a *controlling behavior* to manage a *behavior to be controlled*. Inadequate or poorly scheduled consequences for either of these behaviors can lead to a relapse. Let's look at some examples.

Failure to incorporate everyday rewards into your program.   Many people begin self-control programs with a great deal of enthusiasm. After a while, however, the extra work from recording, graphing, rearranging the environment, and so forth, can become quite burdensome. One way to prevent relapse is to link your self-control program to everyday rewarding activities. One person we know linked his exercise program to his penchant for watching movies on his VCR. His goal was to exercise a minimum of four times a week. On average, he also rented movies about four nights a week. He therefore signed a contract with his wife that he would watch a movie only if he first walked to the rental store to pick up the movie—a distance of approximately 1½ miles. Examine ways that you can incorporate daily rewarding activities into the support of your self-control program.

Consequences that are only cumulatively significant.   Suppose that your dieting program has been successful. You decide that your new slim body can easily handle an extra dessert. And of course, one dessert is not a problem. Rather, it is the accumulation of extra desserts on many occasions that will put the pounds back on. As we described earlier, for many self-control problems, the immediate reinforcement for consumption of harmful substances (such as the extra dessert) is likely to win out over the negative consequences from those substances because the negative effects are noticeable only after they have accumulated over many trials. Individuals with these types of self-control problems are very likely to experience a relapse. One strategy to prevent relapse in such situations is to set specific dates for postchecks and to list specific strategies to follow if the postchecks are unfavorable. For example, if your self-control program was one of weight reduction, you might agree with a friend that you will weigh yourself in your friend's presence once a week. If your weight increases to a specified level, then (with encouragement from your friend) you will immediately return to your program.

Additional Strategies to Make It Last   Additional strategies to prevent relapse and to maintain your gains over the long term involve all three factors of situations, responses, and consequences. One strategy is to practice the self-control steps outlined in this chapter to improve additional behaviors. You are more likely to continue using self-control techniques if you practice them on more than one self-control project (Barone, 1982). Moreover, you are more likely to be able to deal with a relapse if you are skillful in the self-control techniques that brought about the improvement in the first place.

Perhaps the most effective way to make it last is to involve supportive others in your program, both in the short term and in the long term. One strategy is to set up a buddy system. When you start your project, you might find a friend or relative with a similar problem and set mutual maintenance goals. Once a month, you could get together and check each other's progress. If your progress has been maintained, you could celebrate in a previously agreed-upon way. In a study of smokers, for example, Karol and Richards (1978) found that smokers who quit with a buddy and who telephoned encouragement to each other showed greater reduction of smoking in an eight-month follow-up than did smokers who tried to quit on their own.

A particularly effective strategy is to sign a behavioral contract with supportive others. A behavioral contract is a clear, written statement of what behaviors of what individuals will produce what rewards, and who will deliver those rewards. Behavioral contracts were discussed in Chapter 24, and have been used to strengthen desirable target behaviors with children (e.g., Miller & Kelly, 1994) and adults (e.g., Leal & Galanter, 1995). A contract usually involves two or more people, although "self-contracts" have also been used. A form that you might use for your contract is presented in Table 26–2.

A contract serves at least four important stimulus control functions:

1. It ensures that all parties involved agree to the goals and procedures and that they do not lose sight of them during the course of the treatment.
2. Because the goals are specified behaviorally, the contract also ensures that throughout the program all parties will agree on how close they are to reaching the goals.

TABLE 26–2   A FORM FOR A BEHAVIORAL CONTRACT

My specific goals for my self-control program are:
_____
_____
_____
_____

Short-term goals for my self-control program include:
_____
_____
_____
_____

To observe, record, and graph my behavior, I will:
_____
_____

To minimize the causes of the problem, I will:
_____
_____
_____
_____

The details of my treatment plan include:
1. Steps to manage the situation
_____
_____
_____

2. Steps to manage consequences
_____
_____
_____
_____

3. Steps to deal with or change complex behavior
_____
_____
_____
_____

4. Rewards that I can earn for sticking to and/or completing my project include:
_____
_____

Additional steps that I will take to increase and maintain my commitment to the project and to prevent relapse include:
_____
_____

Schedule for review of progress:
_____

Signatures of all involved and the date of the agreement:
_____   _____   _____
(Date)   (Your signature)   (Supporter's signature)

3. The contract provides the client with a realistic estimate of the cost of the program to him or her in time, effort, and money.
4. The signatures on the contract help to ensure that all parties will faithfully follow the specified procedures, because in our society signing a document indicates a commitment.

As we have stressed in previous chapters, behavior modification procedures should be revised in appropriate ways when the data indicate that they are not producing satisfactory results. Thus, your contract should be open to renegotiation at any time. If you find that you simply cannot meet some commitment specified in your contract, you should so inform the other signatories at your next meeting with them. The difficulty can then be discussed, and if it seems desirable, a new contract replacing the previous one can be drafted and signed. Before doing so, however, you might examine the following troubleshooting guide for behavior contracts.

Troubleshooting Guide[2]

The following questions may help you to spot the problems in your contracting system.

The Contract

1. Was the target behavior specified clearly?
2. If the target behavior was complex, did the contract ask for small approximations to the desired behavior?
3. Were specific deadlines identified for the target behavior?
4. Did the contract clearly identify situations where the target behavior should occur?
5. Did the contract provide for immediate reinforcement? Are the reinforcers still important and valuable to you?
6. Could reinforcers be earned often (daily? weekly?)?
7. Did the contract call for and reward accomplishment rather than obedience?
8. Was the contract phrased in a positive way?
9. Do you consider the contract to be fair and in your best interests?

The Mediator (your cosigner)

1. Did the mediator understand the contract?
2. Did the mediator dispense the kind and amount of reinforcement specified in the contract?
3. Did the mediator meet with you on the dates specified in the contract?
4. Is a new mediator required?

Measurement

1. Are the data accurate?
2. Is your data collection system too complex or too difficult?
3. Does your data collection system clearly reflect your progress in achieving the target behavior?
4. Do you need to improve your data collection system?

---

[2]Adapted from DeRisi and Butz, *Writing Behavioral Contracts: A Case Simulation Practice Manual* (Champaign, IL: Research Press, 1975), pp. 58–60.

CIRCUMVENTING THE THERAPIST

Obviously, some personal problems require help from a therapist (as discussed further in Chapters 27 and 28). It should be clear from the preceding sections in this chapter, however, that many people who have mastered some behavior modification principles can use them to control their own behavior. A student who has mastered this and previous chapters should have little difficulty in handling a simple behavior problem that has been bothering him or her (although we recommend seeing a therapist about serious problems). Perhaps the student would like to decrease smoking, nail biting, swearing, or making abusive remarks to others. Or perhaps he or she would like to enhance studying, exercising, eating healthy foods, getting enough rest, personal tidiness, consideration of others, or public speaking. The student probably does not need a therapist to help accomplish these

Note 2 goals. A person who has mastered this book already knows how to take data; a therapist is not needed to help do that. That person knows also how to plan a program and evaluate its effectiveness, how to apply a large number of behavior modification principles and techniques, and how to use a behavioral contract to maintain the controlling behavior. In short, many people can be their own behavior modifiers.

STUDY QUESTIONS

1. What do people seem to mean when they talk about willpower? Is willpower a useful concept? Why or why not?
2. Briefly describe three causes of self-control problems of behavioral excesses, and illustrate each with reference to an example.
3. Briefly describe three causes of self-control problems of behavioral deficiencies, and illustrate each with reference to an example.
4. In two or three sentences, describe the model of self-management presented in this chapter.
5. Consider the model of self-control illustrated in Figure 26–1. In that model, what controls the controlling behavior? Discuss.
6. List five steps that characterize many programs in self-adjustment.
7. List the steps that Mager recommends to "unfuzzify" a vaguely stated problem or self-control goal.
8. How does this book define *commitment*?
9. Describe four steps that you could take to strengthen and maintain your commitment to a program of self-control.
10. Illustrate how Al was inadvertently reinforced for eating numerous times throughout the day.
11. List seven major classes of antecedents that you might consider when planning how to manage the situation in a self-control program.
12. Define and give an example of mastery criterion.
13. In a sentence or two each, describe three different ways of manipulating consequences in self-control programs.
14. In a sentence or two each, describe three different ways of arranging for reinforcers to be earned in a self-control program.
15. Is self-reinforcement an effective self-control strategy? Discuss.

16. Briefly describe four possible causes of relapse in situations, and indicate how each might be handled.
17. Briefly describe three possible causes of relapse in the specification of the response, and indicate how each might be handled.
18. Briefly describe two possible causes of relapse in consequences, and indicate how each might be handled.
19. What is a behavioral contract? Describe its essential features.
20. What important stimulus-control functions does a behavioral contract serve?
21. Is it plausible to suggest that many individuals can become their own behavior therapists? Justify your answer.

APPLICATION EXERCISES

A. Exercise Involving Others

Describe a self-control problem experienced by someone that you know. Is the problem best characterized as a behavioral deficiency or a behavioral excess? What seems to be the cause of the problem?

B. Self-Modification Exercises

1. Using the information in this and the preceding chapters, describe how you might go about following all five steps of a self-control program for bringing about successful self-adjustment for a behavior of yours that you would like to change.
2. Implement your program and take data for a minimum of three weeks. Then write a summary report of the results (approximately 5 to 10 pages, plus graphs).

NOTES AND EXTENDED DISCUSSION

1. A verbal commitment to do something is verbal behavior that corresponds to other behavior that one later engages in if the commitment is kept. A number of studies have been conducted on training a correspondence between stated intentions (commitments) and later behavior (Lloyd, 2002). For example, Ward and Stare (1990) prompted a group of kindergarten children to state that they were going to play in a certain designated area prior to playing there (correspondence training). Specifically, the children were prompted to say, "I'm going to play at the workbench today." The children received a token if they made this statement. After four minutes of play, children who played at the workbench received another token for playing at the workbench after saying that this is what they would do. Compared to a group of children who simply received tokens for playing in the designated area, the group that received correspondence training showed more instances of following through on stated intentions to engage in another activity (playing with toys), even though they received no tokens for following through on this commitment. The results thus

showed that correspondence training on one response can generalize to a new response. This tendency to generalize correspondence training may be what makes it possible for us to keep commitments for behavior change that we have made to ourselves. Correspondence training is also one way that humans learn self-awareness or self-knowledge (Dymond & Barnes, 1997).

2. How effective are self-help manuals? Although a review by Rosen (1987) found major limitations to their usefulness, meta-analysis—a statistical procedure for combining the data analysis of many studies—suggests that somewhat more positive conclusions are in order (Gould & Clum, 1993; Scogin, Bynum, Stephens, & Calhoon, 1990). That does not mean that all self-help books in book stores have been evaluated. However, experiments that examined sophisticated, complex, self-help manuals based on behavioral principles indicated that self-administered treatments stand a good chance of success. The most successful targets for improvement involved study habits, depression, parenting skills, social skills, and overcoming anxiety and fears. Less successful self-treatment programs occurred with the control of alcohol drinking, smoking, and overeating (Gould & Clum, 1993; Seligman, 1994). Also, a number of studies have demonstrated that university students who have read various editions of the self-modification book by David Watson and Ronald Tharp were more successful at completing self-improvement projects than students who did not read the book (Watson & Tharp, 2003).

Study Questions on Notes

1. What is correspondence training? Briefly describe how generalized correspondence was demonstrated in kindergarten children.
2. With which behavior problems are self-help manuals most effective and least effective?

27

Cognitive Behavior Modification

Behavior modification, as described in the preceding chapters, began to emerge in the 1950s and 1960s (this early history is discussed further in Chapter 29). Publications that described an alternative approach to therapy, called *cognitive therapy*, appeared in the 1970s (Beck, 1976; Mahoney, 1974; Meichenbaum, 1977). The word **cognition** means belief, thought, expectancy, attitude, or perception. Accordingly, cognitive therapists regard their approach to be primarily that of helping a client overcome his or her difficulties by getting rid of unproductive, debilitating thoughts or beliefs and adopting more constructive ones. Many behavior modifiers have noted certain similarities between the goals and procedures of cognitive therapists and their own. Cognitive therapists, in turn, have adopted some behavior modification methods. Out of this mutual appreciation has grown an area that has come to be known as **cognitive behavior modification** (Meichenbaum, 1986) or *cognitive behavior therapy* (Ingram & Scott, 1990). Although cognitively oriented and behaviorally oriented therapists disagree on some issues, they have learned from each other (see, e.g., Dougher, 1997; Hawkins & Forsyth, 1997; Wilson, Hayes, & Gifford, 1997). In addition, both approaches are firmly committed to the view that the criterion for judging the effectiveness of any treatment is the amount of measurable improvement that occurs in the client's behavior. Stephen Hayes (2004b) referred to early behavior modification as the first wave of behavior therapy, and to cognitive behavior modification as the second wave. Hayes also described what he referred to as the third wave of behavior therapy—therapeutic approaches that incorporate concepts of "mindfulness," "acceptance," and "values" into the cognitive behavioral tradition. The purpose of this chapter is to describe briefly some of the procedures referred to as cognitive behavior modification, including procedures from the "third wave."

We have organized the different procedures referred to as cognitive therapy or cognitive behavior modification into three categories: (1) treatments that emphasize cognitive restructuring to decrease maladaptive thoughts that are assumed to cause troublesome emotions; (2) self-directed strategies to enhance overt coping skills; and (3) treatments that include "mindfulness," "acceptance," and "values" as important components of therapy.

COGNITIVE RESTRUCTURING METHODS

A major theoretical assumption of some approaches to cognitive therapy is that individuals interpret and react to events in terms of their perceived significance; that is, our beliefs, expectations, and attitudes affect our behavior. The second theoretical assumption of these approaches is that cognitive deficiencies can cause emotional disorders. It follows from these assumptions that the primary focus of therapy is to fundamentally change a client's cognitions. Stated simply, some cognitive therapists believe that faulty thinking is the cause of emotional and behavioral problems, and the primary focus of their approach to therapy is to change faulty thinking. Strategies for doing so are often referred to as **cognitive restructuring.** We emphasize that, from our point of view, these approaches deal mainly with the client's private verbal behavior and imagery relating himself or herself and the surrounding world (see Chapter 15). Moreover, therapists who use these techniques generally also include behavior modification components in their treatments.

Rational-Emotive Behavior Therapy

Do you ever find yourself saying, "I always screw things up," "I'm such a klutz," or "I never do things right"? Some cognitive psychologists consider such self-statements to be irrational (after all, you don't always screw up, you're not always clumsy, and you do some things right). They believe that such irrational thoughts can cause anxiety, sadness, anger, or other troublesome emotions. Their approach to therapy is to help people identify such irrational thoughts or beliefs, and to replace them with more rational self-statements.

Since the 1960s, cognitive behavior modification has received strong impetus from the well-known cognitive therapist Albert Ellis (e.g., Ellis, 1962; Ellis & Bernard, 1985; Ellis & Dryden, 1997). The original name for his approach, *rational-emotive therapy (RET),* was based on the premise that most everyday emotional problems (and related behaviors) stem from irrational interpretations that people make of events in their lives. People tend to think in *absolute terms,* such as a student thinking, "I *must* do well in *all* of my courses." They tend to *overgeneralize,* such as a student thinking, after getting a poor mark on one exam, "I'll *never* be a good student." People also tend to "*catastrophize*": They tell themselves that things are so horrible they can't possibly "stand it." Jim, for example, had slept through his alarm and was going to be late for class. Rushing to get ready, he cut himself while shaving and thought, "I'm a walking disaster! I always screw things up." Later, he got caught in a traffic jam. Thinking, "Why does the worst always happen to me?," he felt angry and frustrated. Ellis considers such self-statements ("I'm a walking disaster," "The worst always happens to me") to be at the root of emotional problems (e.g., Jim's extreme anger and frustration).

Basically, Ellis's approach is to teach his clients to counteract such "irrational" self-statements with more positive and realistic statements. This is accomplished through three main phases. First, Ellis helps the client to identify troublesome thoughts that are based on irrational beliefs, such as Jim's thoughts that he is a walking disaster and that he always screws things up. Second, in a very confrontational, argumentative way, Ellis vigorously challenges the client's irrational beliefs that are thought to be the basis for the problematic self-talk. Jim, for example, might be harboring the irrational belief that he *must* always awake to his alarm, that he *must* never be late for class, and that he *must* never get caught in a traffic jam, a type of irrational thinking that Ellis refers to as "musterbation." To Jim, Ellis might say, "Sooner or later everyone living in a city will get caught in a traffic jam. What makes you so special?," or "What do you mean you always screw things up, you told me that you got an 'A' on your last computer assignment?" Third, the client is taught (through modeling and homework assignments) to replace the "irrational" self-statements with statements based on "rational" beliefs. For example, Jim might be taught to tell himself that there are far worse things than being caught in a traffic jam, and that even though things could be better, they could certainly be a lot worse. His situation may be annoying or inconvenient, but it is not catastrophic, and, moreover, there are usually things that he can do to improve it.

Ellis (1993) later added the word *behavior* to the name of his therapy, now calling it **rational-emotive behavior therapy (REBT).** He did so because, despite being a cognitive therapist, he frequently uses *in vivo* behavioral "homework" assignments. Jim, for example, might be told to write down each time he performs a complex action, such as working at his computer or changing the oil in his car, to prove to himself that he is not a walking disaster. The homework assignments are usually designed to help the client to challenge irrational beliefs and to confront troublesome emotions head on. (For a practical guide to REBT, see Dryden, 1999.)

Evaluation of REBT   To the extent that Ellis's approach is successful, is it because the therapist vigorously disputes the client's irrational beliefs (a "cognitive" component)? Or is it because of the homework assignments (behavioral components)? After all, the homework assignments are likely to influence the client to confront anxiety-evoking situations in real life, which may lead to extinction of the anxiety (see Chapter 28). Or is the improvement the result of a combination of both the correction of faulty thinking and the homework assignments?

Gossette and O'Brien (1989, 1992) examined 107 studies of REBT that (1) focused on therapists' attempts to change clients' irrational beliefs and (2) were not accompanied by other behavioral strategies (such as behavioral rehearsal, reinforced practice). They surveyed all known reports (both published studies and unpublished dissertations) in which REBT was compared with other types of therapy or no treatment at all. Ellis's approach was more effective than the various other comparison conditions in decreasing client's irrational self-talk in only 46% of the cases, and was more effective than the comparison conditions in reducing emotional distress in only 27% of the cases. Finally, REBT had virtually no effect on other behavioral measures (such as the extent to which clients actually approached feared objects). The results of Gossette and O'Brien's review suggest that a big part of the success of REBT may be due to the various homework assignments rather than to the disputation of irrational beliefs.

Beck's Cognitive Therapy

Aaron T. Beck (1976), independently of Ellis, developed a cognitive therapy procedure that is similar to REBT. His cognitive therapy was originally developed for the treatment of depression. However, he subsequently applied it to a wide variety of other problems, including manic states, anxiety disorders, hysteria, obsessional disorders, psychosomatic disorders, and phobias (see Beck, Emery, & Greenberg, 1985). In addition, Beck has written a self-help book for couples that shows how they can use cognitive therapy to improve their relationships (Beck, 1988). Kingdon and Turkington (1994) have extended the approach to cases of schizophrenia.

According to Beck (1976), people with emotional disorders engage excessively in aberrant, fallacious, or dysfunctional thinking, and this is what causes (or exacerbates) their problems. Among the various types of dysfunctional thinking are the following.

1. Dichotomous thinking, which is thinking in absolute terms; for example, assuming that one is a failure if one gets any grade less than an "A"
2. Arbitrary inference, which is drawing a conclusion on the basis of inadequate evidence; for example, misinterpreting a frown on the face of a passerby to mean that the passerby disapproves of him or her
3. Overgeneralization, which is reaching a general conclusion on the basis of too few instances; for example, assuming that a single failure means that one cannot succeed at anything
4. Magnification, which is exaggerating the meaning or significance of a particular event; for example, believing that it is terrible or catastrophic not to obtain something that one wants very badly

Beck's procedure involves three general components. First, clients identify the dysfunctional thoughts and maladaptive assumptions that may be causing debilitating emotions. This is usually accomplished through a series of visualization exercises and easily answerable questions. A client might be encouraged, for example, to recall or imagine situations that elicited such emotions and to focus on the thoughts experienced in those situations. Second, once a thought or dysfunctional assumption has been identified, there are several methods that are used in counteracting it. One such method used by Beck is reality checking or hypothesis testing. After the client has identified the dysfunctional belief or thought and has learned to distinguish it as a hypothesis rather than as a reality, he or she then tests it empirically through homework assignments. For example, if a client believes that everyone he meets turns away from him in disgust, the therapist might help him devise a system for judging other people's facial expressions and body language so that the client can determine objectively if the thoughts behind the problem are indeed accurate. As another example, clients might be encouraged to participate in role-rehearsal sessions. A client who believed that store clerks thought she was inept changed this negative view of herself when she played the role of a salesclerk waiting on her. Third, Beck frequently uses additional homework assignments that contain liberal doses of behavior modification procedures to develop various desirable daily activities. Depressed individuals, for example, frequently neglect various routine tasks such as showering or bathing, bedmaking, and housecleaning. Homework assignments might be directed toward reestablishing these behaviors.

Comparison of the Approaches of Ellis and Beck   There are some obvious similarities between Beck's approach and Ellis's REBT. Both approaches assume that the client's difficulty is caused by some type of inappropriate thought pattern, such as a tendency to exaggerate or catastrophize unpleasant events. Both focus on changing a client's irrational thinking. And both use various behavioral homework assignments. A difference is that Beck does not emphasize the tendency of clients to catastrophize or "awfulize" nearly as much as Ellis. A second difference is that transcripts of sessions with clients conducted by Beck and Ellis suggest that Beck takes a gentler, less confrontational approach than Ellis does when discussing clients' irrational beliefs. A third difference is in their approach to changing irrational beliefs. Ellis attempts to change them by disputing them aggressively through relentless logical arguments. Beck attempts to change them by helping the client develop homework assignments to test them experimentally.

Evaluation of Beck's Cognitive Therapy   Although Beck and his colleagues have applied their approach to a variety of disorders, they consider it to be especially effective for depressed individuals (Beck et al., 1985). Cognitive therapy has been shown to be at least as effective as medication for acute episodes of depression (Antonuccio, Danton, & DeNelsky, 1995), although less effective than medication for chronic depression (Thase et al., 1994). Dobson (1989) concluded from a technique called *meta-analysis* that Beck's cognitive therapy was the treatment of choice for unipolar depression. As indicated previously, meta-analysis is a statistical procedure for combining the data analyses of many different studies to yield the result that one large study containing all the data of the smaller studies would have produced.

In another meta-analysis of published, randomized control trials for treatment of mildly to moderately depressed outpatients, however, overall efficacy was found to be just 46.6% for cognitive therapy, compared to 55.3% for behavior therapy and 52.3% for interpersonal psychotherapy (Depression Guideline Panel, 1993). Morover, evidence from a large-scale, multisite study conducted by the National Institute of Mental Health found that Beck's cognitive therapy was no more effective than a placebo control condition for persons suffering from depression (Elkin et al., 1989). That study has been criticized for having a number of methodological flaws, including the use of newly trained cognitive therapists who may not have been adequately supervised (Elkin, 1994; Otto, Pava, & Sprich-Buckminster, 1995).

Thus, the evidence on the effectiveness of Beck's cognitive therapy is mixed. Given that it may be effective, the question arises as to what its active ingredients and/or components are. A component analysis of Beck's cognitive therapy for treating depression compared behavioral homework assignments to behavioral homework assignments plus cognitive restructuring, and to the previous two components plus the identification and modification of generalized core beliefs that were presumed to be the major causes of dysfunctional thinking and depressive reactions. The behavioral homework assignments focused primarily on identifying specific life problems and prescribing a set of semistructured activities that help participants make contact with natural reinforcers in the environment. Results indicated that, at the end of treatment and at a two-year follow-up, the three treatment conditions were virtually identical on every measure (Jacobson et al., 1996; Gortner, Gollan, Dobson, & Jacobson, 1998). These findings suggest that cognitive restructuring may not be a necessary component in the treatment of depression. In a replication and extension of these findings, researchers compared behavioral homework assignments (referred to as behavioral activation) to cognitive therapy (including cognitive restructuring) to antidepressant medication and to a placebo control group (Dimidjian et al., 2003; and discussed in Martell, Addis, & Dimidjian, 2004). The behavioral activation group performed as well as the antidepressant group on some measures and better than the antidepressant group on other measures. Both the behavioral activation and the antidepressant group significantly outperformed the cognitive therapy group, which was not significantly different from the placebo control group. These results seriously question the necessity of adding cognitive restructuring to behavior activation in the treatment of depression.

Along the same lines, Andrew Sweet and his colleagues examined 29 studies that compared purely behavioral treatments to those same treatments with cognitive components added in order to overcome a variety of disorders (not just depression). They reported that 83% of the studies showed that no more beneficial outcome was achieved by adding therapy components that focused specifically on cognitive restructuring (Latimer & Sweet, 1984; Sweet & Loizeaux, 1991). Thus, while the addition of cognitive restructuring techniques to behavioral treatments may improve outcomes with some individuals suffering from various disorders, a number of studies suggest that it often does not do so.

SELF-DIRECTED COPING METHODS

The previous section described approaches that focus on substituting rational thoughts and appraisal of information for irrational or dysfunctional thinking—referred to as *cognitive restructuring*. Other strategies referred to as *cognitive behavior modification* focus on teaching self-instructional and problem-solving strategies to help clients emit overt behaviors to cope with difficult and often stressful situations.

Self-Instructional Training

Meichenbaum and Goodman (1971) originally developed self-instructional training to help children control impulsive behavior. Self-instructional training with children typically proceeds through these five steps:

1. *Adult demonstration of self-instructing.* For example, an adult might say, "My job is to draw a 10. First I'll draw a straight line like this, and then I'll draw a circle beside it" (while drawing a 10). "I did a good job."

2. *Child performs while adult verbalizes.* For example, the adult would give the child the pencil and repeat the above instructions (and subsequent praise) while the child draws a 10.
3. *The child performs the task and verbalizes out loud.* For example, the child would initate the behavior illustrated by the adult in step 1.
4. *Fading of overt self-instructions.* Over two or three trials, the child would be encouraged to repeat the task while saying the instructions and self-praise more and more softly.
5. *Task performance with covert self-instructions.* Finally, the child would be prompted to perform the task while saying the instructions and the self-praise to himself or herself so that the teacher can't hear them.

An impulsive child receiving self-instructional training would first be encouraged to practice the steps with simple tasks, such as drawing a 10, and then progressing to more complex tasks appropriate for the child's developmental level, such as adding and subtracting.

Meichenbaum (1986) and others have since developed self-instructional training strategies for helping clients to develop coping skills for dealing with stressful situations that are largely out of their control. Often, the emphasis in his approach is more on teaching the client to cope with the negative emotions than on completely eliminating them. For example, following treatment, one phobic client said,

> It [self-instructing] makes me able to be in the situation, not to be comfortable, but to tolerate it. I don't talk myself out of being afraid, just out of appearing afraid. You immediately react to the things you're afraid of and then start to reason with yourself. I talk myself out of panic. (Meichenbaum, 1986, p. 372)

The first step in Meichenbaum's approach to teach a client to cope with stress is to help the client identify certain internal stimuli produced by the stressful situation and by negative statements the client makes to himself or herself (e.g., "I can't deal with this," "I'm no good"). The client learns to use these internal stimuli as S^Ds for engaging in appropriate self-instruction. Next, through modeling and behavioral rehearsal, the client learns self-talk to counteract negative self-statements in the presence of the stressful situation. A client who is nervous about public speaking might be taught to say, "The fact that I'm anxious just before giving a speech doesn't mean I'm going to blow it—my anxiety is just a way of preparing me to be alert and do a good job." Third, the client is taught to self-instruct the steps for taking appropriate action (e.g., "I'll take three deep breaths, smile, then follow my notes and give my speech") while performing those actions. Finally, the client is instructed to make self-reinforcing statements immediately after he or she has coped successfully with the stressful situation (e.g.,"I did it! Wait 'till I tell my therapist about this!").

Stress Innoculations   In an analogy with a physician inoculating a patient with a nonvirulent form of a germ, Meichenbaum (1985) developed what he calls "stress inoculations." This strategy typically proceeds through three phases. In the *reinterpretation phase*, clients are taught that it's not the stressor (such as a student having to give a talk in class) that is the cause of their nervousness or stress reaction, rather it's the way they view that event. Clients are also taught to verbalize that they are capable of learning to take steps to deal with the situation. In the *coping training phase,* clients learn a variety of appropriate coping strategies, such as relaxation, self-instruction, and self-reinforcement (as illustrated above). Finally, in the *application phase,* clients practice their self-talk and coping skills to stressful stimuli, such as having one's arm immersed in freezing water, watching a gruesome film, or recalling a stressful visit to the dentist. Just prior to and during exposure to such stressful situations, the client practices appropriate coping skills. Research indicates that stress innoculations can be particularly helpful for clients with anxiety or stress problems (Meichenbaum & Deffenbacher, 1988).

Evaluation of Self-Instructional Methods   A large number of studies indicate that self-instructional training strategies are effective for such relatively specific tasks as controlling impulsiveness, increasing assertiveness, and improving leisure skills (Meichenbaum, 1986; Spiegler & Guevremont, 2003). Applications to more complex issues, such as social anxiety and personality disorders, have been less successful (Spiegler & Guevremont, 2003). As will be described later in this chapter, self-instructional training appears to rely largely on rule-governed behavior. And as indicated in Chapter 17, rules are often effective when they describe specific circumstances and deadlines for specific behavior that lead to sizable and probable outcomes, even when the outcomes are delayed. Rules that are deficient in any of these components are less likely to be effective.

Problem-Solving Methods

Problem-solving methods focus on teaching people how to proceed through logical reasoning to satisfactory solutions to personal problems. D'Zurilla and Goldfried (1971) outlined the following six general steps in personal problem solving.

1. *General orientation.* The client is encouraged to recognize problems and to realize that it is possible to deal with them by acting systematically rather than impulsively. When faced with a problem, for example, the client might be taught to make such statements as "I know I can work this out if I just proceed step-by-step" or "Let me see how I can rephrase this as a problem to be solved."

2. *Problem definition.* When asked to specify the problem, most clients reply in vague terms—for example, "I've been very upset lately." By specifying the history of the problem and the variables that seem to be controlling it, it is generally possible to define the problem more precisely. For example, a close analysis might indicate that what is upsetting the client is that she shares the apartment with a very untidy roommate and she can't stand the "mess" she feels forced to live in.

3. *Generation of alternatives.* After defining the problem precisely, the client is instructed to brainstorm possible solutions—that is, to "let her mind run free" and to think of as many solutions as she can, no matter how far-fetched. For example, possible solutions might be to (a) move, (b) learn to accept messiness, (c) speak assertively to her roommate about keeping the place neat, (d) try to shape neat behavior in her roommate, (e) negotiate a behavioral contract with her roommate, (f) throw her roommate's things out the window, and (g) throw her roommate out the window.

4. *Decision making.* The next step is to examine the alternatives carefully, eliminating those that are obviously unacceptable, such as (f) and (g) above. She should then consider the likely short-term and long-term consequences of the remaining alternatives. Writing out the positives and negatives of various alternatives has been demonstrated to improve satisfaction with decision making, to increase the likelihood of sticking to decisions, and to lead to more productive choices and fewer regrets (Janis & Mann, 1977; Janis & Wheeler, 1978). On the basis of these considerations, she should select the alternative that seems most likely to provide the optimum solution.

5. *Implementation.* The client then (initially with the help of the therapist) devises a plan for carrying out the best solution to the problem. Sometimes this requires learning new skills. If, for example, the client decided that the best alternative (from those listed above in step 3) was (e), then the client might need to learn about behavioral contracting (discussed in Chapter 26).

6. *Verification.* When the plan is put into effect, the client is encouraged to keep track of progress to ensure that it solves the problem. If it doesn't, the problem-solving sequence must be restarted and another solution attempted.

Evaluation of Problem-Solving Methods   Foxx and Faw (1990) described a program for teaching problem-solving skills to psychiatric patients and discussed how generalization of these skills might be enhanced. In addition, D'Zurilla and Nezu (1999) described how the problem-solving approach might be applied to a variety of clinical problems. Although evidence indicates that adults and children can readily learn problem-solving skills, they do not always apply them appropriately to achieve satisfactory solutions to personal problems.

MINDFULNESS AND ACCEPTANCE

Mindfulness practice is an ancient concept considered to be "at the heart of Buddha's teachings" (Nhat Hanh, 1998, p. 59). **Mindfulness** involves awareness, observation, and description of one's covert and overt behaviors, as they occur, in a nonjudgmental way, as well as (in some cases) observation of the antecedents and consequences of those behaviors. It involves paying close attention to the sights, smells, tastes, and tactile sensations of an experience as it occurs. Suppose, for example, that you made arrangements with a friend of yours to meet outside a particular restaurant at noon. At 12:30, your friend (who is notoriously unreliable) still hasn't arrived. Feeling angry, you might think to yourself, "This really upsets me. I hate it when he's always late! I can't stand it when he's so unreliable! Why do I put up with him? The people in the restaurant must think I'm an idiot for standing here for half an hour." Alternatively, you might practice mindfulness, thinking to yourself, "I'm standing in front of a restaurant. I see cars driving by. I notice that my heart is beating faster. I feel a queasiness in my stomach. I'm clenching my fists and my forearms feel tense. I'm wondering what people in the restaurant are saying about me. I'm visualizing him apologizing to me." As illustrated by this example, mindfulness involves becoming fully aware of one's sensations, thoughts, feelings, and observable behavior on a moment-to-moment basis.

Acceptance refers to a set of behaviors in reaction to mindfulness activities, including refraining from judging one's sensations, thoughts, feelings, and behaviors as good or bad, pleasant or unpleasant, useful or useless, and so on. One's thoughts are viewed as just responses, just passing events. Feelings, both positive and negative, are accepted as part of life. Acceptance procedures are used to teach individuals that they can feel their feelings and think their thoughts, even though they may be aversive, and still take constructive action that is consistent with their values and life goals.

In the early 1990s, several therapists began incorporating mindfulness and acceptance procedures into cognitive behavior therapy (Hayes, Jacobson, Follette, & Dougher, 1994; Linehan, 1993; Teasdale, Segal, & Williams, 1995). As indicated earlier, therapists who incorporate such experiential change strategies in therapy have been described as the third wave of behavior therapists (Hayes, 2004; Hayes, Follette, & Linehan, 2004). One such approach to treatment is Acceptance and Commitment Therapy.

Acceptance and Commitment Therapy

Acceptance and Commitment Therapy (ACT), developed by Hayes and colleagues (Hayes, Strosahl, & Wilson, 1999), proceeds through three main phases. First, through the use of metaphors, paradox, stories, and other verbal techniques by the therapist, the client learns that past attempts to control troublesome thoughts and emotions have not only been unsuccessful, but often served to increase the frequency of such thoughts and emotions. If we tell you, for example, not to think of a pink elephant, what are you likely to think about? A pink elephant. Second, through the use of mindfulness training and acceptance exercises, the client learns to experience and nonjudgmentally embrace thoughts and emotions, including those that are troublesome. In one such exercise, for example, a client is encouraged to imagine his or her thoughts as they "float by like leaves on a stream" (Hayes, 2004). Third, regardless of whether the troublesome thoughts and emotions are eliminated, clients are encouraged to identify values in various life domains, such as work, family, health, intimate relationships, and so forth. The
Note 1 client is then encouraged to translate such values into achievable, concrete goals, and to identify and emit specific behaviors to achieve those goals. This is the commitment portion of ACT—clients are encouraged to identify valued goals in their lives and commit to actions to pursue those goals.

ACT differs from the cognitive therapy (CT) of Ellis and Beck in several ways. First, CT assumes that troublesome thoughts constitute the primary cause of disturbing emotions, whereas ACT considers both thoughts and emotions simply as responses, and assumes that both are caused by various environmental contingencies. Second, a major focus of CT is the use of cognitive restructuring to change
Note 2 troublesome thoughts directly, while ACT uses mindfulness practice and acceptance procedures to teach a client to embrace and accept various thoughts and emotions, rather than judging them as troublesome and trying to change them directly. ACT teaches clients, that, in spite of experiencing troublesome thoughts and aversive feelings, they can still take constructive action to pursue valued goals. A third

difference is in the focus of behavioral homework assignments. With CT, a primary purpose of behavioral homework assignments is to help the client overcome distorted thinking. With ACT, behavioral homework assignments are used to build larger and larger patterns of effective action in the pursuit of valued goals. For all of the above reasons, ACT is considered by some (including perhaps its authors) to be more a form of behavior therapy than of cognitive therapy.

Evaluation of ACT   ACT is a relatively new approach to therapy, and considerable research is needed to clearly establish its efficacy. Nevertheless, early studies have been positive. For example, it has been shown to be equivalent to systematic desensitization (described in Chapter 28) in treating math anxiety (Zettle, 2003), and has been effective for reducing stress in the workplace (Bond & Bunce, 2000). Other outcome studies were reviewed by Hayes, Masuda, Bissette, Luoma, and Guerrero (2004). For additional readings on ACT, see the special issue of *Behavior Therapy* (2004, Vol. 35, No. 4).

A BEHAVIORAL INTERPRETATION OF COGNITIVE BEHAVIORAL TECHNIQUES

As we indicated in Chapter 14, two important categories of behaviors are operant and respondent. As discussed in Chapter 15, much of what we call "thinking" and "feeling" in everyday life can be described in terms of these two fundamental behavioral categories. Also, as indicated in Chapter 15, we assume that the principles and procedures of operant and respondent conditioning apply to private as well as to public behavior. In a number of examples in this book, private behavior was modified to bring about desired changes in public behavior. In no case, however, was it necessary to assume that private behavior is fundamentally different from public behavior. On the contrary, the treatments used were based on the assumption that the same general principles and procedures are applicable to both private and public behavior. From this point let's reexamine some of the methods that others have called cognitive procedures.

Let's start with cognitive restructuring. You will recall that some cognitive therapists believe that faulty thinking is the cause of emotional and behavioral problems, and that the primary focus of cognitive restructuring is to change faulty thinking. As discussed in Chapter 15, it's certainly plausible to suppose that some types of self-statements can function as a CS to elicit the respondent components of anxiety, anger, or some other emotion. Consider, for example, the case of Jim, the student described earlier in this chapter, who overslept, cut himself while shaving, and later got stuck in traffic. Instances of Jim's irrational self-talk (e.g., "I'm a walking disaster! Why does the worst always happen to me?") might function as a CS to elicit the respondent components of anxiety or anger. His self-statements might also be analyzed in terms of rule-governed behavior. You will recall from Chapter 17 that a rule is a description of a situation in which a certain response will produce certain consequences. The statement of a rule (e.g., "If I study my behavior modification text for three hours tonight, I'll get an 'A' on my behavior modification exam tomorrow") can exert control over behavior (it can influence you to study behavior modification for three hours). From a behavioral perspective, cognitive restructuring deals largely with rule-governed behavior (Poppen, 1989; Zettle & Hayes, 1982). Jim's irrational self-talk might be thought of as faulty rules. His statement, "I always screw up," implies the rule: "If I attempt this task I will encounter failure." Such a rule might cause him to avoid a variety of tasks that he is capable of performing. A cognitive therapist might dispute such irrational self-statements, challenge Jim to replace them with rational self-statements, and give him homework assignments that would support rational thinking. For example, Jim might rehearse such rules as "I do some things quite well. I'll follow the computer assignment instructions carefully so that I can complete the assignment by the deadline," or "If I take my time, I can change the oil in my car without making a mess." Such rules would counteract his irrational self-talk ("I always screw up") and would likely lead to behavior that will be reinforced. The therapist will have helped Jim to replace inaccurate rules with more accurate ones, and behavior appropriate to the more accurate rules is likely to be maintained by the natural environment.

But now consider other types of irrational thinking. According to Ellis and Grieger (1977), irrational thinking also includes categories referred to as "awfulizing" (e.g., "It's absolutely awful that I lost my job") and "musterbation" (e.g., "I must get a job or I'm a rotten person"). When a client expresses such thoughts, an REBT therapist might challenge the client ("Why is it awful?" or "Just because you don't have a job doesn't make you a rotten person"). And even though a client may learn (in order to avoid or escape aggressive questioning by the therapist) to express that being without work is not awful or that he or she is not a rotten person, the client is still out of work. In such cases, cognitive restructuring is less likely to be helpful (e.g., see Figure 27–1). The client has not been given a set of rules (e.g., "I'll check the want ads," "I'll go to the employment agency") that are likely to lead to effective action that will be maintained by the natural environment. And even if the client has been given clear rules for effective behavior, he or she may be deficient in the necessary behaviors (time management, assertiveness, persistence, etc.) needed to find a job. Thus, in some cases of cognitive restructuring, the rules may be ineffective because they don't identify specific circumstances for specific behaviors that lead to supportive environmental consequences, or because the client is deficient in the behaviors specified by the rules.

In summary, cognitive restructuring techniques might be effective, from a behavioral point of view, because they decrease the frequency of irrational self-statements that elicit the respondent component of troublesome emotions, and through verbal discourse and homework assignments, they teach a client to rehearse rules that identify specific circumstances for specific behaviors that are likely to be maintained in the natural environment.

What about both self-instruction and problem-solving training? We suggest that these approaches teach rule-governed behavior that leads to effective consequences. Teaching a student who is nervous about giving a speech in class to recognize the fact that she is nervous, to then emit some coping self-statements, and to then self-instruct the steps for taking appropriate action is essentially giving the student a set of rules to follow. If the rules govern the behavior successfully (the student does in fact give the speech and receive some positive feedback), then the use of those rules will have been strengthened. Because there is a focus

Figure 27–1   An exaggerated example of rational-emotive therapy.

on performing the behavior successfully in addition to self-instructions to do so, there is a greater chance of successful behavior change than if the focus had just been on the self-instructions alone. Similarly, in problem solving, whereas the first three steps (general orientation, problem definition, and generation of alternatives) involve self-talk, the last three steps (decision making, implementation, and verification) require the individual to take action and solve the problem. Once again, self-talk that is appropriately linked to overt behaviors and supportive environmental consequences is more likely to be effective than self-talk that is not.

What about mindfulness and acceptance procedures? Why would these be therapeutic? One possibility is that nonjudgmentally observing ongoing sensations is incompatible with and therefore displaces the behavior of irrational thinking and the negative emotions elicited by it. In the case of Jim, for example, when he was caught in traffic on the way to his class, if he had observed mindfully how his heart was racing, how tightly he was gripping the steering wheel, and so forth, then he might have been less likely to make irrational generalizations (e.g., "Why does the worst always happen to me?") that had previously elicited negative emotions.

A second possibility relates to the differences between contingency-shaped and rule-governed behavior. Mindfulness and acceptance involve exposure to natural contingencies, and the awareness and nonjudgmental acceptance of one's sensations would appear to be contingency-shaped behavior (Hayes, 2004). In contrast, as described above, cognitive restructuring deals largely with rule-governed behavior. Contingency-shaped behavior has been described as natural, reactive, and intuitive (Baldwin & Baldwin, 2001), whereas rule-governed behavior tends to be inflexible and rigid (Hayes, 1989). Thus, when a client can accept the sensations characteristic of troublesome thoughts and emotions as experiences to be embraced, then exposure to natural contingencies is more likely to modify that behavior.

A third possibility is that, once the sensations characteristic of troublesome thoughts and emotions are accepted as simply responses, and nothing more, the client may then be more amenable to the identification of various life values, the articulation of concrete goals (i.e, rules) that represent those values, and the commitment to specific behaviors to achieve those goals. Stated simply, it may be that once a client accepts irrational thinking and troublesome emotions as "no big deal," then in spite of them, the client can more easily "get on with life." Thus, it appears that ACT uses strategies to enhance contingency-shaped behavior in the first two phases of therapy, and then capitalizes on both rule-governed and contingency-shaped behavior in the third phase of therapy.

CONCLUDING COMMENTS

Although the behavioral applications we have described briefly in this chapter are usually called cognitive, and although they are often said to be directed toward modifying thoughts, beliefs, and attitudes, their distinguishing characteristic seems to be that they deal with private verbal behavior and imagery as well as with public behavior. They do not appear to involve any behavior principles besides those discussed in the previous chapters of this book. All behavior practitioners should be open to innovative procedures for helping people change their behavior. At the same time, as this chapter has pointed out, there are practical as well as theoretical advantages to looking at such procedures from a consistent behavioral viewpoint. In addition, it is especially important that, whenever possible, practitioners use procedures that have been validated in the research literature and avoid those that have not been validated.

STUDY QUESTIONS

1. What does the word *cognition* mean?
2. What are two major assumptions underlying cognitive restructuring procedures?
3. What are the two main steps of cognitive restructuring methods?

4. In a sentence or two, what are the three main phases of rational-emotive behavior therapy? Who developed it?

5. Why did Ellis change the name of his therapy from RET to REBT?

6. Describe the basic comparisons that were examined and the overall results obtained in the studies on RET reviewed by Gossette and O'Brien.

7. According to Beck, what causes problems for individuals with neuroses? Describe three examples.

8. Describe the three major components of Beck's cognitive therapy.

9. Describe three similarities and three differences between the approaches of Beck and Ellis.

10. Studies in the 1980s indicated that cognitive behavior therapy was the treatment of choice for unipolar depression. Is that therapy effective because of the cognitive restructuring or because of the behavioral homework assignments?

11. Briefly list the five steps of self-instructional training with children used by Meichenbaum and others.

12. Briefly describe the three phases of Meichenbaum's stress innoculation training.

13. In two or three sentences each, outline the six steps of problem solving described by D'Zurilla and Goldfried.

14. What is *mindfulness* as the term is used by cognitive behavior therapists?

15. What is *acceptance* as the term is used by cognitive behavior therapists?

16. Briefly describe the three phases of ACT.

17. What are three differences between cognitive therapy and ACT?

18. Why is ACT considered to be a behavioral therapy?

19. Describe an example of respondent thinking. (You may want to review Chapter 15.)

20. Describe an example of operant thinking. (You may want to review Chapter 15.)

21. Discuss whether reputable behavior modifiers deny the existence and importance of thoughts and feelings.

22. Describe an example that illustrates how cognitive therapists capitalize on rule-governed behavior to help their clients.

23. From a rule-governed behavior interpretation of cognitive therapy, how might we explain effective versus ineffective applications of cognitive restructuring?

24. Do mindfulness and acceptance procedures appear to involve rule-governed behavior or contingency-shaped behavior? Justify your choice.

APPLICATION EXERCISE

Self-Modification Exercise

Consider a situation in which you sometimes experience negative thinking. It could be negative thinking about your future, about a social relationship, about work, about your performance in a university course, and so on. In a sentence, describe the general theme around which negative thinking occurs. Then write down 10 different types of thoughts (these could be self-statements, images, or a mixture of the two) that you experience when thinking negatively on that particular topic or theme. Next, for each negative thought, describe an alternative positive thought or coping self-statement that you might practice to counteract the negative thought. Your coping thoughts should be realistic, positive, and specific, and should relate to specific positive outcomes.

NOTES AND EXTENDED DISCUSSION

1. ACT is based on an approach to the understanding of human language and cognition referred to as **relational frame theory** (RFT; Hayes, Barnes-Holmes, & Roche, 2001). RFT builds on research on the formation of equivalence classes discussed in Chapter 8. In general, relational framing is responding in certain ways to a set of arbitrary stimuli that can be related to each other by some linguistic phrase or "frame"; (e.g., a dime *is worth more than* a nickel). In other words, even though a dime is smaller than a nickel in terms of actual size, we have arbitrarily designated the dime as being worth more. Relational frames exhibit three characteristics. First, they exhibit by *bi-directionality* (also referred to as *mutual entailment*). For example, if you have learned that two nickels equals a dime, then you will know that a dime also equals two nickels. This bi-directionality is involved in all relational frames (such as smaller than and bigger than, slower than and faster than, duller than and brighter than, etc.). Second, relational frames show *combinatorial entailment*. For example, if a child learns that a dime is worth more than a nickel, and a quarter is worth more then a dime, the child will know that a quarter is also worth more than a nickel. (Note that the transitivity relationship of stimulus equivalence, discussed in Note 1 of Chapter 8, is an example of combinatorial entailment). Third, relational frames display *transformation of stimulus functions*. Suppose, for example, that, through training, the written word "dog," the spoken work "dog," and an actual dog have become an equivalence class for a child. Suppose further that a dog approaches the child and barks loudly, scaring the child. The sight of the dog now functions to cause fear. That function will also be transferred to related stimuli so that the child will now feel fear when hearing someone say "dog" or when reading the word "dog." For Hayes and colleagues, relational framing is the essence of verbal behavior, and is the characteristic that sets humans apart from other animals. Nonhuman animals are capable of showing learned stimulus generalization to different stimuli provided that the stimuli have some physical characteristic in common, such as learning the concepts red, tree, or people (see Chapter 8). Humans, however, will show stimulus generalization between members of an equivalence class even though the members are very different, such as learning that "money" and "cash" are the "same," even though the words look very different. This effect, along with the transformation of stimulus functions among related stimuli, leads to relational framing which allows us to talk and think about events that are not present, to analyze pros and cons of possible outcomes, and to select courses of action to solve problems. Unfortunately, relational framing can also cause troublesome emotions with respect to stimuli which are not even present, such as excessive regret or remorse about events in the remote past and excessive and unproductive worrying about potential events in the distant future. For reviews of RFT, see Volume 19 (2003) of *The Analysis of Verbal Behavior,* and Palmer (2004).

2. Another method for treating persistence disturbing thoughts is referred to as *thought-stopping* (Wolpe, 1958). Consider, for example, the case of Carol (Martin, 1982). After being engaged for three years, Carol's boyfriend, Fred, had left her for another woman. Carol suffered from frequent, obsessive thoughts about Fred. She agreed to try thought-stopping. To teach Carol how to use thought-stopping, the therapist first instructed her to close her eyes, think about Fred, and to raise her finger when she was beginning to feel unhappy. When she did so, the therapist yelled,

"STOP!" Carol was startled, immediately opened her eyes, and thoughts about Fred ceased. The therapist and Carol repeated this routine twice more. Carol was then instructed to think about Fred, and when she visualized him clearly, she should yell, "STOP!" herself. Carol followed this routine, and once again, thoughts of Fred immediately ceased. Carol followed this routine on two more trials, the experience of which taught her that she could, at least temporarily, cease thinking about Fred by yelling "STOP!" Carol was then instructed to once more think about Fred, but this time, when clearly visualizing him, she should imagine yelling "STOP!" silently to herself. Carol followed this instruction successfully, and repeated it on two more trials. The therapist then explained to Carol that thought-stopping involves two phases: (a) first terminating the distressing thoughts (which Carol had learned to do); and (b) then thinking competing adaptive thoughts. To implement these phases, Carol agreed that each time she experienced a thought characteristic of those that upset her, she would stop doing what she was doing, clasp her hands, close her eyes, and silently yell "STOP!" to herself. Then she would open her eyes and take from her purse five photographs of herself in a happy mood or situation. She would look at each of the photographs, one at a time, and then turn them over and read statements on the back that prompted her to think positive thoughts. She was also instructed to vary the positive thoughts when viewing the photographs at different times. After following this procedure for several weeks, thoughts about Fred decreased to a very low level, and Carol decided that she no longer needed help. Thought-stopping is often used as a part of a treatment package for decreasing troublesome thoughts.

Study Questions on Notes

1. With an example, illustrate the bi-directionality aspect of relational framing.
2. With an example, illustrate the combinatorial entailment aspect of relational framing.
3. With an example, illustrate how relational framing involves transformation of stimulus functions among related stimuli.
4. Briefly describe the three steps that a therapist might follow in teaching a client to use thought-stopping to terminate distressing thoughts.
5. How would Carol's problem have been treated with ACT?

Areas of Clinical
Behavior Therapy

In this chapter we give a brief overview of the ways in which behavior therapists (behavior modifiers and cognitive behavior modifiers) are applying the principles and techniques described in the preceding chapters to treat some of the most frequently encountered adult psychological disorders. In the field of clinical psychology there has been a move by many therapists away from applying treatments simply because they fit a particular theoretical position. Instead, partly under the instigation of third-party payers (such as insurance companies and governments), emphasis has shifted to *empirically supported therapies* (ESTs)— that is, therapies that have proved to be effective in scientifically conducted clinical trials. Typically, ESTs turn out to be behavioral or cognitive behavioral treatments. This is primarily because—as discussed in Chapter 1—the behavioral approach emphasizes basing treatments on well-established principles, measuring the outcomes of treatments in objectively defined behaviors, and altering treatments that are not producing satisfactory results. As mentioned in the previous chapter, we consider cognitive procedures to be directed toward private or covert behavior, and to be based on operant and Pavlovian conditioning. Thus, although we use the terms *behavioral* and *cognitive* procedures in this chapter, this is merely for convenience rather than indicating any sort of fundamental distinction.

Note 1

Our intention is not to teach you how to assess, diagnose, and treat the disorders discussed in this chapter. This would be far beyond the scope of this text, and these activities must be done only by trained professionals. Instead, our purpose is to provide you with general information about how qualified behavior therapists treat these disorders and to relate that information to the behavioral principles and procedures discussed in previous chapters.Behavioral and cognitive behavioral treatment of the disorders to be discussed has received more detailed coverage in other books (e.g., Antony & Barlow, 2004; Antony & Swinson, 2001; Barlow, 2001; Lambert, 2004).

It should be noted that pharmaceutical treatments (i.e., drugs) are available for some of the problems covered in this chapter. While drugs alone can sometimes be effective treatment, many studies show that it is often more effective to use them in combination with behavior therapy or cognitive behavior therapy. Indeed, drugs may not be necessary when behavior therapy or cognitive behavior therapy is used. Because drugs often have unwanted side effects, it is usually considered desirable to avoid their use when behavioral or cognitive behavior therapy is a viable alternative.

The list of clinical disorders covered in this chapter is clearly not exhaustive; however, the disorders selected are representative of the types of disorders that behavior therapists treat. Because these clinical problems are not independent, clients often have more than one at the same time—a condition known as *co-morbidity*. Treatment is generally not as straightforward when co-morbidity is present as when it is not present. For simplicity, this chapter assumes that the client suffers from only one of the conditions discussed.

SPECIFIC PHOBIAS

Many people have fears that are so intense that they are virtually incapacitated by them. A person might have such an intense fear of heights that he cannot walk up a single flight of stairs or look out of a second-story window without experiencing acute anxiety. Another person might be so terrified of crowds that she cannot bear to go out into public places. Surprising as it may seem, trying to convince these people that their fears are irrational often has no beneficial effect. They usually know that their fears have no rational basis and would like to control them, but they cannot because the fears are automatically elicited by specific stimuli. Such intense, irrational, incapacitating fears are called *specific phobias*. Specific phobias are classed as animal type (e.g., fear of cats, dogs, mice, birds, snakes, spiders), natural environment type (e.g., fear of heights, storms, water), blood–injury–injection type (e.g., fear of seeing blood, receiving an injection, having an operation or dental work), situational type (e.g., enclosed spaces, flying), and other type (any specific phobia not included in the above).

Specific phobias are classified by the *DSM-IV-TR*[1] as a type of anxiety disorder. We discuss other anxiety disorders later in this chapter. We start with a discussion of specific phobias because several well-known behavioral treatments have been developed to treat them.

---

[1]The *DSM-IV-TR*, which you will recall from Chapter 1, is the latest version of the *Diagnostic and Statistical Manual of Mental Disorders* (American Psychiatric Association, 2000).

Systematic Desensitization

Joseph Wolpe (1958) developed the earliest behavioral treatment for specific phobias. His treatment, called **systematic desensitization,** is based on the process of counterconditioning (discussed in Chapter 14). Wolpe hypothesized that the irrational fear characteristic of a phobia is a respondently conditioned response to the feared object or situation. From this hypothesis he reasoned that he could eliminate the irrational fear response if he could establish a response to the feared stimulus that counteracted or opposed the fear response. A fear-antagonistic response that Wolpe found suitable for this purpose was relaxation. Wolpe further reasoned that when counterconditioning the fear response, the therapist should be careful not to elicit the fear response all at once in its full intensity, as too much fear in the therapy session would interfere with the process. This is where the "systematic" part of the procedure comes in. (Further details about the historical rationale behind systematic desensitization are given in Chapter 29.)

In the first phase of systematic desensitization—which, given the above rationale, might also have been called *systematic counterconditioning*—the therapist helps the client construct a fear hierarchy—a list of approximately 10 to 25 stimuli related to the feared stimulus and that also cause fear. The therapist then helps the client order these stimuli from those that cause the least fear to those that cause the most. An actual example of a fear hierarchy constructed with a client is shown in Table 28–1.

In the next phase, the client learns a deep-muscle relaxation procedure that requires tensing and relaxing a set of muscles so that they are more deeply relaxed following the tensing than before. This tension–relaxation strategy is applied to muscles of all major areas of the body (such as arms, neck, face, shoulders, stomach, and legs) and, after several sessions, enables an individual to relax deeply in a matter of minutes. During the third phase, the actual therapy begins. While relaxing, at the direction of the therapist, the client clearly imagines the first (i.e., the least fear-eliciting) scene in the hierarchy for a few seconds, then stops imagining it and continues relaxing for about 15 to 30 seconds. This is repeated with the first scene, then the next scene is presented and repeated in the same way. If at any point the client experiences anxiety (which he or she communicates to the therapist by raising a finger), the therapist returns the client to a previous step or inserts an intermediate scene. When the client finishes the last scene in the hierarchy, he or she can usually encounter the feared objects without distress. The positive reinforcement the client then receives for interacting with the previously feared stimuli helps to maintain continued interactions with those stimuli.

Although systematic desensitization is normally carried out by having the client imagine the feared stimuli, it can also be conducted *in vivo*—from the Latin "in life" or, in other words, in the presence of the actual stimuli that elicit fear in the natural environment. *In vivo* exposure is often used when clients have difficulty imagining scenes. It also has the advantage of eliminating the need to program generalization from imagined scenes to actual situations. However, it is usually less time-consuming and less costly for a client to imagine feared scenes in a hierarchical order (such as sitting in an airplane but not taking off, then riding in airplanes) than to arrange *in vivo* exposure to them.

TABLE 28–1   EXAMPLE OF A FEAR-OF-FLYING HIERARCHY

1. The plane has landed and stopped at the terminal. I get off the plane and enter the terminal, where I am met by friends.

2. A trip has been planned, and I have examined the possible methods of travel and decided "out loud" to travel by plane.

3. I have called the travel agent and told him of my plans. He gives me the times and flight numbers.

4. It is the day before the trip, and I pack my suitcase, close it, and lock it.

5. It is 10 days before the trip, and I receive the tickets in the mail. I note the return address, open the envelope, and check the tickets for the correct dates, times, and flight numbers.

6. It is the day of the flight, I am leaving home. I lock the house, put the bags in the car, and make sure that I have the tickets and money.

7. I am driving to the airport for my flight. I am aware of every plane I see. As I get close to the airport, I see several planes—some taking off, some landing, and some just sitting on the ground by the terminal.

8. I am entering the terminal. I am carrying my bags and tickets.

9. I proceed to the airline desk, wait in line, and have the agent check my tickets and then weigh and check my bags.

10. I am in the lounge with many other people, some with bags also waiting for flights. I hear the announcements over the intercom and listen for my flight number to be called.

11. I hear my flight number announced, and I proceed to the security checkpoint with my hand luggage.

12. I approach the airline desk beyond the security checkpoint, and the agent asks me to choose a seat from the "map" of the plane.

13. I walk down the ramp leading to the plane and enter the door of the plane.

14. I am now inside the plane. I look at the interior of the plane and walk down the aisle, looking for my seat number. I then move in from the aisle and sit down in my assigned seat.

15. The plane is in flight, and I decide to leave my seat and walk to the washroom at the back of the plane.

16. I notice the seat-belt signs light up, so I fasten my seat belt and I notice the sound of the motors starting.

17. Everyone is seated with their seat belts fastened, and the plane slowly moves away from the terminal.

18. I notice the seat-belt signs are again lighted, and the pilot announces that we are preparing to land.

19. I am looking out the window and suddenly the plane enters clouds and I cannot see out the window.

20. The plane has stopped at the end of the runway and is sitting, waiting for instructions to take off.

21. The plane is descending to the runway for a landing. I feel the speed and see the ground getting closer.

22. The plane has taken off from the airport and banks as it changes direction. I am aware of the "tilt".

23. The plane starts down the runway, and the motors get louder as the plane increases speed and suddenly lifts off.

Source: This example is based on a case described by Roscoe, Martin, & Pear (1980).

In recent years, for reasons that are not entirely clear given its proven effectiveness in numerous studies, systematic desensitization has not been as popular among therapists as it once was. One reason might be its emphasis on covert or private behavior (i.e., imagery) in the treatment, as opposed to overt behavior, which tends to be favored by behaviorists. In addition, because of its stimulus–response emphasis, systematic desensitization does not appeal to cognitively oriented therapists. (For further discussion of these points, see McGlynn, Smitherman, & Gothard, 2004).

Flooding

Whereas the model for systematic desensitization is counterconditioning, the model for **flooding** is extinction. That is, the basic assumption behind flooding is that if the client is exposed to the feared stimuli, is not allowed to escape from them, and no aversive event follows, then the fear response to these stimuli will extinguish. Flooding is carried out either *in vivo* or with imagery. Whereas *in vivo* exposure is generally preferred because, in theory, it maximizes generalization, there is evidence that flooding with *in vivo* exposure and flooding with imagery exposure are equally effective (Bordon, 1992).

As the name *flooding* suggests, the treatment involves eliciting the fear at or close to its full intensity. However, the procedure may involve graded levels of exposure if the distress experienced by the client is too overwhelming. A fear of heights, for example, might be treated by having the client look out the window on the first floor, then the third floor, then the seventh floor, and finally the top of a 10-story building. Thus, except for the absence of an explicit relaxation procedure, flooding can be very similar to desensitization.

Participant Modeling

In **participant modeling,** the therapist models approaches to the feared stimulus or stimuli. The approach might simply be called modeling (see Chapter 18); however, the name *participant modeling* emphasizes the fact that both the client and therapist are participating together in the feared situation (as opposed to, for example, the model being provided by video). Participant modeling is typically carried out in a graded fashion. If a client has a fear of birds, for example, the therapist might observe a budgie in a cage from about 10 feet away while the client watches. The client would then be encouraged to imitate this behavior and would be praised for doing so. After several trials, the process might be repeated from a distance of 5 feet from the bird, then 2 feet, then right beside the cage, then with the cage door open, and finally ending with the budgie perched on the client's finger.

Nonexposure Approaches

Systematic desensitization, flooding, and participant modeling are considered
Note 2 *exposure-based therapies,* in that they involve exposure—either in imagination or *in*

vivo—of the client to the feared stimulus or stimuli. There are other approaches that have been used effectively in combination with exposure-based approaches. Cognitive behavior modification may be effective, for example, with a specific phobia such as claustrophobia (fear of being in closed spaces, such as elevators). Individuals with claustrophobia may tell themselves that they are going to suffocate, lose control, or be trapped. Using cognitive therapy to reduce the believability of these self-statements has been found to eliminate or greatly reduce the phobia (Booth & Rachman, 1992; Shafran, Booth, & Rachman, 1993).

Summary of Treatment of Specific Phobias

Comparison studies of systematic desensitization, flooding, and participant modeling have demonstrated no meaningful differences among these different treatments in terms of outcome (Borden, 1992). Also, as indicated in Chapter 27, Acceptance and Commitment Therapy was as effective as systematic desensitization in the treatment of a specific phobia. Further, as we also saw in Chapter 27, adding cognitive components (nonexposure approaches) to behavioral procedures frequently has no detectable benefits.

OTHER ANXIETY DISORDERS

According to the *DSM-IV-TR*, anxiety disorders are characterized by (a) fear/anxiety that results in physiological changes such as sweaty hands, trembling, dizziness, and heart palpitations; (b) the escape and/or avoidance of situations in which the fear is likely to occur; and (c) interference by the unwanted behaviors with the individual's life. The *DSM-IV-TR* classifies anxiety disorders into several broad categories, including specific phobias, panic disorder and agoraphobia, generalized anxiety disorder, obsessive-compulsive disorder, and posttraumatic stress disorder. Having already considered the first, we consider each of the latter four of these in turn.

Panic Disorder and Agoraphobia

Panic disorder is a susceptibility to panic attacks, which are intense fear experiences that seem to come "out of the blue" with no precipitating stimulus or cue. These attacks include four or more of the following symptoms: (a) heart-rate abnormalities, including extremely rapid heart beat, heart palpitations, and pounding heart; (b) sweating; (c) trembling; (d) shortness of breath or feeling of being smothered; (e) feelings of choking; (f) chest pain or discomfort; (g) nausea or extreme abdominal discomfort; (h) dizziness or feeling light-headed or faint; (i) feeling of unreality; (j) numbness or tingling sensation; (k) chills or hot flushes; (l) fear of going crazy or losing control; and (m) fear of dying.

Agoraphobia—which literally means fear of the marketplace—is an intense fear of going out in public or leaving the confines of one's home. People who suffer from panic disorder frequently also have agoraphobia because they are afraid of having a panic attack in public or outside of their home. This can lead to a self-fulfilling prophecy in which the fear of having a panic attack actually generates the attack. To paraphrase Franklin D. Roosevelt's famous words, the thing that a person with panic disorder fears most is fear itself.

Treatment   In general, exposure-based therapy carried out *in vivo* is an effective treatment for panic disorder with agoraphobia (Bouman & Emmelkamp, 1996). This may be accomplished by having the client at first make short trips from the home, followed by gradually longer and longer trips. Alternatively, for an excellent example of contingency management to treat panic disorder, see Guilhardi (2004). Cognitive behavioral treatment is also effective for panic disorder with agoraphobia (Baker, Paterson, & Barlow, 2004). Cognitive behavioral treatment typically includes a behavioral component involving exposure to feared situations, and a cognitive component to help change the client's misconceptions about panic attacks. For example, a client may believe that a panic attack will precipitate a heart attack, whereas in fact this outcome is extremely unlikely. In addition, the client may be taught relaxation and thought-stopping techniques to lessen the intensity of a panic attack. (Thought-stopping was described in Note 2 of Chapter 27).

Generalized Anxiety Disorder

We all know someone who worries too much. A person with generalized anxiety disorder is like that person taken to an extreme degree—constantly worrying and feeling intensely anxious over things, events, and potential events that most people would consider trivial, unimportant, or unlikely. Such a person is so consumed with anxiety that it interferes with normal functioning, often including the ability to sleep at night.

Treatment   The most effective therapies for this problem are treatment packages that combined cognitive and behavioral strategies (Borkovec & Sharpless, 2004; Campbell & Brown, 2004). One of the behavioral components is usually an efficient form of exposure therapy. The therapist teaches the client relaxation techniques (like those used in systematic desensitization) and then has the client use the start of worrying (i.e., exposure to worry itself) as a stimulus to relax, which competes with or suppresses worrying. (It is difficult to worry while relaxed.) In addition, cognitive techniques may be used to challenge and change the client's belief in the importance or likelihood of the things worried about. Acceptance techniques (see Chapter 27) may also help the client realize that worrying or not worrying will not make bad events more likely to occur—that is, the client is taught to make self-statements to the effect that worry by itself has no effect on things worried about.

Obsessive-Compulsive Disorder

A person suffering from an obsessive-compulsive disorder may experience unwanted intrusive thoughts (called an obsession) or feel impelled to engage in unproductive repetitive behaviors (called a compulsion), or both. Unlike a person with generalized anxiety disorder, a person with obsessive-compulsive disorder obsesses or worries about a specific thing. In addition, obsessions and compulsions tend to go together in that obsessions seem to cause anxiety that can only be reduced by engaging in compulsive behavior. For example, a person might obsess about someone breaking into his or her office overnight, feel anxious about it, and then compulsively check that his or her office door is locked before leaving each evening. A person with obsessive-compulsive disorder is not satisfied with just checking once—as would someone who does not have this problem—but will check over and over before finally leaving the workplace.

Some other common examples of obsessive-compulsive behaviors are obsessing about catching a terrible disease from germs, resulting in constant hand washing; obsessing about hitting a pedestrian, leading to constantly retracing one's route while driving to make sure there are no injured pedestrians lying on or beside the road; and obsessing about hurting one's children, leading to avoiding using knives and other potentially dangerous objects in their presence.

Treatment   An effective treatment for obsessive-compulsive disorder is *in vivo* exposure and response prevention (Kozak & Foa, 1996). That is, the client is encouraged to engage in behavior leading to the obsession while being prevented from engaging in the compulsive behavior.Suppose, for example, that a client experiences obsessive thoughts about germs when touching unwashed objects, which causes considerable anxiety. Suppose further that engaging in a variety of compulsive washing rituals appears to be maintained by anxiety reduction. An exposure and response prevention treatment would involve requesting the client to touch particular "contaminated" objects while refraining from performing the washing ritual. The rationale behind this approach is that having the obsession occur without the subsequent anxiety-reducing compulsive behavior allows the anxiety elicited by the obsession to occur in full strength and hence to extinguish. Often a graduated approach is used. For example, a parent who is obsessed with the fear of harming his children with a knife may be encouraged to first hold a butter knife in the presence of the children, then a table knife, then a paring knife, and finally a butcher knife.

Cognitive therapy might also be used to change the self-statements the client makes that help to maintain the obsession (Taylor, Thordarson, & Sochting, 2004). For example, a person who is deathly afraid of germs might be taught to say privately that a normal amount of hand washing is sufficient to protect against any germs he or she is likely to encounter. Acceptance procedures (see Chapter 27) may help an individual learn that thoughts are not powerful controllers of behavior. The parent who obsesses about harming his children may be taught to regard these thoughts simply as normal "mental garbage" or "mental background noise," with no bearing on the parent's actual feelings or behavior toward his children.

Posttraumatic Stress Disorder

The classic cases of posttraumatic stress disorder (PTSD) occurred during World War I, when many soldiers exposed to artillery bombardment exhibited what was then called "shell shock." The ability of these soldiers to function was extremely impaired, and many were branded as cowards. It is now recognized that not only battlefield conditions, but also any extraordinary stressful or traumatic event—such as being physically or sexually abused, being in a serious traffic accident, or witnessing a catastrophic event—can produce PTSD. The impaired functioning by someone with this disorder appears to be due to the individual's attempts to avoid thinking about the traumatic event (or events) and hence to avoid stimuli that remind the individual of the event. Since there are many such stimuli, the effort to avoid them consumes a large proportion of the individual's time and energy.

Treatment   The most effective treatment for PTSD is long-term vicarious exposure to the event or events that caused the problem (Foa, 2000; Resick & Schnicke, 1992). This may be done in imagination, talking about the traumatic event(s) with a therapist, writing about the traumatic event(s), or writing and talking about the event(s). In this way, the emotionality elicited by stimuli related to the trauma will extinguish and the debilitating attempts to avoid those stimuli will decrease. Individuals with PTSD often experience feelings of inadequacy and low self-worth, and some psychologists have suggested that cognitive procedures may be helpful in counteracting these feelings with more positive beliefs. However, there is some evidence that cognitive procedures in combination with exposure techniques may not be helpful and may actually interfere with the beneficial effects of exposure techniques (Foa, 2000). (For recent developments in the treatment of PTSD, see the special issue of *Behavior Modification*, Vol. 29, January 2005).

DEPRESSION

Everyone has felt depressed at some point. Usually the feeling occurs when some significant reinforcer or potential reinforcer has been removed from our lives. A poor grade on a test in a particular course, for example, may cause a student to feel depressed because of the potential loss of the prospect of a good grade in the course. Most people get over their depressions fairly quickly as they find other reinforcers to compensate for the reinforcers they have lost. Some people, however, suffer from chronic depression, that is, depression that lasts for a very long time and never seems to get better. These individuals often seek therapy for their depression.

Given what we know about depression in normal individuals, a reasonable theory about individuals with chronic depression is that they are lacking in reinforcers. Of course, many rich people are depressed. Thus, a reasonable hypothesis is that it is contingent reinforcement—not just reinforcement per se—that is important in stemming depression.

Treatment   Following the above hypothesis, behavioral approaches in the 1970s demonstrated some success treating depression by increasing the contingent reinforcers in chronically depressed individuals' lives (Ferster, 1973; Lewinsohn, 1975). One way they did that was by encouraging depressed individuals to seek out reinforcers—for example, to go to parties, take up hobbies, read books, and go to movies. Encouraging persons with clinical depression to participate in exercise programs is also helpful (Tkachuk & Martin, 1999). Enlisting significant others, such as spouses, to reinforce the behavior of seeking and sampling new reinforcers is another strategy that behavior therapists have tried. Many of our reinforcers are social, that is, they come from other people, and it takes a certain amount of social skills to access these reinforcers. People with depression are often lacking in these skills. Thus a component of therapy for depression often involves teaching the client social skills.

Although a behavioral approach to the treatment of depression had a promising start in the 1970s, that approach lost momentum in the 1980s when Beck's famous cognitive therapy (discussed in the previous chapter) became popular. Beck's theory (Beck et al., 1979) stated that depressed individuals have core beliefs (called cognitive schemas) that influence them to make negative interpretations (or cognitive distortions) of life events, which, lead to depressed behavior. It follows, then, as described in Chapter 27, that a major component of cognitive therapy to treat depression is cognitive restructuring to help clients overcome their faulty thinking. In the late 1990s the behavioral approach in the treatment of depression reemerged (Jacobson, Martell, & Dimidjain, 2001; Martell, Addis, & Jacobson, 2001). Beck's cognitive therapy has always included behavioral homework assignments, and research now indicates that assignments to increase contingent reinforcers (called *behavioral activation*, see Chapter 27) can stand alone in the treatment of depression (Gortner et al., 1998; Jacobson et al., 1996; Martell et al., 2004).

ALCOHOL PROBLEMS

Excessive alcohol drinking is a major health problem, one that costs the economy billions of dollars each year in poor job performance and absenteeism (Taylor, 2003). Most alcohol treatment agencies distinguish between problem drinkers and alcoholics (Taylor, 2003). *Problem drinkers* experience substantial social, occupational or medical problems resulting from alcohol consumption. In addition to these problems, *alcoholics* also show alcohol dependence (more of it is needed to produce the reinforcing effect) and withdrawal symptoms when they stop drinking.

Treatment   As is well known, an organization called Alcoholics Anonymous (AA) has developed a program of social support that has had success in helping individuals with alcohol problems. Not everyone with an alcohol problem, however, is willing to accept the philosophy and regimen of AA, which includes the goal of abstinence for life. Fortunately, research shows that behavior therapy can be as or more effective than AA (Emmelkamp, 2004).

Behavioral treatment procedures have been successful in helping problem drinkers to learn to drink in moderation (Emmelkamp, 2004; Walters, 2000). A program developed by Sobell and Sobell (1993) teaches problem drinkers to use goal setting to drink in moderation, to control "triggers" (S^Ds) for drinking, to learn problem-solving skills to avoid high-risk situations, to engage in self-monitoring to detect controlling cues and maintaining consequences of drinking behaviors, and to practice all of these techniques with various homework assignments.

Behavioral programs have utilized a number of components to treat alcoholics, including: (a) a *motivational interview* in which the therapist asks the client questions about the problem, the answers to which act as motivational establish-
Note 3 ing operations for change (i.e., reduced drinking of alcohol becomes reinforcing

and therefore strengthens behavior that leads to reduced drinking) (Miller, 1996); (b) *coping-skills training* to teach clients to deal with stressors that are thought to cause excessive alcohol consumption; (c) *contingency contracting* (see Chapter 26) to provide reinforcers for work, social, and recreational activities that do not involve alcohol; and (d) *strategies to prevent relapse* (see Chapter 26). These strategies are discussed in more detail in Emmelkamp (2004). In general, however, behavioral treatment programs for alcoholics have achieved only modest success (Taylor, 2003).

EATING DISORDERS AND OBESITY

Several eating disorders have been identified: (a) bulimia nervosa, (b) anorexia nervosa, (c) binge eating disorder, and (d) obesity. In the first two the client is malnourished and obsessed with being thin, the chief difference being that in bulimia the client engages in frequent binges followed by purging or taking laxatives in an attempt to counteract the effects of binging, while in anorexia the client rarely eats or eats very little. In binge eating, the client may be of normal weight or greater-than-normal weight, while in obesity the client is sufficiently overweight enough to cause a health risk.

Treatment Bulimia and anorexia have been extremely resistant to treatment. Some success has been achieved with bulimia by starting with behavioral procedures followed by cognitive procedures (Wilson & Fairburn, 2002). The former might involve reinforcement for going for a specified amount of time, which is gradually increased, between binges, and for eating regular meals at specified times. The cognitive procedures involve attempts to counteract the client's unrealistic beliefs about food and her (most individuals with bulimia are female) weight and appearance. Most individuals with bulimia and anorexia have very poor body images, in that they see themselves as fat when in fact they are thin to the point of being malnourished. Both behavioral and cognitive procedures have been considerably less effective with clients with anorexia than with clients with bulimia. This may be because individuals with anorexia tend to experience extreme anxiety at any attempt to get them to behave in any way that would be less than perfect in their belief systems.

For overweight and obese clients, whether they binge or not, behavioral procedures are effective in weight reduction (Craighead, 2004; Faith, Fontaine, Cheskin, & Allison, 2000). They focus on helping such individuals to adopt long-term lifestyle changes in eating habits and exercise, and in their attitudes toward both (Faith et al., 2000). The programs tend to be more effective if the emphasis is on choosing the right foods rather than on calorie reduction. Behavioral components in such programs are likely to include: (a) *self-monitoring*, including daily records of foods eaten and their caloric contents, and body weight; (b) *stimulus control*, such as restricting eating at home to a specific location (e.g., the kitchen table); (c) *changing rate of eating*, by having clients lay down utensils between bites or take short breaks between courses; (d) *behavioral contracting*, such as having clients sign a contract in which they agree to lose a certain amount of weight in a specified period of time, in return for which they will receive some desired reinforcer (see Chapter 26), and (e) *relapse prevention strategies* (such as those discussed in Chapter 26).

COUPLE DISTRESS

Couple distress occurs when one or both individuals in an intimate (e.g., marital) relationship is experiencing dissatisfaction with the relationship. There are probably as many specific reasons for couple distress as there are distressed relationships. Behavior therapists, however, generally start with the premise that the underlying cause is that there are more negative than positive interactions or communications in the relationship. For example, while communicating, one partner may tend to make sarcastic or other hostile statements that are reciprocated by hostile statements from the other partner, leading to a breakdown in communication (or worse) between the two individuals.

Treatment   Behavioral couple therapy typically includes a number of components, including the following (Snyder & Abbott, 2004): (a) *instigation of positive exchanges*—each individual is asked to increase behaviors that are pleasing to the other partner (such as displaying affection, showing respect, expressing appreciation, see Figure 28–1); (b) *communication training*—each individual is taught to express thoughts and feelings concerning what is liked and appreciated about the other, to help the other express his or her feelings and to be an effective listener; (c) *problem-solving training*—couples learn to use their communication skills to systematically identify and solve problems and conflicts in their relationship (see problem-solving training in Chapter 27); and (d) *programming generality*—clients learn to monitor their relationship for specific critical signs of a relapse, and to continue using the problem-solving and conflict-resolution techniques that they learned in therapy. In an approach called *integrative behavioral couple therapy*, some therapists also incorporate acceptance procedures and exercises (see Chapter 27) to teach partners to accept emotional responses that each

Figure 28–1   What behavioral strategies might be used to help couples increase their rate of positive interactions and decrease their rate of negative interactions with each other?

partner has to the other (Christensen & Jacobson, 2000; Christensen, Sevier, Simpson, & Gattis, 2004).

SEXUAL DYSFUNCTION

There are several types of sexual dysfunction. In males the major types are (a) inability to have an erection and (b) premature ejaculation. In females the major types are (a) vaginismus (involuntary spasms of the vagina musculature that interfere with sexual intercourse), (b) dyspareunia (genital pain related to sexual intercourse), (c) inhibited orgasm, and (d) low sexual desire.

Treatment   A reasonable working hypothesis for many cases of sexual dysfunction is that anxiety is an important factor. In males the anxiety may be fear of performing poorly, which therefore becomes a self-fulfilling prophecy (i.e., the individual performs poorly because he is afraid he will perform poorly). In females the anxiety may be fear of the sex act itself. In either case, exposure programs appear to be most effective. Based on pioneering work by Masters and Johnson (1970), therapists generally recommend that the couple engage in pleasurable stimulation of each other in a relaxing atmosphere without expectation of, or pressure to, engage in intercourse (Leibum & Rosen, 2000; Wincze & Carey, 2001). Masturbation by the woman partner may also be encouraged to help her learn to experience organism if that is one of the issues. Thus, both partners shift the goal from performance to that of experiencing pleasure.

Although behavioral homework assignments have proven effective in treating many cases of sexual dysfunction, we caution you against taking an oversimplistic view of this problem. Sexual dysfunction can result from many causes, including medical diseases, relationship difficulties, lifestyle factors, and age-related changes, to mention a few. Wiegel, Wincze, and Barlow (2004) have described a range of assessments that should be used by a therapist before attempting to treat a case of sexual dysfunction. We also should point out that, since the development of Viagra and other drugs, sexual dysfunction treatment has become increasingly medicalized (Wiegel et al., 2004). Future research is needed to compare the effects of behavior therapies and medical interventions for a variety of sexual dysfunctions.

HABIT DISORDERS

Many people suffer from frequent and repetitive behaviors that are inconvenient and annoying to themselves or others. These may include nail biting, lip biting, knuckle cracking, hair twirling, hair plucking, excessive throat clearing, muscle tics, and stuttering. In many cases these behaviors are similar to the compulsions described earlier in this chapter, except that they are not linked to obsessive thoughts.

Treatment   A method called *habit reversal* has been used effectively to treat a number of these disorders (Azrin & Nunn, 1973; Miltenberger, Fuqua, & Woods, 1998). This method typically consists of three components. First, the client learns to describe and identify the problem behavior. Second, the client learns and practices a behavior that is incompatible with or competes with the problem behavior. The client practices the competing behavior daily in front of a mirror and also engages in it immediately after an occurrence of the problem behavior. Third, for motivation, the client reviews the inconvenience caused by the disorder, records and graphs the behavior, and has a family member provide reinforcement for engaging in the treatment.

STUDY QUESTIONS

1. What is the purpose of this chapter?
2. What are empirically supported therapies? Why do empirically supported therapies often turn out to be behavioral or cognitive-behavioral therapies?
3. List three types of specific phobias, and give two examples of each.
4. Using an example, briefly describe the three phases of systematic desensitization of a specific phobia.
5. Describe the fundamental difference between flooding and systematic desensitization.
6. Briefly describe an example of how *in vivo* flooding might be used to treat a specific phobia.
7. Briefly describe an example of how participant modeling might be used to treat a specific phobia.
8. List and briefly describe four types of anxiety disorder.
9. What is a defining characteristic of exposure-based therapies?
10. Briefly describe an effective treatment for panic disorder with agoraphobia.
11. What is the distinction between obsessions and compulsions, and how might they be related?
12. Briefly describe an effective treatment for obsessive-compulsive disorder.
13. Briefly describe how cognitive therapy and acceptance procedures might be used in the treatment of an obsessive-compulsive disorder. Describe an example of each.
14. In several sentences, describe an effective treatment for posttraumatic stress disorder.
15. Describe a behavioral theory about the cause of depression, and how this suggests a possible treatment for depression.
16. What are the components of Sobell and Sobell's program for problem drinkers?
17. Briefly describe four components of a behavioral treatment for alcoholics.
18. Describe four types of eating disorders. Which has behavior therapy been most effective with?
19. List and briefly describe four behavioral strategies for treating obesity?
20. List and briefly describe four components of behavioral couples therapy.
21. Describe a general behavioral approach to the treatment of sexual dysfunction.
22. Describe the three components of habit reversal used to treat a specific habit disorder.

NOTES AND EXTENDED DISCUSSION

1.   The evolution of managed care organizations (such as health management organizations or HMOs) in the U.S. health care system, and their influence in determining whether psychologists should be paid for providing treatment, has put pressure on psychologists to develop cost-effective treatments for a variety of psychological disorders. In 1993, a task force was developed by the Division of Clinical Psychology of the American Psychological Association to identify empirically supported psychotherapies,

create lists of such therapies, and disseminate that information to various stakeholders (such as HMOs). This task force has become a standing committee known as the Committee on Science and Practice and has published several reports. This Committee established guidelines for a treatment to be judged as an *empirically supported treatment* (EST). Using these guidelines and considering the research evidence, the committee has identified two levels of ESTs: "well established" and "probably efficacious." Treatments considered to be well established have to meet the following criteria: (a) at least two well-controlled studies with random assignment of participants demonstrating that the treatment is better than a pill or psychological placebo (either a therapeutically ineffective pill or a psychological procedure) or is equivalent to an existing, established treatment; (b) the treatment is described precisely in a manual; (c) client characteristics in the research were clearly specified; and (d) research was conducted in at least two independent research settings. The latest list of ESTs can be viewed at http://pantheon.yale.edu/~tat22/empirically_supported/treatments.htm.

   While efforts to establish a list of therapies that have proved to be effective in scientifically conducted clinical trials is laudatory, the effort has been met with criticism and has led to recommendations to improve the scientific viability of the process. Discussion of these topics can be found in a special issue of *Behavior Modification* (2003, Vol. 27, No. 3).

2.   A form of exposure therapy that has become increasingly popular over the past decade, as the cost of computer technology has fallen, is virtual reality therapy, which involves exposing individuals to realistic computer-generated anxiety-eliciting stimuli (such as images of numerous crawling spiders to treat cases of arachnophobia). Although this form of therapy is new, the results so far are encouraging (Lamson, 1997; North, North & Coble, 1997; Riva Wiederhold, & Molinari, 1998; Rothbaum, Hodges, Kooper, et al., 1995 Wiederhold & Wiederhold, 2004; Winerman, 2005).

3.   Substance abuse, not only of alcohol but of even more serious drugs such as cocaine and heroin, is a very destructive problem among many chronically unemployed and homeless people. These individuals often have little or nothing in the way of support groups to help them overcome their problems. Kenneth Silverman and colleagues at Johns Hopkins University Medical School have tackled this problem by implementing a voucher system, whereby individuals earn vouchers (which can be exchanged for goods and services) for drug-free urine samples, and by developing a therapeutic workplace, in which individuals are paid to work at jobs provided that they report to work drug-free (Silverman et al., 1998; Silverman, Svikis, Roblas, Stitzer, & Bigelow, 2001). Data indicate that the voucher system and the therapeutic workplace increase abstinence dramatically in many individuals with drug problems.

Study Questions on Notes

1.   What criteria must a treatment meet to be considered a well-established, empirically supported treatment by the American Psychological Association?
2.   What is virtual reality therapy?
3.   Briefly describe two strategies used by Silverman and colleagues to increase drug abstinence in chronically unemployed individuals.

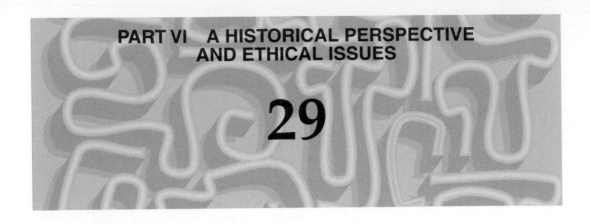

Giving It All
Some Perspective:
A Brief History

This chapter traces some of the highlights of the remarkable early growth of the field of behavior modification. It should be read with the following qualifications in mind:

1. Although we describe behavior modification as developing primarily through two major separate lines of influence, there are obvious cross-influences, blends, and off-shoots, and it might be possible to make a case for somewhat different histories.

Note 1   2. We identify what we consider to be major highlights of the development of behavior modification during its formative years: the 1950s, 1960s, and 1970s; we do not attempt a complete historical account. (For a more complete history of behavior modification, see Kadzin, 1978).

Note 2   3. We describe mainly historical highlights in North America.

In this history, we first consider two major orientations or traditions: one that emphasized operant conditioning and one that emphasized respondent conditioning. Then we discuss mixtures of these with other orientations.

THE OPERANT-CONDITIONING ORIENTATION:
APPLIED BEHAVIOR ANALYSIS

Note 3   In 1938, B. F. Skinner published *The Behavior of Organisms,* in which he described the results of experiments on the lever-pressing behavior of rats for food or water reinforcement and, on the basis of his findings, outlined the basic principles of operant conditioning, which he clearly distinguished from respondent conditioning. This pioneering work gradually influenced other experimental psychologists to begin studying the effects of contingencies of reinforcement on the behavior of rats and other animals.

Note 4
In 1950, Keller and Schoenfeld wrote an introductory psychology text titled *Principles of Psychology*. It was unlike any other text of its kind in that it discussed traditional topics in psychology primarily in terms of operant conditioning (and to a lesser extent, respondent conditioning) principles. Keller and Skinner had been graduate students together at Harvard University, and the Keller and Schoenfeld text was inspired largely by the work and writings of Skinner. *Principles of Psychology* contributed significantly to the development of the field of behavior analysis. Although less well known outside Skinnerian and operant circles, this introductory text had an important impact within the operant tradition.

In 1953 Skinner published *Science and Human Behavior*. In this book he offered his interpretation of how the basic behavior principles (which had been researched on lower organisms and are described in Part II of this text) influence the behavior of people in all kinds of everyday situations. Although little supporting data existed for Skinner's generalizations to humans, his interpretations influenced others to begin examining the effects of reinforcement variables on human behavior in a number of experimental and applied settings. The results of these efforts led to much of what has been described in this text as behavior modification. The highlights of this development prior to the 1980s are presented in the top panel of Table 29–1. (See Chapters 2, 27, and 28 for a discussion of developments in behavior modification since 1980.)

Many of the reports in the 1950s were demonstrations that positive reinforcement and extinction affect human behavior in predictable ways or case demonstrations that an application of a behavioral program could effect a desired behavior change. For example, Fuller (1949) reported a case in which an institutionalized bedridden adult with profound retardation was taught to raise his right arm to a vertical position when arm movements were appropriately shaped and a warm sugar-milk solution was used as the reinforcer. Greenspoon (1955) demonstrated that a simple social consequence (saying "mmm-hmm") could influence college students to say certain types of words. Azrin and Lindsley (1956), two of Skinner's graduate students, demonstrated that jellybean reinforcement could influence pairs of young children to cooperate in playing a simple game. Each of these experiments demonstrated that consequences influence human behavior in predictable ways. None of these experiments, however, was primarily practically oriented. One of the first published reports of the 1950s that concerned practical, applied problems was that of Ayllon and Michael (1959). With Michael as his PhD dissertation advisor, Ayllon conducted a number of behavioral demonstrations at the Saskatchewan Hospital, a psychiatric institution in Weyburn, Saskatchewan, Canada. These demonstrations showed how staff could use procedures such as reinforcement, extinction, and escape and avoidance conditioning to modify patient behaviors such as delusional talk, refusals to eat, and various disruptive behaviors.

Following Ayllon and Michael's article and several subsequent papers published by Ayllon and his colleagues from their work at Weyburn, similar demonstrations of behavioral control began to appear with some frequency in the

TABLE 29–1   SOME HISTORICAL HIGHLIGHTS OF BEHAVIOR
MODIFICATION AND BEHAVIOR THERAPY PRIOR TO 1980

	Pre-1950s	1950s	Early and Middle 1960s
OPERANT CONDITIONING (SKINNERIAN) ORIENTATION	Some basic research and theory (Skinner, 1938)	Two major texts (Keller & Schoenfeld, 1950; Skinner, 1953) Some human studies and applications: profoundly retarded (Fuller, 1949), schizophrenics (Lindsley, 1956), psychotics (Ayllon & Michael, 1959), verbal conditioning (Greenspoon, 1955), stuttering (Flanagan, Goldiamond, & Azrin, 1958) A basic operant research journal, with some applications (*Journal of the Experimental Analysis of Behavior*, 1958–)	Some major university training centers Several books of readings (e.g., Ulrich, Stachnik, & Mabry, 1966) More applications, many to "resistant" populations: e.g., retardation (Birnbrauer, Bijou, Wolf, & Kidder, 1965; Girardeau & Spradlin, 1964), autism (Ferster & DeMyer, 1962; Lovaas, 1966; Wolf, Risley, & Mees, 1964), hyperactivity (Patterson, 1965), delinquency (Schwitzgebel, 1964), psychotics (Isaacs, Thomas, & Goldiamond, 1960; Haughton & Ayllon, 1965) Child development (Bijou & Baer, 1961)
OFFSHOOTS AND MIXTURES			Premack Principle (Premack, 1965) Coverant control (Homme, 1965) Precision teaching (Lindsley, 1966) Modeling (Bandura & Walters, 1963) A major book of readings (Ullmann & Krasner, 1965), An applied journal (*Behavior Research and Therapy*, 1963–) Covert sensitization (Cautela, 1966)
RESPONDENT CONDITIONING (AND HULLIAN AND WOLPEAN) ORIENTATION	Some basic research and theory (Pavlov, 1927; Watson & Rayner, 1920) An early application of fear desensitization (Jones, 1924) An early application of assertion training (Salter, 1949)	Two major texts (Dollard & Miller, 1950; Wolpe, 1958) Applications of systematic desensitization, assertion training, and aversion therapy to a variety of phobias and behavioral excesses Comparisons of behavior therapy and psychotherapy (Eysenck, 1959)	Some major university training centers Several books of readings (e.g., Eysenck, 1960; Franks, 1964) More applications of systematic desensitization, assertion training, and aversion therapy to a variety of classic neurotic behaviors and sexual disorders

(continued)

early 1960s (see Table 29–1). This early work was characterized by two features: (a) Much of it was done with very resistant populations (such as persons with developmental disabilities, children with autism, and severely regressed psychiatric patients), who had not received a great deal of successful input from traditional psychology; and (b) many of the applications took place in institutional or highly controlled settings. A notable exception to this early trend is Bijou and Baer's (1961) interpretation of child development from a strictly behavioral perspective.

In 1965, Ullmann and Krasner published their influential collection of readings, *Case Studies in Behavior Modification* (see the "offshoots and mixtures" panel in Table 29–1). This was the first book with "behavior modification" in its title. In

TABLE 29–1   *(CONTINUED)*

Late 1960s	1970s
Additional major university training centers Isolated undergraduate and graduate courses in many universities Additional books describing applied research and procedures applicable to a variety of areas: e.g., education (Skinner, 1968), parenting (Patterson & Gullion, 1968), community work (Tharp & Wetzel, 1969), mental hospitals (Schaefer & Martin, 1969) Additional applications to a variety of areas, including self-control, delinquency, university teaching, marriage counseling, sexual behaviors, and academic skills An applied journal (*Journal of Applied Behavior Analysis,* 1968–)	Many "how-to-do-it" books in a variety of areas Behavior modification procedures described for many "traditional" areas of psychology (e.g., social, developmental, personality, abnormal, and clinical) Many other helping professions adopting behavior modification procedures (see Chapter 2) Wide variety of individual, institutional, and community applications and research
Token economies (Ayllon & Azrin, 1968) Contingency contracting (Homme, Csanyi, Gonzales, & Rechs, 1969) Formulation of social learning theory (Bandura, 1969) Two major books (Bandura, 1969, Franks, 1969) Implosive therapy (Stampfl & Levis, 1967)	Emergence of cognitive behavior modification, social learning theory, and eclectic behavior therapy Numerous behavior modification–behavior therapy conferences and workshops Concern for behavior modification–behavior therapy as a profession, and for controls against misapplications Mixed paraprofessional and professional organizations (e.g., Association for Behavior Analysis, 1974–) Professional organizations (Association for the Advancement of Behavior Therapy, 1970–; Behavior Research and Therapy Society, 1970–; European Association of Behavior Therapy, 1971–) More journals specializing in behavior modification (see Note 2 in Chapter 2)
Several major university training centers Additional books (e.g., Wolpe, 1969) More applications to phobias, anger, asthmatic attacks, , frigidity homosexuality, insomnia, speech disorders, exhibitionism, and other behaviors	Many additional books, publications and training workshops; much additional research

addition to collecting a number of case histories and research reports by other authors, Ullmann and Krasner compared behavior modification and the behavioral model with more traditional psychotherapeutic strategies and the medical model. Although their book is not solely in the operant tradition, because they also included many studies and discussions in the Pavlovian–Hullian tradition (to be discussed in the next section of this chapter), it undoubtedly had a significant impact on furthering behavior modification and providing, in one source, information on much of the preliminary work in this area.

In the late 1960s, the operant conditioning orientation began to spread throughout the Western Hemisphere. Several university training centers were developed; many universities initiated at least one or two courses in behavior modification at both the graduate and undergraduate levels; and applications spread to normal school settings, to university teaching, to homes, and to other populations and locations.

By the 1970s, the operant orientation had grown considerably. As discussed in Chapter 1, this approach is frequently referred to as *applied behavior analysis*. It is somewhat surprising to find contemporary textbooks that suggest that this approach has been used primarily on client populations with "limited cognitive capacity" and where considerable environmental control is a potential characteristic of the treatment procedures. Although this was true in the 1950s and 1960s, numerous applications now occur in virtually all walks of life (see Chapters 2, 27, and 28).

It has also been claimed that behavior analysts ignore the causes of problem behavior. In the early stages of behavior modification, there was some justification for the charge, for behavior analysts were emphasizing how managing consequences (e.g., powerful reinforcement contingencies) could alleviate problem behavior regardless of its causes. During the 1970s, however, some behavior analysts (e.g., Carr, 1977; Johnson & Baumeister, 1978; Rincover, 1978; Rincover, Cook, Peoples, & Packard, 1979) began to stress the importance of understanding the causes of—that is, the conditions producing or maintaining—problem behavior. This led to the pioneering of functional analysis methodology by Iwata, Dorsey, Slifer, Bauman, and Richman (1982), which a number of prominent behavior analysts hailed as a major new development in the field (e.g., Laties & Mace, 1993). In 1994, the *Journal of Applied Behavior Analysis* published a special issue (Vol. 27, No. 2) devoted to functional analysis approaches to behavioral assessment and treatment. It should be noted, however, that the causes functional analysis attempts to uncover are environmental causes, not the hypothetical inner causes that are often speculated about by nonbehavioral (e.g., psychoanalytic) approaches.

THE RESPONDENT CONDITIONING (AND HULLIAN AND WOLPEAN) ORIENTATION

Late in the 19th century, Russian physiologist I. P. Pavlov conducted experiments on digestion, which won him the Nobel Prize in Medicine in 1904. While doing this research, Pavlov discovered that stimuli paired with food will also elicit salivation, and embarked on a systematic study of what is now called *Pavlovian, classical,* or *respondent conditioning* (see Chapter 14). Results of this work were published in a classic book titled *Conditioned Reflexes* (Pavlov, 1927). (A more accurate translation of Russian would have been "conditional reflexes"—i.e., reflexes that are *conditional* on a pairing process.) In 1913, John B. Watson published an influential paper in which he argued that most human activities could be explained as learned habits. After becoming familiar with the work of Pavlov and another Russian physiologist, V. M. Bechterev (see Note 2), Watson (1916) adopted the conditioned reflex as the unit of habit and argued that most complex activities were due to respondent conditioning (this, of course, was before Skinner distinguished between operant and respondent conditioning). At that time, some of his extreme and unsupported generalizations shook the foundations of much of traditional psychology. Watson followed his 1916 paper with a classic experiment in which he demonstrated that human emotional reactions could be conditioned in an experimental setting (Watson & Rayner, 1920; see also Chapter 15 of this text).

During the next 20 years a number of somewhat isolated reports of the application of respondent conditioning procedures to various behaviors appeared in the literature (for a list of many of these, see Yates, 1970). None of these applications, however, appears to have had any sustained impact on the development of behavior modification as we know it today.

Another influence closely related to the respondent conditioning orientation was the work of American learning theorist Clark Hull (1943, 1952). Hull, an early contemporary of Skinner, developed a learning theory that tended to capitalize on both operant conditioning as described by Skinner and respondent conditioning as described by Pavlov, meshed together in a theory that did not distinguish between the two types of conditioning. According to Hull, reinforcement was involved in Pavlovian as well as in operant conditioning. Hull did not attempt to interpret a wide variety of human behavior to the extent that Skinner did (cf. Hull, 1952, with Skinner, 1953). Two other psychologists, Dollard and Miller (1950), however, translated a variety of Freudian psychodynamic concepts (which, despite their lack of empirical support, were extremely popular in those days) into the language of Hull's learning theory.

Within this Pavlovian–Hullian tradition, two significant developments occurred in the 1950s, both no doubt influenced to some extent by Dollard and Miller's book and by the learning theory of Edwin Guthrie (1935). One development occurred in South Africa, where Joseph Wolpe began some research and theorizing that drew heavily on Pavlovian conditioning, Hullian theory, and the earlier work of J. B. Watson, Mary Cover Jones, and British physiologist, Sir Charles Sherrington. Sherrington (1947) had noted that if one group of muscles is stimulated, an antagonistic muscle group will be inhibited, and vice versa. He called this *reciprocal inhibition* and postulated it to be a general process acting throughout the nervous system. Wolpe extended the principle of reciprocal inhibition to state that if a response that is incompatible with fear or anxiety can be made to occur to a stimulus that normally produces fear or anxiety, then that stimulus will cease to elicit the fear reaction. In 1958, Wolpe published his first book on reciprocal inhibition. It was to provide a major force in the launching of the modern era of the respondent tradition of behavior therapy. Wolpe usually used relaxation responses to reciprocally inhibit fear or anxiety in a procedure called *systematic desensitization* (see Chapter 27).

Also during the 1950s Hans Eysenck in England was instrumental in criticizing traditional Freudian psychoanalytic treatment procedures and advocating learning-theory procedures as alternatives. In 1960 Eysenck published a book of readings, *Behaviour Therapy and the Neuroses*, in which he presented a number of case histories where variations of reciprocal inhibition and respondent conditioning procedures were used in clinical therapy. The respondent conditioning orientation of behavior therapy has occasionally been referred to as the "Wolpe–Eysenck" school.

In the early 1960s Wolpe moved to the United States. He began a program at Temple University in which he trained therapists in his particular version of behavior therapy. In 1963 Eysenck founded the journal *Behaviour Research and Therapy,* which publishes operant-oriented studies as well as studies with a Pavlovian flavor. As indicated in the bottom panel of Table 29–1, behavior therapy within the respondent orientation grew quite rapidly in the 1960s and 1970s and included applications to a variety of phobic and neurotic disorders. On June 30, 1984, the behavior therapy unit at Temple University Medical Center ceased to exist. Wolpe (1985) attributed termination of the unit to misunderstanding of behavior therapy by psychodynamic psychotherapists. Nevertheless, Wolpe continued to contribute actively to the field of behavior therapy until his death in 1997.

MIXTURES AND OFFSHOOTS OF THE TWO MAJOR ORIENTATIONS

Much of the early history of behavior modification and behavior therapy clearly falls within either the operant orientation or the Pavlovian–Hullian–Wolpean orientation. Most other developments tend to be offshoots of one or the other of these traditions or fall in a gray area somewhere in between (see the "offshoots and mixtures" panel of Table 29–1).

In addition to the two major orientations, two broad theoretical models of behavior modification emerged in the 1970s: social learning theory and cognitive behavior modification.

Characteristics of *social learning theory* were outlined by Julian Rotter in 1954 in his book, *Social Learning and Clinical Psychology*. The most influential of the social learning theorists, however, has been Albert Bandura (1969, 1977, 1986, 1996). His approach is "social" in the sense that it places great emphasis on the social contexts in which behavior is acquired and maintained. In addition to basic principles of respondent and operant conditioning, Bandura has strongly emphasized the importance of *observational learning*. By watching other people act and by observing what happens to them, we can then imitate their behavior (see also the previous discussion of modeling in Chapter 18). Bandura also emphasizes *cognitive mediational processes* as an important influence on behavior. Based on prior experience with environmental influences as well as on current perceptions of environmental events, an individual is said to develop cognitive rules and strategies that can serve to determine future actions. An important cognitive mediational process, for example, is what Bandura calls *self-efficacy* (Bandura, 1982, 1996). This refers to a belief that one can perform adequately in a particular situation. In Bandura's words, "Given appropriate skills and adequate incentives . . . efficacy expectations are a major determinant of peoples' choices of activities, how much effort they will expend, and how long they will sustain effort in dealing with stressful situations" (1977, p. 194). (As discussed in Chapter 27, we suggest that cognitions such as self-efficacy can be explained in terms of operant and respondent conditioning.)

A cognitive framework for therapy was contained in Bandura's book, *Principles of Behavior Modification* (1969). However, *cognitive behavior modification,* as represented by individuals such as Ellis and Beck (see Chapter 27), is not to be equated with social learning theory. Social learning theory, with its emphasis on the regulation of behavior by external stimulus events, environmental consequences, and cognitive mediational processes, provides a way of explaining behavior in a variety of contexts. Cognitive behavior modification, however, has focused mainly on explaining maladaptive behaviors in terms of dysfunctional thinking, and it includes cognitive restructuring as a primary treatment component.

In addition to these four theoretical models of behavior modification, a large group of practicing behavior therapists subscribe to an eclectic approach. Lazarus (1971) has been considered as representative of this position. Referring to what he calls *multimodal behavior therapy,* Lazarus (1971, 1976) argued that practicing clinicians should not restrict themselves to a particular theoretical framework but should use a variety of behavior techniques along with psychoanalytic and other traditional clinical techniques, provided that these have some empirical support.

As indicated by this brief discussion of various conceptualizations of behavior modification, there is some disagreement among behavior modifiers on theoretical issues. Nevertheless, there is also considerable agreement.

BEHAVIOR THERAPY, BEHAVIOR MODIFICATION, AND APPLIED BEHAVIOR ANALYSIS

Some writers use the terms *behavior modification* and *behavior therapy* interchangeably. Other writers use either *applied behavior analysis* or *behavior modification* when referring to the principles discussed in the first part of this text. What is the historical use of these terms? It appears that Lindsley, Skinner, and Solomon (1953) were the first to use the term *behavior therapy.* They did so in a report describing some research in which psychotic patients in a mental hospital were reinforced with candy or cigarettes for pulling a plunger. However, those within the operant orientation subsequently made little use of the term (at least, until the 1970s). Although Lazarus (1958) next used the term *behavior therapy* when he applied it to Wolpe's reciprocal inhibition framework, the term became popular among those within the Pavlovian–Hullian–Wolpean orientation after Eysenck (1959) used it to describe procedures published by Wolpe.

The first use of the term *behavior modification* appears to be in a chapter by R. I. Watson (1962). Since that time, many writers have distinguished between behavior modification, with its roots in operant conditioning, and behavior therapy, with its roots in Pavlovian conditioning and Hullian theory. Others, however, have not made that distinction consistently. Ullmann and Krasner (1965), for example, frequently used *behavior modification* and *behavior therapy* interchangeably. Also, critics tended to lump operant psychology with other learning theories (Chomsky, 1959) and behavior modification with Pavlovian conditioning, behavior therapy, conditioning therapy, and learning-based therapies (see, e.g., Breger & McGaugh, 1965). The term *applied behavior analysis* was made popular in 1968 with the founding of the *Journal of Applied Behavior Analysis.* Some of the

TABLE 29–2 A COMPARISON OF THE USES OF THE TERMS *BEHAVIOR THERAPY, BEHAVIOR MODIFICATION,* AND *APPLIED BEHAVIOR ANALYSIS*

1960s and 1970s	
Behavior Therapy	Behavior Modification
1. The term used most often by followers of the Pavlovian–Wolpean orientation and followers of the cognitive orientation (who tended to use it interchangeably with the term *cognitive behavior modification*).	1. The term used most often by followers of the operant orientation.
2. The term tended to be used by behavioral psychologists and psychiatrists who were concerned primarily with treatment in traditional clinical settings. (For a historical time line of behavior therapy in psychiatric settings, see Malatesta, AuBuchon, & Bluch, 1994.)	2. The term tended to be used by behavior specialists in schools, homes and other settings that were not primarily the domain of the clinical psychologist and psychiatrist.
3. The term tended to be used to refer to behavioral treatments conducted in the therapist's office by means of verbal interaction ("talk therapy") between therapist and client.	3. The term tended to be used for behavioral treatments carried out in the natural environment as well as in special training settings.
4. The term was associated with an experimental foundation that was based primarily on human studies in clinical settings.	4. The term was associated with an experimental foundation in basic operant research with animals and humans, in addition to experimental studies in applied settings.

1980s to the Present
• The term **behavior therapy** continues to be used as described above.
• The term **applied behavior analysis** is used increasingly by followers of the operant orientation as described in the right-hand column above.
• The term **behavior modification** tends to have a somewhat broader meaning and includes both behavior therapy and applied behavior analysis.

distinctions that have tended to characterize the uses of these different terms are presented in Table 29–2.

In spite of these historical distinctions, the terms are often used interchangeably. In our view, however, the term *behavior modification* has acquired a broader meaning than the other terms. And, of course, the term *behavior therapy* is clearly less appropriate than *applied behavior analysis* or *behavior modification* when dealing with nondysfunctional behavior, such as the application of a Personalized System of Instruction to normal education or organizational behavior management to the operation of a small business. As indicated in Chapter 1, we suggest that the term *behavior modification* subsume both *behavior therapy* and *applied behavior analysis*. Behavior therapy is behavior modification carried out on dysfunctional behavior, generally in a clinical setting. Applied behavior analysis is behavior modification in which there has been an attempt to analyze or clearly demonstrate controlling variables of the behavior of concern. Behavior modification, we suggest, includes all explicit applications of behavior principles to improve specific behavior—whether or not in clinical settings and whether or not controlling variables have been explicitly demonstrated—which is how we have used the term in this book.

THE FUTURE OF BEHAVIOR MODIFICATION

Behavior modification has been applied to a wide variety of individual and social problems. Moreover, more and more of these applications have been concerned with prevention and social engineering in addition to amelioration of existing problems. There is no doubt that the helping professions are increasingly adopting behavior modification procedures, including such professions as social work, medicine, rehabilitation medicine, nursing, education, preventive dentistry, psychiatric nursing, psychiatry, public health, and clinical and community psychology. Applications are also occurring with increasing frequency in such areas as business, industry, sports, physical education, recreation, and the promotion of healthy lifestyles (see Chapter 2). The future of behavior modification appears to be bright. Someday, a thorough knowledge of behavior techniques may become an accepted necessity in our culture and will be taught to children in elementary school along with good hygiene and physical fitness. Perhaps these children will grow up to see a world in which positive applications of behavior principles will be second nature to everyone and will result in a happy, informed, skillful, productive culture without war, poverty, prejudice, or pollution.

STUDY QUESTIONS

1. How might you answer the question, "What is behavior modification?" (See Chapter 1.)
2. How did Skinner's *Behavior of Organisms* and *Science and Human Behavior* influence the initial development of behavior modification?
3. Discuss Keller's contribution to the development of behavior modification (see text and Note 4).
4. Many of the early reports in the operant tradition in the 1950s were straightforward experiments that demonstrated that consequences influence human behavior. Briefly, describe two such experiments.
5. Briefly describe one of the first published reports (a very influential one) that concerned practical applications within the operant tradition.
6. What is the *Journal of the Experimental Analysis of Behavior*?
7. The publications of the early 1960s within the operant orientation seem to have been characterized by two features. What were they?
8. Was the influential book *Case Studies in Behavior Modification* strictly within the operant orientation? Why or why not?
9. What concept did J. B. Watson adopt from Pavlov? How did Watson use this concept?
10. What behavior therapy procedure do we credit to Joseph Wolpe?
11. What dual role did Hans Eysenck play in the development of behavior therapy in the 1950s?
12. What are the names of four major behavior modification/behavior therapy journals (see Table 29-1 and Note 2)?

13. Briefly describe four conceptual (or theoretical) models of behavior modification from the 1970s.
14. Describe four differences in the usage of the terms *behavior therapy* and *behavior modification* during the 1960s and 1970s. How do the terms *behavior therapy, behavior modification,* and *applied behavior analysis* tend to be used today?
15. If someone suggested, "Behavior modification is okay for some limited types of problems," what would you say?

NOTES AND EXTENDED DISCUSSION

1. The history of behavior modification is as long as the history of psychology, from which it emerged. Some of the more important precursors to the emergence of behavior modification are listed below.

Plato (427–347 B.C.) attributed behavior to something called the psyche (i.e., soul), which he believed is separate from the body and continues to exist even after death. His student Aristotle (384–322 B.C.) argued that the soul is simply the "form" or functioning of the body (including its behavior). Plato's view of the soul had a greater influence than Aristotle's did on early Western European theologians and philosophers.

The French philosopher Rene Descartes (1595–1650) was the first to articulate a clear distinction between the body and the soul. He maintained that the body is essentially a machine operating on the basis of reflexes and guidance from a soul comprised of an immaterial, nonspatially extended substance. His philosophy was contested in Britain by a long line of philosophers—from John Locke (1632–1704) to John Stuart Mill (1806–1873)—known as either the British Associationists or British Empiricists. In their discourses these individuals replaced the word "soul" with the more scientific-sounding term "mind," which stems from an Old English word pertaining to memory or thought. They endeavored to infer the "natural" (i.e., scientific) laws by which the mind forms associations that enable one to relate to the world.

A group of physiologists known as the Russian Reflexologists—most notably Ivan M. Sechenov (1829–1905) and his followers Ivan P. Pavlov (1849–1936) and Vladimir M. Bechterev (1857–1927)—picked up on Descartes' concept of reflexes and the British Empiricists' focus on associations. Bechterev and Pavlov independently performed experiments on establishing new reflexes, which Bechterev called "association reflexes" and Pavlov called "conditional reflexes." As noted in the text, their basic ideas were later incorporated into the behavioral approach.

In the United States, a group of psychologists called functionalists, led primarily by William James (1842–1910) at Harvard and John Dewey (1859–1952) at the University of Chicago, basing their approach on Darwin's theory of evolution, advocated studying the mind's role in the adaptation of the individual to its environment. This included both animal and human studies on learning, such as those of E. L. Thorndike (1874–1949).

John B. Watson (1878–1958), who had received his PhD from the University of Chicago, took functionalism a step further. He asserted that psychology, rather than being about the mind (which he regarded as a fictitious entity), should be purely and simply the science of behavior. Following Watson's exit from academic psychology, the behavioral approach opened to a new generation of leaders, as discussed in the text. For a more complete discussion of the emergence of the behavioral approach, see Pear, 2007).

2. In the 1950s important historical developments in behavior modification occurred concurrently in three countries: in South Africa, where Wolpe conducted his pioneering work on systematic desensitization; in England, where Eysenck spurred on the behavior modification movement by emphasizing dissatisfaction with traditional methods of psychotherapy; and in the United States, where Skinner and his colleagues were working within the operant conditioning orientation. During the 1960s and 1970s, however, most of the major books and research papers in behavior modification and behavior therapy were based on developments in the United States. For example, three of the first four major behavior therapy journals were published in the United States, and most of their articles were written in the United States (*Journal of Applied Behavior Analysis,* 1968–; *Behavior Therapy,* 1970; *Behavior Therapy and Experimental Psychiatry,* 1970–). Although the fourth journal (*Behaviour Research and Therapy,* 1963–) was edited by Eysenck in England, it too contained a large number of U.S. research reports. Since the 1970s, however, behavior modification has become a truly worldwide movement. Significant developments have occurred in Argentina (Blanck, 1983); in Asia (Oei, 1998); in Australia (Brownell, 1981; King, 1996; Schlesinger, 2004); in Brazil (Ardilla, 1982; Grassi, 2004); in Canada (Martin, 1981); in Chile (Ardilla, 1982); in Columbia (Ardilla, 1982; Lopez & Aquilar, 2003); in Costa Rica (Pal-Hegedus, 1991); in Cuba (Dattilio, 1999); in the Dominican Republic (Brownell, 1981); in England (Brownell, 1981); in France (Agathon, 1982; Cottraux, 1990); in Germany (Stark, 1980); in Ghana (Danguah, 1982); in Holland (Brownell, 1981); in Hungary (Tringer, 1991); in Israel (Brownell, 1981; Zvi, 2004); in Italy (Moderato, 2003; Sanivio, 1999); Scrimali & Grimaldi, 1993); in Ireland (Flanagan, 1991); in Japan (Sakano, 1993; Yamagami, Okuma, Morinaga, & Nakao, 1982); in Mexico (Ardilla, 1982); in New Zealand (Blampied, 1999, 2004); in Norway (Brownell, 1981); in Poland (Kokoszka, Popiel, & Sitarz, 2000; Suchowierska & Kozlowski, 2004); in Romania (David & Miclea, 2002); in Singapore (Banerjee, 1999); in Spain (Caballo & Buela-Casal, 1993); in South Korea (Kim, 2003); in Sri Lanka (DeSilva & Simarasinghe, 1985); in Sweden (Brownell, 1981; Carter, 2004); in Thailand (Mikulis, 1983); in the United Kingdom (Dymond, Chiesa, & Martin, 2003); in Uruguay (Zamora & Lima, 2000); and in Venezuela (Ardilla, 1982).

3. Burrhus Frederick Skinner was born on March 20, 1904, in Susquehanna, Pennsylvania. Well before his death on August 18, 1990, in Cambridge, Massachusetts, at the age of 86, Skinner had become the world's best-known living psychologist and its leading behaviorist. After receiving his bachelor of arts degree with a major in English at Hamilton College in upstate New York, Skinner was a somewhat unsuccessful writer during the next two years in New York City's Greenwich Village, and in Europe. He then entered Harvard to study psychology and received his doctorate in 1931. It was at Harvard that he formed a friendship with Fred Keller, a friendship that was to last over 60 years. After being a postdoctoral fellow at Harvard and then teaching at the University of Minnesota and at Indiana University, Skinner returned to Harvard as a professor in 1947. He remained associated with Harvard until his death. Skinner had a remarkable career and received numerous awards, including the Distinguished Scientific Award from the American Psychological Association (1958), the President's National Medal of Science (1968), and the Humanist of the Year Award from the American Humanist Society (1972). In addition to his basic theoretical and experimental contributions, Skinner published a utopian novel, *Walden Two* (1948b), worked on a project to teach pigeons to guide missiles during World War II (Skinner,

1960), and developed the concept of programmed instruction and teaching machines (Skinner, 1958). Skinner continued to be active throughout his academic career, publishing his most recent book in 1989. He leaves a tremendous legacy: His influence on psychology is as significant as Galileo's on physics and Darwin's on biology.

4. Fred S. Keller (1899–1996) made other major contributions. In 1961, he accepted a position at the University of Sao Paulo, Brazil, where he established the first operant conditioning course in that country. With his Brazilian colleagues, Keller also developed the Personalized System of Instruction, a behavior modification approach to university teaching that has the potential to revolutionize education (see Chapter 2). Keller contributed immeasurably to the development of behavior modification in Brazil. Former students of his, their students, and so on, continue to advance behavioral psychology in that country (e.g., see Grassi, 2004).

Study Questions on Notes

1. How did Aristotle's view of the soul differ from that of Plato?
2. What contribution did each of the following make to the behavioral approach:
   a. Descartes?
   b. the British Associationists?
   c. the Russian Reflexologists?
   d. the functionalists?
3. Name three countries that were important in the development of behavior modification in the 1950s and the person most associated with this development in each of these countries.
4. Cite three of Skinner's contributions other than his basic research and theoretical writings.
5. In what Latin American country did Keller accept an academic position in 1961, and what contribution did he make to behavior modification while there?

30

Ethical Issues

Throughout this book we have emphasized the ethical or moral concerns that one should always bear in mind when applying behavior modification. It would be a great tragedy if this powerful scientific technology were somehow to be used in ways that harmed rather than helped humanity. Because this is a real danger, it is fitting that we devote the final chapter of this book to a more detailed discussion of ethical concerns.

The history of civilization is a continuous story of the abuse of power. Throughout the ages, various groups have used the reinforcers and punishers at their disposal to control the behavior of less powerful groups (groups who had fewer reinforcers and punishers to deliver or without the means to deliver them contingent on selected target behaviors). The effect of this tradition has generally been to increase the reinforcements occurring to the more powerful at the expense of those occurring to the less powerful. From time to time, as the proportion of total reinforcement allotted to them steadily dwindled, groups subjected to this abuse of power have successfully revolted against their oppressors and have modified existing social structures, or established new ones, to check or eliminate the possibility of future abuses. Constitutions, bills of rights, and related political documents of modern states can be viewed as formal specifications of contingencies designed to control the behavior of those who control the behavior of others. In Western democracies, for example, we have moved from the era of the divine right of monarchs to one of "government by laws, not people." Moreover, with the

401

introduction of periodic popular elections, the people who are controlled by those who make the laws can exert a certain measure of reciprocal control. They can vote them out of office. In socialist and communist countries the revolutionary process concentrated on eliminating certain economic abuses rather than establishing democracy. In the absence of democracy other abuses developed, however, and many former communist countries are also now becoming more democratic. Nevertheless, the new social designs and practices that have emerged thus far have invariably fallen short of their objective; power continues to be abused throughout the world.

Because of this cultural history and because of people's personal experiences with others who have abused their power (i.e., used it for their own benefit and to the disadvantage of those over whom they exerted control), people have learned to react negatively to overt attempts to manage behavior. It should not be surprising, therefore, that in its early years, the term *behavior modification* evoked many negative reactions, ranging from suspicion to outright hostility. These early reactions were exasperated by the tendency to mistakenly equate behavior modification with such invasive procedures as electroconvulsive shock therapy, brain washing, and even torture. A survey of the *New York Times*, for example, indicated that, over a five-year period in the 1970s, the term *behavior modification* was used incorrectly approximately 50% of the time (Turkat & Feuerstein, 1978). Nowadays, however, as illustrated by reports in newspapers, television, and in movies, the general population is much more aware that behavior modification involves the systematic application of learning principles and techniques to help individuals manage their behavior. It is no secret that such applications are based on two assumptions: (a) Behavior can be controlled; and (b) it is desirable to do so to achieve certain objectives. Whether behavior is completely determined by environmental and genetic factors (everyone agrees that it is at least partially determined by these factors) makes for interesting philosophical discussions. From a practical point of view, however, it makes little difference one way or the other. The important point is that the amount of potential control over behavior is steadily increasing as a result of new discoveries in behavioral science and refinements in behavioral technology.

Extreme wariness is a healthy reaction to any new, far-reaching advance in science or technology. Perhaps civilization would be in less danger if more precautions had been taken early in the development of, say, atomic energy. The solution to the present problems stemming from scientific and technological advances, however, does not lie in attempting to turn the clock back to a seemingly more secure, prescientific era. Science and technology are not the problem. They are merely highly sophisticated means that people have developed for solving problems. The real problem is that people frequently misuse these tools. This is, of course, a behavioral problem. It would seem, therefore, as Skinner (1953, 1971) argued, that the science of behavior is the logical key to the solution of that problem. As with other powerful sciences and technologies, however, behavior modification can be misused. It therefore is important to have ethical guidelines to ensure that it is used for the good of society. In the next section we discuss ethics from a behavioral perspective. Then, we examine some common arguments against deliberately changing behavior. Finally, we turn to the question of how safeguards can be imposed on behavior modification to ensure that it will always be used in the best interests of humanity.

A BEHAVIORAL VIEW OF ETHICS

From a behavioral point of view, the term *ethics* refers to certain standards of behavior that are developed by a culture and promote the survival of that culture (Skinner, 1953, 1971). For example, stealing is considered unethical or wrong in many cultures because of the disruptive effect it has on the culture. Many ethical guidelines, such as "Stealing is wrong," likely evolved in prehistoric times. It might be that among a number of cultures that existed at a particular time before recorded history, behaving honestly in relation to material goods happened to be socially reinforced and stealing happened to be punished in some of these cultures but not in others (just as different cultures happened to reinforce different types of religious beliefs). Cultures in which honest behavior toward material possessions was not reinforced and stealing not punished, however, tended not to survive. There are a number of possible reasons for this. Perhaps the members of these cultures put so much effort into fighting each other that they were fatally vulnerable to invasions from other cultures, or they did not have enough time left over to produce an adequate amount of food for themselves. Perhaps, because of the constant fighting and bickering, these cultures were so unreinforcing to their members that the members defected in large numbers to other cultures, so that their former cultures became extinct due to lack of membership. Whatever the case, many cultures survived that reinforced nonstealing behavior and punished stealing—that is, cultures that considered nonstealing ethical or right and stealing unethical or wrong.

Thus, ethics has evolved as part of our culture in much the same way that the parts of our bodies have evolved; that is, ethics has contributed to the survival of our culture in much the same way that, for example, fingers and an opposable thumb have contributed to the survival of our species. This is not to say that people do not, at times, deliberately decide to formulate ethical rules for their culture. On the contrary, it is part of this cultural evolutionary process that at some point in the process some members of a culture begin to engage in such behavior because they have been conditioned to work toward the survival of their culture. One way in which to work toward the survival of one's culture is to formulate and enforce (through reinforcement as well as punishment) a code of ethics that strengthens that culture.

Ethical guidelines are an important source of behavioral control when immediate reinforcers influence an individual to behave in a way that leads to aversive stimuli for others. For example, whereas a thief is immediately reinforced by possession of the stolen goods, loss of those goods is aversive to the victims. To influence its members to be honest with each other, a culture might therefore develop and enforce the ethical guideline, "Thou shall not steal." Sometimes such guidelines are formulated into rules that specify legal contingencies (e.g., "If you steal another's possessions, you will be fined or sent to jail."). Sometimes such guidelines are expanded into rules that imply contingencies based on religious beliefs (e.g., "If you steal, you will go to hell, rather then heaven, when you die."). When members of a culture learn to follow such ethical guidelines, the guidelines exert rule-governed control over behavior (see Chapter 17). This is one way that people learn to emit behavior that is ethical and to refrain from behavior that is unethical. (For a more detailed discussion of rule-governed control over ethical [moral] behavior, we recommend that you visit www.dickmalott.com.)

With this behavioral view of ethics in mind, let's now examine whether or not behavior modifiers should attempt to deliberately change the behavior of others.

ARGUMENTS AGAINST DELIBERATELY
CONTROLLING BEHAVIOR

As we indicated earlier, because of our knowledge of the abuse of power throughout history, and because of our personal experience with others who have abused their

Note 1   power, we have learned to react negatively to overt attempts to change our behavior. Perhaps for these reasons, it is sometimes argued that all attempts to control behavior are unethical. A little reflection, however, shows that the goal of any social help profession (such as education, psychology, and psychiatry) can be achieved only to the extent that the practitioners of that profession exert control over behavior. The goal of education, for example, is to change behavior so that students will respond differently to their environment than they would had they not been educated. To teach a person to read, for example, is to change her behavior in such a way that she responds to signs, newspapers, books, and so forth in a manner that is different from the way in which she responded prior to being able to read. The goals of counseling, psychological treatment, and psychiatry likewise involve changing people's behavior so that they can function more effectively than they did prior to receiving professional help.

Perhaps because of the negative reactions of people to overt attempts to change behavior, many members of the helping professions do not like to think that they are controlling behavior. They prefer to see themselves as merely helping their clients to achieve control over their own behavior. Establishing self-control, however, is also a form of behavioral control. One simply teaches an individual to emit behavior that controls other behavior in some desired fashion. To do that, it is necessary to manage the behavior involved in self-control. In other words, it is necessary to control the behavior that controls other behavior. The helping practitioner may object that this is nevertheless not control on his or her part because the external influence over the client's behavior is withdrawn as soon as the practitioner is sure that the client is able to manage his or her own behavior. Actually, as we have emphasized repeatedly throughout this book, the practitioner has simply shifted the control to the natural environment. One may speak of this as "withdrawing control," but the control still continues, even though its form has changed. If the practitioner has been successful in achieving the behavioral objectives, the desired behavior will be maintained, and in that sense the practitioner's control or influence over the behavior will persist.

Some people will grant that helping practitioners necessarily engage in the management of behavior but will nevertheless argue that it is wrong to deliberately plan to change behavior. They regard planning to be "cold" and "mechanical" and believe that it interferes with warm, loving, "spontaneous" relationships

Note 2   that should exist between persons. It is difficult to determine where this objection to planning comes from, because we know of no logical or empirical evidence that supports it. On the contrary, most behavior modification programs that we know about are characterized by friendly, warm interactions between the individuals involved. Good behavior modifiers are genuinely interested in their clients as persons, and seem to find the time to interact with them on a personal level, just as other helping practitioners do. There is no doubt that some people show behavior that appears to be cold and mechanical. It is our impression, however, that such people are no more common among behavior modifiers than they are among subgroups with other orientations in the helping professions.

Conversely, a lack of planning, can be disastrous. For illustrations of this, refer to the "Pitfalls" sections in Part II, where we gave numerous examples of how behavior principles and processes can work to the disadvantage of those who are ignorant of them or who do not plan for them. If a behavior practitioner is not skillful in constructing programs for developing desirable behavior, he or she is unwittingly apt to introduce contingencies that develop undesirable behavior.

While it is often necessary to change, manage, influence, or otherwise control behavior, *it is also necessary to ensure that this is done ethically*. We have argued throughout this book that we are likely to achieve desirable behavioral change if we practice research-based principles and procedures of behavior modification. We turn now to ethical guidelines for doing so.

ETHICAL GUIDELINES

Having a set of guidelines that describe ethical applications of behavior modification is important. However, simply resolving to treat various individuals and groups in ethical ways is not a sufficient guarantee that they will be so treated. Contingencies of reinforcement must be arranged to make this happen. One way in which to arrange such contingencies is through *countercontrol*. This is "the reciprocal of control; it is the influence the controllee has on the controller by virtue of access to suitable reinforcers" (Stoltz & Asociates, 1978, p. 19). In a democracy, for example, voters can exert a certain amount of countercontrol over elected officials. If the voters don't like the laws that are passed, they can vote the officials out of office. Similarly, a client can stop seeing a therapist as a form of countercontrol to ensure that the therapist conforms with prearranged treatment guidelines. Some individuals in treatment programs, however, such as children, psychiatric patients, geriatric patients, and persons with severe developmental disabilities, are likely to lack meaningful forms of countercontrol. In such cases, other ethical safeguards may be necessary. These safeguards generally require that the behavior modifier be held accountable (i.e., responsible) to a recognized individual or group for applying acceptable procedures and producing satisfactory results.

Various groups and organizations have addressed the ethical issues involved in the application of behavior modification. Three highly reputable organizations that have done so are the Association for the Advancement of Behavior Therapy (AABT), the American Psychological Association (APA), and the Association for Behavior Analysis (ABA).

In 1977, in its journal *Behavior Therapy*, the AABT published a set of basic ethical questions that one should always ask with regard to any behavior modification or behavior therapy program. These questions are reprinted in Table 30–1 and should

TABLE 30–1 ETHICAL ISSUES FOR HUMAN SERVICES

The focus of this statement is on critical issues of central importance to human services. The statement is not a list of prescriptions and proscriptions.

On each of the issues described, ideal interventions would have maximum involvement by the person whose behavior is to be changed, and the fullest possible consideration of societal pressures on that person, the therapist, and the therapist's employer. It is recognized that the practicalities of actual settings sometimes require exceptions and that there certainly are occasions when exceptions can be consistent with ethical practice.

In the list of issues, the term "client" is used to describe the person whose behavior is to be changed; "therapist" is used to describe the professional in charge of the intervention; "treatment" and "problem," although used in the singular, refer to any and all treatments and problems being formulated with this checklist. The issues are formulated so as to be relevant across as many settings and populations as possible. Thus, they need to be qualified when someone other than the person whose behavior is to be changed is paying the therapist, or when that person's competence or the voluntary nature of that person's consent is questioned. For example, if the therapist has found that the client does not understand the goals or methods being considered, the therapist should substitute the client's guardian or other responsible person for "client," when reviewing the issues listed.

A Have the goals of treatment been adequately considered?
   1 To ensure that the goals are explicit, are they written?
   2 Has the client's understanding of the goals been assured by having the client restate them orally or in writing?
   3 Have the therapist and client agreed on the goals of therapy?
   4 Will serving the client's interests be contrary to the interests of other persons?
   5 Will serving the client's immediate interests be contrary to the client's long term interest?
B Has the choice of treatment methods been adequately considered?
   1 Does the published literature show the procedure to be the best one available for that problem?
   2 If no literature exists regarding the treatment method, is the method consistent with generally accepted practice?
   3 Has the client been told of alternative procedures that might be preferred by the client on the basis of significant differences in discomfort, treatment time, cost, or degree of demonstrated effectiveness?
   4 If a treatment procedure is publicly, legally, or professionally controversial, has formal professional consultation been obtained, has the reaction of the affected segment of the public been adequately considered, and have the alternative treatment methods been more closely reexamined and reconsidered?
C Is the client's participation voluntary?
   1 Have possible sources of coercion on the client's participation been considered?
   2 If treatment is legally mandated, has the available range of treatments and therapists been offered?
   3 Can the client withdraw from treatment without a penalty or financial loss that exceeds actual clinical costs?

(continued)

TABLE 30–1 *(CONTINUED)*

D   When another person or an agency is empowered to arrange for therapy, have the interests of the subordinated client been sufficiently considered?
   1   Has the subordinated client been informed of the treatment objectives and participated in the choice of treatment procedures?
   2   Where the subordinated client's competence to decide is limited, have the client as well as the guardian participated in the treatment discussions to the extent that the client's abilities permit?
   3   If the interests of the subordinated person and the superordinate persons or agency conflict, have attempts been made to reduce the conflict by dealing with both interests?

E   Has the adequacy of treatment been evaluated?
   1   Have quantitative measures of the problem and its progress been obtained?
   2   Have the measures of the problem and its progress been made available to the client during treatment?

F   Has the confidentiality of the treatment relationship been protected?
   1   Has the client been told who has access to the records?
   2   Are records available only to authorized persons?

G   Does the therapist refer the clients to other therapists when necessary?
   1   If treatment is unsuccessful, is the client referred to other therapists?
   2   Has the client been told that if dissatisfied with the treatment, referral will be made?

H   Is the therapist qualified to provide treatment?
   1   Has the therapist had training or experience in treating problems like the client's?
   2   If deficits exist in the therapist's qualifications, has the client been informed?
   3   If the therapist is not adequately qualified, is the client referred to other therapists, or has supervision by a qualified therapist been provided? Is the client informed of the supervisory relation?
   4   If the treatment is administered by mediators, have the mediators been adequately supervised by a qualified therapist?

Note: Adopted May 22, 1977, by the board of directors of the Association for Advancement of Behavior Therapy. This statement on Ethical Issues for Human Services was taken from the Membership Directory of the Association for Advancement of Behavior Therapy and is reprinted by permission of the association.

be examined carefully. As can be seen from the table, most of these points have been made frequently throughout this book, especially in Chapter 24. If you are carrying out a behavior modification program and must answer "no" to any of these questions, it is extremely likely that the ethics of what you are doing would be considered questionable by any recognized group of behavior modifiers or behavior therapists. It should be noted, as well, that these ethical questions are relevant not only to behavior modifiers and behavior therapists, but to all providers of human services.

In 1978, a comprehensive report (Stolz & Associates, 1978) on the ethical issues involved in behavior modification was published by a commission appointed by the APA. A primary conclusion of the commission was that persons engaged in any type of psychological intervention should subscribe to and follow the ethics codes and standards of their professions. For members of the American Psychological Association and the Canadian Psychological Association, the current version of the ethics code is the American Psychological Association's *Ethical Principles of Psychologists and Code of Conduct* (2002). This document includes a set of general principles that are intended to guide psychologists toward the very highest ethical ideals of the profession, and a detailed set of standards to encourage ethical behavior by psychologists and their students.

In 1988, in its journal, *The Behavior Analyst,* the ABA published a statement of clients' rights (Van Houten et al., 1988) to direct both the ethical and appropriate application of behavioral treatment. The following discussion points for the ethical application of behavior modification are based on the reports by Stoltz & Associates (1978) and Van Houten and colleagues (1988).

1. Qualifications of the Behavior Modifier

Behavior modifiers must receive appropriate academic training. They must also receive appropriate supervised practical training to ensure competence in behavioral assessment, designing and implementing treatment programs, evaluating their results, and ensuring a thorough understanding of professional ethics. In cases in which a problem or treatment is complex or may pose risks, Van Houten and colleagues (1988) argue that clients have a right to direct involvement by an appropriately trained doctoral-level behavior modifier. Regardless of the level of training, the behavior modifier should always ensure that the procedures being used are consistent with the most up-to-date literature in the recognized behavior modification and behavior therapy journals.

Steps to Ensure Countercontrol and Accountability   If you are carrying out a behavior modification project and are not a recognized professional, then you should obtain supervision from a recognized professional in the field. Such professionals are likely to be members of the ABA or AABT, or both. Thus far, six states (California, Texas, New York, Florida, Pennsylvania, and Oklahoma) have developed behavior analysis certification programs (Moore & Shook, 2001). In addition, a national certification program, The Behavior Analysis Certification Board (BACB), has been developed (for more information, visit their Web site at www.bacb.com). In addition, practitioners can be certified in behavioral psychology by the American Board of Behavior Psychology, an affiliated board of the American Board of Professional Psychology (Nezu, 2000). The American Board of Professional Psychology develops the examination content and examination instrument used by all 50 states in the United States to license psychologists. For an excellent discussion of the BACB ethical guidelines, including practical advice on how to adhere to them illustrated with numerous examples, see Bailey and Burch (2005).

2. Definition of the Problem and Selection of Goals

Note 3 Target behaviors selected must be the most important for the client and society. There should be an emphasis on teaching functional, age-appropriate skills that will enable the client greater freedom to pursue preferred activities. With individuals with severe handicaps especially, there should be a focus on teaching skills that promote independent functioning. Even when improved functioning requires the elimination of problem behaviors in certain situations, the goals should include desirable alternative behaviors for those situations. The goals should also be consistent with the basic rights of the client to dignity, privacy, and humane care.

Steps to Ensure Countercontrol and Accountability   Defining the problem and selecting the goals are dependent on the values of the individuals involved. For example, some people consider overt gay or lesbian tendencies to be behavior that should be modified; others do not. One form of countercontrol, therefore, is to require the behavior modifier to clearly specify his or her values relating to the client's problems. Ideally, the values on which the goals are based should be consistent with those of the client and with the long-term good of society. A second form of countercontrol is for the client to be an active participant in the selection of goals and identification of target behaviors. In situations in which this is not possible (such as cases of persons with severe developmental disabilities), competent impartial third parties (ombudspersons, representatives of the community) who can act on behalf of a client can ensure accountability by being involved in crucial decisions concerning the selection of goals.

3. Selection of Treatment

Behavior modifiers should use the most effective, empirically validated methods with the least discomfort and fewest negative side effects. To this end it is generally agreed that behavior modifiers should use the least intrusive and restrictive interventions wherever possible; however, there is no clear agreement on a continuum of intrusiveness or restrictiveness. These terms appear to be used in at least three ways. First, interventions based on positive reinforcement are generally considered to be less intrusive than interventions based on aversive control. That does not mean, however, that aversive procedures should never be used. It may not be in the client's best interest for behavior modifiers to apply a slow-acting procedure if available research indicates that more aversive procedures would be more effective. As expressed by Van Houten and colleagues (1988, p. 114), "In some cases, a client's right to effective treatment may dictate the immediate use of quicker-acting, but temporarily more restrictive procedures."

Second, intrusive and restrictive sometimes refer to the extent to which clients are given choices and allowed freedom of movement in a therapeutic environment. In a work-training program for persons with developmental disabilities, for example, the assignment of specific tasks might be considered more intrusive than allowing clients to choose among several optional work activities.

Third, intrusive and restrictive sometimes refer to the extent to which consequences are deliberately managed as opposed to naturally occurring. As indicated in Chapter 3, natural reinforcers are unprogrammed reinforcers that occur in the normal course of everyday living. The desirability of making use of natural contingencies of reinforcement whenever possible was stressed in Chapter 16 and elsewhere in this text. If it is necessary to use contrived or deliberately programmed reinforcers early in a program, then the behavior modifier should transfer control to natural reinforcers as quicky as possible.

While recognizing the desirability of selecting treatments that are the least intrusive and restrictive, based on the three meanings of those terms discussed previously, we must remember that the most effective treatment is likely to be one that is based on a functional assessment of the causes of problem behavior, as discussed in Chapter 22. As expressed by Pyles and Bailey (1990), if the causes of an individual's problem behavior can be identified through functional analysis, and if those causes can be used to implement an effective treatment, undue concern for the intrusiveness/restrictiveness issue may not be particularly helpful.

Steps to Ensure Countercontrol and Accountability   One way to ensure countercontrol is to stipulate that no program is to be carried out on a client who has not given informed consent to participate in that program (i.e., consent based on knowledge of the procedures to be used and their probable effects). Stated differently, the behavior modifier should explain alternative treatments that could be used, state their pros and cons, and give the client a choice. This collaboration between the behavior modifier and an informed client is an essential element of behavior modification, and one that serves to protect clients' rights. A mechanism to facilitate informed consent is the signing of a client–therapist contract that clearly outlines the objectives and methods of treatment, the framework for the service to be provided, and the contingencies for the remuneration that may be forthcoming to the therapist (as described in Chapter 24). There are, however, problems with the concept of informed consent; namely, it involves verbal behavior that, like other behavior, is under the control of the environment. Hence, it may be manipulated in a particular fashion that may not be in the best interests of the client. The stipulation of informed consent probably provides only a partial check on the ethics of a program. In addition, there are many individuals for whom informed consent is inapplicable (e.g., individuals with severe developmental disabilities). Therefore, an additional way to help ensure that clients' rights are protected is through ethical review committees composed of professionals and members of the community who evaluate the ethics of proposed programs.

4. Record Keeping and Ongoing Evaluation

An important component of ensuring ethical treatment of clients is the maintenance of accurate data throughout a program. This includes a thorough behavioral assessment before the intervention is developed, ongoing monitoring of target behaviors as well as possible side effects, and appropriate follow-up evaluation after the treatment is concluded. Whereas behavior modifiers should always take good records, they should exercise utmost discretion in whom they permit to see those records in order to protect the client from undue control. Confidentiality must be respected at all times.

Steps to Ensure Countercontrol and Accountability   Given the above caution, an important form of countercontrol is to provide frequent opportunities for a client to discuss with the behavior modifier the data that tracks progress throughout the program. For this, of course, the client must have access to his or her own records. Another strategy is (with the client's permission) for the behavior modifier to share the client's records with those who are directly concerned with the client's progress. Feedback on the effectiveness of the program from individuals who are concerned directly with the welfare of the client is an important accountability mechanism. As indicated in Chapter 1, the most important characteristic of behavior modification is its strong emphasis on defining problems in terms of behavior that can be measured in some way, and using changes in the behavioral measure of the problem as the best indicator of the extent to which the problem is being helped. Sharing these data with all concerned parties and periodic peer evaluation of the data by all concerned is the cornerstone for ensuring ethical and effective treatment programs by the behavior modifers.

CONCLUSIONS

Behavior modification has great potential to be used for the good of society and may even be used to eliminate the oppression of some humans by others that has characterized all societies from the dawn of recorded history.

An important responsibility of behavior modifiers is to develop ethical safeguards for behavior modification to ensure that it is always used wisely and humanely and does not become a new tool in the oppression that has thus far characterized the human species. Of all the safeguards discussed, the most fundamental is countercontrol. Perhaps the best way for behavior modifiers to help develop effective countercontrol throughout society is to spread their skills as widely as possible, and to help educate the general public with respect to behavior modification. It should be rather difficult to use behavioral science to the disadvantage of any group whose members are well versed in the principles and tactics of behavior modification.

STUDY QUESTIONS

1. Describe in behavioral terms how the history of civilization is a story of the continuous abuse of power. From your knowledge of history or current events, give an example of this abuse.
2. From your knowledge of history or current events, give an example of what often happens when the reinforcements occurring to one group in a society fall below a certain critical level relative to the reinforcements occurring to another group in that society.
3. From a behavioral point of view, how might we account for constitutions, bills of rights, and related political documents of modern states?
4. Explain why we tend to react negatively to all overt attempts to control our behavior.
5. Why and how do people who would control our behavior disguise their aims? Give an example of this that is not in the text.
6. State two propositions on which behavior modification is based.
7. Why is extreme wariness a healthy reaction to any new, far-reaching development in science or technology? Discuss an example of this.
8. What does the term *ethics* mean from a behavioral point of view?
9. Describe how ethics has evolved as a part of our culture.
10. Using an example, explain how ethical guidelines involve rule-governed control over behavior.
11. Explain why all helping professions are involved in the control of behavior, whether or not their practitioners realize it. Give an example.

12. Discuss the relative merits of planning versus not planning for behavior change.
13. Discuss countercontrol. Why is it important?
14. What was a primary conclusion of the comprehensive report by Stolz and associates on the ethical issues involved in behavior modification?
15. What steps can be taken to help ensure that a behavior modifier is appropriately qualified?
16. State two countercontrol measures for clients regarding the definition of problems and selection of goals.
17. What should be the characteristics of intervention methods used by behavior modifiers?
18. Discuss three possible meanings of intrusive and restrictive interventions.
19. Describe a mechanism to facilitate informed consent by the client.
20. What constitutes the cornerstone for ensuring ethical and effective treatment programs by behavior modifiers?
21. Briefly explain why it should be rather difficult to use behavior modification to the detriment of any group whose members are well versed in the principles and tactics of behavior modification.

NOTES AND EXTENDED DISCUSSION

1.   Skinner (1971) argued that we can trace this attitude, at least in part, to the influence of 18th-century revolutionaries and social reformers. To counteract the aversive control utilized by tyrants, these activists developed the concept of freedom as a rallying cry. It was, said Skinner, a worthwhile concept in its time, for it helped to spur people to break away from aversive forms of control. Now, however, we have moved into an era in which positive reinforcement is a more predominant means of control (and will perhaps become increasingly so with the growth of behavior modification). The concept of freedom has therefore outlived its social usefulness. Indeed, it is harmful, in that it tends to prevent us from seeing how our behavior is controlled by positive reinforcement. Many states and provincial governments in North America, for example, have turned to public lotteries as a way to raise funds. Most people who happily buy lottery tickets feel that they are "free" to do so, and they fail to recognize that their behavior is being controlled to the same extent as it would be if they were being "forced" to pay the same amount in taxes. But the mechanism of control is different (i.e., positive reinforcement versus avoidance conditioning). Moreover, the concept of freedom encourages the view that some people deserve more "dignity" than others because of their achievements, whereas in actuality one's achievements (or failures to achieve) are due to one's conditioning history and genetic predispositions. Hence, the title of Skinner's book: *Beyond Freedom and Dignity* (1971).

2.   In fact, in controlled clinical trials, behavior therapists have been rated by observers as significantly more empathic and supportive than nonbehavioral clinicians (Greenwald, Kornblith, Hersen, Bellack, & Himmelhoch, 1981; Sloan, Staples, Cristol, Yorkston, & Whipple, 1975). Moreover, in the absence of a warm and empathic relationship, clients will simply resist complying with the requests by behavior therapists for conducting various self-monitoring and homework assignments (Hersen, 1983; Martin & Worthington, 1982; Messer & Winokur, 1984).

3. Prilleltensky (1989, 1990) has argued that psychology as a whole, including behavior modification, has too readily accepted and promoted the status quo rather than questioning whether the status quo is really always best for human welfare. An example from the early days of behavior modification would be that of teaching children in school to sit quietly at their desks, as though there were some intrinsic merit in this behavior. Perhaps it is the rule that should be changed rather than the children. Prilleltensky argues that we should study how the status quo comes to be accepted and how we can redirect our efforts to changing it, rather than our clients, when this is more consistent with human welfare.

Study Questions on Notes

1. Discuss Skinner's view that we must go "beyond freedom and dignity" if civilization is to solve some of its most difficult problems.
2. Describe an example illustrating how governments use positive reinforcement to control behavior without citizens believing that they are being controlled.
3. Do the data support the notion that behavior modifiers are "cold and mechanical" in their treatment of clients? Explain.
4. Describe two examples in which behavior modification might be used inappropriately, in your opinion, to support the status quo. Why do you think this use of behavior modification would be inappropriate?

Glossary

(The following are the main technical terms used in behavior modification. Please note that many of these terms differ from their standard English dictionary definitions. For further information about these terms, check the index of this text.)

ABAB reversal-replication design. A research design consisting of four phases: baseline (A), intervention (B), reversal to baseline (A), and replication of intervention (B).

ABC assessment. Conducting observations to determine the stimulus antecedents of a behavior, the behavior under the control of those antecedents, and the consequences that maintain that behavior.

Abolishing operation. See motivating abolishing operation.

Acceptance and Commitment Therapy (ACT). A behavior therapy that uses mindfulness and acceptance procedures to teach clients to nonjudgmentally experience thoughts and emotions, including those that are troublesome, and to commit to actions to pursue valued goals in their lives.

Achievement Place. A token economy program for predelinquent teenagers who live with teachers who supervise and administer the program.

Adventitious chain. A behavioral chain in which an earlier response in the chain is maintained by the reinforcement of a later response in the chain even though reinforcement is not contingent on the occurrence of the earlier response.

Adventitious reinforcement. Reinforcement that occurs following a response but that is not contingent on that response.

Alternating-treatments design. A research design in which a baseline and treatment(s) are alternated, typically on successive days or sessions.

Antecedents. Stimuli that precede particular behaviors.

Applied behavior analysis. *Behavior modification* in which there is typically an attempt to analyze or clearly demonstrate controlling variables of the behavior of concern.

Aversive stimulus. A term frequently used to denote either a punisher or a negative reinforcer.

Avoidance conditioning. A contingency in which a response prevents an aversive stimulus from occurring, thereby resulting in an increase in the frequency of the response.

Backup reinforcer. A stimulus that causes other stimuli to become conditioned reinforcers when they are paired with it; typically used to establish and maintain the strength of conditioned reinforcers.

Backward chaining. A method for establishing a behavioral chain in which the last step of the chain is taught first, then the next-to-last step is linked to the last step, and so on, until the entire chain is learned.

Baseline. A measure of behavior in the absence of (i.e., prior to or following) a treatment or intervention program.

Behavior. Any activity (muscular, glandular, or electrical) of an individual.

Behavior analysis. The study of the principles governing human and animal behavior.

Behavior modification. The systematic application of learning principles and techniques to assess and improve individuals' covert and overt behaviors.

Behavior rehearsal. Practicing and receiving feedback on behavior that an individual would like to improve.

Behavior trap. Reinforcers in the natural environment maintain a behavior that was initially developed by programmed reinforcers.

Behavioral assessment. The collection and analysis of information and data in order to identify a specific behavior for treatment, to identify possible causes of the behavior, to select appropriate treatment strategies for the behavior, and to evaluate treatment outcome.

Behavioral chain. A sequence of discriminative stimuli and responses in which each response except the last produces and is reinforced by the S^D for the next response.

Behavioral contract. A written agreement that provides a clear statement of what behaviors of which individuals will produce what consequences and who will deliver those consequences.

Behavioral deficit. Not enough behavior of a particular type.

Behavioral excess. Too much behavior of a particular type.

Biofeedback. Immediate information provided to a person through instrumentation about one or more of his or her own physiological processes, such as heart rate.

Chain. See *behavioral chain*.

Chaining procedures. Procedures to develop behavioral chains (see *backward chaining, forward chaining, and total task presentation*).

Changing-criterion design. A research design in which successive changes in the criterion for application of the treatment occur.

Cognition. Covert verbalizations and imagery, frequently called "believing," "thinking," and "expecting."

Cognitive behavior modification. An approach to treatment that focuses mainly on changing overt behavior by modifying covert behavior, such as dysfunctional thinking.

Cognitive restructuring. Substituting irrational or dysfunctional thinking and inaccurate appraisal of information with rational thinking and accurate appraisal of information.

Competing behaviors. See incompatible behaviors.

Computer-aided personalized system of instruction (CAPSI). A computer-based behavioral approach to education that shares many features with Personalized System of Instruction (PSI), after which it was named.

Concept. A stimulus class that controls a specific behavior.

Conditioned punisher. A stimulus that is a punisher as a result of having been paired with other punishers.

Conditioned reinforcer. A stimulus that is a reinforcer as a result of having been paired with other reinforcers.

Conditioned response. Either a response elicited by a conditioned stimulus or an operant response that has been strengthened by reinforcement.

Conditioned stimulus. A stimulus that elicits a response because that stimulus has been paired with another stimulus that elicits that or a similar response.

Conditioning. Establishing a response through either respondent or operant conditioning.

Contingency. A relationship between two events such that if one event occurs, then the other event is more likely to occur.

Continuous recording. A method of recording behavior in which each instance of a particular response is recorded during a specified period of time.

Continuous reinforcement schedule. A schedule of reinforcement in which each instance of a particular response is reinforced.

Counterconditioning. Conditioning a response to a stimulus that is incompatible with another response elicited by the same stimulus.

Covert behavior. Behavior that is not directly observable by others. Also called *private behavior*.

Covert conditioning. A procedure in which behavior is strengthened or weakened by imagining the components of that behavior being reinforced or punished or by imagining stimuli being paired.

Covert sensitization. A procedure in which an individual imagines pairing a positive reinforcer with an aversive stimulus.

Dependent variable. A measure of behavior that is studied as a function of an independent variable.

Deprivation. The absence of a specific reinforcer for a period of time.

Differential reinforcement of alternative behavior. A procedure that involves extinction of a problem behavior combined with reinforcing a behavior that is topographically dissimilar to, but not necessarily incompatible with, the problem behavior.

Differential reinforcement of incompatible behavior. Extinction of a behavior while concurrently reinforcing a competing behavior.

Differential reinforcement of low rates.   Presenting a reinforcer only if a particular response occurs at a low rate. Can be programmed as limited-responding DRL or space-responding DRL.

Differential reinforcement of other behavior.   Eliminating a behavior by providing a reinforcer if that behavior does not occur during a specified period of time.

Differential reinforcement of zero responding.   Another name for differential reinforcement of other behavior.

Direct assessment.   Obtaining information about a behavior by directly observing it.

Direct-acting reinforcer.   A reinforcer that immediately follows a behavior.

Discrimination training procedure.   Reinforcing a behavior in the presence of one stimulus and not reinforcing it in the presence of another stimulus. Also sometimes referred to as S^D-S^Δ training.

Discriminative stimulus (S^D).   A stimulus in the presence of which a response is reinforced.

Environment.   The totality of all stimuli impinging on an individual.

Equivalence Class.   See stimulus equivalence class.

Error.   A response to an S^Δ or a failure to respond to an S^D.

Errorless discrimination training.   The use of a fading procedure to establish a stimulus discrimination so that no errors occur.

Escape conditioning.   The removal of an aversive stimulus immediately following a response with the effect that the response is strengthened. Also called *negative reinforcement*.

Establishing operation.   See motivating establishing operation.

Exclusionary time-out.   Removing an individual briefly from a reinforcing situation contingent on a response.

External validity.   The extent to which a finding can be generalized to other behaviors, individuals, settings, or treatments.

Extinction (operant conditioning).   The withholding of a reinforcer following a previously reinforced response, with the effect that the response is weakened.

Extinction (respondent conditioning).   Presenting a conditioned stimulus (CS) without further pairings with an unconditioned stimulus, with the effect that the CS loses the ability to elicit the conditioned response.

Extinction burst.   An increase in responding during extinction.

Extra-stimulus prompt.   A stimulus that is added as an antecedent to make a correct response more likely.

Fading.   The gradual change of a stimulus controlling a response so that the response eventually occurs to a new (or partially new) stimulus.

Fear hierarchy.   A list of fear-eliciting events arranged in order from the event that causes the least fear to the event that causes the most fear.

Fixed-duration schedule.   A schedule of reinforcement in which a reinforcer is presented only if a response occurs for a fixed period of time.

Fixed-interval schedule.   A schedule of reinforcement in which a reinforcer is presented following the first instance of a response after a fixed period of time.

Fixed-ratio schedule.   A schedule of reinforcement in which a reinforcer is presented following a fixed number of instances of a particular response.

Flooding.   A method of extinguishing fear by exposure to a strongly feared stimulus for an extended period of time.

Forward chaining.   A method for establishing a behavioral chain in which the initial step of the chain is taught first, then the initial step is linked to the second step, and so on until the entire chain is learned.

Functional analysis.   Discovering controlling variables (antecedents or consequences) for behavior by directly assessing their effects on the behavior.

Functional assessment.   A variety of approaches for attempting to identify antecedents and consequences of a behavior.

Generalized conditioned reinforcer.   A conditioned reinforcer that is paired with more than one backup reinforcer.

Generalized imitation.   Imitating new responses on the first trial as a result of learning to imitate a number of other behaviors.

Habit disorder.   A behavior that has become so frequent or intense that the individual seeks treatment for it.

Habit reversal.   A method to treat habit disorders that involves practicing a competing response and receiving reinforcement.

Higher-order conditioning.   A procedure in which a stimulus becomes a conditioned stimulus by being paired with another conditioned stimulus instead of an unconditioned stimulus.

Imitation.   The performance of some behavior as a result of observing another individual engaged in similar behavior.

Incompatible behaviors.   Two behaviors that cannot be emitted at the same time, such as sitting and standing. Also called *competing behaviors*.

Independent variable.   A treatment or intervention introduced to study its influence on a dependent variable.

Indirect-acting reinforcer.   A reinforcer that follows a response after a long delay and has its effect on the response through verbal behavior instead of by immediately following the response.

Indirect assessment.   Obtaining information about behavior by means other than directly observing it.

Informed consent.   Agreeing to therapy after receiving complete information about what it involves and its potential benefits and side effects.

Intermittent reinforcement.   The maintenance of a behavior by reinforcing it only occasionally rather than every time it occurs.

Internal validity.   Said of an independent variable if it can be shown that it caused the observed changes in the dependent variable.

Interobserver reliability (IOR).   A measure of the extent to which two observers agree on the occurrences of a behavior after independently observing and recording it during a specified period of time.

Interval recording.   A recording method in which a specified behavior is recorded as either occurring or not occurring during equal short-duration intervals throughout an observation period.

Latency.   The time between the onset of a stimulus and the onset of a response.

Limited-responding DRL.   A schedule that specifies the maximum allowable number of responses during a certain time interval in order for reinforcement to occur.

Matching law.   An equation stating that the relative number of responses or time devoted to a behavior is equal to the relative rate of reinforcement for that behavior.

Mindfulness.   Observation of one's covert and overt behaviors as they occur.

Modeling.   Demonstrating a behavior for someone to imitate.

Motivating abolishing operations.   Events or operations that temporarily decrease the effectiveness of consequences as reinforcers or punishers, and decrease the likelihood of behaviors that normally lead to those reinforcers or increase the likelihood of behaviors that normally lead to those punishers.

Motivating establishing operations.   Events or operations that temporarily increase the effectiveness of consequences as reinforcers or punishers, and increase the likelihood of behaviors that lead to those reinforcers or decrease the likelihood of behaviors that lead to those punishers.

Motivating operations.   Events or operations that (a) temporarily alter the effectiveness of consequences as reinforcers or punisher (a value-altering effect), (b) influence behaviors that normally lead to those reinforcers or punishers (a behavior-altering effect).

Multiple-baseline-across-behaviors design.   A research design in which two or more behaviors are monitored concurrently and, in a staggered fashion, the treatment is introduced sequentially to each of the behaviors.

Multiple-baseline-across-people design.   A research design in which a behavior is monitored in two or more individuals concurrently and, in a staggered fashion, the intervention is introduced sequentially to the behavior of each of the individuals.

Multiple-baseline-across-situations design.   A research design in which a behavior is monitored in two or more situations, and in a staggered fashion, the intervention is introduced sequentially to the behavior in each of the situations.

Natural environment.   Setting in which an individual carries out normal, everyday functions outside of a situation explicitly designed for training.

Natural reinforcers.   Reinforcers that follow behavior in the course of everyday living—i.e., reinforcers that occur normally in the natural environment.

Negative reinforcement.   The removal of a negative reinforcer (or aversive stimulus) immediately following a response with the effect that the response is strengthened; another name for escape conditioning.

Negative reinforcer.   A stimulus the removal of which immediately after a response causes the response to be strengthened or to increase in frequency.

Nonexclusionary time-out.   Introducing into a situation, contingent on a response, a stimulus associated with less reinforcement.

Operant behavior.   Behavior that is influenced by its consequences.

Operant conditioning.   The process of strengthening a behavior by reinforcing it; or weakening a behavior by punishing it.

Overt behavior.   Behavior that is observable by others. Also called *public behavior*.

Participant modeling.   A method for decreasing fear in which a client imitates another individual approaching a feared object.

Personalized System of Instruction (PSI).   A method of education based on operant conditioning that involves clearly identifying specific target behaviors in the form of study questions, frequent tests based on the study questions, use of student assistants to mark tests, and mastery criteria. Also called the *Keller plan*.

Physical guidance.   A method of prompting in which the teacher moves the individual through the desired behavior.

Physical prompt.   Another name for physical guidance.

Positive reinforcement.   Presentation of a positive reinforcer immediately following a response with the effect that the response is strengthened or increased in frequency.

Positive reinforcer.   A stimulus the presentation of which immediately after a response causes the response to be strengthened or increased in frequency.

Premack principle.   A principle that states that if the opportunity to engage in a behavior that has a high probability of occurring is made contingent upon a behavior that has a low probability of occurring, the behavior that has a low probability of occurring will be strengthened.

Progressive muscle relaxation.   A method to help an individual relax by having him or her alternately tense and relax various muscle groups, while attending closely to how it feels when they are tensed versus when they are relaxed.

Prompt.   Supplemental antecedent stimuli that are provided to increase the likelihood that a desired behavior will occur, but that are not a part of the final desired stimulus (target stimulus) to control that behavior.

Punisher.   A stimulus the presentation of which immediately after a response causes that response to decrease in frequency.

Punishment.   Presentation of a punisher (or aversive stimulus) immediately following a response with the effect that the response decreases in frequency.

Ratio strain.   A deterioration of responding caused by increasing a ratio schedule too rapidly.

Rational-emotive behavior therapy (REBT).   A method of therapy developed by Albert Ellis that focuses on alleviating emotional problems caused by irrational thinking.

Reactivity.   Change in behavior as a result of knowing that the behavior is being observed.

Relapse.   The return of a treated behavior to its level prior to treatment.

Relational frame theory.   A theory about how we learn to respond to a set of arbitrary stimuli. It involves stimulus equivalence classes and the effects that members of such classes have on each other and the behaviors they control.

Reprimand.   Negative verbal stimuli presented contingent upon behavior.

Resistance to extinction.   A measure of the tendency of a response to continue occurring after being placed on extinction.

Respondent behavior.   Behavior that is elicited by stimuli and that is or can be learned to be elicited by other stimuli through respondent conditioning.

Respondent conditioning.   Teaching a response to a new stimulus by pairing that stimulus with another stimulus that elicits that response.

Response.   A unit of behavior.

Response cost.   The removal of a specified amount of reinforcer following a particular behavior.

Response generalization.   Increased probability of a response as a result of the reinforcement of a similar response.

Role rehearsal.   See *behavior rehearsal*.

Rule.   A desription of a three-term contingency of reinforcement (antecedent—behavior–consequences).

S^D.   See *discriminative stimulus*.

S^Δ.   A stimulus in the presence of which a response will not be reinforced. (Pronounced "ess delta.")

Satiation.   Total ineffectiveness of a specific reinforcer immediately following unrestricted access to it.

Schedule of reinforcement.   A rule specifying which occurrences of a given behavior, if any, will be reinforced.

Self-management.   A strategy for changing one's own behavior by using principles of behavior modification.

Self-monitoring.   Observing and recording one's own behavior.

Shaping.   The reinforcement of successive approximations of a response and the extinction of earlier approximations of that response until a new desired behavior occurs.

Simple conditioned reinforcer.   A conditioned reinforcer that is paired with a single backup reinforcer.

Single-organism research design.   A method used in research in which an experimental effect is demonstrated in single individuals as opposed to groups.

Social validity.   A judgment about the clinical or applied importance of a behavioral change.

Spaced-responding DRL.   A schedule of reinforcement in which a response is reinforced only if it occurs a specified amount of time following the previous response.

Spontaneous recovery.   A temporary recovery of an extinguished behavior following a period of time since the last extinction session.

Stimuli.   Plural of *stimulus*.

Stimulus.   Any physical event that can impinge on the sense receptors.

Stimulus common-element class.   A group of stimuli that have some physical characteristic in common, commonly called a stimulus class.

Stimulus control.   The degree of correlation between the occurrence of a particular stimulus and the occurrence of a subsequent response.

Stimulus equivalence class.   A set of completely dissimilar stimuli in which all members of the class control the same response.

Stimulus equivalence training.   A training method in which different stimuli become functionally equivalent (e.g., control the same response).

Stimulus generalization.   Increased probability of a behavior in the presence of one stimulus as a result of having been reinforced in the presence of another stimulus.

Stimulus–response chain.   Same as *behavioral chain*.

Superstitious behavior.   Behavior that is strengthened and maintained by adventitious reinforcement.

Systematic desensitization.   A procedure for overcoming a phobia (extreme fear) by having a client successively imagine, while in a relaxed state, the items in a fear hierarchy.

Target behavior.   A specific behavior to be improved (increased or decreased) in a behavior modification program.

Task analysis.   The process of breaking a task down into smaller steps or component responses.

Time sampling.   An observational procedure in which a behavior is scored as occurring or not occurring during very brief observation intervals, each of which is separated from the others by a much longer period of time.

Time-out.   Change from a more reinforcing to a less reinforcing situation, typically used as a punisher following inappropriate behavior.

Token economy.   A behavior modification program in which individuals can earn tokens for performing desirable behaviors, and can cash in their tokens for various backup reinforcers.

Tokens.   Conditioned reinforcers that can be accumulated and exchanged for backup reinforcers.

Total-task presentation.   A chaining method in which the individual attempts all of the steps from the beginning to the end of the chain on each trial until the chain is learned.

Unconditioned punisher.   A stimulus that is a punisher without prior learning.

Unconditioned reinforcer.   A stimulus that is a reinforcer without prior learning.

Unconditioned response (UR).   A response elicited by an unconditioned stimulus; an inborn response to a stimulus.

Unconditioned stimulus (US).   A stimulus that elicits a response without prior learning.

Variable-duration schedule (VD).   A schedule of reinforcement in which a reinforcer occurs only if the response occurs for an interval of time that changes unpredictably from one reinforcement to the next.

Variable-interval schedule (VI).   A schedule of reinforcement in which the reinforcer occurs only if the response occurs after an interval of time that varies unpredictably from one reinforcement to the next.

Variable-ratio schedule (VR).   A schedule of reinforcement in which a reinforcer occurs only after a certain number of responses, where the number varies unpredictably from one reinforcement to the next.

Verbal prompt.   A spoken or written hint or cue to increase the likelihood that a desired response will occur.

Warning stimulus.   A stimulus that signals a forthcoming aversive stimulus.

Within-stimulus prompt.   In stimulus discrimination training, an alteration in the characteristics of the S^D or S^Δ to make them more noticeable or distinguishable, thereby easier to discriminate.

References

ADER, R., & COHEN, N. (1982). Behaviorally conditioned immunosuppression and murine systemic lupis erythematosus, *Science, 215,* 1534–1536.

ADER, R., & COHEN, N. (1993). Psychoneuroimmunology: Conditioning and stress. *Annual Review of Psychology, 44,* 53–85.

AGATHON, M. (1982). Behavior therapy in France. 1976–1981. *Journal of Behavior Therapy and Experimental Psychiatry, 13,* 271–277.

AGNEW, J. L. (1998). The establishing operation in organizational behavior management. *Journal of Organizational Behavior Management, 18,* 7–19.

AGRAS, W. S., TAYLOR, C. B., FELDMAN, D. E., LOSCH, M., & BURNETT, K. F. (1990). Developing computer-assisted therapy for the treatment of obesity. *Behavior Therapy, 21,* 99–109.

AIRAPETYANTZ, E., & BYKOV, D. (1966). Physiological experiments and the psychology of the subconscious. In T. Verhave (Ed.), *The experimental analysis of behavior* (pp. 140–157). New York: Appleton-Century-Crofts.

ALBERTO, P. A., & TROUTMAN, A. C. (2004). *Applied behavior analysis for teachers* (6th ed.). Upper Saddle River, NJ: Prentice Hall/Simon & Schuster.

ALBION, F. M., & SALZBURG, C. L. (1982). The effects of self-instruction on the rate of correct addition problems with mentally retarded children. *Education and Treatment of Children, 5,* 121–131.

ALLEN, G. J. (1973). Case study: Implementation of behavior modification techniques in summer camp settings. *Behavior Therapy, 4,* 570–575.

ALLEN, K. D., & STOKES, T. F. (1987). Use of escape and reward in the management of young children during dental treatment. *Journal of Applied Behavior Analysis, 20,* 381–390.

ALLEN, K. D., & WARZAK, D. J. (2000). The problem of parental nonadherence in clinical behavior analysis: Effective treatment is not enough. *Journal of Applied Behavior Analysis, 33,* 373–391.

AMERICAN ASSOCIATION ON MENTAL RETARDATION (AAMR). (1990). Revised policy on aversive procedures. *AAMR News and Notes, 3*(4), 5.

AMERICAN ASSOCIATION ON MENTAL RETARDATION (AAMR). (2002). *Mental retardation: Definition, classification, and systems of supports* (10th ed.). Washington, DC: Author.

AMERICAN PSYCHIATRIC ASSOCIATION. (1952). *Diagnostic and statistical manual of mental disorders: DSM-I.* Washington, DC: Author.

AMERICAN PSYCHIATRIC ASSOCIATION. (1968). *Diagnostic and statistical manual of mental disorders: DSM-II* (2nd ed.). Washington, DC: Author.

AMERICAN PSYCHIATRIC ASSOCIATION. (1980). *Diagnostic and statistical manual of mental disorders: DSM-III* (3rd ed.). Washington, DC: Author.

AMERICAN PSYCHIATRIC ASSOCIATION. (1987). *Diagnostic and statistical manual of mental disorders: DSM-III–R* (3rd ed.). Washington, DC: Author.

AMERICAN PSYCHIATRIC ASSOCIATION. (1993). Practice guidelines for major depressive disorder in adults. *American Journal of Psychiatry, 150*(Suppl. 4), 1–26.

AMERICAN PSYCHIATRIC ASSOCIATION. (1994). *Diagnostic and statistical manual of mental disorders: DSM-IV* (4th ed.). Washington, DC: Author.

AMERICAN PSYCHIATRIC ASSOCIATION. (2000). *Diagnostic and statistical manual of mental disorders: DSM-IV-TR* (4th ed., Text Revision). Washington, DC: Author.

AMERICAN PSYCHOLOGICAL ASSOCIATION (APA). (2002). *Ethical principles in the conduct of research with human participants.* Washington, DC: Author.

ANTONUCCIO, D. O., DANTON, W. G., & DENELSKY, G. Y. (1995). Psychotherapy versus medication for depression: Challenging the conventional wisdom with data. *Professional Psychology: Research and Practice, 26,* 574–585.

ANTONY, M. M., & BARLOW, D. H. (Eds.). (2004). *Handbook of assessment and treatment planning for psychological disorders.* New York: Guilford Press.

ANTONY, M. M., & SWINSON, R. P. (2001). *Phobic disorders and panic in adults: A guide to assessment and treatment.* Washington, DC: American Psychological Association.

ARDILA, R. (1982). International developments in behavior therapy in Latin America. *Journal of Behavior Therapy and Experimental Psychiatry, 13,* 15–20.

ARRICK, C. M., VOSS, J., & RIMM, D. C. (1981). The relative efficacy of thought-stopping and covert assertion. *Behaviour Research and Therapy, 19,* 17–24.

ASH, D. W., & HOLDING, D. H. (1990). Backward versus forward chaining in the acquisition of a keyboard skill. *Human Factors, 32,* 139–146.

ASSOCIATION FOR ADVANCEMENT OF BEHAVIOR THERAPY (AABT). (1994). Some findings from AABT's membership survey. *Behavior Therapist, 17,* 14.

AUBUCHON, P. G., HABER, J. D., & ADAMS, H. E. (1985). Can migraine headaches be modified by operant pain techniques? *Journal of Behavior Therapy and Experimental Psychiatry, 16,* 261–263.

AUSTIN, J. (2000a). Performance analysis and performance diagnostics. In J. Austin & J. E. Carr (Eds.), *Handbook of applied behavior analysis* (449–472). Reno, NV: Context Press.

AUSTIN, J., & CARR, J. E. (Eds.). 2000. *Handbook of applied behavior analysis.* Reno, NV: Context Press.

AUSTIN, L. (2000b). Behavioral approaches to college teaching. In J. Austin & J. E. Carr (Eds.), *Handbook of applied behavior analysis* (pp. 321–350). Reno, NV: Context Press.

AYLLON, T., & AZRIN, N. H. (1968). *The token economy: A motivational system for therapy and rehabilitation.* New York: Appleton-Century-Crofts.

AYLLON, T., & MICHAEL, J. (1959). The psychiatric nurse as a behavioral engineer. *Journal of the Experimental Analysis of Behavior, 2,* 323–334.

AYLLON, T., & MILAN, M. A. (1979). *Correctional rehabilitation and management: A psychological approach.* New York: Wiley.

AZRIN, N. H. (1967). Pain and aggression. *Psychology Today, 1*(1), 27–33.

AZRIN, N. H. (1976). Improvements in the community-reinforcement approach to alcoholism. *Behavior Research and Therapy, 14,* 339–348.

AZRIN, N. H., & LINDSLEY, O. R. (1956). The reinforcement of cooperation between children. *Journal of Abnormal and Social Psychology, 52,* 100–102.

AZRIN, N. H., & NUNN, R. G. (1973). Habit reversal: A method of eliminating nervous habits and tics. *Behaviour Research and Therapy, 11,* 619–628.

AZRIN, N. H., RUBEN, H., O'BRIEN, F., AYLLON, T., & ROLL, D. (1968). Behavioral engineering: Postural control by a portable operant apparatus. *Journal of Applied Behavior Analysis, 1,* 99–108.

AZRIN, N. H., SISSON, R. W., MEYERS, R., & GODLEY, N. (1982). Alcoholism treatment by disulfiram and community reinforcement therapy. *Journal of Behavior Therapy and Experimental Psychiatry, 13*(2), 105–112.

BAER, D. M., PETERSON, R. F., & SHERMAN, J. A. (1967). The development of imitation by reinforcing behavioral similarity to a model. *Journal of the Experimental Analysis of Behavior, 10,* 405–416.

BAER, D. M., & WOLF, M. M. (1970). The entry into natural communities of reinforcement. In R. Ulrich, T. Stachnik, & J. Mabry (Eds.), *Control of human behavior* (Vol. 2, pp. 319–324). Glenview, IL: Scott Foresman.

BAILEY, J. S. (1992). Gentle teaching: Trying to win friends and influence people with a euphemism, metaphor, smoke, and mirrors. *Journal of Applied Behavior Analysis, 25,* 879–883.

BAILEY, J. S., & BURCH, M. R. (2002). *Research methods in applied behavior analysis.* Thousand Oaks, CA: Sage.

BAILEY, J. S., & BURCH, M. R. (2005). *Ethics for behavior analysts: A practical guide to the Behavior Analyst Certification Board Guidelines for Responsible Conduct.* Mahwah, NJ: Lawrence Erlbaum Associates.

BAILEY, J. S., HUGHES, R. G., & JONES, W. E. (1980). *Applications of backward chaining to air-to-surface weapons delivery training.* Williams Airforce Base, AZ: Operations training division, Human Resources Laboratory.

BAILEY, J. S., & PYLES, D. A. M. (1989). Behavioral diagnostics. *Monographs of the American Association on Mental Retardation, 12,* 85–106.

BAILEY, J. S., TIMBERS, G. D., PHILLIPS, E. I., & WOLF, M. M. (1971). Modification of articulation errors of pre-delinquents by their peers. *Journal of Applied Behaviour Analysis, 3,* 265–281.

BAKER, S. L., PATERSON, M. D., & BARLOW, D. H. (2004). Panic disorder and agoraphobia. In M. M. Antony & D. H. Barlow (Eds.), *Handbook of assessment and treatment planning for psychological disorders.* New York: Guilford Press.

BALDWIN, J. D., & BALDWIN, J. I. (1998). *Behavior principles in everyday life* (3rd ed.). Upper Saddle River, NJ: Prentice Hall.

BANDURA, A. (1965). Influence of models' reinforcement contingencies in the acquisition of imitative responses. *Journal of Personality and Social Psychology, 1,* 589–595.

BANDURA, A. (1969). *Principles of behavior modification.* New York: Holt, Rinehart & Winston.

BANDURA, A. (1977). *Social learning theory.* Upper Saddle River, NJ: Prentice Hall.

BANDURA, A. (1982). Self-efficacy mechanism in human agency. *American Psychologist, 37,* 122–147.

BANDURA, A. (1986). *Social foundations of thought and action: A social-cognitive theory.* Upper Saddle River, NJ: Prentice Hall.

BANDURA, A. (1996). Oncological and epistemological terrains revisited. *Journal of Behavior Therapy and Experimental Psychiatry, 27,* 323–345.

BANDURA, A., & WALTERS, R. H. (1963). *Social learning and personality development.* New York: Holt, Rinehart & Winston.

BANERJEE, S. P. (1999). Behavioral psychotherapy in Singapore. *The Behavior Therapist, 22,* 80, 91.

BARKLEY, R. A. (1998). *Attention-deficit hyperactive disorder: A handbook for diagnosis and treatment* (2nd ed.). New York: Guilford Press.

BARKLEY, R. A. (1996). 18 ways to make token systems more effective for ADHD children and teens. *The ADHD Report, 4,* 1–5.

BARLOW, D. H. (2001). *Clinical handbook of psychological disorders* (3rd ed.). New York: Guilford Press.

BARLOW, D. H., & HERSEN, M. (1984). *Single-case experimental design: Strategies for studying behavior change* (2nd ed.). New York: Pergamon Press.

BARONE, D. F. (1982). Instigating additional self-modification projects after a personal adjustment course. *Teaching of Psychology, 9,* 111.

BARRIOS, B. A., & HARTMANN, D. P. (1986). The contributions of traditional assessment: Concepts, issues, and methodologies. In R. O. Nelson & S. C. Hayes (Eds.), *Conceptual foundations of behavioral assessment* (pp. 81–110). New York: Guilford Press.

BECK, A. T. (1976). *Cognitive therapy and the emotional disorders.* New York: International Universities Press.

BECK, A. T. (1988). *Love is never enough: How couples can overcome misunderstandings, resolve conflicts, and solve relationship problems through cognitive therapy.* New York: Harper & Row.

BECK, A. T., EMERY, G., & GREENBERG, R. L. (1985). *Anxiety disorders and phobias: A cognitive perspective.* New York: Basic Books.

BECK, A. T., RUSH, A. J., SHAW, B. F., & EMERY, G. (1979). *Cognitive therapy of depression.* New York: Guilford Press.

BELLACK, A. S. (1986). Schizophrenia: Behavior therapy's forgotten child. *Behavior Therapy, 17,* 199–214.

BELLACK, A. S., & HERSEN, M. (1993). *Clinical behavior therapy with adults.* In A. S. Bellack & M. Hersen (Eds.), *Handbook of behavior therapy in the psychiatric setting* (pp. 3–18). New York: Plenum Press.

BELLACK, A. S., & HERSEN, M. (Eds.). (1998). *Behavioral assessment: A practical handbook* (4th ed.). New York: Allyn & Bacon.

BELLACK, A. S., & MUSER, K. T. (1990). Schizophrenia. In A. S. Bellack, M. Hersen, & A. E. Kazdin (Eds.), *International handbook of behavior modification and behavior therapy* (2nd ed., pp. 353–376). New York: Plenum Press.

BELLACK, A. S., MUSER, K. T., GINGERICH, S., & AGRESTA, J. (Eds.). (1997). *Social skills training for schizophrenia.* New York: Guilford Press.

BELLAMY, G. T., HORNER, R. H., & INMAN, D. P. (1979). *Vocational habilitation of severely retarded adults: A direct service technology.* Baltimore: University Park Press.

BENTALL, R. P., LOWE, C. F., & BEASTY, A. (1985). The role of verbal behavior in human learning. II: Developmental differences. *Journal of the Experimental Analysis of Behavior, 47,* 165–181.

BERGEN, A. E., HOLBORN, S. W., & SCOTT-HUYGHEBART, V. C. (2002). Functional analysis of self-injurious behavior in an adult with Lesch–Nyhan Syndrome. *Behavior Modification, 26,* 187–204.

BERKOWITZ, L. (1988). Frustrations, appraisals, and aversively stimulated aggression. *Aggressive Behavior, 14,* 3–11.

BERKOWITZ, L. (1989). Frustration-aggression hypothesis: Examination and reformulation. *Psychological Bulletin, 106,* 59–73.

BIERMAN, K. L., MILLER, C. L., & STABB, S. D. (1987). Improving the social behavior and peer acceptance of rejected boys: Effects of social skill training with instructions and prohibitions. *Journal of Consulting and Clinical Psychology, 55,* 194–200.

BIJOU, S. W., & BAER, D. M. (1961). *Child development: A systematic and empirical theory* (Vol. 1). New York: Appleton-Century-Crofts.

BIJOU, S. W., & BAER, D. M. (1965). *Child development II: Universal stage of infancy.* Upper Saddle River, NJ: Prentice Hall.

BIRNBRAUER, J. S., BIJOU, S. W., WOLF, M. M., & KIDDER, J. D. (1965). Programmed instruction in the classroom. In L. P. Ullmann & L. Krasner (Eds.), *Case studies in behavior modification* (pp. 358–363). New York: Holt, Rinehart & Winston.

BLAKELEY, E., & SCHLINGER, H. (1987). Rules: Function-altering contingency-specifying stimuli. *The Behavior Analyst, 10,* 183–187.

BLAMPIED, N. (1999). Cognitive-behavior therapy in Aotearoa, New Zealand. *The Behavior Therapist, 22,* 173–178.

BLAMPIED, N. (2004). The New Zealand Association for Behavior Analysis. *Newsletter of the International Association for Behavior Analysis, 27*(2), 27.

BLANCK, G. (1983). *Behavior therapy in Argentina.* Buenos Aires: AAPC Ediciones.

BLIMKE, J., GOWAN, G., PATTERSON, P., & WOOD, N. (1984). Sport and psychology: What ethics suggest about practice. *Sports Science Periodical on Research and Technology in Sport.* Ottawa, Ont.: Coaching Association of Canada.

BLUM, N., & FRIMAN, P. (2000). Behavioral pediatrics. In J. Austin & J. E. Carr (Eds.), *Handbook of applied behavior analysis* (pp. 161–186). Reno, NV: Context Press.

BOND, F. W., & BONCE, D. (2000). Mediators of change in emotion-focused and problem-focused work site stress management interventions. *Journal of Occupational Health Psychology, 5,* 156–163.

BOOTH, R., & RACHMAN, S. (1992). The reduction of claustrophobia: I. *Behaviour Research and Therapy, 30,* 207–221.

BORKOVEC, T. D., & SHARPLESS, B. (2004). Generalized anxiety disorder: Bringing cognitive-behavioral therapy into the valued present. In S. C. Hayes, V. M. Follette, & M. M. Linehan (Eds.), *Mindfulness and acceptance: Expanding the cognitive-behavioral tradition.* New York: Guilford Press.

BORDEN, J. W. (1992). Behavioral treatment of simple phobia. In S. M. Turner, K. S. Calhoun, & H. E. Adams (Eds.), *Handbook of clinical behavior therapy* (pp. 77–94). New York: Wiley.

BOUCHARD, S., VALLIERES, A., ROY, M., & MAZIADE, M. (1996). Cognitive restructuring in the treatment of psychotic symptoms in schizophrenia: A critical analysis. *Behavior Therapy, 27,* 257–277.

BOUMAN, T. K., & EMMELKAMP, P. M. G. (1996). Panic disorder and agoraphobia. In V. B. Van Hasselt & M. Hersen (Eds.), *Sourcebook of psychological treatment manuals for adult disorders* (pp. 23–64). New York: Plenum Press.

BOVJBERG, D. H., REDD, W. H., MAIER, L. A., HOLLAND, J. C., LESKO, L. M., NIEDZWIECKI, D., et al. (1990). Anticipatory immune suppression in women receiving cyclic chemotherapy for ovarian cancer. *Journal of Consulting and Clinical Psychology, 58,* 153–157.

BRAAM, C., & MALOTT, R. W. (1990). "I'll do it when the snow melts": The effects of deadlines and delayed outcomes on rule-governed behavior in preschool children. *Analysis of Verbal Behavior, 8,* 67–76.

BRANTNER, J. P., & DOHERTY, M. A. (1983). A review of time-out: A conceptual and methodological analysis. In S. Axelrod & J. Apsche (Eds.), *The effects of punishment on human behavior* (pp. 87–132). New York: Academic Press.

BRAUKMAN, C., & WOLF, M. (1987). Behaviorally based group homes for juvenile offenders. In E. K. Morris & C. J. Braukman (Eds.), *Behavioral approaches to crime and delinquency: A handbook of application, research, and concepts* (pp. 135–160). New York: Plenum Press.

BREGER, L., & MCGAUGH, J. L. (1965). Critique and reformulation of "learning theory" approaches to psychotherapy and neurosis. *Psychological Bulletin, 63,* 338–358.

BRIGHAM, T. A. (1982). Self-management: A radical behavioral perspective. In P. Karoly & F. H. Canfer (Eds.), *Self-management and behavior change: From theory to practice* (pp. 32–59). New York: Pergamon Press.

BRIGHAM, T. A. (1989a). *Managing everyday problems.* New York: Guilford Press.

BRIGHAM, T. A. (1989b). *Self-management for adolescents: A skills training program.* New York: Guilford Press.

BRISCOE, R. V., HOFFMAN, D. B., & BAILEY, J. S. (1975). Behavioral community psychology: Training a community board to problem-solve. *Journal of Applied Behavior Analysis, 8,* 157–168.

BROMFIELD, R., BROMFIELD, D., & WEISS, B. (1988). Influence of the sexually abused label on perceptions of a child's failure. *Journal of Educational Research, 82,* 96–98.

BROMFIELD, R., WEISZ, J. R., & MESSER, T. (1986). Children's judgments and attributions in response to the "mentally retarded" label: A developmental approach. *Journal of Abnormal Psychology, 95,* 81–87.

BROWN, R. (1973). *A first language: The early years.* Cambridge, MA: Harvard University Press.

BROWNELL, K. D. (1981). Report on international behavior therapy organizations. *The Behavior Therapist, 4,* 9–13.

BUSH, J. P., & CIOCCO, J. E. (1992). Behavioral coding and sequential analysis: The portable computer systems for observational use. *Behavioral Assessment, 14,* 191–197.

BUZAS, H. P., & AYLLON, T. (1981). Differential reinforcement in coaching skills. *Behavior Modification, 5,* 372–385.

CABALLO, V. E., & BUELA-CASAL, G. (1993). Behavior therapy in Spain. *Behavior Therapist, 16,* 53–54.

CALDWELL, L. (1971). Behavior modification with children. Paper presented at the 1st Manitoba Behavior Change Conference, Portage la Prairie, Manitoba, Canada.

CAMERON, J., BANKO, K. M., & PIERCE, W. D. (2001). Pervasive negative effects of rewards on intrinsic motivation: The myth continues. *The Behavior Analyst, 24,* 1–44.

CAMPBELL, L. A., & BROWN, T. A. (2004). Generalized anxiety disorder. In M. M. Antony and D. H. Barlow (Eds.), *Handbook of assessment and treatment planning for psychological disorders.* New York: The Guilford Press.

CARR, E. G. (1977). The origins of self-injurious behavior: A review of some hypotheses. *Psychological Bulletin, 84,* 800–816.

CARR, E. G., NEWSOM, C. D., & BINKOFF, J. A. (1980). Escape as a factor in the aggressive behavior of two retarded children. *Journal of Applied Behavior Analysis, 13,* 101–117.

CARR, J. E., CORIATY, S., & DOZIER, C. L. (2000). Current issues in the function-based treatment of aberrant behavior in individuals with developmental disabilities. In J. Austin & J. E. Carr (Eds.), *Handbook of applied behavior nalysis* (pp. 91–112). Reno, NV: Context Press.

CARTER, N. (2004). Swedish Association for Behavior Analysis. *Newsletter of the International Association for Behavior Analysis, 27*(2), 29.

CATTELL, R. B., EBER, H. W., & TATSUOKA, M. M. (1970). *Handbook for the 16-Personality Factor Questionnaire.* Champagne, IL: Institute for Personality and Ability Testing.

CAUTELA, J. R. (1966). Treatment of compulsive behavior by covert desensitization. *Psychological Record, 16,* 33–41.

CAUTELA, J. R. (1977). *Behavior analysis forms for clinical intervention.* Champaign, IL: Research Press.

CAUTELA, J. R. (1981). *Behavior analysis forms for clinical intervention* (Vol. 2). Champaign, IL: Research Press.

CAUTELA, J. R., KASTENBAUM, R., & WINCZE, J. (1972). The use of the Fear Survey Schedule and the Reinforcement Survey Schedule to survey possible reinforcing and aversive stimuli among juvenile offenders. *Journal of Genetic Psychology, 121,* 255–261.

CAUTELA, J. R., & KEARNEY, A. (1993). *The covert conditioning handbook.* Pacific Grove, CA: Brooks/Cole.

CHARLOP, M. H., BURGIO, L. D., IWATA, B. A., & IVANCIC, M. T. (1988). Stimulus variation as a means of enhancing punishment effects. *Journal of Applied Behavior Analysis, 21,* 89–95.

CHEN, C. P. (1995). Counseling applications of RET in a Chinese cultural context. *Journal of Rational-Emotive and Cognitive Behavior Therapy, 13*, 117–129.

CHOMSKY, N. (1959). A review of B. F. Skinner's *Verbal Behavior. Language, 35*, 26–58.

CHRISTENSEN, A., & JACOBSON, N. S. (2000). *Reconcilable differences.* New York: Guilford Press.

CHRISTENSEN, A., SEVIER, M., SIMPSON, L. E., & GATTIS, K. S., (2004). Acceptance, mindfulness, and change in couple therapy. In S. C. Hayes, V. M. Follette, & M. M. Linehan (Eds.), *Mindfulness and acceptance: Expanding the cognitive behavioural tradition.* New York: Guildford Press.

CHRISTOPHERSEN, E. R., & MORTWEET, S. L. (2001). *Treatments that work: Empirically supported treatments for managing child behavior problems.* Washington, DC: American Psychological Association.

CHUNG, S. H. (1965). Effects of delayed reinforcement in a concurrent situation. *Journal of the Experimental Analysis of Behavior, 8*, 439 444.

CIPANI, E. (2004a). *Classroom management for all teachers; Twelve plans for evidence-based practice.* Upper Saddle River, NJ: Prentice Hall.

CIPANI, E. (2004b). *Punishment on trial.* Reno, NV: Context Press.

COHEN, R., DEJAMES, P., NOCERA, B., & RAMBERGER, M. (1980). Application of a simple self-instruction procedure on adult exercise and studying: Two case reports. *Psychological Reports, 46*, 443–451.

CONE, J. D. (1997). Issues in functional analysis in behavioral assessment. *Behavior Research and Therapy, 35*, 259–275.

CONE, J. D. (Ed.) (1999). Special section: Clinical assessment applications of self-monitoring. *Psychological Assessment, 11*, 411–497.

CONYERS, C., MARTIN, T. L., MARTIN, G. L., & YU, D. C. T. (2002). The 1983 AAMR manual, the 1992 AAMR manual, or the Developmental Disabilities Act: Which is used by researchers? *Education and Training in Mental Retardation and Developmental Disabilities, 37*, 310–316.

COON, D. W., & THOMPSON, L. W. (2002). Family caregivers for older adults: Ongoing and emergent themes for the behavior therapist. *The Behavior Therapist, 25*, 17–20.

COTTRAUX, J. (1990). "Cogito ergo somme": Cognitive behavior therapy in France. *Behavior Therapist, 13*, 189–190.

COWDERY, G. E., IWATA, B. A., & PACE, G. M. (1990). Effects and side-effects of DRO as treatment for self-injurious behavior. *Journal of Applied Behavior Analysis, 23*, 497–506.

COX, B. S., COX, A. B., & COX, D. J. (2000). Motivating signage prompts: Safety belt use among drivers exiting senior communities. *Journal of Applied Behavior Analysis, 33*, 635–638.

CRACKLEN, C., & MARTIN, G. (1983). To motivate age-group competitive swimmers at practice, "fun" should be earned. *Swimming Techniques, 20*(3), 29–32.

CRAIGHEAD, L. W. (2004). Obesity and eating disorders. In M. M. Antony & D. H. Barlow (Eds.), *Handbook of assessment and treatment planning for psychological disorders.* New York: Guilford Press.

CROSBIE J., & GLENN, K. (1993). A computer based personalized system of instruction in applied behavior analysis. *Behavior Research Methods, Instruments and Computers, 25*, 366–370.

CROWELL, C. R., QUINTANAR, L. R., & GRANT, K. L. (1981). Proctor: An online student evaluation and monitoring system for use with PSI format courses. *Behavior Research Methods and Instrumentation, 13*, 121–127.

CUMMINGS, N. A., O'DONOHUE, W. T., & FERGUSON, K. E. (2003). *Behavioral health as primary care: beyond efficacy to effectiveness.* Reno, NV: Context Press.

CUVO, A. J., & DAVIS, P. K. (2000). Behavioral acquisition by persons with developmental disabilities. In J. Austin & J. E. Carr (Eds.), *Handbook of applied behavior analysis* (pp. 39–60). Reno: NV: Context Press.

CUVO, A. J., DAVIS, P. K., O'REILLY, M. F., MOONEY, B. M., & CROWLEY, R. (1992). Promoting stimulus control with textual prompts and performance feedback for persons with mild disabilities. *Journal of Applied Behavior Analysis, 25*, 477–489.

DALY, E. J., III, MARTENS, B. K., KILMER, A., & MASSIE, D. R. (1996). The effects of instructional match and content overlap on generalized reading performance. *Journal of Applied Behavior Analysis, 29,* 507–518.

DANAHER, B. G. (1977). Research on rapid smoking: Interim summary and recommendations. *Addictive Behavior, 2,* 151–166.

DANGUAH, J. (1982). The practice of behavior therapy in West Africa: The case of Ghana. *Journal of Behavior Therapy and Experimental Psychiatry, 13,* 5–13.

DARDIG, J. C., & HEWARD, W. L. (1976). *Sign here: A contracting book for children and their parents.* Kalamazoo, MI: Behaviordelia.

DARUNA, J. H. (2004). Introduction to psychoneuroimmunology. St. Louis, MO: Elsevier, Academic Press.

DATTILO, F. M. (1999). Cognitive behavior therapy in Cuba. *The Behavior Therapist, 22,* 78, 91.

DAVID, D., & MICLEA, M. (2002) Behavior therapy in Romania: A brief history of theory, research, and practice. *The Behavior Therapist, 25,* 181–183.

DECI, E. L., KOESTNER, R., & RYAN, R. M. (1999). A meta-analytic review of experiments examining the effects of extrinsic rewards on intrinsic motivation. *Psychological Bulletin, 125,* 627–668.

DEITZ, S. M., & MALONE, L. W. (1985). Stimulus control terminology. *The Behavior Analyst, 8,* 259–264.

DEITZ, S. M., & REPP, A. C. (1973). Decreasing classroom misbehavior through the use of DRL schedules of reinforcement. *Journal of Applied Behavior Analysis, 6,* 457–463.

DEKKER, E. & GROEN, J. (1956). Reproducible psychogenic attacks of asthma: A laboratory study. *Journal of Psychosomatic Research, 1,* 58–67.

DELEON, I. G., & IWATA, B. A. (1996). Evaluation of a multiple-stimulus presentation format for assessing reinforcer preferences. *Journal of Applied Behavior Analysis, 29,* 519–533.

DELUCA, R. V., & HOLBORN, S. W. (1992). Effects of a variable ratio reinforcement schedule with changing-criteria on exercise in obese and non-obese boys. *Journal of Applied Behavior Analysis, 25,* 671–679.

DEMCHAK, M. (1990). Response prompting and fading methods: A review. *American Journal on Mental Retardation, 94,* 603–615.

DEMCHAK, M. A., & BOSSERT, K. W. (1996). *Innovations: Assessing problem behaviors.* Washington, DC: American Association on Mental Retardation.

DEPAEPE, P. A., SHORES, R. E., JACK, S. L., & DENNY, R. K. (1996). Effects of task difficulty on the disruptive and on-task behavior of students with severe behavior disorders. *Behavioral Disorders, 21,* 216–225.

DEPRESSION GUIDELINE PANEL (1993). *Depression in primary care: Vol. 2. Treatment of major depression* (Clinical Practice Guideline, No. 5, AHCPR Pub. No. 93–0551). Rockville, MD: U.S. Department of Health and Human Services, Public Health Service, Agency for Health Care Policy and Research.

DERENNE, A., & BARON, A. (2002). Behavior analysis and the study of aging. *The Behavior Analyst, 25,* 151–160.

DERICCO, D. A., & NIEMANN, J. E. (1980). In vivo effects of peer modelling on drinking rate. *Journal of Applied Behavior Analysis, 13,* 149–152.

DERISI, W. J., & BUTZ, G. (1975). *Writing behavioral contracts: A case simulation practice manual.* Champaign, IL: Research Press.

DESILVA, P., & SIMARASINGHE, D. (1985). Behavior therapy in Sri Lanka. *Journal of Behavior Therapy and Experimental Psychiatry, 16,* 95–100.

DEVRIES, J. E., BURNETTE, M. M., & REDMON, W. K. (1991). AIDS prevention: Improving nurses' compliance with glove wearing through performance feedback. *Journal of Applied Behavior Analysis, 24,* 705–711.

DICK-SISKIN, L. P. (2002). Cognitive-behavioral therapy with older adults. *The Behavior Therapist, 25*, 3–4, 6.

DIMIDJIAN, S., HOLLON, S., DOBSON, K., SCHMALING, K., KOHLENBERG, R., McGILINCHEY, J., et al. (2003, November). Behavioral activation, cognitive therapy, and antidepressant medication in the treatment of major depression: Design and acute phase outcomes. Presented at the 37th Annual Convention of the Association for Advancement of Behavior Therapy, Boston.

DOBSON, K. S. (1989). Meta-analysis of the efficacy of cognitive therapy for depression. *Journal of Consulting and Clinical Psychology, 57*, 414–419.

DOLEYS, D. M., MEREDITH, R. L., & CIMINERO, A. R. (Eds.). (1982). *Behavioral psychology and medicine and rehabilitation: Assessment and treatment strategies.* New York: Plenum Press.

DOLLARD, J., & MILLER, N. E. (1950). *Personality and psychotherapy.* New York: McGraw-Hill.

DORSEY, M. F., IWATA, B. A., ONG, P., & McSWEEN, T. E. (1980). Treatment of self-injurious behavior using a water mist: Initial response suppression and generalization. *Journal of Applied Behavior Analysis, 13*, 343–353.

DOUGHER, M. J. (1997). Cognitive concepts, behavior analysis, and behavior therapy. *Journal of Behavior Therapy and Experimental Psychiatry, 28*, 65–70.

DOUGHER, M. J. (Ed.). (2000). *Clinical behavior analysis.* Reno, NV: Context Press.

DRYDEN, W. (1999). *Rational-emotive behavior therapy: A training manual.* New York: Springer.

DUNLAP, G., & KINCAID, D. (2001). The widening world of functional assessment: Comments on four manuals and beyond. *Journal of Applied Behavior Analysis, 34*, 365–377.

DUPAUL, G. J., & ERVIN, R. A. (1996). Functional assessment of behaviors related to attention deficit/hyperactive disorder: Linking assessment to intervention design. *Behavior Therapy, 27*, 601–622.

DURLAK, J. A., FUHRMAN, T., & LAMPNAN, C. (1991). Effectiveness of cognitive-behavioral therapy for maladapting children: A meta-analysis. *Psychological Bulletin, 110*, 204–214.

DYMOND, S., & BARNES, D. (1997). Behavior analytic approaches to self-awareness. *The Psychological Record, 47*, 181–200.

DYMOND, S., CHIESA, M., & MARTIN, N. (2003). An update on providing graduate level training in applied behavior analysis in the UK. *Newsletter of the International Association for Behavior Analysis, 26*(3), 10.

DYMOND, S., & REHFELDT, R. A. (2000). Understanding complex behavior: The transformation of stimulus functions. *The Behavior Analyst, 23*, 239–254.

D'ZURILLA, T. J., & GOLFRIED, M. R. (1971). Problem-solving and behavior modification. *Journal of Abnormal Psychology, 78*, 107–126.

D'ZURILLA, T. J., & NEZU, A. M. (1999). *Problem-solving therapy, 2nd ed: A social competence approach to clinical intervention.* New York: Springer.

EKMAN, P. (1972). *Universal and cultural differences in facial expressions of emotions.* In J. K. Cole (Ed.), Nebraska Symposium on Motivation (Vol. 19). Lincoln: University of Nebraska Press.

ELKIN, I. (1994). The NIMH Treatment of Depression Collaborative Research Program: Where we began and where we are. In A. E. Bergin & S. L. Garfield (Eds.), *Handbook of psychotherapy and behavior change* (4th ed., pp. 114–139). New York: Wiley.

ELKIN, I., SHEA, M. T., WATKINS, J. T., IMBER, S. D., SOTSKY, S. M., COLLINS, J. F., et al. (1989). National Institute of Mental Health Treatment of Depression Collaborate Research Program: General effectiveness treatments. *Archives of General Psychiatry, 46*, 971–982.

ELLINGSON, S. A., MILTENBERGER, R. G., STRICKER, J. M., GARLINGHOUSE, M. A., ROBERTS, J., & GALENSKI, T. L. (2000). Analysis and treatment of finger sucking. *Journal of Applied Behavior Analysis, 33*, 41–52.

ELLIS, A. (1962). *Reason and emotion in psychotherapy.* New York: Lyle Stewart.

ELLIS, A. (1993). Changing rational-emotive therapy (RET) to rational-emotive behavior therapy (REBT). *The Behavior Therapist, 16,* 257–258.

ELLIS, A., & BERNARD, M. E. (Eds.). (1985). *Clinical applications of rational-emotive therapy.* New York: Plenum Press.

ELLIS, A., & DRYDEN, W. (1997). *The practice of rational-emotive behavior therapy* (2nd ed.). New York: Springer.

ELLIS, A., & GRIEGER, R. (1977). *Handbook of rational-emotive therapy.* New York: Springer.

EMMELKAMP, P. M. G. (2004). Behavior therapy with adults. In M. J. Lambert (Ed.), *Bergin and Garfield's handbook of psychotherapy and behavior change* (5th ed., pp. 393–446). New York: Wiley.

EMMELKAMP, P. M. G., BOUMAN, T. K., & SCHOLING, A. (1992). *Anxiety disorders: A practitioner's guide.* Chichester, UK: Wiley.

ENGELMAN, K. K., ALTUS, D. E., MOSIER, M. C., & MATHEWS, R. M. (2003). Brief training to promote the use of less intensive prompts by nursing assistants in a dementia-care unit. *Journal of Applied Behavior Analysis, 36,* 129–132.

ERVIN, R. A., & EHRHARDT, K. E. (2000). Behavior analysis and school psychology. In J. Austin & J. E. Carr (Eds.), *Handbook of applied behavior analysis* (pp. 113–136). Reno, NV: Context Press.

EYSENCK, H. J. (1959). Learning theory and behavior therapy. *Journal of Mental Science, 105,* 61–75.

EYSENCK, H. J. (Ed.). (1960). *Behaviour therapy and the neuroses.* London: Pergamon.

FABIANO, G. A., PELHAM, W. E., JR., MANOS, M. J., GNAGY, E. M., CHRONIS, A. M., ONYANGO, A. N., et al. (2004). An evaluation of three time-out procedures for children with attention-deficit/hyperactive disorder. *Behavior Therapy, 35,* 449–469.

FAITH, M. S., FONTAINE, K. R., CHESKIN, L. J., & ALLISON, D. B. (2000). Behavioral approaches to the problems of obesity. *Behavior Modification, 24,* 459–493.

FANTINO, E., & LOGAN, C. A. (1979). *The experimental analysis of behavior.* San Francisco: Freeman.

FARRELL, A. D. (1991). Computers and behavioral assessment: Current applications, future possibilities, and obstacles to routine use. *Behavioral Assessment, 13,* 159–179.

FAVELL, J. E., AZRIN, N. H., BAUMEISTER, A. A., CARR, E. G., DORSEY, M. F., FOREHAND, R., et al. (1982). The treatment of self-injurious behavior. *Behavior Therapist, 13,* 529–554.

FAWCETT, S. B., & MILLER, L. K. (1975). Training public-speaking behavior: An experimental analysis and social validation. *Journal of Applied Behavior Analysis, 8,* 125–135.

FELLNER, D. J., & SULZER-AZAROFF, B. (1984). A behavioral analysis of goal setting. *Journal of Organizational Behavior Management, 6,* 33–51.

FERSTER, C. B. (1993). A functional analysis of depression. *American Psychologist, 28,* 857–870.

FERSTER, C. B., & DEMYER, M. K. (1962). A method for the experimental analysis of the behavior of autistic children. *The American Journal of Orthopsychiatry, 32,* 89–98.

FERSTER, C. B., & SKINNER, B. F. (1957). *Schedules of reinforcement.* New York: Appleton-Century-Crofts.

FISCH, G. S. (1998). Visual inspection of data revisited: Do the eyes still have it? *The Behavior Analyst, 21,* 111–123.

FISCHER, J., & CORCORAN, K. (1994). *Measures for clinical practice: A source book* (2nd ed., Vols. 1 and 2). New York: Free Press.

FISHER, E. B. (1979). Overjustification effects in token economies. *Journal of Applied Behavior Analysis, 12,* 407–415.

FISHER, W. W., KELLEY, M. E., & LOMAS, J. E., (2003). Visual aids and structured criteria for improving visual inspection and interpretation of single-case designs. *Journal of Applied Behavior Analysis, 36,* 387–406.

FIXSEN, D. L., & BLASE, K. A. (1993). Creating new realities: Program development and dissemination. *Journal of Applied Behavior Analysis, 26,* 597–615.

FLANAGAN, B., GOLDIAMOND, I., & AZRIN, N. (1958). Operant stuttering: The control of stuttering behavior through response-contingent consequences. *Journal of the Experimental Analysis of Behavior, 1,* 173–177.

FLANAGAN, C. (1991). Behavior therapy and cognitive therapy in Ireland. *The Behavior Therapist, 14,* 231–232.

FLORA, S. R. (1990). Undermining intrinsic interest from the standpoint of a behaviorist. *The Psychological Record, 40,* 323–346.

FLORA, S. R. (2000). Praise's magic: Reinforcement ratio five-one gets the job done. *Behavior Analyst Today [Online], 1*(4), 64–69. Available: www.behavior.org.

FLORA, S. R., & FLORA, D. B. (1999). Effects of extrinsic reinforcement for reading during childhood on reported reading habits of college students. *The Psychological Record, 49,* 3–14.

FOA, E. B. (2000). Psychosocial treatment of posttraumatic stress disorder. *Journal of Clinical Psychiatry, 61*(Suppl. 5), 43–48.

FOXX, R. M., & FAW, G. D. (1990). Problem-solving skills training for psychiatric inpatients: An analysis of generalization. *Behavioral Residential Treatment, 5,* 159–176.

FOXX, R. M., & SHAPIRO, S. T. (1978). The timeout ribbon: A non-exclusionary timeout procedure. *Journal of Applied Behavior Analysis, 11,* 125–136.

FRANKS, C. M. (1964). *Conditioning techniques in clinical practice and research.* New York: Springer.

FRANKS, C. M. (Ed.). (1969). *Behavior therapy: Appraisal and status.* New York: McGraw-Hill.

FREA, W. D., & VITTIMBERGA, G. L. (2000). Behavior interventions for children with autism. In J. Austin & J. E. Carr (Eds.), *Handbook of applied behavior analysis* (pp. 247–274). Reno, NV: Context Press.

FREDERICK, L. D., DEITZ, S. M., BRYCELAND, J. A., & HUMMEL, J. H. (2003). *Behavior analysis, education, and effective schooling.* Reno, NV: Context Press.

FREDERIKSEN, L. W., & LOVETT, F. B. (1980). Inside organizational behavior management: Perspectives on an emerging field. *Journal of Organizational Behavior Management, 2,* 193–203.

FRIMAN, P. C. (2000). Behavioral family-style residential care for troubled out-of-home adolescents: Recent findings. In J. Austin and J. E. Carr (Eds.), *Handbook of Applied Behavior Analysis.* Reno, NV: Context Press.

FRIMAN, P. C., & VOLLMER, D. (1995). Successful use of the nocturnal urine alarm for diurnal enuresis. *Journal of Applied Behavior Analysis, 28,* 89–90.

FULLER, P. R. (1949). Operant conditioning of a vegetative human organism. *American Journal of Psychology, 62,* 587–590.

GELFAND, D. M., HARTMANN, D. P., LAMB, A. K., SMITH, C. L., MAHAN, M. A., & PAUL, S. C. (1974). Effects of adult models and described alternatives on children's choice of behavior management techniques. *Child Development, 45,* 585–593.

GELLER, E. S., WINETT, R. A., & EVERETT, P. B. (1982). *Preserving the environment: New strategies for behavior change.* New York: Plenum Press.

GENA, A., KRANTZ, P. J., MCCLANNAHAN, L. E., & POULSON, C. L. (1996). Training and generalization of effective behavior displayed by youth with autism. *Journal of Applied Behavior Analysis, 29,* 291–304.

GERSHOFF, E. T. (2002). Corporal punishment by parents and associated child behaviors and experiences: A meta-analytic and theoretical review. *Psychological Bulletin, 128,* 539–579.

GHEZZI, P. M., WILLIAMS, W. L., & CARR, J. E. (Eds.) (1999). *Autism: Behavior analytic perspectives.* Reno, NV: Context Press.

GIMPEL, G. A., & HOLLAND, N. L. (2003). *Emotional and behavioral problems of young children.* New York: Guilford Press.

GIRARDEAU, F. L., & SPRADLIN, J. E. (1964). Token rewards on a cottage program. *Mental Retardation, 2,* 345–351.

GLENWICK, D. S. (1990). Commentary on the special issue: The adolescent identity development of behavioral community psychology. *The Community Psychologist, 23*, 14–16.

GLYNN, E. L., & THOMAS, J. D. (1974). Effect of cueing on self-control of classroom behavior. *Journal of Applied Behavior Analysis, 7*, 299–306.

GOETZ, E. M., & BAER, D. M. (1973). Social control of form diversity and the emergence of new forms in childrens' block building. *Journal of Applied Behavior Analysis, 6*, 105–113.

GOLDIAMOND, I. (1965). Self-control procedures in personal behavior problems. *Psychological Reports, 17*, 851–868.

GOLDSTEIN, L. H. (1990). Behavioral and cognitive behavioral treatments for epilepsy: A progress review. *British Journal of Clinical Psychology, 29*, 257–269.

GORMALLY, J., BLACK, S., DASTON, S., & RARDIN, D. (1982). The assessment of binge eating severity among obese persons. *Addictive Behaviors, 7*, 47–55.

GORTNER, E. T., GOLAN, J. K., DOBSON, K. S., & JACOBSON, N. S. (1998). Cognitive behavior treatment for depression. *Relapse Prevention, 66*, 377–384.

GOSSETTE, R. L., & O'BRIEN, R. M. (1989, May). Efficacy of rational-emotive therapy with children: Fact or artifact? Paper presented at the meeting of the Association for Behavior Analysis, Nashville, TN.

GOSSETTE, R. L., & O'BRIEN, R. M. (1992). The efficacy of rational-emotive therapy in adults: Clinical fact or psychometric artifact? *Journal of Behavior Therapy and Experimental Psychiatry, 23*, 9–24.

GOULD, D. (1998). Goal-setting for peak performance. In J. M. Williams (Ed.), *Applied sport psychology: Personal growth to peak performance* (3rd ed.). Mountainview, CA: Mayfield.

GOULD, R. A., & CLUM, G. A. (1993). A meta-analysis of self-help treatment approaches. *Clinical Psychological Review, 13*, 167–189.

GRASSI, T. C. C. (Ed.) (2004). *Contemporary challenges in the behavioral approach. A Brazilian overview.* Santo André, Brazil: Esetec Editores Associados.

GRAZIANO, A. M. (1975). Futurants, coverants and operants. *Behavior Therapy, 6*, 421–422.

GREENSPOON, J. (1951). The effect of verbal and nonverbal stimuli on the frequency of members of two verbal response classes. Unpublished doctoral dissertation, Indiana University, Bloomington.

GREENSPOON, J. (1955). The reinforcing effect of two spoken words on the frequency of two responses. *American Journal of Psychology, 68*, 409–416.

GREENSPOON, J. (1976). *The sources of behavior: Abnormal and normal.* Monterey, CA: Brooks/Cole.

GREENWALD, D. P., KORNBLITH, S. J., HERSEN, M., BELLACK, A. S., & HIMMELHOCH, J. M. (1981). Differences between social skills, therapists and psychotherapists in treating depression. *Journal of Consulting and Clinical Psychology, 49*, 757–759.

GRESHAM, F. M., & MACMILLAN, D. L. (1997). Autistic recovery? An analysis and critique of the empirical evidence on the early intervention project. *Behavioral Disorders, 22*, 185–201.

GRIFFITH, R. G., & SPREAT, S. (1989). Aversive behavior modification procedures and the use of professional judgment. *Behavior Therapist, 12*(7), 143–146.

GUESS, D., & CARR, E. (1991). Emergence and maintenance of stereotopy and self-injury. *American Journal on Mental Retardation, 96*, 299–319.

GUESS, D., HELMSTETTER, E., TURNBULL, H. R., III, & KNOWLTON, S. (1986). *Use of aversive procedures with persons who are disabled: An historical review and critical analysis.* Seattle, WA: Association for Persons with Severe Handicaps.

GUESS, D., SAILOR, W., RUTHERFORD, G., & BAER, D. M. (1968). An experimental analysis of linguistic development: The productive use of the plural morpheme. *Journal of Applied Behavior Analysis, 1*, 297–306.

GUEVREMONT, D. C., OSNES, P. G., & STOKES, T. F. (1986). Preparation for effective self-regulation: The development of generalized verbal control. *Journal of Applied Behavior Analysis, 19*, 99–104.

GUILHORDI, H. J. (2004). Coersive control and anxiety-A case of "panic disorder" treated by therapy by contingencies of reinforcement. In T. Grassi (Ed.), *contemporary challanges in the behavioral approach: A Brazilian overview*. Santo André, Brazil: Esetec Editores Associados.

GUTHRIE, E. R. (1935). *The psychology of human learning*. New York: Harper & Row.

HAINS, A. H., & BAER, D. M. (1989). Interaction effects in multi-element designs: Inevitable, desirable, and ignorable. *Journal of Applied Behavior Analysis, 22,* 57–69.

HANLEY, G. P., IWATA, B. A., & MCCORD, B. E. (2003). Functional analysis of problem behavior: A review. *Journal of Applied Behavior Analysis, 36,* 147–185.

HANTULA, D. A., BOYD, J. H., & CROWELL, C. I. (1989). Ten years of behavioral instruction with computers: Trials, tribulations, and reflections. *Proceedings of the Academic Microcomputer Conference* (pp. 81–92). Indianapolis, IN: Author.

HARDY, L., MARTIN, G., YU, D., LEADER, C., & QUINN, G. (1981). *Objective behavioral assessment of the severely and moderately mentally handicapped: The OBA*. Springfield, IL; Charles C Thomas.

HARING, T. G., & KENNEDY, C. H. (1990). Contextual control of problem behavior in students with severe disabilities. *Journal of Applied Behavior Analysis, 23,* 235–243.

HARRIS, B. (1979). What happened to little Albert? *American Psychologist, 34,* 151–160.

HARRIS, C. S., & MCREYNOLDS, W. T. (1977). Semantic cues and response contingencies in self-instructional control. *Journal of Behavior Therapy and Experimental Psychiatry, 8,* 15–17.

HARRIS, F. R., WOLF, M. M., & BAER, D. M. (1964). Effects of adult social reinforcement on child behavior. *Young Children, 20,* 8–17.

HATCH, M. L., FRIEDMAN, S., & PARADIS, C. M. (1996). Behavioral treatment of obsessive-compulsive disorder in African Americans. *Cognitive and Behavioral Practice, 3,* 303–315.

HAUGHTON, E., & AYLLON, T. (1965). Production and elimination of symptomatic behavior. In L. P. Ullmann & L. Krasner (Eds.), *Case studies in behavior modification* (pp. 94–98). New York: Holt, Rinehart & Winston.

HAWKINS, R. C., & CLEMENT, P. (1980). Development and construct validation of a self-report measure of binge eating tendencies. *Addictive Behaviors, 5,* 219–226.

HAWKINS, R. P. (1979). The functions of assessment: Implications for selection and development of devices for assessing repertoires in clinical, educational, and other settings. *Journal of Applied Behavior Analysis, 12,* 501–516.

HAWKINS, R. P., & DOTSON, V. A. (1975). Reliability scores that delude: An Alice in Wonderland trip through the misleading characteristics of interobserver agreement scores in interval recording. In E. Ramp & G. Semp (Eds.), *Behavior analysis: Areas of research and application* (pp. 359–376). Upper Saddle River, NJ: Prentice Hall.

HAWKINS, R. P., & FORSYTH, J. P. (1997). Bridging barriers between paradigms: Making cognitive concepts relevant for behavior analysis. *Journal of Behavior Therapy and Experimental Psychiatry, 28,* 3–6.

HAWKINS, R. P., MATHEWS, J. R., & HAMDAN, L. (1999). *Measuring behavioral outcomes*. Norwell, MA: Kluwer Academic/Plenum Publishers.

HAYES, S. C. (1989). *Rule-governed behavior: Cognition, contingencies, and instructional control*. New York: Plenum Press.

HAYES, S. C. (2004a). Acceptance and commitment therapy and the new behavior therapies: Mindfulness, acceptance, and relationship. In S. C. Hayes, V. M. Follette, and M. M. Linehan (Eds.), *Mindfulness and acceptance: Expanding the cognitive behavioral tradition* (pp. 1–29). New York: Guilford Press.

HAYES, S. C. (2004b). Acceptance and commitment therapy, relational frame theory, and the third wave of behavior therapy. *Behavior Therapy, 35,* 639–666.

HAYES, S. C., BARNES-HOLMES, D., & ROCHE, B. (Eds.). (2001). *Relational frame theory: A post-Skinnerian account of human language and cognition*. New York: Plenum Press.

HAYES, S. C., & BISSETT, R. T. (2000). Behavioral psychotherapy and the rise of clinical behavior analysis. In J. Austin & J. E. Carr (Eds.), *Handbook of applied behavior analysis* (pp. 231–245). Reno, NV: Context Press.

HAYES, S. C., FOLLETTE, V. M., & LINEHAN, M. M. (Eds.). (2004). *Mindfulness and acceptance: Expanding the cognitive behavioral tradition.* New York: Guilford Press.

HAYES, S. C., JACOBSON, N. S., FOLLETTE, V. M., & DOUGHER, M. J. (Eds.). (1994). *Acceptance and change: Content and context in psychotherapy.* Reno, NV: Context Press.

HAYES, S. C., MASUDA, A., BISSETTE, R., LUOMA, J., & GUERRERO, L. F. (2004). DBT, FAP, and ACT: How empirically oriented are the new behavior therapy technologies. *Behavior Therapy, 35,* 35–54.

HAYES, S. C., ROSENFARB, I., WULFERT, E., MUNT, E. D., KORN, D., & ZETTLE, R. D. (1985). Self-reinforcement effects: An artifact of social standard setting? *Journal of Applied Behavior Analysis, 18,* 201–214.

HAYES, S. C., STROSAHL, K. D., & WILSON, K. G. (1999). *Acceptance and commitment therapy: An experiential approach to behavior change.* New York: Guilford Press.

HAYNES, S. N. (1998). The changing nature of behavioral assessment. In A. S. Bellack & M. Hersen (Eds.), *Behavioral assessment: A practical handbook* (4th ed., pp. 1–21). Boston: Allyn & Bacon.

HEFFERLINE, R. F., KEENAN, B., & HARFORD, R. A. (1959). Escape and avoidance conditioning in human subjects without their observation of the response. *Science, 130,* 1338–1339.

HERMANN, J. A., MONTES, A. I., DOMINGUEZ, B., MONTES, F., & HOPKINS, B. L. (1973). Effects of bonuses for punctuality on the tardiness of industrial workers. *Journal of Applied Behavior Analysis, 6,* 563–570.

HERRNSTEIN, R. J. (1961). Relative and absolute strength of response as a function of frequency of reinforcement. *Journal of the Experimental Analysis of Behavior, 4,* 267–272.

HERRNSTEIN, R. J., & DEVILLIERS, P. A. (1980). Fish as a natural category for people and pigeons. In G. H. Bower (Ed.), *The psychology of learning and motivation* (Vol. 14, pp. 60–97). New York: Academic Press.

HERRNSTEIN, R. J., & LOVELAND, D. H. (1964). Complex visual concept in the pigeon. *Science, 146,* 549–551.

HERRNSTEIN, R. J., LOVELAND, D. H., & CABLE, C. (1976). Natural concepts in pigeons. *Journal of Experimental Psychology: Animal Behavior Processes, 2,* 285–302.

HERSEN, M. (1976). Historical perspectives in behavioral assessment. In M. Hersen & A. S. Bellack (Eds.), *Behavioral assessment: A practical handbook* (pp. 3–17). New York: Pergamon Press.

HERSEN, M. (Ed.). (1983). *Outpatient behavior therapy: A clinical guide.* New York: Grune & Stratton.

HERSEN, M., & LAST, C. G. (Eds.). (1999). *Child behavior therapy casebook.* New York: Kluwer Academic Publishers/Plenum Press.

HILDEBRAND, R. G., MARTIN, G. L., FURER, P., & HAZEN, A. (1990). A recruitment of praise package to increase productivity levels of developmentally handicapped workers. *Behavior Modification, 14,* 97–113.

HILE, M.G. (1991). Hand-held behavioral observations: The Observer. *Behavioral Assessment, 13,* 187–196.

HOMME, L. E. (1965). Perspectives in psychology: XXIV. Control of coverants, the operants of the mind. *Psychological Record, 15,* 501–511.

HOMME, L. E., CSANYI, A. P., GONZALES, M. A., & RECHS, J. R. (1969). *How to use contingency contracting in the classroom.* Champaign, IL: Research Press.

HONIG, W. K., & STEWART, K. (1988). Pigeons can discriminate locations presented in pictures. *Journal of the Experimental Analysis of Behavior, 50,* 541–551.

HORAN, J. J., & JOHNSON, R. G. (1971). Coverant conditioning through a self-management application of the Premack principle: Its effect on weight reduction. *Journal of Behavior Therapy and Experimental Psychiatry, 2,* 243–249.

HORNER, R. D., & KEILITZ, I. (1975). Training mentally retarded adolescent to brush their teeth. *Journal of Applied Behavior Analysis, 8*, 301–309.

HORNER, R. H. (1994). Functional assessment: Contributions and future directions. *Journal of Applied Behavior Analysis, 27*, 401–404.

HORNER, R. H., SPRAGUE, T., & WILCOX, B. (1982). General case programming for community activities. In B. Wilcox & G. T. Bellamy (Eds.), *Design of high school programs for severely handicapped students* (pp. 61–98). Baltimore: Paul Brookes.

HRYCAIKO, D., & MARTIN, G. L. (1996). Applied research studies with single-subject designs: Why so few? *Journal of Applied Sport Psychology, 8*, 183–199.

HRYDOWY, E. R., & MARTIN, G. L. (1994). A practical staff management package for use in a training program for persons with developmental disabilities. *Behavior Modification, 18*, 66–88.

HUANG, W., & CUVO, A. J. (1997). Social skills training for adults with mental retardation in job-related settings. *Behavior Modification, 21*, 3–44.

HULL, C. L. (1943). *Principles of behavior.* New York: Appleton-Century-Crofts.

HULL, C. L. (1952). *A behavior system.* New Haven, CT: Yale University Press.

HUME, K. M., MARTIN, G. L., GONZALES, P., CRACKLEN, C., & GENTHON, S. (1985). A self-monitoring feedback package for improving freestyle figure skating performance. *Journal of Sport Psychology, 7*, 333–345.

INGRAM, R. E., & SCOTT, W. D. (1990). Cognitive behavior therapy. In A. S. Bellack, M. Hersen, & A. E. Kazdin (Eds.), *International handbook of behavior modification and therapy* (2nd ed., pp. 53–68). New York: Plenum Press.

IREY, P. A. (1972). Covert sensitization of cigarette smokers with high and low extraversion scores. Unpublished master's thesis, Southern Illinois University, Carbondale.

ISRAEL, A. C., STOLMAKER, L., & ADRIAN, C. A. G. (1985). The effects of training parents in general child management skills on a behavioral weight loss program for children. *Behavior Therapy, 16*, 169–180.

ISSACS, W., THOMAS, J., & GOLDIAMOND, I. (1960). Application of operant conditioning to reinstate verbal behavior in psychotics. *Journal of Speech and Hearing Disorders, 25*, 8–12.

IVANCIC, M. T., BARRETT, G. T., SIMONOW, A., & KIMBERLY, A. (1997). A replication to increase happiness indices among some people with profound developmental disabilities. *Research in Developmental Disabilities, 18*, 79–89.

IWAMASA, G. Y. (1999). Behavior therapy and Asian Americans: Is there a commitment? *The Behavior Therapist, 10*, 196–197, 205–206.

IWAMASA, G. Y., & SMITH, S. K. (1996). Ethic diversity in behavioral psychology: A review of the literature. *Behavior Modification, 20*, 45–59.

IWATA, B. A., DORSEY, M. F., SLIFER, K. J., BAUMAN, K. E., & RICHMAN, G. S. (1982). Toward a functional analysis of self-injury. *Analysis and Intervention in Developmental Disabilities, 2*, 3–20.

IWATA, B. A., KAHNG, S. W., WALLACE, M. D., & LINDBERG, J. S. (2000). The functional analysis model of behavioral assessment. In J. Austin & J. E. Carr (Eds.), *Handbook of applied behavior analysis* (pp. 61–90). Reno, NV: Context Press.

IWATA, B. A., PACE, G. M., COWDERY, G. E., & MILTENBERGER, R. G. (1994). What makes extinction work: An analysis of procedural form and function. *Journal of Applied Behavior Analysis, 27*, 131–144.

IWATA, B. A., PACE, G. M., DORSEY, M. F., ZARCONE, J. R., VOLLMER, T. R., SMITH, R. G., et al. (1994). The functions of self-injurious behavior: An experimental-epidemiological analysis. *Journal of Applied Behavior Analysis, 27*, 215–240.

IWATA, B. A., PACE, G. M., KALSHER, M. J., COWDERY, G. E., & CATALDO, M. F. (1990). Experimental analysis and extinction of self-injurious escape behavior. *Journal of Applied Behavior Analysis, 23*, 11–27.

IZARD, C. E. (1991). *The psychology of emotions.* New York: Plenum Press.

JACKSON, D. A., & WALLACE, R. F. (1974). The modification and generalization of voice loudness in a 15-year-old retarded girl. *Journal of Applied Behavior Analysis, 7*, 461–471.

JACOBS, H. (2000). Brain injury rehabilitation. In J. Austin & J. E. Carr (Eds.), *Handbook of applied behavior analysis* (211–230). Reno, NV: Context Press.

JACOBSON, N. S., DOBSON, K. S., TRUAX, P. A., ADDIS, M. E., KOERNER, K., GOLLAN, J. K., et al. (1996). A component analysis of cognitive behavioral treatment for depression. *Journal of Consulting and Clinical Psychology, 64*, 295–304.

JACOBSON, N. S., MARTELL, C. R., & DIMIDJIAN, S. (2001). Behavioral activation for depression: Returning to contextual roots. *Clinical Psychology: Science & Practice, 8*, 255–270.

JANIS, I., & MANN, L. (1977). *Decision-making*. New York: Free Press.

JANIS, I., & WHEELER, D. (1978). Thinking clearly about career choices. *Psychology Today, 11*(12), 66–76, 121–122.

JENSEN, B. J., & HAYNES, S. N. (1986). *Self-report questionnaires and inventories*. In A. R. Ciminero, K. S. Calhoun, & H. E. Adams (Eds.), *Handbook of behavioral assessment* (2nd ed.). New York: Wiley.

JOHNSON, C. M., REDMON, W. K., & MAWHINNEY, T. C. (Eds.). (2001). *Handbook of organizational performance: Behavior analysis and management*. New York: Haworth Press.

JOHNSON, C. R., HUNT, F. M., & SIEBERT, M. J. (1994). Discrimination training in the treatment of pica and food scavenging. *Behavior Modification, 18*, 214–229.

JOHNSON, K. R., & RUSKIN, R. S. (1977). *Behavioral instruction: An evaluative review*. Washington, DC: American Psychological Association.

JOHNSON, S. P., WELCH, T. M., MILLER, L. K., & ALTUS, D. E. (1991). Participatory management: Maintaining staff performance in a university housing cooperative. *Journal of Applied Behavior Analysis, 24*, 119–127.

JOHNSON, W. G. (1971). Some applications of Homme's coverant control therapy: Two case reports. *Behavior Therapy, 2*, 240–248.

JOHNSON, W. L., & BAUMEISTER, A. (1978). Self-injurious behavior: A review and analysis of methodological details of published studies. *Behavior Modification, 2*, 465–484.

JONES, M. C. (1924). The elimination of children's fears. *Journal of Experimental Psychology, 7*, 383–390.

JONES, R. S. P., & MCCAUGHEY, R. E. (1992). Gentle teaching and applied behavior analysis: A critical review. *Journal of Applied Behavior Analysis, 25*, 853–867.

KAHNG, S. W. & IWATA, B. A. (1998). Computerized systems for collecting real-time observational data. *Journal of Applied Behavior Analysis, 31*, 253–261.

KAROL, R. L., & RICHARDS, C. S. (1978, November). Making treatment effects last: An investigation of maintenance strategies for smoking reduction. Paper presented at the meeting of the Association for the Advancement of Behavior Therapy, Chicago.

KAU, M. L., & FISCHER, J. (1974). Self-modification of exercise behavior. *Journal of Behavior Therapy and Experimental Psychiatry, 5*, 213–214.

KAZDIN, A. E. (1973). The effect of vicarious reinforcement on attentive behavior in the classroom. *Journal of Applied Behavior Analysis, 6*, 72–78.

KAZDIN, A. E. (1977a). *The token economy: A review and evaluation*. New York: Plenum Press.

KAZDIN, A. E. (1977b). Assessing the clinical or applied importance of behavior change through social validation. *Behavior Modification, 1*, 427–451.

KAZDIN, A. E. (1978). *History of behavior modification*. Baltimore: University Park Press.

KAZDIN, A. E. (1985). The token economy. In R. M. Turner & L. M. Ascher (Eds.), *Evaluating behavior therapy outcome* (pp. 225–253). New York: Springer.

KAZDIN, A. E., & ERICKSON, L. M. (1975). Developing responsiveness to instructions in severely and profoundly retarded residents. *Journal of Behavior Therapy and Experimental Psychiatry, 6*, 17–21.

KAZDIN, A. E., & POLSTER, R. (1973). Intermittent token reinforcement and response maintenance in extinction. *Behavior Therapy, 4,* 386–391.

KEARNEY, C. A., & SILVERMAN, W. K. (1990). A preliminary analysis of a functional model of assessment and treatment for school refusal behavior. *Behavior Modification, 14,* 340–366.

KELLER, F. S. (1968). Good-bye, teacher . . . . *Journal of Applied Behavior Analysis, 1,* 79–89.

KELLER, F. S., & SCHOENFELD, W. N. (1950). *Principles of psychology.* New York: Appleton-Century-Crofts.

KELLER, F. S., & SHERMAN, J. G. (1982). *The PSI handbook: Essays on personalized instruction.* Lawrence, KS: T.R.I. Publications.

KENDALL, P. C. (Ed.). (2000). *Child and adolescent psychotherapy: Cognitive behavioral procedures* (2nd ed.). New York: Guilford Press.

KERN, L., CHILDS, K. E., DUNLAP, G., CLARKE, S., & FALK, G. D. (1994). Using assessment based curricular intervention to improve the classroom behavior of a student with emotional and behavioral challenges. *Journal of Applied Behavior Analysis, 27,* 7–19.

KIM, J. (2003). History of Korean ABA. *Newsletter of the International Association for Behavior Analysis, 26, (3),* 20–21.

KING, N. (1996). The Australian Association for Cognitive and Behavior Therapy. *The Behavior Therapist, 19,* 73–74.

KINGDON, D. G., & TURKINGTON, D. (1994). *Cognitive-behavioral therapy of schizophrenia.* New York: Guilford Press.

KINSNER, W., & PEAR, J. J. (1988). Computer-aided personalized system of instruction for the virtual classroom. *Canadian Journal of Educational Communication, 17,* 21–36.

KIRBY, F. D., & SHIELDS, F. (1972). Modification of arithmetic response rate and attending behavior in a seventh grade student. *Journal of Applied Behavior Analysis, 5,* 79–84.

KIRCHER, A. S., PEAR, J. J., & MARTIN, G. (1971). Shock as punishment in a picture-naming task with retarded children. *Journal of Applied Behavior Analysis, 4,* 227–233.

KNIGHT, M. F., & McKENZIE, H. S. (1974). Elimination of bedtime thumb-sucking in home settings through contingent reading. *Journal of Applied Behavior Analysis, 7,* 33–38.

KOEGEL, R. L., & WILLIAMS, J. A. (1980). Direct versus indirect response-reinforcer relationships in teaching autistic children. *Journal of Abnormal Child Psychology, 8,* 537–547.

KOHLER, F. W., & GREENWOOD, C. R. (1986). Toward technology of generalization: The identification of natural contingencies of reinforcement. *The Behavior Analyst, 9,* 19–26.

KOHN, A. (1993). *Punished by rewards: The trouble with gold stars, incentive plans, A's, praise, and other bribes.* New York: Houghton Mifflin.

KOKOSZKA, A., POPIEL, A., & SITARZ, M. (2000). Cognitive-behavioral therapy in Poland. *The Behavior Therapist, 23,* 209–216.

KOMAKI, J., & BARNETT, F. T. (1977). A behavioral approach to coaching football: Improving the play execution of the offensive backfield on a youth football team. *Journal of Applied Behavior Analysis, 7,* 199–206.

KONARSKI, E. A., JR., FAVELL, J. E., & FAVELL, J. E. (Eds.). (1997). *Manual for the assessment and treatment of the behavior disorders of people with mental retardation.* Morganton, NC: Western Carolina Center Foundation.

KOOP, S., MARTIN, G., YU, D., & SUTHONS, E. (1980). Comparison of two reinforcement strategies in vocational-skill training of mentally retarded persons. *American Journal of Mental Deficiency, 84,* 616–626.

KOZAK, M. J., & FOA, E. B. (1996). Obsessive-compulsive disorder. In V. B. Van Hasselt & M. Hersen (Eds.), *Sourcebook of psychological treatment manuals for adult disorders* (pp. 65–122). New York: Plenum Press.

KULIK, C.-L., KULIK, J. A., & BANGERT-DROWNS, R. L. (1990). Effectiveness of mastery learning programs: A meta-analysis. *Review of Educational Research, 60,* 265–299.

LALLI, J. S., VOLLMER, T. R., PROGAR, P. R., WRIGHT, C., BORRERO, J., DANIEL, D., et al. (1999). Competition between positive and negative reinforcement in the treatment of escape behavior. *Journal of Applied Behavior Analysis, 32,* 285–296.

LAMBERT, M. J. (Ed.). (2004). *Bergin & Garfield's Handbook of psychotherapy and behaviour change.* New York: Wiley.

LAMSON, R. (1997). *Virtual therapy.* Montreal, Canada: Polytechnic International Press.

LARAWAY, S., SNYCERSKI, S., MICHAEL, J., & POLING, A. (2003). Motivating operations and terms to describe them: Some further reinfinements. *Journal of Applied Behavior Analysis, 36,* 407–414.

LARKIN, K. T., & ZAYFERT, C. (1996). Anger management training with essential hypertensive patients. In V. B. Van Hasselt & M. Hersen (Eds.), *Sourcebook of psychological treatment manuals for adult disorders* (pp. 689–716). New York: Plenum Press.

LATIES, V. G., & MACE, F. C. (1993). Taking stock: The first 25 years of the *Journal of Applied Behavior Analysis. Journal of Applied Behavior Analysis, 26,* 513–525.

LATIMER, P. R., & SWEET, A. A. (1984). Cognitive vs. behavioral procedures in cognitive behavior therapy: A critical review of the evidence. *Journal of Behavior Therapy and Experimental Psychiatry, 15,* 9–22.

LATNER, J. D., & WILSON, G. T. (2002). Self-monitoring and the assessment of binge eating. *Behavior Therapy, 33,* 465–477.

LATTAL, K. A., & METZGER, B. (1994). Response acquisition by Siamese fighting fish with delayed visual reinforcement. *Journal of the Experimental Analysis of Behavior, 61,* 35–44.

LAZARUS, A. A. (1958). New methods in psychotherapy: A case study. *South African Medical Journal, 32,* 660–664.

LAZARUS, A. A. (1971). *Behavior therapy and beyond.* New York: McGraw-Hill.

LAZARUS, A. A. (1976). *Multi-model behavior therapy.* New York: Springer.

LEAL, J., & GALANTER, M. (1995). The use of contingency-contracting to improve outcome in methadone maintenance. *Substance Abuse, 16,* 155–167.

LEBOW, M. C. (1989). *Adult obesity therapy.* New York: Pergamon Press.

LEBOW, M. D. (1981). *Weight control: The behavioral strategies.* New York: Wiley.

LEBOW, M. D. (1991). *Overweight children: Helping your child to achieve lifetime weight control.* New York: Insight Books/Plenum Press.

LEIBLUM, S. R., & ROSEN, R. C. (Eds.). (2000). *Principles and practice of sex therapy: Third edition.* New York: Guilford Press.

LENNOX, D. B., MILTENBERGER, R. G., & DONNELLY, D. (1987). Response interruption and DRL for the reduction of rapid eating. *Journal of Applied Behavior Analysis, 20,* 279–284.

LERMAN, D. C., & IWATA, B. A. (1995). Prevalence of the extinction burst and its attenuation during treatment. *Journal of Applied Behavior Analysis, 28,* 93–94.

LERMAN, D. C., & IWATA, B. A. (1996). Developing a technology for the use of operant extinction in clinical settings: An examination of basic and applied research. *Journal of Applied Behavior Analysis, 29,* 345–382.

LERMAN, D. C., IWATA, B. A., SHORE, B. A., & KAHNG, S. (1996). Responding maintained by intermittent reinforcement: Implications for the use of extinction with problem behavior in clinical settings. *Journal of Applied Behavior Analysis, 29,* 153–171.

LERMAN, D. C., IWATA, B. A., & WALLACE, M. D. (1999). Side effects of extinction: Prevalence of bursting and aggression during the treatment of self-injurious behavior. *Journal of Applied Behavior Analysis, 32,* 1–8.

LERMAN, D. C., & VORNDRAN, C. M. (2002). On the status of knowledge for using punishment: Implications for treating behavior disorders. *Journal of Applied Behavior Analysis, 35,* 431–464.

LESLIE-TOOGOOD, A., & MARTIN, G. L. (2003). Do coaches know the mental skills of their athletes? Assessments from volleyball and track. *Journal of Sport Behavior, 26,* 56–68.

LEWINSOHN, P. M. (1975). The behavioral study and treatment of depression. In M. Hersen, R. M. Eisler, & P. M. Miller (Eds.), *Progress in Behavior Modification* (Vol. 1, pp. 19–65). New York: Academic Press.

LEWIS, T., J., & SUGAI, G. (1996). Descriptive and experimental analysis of teacher and peer attention and the use of assessment-based intervention to improve pro-social behavior. *Journal of Behavioral Education, 6,* 7–24.

LINDSLEY, O. R. (1956). Operant conditioning methods applied to research in chronic schizophrenia. *Psychiatric Research Reports, 5,* 118–139.

LINDSLEY, O. R. (1966). An experiment with parents handling behavior at home. *Johnstone Bulletin, 9,* 27–36.

LINDSLEY, O. R., SKINNER, B. F., & SOLOMON, H. C. (1953). *Studies in behavior therapy: Status report. I.* Waltham, MA: Metropolitan State Hospital.

LINEHAN, M. M. (1993). *Cognitive behavioral treatment of borderline personality disorder.* New York: Guilford Press.

LINES, J. B., SCHWARTZMAN, L., TKACHUK, G. A., LESLIE-TOOGOOD, S. A., & MARTIN, G. L. (1999). Behavioral assessment in sport psychology consulting: Applications to swimming and basketball. *Journal of Sport Behavior, 4,* 558–569.

LINSCHEID, T. R., IWATA, B. A., RICKETTS, R. W., WILLIAMS, D. E., & GRIFFIN, J. C. (1990). Clinical evaluation of the Self-Injurious Behavior Inhibiting System (SIBIS). *Journal of Applied Behavior Analysis, 23,* 53–78.

LINSCHEID, T. R., PEJEAU, C., COHEN, S., & FOOTO-LENZ, M. (1994). Positive side-effects in the treatment of SIB using the Self-Injurious Behavior Inhibiting System (SIBIS): Implications for operant and biochemical explanations of SIB. *Research in Developmental Disabilities, 15,* 81–90.

LIPPMAN, M. R., & MOTTA, R. W. (1993). Effects of positive and negative reinforcement on daily living skills in chronic psychiatric patients in community residences. *Journal of Clinical Psychology, 49,* 654–662.

LLOYD, K. E. (2002). A review of correspondence training: Suggestions for a revival. *The Behavior Analyst, 25,* 57–73.

LOCKE, E. A., & LATHAM, G. P. (1990). *A theory of goal setting and task performance.* Upper Saddle River, NJ: Prentice Hall.

LOGUE, A. W. (1995). *Self-control: Waiting until tommorow for what you want today.* Upper Saddle River, NJ: Prentice Hall.

LOPEZ, W. L., & AGUILAR, M. C. (2003). Reflections on the history of ABA Columbia: Five years of experience and development. *Newsletter of the International Association for Behavior Analysis, 26(3),* 14–15.

LOVAAS, O. I. (1966). A program for the establishment of speech in psychotic children. In J. K. Wing (Ed.), *Early childhood autism* (pp. 115–144). Elmsford, NY: Pergamon Press.

LOVAAS, O. I. (1977). *The autistic child: Language development through behavior modification.* New York: Irvington.

LOVAAS, O. I. (1982, August). An overall evaluation of the young autism project. Paper presented at the annual meeting of American Psychological Association, Washington, DC.

LOVAAS, O. I. (1993). The development of a treatment-research project for developmentally disabled and autistic children. *Journal of Applied Behavior Analysis, 26,* 617–630.

LOVAAS, O. I., NEWSOM, C., & HICKMAN, C. (1987). Self-stimulatory behavior and perceptual development. *Journal of Applied Behavior Analysis, 20*, 45–68.

LOWE, C. F., BEASTY, A., & BENTALL, R. P. (1983). The role of verbal behavior in human learning: Infant performance on fixed interval schedules. *Journal of the Experimental Analysis of Behavior, 39*, 157–164.

LUBETKIN, B. S., RIVERS, P. C., & ROSENBERG, C. N. (1971). Difficulties of disulfiram therapy with alcoholics. *Quarterly Journal of Studies on Alcohol, 32*, 118–171.

LUBOW, R. E. (1974). High-order concept formation in pigeons. *Journal of the Experimental Analysis of Behavior, 21*, 475–483.

LUCE, S. C., DELQUADRI, J., & HALL, R. V. (1980). Contingent exercise: A mild but powerful procedure for suppressing inappropriate verbal and aggressive behavior. *Journal of Applied Behavior Analysis, 13*, 583–594.

LUDWIG, A. M., LEVINE, J. A., & STARK, L. H. (1970). *LDS and alcoholism*. Springfield, IL: Charles C Thomas.

LUTZ, J. (1994). *Introduction to learning and memory*. Pacific Grove, CA: Brooks/Cole.

MACE, F. C., & BELFIORE, P. (1990). Behavioral momentum in the treatment of escape-motivated stereotypy. *Journal of Applied Behavior Analysis, 23*, 507–514.

MACE, F. C., HOCK, M. L., LALLI, J. S., WEST, B. J., BELFIORE, P., PINTER, E., et al. (1988). Behavioral momentum in the treatment of noncompliance. *Journal of Applied Behavior Analysis, 21*, 123–141.

MACE, F. C., LALLI, J., LALLI, E. P., & SHEY, M. C. (1993). Function analysis and treatment of aberrant behavior. In R. Van Houten & S. Axelrod (Eds.), *Behavior analysis and treatment* (pp. 75–99). New York: Plenum Press.

MACE, F. C., McCURDY, B., & QUIGLEY, E. A. (1990). A collateral effect of reward predicted by matching theory. *Journal of Applied Behavior Analysis, 23*, 197–205.

MACE, F. C., & WEST, B. J. (1986). Analysis of demand conditions associated with reluctant speech. *Journal of Behavior Therapy and Experimental Psychiatry, 17*, 285–294.

MADSEN, C. H., BECKER, W. C., THOMAS, D. R., KOSER, L., & PLAGER, E. (1970). An analysis of the reinforcing function of "sit down" commands. In R. K. Parker (Ed.), *Readings in educational psychology* (pp. 71–82). Boston: Allyn & Bacon.

MADSEN, C. H., JR., & MADSEN, C. R. (1974). *Teaching discipline: Behavior principles towards a positive approach*. Boston: Allyn & Bacon.

MAGER, R. F. (1972). *Goal analysis*. Belmont, CA: Fearon.

MAHONEY, K., VANWAGENEN, K., & MEYERSON, L. (1971). Toilet training of normal and retarded children. *Journal of Applied Behavior Analysis, 4*, 173–181.

MAHONEY, M. J. (1974). *Cognition and behavior modification*. Cambridge, MA: Ballinger.

MALATESTA, V. J., AUBUCHON, P. G., & BLUCH, M. (1994). A historical timeline of behavior therapy in psychiatric settings: Development of a clinical science. *Behavior Therapist, 17*, 165–168.

MALETSKY, B. M. (1974). Behavior recording as treatment: A brief note. *Behavior Therapy, 5*, 107–111.

MALOTT, R. W. (1989). The achievement of evasive goals: Control by rules describing contingencies that are not direct-acting. In S. C. Hayes (Ed.), *Rule-governed behavior: Cognition, contingencies, and instructional control* (pp. 269–324). New York: Plenum Press.

MALOTT, R. W. (1992). A theory of rule-governed behavior and organizational behavior management. *Journal of Organizational Behavior Management, 12*, 45–65.

MALOTT, R. W., & WHALEY, D. L. (1983). *Psychology*. Holmes Beach, FL: Learning Publications.

MARION, C., VAUSE, T., HARAPIAK, S., MARTIN, G. L., YU, D., SAKKO, G., et al. (2003). The hierarchical relationship between several visual and auditory discriminations and three verbal operants among individuals with developmental disabilities. *The Analysis of Verbal Behavior, 19*, 91–105.

MARLATT, G. A., & PARKS, G. A. (1982). Self-management of addictive disorders. In P. Karoly & F. H. Kanfer (Eds.), *Self-management and behavior change: From theory to practice* (pp. 443–488). New York: Pergamon Press.

MARR, M. J. (2003). The stitching and the unstitching: What can behavior analysis have to say about creativity? *The Behavior Analyst, 26,* 15–27.

MARTELL, C., ADDIS, M., & DIMIDJIAN, S. (2004). Finding the action in behavioral activation: The search for empirically supported interventions and mechanisms of change. In S. C. Hayes, V. M. Follette, & M. M. Linehan (Eds.), *Mindfulness and acceptance: Expanding the cognitive behavioral tradition* (pp. 152–167). New York: Guilford Press.

MARTIN, G. A., & WORTHINGTON, E. L. (1982). Behavioral homework. In M. Hersen, R. M. Isler, & P. M. Miller (Eds.), *Progress in behavior modification* (Vol. 13, pp. 197–226). New York: Academic Press.

MARTIN, G. L. (1981). Behavior modification in Canada in the 1970's. *Canadian Psychology, 22,* 7–22.

MARTIN, G. L. (1982). Thought stopping and stimulus control to decrease persistent disturbing thoughts. *Journal of Behavior Therapy and Experimental Psychiatry, 13*(3), 215–220.

MARTIN, G. L. (1992). Applied behavior analysis in sport and physical education: Past, present and future. In R. P. West & L. A. Hammerlynk (Eds.), *Designs for excellence in education: The legacy of B. F. Skinner* (pp. 223–287). Longmont, CO: Sopris West.

MARTIN, G. L. (2003). *Sport psychology: Practical guidelines from behavior analysis* (2nd ed.). Winnipeg, Canada: Sport Science Press.

MARTIN, G. L., ENGLAND, G. D., & ENGLAND, K. G. (1971). The use of backward chaining to teach bed-making to severely retarded girls: A demonstration. *Psychological Aspects of Disability, 18,* 35–40.

MARTIN, G. L., ENGLAND, G., KAPROWY, E., KILGOUR, K., & PILEK, V. (1968). Operant conditioning of kindergarten-class behavior in autistic children. *Behaviour Research and Therapy, 6,* 281–294.

MARTIN, G. L., & INGRAM, D. (2001). *Play golf in the zone: The psychology of golf made easy.* San Francisco: Van der Plas.

MARTIN, G. L., KOOP, S., TURNER, C., & HANEL, F. (1981). Backward chaining versus total task presentation to teach assembly tasks to severely retarded persons. *Behavior Research of Severe Developmental Disabilities, 2,* 117–136.

MARTIN, G. L., & OSBORNE, J. G. (Eds.) (1980). *Helping in the community: Behavioral applications.* New York: Plenum Press.

MARTIN, G. L., & OSBORNE, J. G. (1993). *Psychological adjustment and everyday living* (2nd ed.). Upper Saddle River, NJ: Prentice Hall.

MARTIN, G. L., & PEAR, J. J. (1978). *Behavior modification: What it is and how to do it.* Upper Saddle River, NJ: Prentice Hall.

MARTIN, G. L., THOMPSON, K., & REGEHR, K. (2004). Studies using single-subject designs in sport psychology: 30 years of research. *The Behavior Analyst, 27,* 263–280.

MARTIN, G. L., & TKACHUK, G. (2000). Behavioral sport psychology. In J. Austin & J. E. Carr (Eds.), *Handbook of applied behavior analysis* (pp. 399–422). Reno, NV: Context Press.

MARTIN, G. L., TOOGOOD, S. A., & TKACHUK, G. A. (Eds.) (1997). *Behavioral assessment forms for sport psychology consulting.* Winnipeg, Canada: Sport Science Press.

MARTIN, G. L., & YU, C. T. (2000). Research on the Assessment of Basic Learning Abilities Test: A review. *Journal on Developmental Disabilities, 7,* 10–36.

MARTIN, G. L., YU, C. T., & VAUSE, T. (2004). Assessment of Basic Learning Abilities Test. Recent research and future directions. In W. L. Williams (Ed.), *Advances in developmental disabilities: Etiology, assessment, intervention, and integration* (pp. 161–176). Reno, NV: Context Press.

MARTIN, T. L., PEAR, J. J., & MARTIN, G. L. (2002a). Analysis of proctor grading accuracy in a computer-aided personalized system of instruction course. *Journal of Applied Behavior Analysis, 35,* 309–312.

MARTIN, T. L., PEAR, J. J., & MARTIN, G. L. (2002b). Feedback and its effectiveness in a computer-aided personalized system of instruction course. *Journal of Applied Behavior Analysis, 35*, 427–430.

MASIA, C. L., & CHASE, P. N. (1997). Vicarious learning revisited: A contemporary behavior analytic interpretation. *Journal of Behavior Therapy and Experimental Psychiatry, 28*, 41–51.

MASTERS, J. C., BURRISH, T. G., HOLLON, S. D., & RIMM, D. C. (1987). *Behavior therapy: Techniques and empirical findings* (3rd ed.). Orlando, FL: Harcourt Brace Jovanovich.

MASTERS, W. H., & JOHNSON, V. E. (1970). *Human sexual inadequacy.* Boston: Little, Brown.

MATSEN, J. L., BIELECKI, J., MAYVILLE, E. A., SMOLLS, Y., BAMBURG, J. W., & BAGLIO, C. S. (1999). The development of a reinforcer choice assessment scale for persons with severe and profound mental retardation. *Research in Developmental Disabilities, 20*, 379–384.

MATSON, J. L., & VOLLMER, T. R. (1995). *User's guide: Questions About Behavioral Function (QABF).* Baton Rouge, LA: Scientific Publishers.

MAZALESKI, J. L., IWATA, B. A., VOLLMER, T. R., ZARCONE, J. R., & SMITH, R. G. (1993). Analysis of the reinforcement and extinction components in DRO contingencies with self injury. *Journal of Applied Behavior Analysis, 26*, 143–156.

MAZUR, J. E. (1991). Choice with probabilistic reinforcement: Effects of delay and conditioned reinforcers. *Journal of the Experimental Analysis of Behavior, 55*(1), 63–77.

MCEACHIN, J. J., SMITH, T., & LOVAAS, O. I. (1993). Long-term outcome for children with autism who received early intensive behavioral treatment. *American Journal on Mental Retardation, 97*, 359–372.

MCFALL, R. M. (1970). The effects of self-monitoring on normal smoking behavior. *Journal of Consulting and Clinical Psychology, 35*, 135–142.

MCGEE, J. J., MENOLASCINO, F. J., HOBBS, D. C., & MENOUSEK, P. E. (1987). *Gentle teaching: A nonaversive approach for helping persons with mental retardation.* New York: Human Sciences Press.

MCGILL, P. (1999). Establishing operations: Implications for the assessment, treatment, and prevention of problem behavior. *Journal of Applied Behavior Analysis, 32*, 393–418.

MCGINNIS, J. C., FRIMAN, P. C., & CARLYON, W. D. (1999). The effect of token rewards on "intrinsic" motivation for doing math. *Journal of Applied Behavior Analysis, 32*, 375–379.

MCGLYNN, F. D., SMITHERMAN, T. A., & GOTHARD, K. D. (2004). Comment on the status of systematic desensitization. *Behavior Modification, 28*, 194–205.

MCKINNEY, R., & FIEDLER, S. (2004). Schizophrenia: Some recent advances and implications for behavioral intervention. *The Behavioral Therapist, 27*, 122–125.

MEADOWS, S. (1996). *Parenting behavior and childrens' cognitive development.* Hillsdale, NJ: Erlbaum.

MEICHENBAUM, D. H. (1977). *Cognitive behavior modification: An integrative approach.* New York: Plenum Press.

MEICHENBAUM, D. H. (1985). *Stress inoculation training.* New York: Pergamon Press.

MEICHENBAUM, D. H. (1986). Cognitive behavior modification. In F. H. Kanfer & A. P. Goldstein (Eds.), *Helping people change: A textbook of methods* (3rd ed., pp. 346–380). New York: Pergamon Press.

MEICHENBAUM, D., & DEFFENBACHER, J. L. (1988). Stress inoculation training. *Counselling Psychologist, 16*, 69–90.

MEICHENBAUM, D. H., & GOODMAN, J. (1971). Training impulsive children to talk to themselves: A means of developing self-control. *Journal of Abnormal Psychology, 77*, 115–126.

MESSER, S. B., & WINOKUR, M. (1984). Ways of knowing and visions of reality in psychoanalytic therapy and behavior therapy. In H. Arkowitz & S. B. Messer (Eds.), *Psychoanalytic therapy and behavior therapy: Is integration possible?* (pp. 63–100). New York: Plenum Press.

MEYER, L. H., & EVANS, I. M. (1989). *Nonaversive intervention for behavior problems: A manual for home and community.* Baltimore: Paul H. Brookes.

MICHAEL, J. (1982). Distinguishing between discriminative and motivational functions of stimuli. *Journal of the Experimental Analysis of Behavior, 37*, 149–155.

MICHAEL, J. (1986). Repertoire-altering effects of remote contingencies. *Analysis of Verbal Behavior, 4*, 10–18.

MICHAEL, J. (1987). Symposium on the experimental analysis of human behavior: Comments by the discussant. *Psychological Record, 37*, 37–42.

MICHAEL, J. (1988). Establishing operations and the mand. *The Analysis of Verbal Behavior, 6*, 3–9.

MICHAEL, J. (1991). A behavioral perspective on college teaching. *Behavior Analyst, 14*, 229–239.

MICHAEL, J. (1993). Establishing operations. *Behavior Analyst, 16*, 191–206.

MICHAEL, J. (2000). Implications and refinements of the establishing operation concept. *Journal of Applied Behavior Analysis, 33*, 401–410.

MIDGLEY, M., LEA, S. E. G., & KIRBY, R. M. (1989) Algorithmic shaping and misbehavior in the acquisition of token deposit by rats. *Journal of the Experimental Analysis of Behavior, 52*, 27–40.

MIKULIS, W. L. (1983). Thailand and behavior modification. *Journal of Behavior Therapy and Experimental Psychiatry, 14*, 93–97.

MILLER, D. L., & KELLEY, M. L. (1994). The use of goal setting and contingency contracting for improving childrens' homework. *Journal of Applied Behavior Analysis, 27*, 73–84.

MILLER, W. R. (1996). Motivational interviewing: Research, practice and puzzles. *Addictive Behaviors, 21*, 835–842.

MILTENBERGER, R. G., FUQUA, R. W., & WOODS, D. W. (1998). Applying behavior analysis to clinical problems: Review and analysis of habit reversal. *Journal of Applied Behavior Analysis, 31*, 447–469.

MING, S., & MARTIN, G.L. (1996). Single-subject evaluation of a self-talk package for improving figure skating performance. *The Sport Psychologist, 10*, 227–238.

MODERATO, P. (2003). Behaviorism and behavior analysis in Italy. *Newsletter of the International Association for Behavior Analysis, 26*(3), 17–19.

MOHR, B., MULLER, V., MATTES, R., ROSIN, R., FEDERMANN, B., STREHL, U., et al. (1996). Behavioral treatment of Parkinson's disease leads to improvement of motor skills and to tremor reduction. *Behavior Therapy, 27*, 235–255.

MOLLER, A. P., MILINSKI, M., & SLATER, P. J. B. (Eds.). (1998). *Stress and behavior.* New York: Academic Press.

MOORE, J., & SHOOK, G. L. (2001). Certification, accreditation, and quality control in behavior analysis. *The Behavior Analyst, 24*, 45–55.

MORGAN, D. L., & MORGAN, R. K. (2001). Single-participant research design: Bringing science to managed care. *American Psychologist, 56*, 119–127.

MORRIS, R. J., & KRATOCHWILL, T. R. (1983). *Treating childrens' fears and phobias: A behavioral approach.* New York: Pergamon Press.

MULAIRE-CLOUTIER, C., VAUSE, T., MARTIN, G. L., & YU, D. (2000). Choice, task preference, task performance, and happiness indicators with persons with severe developmental disabilities. *International Journal of Practical Approaches to Disability, 24*, 7–12.

MYERSON, J., & HALE, S. (1984). Practical implications of the matching law. *Journal of Applied Behavior Analysis, 17*, 367–380.

NEEF, N. A., MACE, F. C., & SHADE, D. (1993). Impulsivity in students with serious emotional disturbances: The interactive effects of reinforcer rate, delay, and quality. *Journal of Applied Behavior Analysis, 26*, 37–52.

NEEF, N. A., MACE, F. C., SHEA, M. C., & SHADE, D. (1992). Effects of reinforcer rate and reinforcer quality on time allocation: Extensions of the matching theory to educational settings. *Journal of Applied Behavior Analysis, 25*, 691–699.

NEEF, N. A., SHADE, D., & MILLER, M. S. (1994). Assessing influential dimensions of reinforcers on choice in students with serious emotional disturbance. *Journal of Applied Behavior Analysis, 27*, 575–583.

NELSON, R. O. (1983). Behavioral assessment: Past, present, and future. *Behavioral Assessment, 5*, 195–206.

NEVIN, J. A. (1988). Behavioral momentum and the partial reinforcement effect. *Psychological Bulletin, 103*, 44–56.

NEVIN, J. A. (1992). An integrative model for the study of behavioral momentum. *Journal of the Experimental Analysis of Behavior, 57*, 301–316.

NEZU, A. (2000). It's official: To be behavioral is to be special. *The Behavior Therapist, 23*, 181–184, 206.

NHAT HANH, T. (1998). *The heart of the Buddha's teaching: Transforming suffering into peace, joy, and liberation.* Berkeley, CA: Parallax Press.

NORDQUIST, D. M. (1971). The modification of a child's enuresis: Some response-response relationships. *Journal of Applied Behavior Analysis, 4*, 241–247.

NORTH, M. M., NORTH, S. M., & COBLE, J. R. (1997). Virtual reality therapy for fear-of-flying. *American Journal of Psychiatry, 154*, 130.

NORTHUP, J., WACKER, D., SASSO, G., STEEGE, M., CIGRAND, K., COOK, J., et al. (1991). A brief functional analysis of aggressive and alternative behavior in an out-clinic setting. *Journal of Applied Behavior Analysis, 24*, 509–522.

O'BRIEN, S., & REPP, A. C. (1990). Reinforcement-based reductive procedures: A review of 20 years of their use with persons with severe or profound retardation. *Journal of the Association for Persons with Severe Handicaps, 15*, 148–159.

O'CONNOR, R. (1969). Modification of social withdrawal through symbolic modeling. *Journal of Applied Behavior Analysis, 2*, 15–22.

O'DONNELL, J. (2001). The discriminative stimulus for punishment or S^{Dp}. *The Behavior Analyst, 24*, 261–262.

O'DONNELL, J., CROSBIE, J., WILLIAMS, D. C., & SAUNDERS, K. J. (2000). Stimulus control and generalization of point-loss punishment with humans. *Journal of the Experimental Analysis of Behavior, 73*, 261–274.

OEI, T. P. S. (Ed.). (1998). *Behavior therapy and cognitive behavior therapy in Asia.* Glebe, Australia: Edumedia.

OHMAN, A., DIMBERG, U., & OST, L. G. (1984). Animal and social phobias. In S. Reiss & R. Bootzin (Eds.), *Theoretical issues in behavior therapy* (pp. 210–222). New York: Academic Press.

O'LEARY, K. D. (1984). The image of behavior therapy: It is time to take a stand. *Behavior Therapy, 15*, 219–233.

OLENICK, D. L., & PEAR, J. J. (1980). Differential reinforcement of correct responses to probes and prompts in picture-naming training with severely retarded children. *Journal of Applied Behavior Analysis, 13*, 77–89.

OLSEN, R., LARAWAY, S., AUSTIN, J. (2001). Unconditioned and conditioned establishing operations in organizational behavior management. *Journal of Organizational Behavior Management, 21*, 7–35.

OLSON, R. P., & KROON, J. S. (1987). Biobehavioral treatments of essential hypertension. In M. S. Schwartz (Ed.), *Biofeedback: A practitioner's guide.* New York: Guilford Press.

O'NEILL, G. W., & GARDNER, R. (1983). *Behavioral principles in medical rehabilitation: A practical guide.* Springfield, IL: Charles C Thomas.

OSBORNE, J. G., & POWERS, R. B. (1980). Controlling the litter problem. In G. L. Martin & J. G. Osborne (Eds.), *Helping in the community: Behavioral applications* (pp. 103–168). New York: Plenum Press.

OTTO, M. W., PAVA, J. A., & SPRICH-BUCKMINSTER, S. (1995). Treatment of major depression: Applications and efficacy of cognitive behavior therapy. In M. H. Pollack, M. W. Otto, & J. E.

Rosenbaum (Eds.), *Challenges in psychiatric treatment: Pharmacological and psychosocial strategies* (pp. 31–52). New York: Guilford Press.

OTTO, T. L., TORGRUD, L. J., & HOLBORN, S. W. (1999). An operant blocking interpretation of instructed insensitivity to schedule contingencies. *The Psychological Record, 49*, 663–684.

PAGE, T. J., IWATA, B. A., & NEEF, N. A. (1976). Teaching pedestrian skills to retarded persons: Generalization from the classroom to the natural environment. *Journal of Applied Behavior Analysis, 9*, 433–444.

PAGGEOT, B., KVALE, S., MACE, F. C., & SHARKEY, R. W. (1988). Some merits and limitations of hand-held computers for data collection. *Journal of Applied Behavior Analysis, 21*, 429.

PAL-HEGEDUS, C. (1991). Behavior analysis in Costa Rica. *Behavior Therapist, 14*, 103–104.

PALMER D. C. (1991). A behavioral interpretation of memory. In I. J. Hayes & P. N. Chase (Eds.), *Dialogues on verbal behavior* (pp. 259–286). Reno, NV. Context Press.

PALMER, D. C. (2004). Data in search of a principle: A review of Relational Frame Theory: A post-Skinnerian account of human language and cognition. *Journal of the Experimental Analysis of Behavior, 81*, 189–204.

PARADIS, C. M., FRIEDMAN, S., HATCH, M. L., & ACKERMAN, R. (1996). Cognitive behavioral treatment of anxiety disorders in orthodox Jews. *Cognitive and Behavioral Practice, 3*, 271–288.

PASCARELLA, E. T., & TERENZINI, P. T. (1991). *How college affects students: Findings and insights from 20 years of research.* San Francisco: Jossey-Bass.

PASSMAN, R. (1977). The reduction of procrastinative behaviors in a college student despite the "contingency fulfillment problems": The use of external control in self-management techniques. *Behavior Therapy, 8*, 95–96.

PATTERSON, G. R. (1965). An application of conditioning techniques to the control of a hyperactive child. In L. P. Ullmann & L. Krasner (Eds.), *Case studies in behavior modification* (pp. 370–375). New York: Holt, Reinhart & Winston.

PATTERSON, G. R., & GULLION, M. E. (1968). *Living with children: New methods for parents and teachers.* Champaign, IL: Research Press.

PAVLOV, I. P. (1927). *Conditioned reflexes: An investigation of the physiological activity of the cerebral cortex* (G. V. Anrep, Trans.). London: Oxford University Press.

P.D. SUPPORTS BAN ON CORPORAL PUNISHMENT. (1990). *Practitioner Focus, 4*(2), 5, 8.

PEAR, J. J. (1983). Relative reinforcements for cognitive and behavioral terminologies. *Psychological Record, 33*, 20–25.

PEAR, J. J. (2001). *The science of learning.* Philadelphia: Psychology Press.

PEAR, J. J. (2004). A spatiotemporal analysis of behavior. In J. E. Burgos & E. Ribes (Eds.), *Theory, basic and applied research and technological applications in behavior science: Conceptual and methodological issues* (pp. 131–149). Guadalajara: University of Guadalajara Press.

PEAR, J. J. (2007). *A historical and contemporary look at psychological systems.* Mahwah, NJ: Lawrence Erlbaum Associates.

PEAR, J. J., & CRONE-TODD, D. E. (1999). Personalized System of Instruction in cyberspace. *Journal of Applied Behavior Analysis, 32*, 205–209.

PEAR, J. J., & CRONE-TODD, D. E. (2002). A social constructivist approach to computer-mediated instruction. *Computers & Education, 38*, 221–231.

PEAR, J. J., & ELDRIDGE, G. D. (1984). The operant–respondent distinction: Future directions. *Journal of the Experimental Analysis of Behavior, 42*, 453–467.

PEAR, J. J., & KINSNER, W. (1988). Computer-aided Personalized System of Instruction: An effective and economical method for short and long distance education. *Machine-Mediated Learning, 2*, 213–237.

PEAR, J. J., & LEGRIS, J. A. (1987). Shaping of an arbitrary operant response by automated tracking. *Journal of the Experimental Analysis of Behavior, 47*, 241–247.

PEAR, J. J., & MARTIN, T. L. (2004). Making the most of PSI with computer technology. In D. J. Moran & R. W. Malott (Eds.), *Evidence-based educational methods* (pp. 223–243). San Diego: Elsevier Academic Press.

PEAR, J. J., & NOVAK, M. (1996). Computer-aided Personalized System of Instruction: A program evaluation. *Teaching of Psychology, 23*, 119–123.

PERIN, C. T. (1943). The effect of delayed reinforcement upon the differentiation of bar responses in white rats. *Journal of Experimental Psychology, 32*, 95–109.

PERRI, M. G., & RICHARDS, C. S. (1977). An investigation of naturally occurring episodes of self-controlled behaviors. *Journal of Consulting Psychology, 24*, 178–183.

PHILLIPS, E. L., PHILLIPS, E. A., FIXSEN, D. L., & WOLF, M. M. (1973). Behavior shaping works for delinquents. *Psychology Today, 7*(1), 75–79.

PHILLIPS, E. L., PHILLIPS, E. A., WOLF, M. M., & FIXSEN, D. L. (1973). Achievement Place: Development of the elected manager system. *Journal of Applied Behavior Analysis, 6*, 541–546.

PINKER, S. (1994). *The language instinct: How the mind creates language.* New York: William Morrow.

PLIMPTON, G. (1965). Ernest Hemingway. In G. Plimpton (Ed.), *Writers at work: The Paris Review interviews* (2nd series, pp. 215–239). New York: Viking.

POCHE, C., BROUWER, R., & SWEARINGEN, M. (1981). Teaching self-protection to young children. *Journal of Applied Behavior Analysis, 14*, 169–176.

POLENCHAR, B. F., ROMANO, A. G., STEINMETZ, J. E., & PATTERSON, M. M. (1984). Effects of US parameters on classical conditioning of cat hindlimb flexion. *Animal Learning and Behavior, 12*, 69–72.

POLING, A. (2001). Comments regarding Olsen, Laraway, and Austin (2001). *Journal of Organizational Behavior Management, 21*, 47–56.

POLING, A., DICKINSON, A., AUSTIN, J., & NORMAND, M. (2000). Basic and behavioral research in organizational behavior management. In J. Austin & J. E. Carr (Eds.), *Handbook of applied behavior analysis* (pp. 295–320). Reno, NV: Context Press.

POLING, A., METHOT, L. L., & LESAGE, M. G. (1995). *Fundamentals of behavior analytic research.* New York: Plenum Press.

POPPEN, R. L. (1989). Some clinical implications of rule-governed behavior. In S. C. Hayes (Ed.), *Rule-governed behavior: Cognition, contingencies, and instructional control* (pp. 325–357). New York: Plenum Press.

POTTER, B. A. (1980). *Turning around: The behavioral approach to managing people.* New York: AMACOM.

POUTHAS, V., DROIT, S., JACQUET, A. Y., & WEARDEN, J. H. (1990). Temporal differentiation of response duration in children of different ages: Developmental changes in relations between verbal and nonverbal behavior. *Journal of the Experimental Analysis of Behavior, 53*, 21–31.

POWELL, J., MARTINDALE, A., & KULP, S. (1975). An evaluation of time-sample measures of behavior. *Journal of Applied Behavior Analysis, 8*, 463–469.

POWERS, R. B., & OSBORNE, J. G. (1976). *Fundamentals of behavior.* St. Paul, MN: West.

PREMACK, D. (1959). Toward empirical behavioral laws. I: Positive reinforcement. *Psychological Review, 66*, 219–233.

PREMACK, D. (1965). Reinforcement theory. In D. Levin (Ed.), *Nebraska Symposium on Motivation* (pp. 123–180). Lincoln: University of Nebraska.

PRILLELTENSKY, I. (1989). Psychology and the status quo. *American Psychologist, 44*, 795–802.

PRILLELTENSKY, I. (1990). Enhancing the social ethics of psychology: Toward a psychology at the service of social change. *Canadian Psychology, 31*, 310–319.

PURCELL, D. W., CAMPOS, P. E., & PERILLA, J. L. (1996). Therapy with lesbians and gay men: A cognitive behavioral perspective. *Cognitive and Behavioral Practice, 3*, 391–415.

PYLES, D. A. M., & BAILEY, J. S. (1990). Diagnosing severe behavior problems. In A. C. Repp & N. N. Singh (Eds.), *Perspectives on the use of nonaversive interventions for persons with developmental disabilities* (pp. 381–401). Sycamore, IL: Sycamore Press.

QUARTI, C., & RENAUD, J. (1964). A new treatment of constipation by conditioning: A preliminary report. In C. M. Franks (Ed.), *Conditioning techniques in clinical practice and research* (pp. 219–227). New York: Springer.

RAE, A. (1993). Self-paced learning with video for undergraduates: A multimedia Keller Plan. *British Journal of Educational Technology, 24,* 43–51.

RAE, S., MARTIN, G. L., & SMYK, B. (1990). A self-management package versus a group exercise contingency for increasing on-task behavior of developmentally handicapped workers. *Canadian Journal of Behavioral Science, 22,* 45–58.

RASEY, H. W., & IVERSEN, I. II. (1993). An experimental acquisition of maladaptive behavior by shaping. *Journal of Behavior Therapy and Experimental Psychiatry, 24,* 37–43.

REID, D. H., & PARSONS, M. B. (2000). Organizational behavior management in human service settings. In J. Austin & J. E. Carr (Eds.), *Handbook of applied behavior analysis* (pp. 275–294) Reno, NV: Context Press.

REPP, A. C., DEITZ, S. M., & DEITZ, D. E. (1976). Reducing inappropriate behaviors in classrooms and individual sessions through DRO schedules of reinforcement. *Mental Retardation, 14,* 11–15.

REPP, A. C., KARSH, K. G., FELCE, D., & LUDEWIG, D. (1989). Further comments on using hand-held computers for data collection. *Journal of Applied Behavior Analysis, 22,* 336–337.

REPP, A. C., & SINGH, N. (1990). Perspectives on the use of nonaversive and aversive interventions for persons with developmental disabilities. Sycamore, IL: Sycamore Press.

RESICK, P. A., & SCHNICKE, M. K. (1992). Cognitive processing therapy for sexual assault victims. *Journal of Consulting and Clinical Psychology, 60,* 748–756.

REYNOLDS, L. K., & KELLEY, M. L. (1997). The efficacy of a response-cost based treatment package for managing aggressive behavior in preschoolers. *Behavior Modification, 21,* 216–230.

RICHARD, D. C. S., & BOBICZ, K. (2003). Computers and behavioral assessment: Six years later. *The Behavior Therapist, 26,* 219–223.

RICHMAN, G. S., REISS, M. L., BAUMAN, K. E., & BAILEY, J. S. (1984). Training menstrual care to mentally retarded women: Acquisition, generalization, and maintenance. *Journal of Applied Behavior Analysis, 17,* 441–451.

RINCOVER, A. (1978). Sensory extinction: A procedure for eliminating self-stimulatory behavior in psychotic children. *Journal of Abnormal Child Psychology, 6,* 299–310.

RINCOVER, A., COOK, R., PEOPLES, A., & PACKARD, D. (1979). Sensory extinction and sensory reinforcement principles for programming multiple adaptive behavior change. *Journal of Applied Behavior Analysis, 12,* 221–233.

RIVA, G., WIEDERHOLD, B. K., & MOLINARI, E. (1998). *Virtual environments in clinical psychology and neuroscience. Methods and techniques in advanced patient-therapist interaction.* Amsterdam, the Netherlands: IOS Press.

ROBERTS, R. N. (1979). Private speech in academic problem-solving: A naturalistic perspective. In G. Zevin (Ed.), *The development of self-regulation through private speech* (pp. 295–323). New York: Wiley.

ROBERTS, R. N., & THARP, R. G. (1980). A naturalistic study of children's self-directed speech in academic problem-solving. *Cognitive Research and Therapy, 4,* 341–353.

RODRIGUE, J. R., BANKO, C. G., SEARS, S. F., & EVANS, G. (1996). Old territory revisited: Behavior therapists in rural America and innovative models of service delivery. *The Behavior Therapist, 19,* 97–100.

ROMANO, J. M., JENSEN, M. P., TURNER, J. A., GOOD, A. B., & HOPS, H. (2000). Chronic pain patient-partner interactions: Further support for a behavioral model of chronic pain. *Behavior Therapy, 31,* 415–440.

ROSCOE, B., MARTIN, G. L, & PEAR, J. J. (1980). Systematic self-desensitization of fear of flying: A case study. In G. L. Martin & J. G. Osborne (Eds.), *Helping in the community: Behavioral applications* (pp. 345–352). New York: Plenum Press.

ROSEN, G. M. (1987). Self-help treatment books and the commercialization of psychotherapy. *American Psychologist, 42*, 46–51.

ROTHBAUM, B. O., HODGES, L. F., KOOPER, R., et al., (1995), Effectiveness of computer-generated (virtual reality) graded exposure in the treatment of acrophobia. *American Journal of Psychiatry, 152*, 626–628.

ROTTER, J. B. (1954). *Social learning and clinical psychology*. Upper Saddle River, NJ: Prentice Hall.

ROVETTO, F. (1979). Treatment of chronic constipation by classical conditioning techniques. *Journal of Behavior Therapy and Experimental Psychiatry, 10*, 143–146.

SAJWAJ, T., LIBET, J., & AGRAS, S. (1974). Lemon–juice therapy: The control of life-threatening rumination in a six-month-old infant. *Journal of Applied Behavior Analysis, 7*, 557–563.

SAKANO, Y. (1993). Behavior therapy in Japan: Beyond the cultural impediments. *Behavior Change, 10*, 19–21.

SALEND, S. J., ELLIS, L. L., & REYNOLDS, C. J. (1989). Using self-instructions to teach vocational skills to individuals who are severely retarded. *Education and Training in Mental Retardation, 24*, 248–254.

SALMON, D. J., PEAR, J. J., & KUHN, B. A. (1986). Generalization of object naming after training with picture cards and with objects. *Journal of Applied Behavior Analysis, 19*, 53–58.

SALTER, A. (1949). *Conditioned reflex therapy*. New York: Creative Age Press.

SANIVIO, E. (1999). Behavioral and cognitive therapy in Italy. *The Behavior Therapist, 22*, 69–75.

SARWER, D. B., & SAYERS, S. L. (1998). Behavioral interviewing. In A. S. Bellack & M. Hersen (Eds.), *Behavioral assessment: A practical handbook* (4th ed., pp. 63–78). Boston: Allyn & Bacon.

SCHAEFER, C. E., & BRIESMEISTER, J. M. (Eds.). (1998). *Handbook of parent training: Parents as co-therapists for children's behavior.* New York: Wiley.

SCHAEFER, H. H., & MARTIN, p. L. (1969). *Behavioral therapy*. New York: McGraw-Hill.

SCHLEIEN, S. J., WEHMAN, P., & KIERNAN, J. (1981). Teaching leisure skills to severely handicapped adults: An age-appropriate darts game. *Journal of Applied Behavior Analysis, 14*, 513–519.

SCHLESINGER, C. (2004). Australian Association for Cognitive and Behavior Therapy. *Newsletter of the International Association for Behavior Analysis, 27*(2), 20–21.

SCHLINGER, H., & BLAKELEY, E. (1987). Function-altering effects of contingency-specifying stimuli. *The Behavior Analyst, 10*, 41–45.

SCHLOSS, P. J., & SCHLOSS, M. A. (2004). *Applied behavior analysis in the classroom* (2nd ed.). Boston: Allyn & Bacon.

SCHLOSS, P. J., SMITH, M., SANTORA, C., & BRYANT, R. (1989). A respondent conditioning approach to reducing anger responses of a dually-diagnosed man with mild mental retardation. *Behavior Therapy, 20*, 459–464.

SCHREIBMAN, L. (1975). Effects of within-stimulus and extra-stimulus prompting on discrimination learning in autistic children. *Journal of Applied Behavior Analysis, 8*, 91–112.

SCHROEDER, H. E., & BLACK, M. J. (1985). Unassertiveness. In M. Hersen & A. S. Bellack (Eds.), *Handbook of clinical behavior therapy with adults* (pp. 509–530). New York: Plenum Press.

SCHUNK, D. H. (1987). Peer models and children's behavioral change. *Review of Educational Research, 57*, 149–174.

SCHWARTZ, M. S., & ANDRASIC, F. (1998). *Biofeedback: A practitioner's guide*. New York: Guilford Press.

SCHWITZGEBEL, R. L. (1964). *Streetcorner research: An experimental approach to juvenile delinquency.* Cambridge, MA: Harvard University Press.

SCOGIN, F., BYNUM, J., STEPHENS, G., & CALHOON, S. (1990). Efficacy of self-administered treatment programs: Meta-analytic review. *Professional Psychology: Research and Practice, 21*, 42–47.

SCOTT, M. A., BARCLAY, B. R., & HOUTS, A. C. (1992). Childhood enuresis: Etiology, assessment, and current behavioral treatment. In M. Hersen, R. N. Eisler, & P. M. Miller (Eds.), *Progress in behavior modification* (Vol. 28, pp. 84–119). Sycamore, IL: Sycamore Press.

SCOTT, R. W., PETERS, R. D., GILLESPIE, W. J., BLANCHARD, E. B., EDMUNDSON, E. D., & YOUNG, L. D. (1973). The use of shaping and reinforcement in the operant acceleration and deceleration of heart rate. *Behaviour Research and Therapy, 11*, 179–185.

SCRIMALI, T., & GRIMALDI, L. (1993). Behavioral and cognitive psychotherapy in Italy. *The Behavior Therapist, 16*, 265–266.

SEARIGHT, H. R. (1998). *Behavioral medicine: A primary care approach.* Philadelphia: Brunner-Mazel.

SEIGTS, G. H., MEERTENS, R. M., & KOK, G. (1997). The effects of task importance and publicness on the relation between goal difficulty and performance. *Canadian Journal of Behavioural Science, 29*, 54–62.

SELIGMAN, M. E. P. (1971). Phobias and preparedness. *Behavior Therapy, 2*, 307–321.

SELIGMAN, M. E. P. (1994). *What you can change and what you can't.* New York: Knopf.

SEMB, G., & SEMB, S. A. (1975). A comparison of fixed-page and fixed-time reading assignments in elementary school children. In E. Ramp & G. Semb (Eds.), *Behavior analysis: Areas of research and application* (pp. 233–243). Upper Saddle River, NJ: Prentice Hall.

SERKETICH, W. J., & DUMAS, J. E. (1996). The effectiveness of behavioral parent training to modify antisocial behavior in children: A meta-analysis. *Behavior Therapy, 27*, 171–186.

SHAFRAN, R., BOOTH, R., & RACHMAN, S. (1993). The reduction of claustrophobia: II. Cognitive analyses. *Behaviour Research and Therapy, 31*, 75–85.

SHERRINGTON, C. S. (1947). *The integrative action of the central nervous system.* Cambridge, UK: Cambridge University Press.

SHIMOFF, E., MATTHEWS, B. A., & CATANIA, A. C. (1986). Human operant performance: Sensitivity and pseudosensitivity to contingencies. *Journal of the Experimental Analysis of Behavior, 46*, 149–157.

SIDMAN, M. (1953). Avoidance conditioning with brief shock and no exteroceptive warning signal. *Science, 118*, 157–158.

SIDMAN, M. (1960). *Tactics of scientific research.* New York: Basic Books.

SIDMAN, M. (1994). *Equivalence relations and behavior: A research story.* Boston: Authors Cooperative.

SIEDENTOP, D. (1978). The management of practice behavior. In W. F. Straub (Ed.), *Sport psychology: An analysis of athletic behavior* (pp. 42–61). Ithaca, NY: Mouvement.

SIEDENTOP, D., & TANNEHILL, D. (2000). *Developing teaching skills in physical education* (4th ed.). Mountain View, CA: Mayfield.

SILVERMAN, K., SVIKIS, D., ROBLES, E., STITZER, M. L., & BIGELOW, G. E. (2001). A reinforcement-based therapeutic workplace for the treatent of drug abuse: Six-month abstinence outcomes. *Experimental and Clinical Psychopharmacology, 9*, 14–23.

SILVERMAN, K., WONG, C. J., UMBRICHT-SCHNEITER, A., MONTOYA, I. D., SCHUSTER, C. R., & PRESTON, K. L. (1998). Broad beneficial effects of cocaine abstinence reinforcement among methadone patients. *Journal of Consulting and Clinical Psychology, 66*, 811–824.

SIMEK, T. C., & O'BRIEN, R. M. (1981). *Total golf: A behavioral approach to lowering your score and getting more out of your game.* Huntington, NY: B-Mod Associates.

SINGER, G. H., SINGER, J. S., & HORNER, R. H., (1987). Using pretask requests to increase the probability of compliance for students with severe disabilities. *Journal of the Association for Persons with Severe Handicaps, 12*, 287–291.

SKINNER, B. F. (1938). *The behavior of organisms.* New York: Appleton-Century-Crofts.

SKINNER, B. F. (1948a). "Superstition" in the pigeon. *Journal of Experimental Psychology, 38*, 168–172.

SKINNER, B. F. (1948b). *Walden Two.* New York: Macmillan.

SKINNER, B. F. (1953). *Science and human behavior.* New York: Macmillan.

SKINNER, B. F. (1957). *Verbal behavior.* New York: Appleton-Century-Crofts.

SKINNER, B. F. (1958). Teaching machines. *Science, 128,* 969–977.

SKINNER, B. F. (1960). Pigeons in a pelican. *American Psychologist, 15,* 28–37.

SKINNER, B. F. (1968). *The technology of teaching.* New York: Appleton-Century-Crofts.

SKINNER, B. F. (1969). *Contingencies of reinforcement: A theoretical analysis.* New York: Appleton-Century-Crofts.

SKINNER, B. F. (1971). *Beyond freedom and dignity.* New York: Knopf.

SKINNER, B. F. (1974). *About behaviorism.* New York: Knopf.

SKINNER, B. F. (1977). Why I am not a cognitive psychologist. *Behaviorism, 5,* 1–10.

SKINNER, B. F. (1989). *Recent issues in the analysis of behavior.* Columbus, OH: Charles E. Merrill.

SKINNER, B. F., & VAUGHAN, N. E. (1983). *Enjoy old age: A program of self-management.* New York: W. W. Norton.

SMITH, M. T., PERLIS, M., PARK, A., SMITH, M. S., PENNINGTON, J., GILES, G. E., et al. (2002). Comparative meta-analysis of pharmacotherapy and behavior therapy for persistent insomnia. *American Journal of Psychiatry, 159*(1), 5–11.

SMITH, R. E. (1988). The logic and design of case study research. *The Sport Psychologist, 2,* 1–12.

SMITH, R., MICHAEL, J., & SUNDBERG, M. L. (1996). Automatic reinforcement and automatic punishment in infant vocal behavior. *The Analysis of Verbal Behavior, 13,* 39–48.

SNYDER, D. K., & ABBOTT, B. V. (2004). Couple distress. In M. M. Antony & D. H. Barlow (Eds.), *Handbook of assessment and treatment planning for psychological disorders.* New York: Guilford Press.

SNYDER, J., SCHREPFERMAN, L., & ST. PETER, C. (1997). Origins of antisocial behavior: Negative reinforcement and affect disregulation of behavior as socialization mechanisms in family interaction. *Behavior Modification, 21,* 187–215.

SOBELL, L. C., TONEATTO, T., & SOBELL, M. B. (1994). Behavioral assessment and treatment planning for alcohol, tobacco, and other drug problems: Current status with an emphasis on clinical applications. *Behavior Therapy, 25,* 533–580.

SOBELL, M. B., & SOBELL, L. C. (1993). *Problem drinkers: Guided self-change treatment.* New York: Guilford Press.

SOMMER, R. (1977, January). Toward a psychology of natural behavior. *APA Monitor, 8,* 13–14.

SPIEGLER, M. D., & GUEVREMONT, D. C. (2003). *Contemporary behavior therapy* (4th ed.). Belmont, CA: Wadsworth/Thompson Learning.

SPINELLI, P. R., & PACKARD, T. (1975, February). Behavioral self-control delivery systems. Paper presented at the National Conference on Behavioral Self-Control, Salt Lake City, UT.

SPOONER, F. (1984). Comparisons of backward chaining and total task presentation in training severely handicapped persons. *Education and Training of the Mentally Retarded, 19,* 15–22.

SPRAGUE, J. R., & HORNER, R. H. (1984). The effects of single-instance, multiple-instance, and general case training on generalized vending machine use by moderately and severely handicapped students. *Journal of Applied Behavior Analysis, 17,* 273–278.

STAATS, A. W. (1996). *Behavior and personality.* New York: Springer.

STAATS, A. W., STAATS, C. K., & CRAWFORD, H. L. (1962). First-order conditioning of meaning and the parallel conditioning of a GSR. *Journal of General Psychology, 67,* 159–167.

STAINBACK, W. C., PAYNE, J. S., STAINBACK, S. B., & PAYNE, R. A. (1973). *Establishing a token economy in the classroom.* Columbus, OH: Charles E. Merrill.

STAMPFL, T. G., & LEVIS, D. J. (1967). Essentials of implosive therapy: A learning-theory-based psychodynamic behavioral therapy. *Journal of Abnormal Psychology, 72,* 496–503.

STARK, M. (1980). The German Association of Behavior Therapy. *Behavior Therapist, 3,* 11–12.

STEPHENS, C. E., PEAR, J. J., WRAY, L. D., & JACKSON, G. C. (1975). Some effects of reinforcement schedules in teaching picture names to retarded children. *Journal of Applied Behavior Analysis, 8,* 435–447.

STOKES, T. F., & BAER, D. M. (1977). An implicit technology of generalization. *Journal of Applied Behavior Analysis, 10,* 349–367.

STOKES, T. F., & OSNES, P. G. (1986). Programming the generalization of children's social behavior. In P. S. Strain, M. J. Guralnick, & H. Walker (Eds.), *Children's social behavior: Development, assessment, and modification* (pp. 407–443). Orlando, FL: Academic Press.

STOLZ, S. B., & ASSOCIATES. (1978). *Ethical issues in behavior modification.* San Francisco: Jossey-Bass.

STROMER, R., MACKAY, H. A., & REMINGTON, B. (1996). Naming: The formation of stimulus classes, and applied behavior analysis. *Journal of Applied Behavior Analysis, 29,* 409–431.

STUART, R. B. (1971). Assessment and change of the communication patterns of juvenile delinquents and their parents. In R. D. Rubin, H. Fernsterheim, A. A. Lazarus, & C. M. Franks (Eds.), *Advances in behavior therapy* (pp. 183–196). New York: Academic Press.

STUART, R. B. (1975). *Client-therapist treatment contract.* Champaign, IL: Research Press.

STURMEY, P. (1994). Assessing the functions of aberrant behaviors: A review of psychometric instruments. *Journal of Autism and Developmental Disabilities, 24,* 293–303.

STURMEY, P. (1995). Analogue baselines: A critical review of the methodology. *Research in Developmental Disabilities, 16,* 269–284.

SUCHOWIERSKA, M., & KOZLOWSKI, J. (2004). Behavior analysis in Poland: A few words on Polish ABA. *Newsletter of the International Association for Behavior Analysis, 27*(2), 28–29.

SULLIVAN, M. A., & O'LEARY, S. G. (1990). Maintenance following reward and cost token programs. *Behavior Therapy, 21,* 139–149.

SULZER-AZAROFF, B., & REESE, E. P. (1982). *Applying behavior analysis: A program for developing professional competence.* New York: Holt, Rinehart & Winston.

SUNDBERG, M. L. (2004). A behavioral analysis of motivation and its relation to mand training. In W. L. Williams (Ed.), *Advances in developmental disabilities: Etiology, assessment, intervention, and integration* (pp. 199–220). Reno, NV: Context Press.

SUNDBERG, M. L., & MICHAEL, J. (2001). The benefits of Skinner's analysis of verbal behavior for children with autism. *Behavior Modification, 25,* 698–724.

SUNDBERG, M. L., MICHAEL, J., PARTINGTON, J. W., & SUNDBERG, C. A. (1996). The role of automatic reinforcement in early language acquisition. *The Analysis of Verbal Behavior, 13,* 21–37.

SUNDBERG, M. L., & PARTINGTON, J. W. (1998). *Teaching language to children with autism and other developmental disabilities.* Pleasant Hill, CA: Behavior Analysts.

SWEET, A. A., & LOIZEAUX, A. L. (1991). Behavioral and cognitive treatment methods: A critical comparative review. *Journal of Behavior Therapy and Experimental Psychiatry, 22,* 159–185.

TANAKA-MATSUMI, J., & HIGGINBOTHAM, H. N. (1994) . Clinical application of behavior therapy across ethnic and cultural boundaries. *The Behavior Therapist, 17,* 123–126.

TANAKA-MATSUMI, J., HIGGINBAUTHAM, H. N., & CHANG, R. (2002). Cognitive behavioral approaches to counselling across cultures: A functional analytic approach for clinical applications. In P. B. Pedersen, J. G. Draguns, W. J. Lonner, & J. E. Trimble (Eds.), *Counselling across cultures* (5th ed., pp. 337–354). Thousand Oaks, CA: Sage.

TAYLOR, C. B., FRIED, L., & KENARDY, J. (1990). The use of real-time computer diary for data acquisition and processing. *Behavior Research and Therapy, 28,* 93–97.

TAYLOR, S. E. (2003). *Health psychology* (5th ed.). New York: McGraw-Hill.

TAYLOR, S., THORDARSON, D. S., & SOCHTING, I. (2004). Obsessive-compulsive disorder. In M. M. Antony & D. H. Barlow (Eds.), *Handbook of assessment and treatment planning for psychological disorders.* New York: Guilford Press.

TEASDALE, J. D., SEGAL, Z. V., & WILLIAMS, J. M. G. (1995). How does cognitive therapy prevent depressive relapse and why should attentional control (mindfulness) training help? *Behavior Research and Therapy, 33,* 25–39.

TERENZINI, P. T., & PASCARELLA, E. T. (1994). Living with myths: Undergraduate education in America. *Change,* Jan/Feb, 28–32.

THASE, M. E. (1994). After the fall: Perspectives on cognitive behavioral treatment of depression in the "post-collaborative" era. *The Behavior Therapist, 17,* 48–52.

THASE, M. E., REYNOLDS, C. F., FRANK, E., SIMONS, A. D., GARAMONI, G. D., MCGEARY, J., et al. (1994). Response to cognitive-behavioral therapy in chronic depression. *Journal of Psychotherapy Practice and Research, 3,* 204–214.

THIERMAN, G. J., & MARTIN, G. L. (1989). Self-management with picture prompts to improve quality of household cleaning by severely mentally handicapped persons. *International Journal of Rehabilitation Research, 12,* 27–39.

THOMAS, D. L., & MILLER, L. K. (1980). Helping college students live together. Democratic decision-making versus experimental manipulation. In G. L. Martin & J. G. Osborne (Eds.), *Helping in the community: Behavioral applications* (pp. 291–305). New York: Plenum Press.

THOMPSON, R. H., & IWATA, B. A. (2000). Response acquisition under direct and indirect contingencies of reinforcement. *Journal of Applied Behavior Analysis, 33,* 1–11.

THOMPSON, R. H., IWATA, B. A., CONNERS, J., & ROSCO, E. M. (1999). Effects of reinforcement for alternative behavior during punishment of self-injury. *Journal of Applied Behavior Analysis, 32,* 317–328.

THORNDIKE, E. L. (1911). Animal intelligence: An experimental study of the associative processes in animals. *Psychological Review Monograph Supplement 2,* Whole No. 8.

TIFFANY, S. T., MARTIN, C., & BAKER, R. (1986). Treatments for cigarette smoking: An evaluation of the contributions of aversion and counselling procedures. *Behavior Research and Therapy, 24,* 437–452.

TIMBERLAKE, W., & ALLISON, J. (1974). Response deprivation: An empirical approach to instrumental performance. *Psychological Review, 81,* 146–164.

TIMBERLAKE, W., & FARMER-DOUGAN, V. A. (1991). Reinforcement in applied settings: Figuring out ahead of time what will work. *Psychological Bulletin, 110,* 379–391.

TINCANI, M. J., GASTROGIAVANNI, A. & AXELROD, S., (1999). A comparison of the effectiveness of brief versus traditional functional analyses. *Research in Developmental Disabilities, 20,* 327–338.

TKACHUK, G.A., & MARTIN, G.L. (1999). Exercise therapy for psychiatric disorders: Research and clinical implications. *Professional Psychology: Research and Practice, 30,* 275–282.

TODD, F. J. (1972). Coverant control of self-evaluative responses in the treatment of depression: A new use for an old principle. *Behavior Therapy, 3,* 91–94.

TORGRUD, L. J., & HOLBORN, S. W. (1990). The effects of verbal performance descriptions on nonverbal operant responding. *Journal of the Experimental Analysis of Behavior, 54,* 273–291.

TRINGER, L. (1991). Behavior therapy in Hungary. *The Behavior Therapist, 14,* 13–14.

TUCKER, M., SIGAFOOS, J., & BUSHELL, H. (1998). Use of non-contingent reinforcement in the treatment of challenging behavior. A review and clinical guide. *Behavior Modification, 22,* 529–547.

TURK, D. C., & OKIFUJI, A. (1997). Evaluating the role of physical, operant, cognitive, and affective factors in the pain behaviors of chronic pain patients. *Behavior Modification, 21,* 259–280.

TURKAT, I. D., & FEUERSTEIN, M. (1978). Behavior modification and the public misconception. *American Psychologist, 33,* 194.

TURNER, J. R., CARDON, L. R., & HEWITT, J. K. (1995). *Behavior genetic approaches in behavioral medicine.* New York: Plenum Press.

TYRON, W. W. (1998). Behavioral observation. In A. S. Bellack & M. Hersen (Eds.), *Behavioral assessment: A practical handbook* (4th ed., pp. 79–103). Boston: Allyn & Bacon.

TYRON, W. W., & CICERO, S. D. (1989). Classical conditioning of meaning—I. A replication and higher order extension. *Journal of Behavior Therapy and Experimental Psychiatry, 20,* 137–142.

ULLMANN L. P., & KRASNER, L. (Eds.). (1965). *Case studies in behavior modification.* New York: Holt, Rinehart & Winston.

ULRICH, R., STACHNIK, T., & MABRY. J. (Eds.). (1966). *Control of human behavior* (Vol. 1). Glenview, IL: Scott Foresman.

UPPER, D., CAUTELA, J. R., & BROOK, J. M. (1975). Behavioral self-rating checklist. In M. Hersen, R. M. Eisler, & P. M. Miller (Eds.), *Progress in behavior modification* (Vol. 1, pp. 275–305). New York: Academic Press.

VAN HOUTEN, R. (1983). Punishment: From the animal laboratory to the applied setting. In S. Axelrod & J. Apsche (Eds.), *The effects of punishment on human behavior* (pp. 13–44). New York: Academic Press.

VAN HOUTEN, R., AXELROD, S., BAILEY, J. S., FAVELL, J. E., FOXX, R. M., IWATA, B. A., et al. (1988). The right to effective behavioral treatment. *Journal of Applied Behavior Analysis, 21,* 381–384.

VAN HOUTEN, R., & DOLEYS, D. M. (1983). Are social reprimands effective? In S. Axelrod & J. Apsche (Eds.), *The effects of punishment on human behavior* (pp. 45–70). New York: Academic Press.

VAUGHAN, M. (1989). Rule-governed behavior in behavior analysis: A theoretical and experimental history. In S. C. Hayes (Ed.), *Rule-governed behavior: Cognition, contingencies, and instructional control* (pp. 97–118). New York: Plenum Press.

VAUGHAN, M. E., & MICHAEL, J. L. (1982). Automatic reinforcement: An important but ignored concept. *Behaviorism, 10,* 217–227.

VAUGHAN, W., JR., & HERRNSTEIN, R. J. (1987). Choosing among natural stimuli. *Journal of the Experimental Analysis of Behavior, 47,* 5–16.

VOLLMER, T. R., & IWATA, B. A. (1992). Differential reinforcement as treatment for behavior disorders: Procedural and functional variations. *Research in Developmental Disabilities, 13,* 393–417.

VOLLMER, T. R., IWATA, B. A., ZARCONE, J. R., SMITH, R. G., & MAZELESKI, J. L. (1993). The role of attention in the treatment of attention-maintained self-injurious behavior: Non-contingent reinforcement and differential reinforcement of other behavior. *Journal of Applied Behavior Analysis, 26,* 9–21.

VOLLMER, T. R., ROANE, H. S., RINGDAHL, J. E., & MARCUS, B. A. (1999). Evaluating treatment challenges with differential reinforcement of alternative behavior. *Journal of Applied Behavior Analysis, 32,* 9–23.

VYGOTSKY, L. S. (1978). *Mind and society.* Cambridge, MA: Harvard University Press.

WAHLER, R. G., WINKEL, G. H., PETERSON, R. F., & MORRISON, D. C. (1965). Mothers as behavior therapists for their own children. *Behaviour Research and Therapy, 3,* 113–124.

WALKER, H. M., & BUCKLEY, N. K. (1972). Programming generalization and maintenance of treatment effects across time and across setting. *Journal of Applied Behavior Analysis, 5,* 209–224.

WALLACE, I. (1971). *The writing of one novel.* Richmond Hill, Ont., Canada: Simon & Schuster.

WALLACE, I., & PEAR, J. J. (1977). Self-control techniques of famous novelists. *Journal of Applied Behavior Analysis, 10,* 515–525.

WALTERS, G. D. (2000). Behavioral self-control training for problem drinkers: A meta-analysis of randomized control studies. *Behavior Therapy, 31,* 135–149.

WANLIN, C., HRYCAIKO, D., MARTIN, G. L., & MAHON, M. (1997). The effects of a goal-setting package on performance of speed skaters. *Journal of Sport Psychology, 9,* 212–228.

WARD, P. (2005). The philosophy, science, and application of behavior analysis in physical education. In D. Kirk, D. MacDonald, & M. O'Sullivan (Eds.), *The Handbook of Physical Education.* Thousand Oaks, CA: Sage.

WARD, W. D., & STARE, S. W. (1990). The role of subject verbalization in generalized correspondence. *Journal of Applied Behavior Analysis, 23,* 129–136.

WATSON, D. L., & THARP, R. G. (1997). *Self-directed behavior: Self-modification for personal adjustment* (7th ed.). Monterey, CA: Brooks/Cole.

WATSON, D. L., & THARP, R. G. (2003). *Self-directed behavior: Self-modification for personal adjustment* (8th ed.). Monterey, CA: Brooks/Cole.

WATSON, J. B. (1913). Psychology as the behaviorist views it. *Psychological Review, 20,* 158–177.

WATSON, J. B. (1916). The place of the conditioned reflex in psychology. *Psychological Review, 23,* 89–116.

WATSON, J. B. (1930). *Behaviorism* (rev. ed.). Chicago: University of Chicago Press.

WATSON, J. B., & RAYNER, R. (1920). Conditioned emotional reactions. *Journal of Experimental Psychology, 3,* 1–14.

WATSON, R. I. (1962). The experimental tradition and clinical psychology. In A. J. Bachrach (Ed.), *Experimental foundations of clinical psychology* (pp. 3–25). New York: Basic Books.

WATSON, T. S., & GRESHAM, F. M. (1998). *Handbook of child behavior therapy.* New York: Plenum Press.

WATSON, T. S., & STEEGE, M. W. (2003). *Conducting school-based functional behavioral assessments.* New York: Guilford Press.

WEARDEN, J. H. (1988). Some neglect problems in the analysis of human operant behavior. In G. Davey & C. Cullen (Eds.), *Human operant conditioning and behavior modification* (pp. 197–224), Chichester, England: Wiley.

WELCH, M. W., & GIST, J. W. (1974). *The open token economy system: A handbook for a behavioral approach to rehabilitation.* Springfield, IL: Charles C Thomas.

WELCH, S. J., & PEAR, J. J. (1980). Generalization of naming responses to objects in the natural environment as a function of training stimulus modality with retarded children. *Journal of Applied Behavior Analysis, 13,* 629–643.

WELD, E. M., & EVANS, I. M. (1990). Effects of part versus whole instructional strategies on skill acquisition and excess behavior. *American Journal on Mental Retardation, 94,* 377–386.

WETHERELL, J. L. (2002). Behavior therapy for anxious older adults. *The Behavior Therapist, 25,* 16–17.

WEXLER, D. (1981). *Manual for the Wexler Adult Intelligence Scale—Revised.* New York: Psychological Corporation.

WHALEY, D. L., & MALOTT, R. W. (1971). *Elementary principles of behavior.* Upper Saddle River, NJ: Prentice Hall.

WHITAKER, S. (1993). The reduction of aggression in people with learning disabilities: A review of psychological methods. *British Journal of Clinical Psychology, 32,* 1–37.

WHITMAN, T. L., SPENCE, B. H., & MAXWELL, S. (1987). A comparison of external and self-instructional teaching formats with mentally retarded adults in a vocational training setting. *Research in Developmental Disabilities, 8,* 371–388.

WIEDERHOLD, B. K., & WIEDERHOLD, M. D. (2004). *Virtual reality therapy for anxiety disorders: Advances in evaluation and treatment.* Washington, DC: American Psychological Association.

WIEGEL, M., WINCZE, J. P., & BARLOW, D. H. (2004). Sexual dysfunction. In M. M. Antony & D. H. Barlow (Eds.), *Handbook of assessment and treatment planning for psychological disorders.* New York: Guilford Press.

WILLIAMS, C. D. (1959). The elimination of tantrum behavior by extinction procedures. *Journal of Abnormal and Social Psychology, 59,* 269.

WILLIAMS, J. E., & CUVO, A. J. (1986). Training apartment upkeep skills to rehabilitation clients: A comparison of task analysis strategies. *Journal of Applied Behavior Analysis, 19,* 39–51.

WILLIAMS, W. L. (Ed.). (2004). *Advances in developmental disabilities: etiology, assessment, intervention, and integration.* Reno, NV: Context Press.

WILLIAMSON, D. A., CHAMPAGNE, C. M., JACKMAN, L. P., & VARNADO, P. J. (1996). Lifestyle change: A program for long-term weight management. In V. B. Van Hasselt & M. Hersen (Eds.), *Sourcebook of psychological treatment manuals for adult disorders*. New York: Plenum Press.

WILSON, G. T. (1991). Chemical aversion conditioning in the treatment of alcoholism: Further comments. *Behavior Research and Therapy, 29*, 415–419.

WILSON, G. T., & FAIRBORN, C. G. (2002). Eating disorders. In P. E. Nathan & J. M. Gorman (Eds.), *Treatments that work* (2nd ed., pp. 559–592). New York: Oxford University Press.

WILSON, K. G., HAYES, S. C., & GIFFORD, E. V. (1997). Cognition in behavior therapy: Agreements and differences. *Journal of Behavior Therapy and Experimental Psychiatry, 28*, 53–63.

WINCZE, J. P., & CAREY, M. P. (2001). *Sexual dysfunction, second edition: A guide for assessment and treatment*. New York: Guilford Press.

WINERMAN, L. (2004). Back to her roots. *Monitor on Psychology, 35(8)*, 46–49.

WINERMAN, L. (2005). Fighting phobias: A virtual cure. *Monitor on Psychology, 36(7)*, 87–89.

WISOCKI, P. A. (1999). *Handbook of clinical behavior therapy with the elderly client*. New York: Kluwer/Plenum.

WISOCKI, P. A., & POWERS, C. B. (1999). Behavioral treatments for pain experienced by older adults. In D. I. Mostovsky & J. Lomranz (Eds.), *Handbook of pain and aging*. New York: Plenum Press.

WITT, J. C., & WACKER, D. P. (1981). Teaching children to respond to auditory directives: An evaluation of two procedures. *Behavior Research of Severe Developmental Disabilities, 2*, 175–189.

WOLF, M. M. (1978). Social validity: The case for subjective measurement or how applied behavior analysis is finding its heart. *Journal of Applied Behavior Analysis, 11*, 203–214.

WOLF, M. M., HANLEY, E. L., KING, L. A., LACHOWICZ, J., & GILES, D. K. (1970). The timer-game: A variable interval contingency for the management of out-of-seat behavior. *Exceptional Children, 37*, 113–117.

WOLF, M. M., RISLEY, T., & MEES, H. (1964). Application of operant conditioning procedures to the behavior problems of an autistic child. *Behavior Research and Therapy, 1*, 305–312.

WOLFE, V. F., & CUVO, A. J. (1978). Effects of within-stimulus and extra-stimulus prompting on letter discrimination by mentally retarded persons. *American Journal of Mental Deficiency, 83*, 297–303.

WOLFENSBERGER, W. (Ed.). (1972). *Normalization: The principle of normalization in human services*. Toronto: National Institute of Mental Retardation.

WOLKO, K. L., HRYCAIKO, D. W., & MARTIN, G. L. (1993). A comparison of two self-management packages to standard coaching for improving practice performance of gymnasts. *Behavior Modification, 17*, 209–223.

WOLPE, J. (1958). *Psychotherapy by reciprocal inhibition*. Stanford, CA: Stanford University Press.

WOLPE, J. (1969). *The practice of behavior therapy*. Elmsford, NY: Pergamon Press.

WOLPE, J. (1982). *The practice of behavior therapy* (3rd ed.). New York: Pergamon Press.

WOLPE, J. (1985). Requiem for an institution. *Behavior Therapist, 8*, 113.

WOLPE, J. (1990). *The practice of behavior therapy* (4th ed.). New York: Pergamon Press.

WONG, S. E., & LIBERMAN, R. P. (1996). Biobehavioral treatment and rehabilitation for persons with schizophrenia. In V. B. Van Hasselt & M. Hersen (Eds.), *Sourcebook of psychological treatment manuals for adult disorders* (pp. 233–256). New York: Plenum Press.

WOOD, S. J., MURDOCH, J. Y., & CRONIN, M. E. (2002). Self-monitoring and at-risk middle-school students: Academic performance improves, maintains, and generalizes. *Behavior Modification, 25*, 605–626.

WYATT, W. J., HAWKINS, R. P., & DAVIS, P. (1986). Behaviorism: Are reports of its death exaggerated? *Behavior Analyst, 9*, 101–105.

YAMAGAMI, T., OKUMA, H., MORINAGA, Y., & NAKAO, H. (1982). Practice of behavior therapy in Japan. *Journal of Behavior Therapy and Experimental Psychology, 13*, 21–26.

YATES, A. J. (1970). *Behavior therapy*. New York: Wiley.

YU, D., MARTIN, G. L., SUTHONS, E., KOOP, S., & PALLOTTA-CORNICK, A. (1980). Comparisons of forward chaining and total task presentation formats to teach vocational skills to the retarded. *International Journal of Rehabilitation Research, 3,* 77–79.

ZAMORA, R., & LIMA, J. (2000). Cognitive behavioral therapy in Uruguay. *The Behavior Therapist, 23,* 98–101.

ZETTLE, R. D. (2003). Acceptance and commitment therapy (ACT) versus systematic desensitization in treatment of mathematics anxiety. *Psychological Record, 53,* 197–215.

ZETTLE, R. D., & HAYES, S. C. (1982). Rule-governed behavior: A potential theoretical framework for cognitive behavioral therapy. In P. C. Kendall (Ed.), *Advances in cognitive behavioral research and therapy* (Vol. 1, pp. 73–118). New York: Academic Press.

ZIEGLER, S. G. (1987). Effects of stimulus cueing on the acquisition of groundstrokes by beginning tennis players. *Journal of Applied Behavior Analysis, 20,* 405–411.

ZVI, M. B. (2004). IABA: The new Israeli ABA Chapter. *Newsletter of the International Association for Behavior Analysis, 27*(2), 24–25.

Author Index

Subject Index